T0202922

# Lecture Notes in Computer Science    11575

Commenced Publication in 1973
Founding and Former Series Editors:
Gerhard Goos, Juris Hartmanis, and Jan van Leeuwen

## Editorial Board Members

David Hutchison
*Lancaster University, Lancaster, UK*
Takeo Kanade
*Carnegie Mellon University, Pittsburgh, PA, USA*
Josef Kittler
*University of Surrey, Guildford, UK*
Jon M. Kleinberg
*Cornell University, Ithaca, NY, USA*
Friedemann Mattern
*ETH Zurich, Zurich, Switzerland*
John C. Mitchell
*Stanford University, Stanford, CA, USA*
Moni Naor
*Weizmann Institute of Science, Rehovot, Israel*
C. Pandu Rangan
*Indian Institute of Technology Madras, Chennai, India*
Bernhard Steffen
*TU Dortmund University, Dortmund, Germany*
Demetri Terzopoulos
*University of California, Los Angeles, CA, USA*
Doug Tygar
*University of California, Berkeley, CA, USA*

More information about this series at http://www.springer.com/series/7409

Jessie Y. C. Chen · Gino Fragomeni (Eds.)

# Virtual, Augmented and Mixed Reality

## Applications and Case Studies

11th International Conference, VAMR 2019
Held as Part of the 21st HCI International Conference, HCII 2019
Orlando, FL, USA, July 26–31, 2019
Proceedings, Part II

 Springer

*Editors*
Jessie Y. C. Chen
US Army Research Laboratory
Aberdeen Proving Ground, MD, USA

Gino Fragomeni
US Army Research Laboratory
Orlando, FL, USA

ISSN 0302-9743            ISSN 1611-3349  (electronic)
Lecture Notes in Computer Science
ISBN 978-3-030-21564-4       ISBN 978-3-030-21565-1  (eBook)
https://doi.org/10.1007/978-3-030-21565-1

LNCS Sublibrary: SL3 – Information Systems and Applications, incl. Internet/Web, and HCI

This Springer imprint is published by the registered company Springer Nature Switzerland AG
The registered company address is: Gewerbestrasse 11, 6330 Cham, Switzerland

# Foreword

The 21st International Conference on Human-Computer Interaction, HCI International 2019, was held in Orlando, FL, USA, during July 26–31, 2019. The event incorporated the 18 thematic areas and affiliated conferences listed on the following page.

A total of 5,029 individuals from academia, research institutes, industry, and governmental agencies from 73 countries submitted contributions, and 1,274 papers and 209 posters were included in the pre-conference proceedings. These contributions address the latest research and development efforts and highlight the human aspects of design and use of computing systems. The contributions thoroughly cover the entire field of human-computer interaction, addressing major advances in knowledge and effective use of computers in a variety of application areas. The volumes constituting the full set of the pre-conference proceedings are listed in the following pages.

This year the HCI International (HCII) conference introduced the new option of "late-breaking work." This applies both for papers and posters and the corresponding volume(s) of the proceedings will be published just after the conference. Full papers will be included in the *HCII 2019 Late-Breaking Work Papers Proceedings* volume of the proceedings to be published in the Springer LNCS series, while poster extended abstracts will be included as short papers in the HCII 2019 *Late-Breaking Work Poster Extended Abstracts* volume to be published in the Springer CCIS series.

I would like to thank the program board chairs and the members of the program boards of all thematic areas and affiliated conferences for their contribution to the highest scientific quality and the overall success of the HCI International 2019 conference.

This conference would not have been possible without the continuous and unwavering support and advice of the founder, Conference General Chair Emeritus and Conference Scientific Advisor Prof. Gavriel Salvendy. For his outstanding efforts, I would like to express my appreciation to the communications chair and editor of *HCI International News,* Dr. Abbas Moallem.

July 2019                                                                Constantine Stephanidis

# HCI International 2019 Thematic Areas
## and Affiliated Conferences

Thematic areas:

- HCI 2019: Human-Computer Interaction
- HIMI 2019: Human Interface and the Management of Information

Affiliated conferences:

- EPCE 2019: 16th International Conference on Engineering Psychology and Cognitive Ergonomics
- UAHCI 2019: 13th International Conference on Universal Access in Human-Computer Interaction
- VAMR 2019: 11th International Conference on Virtual, Augmented and Mixed Reality
- CCD 2019: 11th International Conference on Cross-Cultural Design
- SCSM 2019: 11th International Conference on Social Computing and Social Media
- AC 2019: 13th International Conference on Augmented Cognition
- DHM 2019: 10th International Conference on Digital Human Modeling and Applications in Health, Safety, Ergonomics and Risk Management
- DUXU 2019: 8th International Conference on Design, User Experience, and Usability
- DAPI 2019: 7th International Conference on Distributed, Ambient and Pervasive Interactions
- HCIBGO 2019: 6th International Conference on HCI in Business, Government and Organizations
- LCT 2019: 6th International Conference on Learning and Collaboration Technologies
- ITAP 2019: 5th International Conference on Human Aspects of IT for the Aged Population
- HCI-CPT 2019: First International Conference on HCI for Cybersecurity, Privacy and Trust
- HCI-Games 2019: First International Conference on HCI in Games
- MobiTAS 2019: First International Conference on HCI in Mobility, Transport, and Automotive Systems
- AIS 2019: First International Conference on Adaptive Instructional Systems

# Pre-conference Proceedings Volumes Full List

1. LNCS 11566, Human-Computer Interaction: Perspectives on Design (Part I), edited by Masaaki Kurosu
2. LNCS 11567, Human-Computer Interaction: Recognition and Interaction Technologies (Part II), edited by Masaaki Kurosu
3. LNCS 11568, Human-Computer Interaction: Design Practice in Contemporary Societies (Part III), edited by Masaaki Kurosu
4. LNCS 11569, Human Interface and the Management of Information: Visual Information and Knowledge Management (Part I), edited by Sakae Yamamoto and Hirohiko Mori
5. LNCS 11570, Human Interface and the Management of Information: Information in Intelligent Systems (Part II), edited by Sakae Yamamoto and Hirohiko Mori
6. LNAI 11571, Engineering Psychology and Cognitive Ergonomics, edited by Don Harris
7. LNCS 11572, Universal Access in Human-Computer Interaction: Theory, Methods and Tools (Part I), edited by Margherita Antona and Constantine Stephanidis
8. LNCS 11573, Universal Access in Human-Computer Interaction: Multimodality and Assistive Environments (Part II), edited by Margherita Antona and Constantine Stephanidis
9. LNCS 11574, Virtual, Augmented and Mixed Reality: Multimodal Interaction (Part I), edited by Jessie Y. C. Chen and Gino Fragomeni
10. LNCS 11575, Virtual, Augmented and Mixed Reality: Applications and Case Studies (Part II), edited by Jessie Y. C. Chen and Gino Fragomeni
11. LNCS 11576, Cross-Cultural Design: Methods, Tools and User Experience (Part I), edited by P. L. Patrick Rau
12. LNCS 11577, Cross-Cultural Design: Culture and Society (Part II), edited by P. L. Patrick Rau
13. LNCS 11578, Social Computing and Social Media: Design, Human Behavior and Analytics (Part I), edited by Gabriele Meiselwitz
14. LNCS 11579, Social Computing and Social Media: Communication and Social Communities (Part II), edited by Gabriele Meiselwitz
15. LNAI 11580, Augmented Cognition, edited by Dylan D. Schmorrow and Cali M. Fidopiastis
16. LNCS 11581, Digital Human Modeling and Applications in Health, Safety, Ergonomics and Risk Management: Human Body and Motion (Part I), edited by Vincent G. Duffy

34. CCIS 1033, HCI International 2019 - Posters (Part II), edited by Constantine Stephanidis
35. CCIS 1034, HCI International 2019 - Posters (Part III), edited by Constantine Stephanidis

**http://2019.hci.international/proceedings**

# 11th International Conference on Virtual, Augmented and Mixed Reality (VAMR 2019)

Program Board Chair(s): **Jessie Y. C. Chen and Gino Fragomeni,** *USA*

- Tamara Griffith, USA
- Fotis Liarokapis, Czech Republic
- Joseph B. Lyons, USA
- Phillip Mangos, USA
- Amar R. Marathe, USA
- Rafael Radkowski, USA
- Maria Olinda Rodas, USA
- Michael S. Ryoo, USA
- Jose San Martin, Spain
- Andreas Schreiber, Germany
- Peter Smith, USA
- Simon Su, USA
- Daniel Szafir, USA
- Tom Williams, USA
- Denny Yu, USA

The full list with the Program Board Chairs and the members of the Program Boards of all thematic areas and affiliated conferences is available online at:

**http://www.hci.international/board-members-2019.php**

# HCI International 2020

The 22nd International Conference on Human-Computer Interaction, HCI International 2020, will be held jointly with the affiliated conferences in Copenhagen, Denmark, at the Bella Center Copenhagen, July 19–24, 2020. It will cover a broad spectrum of themes related to HCI, including theoretical issues, methods, tools, processes, and case studies in HCI design, as well as novel interaction techniques, interfaces, and applications. The proceedings will be published by Springer. More information will be available on the conference website: http://2020.hci.international/.

General Chair
Prof. Constantine Stephanidis
University of Crete and ICS-FORTH
Heraklion, Crete, Greece
E-mail: general_chair@hcii2020.org

**http://2020.hci.international/**

# Contents – Part II

**VAMR in Learning, Training and Entertainment**

# Contents – Part I

**Avatars, Embodiment and Empathy in VAMR**

**Cognitive and Health Issues in VAMR**

**VAMR and Robots**

# Design of Virtual Reality for Humanoid Robots with Inspiration from Video Games

Jordan Allspaw, Lilia Heinold, and Holly A. Yanco(✉)

Computer Science Department, University of Massachusetts Lowell,
Lowell, MA 01854, USA
Jordan_Allspaw@uml.edu, Lilia_Heinold@student.uml.edu, holly@cs.uml.edu

**Abstract.** Advances in robotics have led to breakthroughs in several areas, including the development of humanoid robots. There are now several different models of humanoid robots available, but operating them remains a difficult challenge. Current operator control interfaces for humanoid robots often require very experienced operators and significant amounts of time for planning. A large amount of the planning and cognitive load is attributable to the operator attempting to gain adequate three-dimensional (3D) situation awareness and task awareness while viewing an interface on a flat, two-dimensional (2D) screen. Virtual reality (VR) has enormous potential to provide benefits to allow the operator to quickly and accurately understand the state of a robot in a scanned 3D environment and to issue accurate commands with less cognitive load. In the gaming sphere, VR headsets remain a new and promising interface for playing video games. In some cases, existing video games are being ported over to VR and, in others, brand new games are being designed with VR in mind. Control schemes and best practices for VR are emerging within the video game industry. This paper aims to leverage their lessons learned and to apply them to the teleoperation of humanoid robots.

**Keywords:** Virtual reality · Video games · Robotics ·
Humanoid robotics · Human-robot interaction

## 1 Introduction

Over the past decade, there has been an increase in the development and use of humanoid robots, just as virtual reality (VR) headsets have become more commercially available with improved capabilities. However, VR has not been used extensively with humanoid robots, although it seems that an immersive view could help with the operation of such systems.

Our team performed an analysis of the human-robot interaction (HRI) techniques used at the DARPA Robotics Challenge (DRC) Trials [19] and the DRC Finals [9], both of which had a large collection of humanoid robots used by the

© Springer Nature Switzerland AG 2019
J. Y. C. Chen and G. Fragomeni (Eds.): HCII 2019, LNCS 11575, pp. 3–18, 2019.
https://doi.org/10.1007/978-3-030-21565-1_1

participating teams. Both of these studies examined approaches taken by the teams for interaction design, such as the number of operators, types of control, how information was conveyed to the operator(s), and varying approaches to semi-autonomous task execution. There were a number of strategies employed by the various teams, but teams predominately relied on a combination of mouse, keyboard, and gamepad interfaces.

The only known uses of VR in the DRC Finals were two teams – of the 23 in the competition – utilizing the Oculus Rift Developer Kit (DK) [10] for viewing point clouds. This technique was used as a situation awareness complement to viewing point clouds through traditional means (i.e., on a computer monitor). No teams used VR as their primary interface for either visualization or control. A discussion with a member of one of the teams revealed that they had investigated using the Oculus Rift DK for control but found it to be of limited use and did not end up using it at the DRC Finals.

However, there is a requirement to visualize a great deal of sensor data when teleoperating, or even supervising, a humanoid robot in complex environments. For the visualization of sensor data in the DRC Finals [9], the teams in the study averaged 5.1 active screens, 6.2 camera views, and 2.5 different point cloud visualizations. There were an average of 1.6 active operators (using an input device for robot control) and 2.8 passive operators (watching over the shoulders of active operators, offering strategic advice), representing a large amount of manpower towards the goal of allowing the operator to gain proper situation and task awareness of the remote environment by interpreting sensor data from a 2D interface (the screen) and building a 3D mental model.

Another interesting and common trait was that teams frequently had different visualization and control paradigms depending on the task they were performing. The analysis concluded that this implied that each team spent a significant amount of effort creating a specialized interface for each task, in order to provide enough situation awareness to allow the operator(s) to complete the task within the allotted time.

Much of the work on both the interface design and the operator task load was centered around allowing the operator to gain a proper level of task and situation awareness by interpreting data from the robot, which allowed the operator to give the robot commands in an effective way. This need is why many interfaces had multiple camera views. However, with modern sensors, there is potential for a VR interface to greatly reduce the difficulty of this problem. For example, depth cameras such as the Kinect or Xtion Pro generate 3D point clouds that can be easily rendered inside a virtual world.

In previous work, we proposed an interface where the operator would use a VR headset to teleoperate a humanoid robot [1]. However, in the time since we initially designed our VR interface, a large number of video games have been released for play with VR headsets. Now that VR games are more commonplace, and there are many popular and well tested games available, we are interested in analyzing various VR control techniques used in video games to discover what lessons can be learned.

In this paper, we examine a sample of popular VR video games, analyzing their approach to controls and data visualization. We then categorize common control techniques of the VR games in our sample and discuss how those techniques could be adapted for controlling a humanoid robot. Some of the techniques used in video games will likely not be applicable to robot teleoperation due to the different assumptions and requirements of the domains. However, there should still be enough overlap for improvements to be made. We propose an altered interface from our original design in [1], as well as a series of studies to compare the two interfaces.

## 2 Virtual Reality in Video Game Design

We conducted a survey of current VR video games by reviewing online manuals and watching gameplay on YouTube in order to classify the methods for controlling different aspects of the game. If an online manual was not available, the game was omitted from our survey. Our survey originally included twenty-one VR games[1], of which we found game manuals for fourteen[2]. These fourteen games are included in the analysis discussed in this section, with a summary presented in Table 1.

### 2.1 Use of First vs Third Person

In all of the VR video games that we surveyed, first person was the primary method of interaction between the user and the world. In one game, Job Simulator, the user has the option to move the camera from a first person view to an over the shoulder third person view. However, even when in third person, the user controls the character as if they were still in a first person view, i.e., looking out from the character, not from its side. In all of the multiplayer games that we surveyed, the user could see other players in third person but their character stayed in a first person perspective throughout the game.

When in first person, the user could always see some indication of the location of their hands, usually as gloves on the screen, but sometimes the controllers themselves; however, they could not see the rest of their character.

---

[1] Job Simulator, Star Trek Bridge Crew, Fantastic Contraption, The Lab, Skyrim VR, Fallout 4 VR, Obduction, Subnautica, Rick and Morty: Virtual Rick-ality, The Talos Principle VR, Anshar Wars 2, Settlers of Catan, L.A. Noire: The VR Case Files, Budget Cuts, Arizona Sunshine, Onward, OrbusVR, Space Pirate Trainer, X-Plane 11, IL2 Battle of Stalingrad, and Eve Valkyrie.

[2] Job Simulator, Star Trek Bridge Crew, Fantastic Contraption, Skyrim VR, Fallout 4 VR, Obduction, Subnautica, Rick and Morty: Virtual Rick-ality, The Talos Principle VR, L.A. Noire: The VR Case Files, Arizona Sunshine, Onward, OrbusVR, and X-Plane 11.

Table 1. Characteristics of the VR games surveyed in this paper.

| | 1st Person | 3rd person | Room-scale | Standing | Seated | Real Walking | Joystick | Teleport | Press to Grab | Hold | Button for Menu | Point At Buttons | Permanent HUD | Popup HUD | Wrist HUD |
|---|---|---|---|---|---|---|---|---|---|---|---|---|---|---|---|
| Job Simulator | • | • | • | | • | | | | • | • | • | • | | | |
| Star Trek Bridge Crew | • | | | | • | | | | • | | • | | | | |
| Fantastic Contraption | • | | • | • | • | • | | | • | • | | | | | |
| Skyrim VR | • | | • | • | • | • | • | • | • | • | • | | | • | |
| Fallout 4 VR | • | | • | • | | • | • | • | • | | • | | • | • | |
| Obuduction | • | | | • | • | | • | • | • | | • | • | | | |
| Subnautica | • | | | • | • | • | | | • | | • | | • | • | |
| Rick and Morty: Virtual Rickality | • | | • | | | • | | | • | | • | | | | • |
| The Talos Principle VR | • | | • | • | • | | • | • | • | | | • | | | |
| L.A. Noire: The VR Case Files | • | | • | | | • | • | • | • | • | • | | | • | |
| Arizona Sunshine | • | | • | • | | • | • | • | • | • | | • | | | • |
| Onward | • | | • | • | | • | • | | • | • | • | • | | | |
| OrbusVR | • | | • | • | | • | | | • | • | • | • | • | • | |
| X-Plane 11 | • | | • | • | • | | • | | • | • | • | | | | |

## 2.2 Movement

The second area we examined to categorize the games is movement: how the game allows the player to navigate their character within the virtual world. This includes movement of the player's camera, as well as of the player's character if they are separate. On the gaming platform Steam, VR games are categorized in three ways: Room-scale, Standing, and Seated [7]. In most of the games that we surveyed (71%), the user could choose which method they used. This choice allows the user base to be as wide as possible, allowing each user to choose the method with which they are most comfortable [11]. The terms are defined as follows:

- **Room-scale:** The user moves within a dedicated area in order to move their character. A chaperone is used to let the user know that they have reached the boundaries of the tracked area in the real world. To leave the dedicated area in the game, the user must use an alternate method for movement, such as joystick or teleportation [3].
- **Standing:** The user is standing but stationary. Standing allows for some lateral movement, but the user must stay within a much smaller area than room-scale [15].
- **Sitting:** As with standing, the user is stationary. Because the user is seated, there is less room to move, but the motion controllers usually still track the user's hands [15].

Of the games we surveyed, 71% had the option of room-scale mode. In three of these (21%), the game was limited to a small area, such as a room, and thus did not have an open world that the user could roam freely. This limitation allowed the user to not worry about moving outside the room-scale area and the need for combining movement methods. The games with an open world (43%)

required that the user use a joystick or teleportation to get around outside of the small square in which they were standing. This method allowed the user to bend to pick up objects and to imitate using a weapon such as a gun or bow and arrow.

Eight (57%) of the games used teleportation as one of their movement methods. The user would point one of their joysticks at a location and press a button, then a line and circle would appear indicating the exact location to which they would teleport. When the user would release the button on their joystick, the character would teleport to the specified location. This teleportation allows the user to move around quickly in the VR world without moving in real life. Two games (Rick and Morty, Star Trek Bridge Crew) that did not technically include point to teleport instead allowed the user to move instantly between designated locations, by either using portals or by pressing a button on a menu.

Nine (64%) of the games used joystick control (also known as smooth locomotion) for movement, where the user is stationary and uses a button on the joystick for walking, similar to how a user would use the arrow keys on a computer. Most VR controllers have a trackpad for this purpose. Six of these nine games also had the option to teleport. These games let the user choose their preferred method for movement, mostly because smooth locomotion causes nausea for many users, while teleportation has been reported to reduce nausea compared to smooth locomotion [3].

One of the games had no movement (Star Trek Bridge Crew). This game also only allowed the user to be seated, and the character would be sitting at a station. By moving their hands, the user could select various buttons for their character and switch stations. Similarly, another game (X-Plane 11) based on fighter planes allowed the user only to teleport outside of the plane, but, inside, the user would use their hands to press buttons to control the plane and would not move in real life.

## 2.3   Manipulation

All of the games used the joystick buttons to control manipulation. There were two primary methods for allowing a user to pick up an object. The first, similar to many PC video games, would pop up a menu on the screen when the user was in proximity of an object, indicating which button the user should press to use the object. The second was more VR specific, allowing the user to point their joystick at an object, using a laser pointer to show what object the user wanted to select. Upon release of a joystick button, the player would grab the object.

In 50% of the games, the user had to hold down a button to hold an object. When the user released the button, the character released the object as well. The Vive controller has a dedicated button for this, called the Grip button.

## 2.4   User Interface

Twelve (86%) of the games used a button to bring up a menu in the game. Seven of these allowed the user to point and click to select a menu button, where the user points the controller at a button and a laser appears. The button would also change appearance (e.g., light up, change size, etc.) similar to how buttons change appearance on a computer when you hover over them with a mouse.

Just one game (Star Trek Bridge Crew) used button selection, both on menus and in the game, as one would in real life. The user moved their hand to hover over the correct button in VR, then used a button to select it. This game had the buttons laid out in front of the user like a console, instead of the more traditional menu hovering in front of the user, in order to simulate the look from Star Trek.

The games that did not include the point and click method had the user click buttons on the controller to select options. This method is more similar to a traditional console game where the interface would indicate which button corresponded to which option, and allowed the user to traverse the list with a joystick or arrow button.

### 2.5  Heads Up Display (HUD)

A Heads Up Display (HUD) is commonly used in video games to display stats such as health, amount of ammunition, inventory, etc. [18]. This method seems to be less common in VR, with only three games using a permanent HUD. In two, the HUD was simply a method for displaying information about other players and objects (e.g., a health bar above other players or information hovering above objects). The last of these had optional hints that would hover over objects.

A pop up HUD was marginally more common, used by five of the games. Status bars would pop up in certain instances and locations then disappear again. Sometimes the pop up was not in the user's control (e.g., a health bar when attacking an enemy, or a $-X$ indicating decreasing health), and sometimes the user could choose to view their status whenever they wished.

A wrist accessory HUD (i.e., the user moves their wrist as if they were looking at a watch, allowing them to view their stats, which is sometimes combined with a menu) was as common as a permanent HUD, used by three games. This form of HUD is entirely up to the user as to when they wish to view it.

## 3  Potential Application of VR Game Design to Robotics

While VR game design has the advantage of many more hours of testing with many more users than the typical robot interface, the video game world is not always applicable to robotics. In this section, we discuss the VR game control paradigms from popular video games, described above, in the context of robotics, to determine which ones will be most applicable when designing a VR interface for a robot system.

### 3.1  How Video Games Differ from Robotics

The biggest difference that needs to be considered when comparing VR for robotics and for video games is that in robotics, the world that the user is interacting with is real and not designed. In video games, the designer can bend the rules of physics and create game specific rules that help themselves or the user when it comes to control. For example, in a video game, sometimes the user is allowed to clip through objects that they accidentally run into, to fall from great heights, and to select objects that are not within grasping distance. Many of the surveyed games allowed the user to "summon" an object when they selected it; that is, when the user pressed the correct button, the object would fly into the player's hand.

Real world consequences also have to be considered when designing a VR control system for a robot. With direct control in video games (i.e., when the user is holding the motion controllers in their hands), it does not matter if the user accidentally moves their arm in the wrong direction or needs to make a strange motion to bring up a menu. While controlling a robot, a designer must account for the fact that if a certain motion will bring up a menu, for example, the robot will also attempt to make that motion. This design can be problematic when the motion is impossible for the robot or the robot must hold a certain position.

It is also worth noting that, in a video game, any object or obstacle the user comes across is there by design. The user will not come across anything unexpected (that is, not expected by the designer), so in video games it is much easier to account for all possibilities that could occur while the user is playing. This is definitely not true in the real world where robots must operate.

## 3.2 Applying Common Video Game VR Techniques to Robotics

While the VR control used in video games is not directly applicable to robotics, design guidance can still be drawn from it, especially when it comes to what is most comfortable and intuitive for a user. For example, no game surveyed was exclusively in third person and very few games had the option of third person view. This indicates that in VR, the most intuitive method of control is first person – that is, you are the character. It follows that when designing VR control for a humanoid robot, the user should be able to "be" the robot and see through its eyes. We do believe, however, that third person views will also have relevance to human-robot interaction.

Methods for movement in the games were relatively evenly distributed. Most games offered more than one method so that users could choose a method with which they were comfortable. This provision of multiple movement methods also accounts for players with different gaming setups (e.g., some users cannot afford a full room-scale VR setup or do not have the room for it) and expands the possible user base of the game. Games with room-scale also often combine one-to-one motion, where the character moves exactly with the user, along with locomotion with a joystick or teleportation. This design was usually to account for the fact that even in room-scale, the player has a limited space in which to move. A similar problem is encountered in robotics: even if the operator has a room-scale setup, the robot may have more space to move than the operator. One way to tackle this problem is to allow the user to directly control the robot for smaller motions (e.g., grabbing, reaching, and limited lateral motion) and leave walking to a point and click method. Another way of tackling the limited space in which the operator has to move is to use an omnidirectional treadmill [3], but none of the video games surveyed used this method. This design choice could be attributed to the fact such a treadmill is not accessible to most gamers at home and thus is primarily used in arcade setups.

In the video games that we surveyed, it was extremely common that while the user was holding motion controllers, the game showed a pair of hands instead. When the user pressed a button to grab, the hand would perform a grabbing motion. Since all of the games surveyed used motion controllers to track the users' movements, the users could not physically move, grab, and point with their hands and had to correlate certain buttons to hand movements. A possible application to robotics is that a user could control the robot's hands by using motion controllers, and the buttons could be mapped to preprogrammed hand motions performed by the robot.

In terms of manipulating objects, every video game surveyed which allowed objects to be grabbed used a button on the controller to select the object of interest. It was more evenly distributed which games chose to have the user hold down the "grip button" to keep holding an object or to release the object by tapping a button. Similar to movement, many games also offered settings for object manipulation. The user could choose which method was most intuitive to them, allowing the game to access a larger user base.

Menu access seemed to be tackled in very similar ways across all of the games. The user would press a designated button on the controller to see the menu, then would either use a point and click method of selection or use more buttons on their controller to select. This design can be applied directly to a VR robotics setup, where an operator could use a designated button to access an in-VR menu. This design would account for the fact that current 2D interfaces have many settings and buttons around the view of the robot that would need to be accessed in VR through a menu. A point and click method of selection could also be used, since direct movement could be disabled during menu access.

Most of the games that we surveyed did not include a HUD, but this can be attributed to the fact that many did not need one. Some of the methods of HUD used (e.g., hovering hints and information above other players) would not be applicable to robotics. Since HUDs in video games are usually used to display stats (e.g., health, amount of ammunition, and inventory), it could be used for something similar in robotics. Some applicable statistics to display for robots could include battery power, joint states, and other state of health information.

## 4   Initial Virtual Reality Interface

Our initial interface [1] was designed before VR video games were the norm and while VR best practices were still being developed. Therefore, when designing our interface, we looked to existing 2D interfaces for inspiration. We particularly looked at interfaces used during the DRC, due to the wealth of information available and the fact that the majority of competing robots were humanoid.

While fully autonomous robots are popular in research and have had success in very specific domains, for many complex tasks having a human operator in the loop is still often preferred. For the DRC specifically, many of the teams utilized very little autonomy. The teams that did have some autonomy typically used it in very specific and limited cases. For example, IHMC started with scripts that could perform tasks on their own and over time broke up those scripts into smaller pieces. The end result was a series of steps where the robot would plan a smaller action, and the operator would either confirm the plan or, more often, make adjustments to the robot's state or plan before approving it [6]. Team IHMC allowed their robot operator to "command the robot via interaction with the three-dimensional (3D) graphic tool rather than specifying robot motion or joint positions directly" [6].

With these factors in mind, we designed an interface where the operator retains control of most of the robot functions. Similar strategies were common among several of the teams, albeit all displayed on 2D screen interfaces, with interaction usually through a mouse and keyboard.

After deciding on the level of autonomy that we wished to used in our interface, we decided that building our interface from the lessons learned during the DRC was the best course of action. While the teams competing in the DRC had a specific goal – namely completing a series of structured tasks in a controlled competition – it still represents one of the most significant events in HRI for humanoid robots. We found that the teams used a combination of 2D and 3D imaging. For instance, teams with greater success at performing tasks relied on a fused display of the 3D robot avatar, point cloud, and camera images, in a common reference frame [9]. However, 2D interaction methods, like a mouse and keyboard, were used to maneuver the displays and issue commands. HRI for humanoid robots consists inherently of 3D data, for which VR offers a unified solution for both 3D display and control. Our goal was to create an interface that would leverage VR in order to increase operator situation and task awareness when visualizing a remote location, while also providing adequate control methods to compete with traditional 2D screen with mouse and keyboard interfaces.

## 4.1  Robot Platform

While our interface has been designed to be applicable to any humanoid robot with similar features, we developed and tested it using NASA's Valkyrie R5 [13]. Valkyrie is a 6 foot tall, 300 pound humanoid robot with a pair of four fingered hands attached to 7DOF arms. The robot has several sensors built in, including a Carnegie Robotics Multisense [14], located in its head, capable of generating both high and low density point clouds, depending on bandwidth requirements, as well as a stereo camera view. The robot also has an additional pair of stereo cameras in the lower torso. Finally, in addition to accurate joint state and torque tracking on each joint, the robot has embedded tactile sensors in the fingers and palm to detect grasping success.

The types of actions that the robot performs are to move a foot to a location in 3D space and hold it without taking a step; to move a foot to a location in 3D space and take a step; to command the torso, pelvis, or neck to a commanded position; and to command one of the arms to a location in 3D space.

**Fig. 1.** Screenshot of an operator controlling a robot in VR. On the left is the virtual view that the operator sees; on the right is the real robot with the operator standing behind it.

### 4.2   Software Platform

Valkyrie's sensors and controller interface communicate using ROS [12], a communication middle-ware commonly used in robotics. When this project was started, the Linux driver for the HTC Vive was lacking many important features so we built our application within the Windows operating system. In order to communicate with the Robot we utilized a Unity [17] plugin of ROS.NET [16] which handled all of the communication and conversion between standard ROS topics and types into things that could be uses within Unity. With the infrastructure settled, we were able to use the most supported and feature complete SDK for the HTC Vive, with the added bonus of being able to leverage several other features within Unity.

### 4.3   Design of the Initial Interface

The interface utilizes the HTC Vive [5], a commercially available VR headset combined optionally with the Manus VR [8] gloves, a pair of gloves that allows accurate finger tracking, as well as tracking the wrists' location with the HTC Vive Trackers [5]. As an alternative to the glove, we also use the standard controllers that come with the headset. We also utilized a treadmill so that the operator could walk without leaving the tracking area.

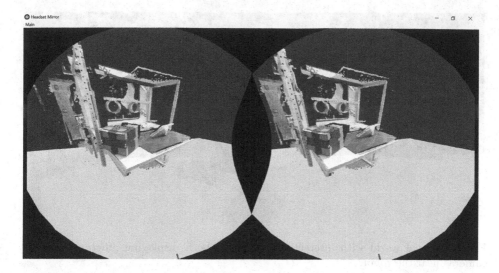

**Fig. 2.** Visualization of the high density point cloud reconstruction.

The operator sees the robot from a third person perspective, and when walking in real life walks around inside the robot's virtual world, allowing them to see the robot from different angles. An example of an operator viewing the robot in VR can be seen in Fig. 1. The operator can also teleport to different locations in the world if they do not wish to walk.

In terms of movement, the way the operator moves the robot is very similar to a 2D interface. While in VR, the operator reaches out and pulls the robot's limbs in a direction, and then the robot uses inverse kinematics to move that part of the robot in the correct direction. The operator can also plan footstep paths that are then visualized in 3D and can view various point cloud visualizations of the world, as seen in Fig. 2. Finally, they can view what is seen by the robot's front camera by movable interactive windows, as seen in Fig. 3. More information on this interface design can be found in Allspaw et al. [2].

## 5    Proposed Redesign Based on VR Video Game Analysis

Currently, our VR interface is very different from the interfaces used in video games. As previously discussed, our interface was designed with the operator existing as a virtual avatar alongside the robot. The operator can then see and interact with the virtual robot from a third person view, sending commands only when desired. In the video games surveyed, the player typically exists in the first person, where there movements directly cause the virtual agent to move. In this case, the user exists in the virtual world as the virtual agent, rather than merely alongside it.

**Fig. 3.** Virtual world with interactable windows, both displaying different external cameras near the robot.

## 5.1  Perspective

Our initial interface was designed for a third person perspective, in contrast to the majority of VR video games, which are first person. One possible reason that first person is so ubiquitous is that many first person video games were easily designed for or ported over to VR. It also has the added benefit of possibly increasing the immersion of the player. We are interested in examining in what situations first person versus third person viewpoints during robot teleoperation would be beneficial.

Our initial decision on the perspective was based upon what was being done at the time in robotics, that is, using VR to get a better idea of the robot's position in space rather than control. In a 2D interface, it can be difficult to tell if the robot is close enough to an object to interact with it, or if the robot is oriented correctly to complete a task. An operator can use VR to "look around" a robot to give them a better idea if the robot is in the correct position for a task. In contrast, the main purpose of perspective in VR is to give the user the best immersion possible. However, this does not mean that a VR interface for robotics should not also have immersion as a goal. With this in mind, we propose a possible change to our interface so that the operator can toggle between first and third person based on their current needs.

It should be noted that in our interface, there is nothing preventing the operator from moving their virtual avatar to the exact position and orientation of the robot, allowing them to gain a first person point of view, which was often used in our pilot testing. However, since the controls were designed for a third person viewpoint, trying to maintain a strictly first person viewpoint would be cumbersome. A better solution might be to allow the operator to switch between a proper first and third person viewpoint, possibly adjusting controls and visualizations to match.

## 5.2    Controls

The common tasks that an operator encounters while controlling our humanoid robot fit into two categories:

1. **Movement:** Tasks that involve moving the robot, whether arms, legs, or the head/sensor systems
   - Instructing the robot to walk forward or backward
   - Positioning arms, hands or fingers in preparation for a task
   - Picking up an object
   - Manipulating an object (such as a handle, a lever or a wheel)
2. **Evaluation:** Tasks that involve ensuring the robot will not be harmed in the next task
   - Evaluating a planned footstep path
   - Evaluating the robot's position before executing a task
   - Evaluating the terrain

Tasks in the evaluation category are not typically relevant in video games. A player usually does not have to worry in a video game if terrain is passable or if their character is too far away to manipulate an object. Typically, the player's virtual character could be considered a near-perfect highly autonomous robot, where the risk of failure is low. If a player commands their character to walk forward, there is a low risk of a catastrophic failure, such as it tripping, except in intentional video game mechanics.

In robotics, evaluation before executing tasks is much more important. If a task is executed improperly, a robot could fall down or break. Evaluation tasks are more easily performed in third person because the user can view the robot and the surrounding from multiple angles and get information that would not otherwise be visible if they could only see in first person.

The tasks in the movement category are much more similar to tasks that also need to be performed in video games. It stands to reason that these tasks could be more easily accomplished from a first person perspective. In our initial interface, the operator would move the robot's limbs in a similar way to a 2D interface: dragging them to an appropriate position in space or using sliders to tune each joint value. However, first person control would allow for greater immersion in VR and potentially more effective control of the robot.

By combining first and third person views into our interface, we hope not only to allow easier movement for the operator (e.g., by allow the robot to move with the operator as in a room-scale video game), but also to allow the operator to evaluate the robot's position and fine tune if needed.

## 5.3    Movement: Walking

Currently, our interface allows for both room-scale and teleportation. The operator can walk around their space to navigate the virtual world for smaller movements, and, if greater distance is needed, they can use the controller to teleport their play area to a new location. For sending movement commands to the robot, the operator points to a location in the virtual world, which prompts the robot to plan, and execute if approved, the footsteps required to reach that location. When considering a first person perspective to the interface, it makes sense to use the similar methods for movement. In first person mode, the robot would imitate the operator moving in real life. As the operator moves around their play area, rather than just move a virtual avatar, the robot would attempt to walk to keep up. In this master slave system, the robot obeys any commands sent by the operator. The alternative method, whereby the operator points to a location and the robot plans and walks on their own, would be problematic due to concerns of motion sickness. As the robot walks to the location, the operator would need to be a slave to the robot's perspective as it walks, which would increase the chances of motion sickness. A method for hiding this movement from the user might be necessary to prevent motion sickness.

Given that a humanoid robot could fall if an incorrect step were taken, we will need to conduct a study to determine the best method for walking control, both for the operator and for the robot.

### 5.4   Movement: Manipulation

Unfortunately, the manipulation techniques used in the surveyed video games are not easily applicable to robotics. Press to grab was overwhelmingly the most popular method of object manipulation, but such a method would require a very high level of consistent autonomy, which is not always available. In video games, objects typically snap into the player's hand when prompted, in a way that is not realistic for the real world. Except in very controlled environments, it is difficult to have a robot capable of grabbing a randomly, and possibly unmodeled, selected object; this is currently an active research problem. However, one important takeaway from the manipulation analysis is that direct manipulation of objects is a large aspect of VR games and thus not something that our interface should ignore.

With this in mind, we propose an alternate design for our manipulation strategy. Instead of using controllers to manipulate the robot's arms and hands, and then watching the robot move to the commanded position, the operator will wear the Manus VR Gloves to provide direct control. The Manus VR Gloves allow for accurate finger tracking for all five fingers, and, when combined with the SteamVR Trackers, we can also track the position of the operator's hands without them holding the controllers. Using this, we can allow control of the robot's hands with inverse kinematics and control the fingers directly. The head can similarly be tied to the operator's headset in a master-slave configuration; as the operator looks in a direction, the robot will do the same. This design goes hand in hand with adding a first person perspective to the interface, as it may be more intuitive to use direct motion to control the robot while in first person.

## 5.5   Planned Studies and Future Work

Despite the wealth of information that we have gained from our analysis, there are many questions that remain unanswered about the best way to implement a VR interface for a humanoid robot. Our next action is to perform a comparison between the first person and third person interface designs. We plan to have participants use both interfaces to perform a series of tasks using a simulated Valkyrie humanoid robot, using simulated environments from previous challenges such as the DRC and the Space Robotics Challenge [4]. We will then analyze the data to determine in what situations the various controls and visualizations were superior. Metrics to be considered include task success, task time, and operator comfort.

While it is possible that one interface would be unanimously superior to the other in every metric, we suspect that the superior interface will be a hybrid of the two, where the operator is able to seamlessly switch between the two modes. After the study, we will adjust our interface accordingly, and run a new study with a similar design; however, this time we will compare the VR interface against a more traditional 2D interface modeled directly on successful interfaces used in the DRC.

## 6   Conclusions

With the advances in both humanoid robots and available VR devices, we believe that there is potential for designing a new type of robot interface that will increase operator success when performing tasks that require situation awareness in a remote 3D environment. In this paper, we have discussed our existing work in designing a VR humanoid robot control interface, as well as discussed possible changes to be made. However, more work is needed to determine what types of controls and visualizations will be the most useful for remote teleoperation, as well as determining when a VR interface versus the standard 2D interface may be desired.

**Acknowledgements.** The work in this paper has been supported in part by NASA (NNX16AC48A) and the Department of Energy's Office of Environmental Management (DE-EM0004482).

## References

1. Allspaw, J., Roche, J., Lemiesz, N., Yannuzzi, M., Yanco, H.A.: Remotely tele-operating a humanoid robot to perform fine motor tasks with virtual reality-. In: Proceedings of the 1st International Workshop on Virtual, Augmented, and Mixed Reality for HRI (VAM-HRI) (2018)
2. Allspaw, J., Roche, J., Norton, A., Yanco, H.: Teleoperating a humanoid robot with virtual reality. In: VAM-HRI 2018 Proceedings, pp. 7–13 (2018)
3. Langbehn, E., Lubos, P., Steinicke, F.: Evaluation of locomotion techniques for room-scale VR: joystick, teleportation, and redirected walking. In: Proceedings of ACM Virtual Reality International Conference, vol. 4, p. 9. ACM (2018)

4. Hambuchen, K.A., et al.: NASA's space robotics challenge: advancing robotics for future exploration missions. In: AIAA SPACE and Astronautics Forum and Exposition, p. 5120 (2017)
5. HTC: Discover virtual reality beyond imagination. https://www.vive.com/us/
6. Johnson, M., et al.: Team IHMC's lessons learned from the DARPA robotics challenge trials: finding data in the rubble. J. Field Robot. **32**(2), 192–208 (2015)
7. Lang, B.: Steam expands VR game listings with supported headsets, play area, and more. Road to VR, February 2016. https://www.roadtovr.com/steam-expands-vr-game-listings-with-supported-headsets-play-area-and-more/
8. ManusVR: Manus VR: the pinnacle of virtual reality controllers. https://manus-vr.com/
9. Norton, A., et al.: Analysis of human-robot interaction at the DARPA Robotics Challenge Finals. Int. J. Robot. Res. **36**(5–7), 483–513 (2017)
10. Oculus Rift, January 2018. https://en.wikipedia.org/wiki/Oculus_Rift
11. Parrish, K.: Stand up or sit down? Many don't take advantage of VR's room-scale experience. Digital Trends, June 2018. https://www.digitaltrends.com/computing/oculus-rift-owners-want-to-sit-for-vr-experiences/
12. Quigley, M., et al.: ROS: an open-source Robot Operating System. In: ICRA Workshop on Open Source Software, Kobe, Japan, vol. 3, no. 2, p. 5 (2009)
13. Radford, N.A., et al.: Valkyrie: NASA's first bipedal humanoid robot. J. Field Robot. **32**(3), 397–419 (2015)
14. Carnegie Robotics: Multisense SL. https://carnegierobotics.com/multisense-sl/
15. Shanklin, W.: Room-scale or standing VR? Why all that walking around may be overrated. https://newatlas.com/room-scale-vs-standing-vr-oculus-rift-htc-vive/48219/
16. UML-robotics: UML-robotics/ros.netunity. https://github.com/uml-robotics/ROS.NET_Unity
17. Unity: Unity. https://unity3d.com/
18. Wilson, G.: Off with their HUDs! Rethinking the heads-up display in console game design. https://www.gamasutra.com/view/feature/130948/off_with_their_huds_rethinking_.php
19. Yanco, H.A., Norton, A., Ober, W., Shane, D., Skinner, A., Vice, J.: Analysis of human-robot interaction at the DARPA Robotics Challenge Trials. J. Field Robot. **32**(3), 420–444 (2015)

# Visualizations for Communicating Intelligent Agent Generated Courses of Action

Jessica Bartik[1(✉)], Heath Ruff[2], Gloria Calhoun[1], Kyle Behymer[2],
Tyler Goodman[1], and Elizabeth Frost[2]

[1] Air Force Research Laboratory, 711 HPW/RHCI, Dayton, OH, USA
{Jessica.Bartik.1,Gloria.Calhoun,
Tyler.Goodman.3}@us.af.mil
[2] Infoscitex, Dayton, OH, USA
{Heath.Ruff.ctr,Kyle.Behymer.1.ctr,
Elizabeth.Frost.6.ctr}@us.af.mil

**Abstract.** Future human-autonomy teams will benefit from intelligent agents that can quickly deliberate across multiple parameters to generate candidate courses of action (COAs). This experiment evaluated the design of an interface to communicate agent-generated COAs to a human operator. Twelve participants completed 14 trials, each consisting of a series of tasks that required participants' selection of the best COA in terms of quality, speed, fuel, and detectability parameters. Trial score and speed of participants' selection were measured as a function of COA visualization (1, 4, or 8 COAs) as well as the type of agent. Supplemental trials in which participants could choose which visualization to employ for COA selection were also conducted. The data showed that presenting multiple COAs were better than a single COA. Differences between the 4 and 8 COA visualizations were not quite as definitive: selections were significantly faster with 4 COAs than 8, but participants' preferences were divided based upon agent comprehensiveness and individual strategy differences. The results also showed that the agent's reasoning process should be communicated more precisely besides just what parameters are being considered in generating COAs.

**Keywords:** Human-autonomy teaming · Intelligent agent ·
Parallel coordinates plot · Plan comparison · Visualization ·
Human autonomy interaction

## 1 Introduction

Given the increasing pervasiveness of adversarial threats and the stable Department of Defense (DoD) workforce numbers, autonomous technologies are being developed that enable a single operator to control multiple autonomous vehicles. One example of such technologies is an intelligent agent that uses a cognitive domain ontology to categorize situations and develop multiple courses of action (COAs) in response to mission events [1]. The agent is capable of analyzing and ranking all of the potential COAs according to multiple optimization criteria for a given high level goal/task. For example, the agent

J. Y. C. Chen and G. Fragomeni (Eds.): HCII 2019, LNCS 11575, pp. 19–33, 2019.
https://doi.org/10.1007/978-3-030-21565-1_2

could determine the vehicle most likely to find a target and expend the least amount of time and fuel in the process.

A significant challenge facing interface designers is determining how to best present agent-generated COAs to an operator, as each one imposes information retrieval costs. Moreover, presented alternatives can potentially mask aspects of the problem space and influence the operator's decision-making [2]. One approach is to present a single solution to the operator, the solution that the agent has determined to be the best. Another approach involves modeling to generate alternatives [3], focusing on generating a small set of alternatives that are "good" in terms of achieving the operator's goal but different in respect to the relevant parameters of the solution space. This approach aims to generate options that can achieve the commander's objective but vary in other parameters. For example, three COAs (A, B, C) might be generated based on the high-level goal of getting a vehicle to a specified location in under 20 min, but COA A minimizes fuel use, COA B maximizes stealth, and COA C minimizes future maintenance costs.

To address this challenge, an experimental testbed was developed in which participants were instructed to achieve the highest score possible (while also avoiding fuel violations and detections) in a specific time window by completing a series of COA selection tasks. For each task, eight possible COAs were generated. Each COA had four associated parameters—quality points, time, fuel, and detection. For example, selecting COA A might give the operator 25 quality points, take 16 min, cost 13 fuel units, and have a 50% chance of being detected, while using COA B might give the operator 10 quality points, take 5 min, cost 12 fuel units, and have a 17% chance of being detected. To enable participants to compare the eight COAs across the four parameters, the testbed included a parallel coordinates plot (see Fig. 1) referred to as the 'Vehicle Comparison Tool' [4]. This tool made the tradeoffs between COAs immediately visible. For example, in Fig. 1, COA G (colored orange) was the highest quality, but consumed the most fuel. COA D (colored green) was the second lowest quality, but was least likely to be detected by enemy forces.

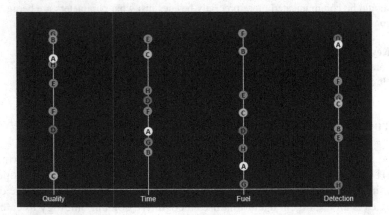

**Fig. 1.** Vehicle Comparison Tool representing eight COAs across four parameters. For each parameter, higher was better (e.g., COA C would generate the least amount of quality points, COA E would take the least amount of time, COA F would use the least fuel, and COA D had the smallest chance of being detected). (Color figure online)

Using this testbed, an experiment was conducted [5] in which participants were tasked with evaluating and selecting the "best" of eight simulated agent-generated COAs. Four visualizations were evaluated, varying in COA number and type: (1) a single COA (highest quality), (2) the four highest quality COAs, (3) the four COAs with the highest value for each parameter (the most quality points, the least time, the least fuel cost, and the least chance of detection), and (4) all eight COAs. Regardless of visualization condition, participants had the ability to call up parameter details of all eight COAs. Data from the experiment indicated that the single COA visualization was significantly less effective than the other visualizations. However, the results did not indicate a clear best option from the other three visualizations.

These findings may reflect limitations of the testbed. Although the testbed provided an engaging test environment that could be rapidly trained, the COA selection tasks did not have high attentional demands compared to operational stations. For instance, participants had as much time as they desired to drill down for COA details not presented, perhaps mitigating differences between visualizations. An additional limitation may have been the lack of a "best COA" for each task. Instead, the eight COAs were balanced across the four parameters making it ambiguous as to which COA was the best option for a specific task. This technique may have led to the lack of significant differences in objective performance measures. Including an agent that could reason across different parameters for the given experimental task and provide participants with one or more recommendations could combat this effect. For example, in one visualization an agent could reason across the four parameters and recommend a single "best" COA. In another visualization, the agent could return the top four solutions.

As such, a follow-on experiment was conducted that employed two intelligent agents. Each was capable of reasoning across multiple parameters to generate and rank COAs, but differed in the number of parameters considered. The testbed and training were also slightly modified to impose more temporal demands. Participants were briefed that their COA selection time was limited to 30 s. To help manage the limited selection time, a digital readout that counted down was added to the testbed. Besides creating a more temporally demanding test environment, these modifications added an interface element that also increased requirements to shift attention. The experiment reported herein utilized this enhanced version of the testbed to examine which of three visualizations was most effective in aiding participant COA selection performance, as well as the impact of agent reasoning comprehensiveness.

## 2   Method

### 2.1   Participants

Twelve volunteer employees working at a U.S. Air Force Base between the ages of 19–51 ($M = 35.08$, $SD = 10.68$) participated in the study. All participants reported normal or corrected normal vision and color vision.

## 2.2   Experimental Design

Six conditions were evaluated, varying in agent type and visualization (see Table 1). The more comprehensive Agent A reasoned across all four parameters (quality, time, fuel, detection) when generating and ranking COAs for a given task. Agent B only reasoned across three of the four parameters (quality, time, and fuel), excluding detection from its reasoning.

**Table 1.** Illustration of the six experimental conditions

|  | Agent A | Agent B |
|---|---|---|
| Visualization | 1 COA | 1 COA |
| Visualization | 4 COAs | 4 COAs |
| Visualization | 8 COAs | 8 COAs |

Trials were blocked by agent type and visualization. For example, a participant completed three blocks of trials (i.e., one per visualization) with one agent and then three more blocks of trials with the other agent. For each participant, the order of the visualization blocks with each agent was the same. However, across participants, the order of the visualizations and two agent types was counterbalanced. Within each of the six blocks, participants completed two trials. For each 480 min (simulated) trial participants were presented a series of generic tasks (i.e., tasks lacked context and were simply labeled "Task 1", "Task 2", etc.) with the number of tasks per trial being dependent upon participants' COA selections (ranged from 12 to 21, $M = 14.65$, $SD = 1.55$). To complete each task, participants were trained to select one of the eight COAs (i.e., vehicles) labeled A–H within 30 s. Each COA differed on four parameters: quality (i.e., the number of points the participant could accumulate for selecting this COA), time to complete the task using this COA, fuel used, and probability of detection.

In addition to the series of experimental trials described above, participants completed two supplemental trials, one with each agent type (order counterbalanced across participants). For each of the tasks within these trials, participants selected which visualization (1, 4, or 8 COAs) they wanted to have presented (and they could switch as much as they desired between the different visualizations). Unlike the prior experimental trials, participants had an unlimited amount of time to make decisions.

## 2.3   Test Stimuli

Figure 2 illustrates how the same data set was depicted in the Vehicle Comparison Tool for each of the six conditions. Panes 1–3 show COAs suggested by Agent A. In (1), the top COA (F) is shown. In (2), the top four COAs are shown (adding B, D, and E to F). In (3), all eight COAs are shown. COAs suggested by Agent B are shown in Panes 4–6. In (4), the top COA (E) is shown. In (5), the top four COAs are shown (adding B, F, and G to E). In (6), all eight COAs are shown.

A range of possible values was determined for each of the four parameters and assigned to the eight COAs according to the method outlined in [5]: quality 10–60 points, time 15–45 min, fuel 5–22 gallons, and detection probability 5%–60%. Upon COA selection, a random number between 1–100 was generated. If that number was below the chosen COA's detection probability, the selection would result in a detection. If the number was above the chosen COA's detection probability, the COA selection would not result in a detection and the quality points for that task would be awarded. For example, if a COA with a 20% chance of being detected was selected and the random number generated was "19", the result would be a detection.

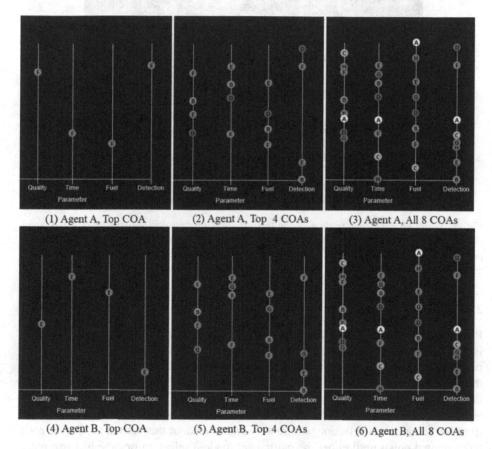

|  (1) Agent A, Top COA  |  (2) Agent A, Top 4 COAs  |  (3) Agent A, All 8 COAs  |
|  (4) Agent B, Top COA  |  (5) Agent B, Top 4 COAs  |  (6) Agent B, All 8 COAs  |

**Fig. 2.** Six experimental conditions differing in agent type (A or B) and visualization (1, 4, or 8 COAs)

Regardless of agent type or the number of COAs shown, participants were provided the top agent COA for each task via a text readout located directly below the Vehicle Comparison Tool (e.g., "The agent recommends Vehicle C"; see Fig. 3). Participants also were provided the ability to 'drill down' to see the associated values for all eight COAs. Two drill down methods were available (see Fig. 3 for the results of both methods). One allowed participants to use a mouse to hover over a parameter in the Vehicle Comparison Tool to see the values of each of the eight COAs for that parameter. The second method allowed participants to hover over a COA/vehicle button to see that vehicle's values for each of the four parameters.

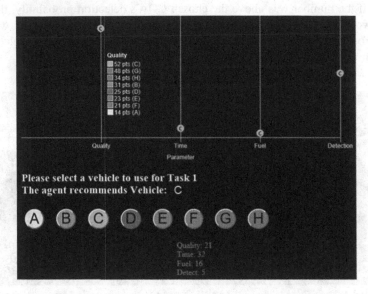

**Fig. 3.** Close up view of a portion of the testbed showing two drill down methods and agent recommended COA text readout. Hovering over a parameter (e.g., Quality) showed the parameter's specific value for all eight COAs, from highest to lowest. Hovering over a vehicle selection button (e.g., F) showed the values of all four parameters for that specific COA.

## 2.4   Trial Procedure

Participants were seated in front of the testbed (see Fig. 4) that was presented on a 24 inch monitor. A mouse was used for inputs. To start each experimental trial, participants clicked a button on the monitor labeled *BEGIN*. Participants were trained to use the *Vehicle Comparison Tool* (see Fig. 4) to determine which COA to select for each task within the trial. Participants indicated their selected COA/vehicle by clicking on the corresponding lettered circle (see *Vehicle Selection Buttons* in Fig. 4). The time limit for making each selection was 30 s. A digital readout that started at 30 s for each task counted down until either the participant made a selection or time had expired.

Upon COA selection, the *Scoreboard* (see Fig. 4) updated based on the results of the participant's selection. *Score* increased by the chosen COA's associated quality value if the vehicle wasn't detected. If detected, *Score* remained the same and *Detections* increased by one. *Time Remaining* decreased based on the amount of time associated with that COA selection. If participants took more than 30 s to make a decision *Time Remaining* decreased by an additional 25 min. Similarly, if participants had to refuel a vehicle, *Time Remaining* decreased by 25 min. The *Fuel Status Display* (see Fig. 4) updated to reflect the amount of fuel used. If selecting a COA resulted in a vehicle having less than 50 gallons of fuel, *Fuel Violations* increased by one. Participants continued to receive new tasks until there were no COAs whose associated time requirement was less than the *Time Remaining*, at which point the trial ended.

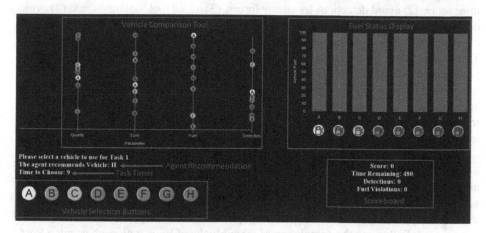

**Fig. 4.** Screenshot of the experimental testbed with key elements annotated

The supplemental experimental trials followed a similar procedure but there was no timer and participants could use the buttons (labeled 1, 4, and 8 in Fig. 5) to choose, as well as flip between, the visualization(s) presented for each task.

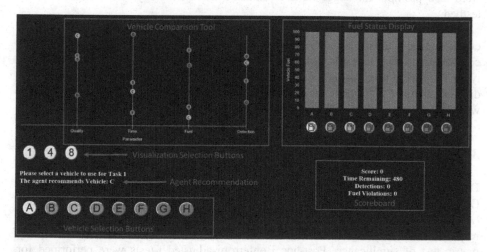

**Fig. 5.** Screenshot of the experimental testbed configured for the supplemental trials with key elements annotated

## 2.5  Test Sessions

Upon arrival, participants read the informed consent document and completed a demographics questionnaire. Next, participants were trained on the COA selection task, beginning with a discussion of the four parameters they needed to consider when selecting a COA. Participants learned they had four equally important goals: (1) maximize score, (2) avoid detections by enemy forces, (3) avoid fuel violations, and (4) avoid timeouts. Participants were then briefed on the major testbed components for the experimental trials to include the Vehicle Comparison Tool, Agent Recommendation, Timer, Fuel Status Display, Vehicle Selection Buttons, and Scoreboard (Fig. 4). Finally, participants were trained on the four visualizations, two agent types, and both drill down methods. After conducting a series of training trials and being trained to a level deemed appropriate by the experimenter, the participants began the experimental trials. A similar training procedure was used for the supplemental trials, highlighting the changes in the testbed and requirement to select a visualization at the start of each task.

After each block (6 total), participants were given a Post-Block questionnaire asking about their perceived performance, workload, ability to identify the best COA, ability to identify the best COA for a specific parameter, how often they drilled down, and the strategy they used for the visualization they just experienced. All questions used a five point Likert scale, with the exception of the strategy question, which was open-ended. Following the completion of three blocks of trials with each agent, a Post-Agent questionnaire was administered asking the participants to rank the visualizations from 1–3 (1 = best, 3 = worst) in terms of performance, response time, accuracy, and trust. After trials with all six conditions were finished, participants completed a Post-Experiment questionnaire containing open-ended questions asking participants which visualization they most and least preferred, whether or not their strategy changed depending on the visualization, and which drill down method they preferred. There were also prompts for suggestions to enhance the symbology and elements of the testbed.

Lastly, after the supplemental trials, a questionnaire was administered with open-ended questions asking which visualization participants tended to select most often to complete the COA selection tasks and whether that tendency changed based on agent type. They were also queried on whether they preferred having the ability to call up a different number of COAs versus having a default number of COAs in conjunction with drill down capabilities. Total session time, per participant, was approximately 2 h.

## 3  Results/Discussion

Data for each participant were collapsed across the two trials for each visualization. Objective data were analyzed with a repeated measures Analysis of Variance (ANOVA) model. An ANOVA model was also applied to the Post-Block questionnaire responses. The Post-Agent ranking data were analyzed using the Friedman nonparametric test of significance. Post-hoc Bonferroni-adjusted t-tests were performed for significant ANOVA and Friedman results. Error bars in figures are standard errors of the mean.

## 3.1 Performance

Score, response time (amount of time between visualization presentation and COA selection), and detection data were analyzed as objective measures of performance. The results of an ANOVA indicated that there was a significant interaction between agent type and visualization on mean score ($F(2,22) = 7.45$, $p = .003$, $\eta_p^2 = .40$). When utilizing the less comprehensive Agent B, participants scored lower with the 1 COA visualization, compared to when 4 COAs were presented ($t(11) = 3.80$, $p = .05$, $d = 1.35$, see Fig. 6). Rankings from the Post-Agent questionnaires were aligned with these results. Participants ranked their COA selections less accurate with the 1 COA visualization compared to the 4 COA visualization (Agent B) and the 4 COA and 8 COA visualizations (Agent A). Overall performance was also ranked worse with the 1 COA visualization versus the 4 COA visualization (Agent B) (see Tables 2 and 3).

These performance results are aligned with participants' ratings on their ability to make COA selections with the three visualizations. For example, their ratings indicated that it was more difficult to select the best vehicle when only 1 COA was presented compared to the 8 COA visualization ($t(11) = 4.45$, $p = .003$, $d = 0.44$). In contrast, differences in vehicle selection ability/performance between the 4 COA and 8 COA visualizations were not clear. In fact, participants' ratings were divided with respect to these visualizations. Seven of twelve participants indicated a preference for 4 COAs commenting that it provided a variety to choose from but was less cluttered and eliminated undesirable options, compared to 8 COAs. Another four participants preferred the 8 COA option, noting that presentation of more options provided a "big picture" and an ability to judge COAs just by their relative positioning on the axes of the Vehicle Comparison Tool, with less drilling down for exact numeric parameter values. Finally, one participant's preference depended on the agent in effect, desiring 4 COAs for the more comprehensive Agent A and 8 COAs for Agent B that didn't consider detection.

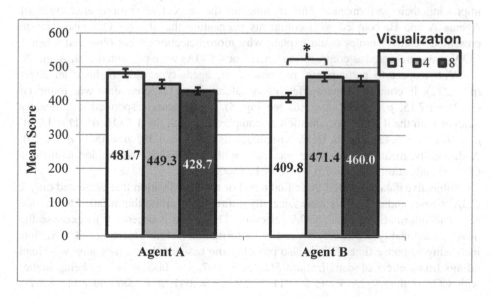

**Fig. 6.** Mean score by agent type and visualization

**Table 2.** Post-Agent questionnaire Friedman results

| Variable name | $\chi^2(2)$ | $p$ | $W$ |
|---|---|---|---|
| Performance (Agent B) | 9.5 | .009 | .34 |
| Accuracy (Agent B) | 6.0 | .05 | .25 |
| Accuracy (Agent A) | 10.2 | .006 | .42 |

**Table 3.** Post-Agent questionnaire post-hoc results

| Variable name | One COA | | Four COAs | | All eight COAs | | $t(11)$ | $p$ | $d$ |
|---|---|---|---|---|---|---|---|---|---|
| | $M$ | $SE$ | $M$ | $SE$ | $M$ | $SE$ | | | |
| Performance (Agent B) | 2.67 | 0.19 | 1.42 | 0.15 | | | 5.00 | .001 | 2.13 |
| Accuracy (Agent B) | 2.50 | 0.23 | 1.50 | 0.15 | | | 3.32 | .021 | 1.48 |
| Accuracy (Agent A) | 2.75 | 0.13 | 1.58 | 0.19 | | | 4.84 | .002 | 2.04 |
| Accuracy (Agent A) | 2.75 | 0.13 | | | 1.67 | 0.23 | 3.46 | .016 | 1.70 |

Similarly, the mean number of detections differed as a function of agent type and visualization ($F(2,22) = 6.94$, $p = .005$, $\eta_p^2 = .39$). For the more comprehensive Agent A, participants' COA selection resulted in a higher number of detections when 8 COAs were presented compared to the other two visualizations: 1 COA ($t(11) = 5.61$, $p = .002$, $d = 1.69$) and 4 COAs ($t(11) = 4.53$, $p = .013$, $d = 1.13$, see Fig. 7). This finding was unexpected as it was anticipated that there would be more detections with Agent B, the agent that doesn't consider detections in its reasoning, than with Agent A. However, the fact that participants were trained on Agent B's shortcoming might have made them more acutely aware of detections for trials supported by Agent B, thus improving their performance. This training on the respective comprehensiveness of Agents A and B, coupled with comments suggesting that the 8 COA visualization presented "clutter" issues could explain why more detections were observed when 8 COAs were presented as compared to when 1 or 4 COAs were presented with Agent A.

With respect to participants' response time, agent type did not have an effect ($p = .221$). In contrast, a main effect of visualization on response time was found ($F(2,22) = 67.15$, $p < .001$, $\eta_p^2 = .86$, see Fig. 8). Participants responded significantly quicker with the 4 COA visualization as compared to both the 1 COA ($t(11) = 14.34$, $p < .001$, $d = 6.42$) and 8 COA visualizations ($t(11) = 4.38$, $p = .003$, $d = 2.10$). Additionally, mean response time was faster with the 8 COA visualization than the 1 COA visualization ($t(11) = 7.63$, $p < .001$, $d = 2.08$).

Subjective data supported these findings. For the visualization that presented only 1 COA, ratings and comments were generally unfavorable, citing that it failed to provide adequate information to base COA selection. This made it necessary to exercise the hover functionality repeatedly to call up information before selecting a COA, thus increasing response time. This is also probably the basis of the participants' workload ratings (main effect of visualization: $F(2,22) = 6.67$, $p = .006$, $\eta_p^2 = .38$) being higher with COA 1 than COA 4 and 8 ($t(11) = 2.93$, $p = .041$, $d = 1.06$ and $t(11) = 3.19$,

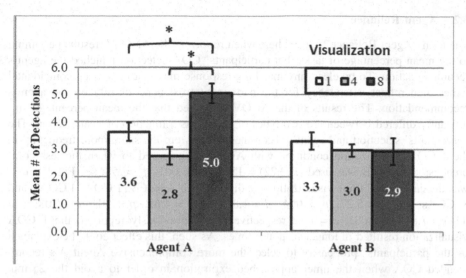

**Fig. 7.** Mean number of detections for each visualization by agent type

$p = .026$, $d = 1.21$, respectively). In contrast, the visualizations with 4 and 8 COAs provided more information.

Likewise, participants' frequency in using hovers to drill down for additional information significantly differed across visualizations ($F(2,22) = 9.52$, $p = .003$, $\eta_p^2 = .46$). The drill down functionality (with Agent A) was utilized more with 1 COA than with visualizations that had 4 COAs and 8 COAs ($t(11) = 3.08$, $p = .031$, $d = 1.46$ and $t(11) = 4.21$, $p = .004$, $d = 2.23$, respectively). Similar results pertaining to drill down frequency were shown in the ranking of the visualizations on the Post-Agent questionnaire ($\chi^2(2) = 12.17$, $p = .002$, $W = .51$).

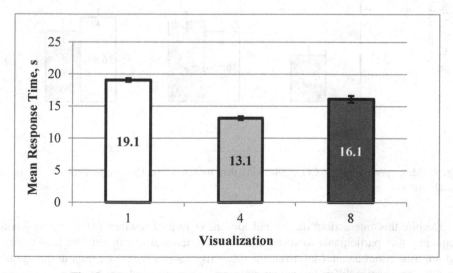

**Fig. 8.** Mean response time for each of the three visualizations

## 3.2   Agent Reliance

The term "Agent Reliance" is used here when reporting the ANOVA results pertaining to the mean percentage of tasks that participants' COA selection matched the agent's recommendation. To be clear, any matching response may just have been coincidental rather than reflect a tendency for the participant to depend or rely on the agent's recommendation. The results of the ANOVA showed that the mean percentage significantly differed between the two types of agents, as a function of visualization. The participants' selection and agent's recommendation were the same more frequently in the 1 COA visualization condition with Agent A compared to when the less comprehensive Agent B was used ($F(2,22) = 15.16$, $p = .001$, $\eta_p^2 = .58$; see Fig. 9). This was the case for all three visualization conditions with Agent B (1 COA, 4 COAs, and 8 COAs; ($t(11) = 5.27$, $p = .004$, $d = 1.81$; $t(11) = 4.68$, $p = .01$, $d = 1.08$; and $t(11) = 7.81$, $p < .001$, $d = 1.12$ respectively). As previously reported, the 1 COA visualization resulted in longer response times. As such, this effect could be explained by the participants' propensity to select the more comprehensive Agent A's recommended COA when the timer approached expiration in order to avoid the 25 min simulated time penalty associated with a timeout. Overall, participants completed COA selections before the timer expired on 85.42% of trials.

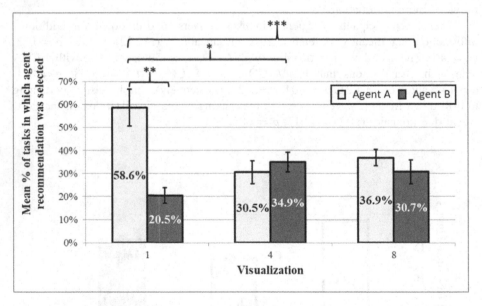

**Fig. 9.** Mean percentage of COA selections that matched agent's recommendation for each visualization

Despite this interaction, the overall low mean rate of reliance ($M = 35.35\%$) and frequency that participants used the drill down functionality suggest that participants did not trust either agent. Moreover, the subjective ratings regarding trust in the agents did not significantly differ. Instead, participants' comments indicated that many did not rely on either agents' recommendations (e.g., "I didn't trust either agent to rely on them"). Even for Agent A that considered all four parameters, participants raised questions on the degree to which the agent's algorithm took each parameter into account (e.g., several commented that the agent weighted fuel remaining too high). The recorded comments imply that participants' knowledge of which parameters were considered by the agent was inadequate – many wanted more transparency into the agent's processing (e.g., the relative weights and parameter thresholds each agent took into account in coming up with the recommended COA).

### 3.3   Visualization Usage in Supplemental Trials

The supplemental trials provided data on participants' preference when they were free to choose and switch between the 1, 4 and 8 COA visualizations. In the questionnaire data, nine of the twelve participants indicated they preferred having the option to change the number of COAs presented. The results of an ANOVA examining actual selections made by the participants revealed a significant effect of agent type on visualization choice ($F(1,11) = 6.61$, $p = .03$, $\eta_p^2 = .40$, see Fig. 10). (This ANOVA did not include instances when the single COA option was selected ($n = 1$)). The 4 COA visualization was chosen more often by participants for trials with the more comprehensive Agent A. With Agent B, the 8 COA visualization was chosen more frequently. It is possible that participants felt they needed more information with the less comprehensive Agent B to make a decision and thus they preferred the 8 COA visualization's more detailed information over having only 4 options.

The number of times participants changed the visualization for each task was also examined. The difference between the number of changes with Agent A and Agent B was not significant ($t = .11$) and ranged from 0 to 33 times per trial ($M = 7.50$, $SD = 8.80$).

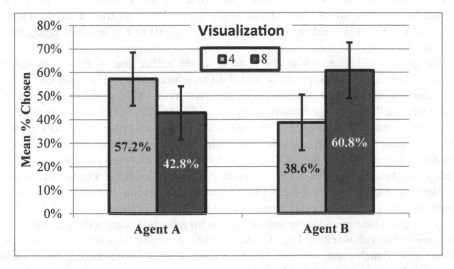

**Fig. 10.** Mean percentage of tasks in which participants chose the 4 COA and 8 COA visualization with each agent type

## 3.4 Drill Down Functionality

Contrary to the different preferences for 4 versus 8 COAs, participants' opinions were generally in agreement about the two methods of drilling down for information. Most preferred using the hover functionality on the Vehicle Comparison Tool that called up the specific values, listed in order from best to worst, for all 8 vehicles for the corresponding parameter (see Fig. 3). These participants commented that it was easy to jump between different parameters with this method and appreciated it giving values for all the vehicles for that parameter at the same time. The hover functionality on the individual vehicle buttons that called up all four parameters for that specific vehicle/COA was less preferable. Only a single participant preferred this method citing that it facilitated evaluating each vehicle as a whole. Experimenter observations indicated that most participants used both methods during the course of trials, probably because both required participants' recall of other pertinent information to inform their selections. Specifically, each hover function either did not provide information on other parameters (Vehicle Comparison Tool) or information on other COAs/vehicles (Vehicle Selection Buttons).

# 4 Summary

The present experiment confirmed the results from an earlier study examining autonomous vehicle management [5]—presenting multiple COAs was better than a single COA. Even though a more temporally demanding task environment was employed in the present experiment, both the objective and subjective data were more favorable with the 4 and 8 COA visualizations compared to data with the single COA visualization, regardless of agent comprehensiveness. It should be noted, though, that it could be that a single COA visualization would be advantageous if participants had a complex multi-task environment or if COA selection had even more severe temporal constraints. In other words, participants might have elected to trust a single agent-generated COA as best (and the only information needed) in a more challenging task environment.

The present experiment was also similar to the earlier one as there was not a definitive best option between the 4 and 8 COA visualizations. For instance, mean score did not significantly differ between the two multi-COA visualizations. While mean response time was significantly faster with 4 COAs than 8, it could be argued that 3 s is not a practical difference. There were also no noteworthy differences in the subjective data; participants' ratings were divided between the two multi-COA presentations. Some preferred the 4 COA visualization, a less cluttered presentation of the agent's four best alternatives, with additional information available via the drill down functionality. Others preferred the 8 COA visualization, stating it provided an overall comparison of a high number of alternative COAs with less need to drill down.

When given the option to choose amongst the visualizations during the supplemental trials, participants chose either 4 or 8 COAs depending on agent comprehensiveness. The participants' visualization preferences and strategies used in comparing parameters across COAs illustrate that individual differences and agent comprehensiveness need to be considered in future interface design. One approach would be to employ a procedure similar to that examined in the supplemental trials: display the user's pre-selected default COA visualization, but also allow that view to be switched, by the user, to alternative visualizations. Indeed, the ability to rapidly switch between different visualizations (such as 4 and 8 COAs) may reduce the need to use hover functionality to call up additional information. Another approach would be to scope the visualization based upon agent comprehensiveness. Thus a system utilizing an agent with a highly comprehensive reasoning scheme would employ a more minimal visualization approach (such as 4 COAs) than a system using an agent with a limited reasoning scheme.

Lastly, this experiment demonstrated that for the human teammate to have an appropriate calibrated trust in the agent partner, more information about the agent's reasoning needs to be communicated (i.e., how the agent arrived at recommended solution(s)). Participants' comments indicated that many of them compared the result of their personal decision-making with the agents' recommendations and assessed plausible differences in their respective reasoning. This explains participants' requests for more insight into how agents utilized each COA parameter in tradeoff analyses. Control functionality that enables certain vehicles/parameters/COAs to be grouped together on the visualization might also facilitate comparisons and inform selections. Any new visualization and control functionality technique would need to be evaluated, though, to ensure that it enhances accurate and timely decision making.

**Acknowledgment.** This work was funded by the Air Force Research Laboratory.

# References

1. Hansen, M., Calhoun, G., Douglass, S., Evans, D.: Courses of action display for multi-unmanned vehicle control: a multi-disciplinary approach. In: The 2016 AAAI Fall Symposium Series: Cross-Disciplinary Challenges for Autonomous Systems, Technical Report FS-16-03 (2016)
2. Smith, P.J.: Making brittle technologies useful (Chap. 10). In: Smith, P.J., Hoffman, R.R. (eds.) Cognitive Systems Engineering: The Future for a Changing World, pp. 181–208. CRC Press, New York (2018). https://doi.org/10.1201/9781315572529
3. Brill, E., Flach, J., Hopkins, L., Ranjithan, S.: MGA: a decision support system for complex, incompletely defined problems. IEEE Trans. Syst. Man Cybern. **20**(4), 745–757 (1990). https://doi.org/10.1109/21.105076
4. Behymer, K.J., Mersch, E.M., Ruff, H.A., Calhoun, G.L., Spriggs, S.E.: Unmanned vehicle plan comparison visualizations for effective human-autonomy teaming. Proc. Manuf. **3**, 1022–1029 (2015). https://doi.org/10.1016/j.promfg.2015.07.162
5. Behymer, K., Ruff, H., Calhoun, G., Bartik, J., Frost, E.: Presentation of autonomy-generated plans: determining ideal number and extent differ. In: Chen, J. (ed.) AHFE 2018. AISC, vol. 784, pp. 90–101. Springer, Cham (2019). https://doi.org/10.1007/978-3-319-94346-6_9

# Using HMD for Immersive Training of Voice-Based Operation of Small Unmanned Ground Vehicles

Daniel W. Carruth[1]([&#9993;]) [iD], Christopher R. Hudson[1] [iD], Cindy L. Bethel[1] [iD], Matus Pleva[2] [iD], Stanislav Ondas[2] [iD], and Jozef Juhar[2] [iD]

[1] Mississippi State University, Starkville, MS 39759, USA
{dwc2,chudson}@cavs.msstate.edu, cbethel@cse.msstate.edu
[2] Technical University of Kosice, Letna 9, 042 00 Kosice, Slovakia
{matus.pleva,stanislav.ondas,jozef.juhar}@tuke.sk
http://www.cavs.msstate.edu/, http://www.kemt.fei.tuke.sk/

**Abstract.** Voice recognition systems provide a method of hands-free control of robotic systems that may be helpful in law enforcement or military domains. However, the constraints of the operational environment limit the capabilities of the on-board voice recognition system to a keyword-based command system. To effectively use the system, the users must learn the available commands and practice pronunciation to ensure accurate recognition. Virtual reality simulation provides users the opportunity to train with the voice recognition system and the robot platform in realistic interactive scenarios. Training using virtual reality with a head-mounted display may increase immersion and sense of presence compared to using a keyboard and monitor. A small pilot study compared user experience in the desktop mode and the virtual reality mode of our voice recognition system training tool. Participants controlled a simulated unmanned ground vehicle in two different modes across four different environments. The results revealed no significant differences in simulator sickness, sense of presence, or perceived usability. However, when asked to choose between the desktop mode and the head-mounted display mode, results indicate users' overall preference for the head-mounted display. However, the users also perceive the head-mounted display to be more complex, less consistent, and more difficult to learn to use. The desktop mode was perceived as easier to use and users reported being more confident when using it.

**Keywords:** Virtual reality · Usability · Human-robot interaction · Speech recognition

Supported by the Center for Advanced Vehicular Systems, Mississippi State University and by the Slovak Research and Development Agency - APVV-15-0731, APVV-SK-TW-2017-0005, Ministry of Education, Science, Research and Sport of the Slovak Republic under the research project VEGA 1/0511/17 and by Cultural and Educational Grant Agency of the Slovak Republic, grant No. 009TUKE-4/2019.

J. Y. C. Chen and G. Fragomeni (Eds.): HCII 2019, LNCS 11575, pp. 34–46, 2019.
https://doi.org/10.1007/978-3-030-21565-1_3

# 1   Introduction

Voice recognition systems provide a powerful potential method of control for robotic systems. In law enforcement, communication between team members is verbal and gestural. By providing a verbal interface for a small unmanned ground vehicle (sUGV) for special weapons and tactics (SWAT) operations, team members can operate the sUGV hands-free and maintain situation awareness [1]. However, the constraints of the operational environment limit the network connectivity and on-board computational power available to the voice recognition system and thereby limit its capabilities to a keyword-based command system. In the keyword-based command system, the officers must learn the available commands and how to pronounce them to ensure proper recognition. Then, the officers must accurately recall the commands and say them correctly in highly stressful and dynamic situations. In an early test of our voice recognition system, officers failed to recall the commands [1]. To address recall failures and to assist with recognizable pronunciation of commands, we developed training tools that allowed officers to practice issuing verbal commands to the voice recognition system [2,3]. Our most recent virtual environment training tool includes an operating environment, a simulated sUGV, and supports both virtual reality and desktop computer-based training [3].

Virtual reality provides a more immersive training environment that increases engagement and retention [4,5]. However, VR requires users to wear a head-mounted display, isolate themselves from their surroundings, and set aside time dedicated to VR training. The desktop training system has lower computational requirements, requires less start-up time, and better supports drop-in/drop-out training. It is not known whether the benefits of VR training outweigh the limitations.

# 2   Related Work

Virtual reality using head-mounted displays is an emerging technology with many potential applications [5–10]. The most recent generation of VR HMDs has made significant progress in addressing technological issues that have previously limited adoption of the technology. Improved tracking, reduced latency, high resolution displays, and advanced graphics capability have converged to provide powerful, immersive simulations. The technology is not only effective for gaming or data visualization. The technology has been rapidly adopted for education and training by the military, industry, and sports [4,8]. VR training can increase retention of knowledge and improve task performance.

Despite its advantages, there are drawbacks to VR HMDs that may limit use of the technology. HMDs can cause user discomfort in many forms: eyestrain, heat, neck and head pain, fatigue, and simulator sickness [11–15]. Many of the advances in HMD technology have helped to address factors known to contribute to simulator sickness: low frame rates, low quality displays, high latency, poor tracking. However, movement through virtual spaces can lead to simulator sickness and there is no solution available that fully addresses the issue. Often, the user has limited space to move either because of the limitations of the physical space (room size, obstacles) or because of the limitations of the VR system. Many of the methods that allow the user to move through a virtual space larger than the physical space will contribute to simulator sickness [15,16]. Steering movement, with a joystick in VR and/or with a keyboard and mouse in games, often leads to simulator sickness in VR [14]. Some methods, like teleportation or portaling [17–19], modify how the user moves through space. Some methods apply visual effects to reduce simulator sickness [20,21]. Others use physical motions to drive virtual motions and provide physical cues to the user's sensory system [22,23]. Another popular technique, redirected walking, takes advantage of control of all visual inputs to the user and manipulates the user into walking in circles while believing they are walking straight [24]. The different methods available each have strengths and weaknesses that may depend on the context and the tasks to be performed in the virtual environment.

VR HMDs are also not always convenient. The HMD is not an integral part of the computer. It is an optional add-on purchased for special applications. Typically, a user will use a keyboard and monitor for most tasks and then start their specific VR application, wear the HMD, and then interact with the virtual environment. In the VR HMD, the user is often blind to the outside environment and may have difficulty communicating with those in their physical space [25]. For any task outside of the specific application, the user may have to remove the HMD, perform the task with the keyboard and mouse, put the HMD back on, and return to the VR application. This switching cost may also reduce the perceived usability of a VR training tool or application.

The differences in VR and desktop modes for training and learning have been previously explored by many researchers, but the results have been inconsistent. In some cases, there is no difference found in quantitative assessments, but participants self-report special benefits (improved spatial insights, more realistic) and increased difficulties in the VR mode [26]. Others show only slight improvements for VR in quantitative metrics [27]. In a navigation task, users reportedly prefer the VR mode but measures of performance are better in a desktop mode [28]. These results suggest that the strengths of VR may be offset by the weaknesses associated with VR. The advantages of VR may be context dependent and limited to benefits in specific aspects of the training task.

The current study compares VR and desktop modes for a training tool to evaluate potential differences in simulator sickness, sense of presence, usability, and user preferences for the two modes.

## 3   Apparatus

We developed the desktop and VR training tool using Unity 2017. The tool was designed to provide more realistic and immersive training with the voice recognition system. In the training tool, participants were directed to search virtual environments for boxes containing contraband (e.g., drugs) and find and disarm a small bomb. Participants interacted with the simulation in VR using an HMD and on a desktop system using a standard display.

## 3.1 Robot and Environment

We imported a virtual sUGV model based on Dr. Robot's Jaguar V4 Mobile Robotic Platform [29]. A physical robot of the same design is used in our laboratory and in training activities with local law enforcement officers. Four virtual environments were used in the study. We acquired two complete virtual environments from the Unity Asset Store: a desert city environment [30] and a shooting range [31]. We developed two additional environments for the project: a school environment consisting of a single hallway lined with lockers and two classrooms and an office space with three rows of cubicle desks. See Fig. 1 for top-down renderings of the four virtual environments.

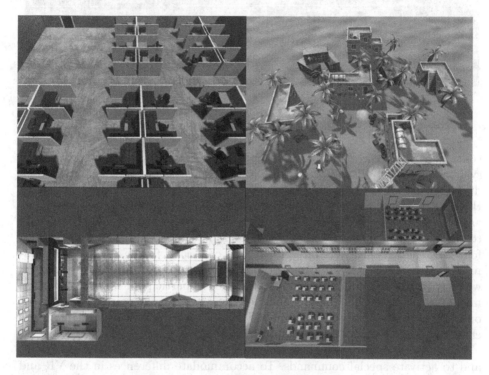

**Fig. 1.** Renderings of the four virtual environments used in the study: desert city, shooting range, school, and offices.

For this study, participants were told to search for boxes of contraband and a bomb (see Fig. 2). We placed two boxes of contraband and a single bomb in each of the environments. In each environment, the items were placed in two configurations: one for the VR mode and one for the desktop mode.

## 3.2 Command and Control

The basic functions of the robot (move forward, backward, turn left, turn right, activate lights, activate sirens, etc.) were implemented using both physical

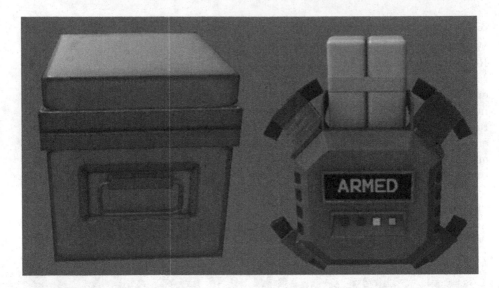

**Fig. 2.** Renderings of the contraband box (left) and bomb (right).

controls and voice commands. Participants used voice commands to activate systems on the robot. Table 1 lists the voice commands available to participants during the study. In the study, participants used a 'push-to-confirm' model. In this model, the recognizer was always running and attempting to interpret utterances made by the participant. Participants used a keyword, 'Apple', to indicate to the recognizer that a command was being issued to the robot. The word(s) following the keyword were interpreted as a command to the robot. If no command was recognized in an utterance, the utterance was ignored. If a command was recognized, the command was displayed to the participant via the voice command user interface. The participant then must confirm the voice command and only then will the action be performed. The 'push-to-confirm' model reduced the chances of an accidental activation of one of the robot systems.

Participants used physical controls to select menu items, to drive the robot, and to activate special commands. To accommodate differences in the VR and desktop systems, controls were varied slightly between the two modes.

In VR, participants wore the HMD (Oculus Rift virtual reality headset) and held two controllers (Oculus Touch controllers). Participants used the built-in microphone on the HMD to issue voice commands. Three Oculus cameras were used to provide full 360-degree tracking of the participants. Participants selected menu commands by pointing at the menu items and pressing the left controller joystick. Once in the environment, participants directed movement of the robot using a joystick on the controller held in their left hand. Locomotion in VR could lead to simulator sickness. However, the study environments are large and include multiple rooms. For this study, we chose to use a common method of movement in VR: teleportation. Participants press down on the right controller's joystick,

**Table 1.** Voice commands available to participants.

| Voice commands | Action performed |
|---|---|
| Apple Off | Turn off all lights |
| Apple Front On | Turn on spotlight |
| Apple Front Off | Turn off spotlight |
| Apple Siren | Activates a repeating alarm |
| Apple Quiet | Deactivates all active sounds |
| Apple Photo | Take a photo of area in front of the robot |
| Apple Scan | Perform a scan for contraband or a bomb (2m radius) |
| Apple Disarm | If a bomb is nearby, disarm the bomb |

point to where they want to move to, and release the joystick. Upon release, the participant's camera is instantly re-positioned above the target position. This method allows participants to control their view and minimizes simulator sickness. At times, the robot could become stuck in the environment. Participants could reset the robot position by pressing and holding the right controller's grip button.

In the desktop mode, participants used a keyboard and touchpad for the physical controls. Participants wore a headset microphone (Logitech Wireless Gaming Headset G930) to issue voice commands and used the touchpad only at the start of a scenario to make their selections from menus. They directed the movements of the robot using the 'W-A-S-D' keys, a common configuration for gaming. A significant difference from the VR environments was that the participant's point of view was always locked to the robot's position. Participants could select between two views: a first-person view as if they were viewing the scene through the robot's camera and a third-person view as if they were viewing from a chase camera just behind and above the robot. Participant's used the 'Z' key to switch between the views. On the desktop system, participants reset the robot using the 'R' key (Table 2).

**Table 2.** Physical controls.

| VR Control | Desktop control | Action performed |
|---|---|---|
| Left Joystick Press | Tap Left Touchpad | Select Menu Item |
| Left Joystick Up | 'W' Key Press | Robot Drive Forward |
| Left Joystick Up | 'A' Key Press | Robot Rotate Left |
| Left Joystick Up | 'S' Key Press | Robot Rotate Right |
| Left Joystick Up | 'D' Key Press | Robot Drive Backward |
| Right Joystick Press | – | Select and Move to Location (VR) |
| Right Joystick 'A' Button | 'Enter' Key Press | Confirm Voice Command |
| Right Joystick Grip | 'R' Key Press | Reset Robot Position |
| – | 'Z' Key Press | Switch Camera View (Desktop) |

# 4    Method

## 4.1    Participants

Participants were recruited from the general population in and around Starkville, MS. Five participants completed the preliminary study (3 men, 2 women). The average age of participants was 27.4 (SD: 7.16). All of the participants reported familiarity with virtual reality and reported at least some experience playing video games (80% sometimes play and 20% often play). Two participants wore corrective lenses. With regard to frequency of simulation or motion sickness, 1 reported that it occurred often, 2 sometimes, and 2 never.

## 4.2    Procedure

All procedures were reviewed and approved by the Mississippi State University Institutional Review Board. We observed participants as they completed training in both environments (desktop and VR) to evaluate user preferences and usability of VR training compared to desktop training for learning voice controls for a sUGV in a law enforcement domain.

Participants completed a short demographics survey and an initial simulator sickness questionnaire (SSQ) [15]. The initial SSQ score provided a baseline score for comparison. Participants were randomly assigned to start with the VR mode or the desktop mode. Participants opened the training tool using a shortcut on the desktop. In VR mode, participants put on the HMD and picked up the controllers. In desktop mode, participants put on the headset microphone. In both the VR mode and desktop mode, participants began by completing an unscored trial in the desert city environment to familiarize themselves with the display and the controls used in the current mode. The remaining three environments were presented in random order. In each trial, participants searched the environment for two boxes of contraband and a single bomb. We instructed participants to perform the following tasks: (1) find the items, (2) use the robot's 'scan' function to verify that the object was contraband or a bomb, (3) take a photo using the robot's 'photo' function, and (4) in the case of a bomb, use the robot's 'disarm' command to disable the bomb. We further instructed participants that the highest priority was to find and disarm the bomb. Participants were given up to eight (8) minutes to search the environment. When participants disarmed the bomb, the trial ended, whether they had discovered the contraband boxes or not.

After each trial, participants removed the HMD or the headset microphone and completely closed the training tool application. Participants then completed a SSQ and a system usability survey (SUS) [32]. After completing all four trials in VR mode or desktop mode, participants completed a 30-question presence survey [33, 34] then switched to the other mode. After completing all trials for both modes, participants were asked to indicate their preferred mode: VR, desktop, or both on 10 usability items (adapted from the SUS) [32].

# 5  Results

Survey data was collected on-site using a Qualtrics web-based survey. Overall, the results revealed no significant differences between the desktop and HMD modes for simulator sickness, sense of presence, or perceived usability. When participants were asked to choose between the desktop mode and the HMD mode, results indicated that, overall, participants preferred the head-mounted display. However, participants also reported that the head-mounted display was more complex, less consistent, and more difficult to learn to use. The desktop mode was perceived as easier to use and participants reported being more confident when using it.

## 5.1  Simulator Sickness

The SSQ consists of 16 items that describe symptoms associated with simulator sickness (e.g., headache, eyestrain, etc) [15]. Participants responded by indicating their current feelings with respect to the symptoms with possible responses including None (0), Slight (1), Moderate (2), and Severe (3). We calculated the total simulator sickness score according to [15] for each trial. The average and maximum total score for the VR and desktop are listed in Table 3. There was no significant difference in simulator sickness symptoms between baseline, VR mode, and desktop mode, $F(2,8) = .942$, $p = .48$.

**Table 3.** Descriptive statistics for SSQ for baseline, VR, and Desktop

| Condition | $M$ | $SD$ | Min | Max |
|---|---|---|---|---|
| Baseline | 4.49 | 4.88 | 0.0 | 11.22 |
| VR | 5.24 | 7.76 | 0.0 | 18.70 |
| Desktop | 0.75 | 1.67 | 0.0 | 3.74 |

## 5.2  Presence

The presence survey consisted of 30 items that taken together attempt to assess the level of immersion in the virtual environment. Our survey was based on [33] with two questions related to haptic interaction removed. A presence survey was completed at the completion of the VR mode trials and the desktop mode trials. Table 4 lists descriptive statistics for the presence survey. As with the SSQ, there was no significant difference between the VR and desktop modes.

Table 4. Descriptive statistics for Presence for VR and Desktop

| Condition | M | SD | Min | Max |
|---|---|---|---|---|
| VR | 162.2 | 20.28 | 133.0 | 186.0 |
| Desktop | 151.2 | 15.83 | 130.0 | 169.0 |

## 5.3   Usability

Participants were asked about usability of the VR mode and the desktop mode in two different ways: First, participants completed the SUS [32] after each trial. Second, after all trials were completed, participants were asked to select their preferred mode for 10 items based on the SUS items. The SUS is a 10-item survey designed to evaluate the usability of a system. We scored the SUS for each trial and then combined the VR and desktop scores to compare the overall means. As with the SSQ results, there was not a significant difference between the mean reported usability for the VR and desktop systems, $t(4) = -1.793$, $p = .147$. In Table 5, there did appear to be a large difference in minimum reported usability. In our preliminary data set, there was a single outlier participant that particularly disliked the VR system ($M = 11.67$ SUS) but appeared to find the desktop more usable ($M = 31.67$ SUS). This is the only participant with a large difference in SUS scores for the two modes. This difference also was only observed for SUS; there was not a large difference in participant's SSQ and presence results for the two modes. For all other participants, the mean SUS for VR and desktop were roughly the same.

Table 5. Descriptive statistics for SUS for VR and Desktop

| Condition | M | SD | Min | Max |
|---|---|---|---|---|
| VR | 64.5 | 32.46 | 11.67 | 100.0 |
| Desktop | 72.5 | 25.52 | 31.67 | 97.5 |

After completing all trials, participants were asked a series of questions based on the SUS items. For each of the 10 items, participants chose between the VR mode, the desktop mode, or both. Table 6 lists the item text and the proportion of responses for each item.

## 6   Discussion

This preliminary study revealed clear differences in user perception of the VR and desktop modes of the training tool. Both modes of training (VR and desktop) showed no signs of simulator sickness despite requiring participants to explore four separate scenarios, each one lasting up to 8 min. Neither virtual environment

**Table 6.** User selections for usability items.

| Item | VR | Desktop | Both |
|---|---|---|---|
| Which system would you prefer to use frequently? | 40% | 20% | 40% |
| Which system was more complex? | 100% | 0% | 0% |
| Which system was the easiest to use? | 20% | 80% | 0% |
| Which system would require more support for you to use? | 80% | 0% | 20% |
| Which system's functions were most well integrated? | 20% | 40% | 40% |
| Which system was more inconsistent? | 60% | 20% | 20% |
| Which system would most people learn to use quickly? | 0% | 40% | 60% |
| Which system was more cumbersome to use? | 40% | 20% | 40% |
| Which system were you most confident in using? | 20% | 80% | 0% |
| Which system required you to learn the most before you could use it? | 80% | 0% | 20% |

imparted any significant symptoms of simulator sickness to the participants and was likely not a factor in their perceived usability of the system.

When comparing the VR and desktop versions, the majority of participants preferred to use VR or both systems. Only one participant preferred only the desktop version. The increased complexity of the VR mode reported by participants was likely due to the added complexity of the navigation system used by the participant to move in the VR environment. VR was also perceived to be inconsistent and to be poorly integrated into the system. Again, the added complexity of the movement system in VR likely contributed to this perception. In addition, the mapping of actions to controller buttons could also be improved. There was some inconsistency in use of the joystick button for menu selection (push button + pull trigger) and for movement (push button + release button). This may also have contributed to perception of complexity in the VR mode.

The increased complexity of the VR training tool likely contributed to the increase in the participants expectation that additional support and learning would be required to use the VR system for training. The combination of these factors likely contributed to the overall sense that, in comparison to the VR training, the desktop mode was perceived as easier to use and imparted a higher sense of overall user confidence.

Overall, the users were able to use both modes to interact with the voice recognition system and the training tool appears to have potential regardless of which mode users prefer.

## 7   Conclusions and Future Work

This small pilot study compared participant experience in two modes: VR and desktop. We believed that the VR mode would provide additional immersion and sense of presence to participants but would also be more difficult to use and could cause participants to suffer symptoms of simulator sickness. Participants' responses indicated that the two modes provided similar sense of presence and usability. When asked to select between the systems, participants' responses indicated a preference for the VR mode but also identified challenges that may limit use of the VR mode. Overall, the training tool scored well on usability. Future work should expand the sample size. The single participant that reported a poor experience could be a true outlier or could represent a minority group that would strongly prefer the desktop mode. Future research should also evaluate participant performance with the voice recognition system, progress throughout training, and long-term retention and transfer from the training tool to the real world.

# References

1. Pleva, M., Juhar, J., Cizmar, A., Hudson, C., Carruth, D., Bethel, C.: Implementing English speech interface to Jaguar robot for SWAT training. In: IEEE 15th International Symposium on Applied Machine Intelligence and Informatics (SAMI), Herl'any, Slovakia, pp. 105–110. IEEE (2017)
2. Hudson, C.R., Carruth, D.W., Bethel, C., Pleva, M., Juhar, J., Ondas, S.: A training tool for speech driven human-robot interaction applications. In: 15th International Conference on Emerging eLearning Technologies and Applications (ICETA), Stary Smokovec, Slovakia, pp. 1–6. IEEE (2017)
3. Hudson, C.R., Bethel, C.L., Carruth, D.W., Pleva, M., Ondas, S., Juhar, J.: Implementation of a speech enabled virtual reality training tool for human-robot interaction. In: 2018 World Symposium on Digital Intelligence for Systems and Machines (DISA), Kosice, Slovakia, pp. 309–314, IEEE (2018)
4. Bailenson, J.: Experience on Demand: What Virtual Reality is, How it Works, and What it Can Do. W. W. Norton & Company, New York (2018)
5. Stratos, A., Loukas, R., Dimitris, M., Konstantinos, G., Dimitris, M., Chryssolouris, G.: A virtual reality application to attract young talents to manufacturing. Proc. CIRP **57**, 134–139 (2016)
6. Bout, M., Brenden, A. P., Klingegård, M., Habibovic, A., Böckle, M.-P.: A head-mounted display to support teleoperations of shared automated vehicles. In: 9th International Conference on Automotive User Interfaces and Interactive Vehicular Applications Adjunct, pp. 62–66, ACM, New York (2017)
7. Feeman, S.M., Wright, L.B., Salmon, J.L.: Exploration and evaluation of CAD modeling in virtual reality. Comput.-Aided Des. Appl. **15**(6), 892–904 (2018)
8. Feloni, R.: Walmart is using virtual reality to train its employees. http://www.businessinsider.com/walmart-usingvirtual-reality-employee-training-2017-6. Accessed 6 Apr 2018
9. Jensen, L., Konradsen, F.: A review of the use of virtual reality head-mounted displays in education and training. Educ. Inf. Technol. **23**(4), 1515–1529 (2018)
10. Clifford, R.M.S., Khan, H., Hoermann, S., Billinghurst, M., Lindeman, R.W.: The effect of immersive displays on situation awareness in virtual environments for aerial firefighting air attack supervisor training. In: 2018 IEEE Conference on Virtual Reality and 3D User Interfaces (VR), pp. 1–2, IEEE (2018)
11. Souchet, A. D., Philippe, S., Zobel, D., Ober, F., Lévêque, A., Leroy, L.: Eyestrain impacts on learning job interview with a serious game in virtual reality: a randomized double-blinded study. In: 24th ACM Symposium on Virtual Reality Software and Technology, pp. 15:1–15:12, ACM, New York (2018)
12. Wang, Z., Chen, K., He, R.: Study on thermal comfort of virtual reality headsets. In: Ahram, T. (ed.) AHFE 2018. Advances in Intelligent Systems and Computing, vol. 795, pp. 180–186. Springer, Cham (2019). https://doi.org/10.1007/978-3-319-94619-1_17

13. Sharples, S., Cobb, S., Moody, A., Wilson, J.R.: Virtual reality induced symptoms and effects (VRISE): comparison of head mounted display (HMD), desktop and projection display systems. Displays **29**(2), 58–69 (2008)
14. McCauley, M.E., Sharkey, T.J.: Cybersickness: perception of self-motion in virtual environments. Presence: Teleoper. Virtual Environ. **1**(3), 311–318 (1992)
15. Kennedy, R.S., Lane, N.E., Berbaum, K.S., Lilienthal, M.G.: Simulator sickness questionnaire: an enhanced method for quantifying simulator sickness. Int. J. Aviat. Psychol. **3**(3), 203–220 (1993)
16. So, R.H., Lo, W.T., Ho, A.T.: Effects of navigation speed on motion sickness caused by an immersive virtual environment. Hum. Factors **43**(3), 452–461 (2001)
17. Bozgeyikli, E., Raij, A., Katkoori, S., Dubey, R.: Point & teleport locomotion technique for virtual reality. In: 2016 Annual Symposium on Computer-Human Interaction in Play, pp. 205–216, Austin, Texas, USA (2016)
18. Weißker, T., Kunert, A., Fröhlich, B., Kulik, A.: Spatial updating and simulator sickness during steering and jumping in immersive virtual environments. In: IEEE Conference on Virtual Reality and 3D User Interfaces (VR), pp. 97–104 (2018)
19. Smink, K., Carruth, D.W., Swan, W., Davis, E.: A new traversal method for virtual reality: overcoming the drawbacks of commonly accepted methods. In: Human Computer Interaction International, Orlando, FL, USA (2019)
20. Norouzi, N., Bruder, G., Welch, G.: Assessing vignetting as a means to reduce VR sickness during amplified head rotations. In: SAP 2018: ACM Symposium on Applied Perception 2018, p. 8. ACM, Vancouver (2018)
21. Farmani, Y., Teather, R.J.: Viewpoint snapping to reduce cybersickness in virtual reality. In: Graphics Interface, pp. 1–8 (2018)
22. Whitton, M.C., et al.: Comparing VE locomotion interfaces. In: IEEE Virtual Reality 2005, VR 2005, pp. 123–130. IEEE, Bonn (2005)
23. Loup, G., Loup-Escande, E.: Effects of travel modes on performances and user comfort: a comparison between ArmSwinger and teleporting. Int. J. Hum.-Comput. Interact. (2018)
24. Razzaque, S., Kohn, Z., Whitton, M.C.: Redirected walking. In: EUROGRAPHICS 2001 (2001)
25. Chan, L., Minamizawa, K.: FrontFace: facilitating communication between HMD users and outsiders using front-facing-screen HMDs. In: 19th International Conference on Human-Computer Interaction with Mobile Devices and Services, pp. 22:1–22:5. ACM, New York (2017)
26. Greenwald, S.W., Corning, W., Funk, M., Maes, P.: Comparing learning in virtual reality with learning on a 2D screen using electrostatics activities. J. Univ. Comput. Sci. **24**(2), 220–245 (2018)
27. Shu, Y., Huang, Y.-Z., Chang, S.-H., Chen, M.-Y.: Do virtual reality head-mounted displays make a difference? A comparison of presence and self-efficacy between head-mounted displays and desktop computer-facilitated virtual environments. In: Virtual Reality (2018)
28. Sousa Santos, B., et al.: Head-mounted display versus desktop for 3D navigation in virtual reality: a user study. Multimed. Tools Appl. **41**(1), 161–181 (2009)
29. Dr Robot: Jaguar V4 Mobile Robot Platform. http://jaguar.drrobot.com/specification_V4.asp. Accessed 31 Jan 2019
30. Troth, S.: Desert Environment. http://devassets.com/asscts/desert-environment/. Accessed 31 Jan 2019
31. Miguel, J.C.: Shooting Gallery. https://assetstore.unity.com/packages/3d/environ-ments/shooting-gallery-enviroment-pack-105306. Accessed 31 Jan 2019

32. Brooke, J.: SUS: a "quick and dirty" usability scale. In: Jordan, P.W., Thomas, B., Weerdmeester, B.A., McClelland, A.L. (eds.) Usability Evaluation in Industry. Taylor and Francis, London (1996)
33. Witmer, B.G., Jerome, C.J., Singer, M.J.: The factor structure of the presence questionnaire. Presence: Teleoper. Virtual Environ. **14**(3), 298–312 (2005)
34. Witmer, B.G., Singer, M.J.: Measuring presence in virtual environments: a presence questionnaire. Presence: Teleoper. Virtual Environ. **7**(3), 225–240 (1998)

# Scalable Representation Learning for Long-Term Augmented Reality-Based Information Delivery in Collaborative Human-Robot Perception

Fei Han, Sriram Siva, and Hao Zhang$^{(\boxtimes)}$

Human-Centered Robotics Lab, Colorado School of Mines,
1500 Illinois Street, Golden, CO 80401, USA
{fhan,sriramsiva,hzhang}@mines.edu

**Abstract.** Augmented reality (AR)-based information delivery has been attracting an increasing attention in the past few years to improve communication in human-robot teaming. In the long-term use of AR systems for collaborative human-robot perception, one of the biggest challenges is to perform place and scene matching under long-term environmental changes, such as dramatic variations in lighting, weather and vegetation across different times of the day, months, and seasons. To address this challenge, we introduce a novel representation learning approach that learns a scalable long-term representation model that can be used for place and scene matching in various long-term conditions. Our approach is formulated as a regularized optimization problem, which selects the most representative scene templates in different scenarios to construct a scalable representation of the same place that can exhibit significant long-term environment changes. Our approach adaptively learns to select a small subset of the templates to construct the representation model, based on a user-defined representativeness threshold, which makes the learned model highly scalable to the long-term variations in real-world applications. To solve the formulated optimization problem, a new algorithmic solver is designed, which is theoretically guaranteed to converge to the global optima. Experiments are conducted using two large-scale benchmark datasets, which have demonstrated the superior performance of our approach for long-term place and scene matching.

**Keywords:** Collaborative human-robot perception ·
Representation learning · Augmented Reality ·
Long-term information delivery

## 1 Introduction

Augmented Reality (AR) has been attracting an increasing attention in industry and academia, which provides a revolutionary technology to insert virtual objects into the real world through the use of a head-mounted display or a hand-held

© Springer Nature Switzerland AG 2019
J. Y. C. Chen and G. Fragomeni (Eds.): HCII 2019, LNCS 11575, pp. 47–62, 2019.
https://doi.org/10.1007/978-3-030-21565-1_4

mobile device [1,2]. In particular, by overlaying digital information on top of the real scene, AR provides a promising solution to more intuitively and interactively deliver information to humans, which can be applied to improve communications between robots and humans in the critical application of human-robot teaming. For example, such information may include restaurant ratings and descriptions of a building in a city's downtown area, or a tagged damage for further inspection or repair in indoor or underground infrastructure (e.g., power plant boilers, subway tunnels, and pipeline networks), collected by mobile robots and labeled by other teammates. To tether the robot-collected information correctly and stably to reality, the AR system, as a component of communication in human-robot teams, must either estimate the location and orientation of the user, or match the real scene with a database that includes information of the same scene from previous visits. Place and scene matching is especially essential, when human-robot teams work in GPS-denied (e.g., underground infrastructure) and GPS-limited (e.g., a downtown area with tall buildings) areas. With accurate matches of the current scene with previous scenes in the database, labels associated with previous scenes can be displayed over the current scene (Fig. 1).

Scenes and labels collected by robots                    Currently observed scene

**Fig. 1.** A motivating example of long-term place and scene matching for long-term AR-based information delivery in collaborative human-robot perception applications. Due to long-term environment changes such as weather, lighting, and vegetation variations, the current scene observed by a camera of AR systems may look significantly different from stored scenes of the same place collected previously by robots.

One biggest challenge of matching a currently observed scene and place with previous scenes is to address long-term changes of the environment during long-term use of an AR system. Occlusion and viewpoint differences are typical problems in conventional scene matching problems. Besides those, the long-term scene and place matching problem is even more challenging since the AR system needs to operate in various scenarios. The appearance of the same place can drastically change in different times of the day, months and seasons. Many factors can cause the appearance changes, for example, lightening changes, weather changes, and vegetation condition changes. In addition, multiple places could have a similar appearance (e.g., two chain stores in Colorado and California may look similarly), which is usually called perceptual aliasing. It is another challenge that makes the long-term scene and place matching problem hard for AR-based information delivery in collaborative human-robot perception applications.

Due to its importance, several approaches on the long-term scene and place matching were investigated, mainly by researchers from robotics and computer vision communities [3–5], for example, to perform camera localization and loop closure detection for simultaneous localization and mapping (SLAM) [6–9]. Many previous techniques formulate long-term scene and place matching into an image-vs-image matching problem using either local features or global features. Typical local features used in long-term scene matching include SIFT [10], SURF [11], ORB [12], while HOG [13], GIST [14], and CNN [15] are widely used global features. However, scene and place matchings based upon single images cannot address perceptual aliasing well. As an improved paradigm, sequence-vs-sequence matching was demonstrated to have better performance to address perceptual aliasing, by introducing additional temporal and spatial information of scenes and places [16,17]. However, image-vs-image and sequence-vs-sequence matchings cannot incorporate the rich information recorded from different scenarios. The methods only compare the currently query scene with *one and only one* existing template acquired from a specific scenario in the database.

In this paper, we propose a novel approach of learning a scalable long-term representation model that adaptively integrates information extracted from multiple environmental conditions to improve encoding power of long-term perceptual variations in order to enable scene matching for long-term use of AR systems. Given its advantage, we refer to the approach as *Learning Of Representation with Scalability* (LORS). Formulated as a regularized optimization problem, LORS learns the representativeness of multiple scene templates (instead of only one template as in conventional methods) recorded in multiple scenarios of the each place. Then LORS adaptively selects the most representative subset of templates to build the representation model for that place, which incorporates representative place information in different scenarios, as shown in Fig. 2. Since LORS is capable of selecting a small subset of the most representative templates, it scales well to large-scale real-world AR applications when identifying a big number of places from observations collected from a big number of long-term scenarios.

The contributions of this research are twofold:

- We propose the novel LORS approach to learn a representation model that adaptively integrates a set of sequence templates extracted under multiple environmental scenarios, which provides a comprehensive representation of long-term perceptual variations for more robust place and scene in long-term use of AR systems. The existing scene matching methods based upon single images and sequences are special cases of the proposed LORS method.
- We introduce a novel formulation to construct the representation model under the general regularized optimization framework, in order to select only a small number of most representative templates, which makes it applicable to large-scale long-term AR-based information delivery in collaborative human-robot

perception applications. A new optimization solver is also implemented to address the formulated problem with a convergence guarantee.

The remainder of the paper is organized as follows. In Sect. 2, we discuss our LORS approach in detail. In Sect. 3, experimental results are presented. Finally, we conclude our paper in Sect. 4.

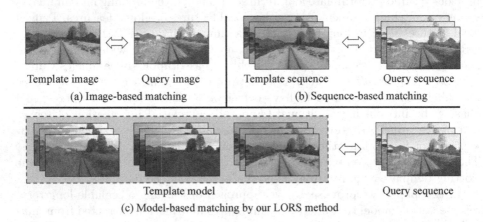

Fig. 2. Overview of the proposed LORS approach to learn an representation model for each place that integrates multiple sequence scene templates extracted in various environmental conditions for long-term AR-based information delivery. Our representation model is constructed by adaptively selecting a small number of the most representative sequence templates. LORS is more general and representative than the previous image-based (Fig. (a)) and sequence-based (Fig. (b)) matching techniques that only use one and only one template to match with the query observation. In addition, LORS is scalable in real-world long-term autonomy applications due to its adaptive, representative sequence selection capability.

## 2    LORS for Long-Term Scene and Place Matching

In this section, we introduce our novel LORS approach to learn the representation model for each place, which is adaptively constructed by representative templates recorded in different scenarios in a long period of time. We formulate the problem into a novel optimization problem with structured sparsity regularization. In addition, we also developed a new optimization algorithm to solve the formulated non-smooth optimization problem, with the theoretical convergence guarantee.

Notations in this paper follow the following standards: Vectors are denoted as boldface lowercase letters, while matrices use boldface capital letters. For a given matrix $\mathbf{M} = \{m_{ij}\} \in \mathbb{R}^{n \times m}$, its $i$-th row and $j$-th column are referred as $\mathbf{m}^i$ and $\mathbf{m}_j$, respectively. The $\ell_1$-norm of a vector $\mathbf{v} \in \mathbb{R}^n$ is defined as $\|\mathbf{v}\|_1 = \sum_{i=1}^n |v_i|$, and the $\ell_2$-norm of $\mathbf{v}$ is defined as $\|\mathbf{v}\|_2 = \sqrt{\mathbf{v}^\top \mathbf{v}}$. The $\ell_{2,1}$-norm of the matrix $\mathbf{M}$ is defined as: $\|\mathbf{M}\|_{2,1} = \sum_{i=1}^{n} \sqrt{\sum_{j=1}^{m} m_{ij}^2} = \sum_{i=1}^{n} \|\mathbf{m}^i\|_2$, and the Frobenius norm is defined as $\|\mathbf{M}\|_F = \sqrt{\sum_{i=1}^{m} \sum_{j=1}^{n} m_{ij}^2}$.

## 2.1   Problem Formulation

To solve the critical long-term place and scene matching problem, a sequence of frames are collected to represent the place in different scenarios (e.g., different times of the day, months, or seasons). For a specific place $p$, the feature vectors extracted from the sequential frames in different scenarios are represented as $\mathbf{X}(p) = [\mathbf{x}_1(p), \cdots, \mathbf{x}_s(p)] \in \mathbb{R}^{d \times s}$, where $\mathbf{x}_i(p) = \left[ (\mathbf{x}_i^1(p))^\top, \cdots, (\mathbf{x}_i^f(p))^\top \right]^\top \in \mathbb{R}^{d \times 1}$ is a concatenated feature vector of $f$ images in scenario $i$, and the feature length for each image $\mathbf{x}_i^j(p), j = 1, \cdots, f$ is $d^j$ satisfying $d = \sum_{j=1}^{f} d^j$. $s$ denotes the number of scenarios in the long-term span.

Though sequences of the same place in different $s$ scenarios are recorded for the representation, it is obvious that not all of them are unique and representative. For example, the sequences captured when passing through a tunnel in summer and winter can be largely identical, though it is not true for those on open roads. We are interested in seeking representative sequences that can represent the place in various scenarios in a long period. According to the formulation above, we are trying to select $r(r \leq s)$ template sequences that are most representative in long-term for each place $p$, respectively, which can be formulated to solve:

$$\min_{\mathbf{W}(p)} \|\mathbf{X}(p)\mathbf{W}(p) - \mathbf{X}(p)\|_F^2 + \lambda \|\mathbf{W}(p)\|_{2,1}, p = 1, \cdots, c \qquad (1)$$

where $\mathbf{W}(p) = [\mathbf{w}_1(p), \cdots, \mathbf{w}_s(p)] \in \mathbb{R}^{s \times s}$, and $\mathbf{w}_i(p)$ is the weight of the sequence template candidates to represent the $i$-th candidate ($i$-th column) in $\mathbf{X}(p)$. The $\ell_{2,1}$-norm based regularization enforces the sparsity among all sequence template candidates, which means only part of representative sequences are selected to represent all other sequences. $c$ is the total number of places to be distinguished. There is a specific weight matrix $\mathbf{W}(p)$ for place $p$. For simplicity, we omit $p$ in $\mathbf{X}(p)$ and $\mathbf{W}(p)$ as $\mathbf{X}$ and $\mathbf{W}$ in the following presentation, respectively.

After solving Eq. (1), the rows $\mathbf{w}^i, i = 1, \cdots, s$ are sorted by the value of $\|\mathbf{w}^i\|_1$ in decreasing order, and the resulted row-sorted matrix $\mathbf{W}'$ is obtained. Then, our LORS model enables to adaptively select the most representative sequence templates. This encodes our *insight* that the number of templates in the model should vary according to the degree of the appearance variation of a specific place. For example, a place inside a tunnel requires fewer sequence templates as the appearance does not show significant long-term variations (e.g., it is not affected by snow or sunshine); on the other hand, places on the road in an open area require more templates to represent long-term changes in different times of a day and seasons. Given $\mathbf{W}'$, our model determines the minimum value of $r$ that satisfies $\frac{1}{s}\sum_{i=1}^{r}\|\mathbf{w}'^{i}\|_1 \geq \gamma$. Then, the $r$ sequence template candidates (columns of $\mathbf{X}$) are selected corresponding to the top $r$ rows of $\mathbf{W}'$, where $\gamma$ is a threshold encoding the expected overall representativeness of the selected sequence template candidates, called the *representativeness threshold*. By this mechanism, not all captured sequences will be treated as the sequence templates, which makes our model highly scalable in real-world applications while still keeps the representativeness among different places and the robustness under different environmental conditions.

Intuitively, when there are no appearance changes during the long-term navigation period, only one sequence template candidate will obtain a high row-sum value (Others have a value close to 0 due to the sparsity effect by the $\ell_{2,1}$-norm regularization), which will be selected as the single template for this place. On the other hand, when the place experiences significant appearance variations, no single sequence template candidate can well represent others. In this case, the rows of $\mathbf{W}$ will become much less sparse and a set of sequence templates can have a high row-sum value, resulting in multiple sequence templates in the top rows of $\mathbf{W}'$ to be selected as templates. Therefore, the proposed LORS model is able to adaptively select a varying number of sequence template candidates based on their different appearance variation degree. Since LORS only requires a subset of templates instead of all, it is highly storage efficient in real-world applications.

Our LORS model is different from the traditional Bag of Words (BoWs) technique. Firstly, the sequence-based representation is applied in our model, which incorporates temporal information while BoWs approaches discard it. Sequence-based scene and place matching has be demonstrated to have better performance than image-based methods [16,18,19]; Secondly, our LORS model enables to select the top representative sequence templates, while BoWs cannot. The LORS mechanism scales well when places are recorded in various scenarios.

## 2.2  Long-Term Scene and Place Matching

The optimal weight matrix $\mathbf{W}^* = \left[(\mathbf{w}^1)^*; \cdots ; (\mathbf{w}^s)^*\right] \in \mathbb{R}^{s \times s}$ can be obtained after solving the optimization problem in Eq. (1) using Algorithm 1, which is detailed in Sect. 2.3. Then, the representative sequence templates $\mathbf{X}^* \in \mathbb{R}^{d \times r}$ for place $p$ are selected according to the corresponding top $r$ rows satisfying $\frac{1}{s}\sum_{i=1}^{r}\|\mathbf{w}^i\|_1 \geq \gamma$.

For long-term scena and place matching in the testing phase, we are given a new query sequence represented by the feature $\mathbf{x}_q \in \mathbb{R}^{d \times 1}$. We then calculate the matching score $\text{score}_{p,i}, p = 1, \cdots , c, i = 1, \cdots , r$ between the query observation sequence and each sequence template $i$ for each place $p$ by feature similarity. Then, the query place $q$ can be identified as

$$q = \underset{p}{\operatorname{argmax}} \, \text{score}_{p,i} \qquad (2)$$

---

**Algorithm 1.** An iterative algorithm to solve the sparse optimization problem in Eq. (1).

---

**Input** : Sequence-based features w.r.t. observations in different scenarios
$\mathbf{X} \in \mathbb{R}^{d \times s}$
**Output:** The weight matrix $\mathbf{W} \in \mathbb{R}^{s \times s}$

1: Let $t = 1$, and initialize $\mathbf{W}(t) \in \mathbb{R}^{s \times s} = \mathrm{argmin}_{\mathbf{W}} \|\mathbf{XW} - \mathbf{X}\|_F^2$;
2: **while** *not converge* **do**
3:     Calculate the diagonal matrix $\mathbf{D}(t + 1)$ with the $i$-th diagonal element as $\frac{1}{2\|\mathbf{w}^i(t)\|_2}$, where $\mathbf{w}^i(t)$ is the $i$-th row of $\mathbf{W}(t)$;
4:     For each $\mathbf{w}_i$ $(1 \le i \le s)$, calculate $\mathbf{w}_i(t+1) = \left(\mathbf{X}^\top\mathbf{X} + \lambda\mathbf{D}(t+1)\right)^{-1}\mathbf{X}^\top\mathbf{x}_i$;
5:     $t = t + 1$.
6: **end**
7: **return** $\mathbf{W} \in \mathbb{R}^{s \times s}$.

---

## 2.3  Optimization Algorithm

The optimization problem in Eq. (1) is convex and can be reformulated and solved as a second-order cone programming (SOCP) or semidefinite programming (SDP) problem. However, solving SOCP or SDP is computationally expensive in general. In this section, we propose an algorithm to solve the formulated optimization in Eq. (1) efficiently with theoretical convergence guarantee.

Taking the derivative of Eq. (1) for each place $p$ with respect to each column of $\mathbf{W}$ and setting it to $\mathbf{0}$, we have

$$\mathbf{X}^\top\mathbf{Xw}_i - \mathbf{X}^\top\mathbf{x}_i + \lambda\mathbf{Dw}_i = \mathbf{0}, \tag{3}$$

where $\mathbf{D}$ is a diagonal matrix with the $i$-th diagonal element as $\frac{1}{2\|\mathbf{w}^i\|_2}$, $i = 1, \cdots, s$.

Therefore, $\mathbf{w}_i$ can be calculated by

$$\mathbf{w}_i = \left(\mathbf{X}^\top\mathbf{X} + \lambda\mathbf{D}\right)^{-1}\mathbf{X}^\top\mathbf{x}_i. \tag{4}$$

It is observed that the matrix $\mathbf{D}$ in Eq. (4) depends on the weight matrix $\mathbf{W}$, which is also unknown. In order to solve this problem, an iterative solver is presented in Algorithm 1. Algorithm 1 can be proved to guarantee the theoretical convergence to the global optima.

## 3  Experiments

To evaluate the performance of our LORS approach, we conducted experiments on two public benchmark datasets: CMU-VL dataset and Nordland dataset. Our prior work [5] has shown that HOG descriptors can achieve significant performance in comparison to other descriptors (e.g. color, CNN, GIST, etc.) in these two datasets for long-term scene and place matching. Thus, we select the HOG descriptor for every single frame in both experiments. It aims to ensure that the performance increase results from the proposed LORS approach instead of raw feature engineering. Though the HOG descriptor is selected in our experiments, any descriptor can be used in our LORS approach. In addition, multimodal representations by combining multiple descriptors also work in our LORS approach.

## 3.1   Results over Different Months

The CMU Visual Localization (CMU-VL) dataset [20] is a public benchmark dataset that recorded a 8.8 Km route under a variety of scenarios across different months throughout the entire year. It was recorded by a car with two cameras mounted on the roof of the it and oriented to left and right respectively. GPS data were also measured and recorded to be used as the ground truth of the recorded places. The environmental conditions in the CMU-VL dataset vary a lot across different months of the year (e.g. sunny, snowy, partial cloudy, with green vegetation or reduced colored vegetation, etc.), which makes it very challenging to recognize the same place in such a long period of time. Since multiple recordings of the same route are used to evaluate the proposed LORS method, we have to align them strictly before the experiments. We use the GPS information w.r.t. each frame of different recorded videos to find the same place under different scenarios.

**Fig. 3.** Three example places and their scenes in five different scenarios in the experiment using the CMU-VL dataset.

The scenarios considered in the experiment via the CMU-VL dataset include:

1. Mid September: sunny with abundant green vegetation and vertical shadows
2. Early November: sunny with reduced colored vegetation and fallen leaves
3. Late November: sunny with strong slanted shadows

4. Late December: cloudy with lots of snow on ground
5. Early March: partially cloudy with some shadows

which is also illustrated in Fig. 3. The five videos recorded in these five scenarios respectively are used to train the LORS model. Without loss of generality, a new video recorded in the same first scenario (Mid September) is used as the testing data to evaluate the performance of our proposed LORS method.

The representative templates of each place are obtained during the training phase using the proposed LORS method. After that, the new unseen query observations recorded in Scenario #1 is used to assess the performance. The qualitative evaluation is illustrated in Fig. 4(a), where Fig. 4(a) shows all templates recorded in five different scenarios as illustrated in Fig. 3. Instead of applying all five templates in the testing phase, three representative ones (Scenario #1, 3, and 4, shown in Fig. 4(b)) are identified by our LORS method and are used to represent the place. In the testing phase, the same place has been successfully recognized as shown in Fig. 4(b). The representativeness of each template is quantified in Fig. 4(c), where we can see the templates in Scenario #1, 3 and 4 are three top representative ones for the place when the threshold $\gamma = 40\%$.

We also quantitatively evaluate our LORS method in Fig. 5, where Fig. 5(a) and (b) show the precision-recall curves with respect to different number of templates for place representation and different representativeness threshold in

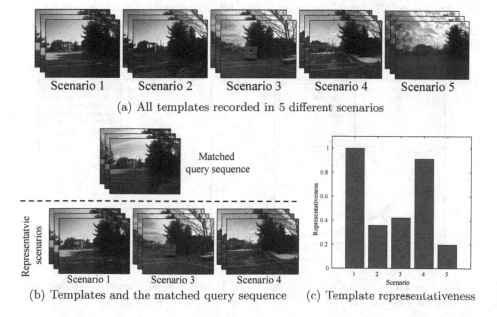

(a) All templates recorded in 5 different scenarios

(b) Templates and the matched query sequence      (c) Template representativeness

**Fig. 4.** Qualitative evaluation of our LORS approach over the CMU-VL dataset across different months.

the LORS method, respectively. From Fig. 5(a) we observe that the best performance is achieved when all 5 templates are used for the place representation, which provides the largest amount of information for each place. Figure 5(a) also shows our LORS method almost has the same performance when the representativeness threshold $\gamma = 20\%$. In addition, our LORS method outperforms other cases when the single template is used for the place representation. Using the single template recorded in Scenario #1 has much better performance than those recorded in Scenario #2, 3, 4 and 5. That is because the query observations in testing are also recorded in Scenario #1, which means it reduces to the 'short-term' place matching problem in this case. On the other hand, the performance is decreased significantly when the training and testing scenarios are inconsistent, showing the poor robustness of the traditional single-scenario-based methods in the long-term scene and place matching problem.

Figure 5(a) demonstrates that incorporating more place information (with more templates) results in better place recognition performance. However, it will require a lot of data storage and suffer from the processing speed. Our LORS method enables to select most representative templates while does not have too much performance decrease. Figure 5(b) and Table 1 further evaluate the LORS performance with respect to different representativeness threshold. Higher representativeness threshold $\gamma$ indicates more templates (templates with representativeness less than $\gamma$) will be discarded for the place representation. From Fig. 5(b) and Table 1, it is observed that the performance (area size below the precision-recall curves) decrease is significantly smaller than the percentage of templates that are discarded, demonstrating the superior place representation capability by our LORS method.

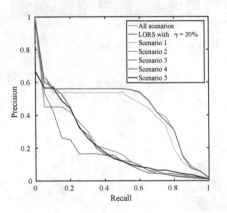
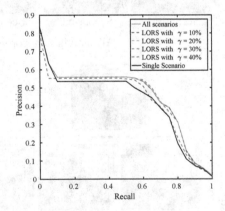

(a) Precision-recall curves computed using different training scenarios

(b) Precision-recall curves computed using varying representativeness threshold

**Fig. 5.** Quantitative evaluation of our LORS approach on the CMU-VL dataset across different months.

**Table 1.** Performance decrease with respect to different degrees of information loss (Representativeness threshold $\gamma$) over the CMU-VL and Nordland dataset.

| Representativeness threshold $\gamma$ | Performance decrease over CMU-VL | Performance decrease over Nordland |
|---|---|---|
| 10% | 0 | 0 |
| 20% | 0.132% | 0 |
| 30% | 0.375% | 0 |
| 40% | 5.05% | 2.05% |
| 50% | 12.5% | 2.22% |
| 60% | 15.6% | 3.29% |

## 3.2 Results over Different Seasons

We also evaluate the performance of LORS via the Nordland dataset. Nordland dataset [4] is another public benchmark dataset that records the scenes recorded by a self-driving train in a ten-hour long trip traveling around 3000 km in Nordland. Visual data in four seasons were recorded and aligned strictly frame by frame in the dataset. The video has a 1920 × 1080 resolution and 25 frames per second (FPS).

There are significant appearance changes in the Nordland dataset, which are caused by various weather, vegetation and illumination conditions in four seasons. For example, there is almost full snow coverage on the ground in winter while with green vegetation in summer. In addition, the journey passes through many wild places with similar appearances, which means the dataset has strong perceptual aliasing problem. All these difficulties make the Nordland one of the most challenging dataset for long-term place and scene matching. In this experiment, the videos are downsampled with 640 × 360 resolution and 5 FPS.

The previous experiment via the CMU-VL dataset demonstrates significant performance of the proposed LORS approach when the testing scenario is the same as the one of the training scenarios, that is, the testing environmental condition is experienced in the training process. On the other hand, we are also interested in the case when the testing scenario is never experienced during training, since there are numerous combinations of environmental conditions in real-world collaborative human-robot perception applications. In this experiment over the Nordland dataset, the videos recorded in Summer, Autumn and Winter are used in the representation model learning by our LORS method, which are shown in Fig. 6, and the video recorded in Spring is used for testing, which is never experienced before.

The representative templates of each place are obtained during the training phase using the proposed LORS method. After that, the new unseen query observations recorded in Spring is used to assess the performance. The qualitative evaluation is illustrated in Fig. 7, where Fig. 7(a) shows all seasonal templates recorded in Summer, Autumn, and Winter. Instead of applying all three templates in the testing phase, two representative ones (Summer and Autumn shown in Fig. 7(b)) are identified by our LORS method and are used to represent the

**Fig. 6.** Three example places and their scenes in three different seasons in the experiment over the Nordland dataset.

place. In the testing phase, the same place has been successfully recognized as shown in Fig. 7(b) though the Spring scenario is never experienced in the training process. The representativeness of each template is quantified in Fig. 7(c), where we can see templates in Summer and Autumn are two top representative ones for the place when the threshold $\gamma = 60\%$.

Similar to the experiment over the CMU-VL dataset, we also quantitatively evaluate our LORS method via the Nordland dataset in Fig. 8, where Fig. 8(a) and (b) show the precision-recall curves with respect to different number of templates for place representation and different representativeness threshold in the LORS method, respectively. From Fig. 8(a) we observe that the best performance is achieved when all 3 seasonal templates are used for the place representation, which provides the largest amount of information for each place. Figure 8(a) also shows our LORS method almost has the same performance when the representativeness threshold $\gamma = 35\%$. In addition, our LORS method outperforms other cases when the single template is used for the place representation, showing the great benefits from multiple template adoption as well as representative template learning even when the environmental condition in testing phase is never experienced before. Different from the previous experiment over the CMU-VL dataset, using the single template recorded in any single season cannot perform well in the long-term scene and place matching (low precision and recall values as shown in Fig. 8(a)). That is because the query observations in testing are recorded in Spring, which is never experienced during training.

Figure 8(b) and Table 1 also evaluate the LORS performance with respect to different representativeness threshold $\gamma$, from which it is observed that the performance (area size below the precision-recall curves) decrease is significantly smaller than the percentage of templates that are discarded, demonstrating the superior place representation capability by our LORS method. We are able to balance the long-term place matching performance and scalability degree for

(a) All templates recorded in three different seasons

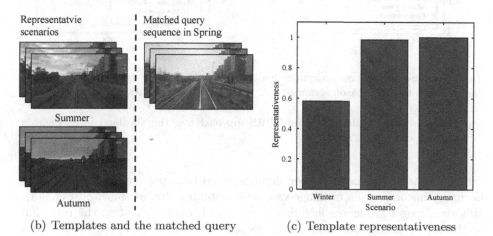

(b) Templates and the matched query       (c) Template representativeness

**Fig. 7.** Qualitative evaluation of our LORS approach over the Nordland dataset across different seasons.

real-world AR-based information delivery in human-robot collaboration applications by the $\gamma$ parameter of the proposed LORS method.

### 3.3 Discussion

The main parameters of the LORS approach are discussed and analyzed in this subsection. Without loss of generality, the experimental results via the Nordland dataset is selected to evaluate the effects of the parameter selection in our LORS method, which are illustrated in Fig. 9. We have similar results over the CMU-VL dataset.

The sequence length $f$ is one of the most important parameter in our LORS method. The precision-recall curves in Fig. 9(a) indicate that better long-term place and scene matching accuracy can be achieved when the sequence length $f$ is increased. There is more comprehensive information contained in longer sequences, especially in the Nordland dataset that has strong perceptual aliasing problems. When $f = 1$, the sequence-based place representation reduces to the single image-based representation losing the temporal information, making the performance even worse. Our LORS method is a model-vs-sequence scene

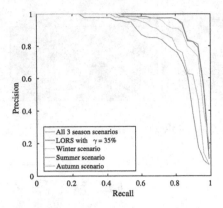 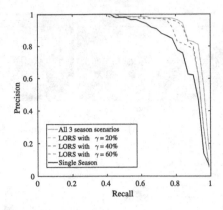

(a) Precision-recall curves computed using different training season scenarios

(b) Precision-recall curves computed using varying representativeness threshold

**Fig. 8.** Quantitative evaluation of our LORS approach over the Nordland dataset across different seasons.

matching method, which has been demonstrated to improve the place matching accuracy in comparison to image-vs-image matching [16], as shown in Fig. 9(a). However, longer sequences include more image frames, indicating the precision of the represented place is low. For example, assuming the speed of the train is 130 km/h, the localization precision when $f = 1$ is 7.2 m, while it is 36.0 m when $f = 5$.

Besides the sequence length $f$, the LORS's performance will also be affected by the hyperparameter $\lambda$ in Eq. (1) as all techniques based on optimization with regularization terms [5]. In Fig. 9(b), we compare the LORS approach with different values of $\lambda$ using the challenging Nordland dataset. In the comparisons in Fig. 9(b), the sequence length $f = 5$ and the representativeness threshold $\gamma = 90\%$ are applied. It is observed from 9(b) that the best performance is achieved when $\lambda = 1$ when the full version LORS is introduced ($\lambda \neq 0$). When $\lambda = 0$, the LORS method reduces to the naive case that all templates in every scenario are used for the place representation. Although it has the highest long-term place matching performance due to the full information utilization, it cannot receive the benefits by the LORS method, including the scalability in real world long-term AR-based information delivery applications.

Our LORS method is a general representation learning framework. The raw feature engineering is not the focus of our LORS method. In our experimental evaluations, the same HOG descriptor is applied based on the prior knowledge that it performs well in both CMU-VL and Nordland datasets [5]. The performance may be further improved if other advanced features (either single feature or multimodal features) are applied in our LORS method.

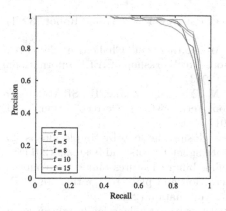 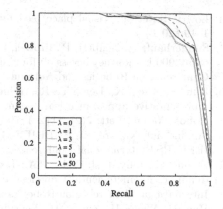

(a) Precision-recall curves computed using different sequence length $f$

(b) Precision-recall curves computed using different hyperparameters $\lambda$

**Fig. 9.** Parameter analysis of the proposed LORS approach over the Nordland dataset across different seasons.

## 4 Conclusion

In this paper, we propose the novel LORS approach that integrates information from multiple environmental scenarios to build a comprehensive representation model to improve long-term place and scene matching, with the ultimate goal to enable long-term AR-based information delivery in collaborative human-robot perception applications. LORS is formulated as a regularized optimization problem, in order to adaptively select only a small subset of most representative scene templates and fuse them into a representation for place representation, which makes LORS highly scalable to long-term changes in real-world AR-based information delivery applications. We further develop an optimization solver that possesses a guarantee to converge to the global optima theoretically. We conduct experiments based upon two public datasets for benchmarking long-term place and scene matching. The promising results have shown performance improvement resulted from the LORS approach.

**Acknowledgments.** This work was partially supported by NSF CNS-1823245, DOE DE-FE0031650, ARO W911NF-17-1-0447, USAFA FA7000-18-2-0016, and DOT PHMSA 693JK31850005CAAP.

## References

1. Billinghurst, M., Clark, A., Lee, G., et al.: A survey of augmented reality. Found. Trends® Hum.-Comput. Interact. **8**(2–3), 73–272 (2015)
2. Chatzopoulos, D., Bermejo, C., Huang, Z., Hui, P.: Mobile augmented reality survey: from where we are to where we go. IEEE Access **5**, 6917–6950 (2017)

3. Lowry, S., et al.: Visual place recognition: a survey. IEEE Trans. Robot. **32**(1), 1–19 (2016)
4. Sünderhauf, N., Neubert, P., Protzel, P.: Are we there yet? Challenging SeqSLAM on a 3000 km journey across all four seasons. In: Workshop of IEEE International Conference on Robotics and Automation (2013)
5. Han, F., Yang, X., Deng, Y., Rentschler, M., Yang, D., Zhang, H.: SRAL: shared representative appearance learning for long-term visual place recognition. IEEE Robot. Autom. Lett. **2**(2), 1172–1179 (2017)
6. Sünderhauf, N., Protzel, P.: BRIEF-Gist - closing the loop by simple means. In: IEEE/RSJ International Conference on Intelligent Robots and Systems (2011)
7. Zhang, G., Lilly, M.J., Vela, P.A.: Learning binary features online from motion dynamics for incremental loop-closure detection and place recognition. In: IEEE International Conference on Robotics and Automation (2016)
8. Han, F., Wang, H., Zhang, H.: Learning of integrated holism-landmark representations for long-term loop closure detection. In: AAAI Conference on Artificial Intelligence (2018)
9. Siva, S., Zhang, H.: Omnidirectional multisensory perception fusion for long-term place recognition. In: IEEE International Conference on Robotics and Automation (ICRA) (2018)
10. Valgren, C., Lilienthal, A.J.: SIFT, SURF and seasons: long-term outdoor localization using local features. In: European Conference on Mobile Robotics (2007)
11. Cummins, M., Newman, P.: FAB-MAP: probabilistic localization and mapping in the space of appearance. Int. J. Robot. Res. **27**(6), 647–665 (2008)
12. Mur-Artal, R., Tardós, J.D.: Fast relocalisation and loop closing in keyframe-based SLAM. In: IEEE International Conference on Robotics and Automation (2014)
13. Naseer, T., Spinello, L., Burgard, W., Stachniss, C.: Robust visual robot localization across seasons using network flows. In: AAAI Conference on Artificial Intelligence (2014)
14. Latif, Y., Huang, G., Leonard, J., Neira, J.: An online sparsity-cognizant loop-closure algorithm for visual navigation. In: Robotics: Science and Systems (2014)
15. Sünderhauf, N., Shirazi, S., Dayoub, F., Upcroft, B., Milford, M.: On the performance of convnet features for place recognition. In: IEEE/RSJ International Conference on Intelligent Robots and Systems (2015)
16. Zhang, H., Han, F., Wang, H.: Robust multimodal sequence-based loop closure detection via structured sparsity. In: Robotics: Science and Systems (2016)
17. Han, F., Yang, X., Zhang, Y., Zhang, H.: Sequence-based multimodal apprenticeship learning for robot perception and decision making. In: IEEE International Conference on Robotics and Automation (ICRA) (2017)
18. Arroyo, R., Alcantarilla, P.F., Bergasa, L.M., Romera, E.: Towards life-long visual localization using an efficient matching of binary sequences from images. In: IEEE International Conference on Robotics and Automation (2015)
19. Johns, E., Yang, G.-Z.: Feature co-occurrence maps: appearance-based localisation throughout the day. In: IEEE International Conference on Robotics and Automation (2013)
20. Badino, H., Huber, D., Kanade, T.: Real-time topometric localization. In: IEEE International Conference on Robotics and Automation (2012)

# Robot Authority in Human-Machine Teams: Effects of Human-Like Appearance on Compliance

Kerstin S. Haring[1,4](✉) [iD], Ariana Mosley[1], Sarah Pruznick[1], Julie Fleming[2],
Kelly Satterfield[3], Ewart J. de Visser[1] [iD], Chad C. Tossell[1] [iD],
and Gregory Funke[3]

[1] United States Air Force Academy, Warfighter Effectiveness Research Center,
AF Academy, CO 80840, USA
{kerstin.haring,ewart.devisser.nl.ctr,chad.tossell}@usafa.edu
[2] Adler University, Chicago, IL 60602, USA
[3] Air Force Research Laboratory, Wright-Patterson Air Force Base,
Dayton, OH 45433, USA
{kelly.satterfield.ctr,gregory.funke1}@us.af.mil
[4] Daniel Felix Ritchie School of Engineering and Computer Science,
University of Denver, Denver, CO 80210, USA

**Abstract.** Current technology allows for the deployment of security patrol and police robots. It is expected that in the near future robots and similar technologies will exhibit some degree of authority over people within human-machine teams. Studies in classical psychology investigating compliance have shown that people tend to comply with requests from others who display or are assumed to have authority. In this study, we investigated the effect of a robot's human-like appearance on compliance with a request. We compared two different robots to a human control condition. The robots assumed the role of a coach in learning a difficult task. We hypothesized that participants would have higher compliance with robots high compared to robots low in human-like appearance. The coach continuously prompts the participant to continue to practice the task beyond the time the participant wishes to actually proceed. Compliance was measured by time practiced after the first prompt and the total number of images processed. Results showed that compliance with the request was the highest with a human and compliance with both robots was significantly lower. However, we showed that robots can be used as persuasive coaches that can help a human teammate to persist in training task. There were no differences between the High and Low Human-Like robot for compliance time, however the Low Human-Like robot has people practise on more images than the High Human-Like robot. The implication of this study is that robots are currently inferior to humans when it comes to compliance in a human-machine team. Future robots need to be carefully designed in an authoritative way if maximizing compliance to their requests is the primary goal.

This work was supported by the Air Force Office of Scientific Research under grant number 16RT0881 and award 16RHCOR360.

© Springer Nature Switzerland AG 2019
J. Y. C. Chen and G. Fragomeni (Eds.): HCII 2019, LNCS 11575, pp. 63–78, 2019.
https://doi.org/10.1007/978-3-030-21565-1_5

64   K. S. Haring et al.

**Keywords:** Human-robot interaction · Human-machine teaming · Anthropomorphism · Machine authority · Compliance

## 1   Introduction

With the emergence of Human-Machine Teams, machines have already obtained some degree of authority over humans. For example, drivers mostly comply with GPS (Global Positioning System) requests to follow a certain route when navigating unknown areas [1]. We soon expect the current interfaces that make such requests, like computers or phone apps, to switch to physical robots. For example, the first security robots are already patrolling areas adding to surveillance of public spaces [2, 3]. A next logical step of such a robot in a range of authority positions will be to issue requests to humans in their environment to support military or local law enforcement objectives. Robots and autonomous systems are at least partly starting to execute decisions autonomously [4–6]. Yet, it is not clear how people react to and interact with this kind of machine authority. For example, current technology already allows for the deployment of police robots and robotic peacekeepers that at least in theory exhibit some degree of authority over people [7]. Recent studies found that people in compliance with a robot's instruction found a robot to be more safe and human-like than people that disobeyed the robot [8]. Another study found that robots have some authority to prevent cheating, although people felt less guilty when they cheated in a robot's presence when compared to a human [9]. A robot's appearance has shown to influence trait inferences and evaluative responses (i.e. willingness to interact) to varying degrees given the robot's role [10]. A robot in the role of a peacekeeper, and therefore in a kind of authoritative role, has been identified to be more threatening than a robot role that explains the reason for its decisions [11]. In a non-threatening environment, a robot has shown enough authority to keep people engaged in a mindless file-renaming task after they expressed a desire to quit [12].

Classical psychology studies investigating obedience and compliance [13–16] and their more recent replications [17] have shown that people tend to comply with requests from others who display or are assumed to have authority. For instance, in the Milgram studies series, participants were made to believe that they were physically harming a learner in an adjacent room through administering shocks under the direction of an authority figure. Despite the clear pain of the learner and participant's agitation, 65% of participants continued to steadily increase the level until the maximum shock level was reached. Unbeknownst to the participants, the learner was a confederate actor and not actually hurt in the experiments. The studies showed that obedience seems to be ingrained in humans and that people tend to obey orders from another human even if they merely appeared as having authority. Milgram achieved an authority effect by dressing an experimenter in a lab coat, which was perceived as authoritative and comparable to the effect that uniforms have in establishing authority [18]. However, these kinds of obedience studies have placed participants in highly objectionable situations and are in this form considered unethical. The Milgram studies contradict protection measures of human participants and have become essential in the establishment of the internal review board [19].

The replication of an experimental task inspired by Milgram and the application of compliance concepts to robots is a largely unexplored unknown area in Human Robot Interaction (HRI). Therefore, we examined how a robot's anthropomorphic appearance effects compliance. With regard to the strict ethical guidelines we were following in this experimental study, we made adjustments to Milgram's obedience study and created an experimental task measuring compliance with a robot's request. Similar to using lab-coats or uniforms as display of authority, we believed that a robot's appearance would show the robot's degree of authority. The appearance of a robot has been linked to a (biased) expectation of the robot's functions [20] and it also has been found that highly human-like robots like android robots [21] and small human-like robots [22] elicit significant perception changes in short-term interactions. Previous studies suggest a link between anthropomorphism and human-likeness to obedience [8]. Furthermore, anthropomorphized robots are attributed responsibility for their work in collaborative tasks with humans [23] and are perceived as more understandable and predictable [24]. This emerges from the assumed mind perception of robots [25]. One of the consequences of ascribing mind is that it makes actions more meaningful, a component we believe to be crucial to elicit compliance with a request.

We hypothesized therefore that robots high in anthropomorphic appearance would have higher compliance than robots low in anthropomorphic appearance. Our study compared two different kinds of robots (see Fig. 1) to a human control condition where the robots and the human take the role of a coach. Participants were asked to learn a difficult task together with the coach. The coach continuously prompted the participant to continue with the practice of the task beyond the time the participant wished to actually proceed. The prompts used here were adapted from the original Milgram study and consistent throughout all conditions.

To summarize, we hypothesized that:

1. The human control condition would elicit the highest compliance rates.
2. The High Human-like Robot Coach would elicit more compliance than the Low Human-like Robot Coach.
3. There would be equal compliance rates across to the four prompts in the human conditions and declines of compliance rates over the four prompts in the robot conditions.

For the purpose of this study, we distinguished between obedience and compliance: Obedience has been defined as following orders contrary to one's moral beliefs and values [26]; compliance has been defined as following requests of continuation of a task beyond one's initial willingness using a specific experimental design employing logical reasoning and persuasion [26]. Compliance with a robot's request can be beneficial if people are trusting and willing to work with the robot. However, compliance, if not well-calibrated, can have a variety of negative consequences such as low acceptance or rejection of the robot technology or overtrust in the robot's expertise and following a potentially wrong request.

**Fig. 1.** The robot coaches used in the study. The High Human-Like (Aldebaran Nao) robot on the left and the Low Human-Like (3D print modified Roomba) on the right.

## 2    Methodology

### 2.1    Participants

Seventy-five participants (48.1% Females; M = 18.6, SD = 0.75) from the US Air Force Academy participant pool participated in the study in exchange for course credit. Participants were screened for awareness of the original Milgram experiments. Based on this screening, three participants were excluded as they either suspected the experimental manipulation, recognized the prompts or because the study was interrupted. The remaining 72 complete data sets were analyzed in this study with 20 participants in the Human condition, 24 participants in the High Human-like Robot condition (ABOT score = 45.92 [27]) and 28 participants in the Low Human-like Robot (ABOT est. score = 0.37) condition. Informed consent was obtained from each participant. This research complied with the tenets of the Declaration of Helsinki and was approved by the Institutional Review board at the US Air Force Academy.

### 2.2    Experimental Design

Participants were randomly assigned to one of the coaching conditions: Human, High Human-like robot (Aldebaran Nao robot), and Low Human-like robot (modified Roomba robot) (see Fig. 1). The Human condition served as the control condition. Human-likeness was verified with the ABOT Database, which houses an array of images of human-like robots that have been scored psychometrically on their degree of human-likeness from 0 to 100 (ABOT [27]. Using

**Fig. 2.** Example of a SAR image. The left image shows three targets identified by the participant with a mouse click, which creates a yellow circle directly on the picture. On the right image, target accuracy feedback was provided with red circles that confirmed whether participants had correctly identified a hostile. (Color figure online)

this measure, the High Human-like robot scored 45.92 whereas the Low Human-like robot scored 0.37. The experimental procedure and task were the same for all conditions.

## 2.3  Experimental Task

For the experimental task, participants were shown synthetic-aperture radar (SAR) images on a screen and were asked to identify all hostile targets (tanks) present in the pictures. Hostiles on these SAR images were difficult to identify because targets were low-resolution, blurry and often looked similar to distractor vehicles or trees (see Fig. 2). The goal for participants in the practice phase was to identify which vehicles are targets without missing targets or making false alarms. They were instructed to practice until they met or exceeded the passing score. In this phase, they received verbal feedback from the coach in addition to the red circles from the respective coach. Then, they were told they would move on to the testing phase.

**Table 1.** The four verbal prompts the participant is told after each time they click the "Advance to Testing" button on the screen. When they try to advance to testing for a 5th time, the program terminates without a testing phase.

| Prompt | Description |
|---|---|
| Prompt 1 | Please continue with practice |
| Prompt 2 | Your performance could be improved. You should continue with practice |
| Prompt 3 | Your performance is adequate. However, you should continue with practice |
| Prompt 4 | Your performance is sufficient. But it is essential that you continue with practice |

The experiment began when participants commenced practicing the task. After evaluating 25 images, the task was interrupted and a score was displayed. Every time the score was displayed, participants needed to make a choice between either "Advance to Testing" or "Continue Practicing" (see Fig. 3). The "Advance to Testing" button was also available anytime during the task. Once participants tried to advance to testing with the button click, they heard one of the four adapted Milgram prompts in the order displayed in Table 1. The task terminated after the fifth time they clicked the "Advance to Testing" button.

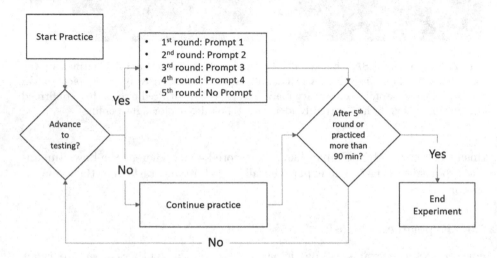

**Fig. 3.** Diagram showing prompts and decision loop for participants.

Extensive pilot testing without the scoring system revealed that participants felt this task was too difficult and they did not perform well enough throughout the entire study time (up to 103 min) to advance to testing for even the first time. The pilot tests of 20 participants ran for an average of 92.1 min (SD = 21.9 min) and participants completed 175.1 pictures (SD = 80.9). We scheduled approximately 90 min per pilot participant, meaning that the majority of the pilot tests did not complete the four prompts with some not even getting to the first one. However, the attempt to move on to the testing phase was the crucial part of the study to test compliance with the four requests made by the coach (see Table 1). We therefore altered the score based on how well they performed the task. Participants were told that the performance score was computed using a formula combining correctly identified targets, missed targets, and false positives. The formula provided to participants was deliberately complicated to obscure that the scores reported back to the participants were manipulated. Participants were told scores would rank from 700–1015 with 850 being a passing score in the testing phase. In reality, participants were given a random score between 851 and 900 every 25 images to reassure them that their performance was adequate.

After several pilot iterations testing slightly easier images and the introduction of the score participants average task time was around 35 min in the human pilot condition.

A form of mild deception was used in this study, which was necessary to explore how people would respond naturally to compliance requests in our task setting [18]. Participants were told there would be a testing phase, which never actually occurred in the experiment. The program simply terminated when participants were ready to advance to testing and finished all prompts. We checked through post-study interviews if participants suspected or knew that they were observed for their compliance behaviors and excluded their data from evaluation if participants had guessed the nature of the experiment.

## 2.4 Procedure

Participants submitted their informed consent providing the individual with adequate information about the research project and time to make an informed decision. In light of the ethical considerations of the studies serving as inspiration to the present study, the study underwent a rigorous review process at a local IRB (Institutional Review Board) and was approved to be conducted in the way described here. The experimenter then started the study with a pre-survey which measured demographics on a screen. Upon completion, participants were brought by the experimenter in an adjacent separated space where they met their coach. In the human condition, the experimenter acted as the coach. In the other conditions participants were told they were free to get started and the experimenter left the room and remotely watched the participant over a camera live-feed to intervene if necessary. The robots were not remote controlled and programmed to give feedback in always the same way. In all conditions, the coach started with an initial friendly greeting and introduced herself as Alex (a gender neutral name). Participants in all conditions then proceeded with the experimental task. After they tried to advance for the fifth time, the program terminated and the experimenter returned. When participants asked about the testing phase, the experimenter simply told them there was another survey planned in the study.

After completion of the experiment participants received a guided interview debrief. This included a manipulation check and the debrief about the details of the study. The debrief further explained the false pieces of information and described why we decided to conduct the study in this fashion. After hearing this information, participants had the option to withdraw all data associated with their participant number. They received a copy of the informed consent document and the debriefing statement and then left the experimental site.

## 2.5 Measures

**Performance.** Performance was calculated using two measures, hit rate and error rate. Hit rate was calculated by summing the total number of correctly identified targets and dividing them by the sum of the correct and missed targets.

The error rate was calculated by dividing the sum of misidentified and missed targets by the total number of targets.

**Compliance Time.** Compliance time was measured as the amount of time participants adhered to the coach's request to continue practice until the next time the participant tried to advance to testing (see Fig. 3). This was then summed for the four instances and is referred to as the total compliance time throughout the experiment (i.e. the total amount of time continued in practice) and the compliance time by prompt (i.e. the amount of continued practice time after each prompt). In case the participant clicked twice or several times in a row on the "Advance to testing" button after listening to the respective prompt, the time between prompts was scored as 0.

**Verified Images.** Verified images was a measure calculated by either summing or averaging the total number of target identification images processed by the participant.

## 3    Results

### 3.1    Performance

A one-way ANOVA was conducted to determine significant performance effects between the conditions. There was no significant effect [$F(2, 68) = .38$, $p = .68$]. Hit rate hovered around 77% (SE = 0.01). Similar for the error rate, no significant effect was found [$F(2, 68) = 23.3$, $p = .54$] (see Fig. 4). With the error rate being close to significance levels, pairwise comparisons showed that the differences between Human (M = 29.7%, SD = .10) and High Human-Like (M = 34.4%, SD = .07) as well as Human and Low Human-Like (M = 33.3%, SD = .08) were also close to $p < .05$ significance levels.

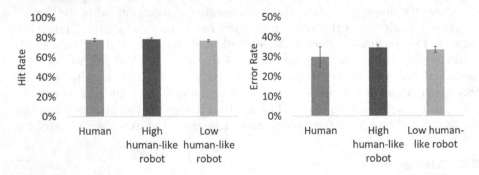

**Fig. 4.** The hit rate of the number of correctly identified hostiles in the target detection task and the error rate combining misidentified and missed hostiles.

## 3.2  Compliance Time

After the first prompt, participants continued for an average of 27.6 min with the human, 9.7 min with the High Human-Like robot and 11.4 min with the Low Human-Like robot (see left hand side Fig. 5). This is reflected by a similar trend of verified images with 120.6 images with the human, 31.1 with the High Human-Like robot and 44.0 with the Low Human-Like robot.

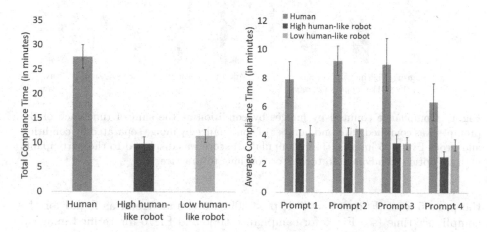

**Fig. 5.** Compliance time in minutes by condition as the sum of time each of the prompts was complied with and compliance time separated by condition and prompt.

A one-way between subjects ANOVA was conducted to compare the effect of robot type on compliance time for the High Human-Like robot, Low Human-Like robot, and Human control condition. There was a significant effect of robot type on compliance time at the $p < .05$ level for the three conditions [$F(2, 68)$ = 30.9, $p < .001$]. Bonferroni corrected post hoc comparisons showed that the differences between Human (M = 27.6 min, SD = 10.7) and High Human-Like (M = 9.7 min, SD = 7.1) as well as Human and Low Human-Like (M = 11.4 min, SD = 6.9) conditions were significant. No significant differences were found between the High and Low human-like robots.

Figure 5 shows the compliance time grouped by each of the prompts. We did not submit these data to formal analyses because of unequal group sizes for each of the prompts. The highest number of people continued practice after the first prompt. This number declined for each consecutive prompt with the lowest number of participants continuing with the last prompt. Nonetheless, Fig. 5 shows the trend that compliance time remained higher with human compared to robotic coaches throughout the session.

## 3.3  Verified Images

A one way ANOVA was conducted to compare the effect of prompt on number of images. There was a significant effect the condition on number of images at

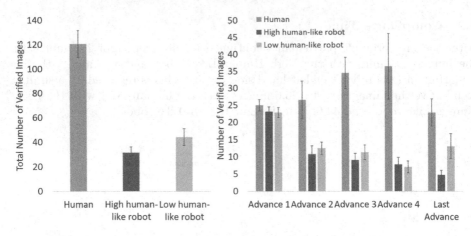

**Fig. 6.** Compliance counted by images by condition as the sum of time each of the prompts was complied with and number of compliance by image separated by condition and prod. Every 25 images, the (manipulated) score was displayed to the participants with an option to advance to testing or continue to practice.

the p < .05 level [F(2, 69) = 37.1, p < .001], a similar trend as found for the compliance time (see Fig. 5 for compliance time and Fig. 6 for verified images). Bonferroni corrected post hoc comparisons showed that the difference between Human (M = 120.6 min, SD = 49.5) and High Human-Like (M = 31.1 min, SD = 24.3) as well as Human and Low Human-Like (M = 44.9 min, SD = 35.5) conditions were significant and the difference between high and Low Human-Like robots trended towards significance, p = 0.055. Number of verified images with the Low Human-Like robot was higher (M = 44.9 min, SD = 35.5) compared to the High Human-Like robot (M = 31.1 min, SD = 24.3).

Also similar to the results found for compliance time, the separation by prompts consists of different group sizes. The graph on the right in Fig. 6 shows additionally the number of images complied with after the fourth prompt and before the study terminates with the last advance to testing attempt. For this particular graph, it has to be taken into account that the (manipulated) performance score was displayed every 25 images giving participants the option to advance to testing right then or continue with practice. The graphs reflects the choice of many participants to advance to testing around the 25 images mark for the first time. Only within the human condition an initial increase in verified images was observed as both the high and Low Human-Like robot conditions showed a decrease in verified images.

## 4   Discussion

The goal of this study was to examine the effects of different types of robots on trainees' compliance levels in a target detection task. Without a human present, each type of robot produced a compliance effect ranging from 10 to 11.5 min.

Participants continued practicing the target detection task based on the robots' instructions despite their own perceptions that they achieved the desired level of readiness to move forward. Even though participants complied to human instructions to a much greater degree, human-machine teams should be designed with these results in mind. Robots can be used as persuasive coaches that can help a human teammate to persist in training tasks. Beyond training, the design of human-machine teams should carefully consider the roles and levels of authority desired from robot teammates in addition to levels and degrees of automation [28–30].

Contrary to our second hypothesis, the more human-like robot did not elicit higher compliance relative to the low human-like robot. Somewhat surprisingly, the low human-like robot seemed to have had a higher influence on participants to continue with their training. Participants completed more images with the low human-like robot than the more human-like robot, though these effects did not quite reach the level of significance. Participants in the High Human-Like robot condition commented in the guided interview debrief that they expected better, more intelligent feedback from the robot. This was not a prevalent comment in the Low Human-Like robot condition. It seemed that the expectations towards the Low Human-Like robot matched the system's capabilities more than the other conditions which could be an explanation for the higher number of verified images. The general lack of significant differences in compliance times across robot conditions could be due to a number of factors. First, human likeness by itself may not be important in provoking humans to comply to robots. The both robots used here are similar in size (i.e., small) and shared other features (e.g., voice qualities and volume). It could be more important for the form to match the function in order to influence humans to respond to directions [20]. Additionally, physical size of the robot could be more important than anthropomorphic features for influencing humans to comply. Indeed, previous research has found that the physical size of humans is a primary factor in determining a prospective foe's formidability [31]. Future research will examine the larger Baxter robot within this paradigm (ABOT score = 27.3 [27]). Another reason we did not see differences in compliance levels across robot differences could be due the population studied in this research. Cadets are trained to follow orders and effective followership is strongly encouraged their freshman/first year at USAFA. Given most of our participants were freshman/first-year students, they complied with more senior cadets' instructions much more than robots. Recall that the robot instructions were standardized and not personalized to the actual performance of the trainees (i.e., participants). The similarity in perceived competence levels across the Low and High Human-Like robots could have been an important factor in yielding similar compliance rates.

The human coach, ultimately, induced the most compliance in participants. Even though most of our participants were freshman cadets, other studies with a civilian undergraduate population yielded similar results [32]. Thus, if compliance to mundane tasks is required, human instructors are more effective than robots in encouraging trainees to continue practicing undesired tasks.

Participants continued the task for much longer and continued to make errors after they perceived they were ready to progress to the testing phase. This could have indicated the trainees were overconfident and needed the additional training time. Indeed, the number of errors they committed under the instruction of human instructors far exceeded the number of errors they made with the robot instructors given the increased length of training.

The lower compliance levels elicited by the robots in this study may better match the desired function of the technology. For example, if the intelligence of the robot is low and higher decision authority is desired for the human trainee, then a smaller robot might make more sense for self-paced learning. This might be an important design feature for training that is not vital relative to other types of training. For training that is requisite to important missions or critical for safety, human instructors might be better and this is especially the case if continued practice is desired beyond trainee' preferences.

Of course, the human instructor could have influenced performance in a way that was undesired and led to more errors. It is possible that participants felt more observed or supervised in the human condition compared to the robot conditions and as a result increased their efforts to find targets, akin to a Hawthorne effect [33–35]. This conclusion is consistent with other findings that have shown that people feel less judged when evaluated by an automated avatar compared to an avatar controlled by a human [36]. It is thus important to evaluate a number of measures to evaluate the overall effect of compliance with human or robotic agents on human-machine teaming performance. The low authority observed with smaller robots may not be a good fit for urgent or high-performance tasks where the robot does not have high confidence in guidance provided to human teammates. However, based on the results of future studies with larger robots, the Baxter or similarly-sized robots could be more effective in urgent tasks. Robots working with more novice teammates could be larger in size or substituted for human experts. As expertise increases, the human instructor/mentor could be replaced with a smaller robot given the human teammate's increased capabilities. There are a number of other factors to consider as robots penetrate society and influence humans. For example, when designing robot features for education and training, a robot's persuasiveness and authority could stimulate longer practise on initially considered undesirable tasks [12], increases in a student's motivation [37], enhance interest [38], and have a positive effect on learning performance [39]. In addition, compliance rates and overall trust in robots could be increased or repaired by using politeness strategies [11,40–44] as long as the robot responses are not miscalibrated and perceived as inappropriately polite [45].

This study had several limitations. First, the robot was not providing intelligent or individualized feedback. The feedback was not specific to the task and the same across all conditions. Semi-structured interviews in the debriefing revealed that participants felt that the coaching, regardless of condition, was not realistic or helpful. Future studies could examine the use of intelligent and adaptive robot behaviors that are helpful. The increased perceived competence of robot instructors would have likely increased compliance levels. Second, there may have been a mismatch between people's expectations of the robot and its behavior. Given the expectations people form from a robot's appearance [20] we believe that the interaction capabilities matched the low human-like robot better compared to the high human-like robot. As mentioned above, incorporating awareness of social norms or additional manners into a robot may close this expectation gap [11]. Future research should focus on assessing strategies to address these issues by establishing rapport with the robot prior the experimental task and change the monotone answers to a larger variety of feedback. With prior research showing that the responsiveness and not the level of aggressiveness of a security guard robot influenced human compliance [8], we believe that increased responsiveness of the robots will increase compliance with their requests. Third, compliance in this study was highly task specific. Extensive pilot testing was required to create a situation in which participants would ignore a prompt and stop practice with the task. Therefore, our results can not be universally translated to other tasks. Lastly, this study did not account for long term effects of compliance. We predict that the effect of initial compliance with a robot will eventually wear off over time. Given the high compliance rates to a human in Milgram's original experimental series and its more recent replications [14,17], the goal of achieving higher compliance rates with a robot should be carefully considered from an ethical perspective. Finally, we physically separated the automated tutor from the computer where the task was performed. Many intelligent tutors have integrated the function of tutors within the training system. Constraints can be built in that prevent progress until a certain quiz score or training criterion is met. Thus, if continued training is required, designing these constraints into the system would take the decision away from the trainee and remove the need for instructors to influence their trainees. Additional training would be required instead of encouraged by a physical instructor. Yet, as robots become more commonplace in work environments, having a robot mentor or instructor might produce trust in robotic systems and lead to more effective teaming in other tasks and environments.

## 5   Conclusion

Shared and flexible authority between robots and humans for tasks and commands remains a fundamental feature in the design, role distribution, and organization of human-machine teams. In some circumstances, final authority should rest firmly in human hands; however, obtaining compliance through a robot's request is possible. The design of robots within human-machine teams should incorporate and calibrate the right amount of features that inspire the desired level of authority within such teams.

# References

1. Salem, M., Dautenhahn, K.: Evaluating trust and safety in HRI: practical issues and ethical challenges. In: Emerging Policy and Ethics of Human-Robot Interaction (2015)
2. Sharkey, N.: The robot arm of the law grows longer. Computer **42**(8), 115–116 (2009)
3. Pennisi, A., et al.: Multi-robot surveillance through a distributed sensor network. In: Koubâa, A., Martínez-de Dios, J.R. (eds.) Cooperative Robots and Sensor Networks 2015. SCI, vol. 604, pp. 77–98. Springer, Cham (2015). https://doi.org/10.1007/978-3-319-18299-5_4
4. Dennis, L.A., Fisher, M., Lincoln, N.K., Lisitsa, A., Veres, S.M.: Practical verification of decision-making in agent-based autonomous systems. Autom. Softw. Eng. **23**(3), 305–359 (2016)
5. Li, L., Ota, K., Dong, M.: Humanlike driving: empirical decision-making system for autonomous vehicles. IEEE Trans. Veh. Technol. **67**(8), 6814–6823 (2018)
6. Cunningham, A.G., Galceran, E., Mehta, D., Ferrer, G., Eustice, R.M., Olson, E.: MPDM: multi-policy decision-making from autonomous driving to social robot navigation. In: Waschl, H., Kolmanovsky, I., Willems, F. (eds.) Control Strategies for Advanced Driver Assistance Systems and Autonomous Driving Functions. LNCIS, vol. 476, pp. 201–223. Springer, Cham (2019). https://doi.org/10.1007/978-3-319-91569-2_10
7. Long, S.K., Karpinsky, N.D., Bliss, J.P.: Trust of simulated robotic peacekeepers among resident and expatriate Americans. In: Proceedings of the Human Factors and Ergonomics Society Annual Meeting, vol. 61, no. 1, pp. 2091–2095. SAGE Publications, Los Angeles (2017)
8. Agrawal, S., Williams, M.-A.: Robot authority and human obedience: a study of human behaviour using a robot security guard. In: Proceedings of the Companion of the 2017 ACM/IEEE International Conference on Human-Robot Interaction, pp. 57–58. ACM (2017)
9. Hoffman, G., et al.: Robot presence and human honesty: experimental evidence. In: Proceedings of the Tenth Annual ACM/IEEE International Conference on Human-Robot Interaction, pp. 181–188. ACM (2015)
10. Benitez, J., Wyman, A.B., Carpinella, C.M., Stroessner, S.J.: The authority of appearance: how robot features influence trait inferences and evaluative responses. In: 2017 26th IEEE International Symposium on Robot and Human Interactive Communication (RO-MAN), pp. 397–404. IEEE (2017)
11. Inbar, O., Meyer, J.: Manners matter: trust in robotic peacekeepers. In: Proceedings of the Human Factors and Ergonomics Society Annual Meeting, vol. 59, no. 1, pp. 185–189. SAGE Publications, Los Angeles (2015)
12. Geiskkovitch, D.Y., Cormier, D., Seo, S.H., Young, J.E.: Please continue, we need more data: an exploration of obedience to robots. J. Hum.-Robot Interact. **5**(1), 82–99 (2016)
13. Milgram, S.: Behavioral study of obedience. J. Abnormal Soc. Psychol. **67**(4), 371 (1963)
14. Milgram, S., Gudehus, C.: Obedience to authority (1978)
15. Meeus, W.H., Raaijmakers, Q.A.: Obedience in modern society: the Utrecht studies. J. Soc. Issues **51**(3), 155–175 (1995)
16. Haney, C., Banks, W.C., Zimbardo, P.G.: A study of prisoners and guards in a simulated prison. Naval Res. Rev. **9**, 1–17 (1973)

17. Burger, J.M.: Replicating milgram: would people still obey today? Am. Psychol. **64**(1), 1 (2009)
18. Weiss, D.J.: Deception by researchers is necessary and not necessarily evil. Behav. Brain Sci. **24**(3), 431–432 (2001)
19. Masters, K.S.: Milgram, stress research, and the institutional review board (2009)
20. Haring, K.S., Watanabe, K., Velonaki, M., Tossell, C.C., Finomore, V.: FFAB-the form function attribution bias in human-robot interaction. IEEE Trans. Cogn. Dev. Syst. **10**(4), 843–851 (2018)
21. Haring, K.S., Matsumoto, Y., Watanabe, K.: How do people perceive and trust a lifelike robot. In: Proceedings of the World Congress on Engineering and Computer Science, vol. 1 (2013)
22. Haring, K.S., Watanabe, K., Silvera-Tawil, D., Velonaki, M., Takahashi, T.: Changes in perception of a small humanoid robot. In: 2015 6th International Conference on Automation, Robotics and Applications (ICARA), pp. 83–89. IEEE (2015)
23. Hinds, P.J., Roberts, T.L., Jones, H.: Whose job is it anyway? A study of human-robot interaction in a collaborative task. Hum.-Comput. Interact. **19**(1), 151–181 (2004)
24. Waytz, A., Morewedge, C.K., Epley, N., Monteleone, G., Gao, J.-H., Cacioppo, J.T.: Making sense by making sentient: effectance motivation increases anthropomorphism. J. Pers. Soc. Psychol. **99**(3), 410 (2010)
25. Waytz, A., Gray, K., Epley, N., Wegner, D.M.: Causes and consequences of mind perception. Trends Cogn. Sci. **14**(8), 383–388 (2010)
26. Constable, S., Shuler, Z., Klaber, L., Rakauskas, M.: Conformity, compliance, and obedience (1999). [Online]. https://www.units.miamioh.edu/psybersite/cults/cco.shtml
27. Phillips, E., Zhao, X., Ullman, D., Malle, B.F.: What is human-like?: Decomposing robots' human-like appearance using the anthropomorphic robot (abot) database. In: Proceedings of the 2018 ACM/IEEE International Conference on Human-Robot Interaction, pp. 105–113. ACM (2018)
28. Parasuraman, R., Sheridan, T.B., Wickens, C.D.: A model for types and levels of human interaction with automation. IEEE Trans. Syst. Man Cybern.-Part A: Syst. Hum. **30**(3), 286–297 (2000)
29. Beer, J.M., Fisk, A.D., Rogers, W.A.: Toward a framework for levels of robot autonomy in human-robot interaction. J. Hum.-Robot Interact. **3**(2), 74–99 (2014)
30. Onnasch, L., Wickens, C.D., Li, H., Manzey, D.: Human performance consequences of stages and levels of automation: an integrated meta-analysis. Hum. Factors **56**(3), 476–488 (2014)
31. Fessler, D.M., Holbrook, C., Snyder, J.K.: Weapons make the man (larger): formidability is represented as size and strength in humans. PloS One **7**(4), e32751 (2012)
32. Satterfield, K., et al.: Investigating compliance in human-robot teaming. In: 2nd International Conference on Intelligent Human Systems Integration (IHSI 2019): Integrating People and Intelligent Systems (2019)
33. McCambridge, J., Witton, J., Elbourne, D.R.: Systematic review of the Hawthorne effect: new concepts are needed to study research participation effects. J. Clin. Epidemiol. **67**(3), 267–277 (2014)
34. Wickström, G., Bendix, T.: The Hawthorne effect-what did the original Hawthorne studies actually show? Scand. J. Work Environ. Health **26**, 363–367 (2000)

35. Parsons, H.M.: What happened at Hawthorne?: New evidence suggests the Hawthorne effect resulted from operant reinforcement contingencies. Science **183**(4128), 922–932 (1974)
36. Lucas, G.M., Gratch, J., King, A., Morency, L.-P.: It's only a computer: virtual humans increase willingness to disclose. Comput. Hum. Behav. **37**, 94–100 (2014)
37. Linder, S.P., Nestrick, B.E., Mulders, S., Lavelle, C.L.: Facilitating active learning with inexpensive mobile robots. J. Comput. Sci. Coll. **16**(4), 21–33 (2001)
38. Hashimoto, T., Kato, N., Kobayashi, H.: Development of educational system with the android robot SAYA and evaluation. Int. J. Adv. Robot. Syst. **8**(3), 28 (2011)
39. Saerbeck, M., Schut, T., Bartneck, C., Janse, M.D.: Expressive robots in education: varying the degree of social supportive behavior of a robotic tutor. In: Proceedings of the SIGCHI Conference on Human Factors in Computing Systems, pp. 1613–1622. ACM (2010)
40. Srinivasan, V., Takayama, L.: Help me please: robot politeness strategies for soliciting help from humans. In: Proceedings of the 2016 CHI Conference on Human Factors in Computing Systems, pp. 4945–4955. ACM (2016)
41. Hayes, C.C., Miller, C.A.: Human-Computer Etiquette: Cultural Expectations and the Design Implications they Place on Computers and Technology. CRC Press, Boca Raton (2010)
42. Parasuraman, R., Miller, C.A.: Trust and etiquette in high-criticality automated systems. Commun. ACM **47**(4), 51–55 (2004)
43. de Visser, E.J., Pak, R., Shaw, T.H.: From 'automation' to 'autonomy': the importance of trust repair in human-machine interaction, Ergonomics **61**, 1409–1427 (2018)
44. de Visser, E.J., et al.: Almost human: anthropomorphism increases trust resilience in cognitive agents. J. Exp. Psychol.: Appl. **22**(3), 331 (2016)
45. Jackson, R.B., Wen, R., Williams, T.: Tact in noncompliance: the need for pragmatically apt responses to unethical commands (2019)

# Augmented Reality for Human-Robot Teaming in Field Environments

Christopher Reardon[1]([✉]), Kevin Lee[2], John G. Rogers III[1],
and Jonathan Fink[1]

[1] U.S. Army Research Laboratory, Adelphi, MD 20783, USA
{christopher.m.reardon3,john.g.rogers59,jonathan.r.fink3}.civ@mail.mil
[2] U.S. Army Research Laboratory Research Associateship Program administered by
Oak Ridge Associated Universities, Oak Ridge, USA
klee23456@gmail.com

**Abstract.** For teams of humans and mobile robots to work together,
several challenges must be overcome, including understanding each others' position, merging map information, sharing recognition of salient features of the environment, and establishing contextually-grounded communication. These challenges are further compounded for teams operating in field environments, which are unconstrained, uninstrumented, and
unknown. While most modern studies that use augmented reality (AR) in
human-robot teaming side-step these challenges by focusing on problems
addressable in instrumented environments, we argue that current AR
technology combined with novel approaches can enable successful teaming in such challenging, real-world settings. To support this, we present
a set of prototypes that combine AR with an intelligent, autonomous
robot to enable better human-robot teaming in field environments.

**Keywords:** Human-robot teaming · Augmented reality ·
Field robotics

## 1 Introduction

Intelligent robots working cooperatively alongside human teammates in unconstrained, uninstrumented, and unknown field environments represents a
formidable vision with the potential to impact application domains such as disaster relief, search and rescue, environmental monitoring, and military operations.
Particularly in disaster and search and rescue work, the need for robots need to
perform better alongside humans is well-recognized [8,10].

A specific technical challenge to achieving this vision is the need to cooperate
in a natural, non-invasive manner. We believe that this challenge is important
for co-located human-robot teams, and can be addressed by using augmented
reality (AR). Indeed, a number of recent works have used AR to demonstrate
improved human-robot teaming – albeit in structured [5] or instrumented [16]
environments.

J. Y. C. Chen and G. Fragomeni (Eds.): HCII 2019, LNCS 11575, pp. 79–92, 2019.
https://doi.org/10.1007/978-3-030-21565-1_6

We believe that it is not only possible but important to transition from this reliance on highly-structured environments to begin using AR for building and studying teams of humans and intelligent mobile robots capable of operating outside the laboratory. Conclusions drawn under the imposition of the constraints of instrumentation could be strengthened and clarified in the transition to creating a human and robot team operating in the real world. To support this argument, we present four approaches that enable essential abilities for humans and robots to work together in these situations through the sharing of metric and symbolic information:

1. Understanding teammate position (i.e., where the teammates are),
2. Merging map information (i.e., where they have been),
3. Recognizing and sharing salient information about objects in their environment (i.e., what they have seen),
4. Communicating understanding and receiving feedback (i.e., deciding what to do next).

To explore these capabilities, we equip a human teammate with an augmented reality head-mounted device (AR-HMD), which we use to collect metric information from the human's task performance, share through visualization metric and symbolic information from the robot's reasoning system, and communicate using augmented reality visualizations and simple dialogue to achieve shared semantic understanding. We present our approaches to enabling each capability, share exemplar experimental results for each, and discuss outcomes.

## 2 Background and Related Work

With the recent advent of inexpensive, commercial-off-the-shelf AR-HMDs there is a growing interest in using such devices for human-robot teaming tasks [17]. There is growing consensus that AR can be used to provide humans with insight into the perception and reasoning of their robot teammates.

The potential for augmented reality is recognized in several related fields. Versions of augmented reality for supporting maintenance has been a research topic for 50 years. A review of that research is presented in [9]. Several recent papers have examined AR for human-robot teaming in scenarios inspired by maintenance and assembly. For example, using AR to visualize the planned motion of a Baxter robot for faster, more accurate performance of a manipulation task [13]. Mixed reality was used in [5] with armed robot performing object manipulation in a shared workspace. Recent works have used projected light in structured environments such as assembly lines [1] and factory floors [2]. How a robot's ability to reveal intentions via AR affects plan cost, termed projection-aware planning, was explored in [3], and illustrated through object manipulation tasks. AR for medical robotics, for example overlaying stiffness information in surgical applications [18], is also believed to have significant potential.

This paper focuses on using AR with mobile robots to improve human-robot teaming in field environments. Recent work has examined using AR with mobile robots and shown great potential for enabling human-robot teaming. For example, AR was used to visually signal robot motion intent for UAVs performing an assembly task in [16] and found to improve task efficiency and human understanding of intent. Robot video data was projected to allow humans to "see through walls" in [4] and thereby improve human situational awareness. Methods of communicating robot field of view via AR to improve teleoperation were examined in [7]. [19] used AR via a screen to convey an understanding of a team of robot soccer players' behavior.

However, these previous works were limited to instrumented environments, e.g., using motion capture to localize and perform the coordinate transformations necessary to share any information between the human and robot or robots. Preliminary work by the authors [11], which presented a method using AR to enable human-robot cooperative search, eschewed an instrumented environment and is reviewed as part of this work.

## 3   AR-Based Approaches to Enabling Human-Robot Teaming

In this section, we present technical approaches to enable each of the four capabilities outlined in Sect. 1. For each approach, a corresponding experimental validation in a motivational application scenario that is enabled by each capability and is relevant to the human-robot teaming in field environments domain is presented in Sect. 4.

### 3.1   Dynamic Frame Alignment to Understand Teammate Position

In scenarios multiple physical agents working together, an important first step is for each agent to understand where the other agents are. Practically, this requires aligning the coordinate frames of each agent. Environmental instrumentation is often used as a shortcut to bypass this problem, e.g., using motion capture or fiducial markers to trivially locate and directly compute the transforms between agents. While this approach is perfectly valid in constrained environments such as laboratory and factory settings, we believe there is a great potential for impact in unconstrained field environments, for example in cooperative search and rescue in resource-denied locations, such as disaster scenarios.

In these scenarios, teammates perform SLAM independently and the transformation between agents' frames must be computed online. To accomplish this, we take advantage of modern AR-HMD devices' (i.e., Microsoft HoloLens - see Sect. 4.1) ability to localize itself and its wearer through the performance vision-based SLAM, and team a human wearing such a device with a mobile robot performing LiDAR-based SLAM.

In particular, we use the approach presented in previous work [11] to align the human and robot teammates' coordinate frames. We assume that both the robot and the AR-HMD generate a geometric representation of the environment in point cloud format, and compute the homogeneous transformation matrix between the robot and human point clouds using the Iterative Closest Point (ICP) algorithm [14]. This is initially performed on a coarse estimate provided by the human. It is recomputed online thereafter as the robot and human move throughout the environment.

Knowing this transform allows the robot teammate to understand and reason about the human's position. We previously demonstrated that this capability enables a robot to perform cooperative search with a human teammate [11]. We review the outcomes of enabling this capability in Sect. 4.2.

## 3.2   Merging Robot and AR-HMD Map Information

In addition to understanding where other agents are, a second critical capability in cooperative teaming tasks is to understand where one's teammates have been. In field applications where teammates must maneuver in the same environment, fusing of map information allows each agent to reason over the other's map information. Our human and robot teammates generate maps using different sensor modalities and at different scales. The challenge is to fuse these heterogeneous maps - one generated by a human wearing an AR-HMD performing vision-based SLAM and another by a mobile ground robot performing SLAM with a LiDAR sensor.

The ground robot uses an OmniMapper-based [15] mapping system, which uses pose graph vertices to represent the robot's location and sensor measurements. Sensor measurements associated with pose graph vertices are then used to generate local occupancy grid maps by iterating through the point cloud and setting an obstacle for points which fall within a height filter. Local occupancy grid maps are generated from the vertices of a pose graph, as points in the point cloud which fall within a height filter are treated as occupied.

The AR-HMD uses an onboard, proprietary SLAM system to generate a model of the environment and localize the wearer within that model. We translate the internal mesh-based representation into a point cloud, from which we are able to similarly generate an occupancy grid for compositing with the robot's map. We use the relative transform method from Sect. 3.1 to effect this transform, and composite the AR-HMD occupancy grid information only into the unmapped area of the robot's occupancy grid.

With this composite map, each teammate is effectively able to make use of the other teammate's exploration efforts in addition to its own when making decisions. We demonstrate this ability in experiments where the robot and the human perform cooperative exploration of an unknown, uninstrumented environment in Sect. 4.3.

## 3.3   Shared Object Recognition

A third significant capability for enhancing human-robot teaming that can be enabled with AR is the ability to reason about other objects in the team's environment. Building upon the abilities to understand and reason about teammate position and fused map information, we explore how recognizing objects and localizing them in the shared reference frame can be used to facilitate shared semantic understanding.

An initial implementation of a modern online classifier [12] allows the robot to classify objects from its video feed. Then, as a first step, we achieve semantic understanding for the human through visualizing via the AR-HMD objects recognized by the robot teammate. Visualized objects are highlighted and annotated with information about the robot's knowledge of those objects. For example, at the most basic level this could be object class and a unique index. Sharing this information to the human teammate gives the human insight into the robot's semantic understanding of the environment.

We show in Sect. 4.4 that with this understanding, the human is able to provide clear instruction with regard to the objects in the environment.

## 3.4   AR-Enhanced Dialogue

A fourth and final powerful capability enabled by AR for human-robot teaming is through the incorporation of basic dialogue for human-robot team cooperative decision making. This capability is particularly complimentary to the shared object recognition capability (Sect. 3.3), as sharing recognized objects with the human allows the human insight into robot's perception and provides a corpus over which dialogue can occur.

We construct this preliminary basic dialogue system by combining commands for basic mobile robot capabilities (e.g., "go to," "explore," "examine") with the set of known object classes to form a dialogue corpus. Then, we use basic speech recognition through the AR-HMD to allow the robot to follow the commands of the human teammate. This allows the human to give instruction in the context of objects, for example, "go to the door." It also makes dialogue particularly powerful in resolving situations of ambiguous semantic grounding, as the robot is able to request feedback in scenarios where instructions are ambiguous.

In Sect. 4.5, we present a scenario where such dialogue is used to clarify ambiguous instructions and correctly perform the command, showing that incorporating dialogue with AR in this way allows a human-robot team to rapidly achieve mutual understanding in decision-making situations.

## 4   Experiments

### 4.1   AR and Robot Hardware Implementation

The human teammate's AR-HMD used for these experiments is the Microsoft HoloLens[1] shown in Fig. 1a. The HoloLens performs vision-based SLAM onboard using a forward-facing camera array and internal IMU.

For these experiments, the human is paired with a robot teammate. A Clearpath Robotics Jackal (Fig. 1b) is equipped with a Velodyne VLP-16 LiDAR, Microstrain 3DM-GX4 inertial measurement unit (IMU) and an Orbbec Astra

---

[1] www.microsoft.com/en-us/hololens.

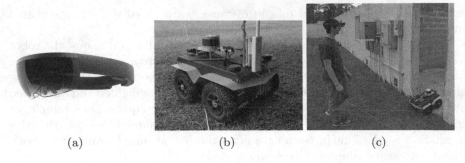

(a)                        (b)                        (c)

**Fig. 1.** The hardware used for these experiments: (a) Microsoft HoloLens AR-HMD, and (b) Clearpath Robotics Jackal. In (c), the human and robot teammates enter an experiment environment.

Pro camera. The robot is capable of both simultaneous localization and mapping as well as autonomous navigation as described in [6].

### 4.2 Understanding Teammate Position Enables Cooperative Navigation

Through communication of the mapping information from the AR-HMD and subsequent alignment of that map with the robot's map, the robot is able to understand where the human is relative to the robot. This understanding enables the human-robot team to perform cooperative navigation, where the robot is able to both share search results and provide navigation assistance to the human to each search target.

We demonstrated this ability in a search scenario, where the human and robot are searching an environment for targets, which could be disaster victims, infrastructure needing repairs, etc., which when found by the robot require the attention of the human teammate. Because this is not a visual classification task, in our case we use AprilTags[2] to represent these targets. The targets are hidden in uninstrumented indoor and outdoor field environments (Fig. 2).

The human and robot split up to search. As illustrated in Fig. 3, when the robot identifies and localizes a target, using its understanding of the human position, the robot is able to share the target location via AR. Using its onboard navigation planning, the robot is also able to provide navigation direction via AR to bring the human to the correct target. This cooperative navigation is possible even if the human has not explored the environment where the target is located – the human teammate receives easy to follow navigation direction in the form of a highlighted path through the environment that is updated as the human moves.

We believe these experiments in cooperative search illustrate the general potential impact for robot teammates providing increased situational awareness

---

[2] april.eecs.umich.edu/software/apriltag.

(a)                                            (b)

**Fig. 2.** Indoor/outdoor field environment (a) and example target placement in the environment (b).

to human teammates, through enabling the critical capability of robot under-standing of human position.

### 4.3  Merging Map Information Enables Cooperative Exploration

Building upon understanding of human teammate position, the ability to merge heterogeneous human and robot maps allows *both* the human and the robot to reason about where the other has been.

With this capability, knowledge of each teammate's map is available to the other, but clearly each teammate is able to use this information in different ways. The robot is able to plan its exploration strategy over the map explored by the team, not just the robot. Likewise, the human is able to see detailed information about the team's exploration progress and the robot's reasoning, which we present via AR and illustrated in Fig. 4. This includes visualization of the unexplored regions (yellow spheres), unexplored frontiers and projected information gain for exploring them (orange polygons best seen in Fig. 4b), and the robot's plan (green path showing intended navigation route and purple discs showing navigation goals to explore corresponding frontiers in Fig. 4c).

Using this information, the robot is able to explore only areas that the human has not explored, increasing team exploration efficiency. Likewise, the human is able to do the same, using visualizations showing the explored and unexplored regions. In addition, as the human teammate also has access to the robot's planned path, he/she can select areas to explore that are not along the robot's route. Further, by being able to see the robot's *future* plans and expected infor-mation gains for each, the human can choose to exploit this information to fur-ther deconflict his/her exploration actions while maximizing exploration infor-mation gained, e.g., by exploring the frontier with the highest information gain that is not in the robot's immediate plan.

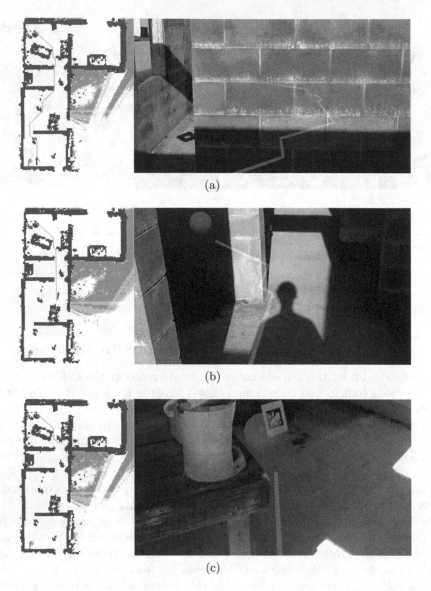

**Fig. 3.** Cooperative navigation in a search task: (a)–(c) show a sequence of human navigation to a target detected by the robot teammate. In this scenario, the human and robot search independently. When the robot discovers a target, it plans a path from the human's current position to the target. That navigation plan is communicated and visualized to the human (cyan blue line) as well as the target location (red sphere). The navigation plan is updated online as the human moves through the environment, as shown in the robot-generated map on the left, where the red arrow indicates the current location of the human. Through understanding of teammate position in this way, the robot is able to provide navigation assistance to the human teammate, even through parts of the environment that the human has not yet visited. (Color figure online)

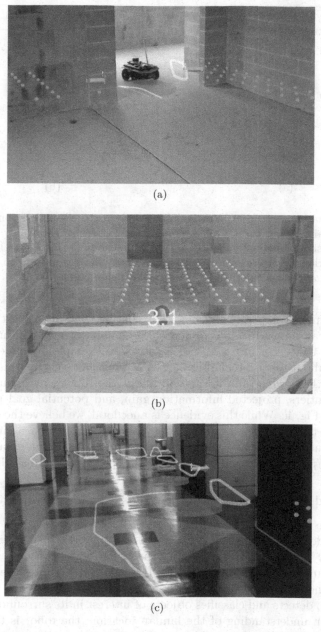

(a)

(b)

(c)

**Fig. 4.** Heterogeneous map composition allows sharing autonomous robot information-theoretic-based exploration plans, including visualizing unexplored regions (yellow spheres), exploration frontiers and estimated potential information gain (orange polygons with arrows and white numerical text), selected points to begin frontier exploration (purple circles), and robot planned path (green line) via AR for cooperative exploration. Using this information, the human teammate is able to understand the robot's reasoning about the exploration task and explore areas of high reward (information gain) that do not conflict with the robot teammate's plan. (Color figure online)

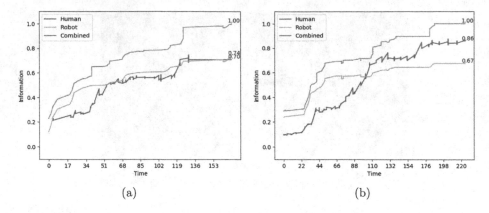

**Fig. 5.** Information gain from human, robot, and combined exploration. (a) shows information gain in the presence of communication of robot intent only (green lines in Fig. 4). (b) shows information gain from communication of all information (Fig. 4c). Note that overlaps in exploration result in combined information gain that is not the sum of human and robot information gain. (Color figure online)

Our preliminary experiments show that sharing this sort of past and future information can be used to inform and shape human behavior in human-robot collaborative tasks. For example, Fig. 5 shows an example outcome of sharing information about robot intent (Fig. 5a), as in the robot's current planned path, compared with showing full information about the robot's reasoning (Fig. 5b), including frontiers, projected information gain, and potential goal positions as illustrated in Fig. 4c. While this evidence is anecdotal, we believe the observation that sharing the robot's reasoning about complex tasks such as information-based exploration can shape the behavior of human teammates and thereby improve task performance will be supported by planned future studies.

### 4.4   Shared Object Recognition Enables Semantic Understanding

The ability to provide immediate, transparent insight into the robot teammate's semantic understanding of its environment is a powerful tool to enable team coordination. We validate this capability through proof-of-concept experiments, where the human teammate is able to select, via the AR interface, objects of interest for the robot to visit.

The robot detects and classifies objects of interest in its surroundings. Again building upon understanding of the human location, the robot is then able to provide information about those objects (location, size, orientation) so that the objects can be highlighted (e.g., with a bounding box) and annotated (e.g., with text) via AR. Then, the human teammate is able to use the AR-HMD interface to select an object for the robot to visit. This is done using the cursor in the center of the HMD field of view and the "click" gesture provided by the HoloLens interface. The selected object is set as a goal position for the robot to visit using its onboard autonomous navigation.

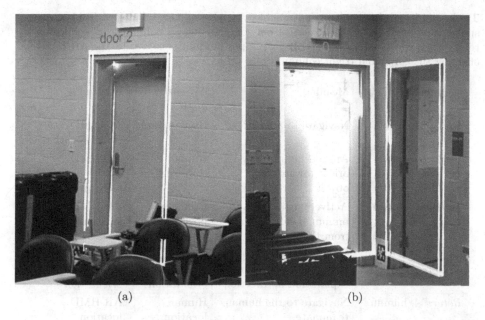

(a)                                    (b)

**Fig. 6.** Shared object recognition allows object (doorway) location and semantic labeling. (a) shows the case of a single door label and index ("door 2"). (b) shows the case of two doors detected in the same vicinity ("door 0" and "door 1"). Note that the bounding box in these images have been manually adjusted to best account for the AR-HMD viewing angle. Automatically finding and displaying the most useful and human-interpretable placement of such 3D visualizations from the human/AR-HMD perspective is an open research question.

For example, illustrated in Fig. 6a, the human is able to give direction to visit the doorway ("door 2"), knowing that the robot has detected and labeled a doorway. The robot can then take appropriate action. While in this case that action is to simply approach the doorway opening, one could imagine more complicated robot behaviors tied to object classification types, commands, and the combinations thereof.

For example, if the robot recognized a potentially dangerous object (e.g., fire, leaking pipe, explosive device), it could be instructed to *take measurements* of that object. Because the human teammate is aware that the robot has classified the object as dangerous, he or she would know that the *take measurements* command would result in the robot keeping a safe distance while recording sensor data, without having to instruct the robot to maintain a safe distance explicitly, thus simplifying the interaction requirements.

We envision this sort of mutual semantic understanding through shared object recognition, which is readily enabled by AR, will improve human-robot team coordination. By knowing what the robot teammate has seen because he or she can see the same information visualized in augmented reality, the human

**Table 1.** List of simple commands enabled by AR-enhanced dialogue. Table contains spoken command (italics) and non-verbal component (left column), interpretation by robot teammate (center column), and the input modality enabled by the AR-HMD for effecting the command (right column).

| Command | Meaning | AR-enabled input | Source |
|---|---|---|---|
| *Go to* + cursor | Navigate to a position | Human gaze | AR-HMD cursor location |
| *Go to [object]* | Approach an object & orient towards that object | Human command | AR-HMD Speech recognition |
| *Follow* + human | Actively maintain a minimum safe distance from the human teammate | Human position | AR-HMD location |
| *Explore* + direction | Begin information-based exploration in direction | Human orientation | AR-HMD orientation |
| *Return* + human | Navigate to the human teammate | Human location | AR-HMD location |
| *Stop* | Cease movement | | |

will be able to communicate to the robot in that context and know if he or she can expect contextually appropriate behavior.

### 4.5   AR-Enhanced Dialogue Enables Team Decision Making

Finally, we further build upon the previous capabilities to show how AR-enhanced dialogue can be used for team decision making.

Using a basic fixed dialogue consisting of commands and object annotations as discussed in Sect. 3.4, the human teammate is able to give the robot basic commands. The semantic understanding of objects (Sect. 4.4) is particularly valuable in that the human is able to use the classifications of objects in commands, e.g., to "go to door 2" as in Sect. 4.4, except using spoken dialogue instead of pointing and clicking. This dialogue is made more impactful by both the visualization of information from the robot via AR (semantic labeling of objects), and by the use of human teammate information (position and head orientation from the AR-HMD). A table of basic commands is shown in Table 1, showing the command, command meanings, and input modality from the AR-HMD used in the command context.

While this is indeed a useful, if basic, capability, the significance of this capability is even more apparent when dialogue can be used to clarify ambiguity in the robot's understanding of human commands.

For example, Fig. 6b shows a situation where the robot detects multiple doorways. In this situation, if the human directs the robot to go to the doorway, the robot must make a decision about which doorway. Using the AR-HMD and audio and visual text prompts, the robot can ask the human teammate for clarification – i.e., which doorway. The human can respond with a simple vocal command (e.g., "door 0"), to disambiguate and identify the correct doorway object.

This capability, combined in this way with the object recognition capability from Sect. 4.5, results in a powerful method of rapidly disambiguating communication, through communicating the presence of and resolution to the ambiguity. We believe this capability will be particularly impactful as human-robot teams operate in increasingly complex, cluttered environments.

# 5 Conclusion

Motivated by the vision of humans and robots operating together as teammates in challenging field environments, we have presented four approaches to using AR to share metric and symbolic information between human and robot teammates: understanding of teammate position, composition of heterogeneous mapping information from teammates, shared understanding of object recognition, and AR-enhanced dialogue. The combination of these AR-enabled abilities beings to address critical requirements for human-robot teaming in field environments. While the results presented in this work are limited, and engineering effort is still required to create robust systems, the technological approaches presented can begin to enable these capabilities, and these limitations will be addressed with future studies. The realization of these capabilities supports the argument that current AR technology, combined with novel approaches, can enable teams of humans autonomous mobile robots to work together in field environments.

# References

1. Andersen, R.S., Madsen, O., Moeslund, T.B., Amor, H.B.: Projecting robot intentions into human environments. In: 2016 25th IEEE International Symposium on Robot and Human Interactive Communication (RO-MAN), pp. 294–301. IEEE (2016)
2. Chadalavada, R.T., Andreasson, H., Krug, R., Lilienthal, A.J.: That's on my mind! robot to human intention communication through on-board projection on shared floor space. In: 2015 European Conference on Mobile Robots (ECMR), pp. 1–6. IEEE (2015)
3. Chakraborti, T., Sreedharan, S., Kulkarni, A., Kambhampati, S.: Alternative modes of interaction in proximal human-in-the-loop operation of robots. arXiv preprint arXiv:1703.08930 (2017)
4. Erat, O., Isop, W.A., Kalkofen, D., Schmalstieg, D.: Drone-augmented human vision: Exocentric control for drones exploring hidden areas. IEEE Trans. Vis. Comput. Graph. 24(4), 1437–1446 (2018)
5. Frank, J.A., Moorhead, M., Kapila, V.: Mobile mixed-reality interfaces that enhance human-robot interaction in shared spaces. Front. Robot. AI 4, 20 (2017)

6. Gregory, J., et al.: Application of multi-robot systems to disaster-relief scenarios with limited communication. In: Wettergreen, D.S., Barfoot, T.D. (eds.) Field and Service Robotics. STAR, vol. 113, pp. 639–653. Springer, Cham (2016). https://doi.org/10.1007/978-3-319-27702-8_42

7. Hedayati, H., Walker, M., Szafir, D.: Improving collocated robot teleoperation with augmented reality. In: Proceedings of the 2018 ACM/IEEE International Conference on Human-Robot Interaction, pp. 78–86. ACM (2018)

8. Murphy, R.R.: Disaster Robotics. MIT Press, Cambridge (2014)

9. Palmarini, R., Erkoyuncu, J.A., Roy, R., Torabmostaedi, H.: A systematic review of augmented reality applications in maintenance. Robot. Comput.-Integr. Manuf. **49**, 215–228 (2018)

10. Park, S., Oh, Y., Hong, D.: Disaster response and recovery from the perspective of robotics. Int. J. Precis. Eng. Manuf. **18**(10), 1475–1482 (2017)

11. Reardon, C., Lee, K., Fink, J.: Come see this! augmented reality to enable human-robot cooperative search. In: Proceedings of the 2018 IEEE Symposium on Safety, Security, and Rescue Robotics (2018)

12. Ren, S., He, K., Girshick, R., Sun, J.: Faster R-CNN: towards real-time object detection with region proposal networks. In: Advances in Neural Information Processing Systems, pp. 91–99 (2015)

13. Rosen, E., et al.: Communicating robot arm motion intent through mixed reality head-mounted displays. In: Proceedings of the 2017 International Symposium on Robotics Research (ISRR) (2017)

14. Segal, A., Haehnel, D., Thrun, S.: Generalized-ICP. In: Robotics: Science and Systems, vol. 2, p. 435 (2009)

15. Trevor, A.J.B., Rogers, J.G., Christensen, H.I.: OmniMapper: a modular multi-modal mapping framework. In: 2014 IEEE International Conference on Robotics and Automation (ICRA), pp. 1983–1990, May 2014. https://doi.org/10.1109/ICRA.2014.6907122

16. Walker, M., Hedayati, H., Lee, J., Szafir, D.: Communicating robot motion intent with augmented reality. In: Proceedings of the 2018 ACM/IEEE International Conference on Human-Robot Interaction, pp. 316–324. ACM (2018)

17. Williams, T., Tran, N., Rands, J., Dantam, N.T.: Augmented, mixed, and virtual reality enabling of robot deixis. In: Proceedings of the 10th International Conference on Virtual, Augmented, and Mixed Reality (2018)

18. Zevallos, N., et al.: A real-time augmented reality surgical system for overlaying stiffness information. In: Robotics Science and Systems (RSS) (2018)

19. Zhu, D., Veloso, M.: Visualizing robot behaviors as automated video annotations: a case study in robot soccer. In: 2017 IEEE/RSJ International Conference on Intelligent Robots and Systems (IROS), pp. 6408–6413. IEEE (2017)

# Augmented Reality Based Actuated Monitor Manipulation from Dual Point of View

Ying Ren[✉] and Jiro Tanaka

Graduate School of Information, Production and System, Waseda University,
Kitakyushu, Japan
m18302962396@163.com, jiro@aoni.waseda.jp

**Abstract.** The mobile robots are increasingly used in domestic space for room surveillance. However, joystick based controller dose not realize direct and intuitive motion control for monitor. To solve this problem, we propose an augmented reality based interface to control monitor from dual point of view, referring to the third-person view and rear first-person view. In this system, augmented reality models used to represent monitor are superimposed on the dual point of view, which enables users to control each part of actuated monitor intuitively with interaction of augmented reality models on screen. Through augmented reality models, our system realized the concept of user-centered manipulation since the control of target object is described in user's coordination system. In addition, we carried out a preliminary user study to evaluate our design and the performance of the system, and a positive feedback has been received.

**Keywords:** Robot control · Augmented reality · Dual point of view · Direct control

## 1 Introduction

Recent years, mobile robots are increasingly utilized in domestic space for room surveillances. Since the complex motion control of monitor in diverse working environments, it is necessary to develop a natural Human-Robots Interaction system to realize intuitive manipulation [8]. Especially for inexperienced user, understand the function of button may burden their thinking.

Traditionally, joystick based controller is most commonly used for robot control. However, the limitation of button operation cannot enable user to realize direct and intuitive operation. On the one hand, complicated motion manipulation implemented on the multiple buttons is not a direct way to indicate the controlling relationship between controller and robot. Especially for inexperienced user, it may demand more effort for them to get familiar with the function of controller. Moreover, by using joystick based control, the gap between user's coordinate system and robot's coordinate system may led to mapping

© Springer Nature Switzerland AG 2019
J. Y. C. Chen and G. Fragomeni (Eds.): HCII 2019, LNCS 11575, pp. 93–107, 2019.
https://doi.org/10.1007/978-3-030-21565-1_7

errors between users' input and robot's motion. Therefore, extra calculation is required for user to map the relative direction between themselves and robot.

Recent years, however, compared to conventional button controller, video-based interface like smartphone and PC are widely used which can provide unlimited interaction designed by software [4]. Commonly, their control is based on single view, such as third-person view or first-person view. For operation on these two views respectively, however, some disadvantages cannot be solved. Specifically, in the third-person view provided by fixed camera, robot cannot be manipulated in dead zone of view. In the first-person view, since the narrow vision of robot-mounted camera, user cannot understand the situation of entire working space.

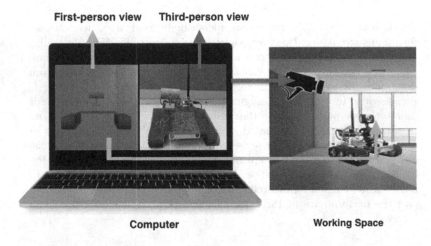

**Fig. 1.** Augmented reality based robot manipulation system.

In this study, we propose a robot manipulation system which enables users to control the actuated monitor intuitively with interaction of augmented reality model from dual point of view, which refers to the third-person view and rear first-person view. As shown in Fig. 1, the screen of PC displays two live videos acquired from fixed setting camera observing the robot from third-person view, and robot-mounted camera observing the working space from first-person view. On dual point of view, augmented reality models are applied to monitor control which allow users to manipulate each part of monitor by directly dragging the corresponding models to target position or direction. With these models, we can realize the spatially consistent relation between virtual world and real world for more intuitive operation. Furthermore, augmented reality based manipulation eliminates the difference of view point between users and monitor since manipulation is described in user's coordinate and it is unnecessary to consider relative position and direction between monitor and themselves.

In addition, our system is based on dual point of view. In the third-person view, users can catch the sight of entire working space including controlled monitor, target objects for observing and surrounding obstacles. With this, it is more efficient to determine the motion of monitor and much easier to avoid collisions. However, in specific situation such as dead zone of the view from fixed setting camera, user need to operation in first-person view. In practical work, two point of view are complementary to each other in diverse settings to provide users with all-around view.

## 2   User Interaction

Our system is an augmented reality interaction interface for users' operation on monitor. The two cameras capture the live videos of the working space in different view point which show on the screen simultaneously. Physical monitor in live video is overlaid with augmented reality models on dual point of view. In the way of mouse control, the user select the part of virtual model they want to control, and then drags it to the target position and direction. As user control the virtual model in real time, the system drives the physical monitor so that it matches with the motion of augmented reality model.

### 2.1   Dual Point of View

In order to provide user with all-around view, our system allows the operation on monitor from two point of view: third-person view and first-person view.

**Third-Person View.** Surveillance by fixed setting camera in different places is the most commonly way for safety supervision. Usually, the camera is mounted in appropriate position without much obstructions on view. In addition, the height of camera is exceeded the person's eye level in order to obtain a broad vision. In our system, a fixed camera is installed in the working space, the view from this camera is considered as the third-person view. With this, a stable view can be obtained for knowing the layout of space and finding target objects for observing efficiently. However, the camera is limited to its fixed position without flexible movement. Although the wide-angle camera can be applied and the camera can be rotated in a given angle range, the dead zone of view and the problem of occlusion are inevitable and difficult to resolve.

**First-Person View.** The actuated monitor is equipped with a camera, and we define the view from this camera as the first-person view. The camera is mounted on a pan-tilt, which can be drove to rotate in two perpendicular orientations. When monitor is employed in a working space, the camera can follow the movement of the monitor to surveilling different places. In addition, the 2DOF (degree of freedom) pan-tilt means even in the fixed position, the direction of vision can also be adjusted to various angle, which provide user with all-around vision.

## 2.2  Augmented Reality Model

For intuitive manipulation, in dual point of view the augmented reality models are built on screen to operate the direction and position of two controlled parts on monitor: 2 DOF pan-tilt and caterpillar band.

**Fig. 2.** Augmented reality model in third-person view.

In the third-person view, aiming to indicate the relation between virtual models and controlled parts, the real objects showing on the screen will be overlapped with augmented reality model described in the fixed camera's coordinate system. As shown in Fig. 2, the virtual models are completely superimposed on camera and caterpillar band with the comparable size and same shape. In addition, the virtual model shows in semi-transparent for avoiding shading the vision of user.

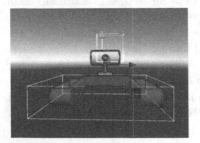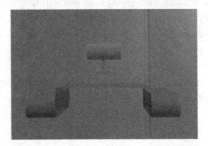

**Fig. 3.** Augmented reality model in rear first-person view.

In the first-person view, in order to realize consistent manipulation interface, the same augmented reality model is made use of on screen for operation (Fig. 3). In general, however, in the vision of the monitor-mounted camera, the pan-tilt and caterpillar band cannot show on its view. In our system, the virtual model reveals on screen just like the view from the back side of the first-person view.

Therefore, we rename this view as the rear first-person view. In each operation, the virtual models representing camera and caterpillar band will be place in the fixed location initially for control. Furthermore, when user manipulate the model of caterpillar band, the virtual model of camera will make synchronous motion since these two parts are connected with each other.

In dual point of view, following the control of mouse, the virtual model of camera on screen, which indicates the direction of 2 DOF pan-tilt, can be dragged to up and down for vertical rotation, or right and left for horizontal rotation. In the same way, the model of caterpillar band, revealing the position and direction of the physical monitor, can be controlled to go forward and back, or make right/left handed rotation.

In real world, the controlled parts of monitor follow the on-screen models to make corresponding motion. User can see the results through the live video on screen.

## 3    System Implementation

Our system is an augmented reality based interface for robot manipulation. By using augmented reality technology, the operation of models' position and orientation on screen can be projected to three-dimensional space for physical monitor control. Moreover, the system has two manipulation methods, one is the third-person view manipulation, the other is the first-person view manipulation.

### 3.1    System Hardware Overview

The hardware of our system consists of the three parts: the actuated monitor, the wireless communication equipment and the host computer. As shown in Fig. 4, the robotic vehicle, whose microprocessor is Arduino, is equipped with a camera connecting with 2 DOF pan-tilt to work as the actuated monitor. The vehicle has a mechanism for locomotion by using caterpillar band, which allows

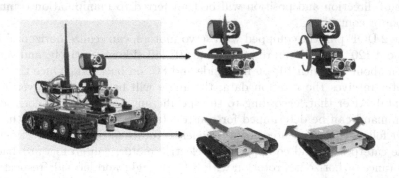

**Fig. 4.** The actuated monitor.

the monitor to rotate and move forward or backward. In addition, the pan-tilt with two servo motors connecting with camera has 2 degree of freedom, vertical rotation and horizontal rotation. In terms of communication part, bluetooth is used to realize serial communication for transmitting manipulation command from host computer to single chip microcomputer.

### 3.2   Vuforia Object Scanner

In the third-person view manipulation, in order to register the position between the real monitor and virtual model, an Android application, Vuforia Object Scanner, is used to scan a physical 3D object [9].

Once user Launch the Vuforia Object Scanner, the target object need to be placed in the grid region of a paper named Object Scanning Target, and the coordinate system will be shown on the screen. According to the size of the target object, it will be a polyhedron covering on the object. Move the camera around the object to scan the vantage points on the surface of the object. Initially, all surface regions are in gray. When a surface region has been successfully captured, it will turn green. Once all of the surface areas are captured, we can press the stop button to terminate the scanning process. Since then, once the target object comes into the view of camera, it can be recognized automatically and its position and orientation in three-dimensional space can be mapped on screen. In addition, the accuracy rate of recognition is related to the number of vantage point on surface, which means the more vantage points you get, the higher accuracy it will be.

### 3.3   Actuated Monitor Manipulation

The system provide users with two manipulation method: third-person view manipulation and rear first-person view manipulation.

**Third-Person View Manipulation.** After controlling the AR model, the change of direction and position will be transferred to manipulation command for monitor control.

The 2 DOF pan-tilt equipped with servo motors, can realize horizontal rotation about 120° with 60° on right side and 60° left side respectively, and vertical rotation about 90° with 10° on front side and 80° on back side. Once the upper computer receives the rotation data, the angle will be judged into vertical or horizontal. After that, according to the specific angle we drag the corresponding command can be determined for control. In the Fig. 5 we can see that the pan-tilt follow the augmented reality model to rotate in different directions.

The caterpillar band equipped with electric motor, can go forward/back in any distance or horizontal rotation with 360° on right and left side respectively. For translation, the upper computer reads the initial position and current position of AR model in coordinate system in Unity and calculates the movement

(a) Vertical rotation

(b) Horizontal rotation

**Fig. 5.** The rotation of 2 DOF pan-tilt

(a) Go forward/back

(b) Left/right handed rotation

**Fig. 6.** The rotation and translation of caterpillar band

distance. If the value is positive, it means the model moves to front side. If negative, the model moves to the back side comparing the previous position. Then the upper computer according to the specific value to determine the corresponding command and send to lower computer. For rotation control, the difference value of current orientation and previous orientation will be calculated to positive or negative corresponding to the right handed or left handed. Then based on the specific angle the upper computer will determine the operation command. After each dragging, the new position and direction data will overlap the old one as the origin point in the monitor's coordinates system. The Fig. 6 shows the translation and rotation of caterpillar band in third-person view.

**Rear First-Person View Manipulation.** In the same way, the system realize the rear first-person view manipulation of two controlled part.

For 2 DOF pan-tilt, we drag the AR model in different direction around two axes, and the change of angle indicates the target direction of camera. As shown in Fig. 7, the smile face shows in different positions in these four pictures, which illustrate the rotation of camera.

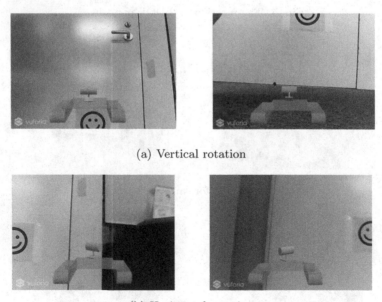

(a) Vertical rotation

(b) Horizontal rotation

**Fig. 7.** The rotation of 2 DOF pan-tilt

Follow the virtual model on screen, in Fig. 8 the caterpillar band can be drove to go forward/back in any distance or horizontal rotation degree with 360° on right and left side respectively.

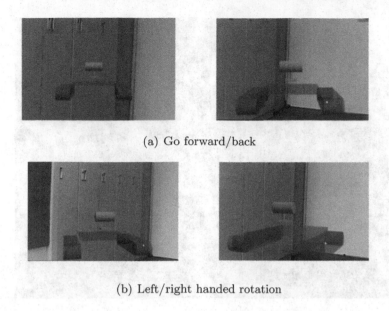

(a) Go forward/back

(b) Left/right handed rotation

**Fig. 8.** The rotation and translation of caterpillar band

# 4    Preliminary Evaluation

We conducted a preliminary user experiment to evaluate the performance of our system. Our target is to test whether our system could achieve an intuitive manipulation of monitor by using augmented reality model in dual point of view.

## 4.1    Participants

We recruited 8 participants including 4 females and 4 males. Before experiment, we asked each participant to confirm all of them have the experience of using joystick to control robot, and they were not familiar with our robot. The experiment took approximately 25 min.

## 4.2    Method

We conducted our user experiment in a prepared working space with the monitor like the Fig. 9 shows. The fixed setting camera was placed at 80 cm high from the floor. No participant was allowed to enter or see the working space before experiment, therefore the working space was a completely unknown environment for them. All objects and the monitor were placed in their initial positions for each trial.

When the test began, we explained to all participants how to control the robot, and the DOF of the robot. Before taking the experiment, the participants were asked to practice using our system for about 15 min. During the experiment,

**Fig. 9.** The experimental working space.

participants were divided into 2 groups. In group 1, they were asked to use third-person view manipulation at first and next rear first-person view. In group 2, the participants were allowed to use two point of view in reverse order. All participants in each group were given 10 min to complete the following task:

(a) Control the caterpillar band to translate from Place A to Place B.
(b) Control the caterpillar band for horizontal rotation.
(c) Control the 2 DOF pan-tilt for horizontal rotation.
(d) Control the 2 DOF pan-tilt for vertical rotation.

After finishing the task, all participants were asked to fill a questionnaire in Table 1. They needed to answer the Q1–Q3 by grading from 1 to 5 (1 = very negative, 5 = very positive) for third-person view manipulation, and Q4–Q6 for rear first-person view manipulation. Finally, in Q7 they need to chose the prefer one in two point of view with three options: (a) third-person view; (b) rear first-person view; (c) using both view.

### 4.3 Results

All participants succeeded in completing task within the stipulated time. After collecting the questionnaires result from all participants, we calculated the average scores of each question from participants in each group respectively. The results from the questionnaire are shown in Fig. 10.

Question 1 to question 6 are related to the practicability of augmented reality based manipulation in two point of view. In each question, the average score of

**Table 1.** Questionnaire

| Third-person view | |
|---|---|
| Q1 | Do you think this interface is intuitive to manipulate monitor in domestic working space |
| Q2 | Do you think using augmented reality model is better than button to control monitor? |
| Q3 | Do you have difficulty to get accustomed to our system to manipulate monitor? |
| **Rear first-person view** | |
| Q4 | Do you think this interface is intuitive to manipulate monitor in domestic working space |
| Q5 | Do you think using augmented reality model is better than button to control monitor? |
| Q6 | Do you have difficulty to get accustomed to our system to manipulate monitor? |
| **Dual point of view** | |
| Q7 | which point of view do you prefer to manipulate monitor? |

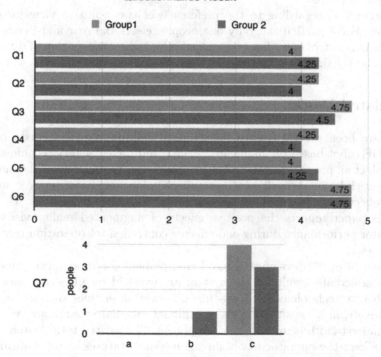

**Fig. 10.** The results of the questionnaire.

two groups are higher than 4 points, which prove that our design can realize intuitive manipulation to some extent.

For question 1 and question 4, the results are opposite. In the post-task interviews we find that it may related to the inverse manipulation order of the two groups. In group 1 participants operated the monitor in the third-person view at first, by which they can understand the entire working space. After that, when they use the rear first-person view later, they can better know the target place for translation. However, for participant in group 2 who did not know the working space before, they may spend longer time to determine target place for translate or rotate. The question 2 and question 5 is related to the comparison between our method with the way of button manipulation. The positive result means our system enable users better manipulation experience than the previous way of joystick control.

Question 3 and question 6 are used to judge the ease of use of our system. The result suggests that the user can easily learn how to use and get accustomed to our system without much difficult. In the post-task interviews, the majority of participants thought other than joystick based control by which user need to know the function of various buttons, using augmented reality model is more direct and simple. Besides, the user indicated that they have successfully learned how to use it in a very short time and our system is very suitable for inexperienced people.

Question 7 is regarding to the preference of two point of view for different people. For 8 participant, only one people selects the rear first-person view manipulation control only. The other people think the combination of dual point of view is better since they can choose more efficient view in different situations.

## 5    Related Work

There have been several studies for intuitive manipulation system to control multi-DOF robot based on augmented reality and mixed reality techniques.

Nawab et al. proposed a system which allows user to understand the mapping of the joystick based controller by overlaying a color-coded coordinate system on the end-effector of the robot by using augmented reality technology [7]. Moreover, this paper reports the positive effects of augmented reality visual cues on operator performance during end-effector controlled teleoperation using only camera views.

Kobayashi et al. developed a novel environment for robot development, in which intermediate results of the system are overlaid on physical space using Mixed Reality technology [6]. Real-time observation enables the developers to see intuitively, in what situation the specific intermediate results are generated, and to understand how results of a component affected the total system. Their method allows the operator to obtain the internal statuses of robot intuitively, which is useful for operation in practical work.

Chen et al. proposed a mixed reality environment for performing robot simulations based on the concept of Mixed Reality [1]. Robot developers can create scenarios for evaluating robot tasks by mixing virtual objects into a real physical environment to create an MR simulation with varying level of realism. The simulation environment can be displayed to users in both an AR and an AV view.

Drascic et al. developed a display system named ARGOS (Augmented Reality through Graphic Overlays on Stereo-video) [2]. In order to enhancing human-robot interaction, an augmented reality through graphic overlaying on a stereo video. In their design, user controls a robotic arm by operate the virtual cursor superimposed on the video image. A tele-robotic system based on augmented reality to control a robotic arm is introduced by Xiong et al. [10]. They designed a virtual robot works as an interface to control the physical robot by using the operator, which can reduce the time-delay between user operation and the action of robot. In addition, they present the advantages of predictive display. Simulation of virtual robot's tasks in the augmented environment improves the safety of the robot when it executes the planned tasks.

Hashimoto et al. propose "TouchMe", a tele-operating system which allows the user to manipulate a multi-DOF robot intuitively with touch interaction from a third-person view [3]. TouchMe de has two elements to realize more intuitive control: (1) Using a third-person view camera because it allows the user to understand the situation of the entire work space. With this, it is easy to avoid collisions with obstacles on the side or behind the robot when the robot is rotating or moving backwards and clear to find target objects for observing and specify the distance of movement and angle of rotation. (2) Building computer graphics (CG) model superimposed on multi-DOF robot to help the user predict how the robot will move and understand the controllable direction of the mounted part. In this work, the camera captures the image of the workspace in real-time, and the image is shown on the touch screen with a CG model overlaid on the real robot. The user controls the robot by touching the part of the CG model where he/she wants to move, and he/she then drags it to the desired position and direction. Although the system eliminates the difference of view point between user and robot, the TouchMe cannot solve the problem of dead zone manipulation. In addition, four markers (ARToolKit [5]) on the top of robot are used to locate the initial state of the robot and also for visual feedback when the robot moves to the specific position or rotates to specific direction. However, marker recognition can be influenced by the shooting angle of the camera. For example, in the angle that four makers are shield by obstacles, robot cannot be recognized successfully.

Comparing with TouchMe, our system has advantages in following two aspects. Firstly, based on third-person view our system add first-person view provided by a robot-mounted camera, which means when robot moves into the dead zone of the third-person view, user can switch to the first-person view for operation. The two point-of-view manipulation systems are running simultaneously and user can switch according to the different situations. What's more, instead of using marker for registration between the real robot and the CG model, an application named Vuforia Object Scanner are used to scan and recognize the robot automatically. It means after scanning the target object and getting enough feature points from its surface, when the target object comes into the view of the camera it can be recognized automatically.

## 6    Conclusion

In this paper, we have presented the design, implementation and an preliminary evaluation of an augmented reality based system for controlling a multi-DOF monitor. Our system allows the user to manipulate each part of the monitor by directly dragging corresponding augmented reality models from dual point of view, which refers to the third-person view provided by a fixed setting camera in working space, and the rear first-person view seen by the camera mounted on monitor. In addition, by using augmented reality models we can realize the spatially consistent relation between virtual world and real world, which means the action of target object is consistent in augmented reality models described in the user's coordination system. Our system have received a positive feedback from the preliminary experiment. The result indicates that user could achieve an intuitive manipulation of monitor by using augmented reality model to some extent. Although in this paper we test our system in a working space with simple environment, it is also suitable for other domestic space with more complex environment.

## References

1. Chen, I.Y.-H., MacDonald, B., Wunsche, B.: Mixed reality simulation for mobile robots. In: Proceedings of the International Conference on Robotics and Automation (ICRA 2009), pp. 232–237. IEEE (2009)
2. Drascic, D., Grodski, J.J., Milgram, P., Ruffo, K., Wong, P., Zhai, S.: ARGOS: a display system for augmenting reality. In: Proceedings of the INTERACT and CHI Conference on Human Factors in Computing Systems (CHI 1993), p. 521. ACM (1993)
3. Hashimoto, S., Ishida, A., Inami, M., Igarashi, T.: TouchMe: an augmented reality based remote robot manipulation. In: Proceedings of the International Conference on Artificial Reality and Telexistence (ICAT 2011), pp. 61–66 (2011)
4. Kasahara, S., Niiyama, R., Heun, V., Ishii, H.: exTouch: spatially-aware embodied manipulation of actuated objects mediated by augmented reality, pp. 223–228 (2013)
5. Kato, H., Billinghurst, M.: Marker tracking and HMD calibration for a video-based augmented reality conferencing system. In: Proceedings of the IEEE and ACM International Workshop on Augmented Reality (IWAR 1999), pp. 85–94. IEEE (1999)
6. Kobayashi, K., Nishiwaki, K., Uchiyama, S., Yamamoto, H., Kagami, S., Kanade, T.: Overlay what humanoid robot perceives and thinks to the real-world by mixed reality system. In: Proceedings of the IEEE and ACM International Symposium on Mixed and Augmented Reality (ISMAR 2007), pp. 1–2. IEEE Computer Society (2007)

7. Nawab, A., Chintamani, K., Ellis, D., Auner, G., Pandya, A.: Joystick mapped augmented reality cues for end-effector controlled tele-operated robots. In Proceedings of the IEEE Conference on Virtual Reality (VR 2007), pp. 263–266. IEEE (2007)
8. Rossi, A., Dautenhahn, K., Koay, K.L., Walters, M.L.: Human perceptions of the severity of domestic robot errors. In: Kheddar, A., et al. (eds.) ICSR 2017. LNCS, vol. 10652, pp. 647–656. Springer, Cham (2017). https://doi.org/10.1007/978-3-319-70022-9_64
9. Vuforia Object Scanner (2018). https://library.vuforia.com/articles/Training/Vuforia-Object-Scanner-Users-Guide
10. Xiong, Y., Li, S., Xie, M.: Predictive display and interaction of telerobots based on augmented reality. Robotica **24**(4), 447–453 (2006)

# Exploring Temporal Dependencies
# in Multimodal Referring Expressions
# with Mixed Reality

Elena Sibirtseva[1(✉)], Ali Ghadirzadeh[1,2], Iolanda Leite[1], Mårten Björkman[1],
and Danica Kragic[1]

[1] Division of Robotics, Perception and Learning,
EECS at KTH Royal Institute of Technology, Stockholm, Sweden
{elenasi,algh,iolanda,celle,dani}@kth.se
[2] Intelligent Robotics Research Group, Aalto University, Espoo, Finland

**Abstract.** In collaborative tasks, people rely both on verbal and non-verbal cues simultaneously to communicate with each other. For human-robot interaction to run smoothly and naturally, a robot should be equipped with the ability to robustly disambiguate referring expressions. In this work, we propose a model that can disambiguate multimodal fetching requests using modalities such as head movements, hand gestures, and speech. We analysed the acquired data from mixed reality experiments and formulated a hypothesis that modelling temporal dependencies of events in these three modalities increases the model's predictive power. We evaluated our model on a Bayesian framework to interpret referring expressions with and without exploiting the temporal prior.

**Keywords:** Multimodal interaction · Human-robot interaction · Referring expressions · Mixed reality

## 1 Introduction

In most industrial applications, robots typically work in isolation from humans in repetitive tasks with or without very little interaction with humans. There has been however, the need for developing collaborative robots that can communicate their intent to humans, but also understand human communicative behaviours [21]. This means that we need to go beyond designing classical pre-scripted robots for industrial settings, and more towards assistive robot co-workers with interaction capabilities that empower human workers. For humans to establish successful communication with robotic agents, robots need to use multisensory approaches to perceive human multimodal data and *interpret social cues that communicate humans' intent.*

One of the challenges in understanding human intent is the multisensory fusion problem [11,23]. The goal of multisensory fusion is to get data from different sensors, combine it in some fashion and, ultimately, a come up with a model

© Springer Nature Switzerland AG 2019
J. Y. C. Chen and G. Fragomeni (Eds.): HCII 2019, LNCS 11575, pp. 108–123, 2019.
https://doi.org/10.1007/978-3-030-21565-1_8

of the user's intentions. The main problem is interpretation of each modality in combination with each other. Our focus in this research is currently on the following modalities: head movements, hand gestures and speech. The interaction scenario we are interested in is a fetching task, where a human participant explains which object he/she needs from the shared workspace and the robot has to interpret the request from the multimodal sensor observations (Fig. 1).

**Fig. 1.** Interaction scenario. The human agent is requesting a robot to give them Lego blocks. Any modality can be used in a natural way, no restriction to the interaction is applied. The only tracked modalities are head movements, hand gestures and speech. The participant wears a mixed reality headset to see which block to request and what is the robot's estimation of their command.

Recent studies focused on intent recognition by combining different features from speech with gaze fixations [1], head movements [25], and gestures [6]. However, in non-guided natural human-robot interaction this approach has its own limitations. Our previous human study [10] showed that participants often look at each other more than at the target object or spend more time looking at the next object in the sequence while still describing the previous one. This lead us to look for more high level behaviour patterns that consist of events happening in all the modalities. Our hypothesis is that it is important to look at *when* a certain event happened (e.g. head fixation, pointing gesture) given events in other modalities and *not for how long*. This way we assume that individual events in modalities can be combined in higher level behaviour patterns based on temporal dependencies.

In this paper we present our findings on the answers to the following questions:

- **Q1:** Do common temporal patterns emerge in participants' behaviour during the fetching request task?
- **Q2:** If we encode these patterns as temporal priors, will they be helpful in inferring the intended object from multimodal referring expressions?
- **Q3:** Are temporal patterns common across most participants or are they person-dependent?

We discuss what we learned from the analysis of a human study and how we see the future development of efficient and natural human-robot interaction in shared workspaces.

## 2    Related Work

Disambiguation of referring expressions is a well-researched topic in the human-robot interaction community. While written text understanding can be performed in batches, real-time interaction requires continuous reference resolution.

Many works focused exclusively on the language part of the request through incremental reference resolution [4,7]. However incremental reference resolution is sometimes not enough to completely disambiguate a verbal request. Additional information can be inferred from other modalites, since studies show that people convey considerable amount of information through non-verbal cues [21]. For instance, through gaze [1,13], head movements [25], and gestures [6]. Our focus is on combining three modalities - speech, head movements, and pointing gestures.

While originally relationships between modalities were encoded through a heuristic approach [3], currently probabilistic graphical models [17,20] and deep learning [24,27] are the most common ways to handle the multimodal representation. We are interested in investigating multimodal behaviour patters and modelling them explicitly in a probabilistic manner. Thus we implemented multimodal fusion as a Bayesian filter, which already showed promising results for reference resolution [26].

More specifically, Whitney et al. [26] developed a Bayesian filter to calculate the belief of an object being the target given observed person's gestures and speech. In this approach, the longer a person is pointing at an object, the more probable it is to be the target. Basing prediction on the longest fixation in continuous modalities such as pointing and gaze [9] are a common way to model them. However, as was shown in our previous study [10], when the complexity of the task is increased, nosiness of these modalities increases accordingly to such an extent that it becomes nearly impossible to make a prediction solely from the longest fixation.

Behaviour studies [2] showed that gestures are temporally coordinated with speech, when people are retelling a scene from their favourite movie. Based on these finding, we hypothesise that by incorporating timing of gestures and head fixations with relation to speech in our model, we can filter out unrelated to the request non-verbal behaviour. In our work, we expand Whitney's framework [26] by learning a temporal prior and adding it to the observations update. Our focus is on the temporal relationships between events in modalities and whether this prior can increase filter's accuracy.

## 3   Methodology

### 3.1   Bayesian Filter

Having three continuous modalities, we want to fuse them together in order to get a probability distribution over all objects ($\mathcal{X}$), given observed speech, head, and pointing inputs ($\mathcal{Z}$) at each time step ($t$). We apply probabilistic inference based on Bayesian filtering [22]. The hidden state, $x_t \in \mathcal{X}$, is the target object in the scene that the person is currently referencing. The robot observes the user's non-verbal actions and speech, $\mathcal{Z}$, and at each time step estimates a distribution over the current state, $x_t$ (Fig. 2):

$$p(x_t|z_{0:t}). \tag{1}$$

First, a prediction about current state is made based only on previous observations and then two types of update are made: time update without any contextual information and observation update, as proposed in [26].

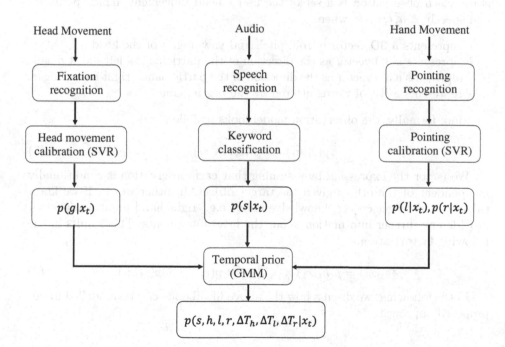

**Fig. 2.** Observation update with a temporal prior

## 3.2   Observation Update

The posterior distribution of $x_t$ given a history of observations, $p(x_t|z_{0:t})$, also known as the belief $\mathcal{B}(x_t)$, is obtained using the Bayesian rule:

$$\mathcal{B}(x_t) = p(x_t|z_{0:t}) = \frac{p(z_t|x_t) \times p(x_t|z_{0:t-1})}{p(z_t|z_{0:t-1})} \propto p(z_t|x_t)p(x_t|z_{0:t-1}). \quad (2)$$

By substituting $p(x_t|z_{0:t-1}) = \sum_{x_{t-1} \in \mathcal{X}} p(x_t|x_{t-1})p(x_{t-1}|z_{0:t-1})$ in the above equation (considering Markovian properties), the Bayes filter algorithm can be used to obtain a recursive update rule:

$$\mathcal{B}(x_t) = p(z_t|x_t) \sum_{x_{t-1} \in \mathcal{X}} p(x_t|x_{t-1})\mathcal{B}(x_{t-1}), \quad (3)$$

where, $p(x_t|x_{t-1})$ is the transition probability found similarly as in [26],

$$p(x_t|x_{t-1}) = \begin{cases} c, & \text{if } x_t = x_{t-1}. \\ \frac{1-c}{|\mathcal{X}|-1}, & \text{otherwise.} \end{cases} \quad (4)$$

where $c$ is a constant value.

The observation model calculates the probability of the observation given the state. Each observation is a set of the user's head movement, hands pointing, and speech, $< h, l, r, s >$ where:

– $h$ represents a 3D vector of roll, pitch and yaw angles of the head.
– $l$ represents a 3D vector as the direction of the participant's left index finger.
– $r$ represents a 3D vector as the direction of the participant's right index finger.
– $s$ represents a list of words uttered by the participant.

More formally, the observation model looks as follows:

$$p(z_t|x_t) = p(h, l, r, s|x_t). \quad (5)$$

We factor the expression by assuming that each observation is conditionally independent of the others given the target object. In other words, if we know the intended target object, knowledge about e.g., right hand pointing does not provide any further information about the head movements. This results in the following factorization:

$$p(z_t|x_t) = p(h_t|x_t) \times p(l_t|x_t) \times p(r_t|x_t) \times p(s_t|x_t). \quad (6)$$

In the following, we discuss how the above likelihoods can be modelled in our proposed approach.

**Head Movement.** We first learn a model p $\leftarrow f_h(h)$ that maps an angular position of the participant head ($h$) into a 2D position on the table ($p$) where the participant is looking at. Following the guidelines of the device [8], we calibrated it as an eye-tracker by training a Support Vector Regression (SVR) [19] with a RBF kernel (C = 10, gamma = 5) on 14 known points on the table. Participants were asked to look at each point for a duration of 1950 ms out of which the first 700 ms period was ignored. This calibration process results in ±4.85 cm gaze positioning error.

Similar to the earlier study [26], we assign distributions over different head angular positions according to the distance between the corresponding gaze location and the target object location, i.e.,

$$p(h_t|x_t = i) \propto \exp\left[-(f_h(h_t) - p_i)^T \Sigma_h (f_h(h_t) - p_{x_t})\right], \tag{7}$$

where, $p_i$ is the position of the $i_{th}$ object on the table, and $\Sigma_h$ is a diagonal co-variance matrix with trainable parameters.

**Hand Gestures.** Similarly, two separate SVM models are trained to map the directions of the left ($p \leftarrow f_l(l)$) and right ($p \leftarrow f_r(r)$) hands to the corresponding 2D positions on the table. Pointing detection is made with the help of LeapMotion device. The same expression as in Eq. 7 is used to assign probability distributions over left $l_t$ and right $r_t$ hand pointing directions conditioned on the target object $x_t$.

**Speech.** First, we use speech recognition to convert audio to text and then perform keywords dictionary-based classification to identify the following speech events:

- attribute - adjectives that describes size, shape or colour of a Lego block from the workspace, e.i. *red, large, cylinder*, etc.
- deictic - i.e. *here, there, this, that*, etc.
- other - any other word that is not included into the previous two categories

As an extra speech event, the beginning of a verbal request is detected from the audio directly. These specific classes were inferred from the initial data collection. The highest correlation was shown between them and events in other modalities.

After detecting speech events, we represent it with a unigram model. Namely, we take each word $w$ in a given speech input $s$ and calculate the probability that, given state $x_t$, that word would have been spoken.

$$p(s|x) = \prod_{w \in s} p(w|x) \tag{8}$$

### 3.3  Temporal Priors

The main hypothesis of this paper, is whether incorporating the knowledge of temporal correlations between high-level events in the input modalities can help the robot to better understand the intentions of a human while the person is referring to something. In order to validate this hypothesis, we propose to use temporal conditional probabilities to represent the observation likelihood introduced in Eq. 2. This yields,

$$
p(s_t, h_t, \Delta T_h, l_t, \Delta T_l, r_t, \Delta T_r | x_t) =
$$
$$
= p(s_t|x_t) \times p(h_t|x_t) \times p(l_t|x_t) \times p(r_t|x_t) \times p(\Delta T_h, \Delta T_l, \Delta T_r | x_t), \quad (9)
$$

where $\Delta T_h = T_s - T_h$, i.e., the time difference between the speech and head movement events. Similarly, $\Delta T_l = T_s - T_l$ and $\Delta T_r = T_s - T_r$. We used $T_s$ as the time reference, since it is less affected by noises compared to the other modalities. Furthermore, we assumed independence between, e.g., the current value of the head position and its event time. However, the time differences between the events are highly correlated.

In this paper, multivariate Gaussian Mixture Models (GMMs) are used to represent the PDF of $p(\Delta T_h, \Delta T_l, \Delta T_r | x_t)$. We assume that modalities are temporally dependent; thus, the co-variance matrix is learned alongside kernels' means. We train GMMs with an Expectation Maximisation (EM) algorithm. Online adaptation of the model is performed via Maximum A Posteriori (MAP) estimation approach, as in Reynolds' work [16], due to a limited number of samples that we are able to collect during the interaction.

## 4  Data Collection

In order to test our hypothesis of existing temporal dependencies in behaviour patterns, we collected data of people interacting with a robot controlled by a wizard of Oz.

Our previous experiments showed that human behaviour varies dramatically in human-human interaction versus human-robot interaction. For instance, if the person has a human partner, they were more prone to use gestures and look at their partner. On the other hand, with a robot partner, participants favoured other modalities, like speech and exaggerated head movements. Moreover, robots can interpret some modalities with more precision than humans do. For humans, it is easier to understand where the person is pointing at than where they are looking. For robots using head movement tracking sensors, this modality becomes much more precise and easy to interpret than hand gestures. Our goal is to recreate the data collection scenario as close as possible to the target settings of the real human-robot interaction we plan our robot to operate in.

**Fig. 3.** First person view of the mixed reality interface. The participant is instructed to request an Lego block, that has an augmented orange circle around it. Robot's guess is indicated as a white cylinder. The virtual robot shows the future trajectory of a picking up motion before the participant confirms whether the object was disambiguated correctly. (Color figure online)

### 4.1  Scenario

In our study, participants are instructed though a projection in a mixed reality headset to request Lego blocks (see Fig. 3) from the robot in an ambiguous environment, i.e., there are several blocks of the same colour and shape. Thus, it is impossible to disambiguate a human request only from speech and the interpretation of other modalities is necessary. Mixed reality was chosen as the way to convey robot's current belief and augment additional information on the shared workspace, based on the results of our previous human study [18]. A human wizard interprets the human requests by looking at what a robot would be able to sense and tries to infer the intended object. When the human participant acknowledges that the robot understood which object the participant meant, the mixed reality headset suggests the next object for the participant to describe to the wizard. The wizard's interface contains data from all the sensors. Namely,

- 3D position and rotation of the participant's head tracked by the headset[1] and updated at frequency 60 Hz;
- Projection from the centre of their head on the table;
- 3D coordinates of both hands, a projection from the index finger on the table when pointing occurs. The original frame rate of the sensor is 120 Hz but to align data streams of head and hand tracking, we record only each second

---

[1] https://www.microsoft.com/en-us/hololens.

frame, resulting in 60 Hz frequency. Tracking is performed by the Leap Motion sensor[2];

- Speech recognition represented as text, acquired from using Microsoft Speech Platform[3]. Speech data is recorded every time the dictation hypothesis is updated. We don't wait for the utterance to be completed, and instead employ a riskier but also faster approach (Fig. 4).

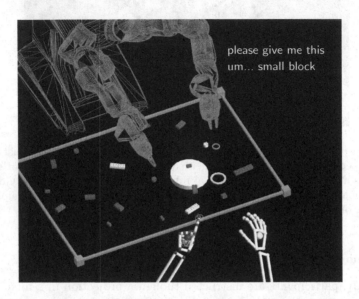

**Fig. 4.** Wizard interface with wizard's guess visualised as a white cylinder around an object. Multimodal input is represent as (a) text from speech recognition; (b) white rectangle being participant's head position and rotation, while a blue circle on the table surface is a projected vector from the centre of the head; (c) skeleton of a hand and a projected position from its finger on the table plane as a green circle. (Color figure online)

## 4.2 Participants

Subjects were recruited using mailing lists and flyers on the university campus. A total of 30 subjects (16 female, 14 male), ages between 23 and 34 ($M = 27.7$), participated in the data collection. All participants had to meet the following requirements: to be fluent in English, not require glasses to see objects 1.5-2 away from them (due to the mixed reality head-mounted display) and not have any colour vision deficiencies. In general, participants indicated their experience with digital technology as $M = 1.3$ on a scale from 5 to 1 (where 1 denotes "very

2   https://www.leapmotion.com/.
3   https://msdn.microsoft.com/en-us/library/hh361572(v=office.14).aspx.

highly"). Moreover, 57% had some experience with virtual reality and only 10% tried augmented/mixed reality head-mounted displays before.

## 4.3   Dataset

Each participant made a total of 20 fetching requests. The time of each request was not fixed; the start time of the request is considered to be the moment a participant was shown a new object in the Mixed Reality interface, and the request was considered resolved when a participant verbally confirmed the robot's guess. Thus, enabling the data collection to proceed to the next randomly selected object and marking the current timestamp as the end of the request. Overall, 600 requests were collected with a total duration of 429 min of uninterrupted recording. Each request consisted of multiple datapoints with the following fields: a timestamp, a 3D vector of *head position*, a boolean variable representing whether the current head movement is a *fixation*, a 3D vector of each hand index *finger positions*, a boolean variable indicating whether the current gesture was *pointing*, the *text of the verbal request* so far from speech recognition, the current *target object*, and current *wizard's guess* of the target object. The final dataset contains $N = 30705$ datapoints.

## 5   Results

This section presents our findings on the questions **Q1 - Q3**.

***Q1: Do common temporal patterns emerge in participants' behaviour during the fetching request task?***

A pre-processing step is performed before training temporal priors encoded as GMMs. All fixations from both head movements and gestures are labelled as intentional or accidental. By intentional, we imply a fixation on the target object. All the other fixations are considered accidental, or noise. In a request, fixations on the minimum distance from the ground truth target object are labelled as intended. Moreover, time intervals of head fixations and pointing gestures are computed relative to the events in the speech modality. As a result, the training data set consists of time intervals and labels of head fixations, gestures and types of the corresponding event in the speech modality. Finally, through leave-one-participant-out cross validation, we train GMMs temporal priors on the training dataset. Analysis of the GMMs densest regions discovers three most common temporal patterns in participants' behaviour, namely:

- **P1** Head fixation + beginning of the verbal request
- **P2** Head fixation + deictic keyword + pointing gesture
- **P3** Object attribute keyword + head fixation

Let's observe how these patterns appear in the human-robot interaction during a fetching request. On the Fig. 5, we visualise a timeline of events in each modality during one of the participant's request. This request contains all three of the common patterns (highlighted with rectangles). In the beginning of the request, the participant, firstly, fixates his/her head on an unrelated to the request object. Then, he starts to verbalise his request with words "please gimme...". Just before the beginning of the utterance, the first common pattern occurs (**P1**) - the participant fixates on the target object. After that several unintentional head fixations are detected alongside with the left hand pointing gesture in an uninformative direction. At the timestamp 800 ms the second pattern (**P2**) is detected - deictic keyword "this" with an intended head fixation and the left hand pointing at the target object. Later on, at timestamps 1300 ms and 1800 ms we can observe **P3**. The participant clarifies his request by saying an attribute key-word "small" and "blue" simultaneously with head fixations on the target object.

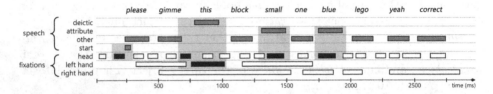

**Fig. 5.** A timeline of events in each modality during request 3 from participant 27. The top line is speech recognition of participant's request. Black rectangles represent fixations on the target object, white on any other. Grey rectangles indicate common behaviour patters. (Color figure online)

**Q2: If we encode these patterns as temporal priors, will they be helpful in inferring the intended object from multimodal referring expressions?**

To answer this question, we compare performance of Bayesian filter with (**BF+TP**) and without (**BF**) temporal priors through leave-one-participant-out cross validation. Bayesian filter without temporal priors (**BF**) is considered as a control condition. Our evaluation consists of two measures - **accuracy** (%) and decision making **time** (sec). Accuracy is measured as a ratio of correctly disambiguated target objects to the total number of requests. Decision making time is computed from the moment a person started speaking and until the robot makes a final decision which object is the target.

There are two possible scenarios of how a model can make a decision.

- *Voluntary decision.* We define a decision making line as 85%, a commonly used value for such scenarios [26]. This means that if probability of an object being the target reaches 85% or higher, given all previous multimodal observations, then the model selects it as a target object.
- *Forced decision.* If during a request no object's probability to be the target one crossed the decision line and there are no datapoints left in this request, then the object with the highest probability is chosen the target.

Models have to make forced decisions due to the way we collected the dataset. A human wizard was imitating a robot during the data collection process; therefore, a request was considered resolved when the wizard guessed the correct target object. However, our models have a limited understanding of multimodal human behaviour and are not as sophisticated as a human wizard reasoning.

To find out what causes the main issues for the models, compared to the human wizard, we analysed only cases where models had to make forced decisions. We manually checked video recordings of the interactions and discovered that the majority of such cases contained utterances such as "to the left", "in the corner", "he same as the previous one" A human is able to infer much more information from such phrases, while our speech system is only corpus-based. This bottleneck can be addressed by implementing a more sophisticated natural language recognition system, for instance, BERT [5].

For models' evaluation we take into account both voluntary and forced decisions.

Two types of evaluation is performed. In the first case, only the first attempt of the model to make a decision is considered. In the second, though, we employ the same way of interaction as during the data collection phase. The model can make several attempts to guess the target object while there is still data left in the request. After each guess it gets feedback whether the guess is correct or not. If it is incorrect, the model excludes the previous object from the possible objects set and proceeds disambiguation participant's request as before. For the multiple attempts case, the decision making time is measured from the beginning and until the guess is either correct or the request is over and the model is forced to make the final guess.

We performed a repeated measurement one-tailed t-test to test significance of our results on the 95% interval. According to the Table 1, **BF+TP** dramatically ($p < 0.00$) decreases decision making time from $24.99 \pm 7.94$ sec to $15.32 \pm 3.08$ sec. Accuracy of the Bayesian Filter with Temporal Priors ($M = 68.45, SE = 5.73$) is also significantly ($p < 0.00$) higher than without ($M = 55.83, SE = 12.01$).

In the multiple attempts case (Table 2), the tendency of **BF+TP** ($M_{time} = 18.85, SE_{time} = 3.73, M_{acc} = 86.22, SE_{acc} = 4.34$) outperforming BF on both measurements is even more evident. Time and accuracy of **BF** does not significantly ($p > 0.05$) change from the first attempt. Number of attempts per request gives us insight into why this is the case. For BF, number of attempts is nearly one per request ($M = 1.14$), while **BF+TP** can make 2.58 on average. An explanation to this can be drawn from the Table 2, specifically the decision making time. **BF** takes approximately 1.6 times more to make the first decision and it does not have enough time left of the request to make an accurate guess on the second attempt. In a multiple attempt scenario **BF+TP** model can potentially make more guesses on the same amount of data, while being more accurate than the control condition.

Therefore, we can conclude that temporal priors have a significant positive influence on both decision making time and accuracy for the both evaluation scenarios.

**Table 1.** Models evaluation on the first attempt at disambiguating a multimodal referring expression

| Model | Time (sec) | Accuracy |
|---|---|---|
| BF | 24.99 ± 7.94 | 55.83% ± 12.01% |
| BF+TP | 15.32 ± 3.08 | 68.45% ± 5.73% |
| BF+TP+OA | **13.41 ± 2.93** | **76.58% ± 5.65%** |

**Table 2.** Models evaluation on multiple number of attempts at disambiguating a multimodal referring expression

| Model | Time (sec) | Accuracy | # Attempts |
|---|---|---|---|
| BF | 25.50 ± 8.11 | 57.38% ± 12.24% | 1.14 |
| BF+TP | 18.85 ± 3.73 | 86.22% ± 4.34% | 2.58 |
| BF+TP+OA | 18.92 ± 3.70 | **89.16% ± 4.28%** | 2.63 |

### Q3: Are temporal patterns common across most participants or person-dependent?

Our approach to **Q3** is to evaluate what is the effect of online adaptation (**BF+TP+OA**) on the decision making time and accuracy versus no participant-based adaptation (**BF+TP**). The model with online adaptation of temporal priors is performed in the same fashion as in the previous section, through leave-one-participant-out cross validation. However, we iteratively update the GMMs temporal priors by feeding them datapoints from the previously resolved request. The following request disambiguation is made with the refitted with all the previous requests model. This implies that with time, the GMMs become more fitted to the temporal patterns of this particular participant. The first requests of each participant in both models with and without adaptation are based on the same temporal priors GMMs.

Our results show that while **BF+TP+OA** accuracy ($M = 76.58, SE = 5.65$) increases significantly ($p = 0.04$) in comparison to the temporal priors without online adaption during the first attempt (Table 1). Decision making time ($M = 13.41, SE = 2.93$), even though has a decreasing trend, is not statistically significant (p = 0.13).

For the multiple attempts case (Table 2), adaptation results also show the best accuracy ($M = 89.16, SE = 4.28$) out of the evaluated models. In regards of decision making time ($M = 18.92, SE = 4.28$) and number of attempts, there was no statistically significant difference found between models **BF+TP** and **BF+TP+OA**.

We can reason that adaptation has a positive effect on model's accuracy, slightly adjusting temporal priors for each participant. The structure of the common patterns stays mostly the same between participants, while the Gaussian Mixtures shift to accommodate to the different timing of each participant individually.

# 6    Conclusion

In this paper, we explored temporal dependencies in multimodal human-robot interaction and developed a Bayesian-based model to evaluate our hypothesis. We developed a system in Mixed Reality to efficiently collect data of humans interacting with a robot in a fetching scenario. As our results showed, taking temporal dependencies between high-level events in all input modalities (i.e. fixations in head movements, key words in speech, etc.) increases the model's speed and accuracy of the person's intention predictions. Moreover, we tested how online adaptation influences results of the prediction and found out that, while both speed and accuracy increase, the change is not as dramatic as between using a Bayesian filter with or without temporal priors. Thus, we came to a conclusion that common temporal patterns exist in human behaviour during referencing objects and have a significant impact on the intention prediction. We encoded temporal priors as a Gaussian Mixture Model and used it with the Bayesian filter to compute probabilities of objects being the target ones.

The next step for this project is to test how scalable our approach is to more complex tasks. Our initial motivation to explore temporal dependencies comes from our previous work [10], where participants where building furniture together. The main challenge there came from the nosiness of input modalities. And the more complex the interaction, the nosier participant's behaviour is. In other words, participants are less distracted and more focused on the task during simple interactions, such as fetching requests. We see the potential benefits of employing temporal priors to tackle nosiness in the more complex interactions.

Another direction will be to add more modalities and explore how they can be represented as high-level events and encoded into temporal behaviour patterns. For instance, body posture and gaze tracking. A more nuanced, not key-words based, approach to natural language understanding can also enrich the possibilities for diverse interactions.

And finally, in the future we would like to focus more on the deep reinforcement learning approaches to multimodal human-interaction. So far our study was necessary for gaining a deeper understanding of human behaviour and multimodal data. However, we want to move away from feature engineering and formulate our human-robot interaction scenario as a deep reinforcement learning problem. Recent studies in HRI showed impressive results in employing deep reinforcement learning for various applications [12,14,15]. The main challenge for deep learning approaches is the lack of training data from human studies but we plan to tackle this problem using our current Bayesian-based model to simulate human behaviour data as a prior for the deep reinforcement learning model.

**Acknowledgements.** This work is supported by the SSF (Swedish Foundation for Strategic Research) projects COIN.

# References

1. Admoni, H., Srinivasa, S.: Predicting user intent through eye gaze for shared autonomy. In: Proceedings of the AAAI Fall Symposium Series: Shared Autonomy in Research and Practice (AAAI Fall Symposium), pp. 298–303 (2016)
2. Bavelas, J., Gerwing, J., Healing, S.: Hand and facial gestures in conversational interaction. In: Holtgraves, T.M. (ed.) The Oxford Handbook of Language and Social Psychology, pp. 111–130. Oxford University Press, Oxford (2014)
3. Bolt, R.A.: "Put-that-there": voice and gesture at the graphics interface, vol. 14. ACM (1980)
4. Chai, J.Y., et al.: Collaborative effort towards common ground in situated human-robot dialogue. In: Proceedings of the 2014 ACM/IEEE International Conference on Human-Robot Interaction, pp. 33–40. ACM (2014)
5. Devlin, J., Chang, M.W., Lee, K., Toutanova, K.: Bert: pre-training of deep bidirectional transformers for language understanding. arXiv preprint arXiv:1810.04805 (2018)
6. Duarte, N., Tasevski, J., Coco, M., Raković, M., Santos-Victor, J.: Action anticipation: reading the intentions of humans and robots. arXiv preprint arXiv:1802.02788 (2018)
7. Funakoshi, K., Nakano, M., Tokunaga, T., Iida, R.: A unified probabilistic approach to referring expressions. In: Proceedings of the 13th Annual Meeting of the Special Interest Group on Discourse and Dialogue, pp. 237–246. Association for Computational Linguistics (2012)
8. Harezlak, K., Kasprowski, P., Stasch, M.: Towards accurate eye tracker calibration-methods and procedures. Proc. Comput. Sci. **35**, 1073–1081 (2014)
9. Huang, C.M., Andrist, S., Sauppé, A., Mutlu, B.: Using gaze patterns to predict task intent in collaboration. Front. Psychol. **6**, 1049 (2015)
10. Kontogiorgos, D., Sibirtseva, E., Pereira, A., Skantze, G., Gustafson, J.: Multi-modal reference resolution in collaborative assembly tasks. In: Proceedings of the 4th International Workshop on Multimodal Analyses Enabling Artificial Agents in Human-Machine Interaction, pp. 38–42. ACM (2018)
11. Lalanne, D., Nigay, L., Robinson, P., Vanderdonckt, J., Ladry, J.F., et al.: Fusion engines for multimodal input: a survey. In: Proceedings of the 2009 international conference on Multimodal interfaces, pp. 153–160. ACM (2009)
12. Lathuilière, S., Massé, B., Mesejo, P., Horaud, R.: Neural network based reinforcement learning for audio-visual gaze control in human-robot interaction. Pattern Recogn. Lett. **118**, 61–71 (2018)
13. Mehlmann, G., Häring, M., Janowski, K., Baur, T., Gebhard, P., André, E.: Exploring a model of gaze for grounding in multimodal HRI. In: Proceedings of the 16th International Conference on Multimodal Interaction, pp. 247–254. ACM (2014)
14. Minh, V., et al.: Human-level control through deep reinforcement learning. Nature **518**(7540), 529 (2015)

15. Qureshi, A.H., Nakamura, Y., Yoshikawa, Y., Ishiguro, H.: Robot gains social intelligence through multimodal deep reinforcement learning. In: 2016 IEEE-RAS 16th International Conference on Humanoid Robots (Humanoids), pp. 745–751. IEEE (2016)
16. Reynolds, D.A., Quatieri, T.F., Dunn, R.B.: Speaker verification using adapted gaussian mixture models. Digit. Sig. Process. $10$(1–3), 19–41 (2000)
17. Savran, A., Cao, H., Nenkova, A., Verma, R.: Temporal bayesian fusion for affect sensing: combining video, audio, and lexical modalities. IEEE Trans. Cybern. $45$(9), 1927–1941 (2015)
18. Sibirtseva, E., et al.: A comparison of visualisation methods for disambiguating verbal requests in human-robot interaction. arXiv preprint arXiv:1801.08760 (2018)
19. Smola, A.J., Schölkopf, B.: A tutorial on support vector regression. Stat. Comput. $14$(3), 199–222 (2004)
20. Srivastava, N., Salakhutdinov, R.: Learning representations for multimodal data with deep belief nets. In: International Conference on Machine Learning Workshop, vol. 79 (2012)
21. Thomaz, A., Hoffman, G., Cakmak, M., et al.: Computational human-robot interaction. Found. Trends® Robot. $4$(2–3), 105–223 (2016)
22. Thrun, S., Burgard, W., Fox, D.: Probabilistic Robotics. MIT Press, Cambridge (2005)
23. Turk, M.: Multimodal interaction: a review. Pattern Recogn. Lett. $36$, 189–195 (2014)
24. Venugopalan, S., Xu, H., Donahue, J., Rohrbach, M., Mooney, R., Saenko, K.: Translating videos to natural language using deep recurrent neural networks. arXiv preprint arXiv:1412.4729 (2014)
25. Veronese, A., Racca, M., Pieters, R.S., Kyrki, V.: Probabilistic mapping of human visual attention from head pose estimation. Front. Robot. AI $4$, 53 (2017)
26. Whitney, D., Eldon, M., Oberlin, J., Tellex, S.: Interpreting multimodal referring expressions in real time. In: 2016 IEEE International Conference on Robotics and Automation (ICRA), pp. 3331–3338. IEEE (2016)
27. Yao, L., et al.: Describing videos by exploiting temporal structure. In: Proceedings of the IEEE International Conference on Computer Vision, pp. 4507–4515 (2015)

# Mediating Human-Robot Interactions with Virtual, Augmented, and Mixed Reality

Daniel Szafir$^{(\boxtimes)}$ (iD)

Department of Computer Science and ATLAS Institute,
University of Colorado Boulder, Boulder, CO 80309, USA
`daniel.szafir@colorado.edu`
`http://danszafir.com`

**Abstract.** Effective human-robot interaction (HRI) remains a critical barrier to the successful and widespread deployment of robotic technologies. Fundamentally, HRI problems represent breakdowns in *communication*, where poor information exchange between people and robots leads to disfluencies, incorrect mental models, poorly calibrated trust, inadequate situational awareness, etc. In this paper, I argue that the emergence of a new generation of virtual, augmented, and mixed reality (VAMR) technologies is creating an exciting new design space in which to address these problems in communication. To support this argument, I present the results of three experiments demonstrating the value in using modern VAMR technologies to mediate human-robot interactions and discuss various challenges and opportunities in this emerging space at the intersection of several communities, including robotics, VR, graphics, and human-computer interaction.

**Keywords:** Human-robot interaction (HRI) · Robotics ·
Virtual reality (VR) · Augmented reality (AR) · Mixed reality (MR) ·
VAMR · 3D user interfaces (3DUI)

## 1 Overview

Robots hold significant promise in benefitting society by supporting human activities across a variety of critical domains, including manufacturing, construction, healthcare, and space exploration. However, in practice, robot deployments remain quite limited because *robots are extremely difficult for people to work with*. A primary source of these difficulties is that humans and robots do not communicate well; people often find robots incomprehensible and have difficulties understanding what a robot can or will do, while robots lack computational models for reasoning about complex human behaviors.

At their core, these issues (aside from purely technical challenges such as limited battery lifetime) are the result of poor information exchange: either the human does not understand the information the robot is conveying, the robot

© Springer Nature Switzerland AG 2019
J. Y. C. Chen and G. Fragomeni (Eds.): HCII 2019, LNCS 11575, pp. 124–149, 2019.
https://doi.org/10.1007/978-3-030-21565-1_9

cannot understand the user's input, or both. These problems are analogous to the *Gulf of Execution* and *Gulf of Evaluation* concepts within the *Human Action Cycle* (Fig. 1), a proposed model describing human interactions with complex systems from the cognitive engineering and human-computer interaction communities [44–46]. At a high level, gulfs of execution arise when users have difficulty translating their high level goals into inputs that a system understands (often because there is a gap between the user's mental model of how a system works and the actual controls/inputs/sequences that the system provides), while gulfs of evaluation occur when users do not understand system feedback and/or have trouble assessing system state.

Translating these concepts to the realm of human-robot interaction, an example of a gulf of execution would be a user attempting to direct a humanoid robot that lacks speech recognition via voice dialog, while an example of a gulf of evaluation would be a user believing that a robot with visually apparent eyes was actively perceiving and tracking the user and the surrounding environment, even if the robot had no actual cameras or visual system. These gulfs are often readily apparent when considering human interaction with humanoid robots due to inaccurate assumptions users commonly hold regarding the link between robot functionality and morphology (e.g., assuming one can talk to a humanoid robot and that the robot will understand), although they may arise with non-humanoid and non-zoomorphic robots as well [22, 36].

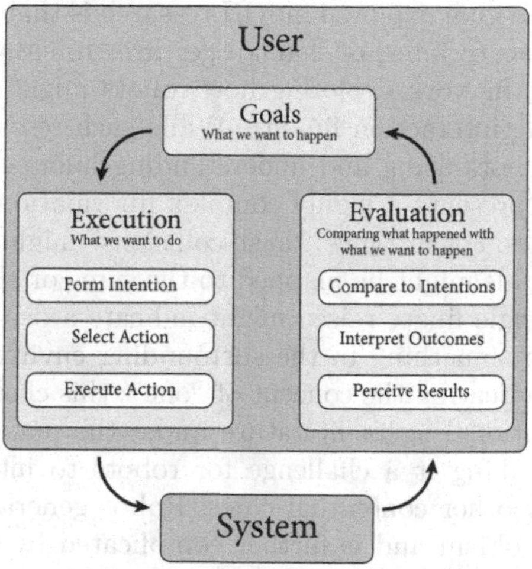

Breakdowns in human-robot interactions can arise from gulfs of execution, gulfs of evaluation, or both. As a result, a great deal of research in the HRI community has examined how to improve human-robot communication.

**Fig. 1.** The Human Action Cycle, a model describing user interaction with complex systems, adapted from [44–46]. This model can also be useful in considering human interactions with robots as breakdowns may occur in both the execution stage (inputting information in an attempt to operate or work with a robot to accomplish some goal) and the evaluation stage (understanding what the robot does and whether that advances the user's goal). Breakdowns in different stages of the cycle will likely require different solutions.

For instance, prior work has examined how to reduce gulfs of execution through the development of computational models that enable robots to interpret a large body of potential human inputs such as gaze (e.g., [1, 2, 30, 31]), gestures (e.g., [53, 72]), natural language (e.g., [49, 71]), and multimodal cues (e.g., [48, 57]), enabling users to interact with robots more naturally and intuitively using methods with which they are already familiar.

Other work has focused on reducing gulfs of evaluation by conveying robot state and plans via expressive and legible motion [19,61], LED lights [5,62], or other methods (see [15] for a survey). Overall, such research typically must address (at least) two fundamental challenges in identifying (1) the *information content* regarding what information should be communicated and (2) the *information medium* in terms of how the information can be communicated effectively[1].

One of the difficulties in HRI research is that these two challenges of what and how to communicate cannot generally be addressed independently, for the medium chosen will necessarily encode the information content, potentially in a lossy manner or in one that is not easy to decode. For instance, one common medium explored in HRI research is that of gestures, either in research exploring how to interpret human gestures to enhance robot comprehension of user goals or in work exploring how robots might utilize gestures as a means of enhancing interaction fluidity. While such research has shown a variety of benefits for robots using and understanding human gestures, gesture communication itself represents a highly complex information medium with many potential difficulties. For instance, "hash collisions" might occur as many different communicative goals might be mapped to the same or similar gestures (e.g., a closed fist with a single finger raised might indicate a deictic pointing gesture to direct attention to something in the surrounding environment or be used as an iconic gesture indicating the concept of "one"; this challenge has been identified in the conversational agent literature under the maxim "behaviors are not functions" [14]), making it a challenge for robots to interpret human gestures in the absence of other contextual clues. Robot generation of gestures suffers from this same problem and is further complicated by our current lack of standardized robot hardware, meaning desired gestures may be difficult or impossible to implement on a given platform or generalize across platforms. Overall, gesture communication among humans is still not fully understood, thus developing a general framework of gesture modeling and production for robots remains an extremely challenging and open problem.

The fundamental difficulties in communication modeling and understanding described above are not unique to gestural interaction, but are common across any medium used for information exchange (for example, consider the analogous problem of understanding *channel capacity* in information theory). However, different mediums make trade-offs regarding various aspects of communication; for instance verbal communication might be used to communicate larger and more complex ideas than purely gestural communication, but may also require more direct attention be less effective for exchanging immediate or low-level ideas (e.g., a deictic gesture may better direct attention and convey spatial information than a verbal description of where to look). One of the major goals of the HRI field is to bring human-robot interactions to the same level of naturalness and

---

[1] Here "effectively" may take many different meanings depending on context, for instance scenarios involving robots in emergency response might prioritize the speed and accuracy of information exchange, while robots in social settings might prioritize fluidity and naturalness.

effectiveness as human-human interactions (or one day, potentially even surpass them), where interactants commonly switch between mediums and often leverage multiple mediums simultaneously in synchronicity to effectively communicate and identify and repair communicative breakdowns as they occur.

Towards this end, new methods of communication may be highly valuable in enhancing HRI because robots are not limited to only communicating in a manner similar to humans (i.e., using traditional verbal and nonverbal cues). For example, prior work has found that various electronic and computer-mediated methods may be highly beneficial, ranging from the use of enhanced graphical displays to improve robot control (reducing gulfs of execution) [43] to the previously raised example of LED lights that communicate various robot signals (reducing gulfs of evaluation). Recently, the rise of consumer-grade, standardized virtual, augmented, and mixed reality (VAMR) technologies (including the Microsoft HoloLens, Meta 2, Magic Leap, Oculus Rift, HTC Vive, etc.) are creating a promising new medium for information exchange between users and robots. This medium seems particularly well suited to human-robot communication for a variety of reasons. For example, robots often collect 3D spatio-temporal data that may be useful to transmit to users for analysis, which aligns well with one of the primary benefits of the emerging ecosystem of modern VAMR head-mounted displays (HMDs), namely the ability to provide users with 3D virtual imagery with accurate stereoscopic depth cues. In addition, modern HMDs are typically hands-free (and thus may easily integrate with existing solutions for managing human-robot interactions) and can even provide additional communicative channels beyond the visual (e.g., providing 3D spatial audio or microphones for speech recognition).

In this paper, I trace the development of early work merging HRI and VAMR (which, while promising, was often hampered by limitations in underlying VAMR technologies) and highlight more recent work that leverages modern systems. To highlight the potential of VAMR as a communicative medium for mediating HRI, I further detail the results of three laboratory experiments with 126 participants: one experiment examining how VAMR might reduce a gulf of evaluation by presenting users with visualizations of planned robot trajectories, one experiment exploring how VAMR might reduce a gulf of execution by enhancing robot teleoperation, and one experiment examining an integrative VAMR approach towards reducing both gulfs in the design of a new robot supervisory control interface. In each experiment, solutions that utilize VAMR significantly outperform commercially available systems in common use today. I close with a discussion of the current state of VAMR-HRI research and the opportunities and challenges I have observed conducting this research, which sits at the intersection of several communities, including robotics, graphics, and human-computer interaction, that have historically developed largely independent from one-another.

## 2    Background

The development of VAMR technologies typically trace back to Sutherland's vision of "The Ultimate Display" (itself influenced by Vannevar Bush's conception of the Memex) [59] and later developments with the Sword of Damocles system [60]. A full review of the development of VAMR technologies and user experience since the 1960's is beyond the scope of this article, although helpful surveys can be found in [4,8,54]. Instead, below I concentrate on tracing early efforts aimed at improving human-robot interaction by integrating VAMR technologies.

## 2.1  VAMR and HRI

The earliest major work leveraging VAMR for HRI appears to date back to a push in the late 1980's and early 1990's with various work exploring robot teleoperation systems [7,10,26,32,34,56,58,73] that largely originated in the IEEE IROS, ICRA, and SMC communities, although contemporaneously the SIGGRAPH community also noted this as an promising area for future overlapping work [9]. Perhaps the most fully-developed instance of these early systems was the ARGOS interface for augmented reality robot teleoperation [40]. While the ARGOS interface used a stereo monitor, rather than the head-mounted displays in vogue today, the system introduced several design elements for displaying graphical information to improve human-robot communication and introduced concepts such as virtual pointers, tape measures, tethers, landmarks, and object overlays that would influence many subsequent designs (Fig. 2).

Later developments throughout the 1990's introduced several other important concepts, such as the use of virtual reality for both actual robot control and teleoperator training [28,41], the integration of HMDs (including the first use of an HMD to control an aerial robot [66]), projective virtual reality where user "reaches through" a VR system to control a robot that manipulates objects in the real world [24,63], the rise of VAMR applications for robotics in medicine and surgery [11], and continued work on ARGOS and ARGOS-like systems [39,50]. At a high level, major themes appear to be work focused on using VR for simulation or training purposes, VR and/or AR as new forms of information displays (e.g., for data from robot sensors), and generally VAMR-

**Fig. 2.** The ARGOS system represented one of the earliest robot teleoperation interfaces that leveraged VAMR technology. Here, a "virtual tether" concept is illustrated, which might visualize potential constraints or information about the position and orientation of the manipulator and target. Image reproduced from [40].

based robotic control interfaces. While many of these developments appear initially promising, it is interesting to note that following an initial period of intense early research on HRI and VAMR, later growth throughout the 1990's appears

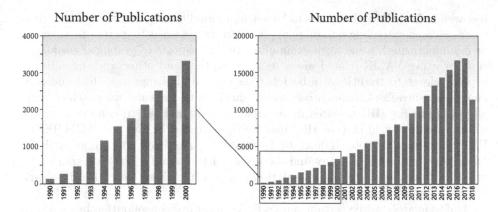

**Fig. 3.** Publication rates from Google Scholar under the query "'robot' AND 'virtual reality' OR 'augmented reality' OR 'mixed reality'" since 1990 as a rough approximate of research productivity in the VAMR-HRI space. Rates appear to have fairly constant growth between 1990 and 2000 (left), but the full picture (right) indicates we may actually be close to the inflection point for exponential growth and are entering an exciting time for the field. The relatively low numbers for 2018 are likely due to proceedings from 2018 having yet to be archived in Scholar.

to have happened at a relatively stable rate, rather than rapidly expanding (Fig. 3). In addition, efforts to take research developments beyond laboratory environments into commercial/industrial systems appear to have been largely unsuccessful (indeed, even today robot teleoperation interfaces are still typically based on standard 2D displays rather than leveraging VAMR).

In general, I speculate that several key challenges towards VAMR-HRI research may have inhibited the initial growth of the area. First, the lack of any standardized VAMR or robotics hardware at this time introduced an incredibly high barrier towards conducting VAMR-HRI research as essentially all of the research of this time period required laboratories to have the expertise to build both robotics and VAMR equipment, two already highly specialized areas. Moreover, hardware specialization may have introduced difficulties generalizing findings across systems or extending prior work. Second, the general failure of VAMR technologies in the commercial entertainment market of the early 1990's may have soured both industry and academic researchers on conducting further explorations of such systems. This issue may have been exacerbated by the general lack of formal system evaluations in the research developments at this time (i.e., user studies for VAMR-HRI systems of this time period are exceedingly rare, with research papers written largely as system implementations), making it difficult to quantify the value of developments such as those produced in the ARGOS interface.[2] Finally, rather than developing in a cohesive manner,

---

[2] This issue was not unique to VAMR-HRI, as formal evaluation methods have taken time to integrate into many research communities even though they inherently deal with some form of human interaction, including robotics more generally.

research in VAMR-HRI appears to have fragmented throughout the 1990's, with some research extending into more application-driven areas (e.g., robotic surgery or manufacturing), some work examining specific aspects of graphics, visualization, or other VAMR-related areas such as haptics, and other work examining aspects closer to traditional robotics. One critical challenge may have been a lack of a centralized research community and venue for such work, which was also an issue for HRI research more broadly as it had yet to consolidate into its own distinct field (a time that may be demarcated by the first ACM/IEEE HRI conference in 2006). Indeed, by 1999 there was already concern about how "to a large extent the robotics and the newer virtual reality (VR) research communities have been working in isolation" even while there were already clear, promising ideas for their integration [12].

Unfortunately, while certain venues for community consolidation have arisen (e.g., HCII VAMR for both the VAMR and HCI communities), VAMR-HRI work continued in a largely fragmented manner throughout the 2000's, with work scattered across the traditional VAMR communities (IEEE VR, ISMAR, 3DUI, etc.), robotics communities (ICRA and IROS, and eventually HRI and RSS, etc.), and HCI communities (ACM SIGCHI, UIST, etc.) as well as relevant journals (including domain-focused venues, such as for surgical robotics). [25] provides a review of major developments in the early 2000's and a vision for augmented reality HRI as HRI research increasingly focused on various aspects of social interaction and human-robot collaboration. In addition, MiRAs (mixed reality agents) and AuRAs (augmented reality agents) represent a major relevant development during this period, in which robots may interact with or be augmented by virtual agents (e.g., a robot might be shown to a user as driven by a virtual character or have its planned path rendered in physical space) [13,29].

Overall, while we see an exciting trend in the production of VAMR-HRI papers (in Fig. 3, examining publication rates from 1990 to the present reveals what appears to be the start of an exponential curve, rather than linear growth) and many of the technical limitations in conducting earlier research have been reduced (e.g., due to the increasing prevalence of common/commercially available robot and VAMR platforms), the lack of a centralized research community remains a critical challenge. Towards addressing this issue, the first International Workshop on Virtual, Augmented, and Mixed Reality for Human-Robot Interaction (VAMR-HRI)[3] was held in 2018 in conjunction with the IEEE/ACM HRI conference, with a followup workshop to occur in March 2019, but it remains to be seen whether this (or other efforts) will help the community converge. Although research fragmentation remains an issue, the overall trajectory for VAMR-HRI research appears very promising, and it is my hope that we are now truly poised to make good on the exciting initial research from the early 1990's. Below, I describe some of my own recent work aligned towards these ends.

---

[3] See http://vam-hri.xyz/.

# 3    Case Studies

To further build the case for how VAMR can support HRI and how the time is now ripe for a convergence of research that takes advantage of modern hardware in doing so, below I detail some of my own recent work examining the utility of modern VAMR technologies for mediating human-robot interactions. These studies, more fully described in [27, 67, 68], each examine an aspect of how VAMR might specifically support the Human Action Cycle within the context of a longstanding HRI problem. The first study explores how VAMR can provide visual information to help bridge a gulf of evaluation for users presented with the *motion inference* problem, where people fail to understand when, where, and how a robot teammate will move. The second study explores VAMR in bridging a gulf of execution within the context of *perspective-taking*, i.e., determining what information, and how to convey it, to support robot operators and supervisors in gaining accurate perceptions of the robot and sufficient situational awareness of the robot's working environment to enable precise, and efficient control. The final study harkens back to the early work on VAMR robot teleoperation from the 1990's and combines information gained in the first two experiments towards the design of a comprehensive, modern VAMR teleoperation system that provides new forms of bidirectional information exchange.

## 3.1    Visualizing Robot Information

One primary challenge towards achieving safe and usable robotic systems is known as the *motion inference* problem, a gulf of evaluation that arises as humans encounter difficulties understanding when, where, and how a robot teammate will move. A great deal of prior HRI work has examined methods for mediating this issue, such as by having robots use human-inspired social cues (e.g., gaze, gestures, etc.) to communicate their intentions [22, 42, 51], altering robot trajectories to be more legible [19] or expressive [61], or using various other means such as light or auditory indicators [3, 6, 16, 33, 47, 52, 55, 62, 64, 69]. While such advances have shown promise in enhancing interaction safety and fluidity, a variety of constraints arising from environmental, task, power, computational, and platform considerations may limit their feasibility or effectiveness in certain contexts. For example, some robots may not be able to reproduce human-based cues due to their morphology, while altering robot motions for legibility or expressiveness may not always be possible in dynamic or cluttered environments, and auditory indicators may not be a practical form of feedback in noisy environments (e.g., manufacturing warehouses or construction sites) or for robotic platforms that generate a great deal of noise (e.g., aerial robots). Instead, we explored VAMR (specifically augmented reality) as an alternative design space for resolving motion inference.

**A Design Framework.** We began our research process with an analysis how modern VAMR technologies, in particular HMDs that have the advantage of being hands-free, might mediate HRI. Synthesizing information from past VAMR work, including mixed-reality projection systems, VR/AR entertainment applications, and augmented virtuality educational software, we developed a high-level framework for considering how augmented reality HMDs (ARHMDs) might enhance human-robot interactions. Our framework classifies potential designs for augmenting human-robot interactions with virtual imagery into three main categories, regarding whether additional information is communicated to the user by (1) *augmenting the environment*, (2) *augmenting the robot*, or (3) *augmenting the user interface*.

Briefly, in the first paradigm, virtual imagery is represented as new cues directly embedded into the context of a shared work area using an *environment-as-canvas* metaphor. In the second paradigm, virtual imagery is directly connected to the robot platform to alter robot morphology in a *robot-as-canvas* metaphor. This technique may alter robot form and/or function by creating new "virtually/physically embodied" cues, where cues that are traditionally generated using physical aspects of the robot are instead generated using indistinguishable virtual imagery, or be used to add full-fledged virtual avatars to physical robots along the MiRA (Mixed Reality Agent) approach [20,29]. In the third paradigm, virtual imagery is provided directly in front of the user, giving them an interface to the physical world, inspired by "window-on-the-world" AR applications [21] and heads-up display technologies used for pilots [23,37]. This third *interface-as-canvas* metaphor may uniquely supply egocentric cues, either directly in front of the user's view or in their periphery, compared to the exocentric feedback provided by augmenting the environment or robot [65]. Overall, we found this augmenting environment/robot/interface framework helpful in surveying the landscape of possible AR interfaces to categorize broad design concepts and in providing us with a structure for reasoning about requirements, benefits, and trade-offs in integrating AR (and possibly, more broadly VAMR) with HRI.

**Design Prototypes.** We used the design framework described above to develop several reference designs for AR visualizations that might convey robot intent and thus address the motion inference problem. While we prototyped a large number of visualizations, we ultimately ended up evaluating four main designs: *NavPoints* (augmenting environment), *Arrows* (augmenting environment), *Gaze* (augmenting robot), and *Utilities* (augmenting UI). These designs, which sample from each paradigm in our design framework and offer potential trade-offs in terms of information conveyed, information precision, generalizability, and possibility for distraction/interface overdraw, can be seen in Fig. 4. At a high level, the NavPoints shows the robot's planned path as 3D waypoints with timers indicating arrival and departure times, the Arrows design provides an arrow showing the immediate future motion of the robot, the Gaze design provides virtual imagery that alters the robot's morphology such that the robot can make use of gaze behaviors to indicate planned motion in a similar manner as humans, and the Utilities design provides the user with a minimap showing where the robot is in relation to them and gives off-screen indicators if the robot is not currently in view. For more details on each design (including parameters needed for replication), please see [67].

**Evaluation.** We conducted a $5 \times 1$ between-participants experiment to evaluate how our VAMR designs might improve user motion inference when interacting with an autonomous robot in a shared workspace. The independent variable in this study was the type of AR feedback the user received (five levels: a baseline and the four designs described above). In the baseline condition, participants still wore an ARHMD (in this study, we used the Microsoft HoloLens), but did not see any virtual imagery. Instead, participants in this condition were informed that the robot had a distinct "front," which always indicated its direction of flight; this baseline behavior meant the robot would always orient itself to the direction of travel, leveraging the only physically-embodied cue that the robot's default morphology provides. All conditions shared this baseline orientation behavior. Dependent variables included objective measures of task performance and efficiency as well as subjective ratings of communication clarity and robot usability.

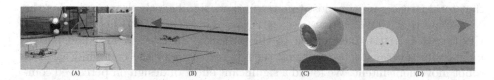

**Fig. 4.** We explored how augmented reality might address the motion inference problem in HRI by visually conveying robot motion intent. We evaluated four reference prototypes for cuing aerial robot flight motion: (A) NavPoints, (B) Arrows, (C) Gaze, (D) Utilities.

In the experiment, participants had to navigate between several different workstations to collect materials (Fig. 5). These workstations were also used by the robot, who was given priority over the participant, thus participants had to balance their use of the shared resources with being interrupted by the robot. At a high level, the task was set up such that the better participants were at predicting which stations the robot planned to use (i.e., inferring the robot's motion intent), the better they would be able to plan which stations they should use themselves in order to reduce their interruptions and maximize task efficiency.

We recruited a total of 60 participants (40 males, 20 females, evenly balanced across conditions) from the University of Colorado Boulder campus to take part in this study. Each experiment lasted approximately 30 min, which included a 60 s tutorial video that provided a brief instruction on the AR feedback participants would receive if they were not in the baseline condition.

In this experiment, we found that most of our designs were helpful in improving robot motion inference, enabling participants to more quickly and accurately deduce robot intent in order to plan their own activities more effectively. Analyzing our objec-

**Fig. 5.** We conducted a laboratory experiment to evaluate the effectiveness of our VAMR designs in improving human-robot interaction. Above, a participant wearing a HoloLens receives AR feedback informing him of the intentions of a nearby robot, helping to bridge a gulf of evaluation.

tive measure of task performance with a one-way Analysis of Variance (ANOVA) using experimental condition (i.e., interface design) as a fixed effect, we found a significant main effect of ARHMD interface design on total time participants spent interrupted, $F(4, 55) = 12.56$, $p < .001$. Comparing the performance of each design to the baseline with Dunnett's multiple comparison test, we found that total participant time lost to interruptions significantly decreased using the NavPoints ($p < .001$), Arrow ($p < .001$), and Gaze ($p = .003$) designs, but not Utilities ($p = .104$). In addition to this objective metric, we also had participants rate several facets regarding their perceptions of the communication of robot movement intent. We found a significant effect of design on perceived communication clarity, $F(4, 55) = 11.04$, $p < .001$, with post-hoc comparisons using Dunnett's test revealing that only the NavPoints design was rated significantly higher than the baseline ($p < .001$). Finally, we compared the designs directly to one another by having participants in all but the baseline condition rate the usability of the displayed virtual imagery for understanding of robot movement intent. We found a significant main effect of design on perceived usability, $F(3, 44) = 25.32$, $p < .001$. Post-hoc comparisons using Tukey's HSD found that NavPoints ($M = 6.96$), $p < .001$, Arrow ($M = 6.67$), $p < .001$, and Gaze ($M = 5.83$), $p < .001$, were ranked as significantly more helpful than Utilities ($M = 4.21$). We also found that NavPoints was rated as significantly more helpful than Gaze, $p = .012$, with Arrow ranked marginally more helpful than Gaze, $p = .092$. Figure 6 visually summarizes these results.

Overall, we found strong support for the ability of VAMR technology to improve HRI by addressing the motion inference problem. Despite their lack of prior familiarity with VAMR technologies or robots, participants were quickly able to use VAMR feedback displaying robot motion intent and integrate it into their own planning processes, likely due to the intuitive and visual nature of the

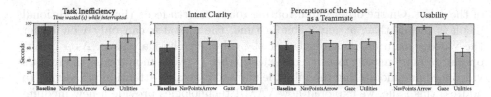

**Fig. 6.** Objective results show that the NavPoints, Arrows, and Gaze designs improved task performance by decreasing inefficiencies and wasted time. Subjective results reveal that NavPoints outperformed other designs in terms of user preferences and perceptions of the robot.

VAMR designs. We found that our designs that provided more specific information (NavPoints) generally outperformed designs that communicated information in a more implicit manner (Gaze), and that all designs outperformed the Utilities design, which emphasized current robot position relative to the user rather than displaying cues that helped users predict the robot's future destinations. While open questions remain about scalability to scenarios involving larger team interactions with multiple robots and/or multiple people, our results provide strong evidence for the value and potential of the VAMR-HRI design space and showcase the design of novel interface techniques that can provide intuitive, visual cues.

## 3.2   Information for Control and Supervision

Another critical challenge for HRI is developing interfaces that support effective robot teleoperation and supervision. A substantial body of past research has explored human performance issues in various forms of robotic teleoperation interfaces and mixed teleoperation/supervisory control systems (see [17] for a survey). In particular, prior work has highlighted the issue of *perspective-taking*— the notion that poor perceptions of the robot and its working environment may degrade situational awareness and thus have a detrimental effect on operation effectiveness [17, 38].

Mastering perspective taking, where users must rapidly and accurately synthesize information provided directly from the robot (commonly provided via one or more live camera feeds) with an understanding of where the robot is located within the larger context of the environment, is a challenging task, meaning that most robot deployments involving teleoperation still require skilled experts. Current interface designs, particularly for aerial robots (the context we explored in this research), can often exacerbate this problem as live robot camera feeds are typically presented in one of two ways: viewed directly in display glasses or on a traditional screen (e.g., a mobile device, tablet, or laptop computer). While video display glasses may help users achieve an egocentric understanding of what the robot can see, they may degrade overall situational awareness by removing a third-person perspective that can aid in understanding operating context, such as identifying obstacles and other surrounding objects that are not in direct view of the robot. On the other hand, routing robot camera feeds through traditional displays means that, at any point in time, the operator can only view either the video stream on their display or the robot in physical space. As a result, operators must make constant context switches between monitoring the robot's video feed and monitoring the robot, leading to a divided attention paradigm. To address this issue, we explored how VAMR technologies provide a new medium for designing teleoperation interfaces that can merge viewpoints, enabling teleoperators to monitor the robot in the environment while synchronously monitoring a robot video feed.

**Design Prototypes.** In exploring perspective-taking, we once again focused on leveraging modern ARHMD technology in the form of the Microsoft HoloLens and utilized the same VAMR-HRI design framework for interfaces that augment the environment/robot/UI described above. Although ARHMD interfaces might provide feedback on many different aspects relevant to robot teleoperation, we focused our design exploration specifically on how to convey information about the robot's camera, as this is typically the most critical information for robots operators.

We developed three primary prototypes, each of which falls within one of the major paradigms in our design framework. We refer to these three design prototypes as *Frustum*, an example of augmenting the environment, *Callout*, an example of augmenting the robot, and *Peripherals*, an example of augmenting the user interface. These designs are each based on prior robot interface designs or other metaphors that may be common to user experiences, adjusted and extended to take advantage of VAMR technology. The Frustum design provides virtual imagery that displays the robot's camera frustum as a series of lines and points, similar to what might be seen emanating from a virtual camera in computer graphics and modeling applications (e.g., Maya, Unity, etc.). The Callout design displays the robot's live camera feed on a panel connected to the top of the robot with an orientation corresponding to the orientation of the camera on the physical robot using a metaphor inspired by speech balloons and thought bubbles. The Peripherals design displays a live robot video feed within a fixed window within the user's view, which was affixed to the periphery of the UI to enable users to monitor the feed while maintaining visual focus on the physical robot in a manner inspired by ambient displays. Each design offers potential tradeoffs in terms of how they support perspective-taking, the total information conveyed, potential scalability across interaction distances, and possibility for user distraction and/or interface overdraw. Figure 7 showcases these interface designs, which are presented in more detail with a discussion of specific design elements in [27].

**Evaluation.** We conducted a $4 \times 1$ between-participants experiment to evaluate how our designs might improve robot teleoperation by improving perspective-taking. The study tasked participants with operating a quadcopter to take several pictures of various targets in a laboratory environment as an analog to aerial

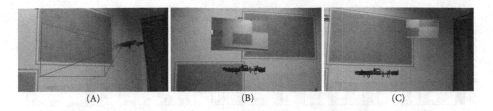

(A)                              (B)                              (C)

**Fig. 7.** In this research, we explored how to leverage augmented reality (AR) to improve robot teleoperation. We developed and evaluated 3 design prototypes: (A) the Frustum design augments the environment giving users a clear view of what real-world objects are within the robot's FOV; (B) the Callout design augments the robot like a thought-bubble, attaching a panel with the live video feed above the robot; (C) the Peripheral design provides a window with the live video feed fixed in the user's periphery.

robot inspection and environmental survey tasks. The independent variable in this study corresponded to what type of teleoperation interface the participant used (four levels: Frustum, Callout, and Peripherals designs plus a baseline). In the baseline condition, participants still wore an ARHMD (to control for possible effects of simply wearing a HMD), but did not see any augmented reality imagery. Instead, participants used the Freeflight Pro application[4], the official commercial teleoperation interface supplied by the robot manufacturer. Dependent variables included objective measures of task completion and subjective ratings of operator comfort and confidence.

We recruited a total of 48 participants (28 males, 19 females, 1 self-reported non-binary) from the University of Colorado Boulder campus to participate in our experimental evaluation. Each experiment lasted approximately 30 min, which included two minutes of time spent practicing operating the robot.

The results from our experiment revealed that our VAMR designs outperformed the commercially-available interface across nearly all of our measures. Our objective metrics included task accuracy in terms of the pictures participants took of the experimental targets, task completion time, and number of crashes, each of which we analyzed with a one-way ANOVA with experimental condition as a fixed effect. We found a significant main effect of design on task performance scores for accuracy, $F(3, 44) = 25.01$, $p < .0001$. Comparing designs, Tukey's HSD revealed that the Frustum ($M = 63.2\%$) and Callout ($M = 67.0\%$) interfaces significantly improved inspection performance over the baseline interface ($M = 31.33\%$), with the Peripheral design ($M = 81.1\%$) showing even further benefits by significantly outperforming both Frustum and Callout (all post-hoc results with $p < .0001$). We also found a significant main effect of design on task completion time, $F(3, 44) = 3.83$, $p = .016$. Post-hoc comparisons against the baseline ($M = 239.70$ s) revealed that participants were able to complete the task significantly faster using the Frustum ($M = 140.69$ s), $p = .017$, and Peripherals

---

[4] This popular commercial application can be downloaded from https://itunes.apple.com/us/app/freeflight-pro/id889985763?mt=8.

138     D. Szafir

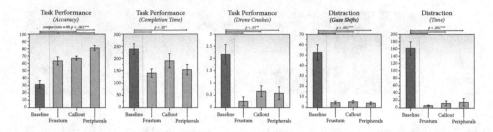

**Fig. 8.** Objective results show that the augmented reality interface designs improved task performance in terms of accuracy and number of crashes, while minimizing distractions in terms of number of gaze shifts and total time distracted. (\*), (\*\*), and (\*\*\*), denote comparisons with $p < .05$, $p < .01$, and $p < .001$ respectively.

($M = 154.44$ s), $p = .050$, but not the Callout ($M = 191.09$ s), $p = .434$. Examining occurrences when users crashed the robot, we found a significant effect of interface design on operational errors, $F(3, 44) = 9.24$, $p < .001$ with each of our AR designs significantly reducing the number of crashes compared to the baseline (Frustum: $M = .250$, $p < .0001$; Callout: $M = .667$, $p = .003$; Peripherals: $M = .584$, $p = .001$; Baseline: $M = 2.17$).

To better understand these results, we analyzed first- and third-person videos that we recorded of each experiment to look for behavioral patterns. Two coders annotated video data from each interaction based on when participants were able to view the robot and when they were not. Data was divided evenly between coders, with an overlap of 15% of the data coded by both. Inter-rater reliability analysis revealed substantial agreement between raters (Cohen's $\kappa = .92$) [35]. This coding enabled us to calculate *distracted gaze shifts*—the number of times the participant was distracted looking away from the robot during the task; and *distraction time*—the total time spent not looking at the robot. Analyzing this data, we found a significant main effect of interface design on number of distracted gaze shifts, $F(3, 44) = 40.28$, $p < .001$, and on total distraction time, $F(3, 44) = 48.72$, $p < .001$. Post-hoc tests showed that all three VAMR designs significantly decreased both the number and length of distractions compared to the baseline (all comparisons at $p < .0001$), which we take to be evidence that our VAMR prototypes were indeed successful in addressing the perspective-taking issue, thus leading to the performance enhancements found in task accuracy, time, and number of crashes. Figure 8 visualizes these results, while additional analysis of several subjective metrics regarding interface usability, comfort, confidence, etc. that provide further evidence for our conclusions can be found in [27].

Overall, our novel VAMR interface designs that provided users with augmented reality feedback while teleoperating an aerial robot demonstrated significant improvements over a modern interface that is representative of popular designs currently in use. In addition, users rated our designs as more favorable, even though they had a relatively short amount of time with which to practice and may have found the baseline interface, which simply uses a traditional tablet, more familiar. Once again we believe that these results showcase that interfaces leveraging modern VAMR technologies can be readily integrated with robots to produce highly intuitive user experiences that significantly reduce breakdowns common in human-robot interactions.

## 3.3  Bidirectional Communication

While each of the studies above showed that VAMR technologies hold promise in helping users bridge a gulf of execution or evaluation, they examined individual aspects of interaction and communicated information in a singular direction (robot-to-human). To more fully examine VAMR-HRI integration within the context of the full Human Action Cycle, we endeavored to design an end-to-end VAMR teleoperation interface. Inspired by the "phantom robot" of [7], our key insight was that VAMR may be used in conjunction with prior work on predictive graphical interfaces such that a teleoperator controls a three-dimensional *virtual robot surrogate*, rather than directly operating the robot itself, providing the user with foresight regarding where the physical robot will end up and how it will get there.

In this system, we provide users with a VAMR robot surrogate—virtual imagery in the form of a "ghost" of the real robot that is embedded within the same operational environment, with accurate stereoscopic depth cues and a matching dynamics model, but that cannot physically interact with the environment (i.e., cannot be damaged or present a hazard to other physical objects or users). This robot avatar serves as a middleman, enabling bidirectional communication of information from human-to-avatar-to-robot and robot-to-human/avatar-to-human. At a theoretical level, we believe that such an interface may help with both gulfs of execution and evaluation by enabling teleoperators to more rapidly iterate through the goal/action/evaluation phases of the Human Action Cycle without the potential of an action that leads to a negative consequence that is realized only after evaluation (e.g., a robot colliding with an obstacle or person). In other words, the system provides users with visuals that let them "test" different inputs and preview results, helping them understand how to pilot the robot to their desired location and providing real-time feedback to understand if course corrections are needed. This system can help reveal mappings between operator input and robot dynamics, information that traditional teleoperation hides in implicit system encodings that users must learn indirectly through experience (e.g., learning the relationship between joystick angle and motor torque).

**Design and Evaluation.** Robot actions might be tied to actions of a virtual surrogate in a variety of ways. In this research, we explored two main control paradigms: (1) *Realtime Virtual Surrogate (RVS)* operation where the virtual robot responds instantaneously to user input (matching standard forms of teleoperation) while the physical robot, connected to the surrogate with a virtual "fishing line" follows the surrogate after a short delay and (2) *Waypoint Virtual*

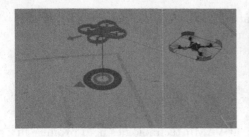

**Fig. 9.** Two VAMR teleoperation interfaces designed in this work: Left - Realtime Virtual Surrogate (RVS), Right - Waypoint Virtual Surrogate (WVS).

*Surrogate (WVS)* operation, a delayed form of control that lets the user pilot the surrogate to create a flight plan of various waypoints for the physical robot to traverse, also providing pause/resume and live waypoint editing features that overall leverage AR's ability to place virtual information and objects within the user's environment (see Fig. 9 for visualizations of these interface designs). More specific details on the implementation of each design can be found in [68].

We conducted a $3 \times 1$ within-participants experiment to evaluate, relative to a baseline, how our RVS and WVS designs might affect user experiences when teleoperating a collocated aerial robot. In the experiment, participants teleoperated a physical quadcopter to various points of interest (POIs) in a laboratory environment in a task that simulated real-time collection and analysis of environmental data. The independent variable in this study corresponded to what type of teleoperation interface the participant used: a baseine teleoperation system in which the handheld controller input directly controlled the physical robot (i.e., the most common teleoperation system in use today, found in tasks ranging from drone-racing to search-and-rescue), the realtime virtual surrogate design, or the waypoint virtual surrogate system. The same handheld controller and control mapping were utilized across all conditions, although in the RVS and WVS conditions control was rerouted to the surrogate rather than the physical robot. Dependent variables included objective measures of completion time, response time, and interface usage, as well as subjective rankings directly comparing each interface and their perceived multitasking ability, stress, and ease of use.

We recruited a total of 18 participants (11 males, 7 females) from the University of Colorado Boulder campus to take part in this experiment. In our previous two studies, users were largely unfamiliar with either VAMR technologies or robots. While this may be representative of certain target user populations (e.g., users of commercial drones for hobby or entertainment purposes), robot teleoperators in many settings (disaster response, search-and-rescue, etc.) often have a high degree of expertise. As a result, in this experiment we worked to ensure our population sample contained a greater representation of both novices and users experienced at piloting aerial robots. In total, 7 of our participants represented expert users who were recruited from a local "Drone Club," 8 participants reported moderate familiarity with aerial robots, while 3 participants had little to no experience operating flying robots.

For each participant, the experiment lasted approximately 80 min and consisted of four trials. The first three trials corresponded to the participant using one of the three main interface designs (baseline, RVS, or WVS), with the presented order of interfaces counterbalanced across participants. In the fourth trial, participants were free to use any of the three interfaces and could switch between them at will. Prior to each of the first three trials, participants watched a short 60 s tutorial video that presented the interface design they were going to use, covering both the controls and what the visual feedback looked like (if any). In addition, participants were given two minutes to test each interface before each main trial began, giving them time to become familiar with the controller, augmented reality imagery, and the robot. Participants wore an ARHMD (the Microsoft HoloLens) during all trials as virtual imagery was also used to mark the POIs and show a progress bar corresponding to robot collection of environmental data (even in the baseline condition).

We collected data using a variety of objective and subjective measures to analyze the performance of our two VAMR teleoperation interface designs relative to the baseline of traditional teleoperation. Objective metrics included task completion time and design usage, measured by the percent of total task time that participants used each interface design during the fourth trial in which they were free to switch between interfaces as will (and would presumably use the design(s) they found most helpful). Subjective metrics included the System Usability Scale (SUS), an industry standard ten-item attitude survey for measure perceived usability, several constructed scales to measure aspects of user experience such as stress, and direct rankings to compare each interface in terms of "easy to learn" and "would want to use in the future." We analyzed the objective measures, SUS, and constructed rating scales using a repeated-measures analysis of variance with experimental condition (i.e., interface design) as a fixed effect and condition order included as a covariate to control for potential variance that might arise from ordering effects. Post-hoc tests used Tukey's Honestly Significant Difference (HSD) to control for Type I errors in comparing effectiveness across each interface. Participant rankings of each interface were analyzed with a nonparametric Kruskal-Wallis Test with experimental condition as a fixed effect. Post-hoc comparisons used Dunn's Test for analyzing design sample pairs for stochastic dominance.

Our measures once again revealed the positive benefit that VAMR technologies can have for HRI (see Fig. 10). We found a significant main effect of robot interface design on task completion time, $F(2, 45) = 13.65$, $p < 0.001$, where the RVS ($M = 186.39$ s, $p = .001$) and WVS ($M = 184.39$ s, $p = .001$) designs significantly improved completion time over the baseline interface ($M = 260.11$ s). We also found a significant main effect in regard to design usage during the final trial where participants could switch between designs at will, $F(2, 51) = 34.92$, $p < .001$. Tukey's HSD revealed participants used WVS ($M = 81.94\%$) significantly more than the Virtual Surrogate ($M = 18.06\%$) and Baseline ($M = 0\%$)

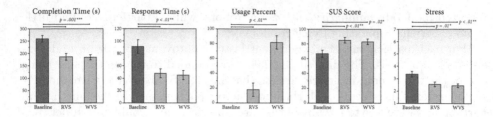

**Fig. 10.** The RVS and WVS systems showed improvement over the baseline along all objective measures as well as improving subjective user experience (error bars encode standard error).

designs (all comparisons at $p < .001$), with not a single participant ever using the baseline design at any point. We believe this represents extremely strong evidence for the utility of VAMR systems given that even users who were experts in the baseline system (i.e., participants recruited from our local Drone Club) chose to use the VAMR interfaces rather that the control system with which they had prior familiarity. Our subjective results provide additional supporting evidence for the perceived usefulness of the VAMR designs over the baseline (for a full discussion of these results, please see [68]), while highlighting some qualitative differences between RVS and WVS. Although the WVS design was consistently ranked highest in terms of the system users most wanted to use again and by a wide margin the most-used system during the summary evaluation in which users were free to use whichever interface they preferred, it received mixed feedback in open-ended responses where users were asked to comment on each interface. In particular, some users found the WVS system to create too much of a control disconnect between them and the robot. Synthesizing our results and feedback suggests that the RVS system may be most appropriate for hobby use, non-critical tasks, or when users prefer more direct control as it struck a balance between being an enjoyable, responsive, and effective system, while the WVS system may be more useful in professional or multitasking applications where performance trumps user preference.

While the aim of this study was not to design an "optimal" interface, we were nevertheless encouraged by the strong results showing the benefits of integrating VAMR and robotics, building upon prior work in 2D graphical predictive interfaces and the vision of early VAMR teleoperation systems from the 1990's. As mixed, collocated teams of humans and robots become increasingly prevalent in our society, we envision interfaces, such as those evaluated in this and our previous studies, assisting across a variety of human-robot interaction contexts, ranging from robot inspection of equipment and structures, teleoperation on factory floors, and all the way to space exploration where astronauts and/or ground control may be in direct contact or exert supervisory control of various ground and aerial robots.

# 4    Discussion

In each of these three efforts, we have demonstrated that VAMR designs can lead to significant performance benefits over existing solutions. Much of this work was inspired by ideas first introduced in the early 1990's that can now be more fully realized with modern hardware and validated through empirical experimentation. Such validation is critical for the field to advance beyond technical curiosities and into commercially viable interfaces and software.

In general, we have found that modern VAMR HMDs have several benefits over past systems, including enabling a standardized approach for presenting stereographic imagery, simple or automatic calibration, modern development environments (e.g., Unity and Unreal Engine), onboard (and often built-in) solutions for SLAM, additional built-in sensors and devices such as microphones and speakers, and the capacity for hands-free operation enabling integration with prior systems (e.g., existing teleoperation controllers). However, such systems are not without limitations; for instance, most systems are still limited by field of view (e.g., the HoloLens provides a $30° \times 17.5°$ FOV for virtual imagery), the ability to properly show occlusions with real-world objects, and the ability to be used in bright and/or outdoor environments (although these last two limitations can be mitigated by modern video pass-through technologies, such as the Zed Mini).

One major hurdle we had to face in our research is that there is very limited (or no) support for linking VAMR development libraries with standard robotics development systems (i.e., ROS). In our work, we followed a network communication approach similar to that outlined in [18] to pass data between each system, although new efforts such as ROSBridgeLib[5] and ROS Reality [70] aim to address this issue. However, once a communication layer is established, modern VAMR technologies provide an unprecedented ability for researchers and developers to rapidly prototype HRI designs. For example, in our first study we only ended up evaluating four VAMR designs in our final experiment, but these four designs were downselected through pretesting from an initial candidate set of eight prototypes that each sampled different areas within our design framework.

Another major challenge we have faced is the lack of a theoretical framework to ground VAMR-HRI work. In our research, we have grounded our work in two ways: first, we have leveraged the Human Action Cycle to reason about potential HRI breakdowns that VAMR might address, and second we have developed our model of cues that augment the environment/robot/UI to reason over potential solutions and categorize past work. However, our model is clearly preliminary and may fail to capture nuances across designs and miss other important axis (for instance, it is focused on AR and may be of less use as newer systems increasingly provide the ability to dynamically move along the reality-virtuality continuum). In addition, we have leveraged prior work, where appropriate, to

---

[5] ROSBridgeLib can be downloaded from https://github.com/MathiasCiarlo/ROSBridgeLib.

inspire our design process (e.g., research in graphical predictive interfaces helped motivate our third study). Further work in this area could be greatly aided by a more thorough review of past VAMR-HRI work (at present, no such survey exists) and a cohesive framework to anchor the burgeoning field. In addition, as discussed above, future work would be aided by a greater cohesion across various communities interested in this space, including integrating work from other related fields, such as the graphics and visualization communities, and clear venues to target for publication; at current such work still feels ancillary in either robotics or VAMR venues.

Overall, our work is still limited in many ways. For example, each of our three studies was limited to exploring interactions between a single user and robot in a controlled laboratory environment. As a result, more work is needed to explore scalability to larger, more complex interactions in more realistic conditions (e.g., via field deployments). There are many additional open questions for the research community interested in this space, including developing technical solutions for live, dynamic registration between VAMR technologies and robots, understanding use contexts in which VAMR technologies are and are not appropriate for HRI, improving the development process for VAMR and robotics, integrating additional, related methods of feedback such as haptics, and building information theoretic understandings regarding VAMR, HRI, and communication flow. However, overall we are seeing increasing activity in this space (at least using rough metrics as in Fig. 3) and the time seems ripe for increased innovation, efforts at community-building (e.g., the 2018 and upcoming 2019 VAMR-HRI workshop), and integration across developments from robotics, VAMR, HCI, graphics, and visualization.

## 5    Conclusion

In this paper, I have briefly traced the origins of work integrating virtual, augmented, and mixed reality technologies with robotics with the goal of improving human-robot interaction. Through three case studies from my own research, I have demonstrated the utility of reviving some of these initial ideas on modern VAMR hardware, leading to objective and experiential improvements over existing commercial systems. In addition, I have introduced the Human Action Cycle as a valuable model borrowed from the cognitive engineering and the HCI communities that can be adapted to reasoning about HRI in general and VAMR-HRI specifically. I have also proposed a preliminary framework for VAMR-HRI developments in terms of providing visual cues that augment the shared environment, the robot(s), or the user interface that, while limited, may serve as a useful starting point in building more formal models for the field. In both my work and VAMR-HRI more broadly, several themes have emerged, including common approaches for leveraging VAMR as a robotics visualization tool, as a control system, or as a training platform as well as common challenges, such as the lack of research cohesion due to fragmentation across several fields. While a formal survey and thematic analysis of the VAMR-HRI research space over the past thirty years is left for future work, I hope this paper can serve as a rallying cry (or a call to action) for increasing attention to this exciting and growing research area and the need for increased cooperation and interdisciplinary research among the robotics, VAMR, HCI, graphics, and visualization communities.

**Acknowledgements.** An Early Career Faculty grant from NASA's Space Technology Research Grants Program under award NNX16AR58G and NSF Award #1764092 provided support for various aspects of this research. I thank Hooman Hedayati, Michael Walker, Jennifer Lee, Andrew Gorovoy, and Adrienne Stenz for their help in the studies described above.

# References

1. Admoni, H., Scassellati, B.: Social eye gaze in human-robot interaction: a review. J. Hum.-Robot Interact. **6**(1), 25–63 (2017)
2. Admoni, H., Srinivasa, S.: Predicting user intent through eye gaze for shared autonomy. In: Proceedings of the AAAI Fall Symposium Series: Shared Autonomy in Research and Practice (AAAI Fall Symposium), pp. 298–303 (2016)
3. Andersen, R.S., Madsen, O., Moeslund, T.B., Amor, H.B.: Projecting robot intentions into human environments. In: IEEE International Symposium on Robot and Human Interactive Communication (RO-MAN 2016), pp. 294–301 (2016)
4. Azuma, R.T.: A survey of augmented reality. Presence: Teleoperators Virtual Environ. **6**(4), 355–385 (1997)
5. Baraka, K., Paiva, A., Veloso, M.: Expressive lights for revealing mobile service robot state. Robot 2015: Second Iberian Robotics Conference. AISC, vol. 417, pp. 107–119. Springer, Cham (2016). https://doi.org/10.1007/978-3-319-27146-0_9
6. Baraka, K., Rosenthal, S., Veloso, M.: Enhancing human understanding of a mobile robot's state and actions using expressive lights. In: IEEE International Symposium on Robot and Human Interactive Communication (RO-MAN 2016), pp. 652–657 (2016)
7. Bejczy, A.K., Kim, W.S., Venema, S.C.: The phantom robot: predictive displays for teleoperation with time delay. In: IEEE International Conference on Robotics and Automation (ICRA 1990), pp. 546–551 (1990)
8. Billinghurst, M., Clark, A., Lee, G., et al.: A survey of augmented reality. Found. Trends Hum.-Comput. Interact. **8**(2–3), 73–272 (2015)
9. Bricken, W.: Virtual Reality: Directions of Growth Notes from the SIGGRAPH 1990 Panel. Virtual Reality: Directions of Growth, p. 16 (1990)
10. Browse, R., Little, S.: The effectiveness of real-time graphic simulation in telerobotics. In: Proceedings of the IEEE International Conference on Systems, Man, and Cybernetics, pp. 895–898 (1991)
11. Burdea, G.C.: Virtual reality and robotics in medicine. In: IEEE International Workshop on Robot and Human Communication, pp. 16–25 (1996)
12. Burdea, G.C.: Invited review: the synergy between virtual reality and robotics. IEEE Trans. Rob. Autom. **15**(3), 400–410 (1999)
13. Campbell, A.G., Stafford, J.W., Holz, T., O'Hare, G.M.: Why, When and How to use Augmented Reality Agents (AuRAs). Virtual Reality **18**(2), 139–159 (2014)
14. Cassell, J.: Embodied conversational agents: representation and intelligence in user interfaces. AI Mag. **22**(4), 67 (2001)

15. Cha, E., Kim, Y., Fong, T., Mataric, M.J.: A survey of nonverbal signaling methods for non-humanoid robots. Found. Trends Rob. **6**(4), 211–323 (2018)
16. Chadalavada, R.T., Andreasson, H., Krug, R., Lilienthal, A.J.: That's on my mind! Robot to human intention communication through on-board projection on shared floor space. In: European Conference on Mobile Robots (ECMR 2015), pp. 1–6 (2015)
17. Chen, J.Y., Haas, E.C., Barnes, M.J.: Human performance issues and user interface design for teleoperated robots. IEEE Trans. Syst. Man Cybern. Part C (Appl. Rev.) **37**(6), 1231–1245 (2007)
18. Codd-Downey, R., Forooshani, P.M., Speers, A., Wang, H., Jenkin, M.: From ROS to unity: leveraging robot and virtual environment middleware for immersive tele-operation. In: IEEE International Conference on Information and Automation (ICIA 2014), pp. 932–936 (2014)
19. Dragan, A.D., Lee, K.C., Srinivasa, S.S.: Legibility and predictability of robot motion. In: Proceedings of the HRI 2013, pp. 301–308 (2013)
20. Dragone, M., Holz, T., O'Hare, G.M.: Using mixed reality agents as social interfaces for robots. In: IEEE International Symposium on Robot and Human interactive Communication (RO-MAN 2007), pp. 1161–1166 (2007)
21. Feiner, S., MacIntyre, B., Haupt, M., Solomon, E.: Windows on the world: 2D windows for 3D augmented reality. In: Proceedings of the 6th Annual ACM Symposium on User Interface Software and Technology, pp. 145–155 (1993)
22. Fong, T., Nourbakhsh, I., Dautenhahn, K.: A survey of socially interactive robots. Rob. Auton. Syst. **42**(3–4), 143–166 (2003)
23. Foyle, D.C., Andre, A.D., Hooey, B.L.: Situation awareness in an augmented reality cockpit: design, viewpoints and cognitive glue. In: Proceedings of the 11th International Conference on Human Computer Interaction, pp. 3–9 (2005)
24. Freund, E., Rossmann, J.: Projective virtual reality: bridging the gap between virtual reality and robotics. IEEE Trans. Rob. Autom. **15**(3), 411–422 (1999)
25. Green, S.A., Billinghurst, M., Chen, X., Chase, J.G.: Human-robot collaboration: a literature review and augmented reality approach in design. Int. J. Adv. Rob. Syst. **5**(1), 1 (2008)
26. Grodski, J.J., Milgram, P., Drascic, D.: Real and virtual world stereoscopic displays for teleoperation. In: NATO DRG Seminar: Robotics in the Battlefield (1991)
27. Hedayati, H., Walker, M., Szafir, D.: Improving collocated robot teleoperation with augmented reality. In: ACM/IEEE International Conference on Human-Robot Interaction (HRI 2018), pp. 78–86 (2018)
28. Hine, B., Hontalas, P., Fong, T., Piguet, L., Nygren, E., Kline, A.: VEVI: a virtual environment teleoperations interface for planetary exploration. SAE Trans. 615–628 (1995)
29. Holz, T., Campbell, A.G., O'Hare, G.M., Stafford, J.W., Martin, A., Dragone, M.: MiRA: mixed reality agents. Int. J. Hum.-Comput. Stud. **69**(4), 251–268 (2011)
30. Huang, C.M., Andrist, S., Sauppé, A., Mutlu, B.: Using gaze patterns to predict task intent in collaboration. Front. Psychol. **6**, 1049 (2015)
31. Huang, C.M., Mutlu, B.: Anticipatory robot control for efficient human-robot collaboration. In: ACM/IEEE International Conference on Human Robot Interaction (HRI 2016), pp. 83–90 (2016)
32. Ince, I., Bryant, K., Brooks, T.: Virtuality and reality: a video/graphics environment for teleoperation. In: Proceedings of the IEEE International Conference on Systems, Man, and Cybernetics, pp. 1083–1089 (1991)

33. Ishii, K., Zhao, S., Inami, M., Igarashi, T., Imai, M.: Designing laser gesture interface for robot control. In: Gross, T., et al. (eds.) INTERACT 2009. LNCS, vol. 5727, pp. 479–492. Springer, Heidelberg (2009). https://doi.org/10.1007/978-3-642-03658-3_52

34. Kim, W., Tendick, F., Stark, L.W.: Visual enhancements in pick-and-place tasks: human operators controlling a simulated cylindrical manipulator. IEEE J. Rob. Autom. **3**(5), 418–425 (1987)

35. Landis, J.R., Koch, G.G.: The measurement of observer agreement for categorical data. Biometrics **33**, 159–174 (1977)

36. Li, D., Rau, P.P., Li, Y.: A cross-cultural study: effect of robot appearance and task. Int. J. Soc. Rob. **2**(2), 175–186 (2010)

37. Li, H., Zhang, X., Shi, G., Qu, H., Wu, Y., Zhang, J.: Review and analysis of avionic helmet-mounted displays. Opt. Eng. **52**(11), 110901–110901 (2013)

38. Menchaca-Brandan, M.A., Liu, A.M., Oman, C.M., Natapoff, A.: Influence of perspective-taking and mental rotation abilities in space teleoperation. In: ACM/IEEE International Conference on Human-Robot Interaction (HRI 2007), pp. 271–278 (2007)

39. Milgram, P., Rastogi, A., Grodski, J.J.: Telerobotic control using augmented reality. In: IEEE International Workshop on Robot and Human Communication (RO-MAN 1995), pp. 21–29 (1995)

40. Milgram, P., Zhai, S., Drascic, D., Grodski, J.: Applications of augmented reality for human-robot communication. In: Proceedings of the IEEE/RSJ International Conference on Intelligent Robots and Systems (IROS 1993), vol. 3, pp. 1467–1472 (1993)

41. Miner, N.E., Stansfield, S.A.: An interactive virtual reality simulation system for robot control and operator training. In: IEEE International Conference on Robotics and Automation (ICRA 1994), pp. 1428–1435 (1994)

42. Nehaniv, C.L., Dautenhahn, K., Kubacki, J., Haegele, M., Parlitz, C., Alami, R.: A methodological approach relating the classification of gesture to identification of human intent in the context of human-robot interaction. In: IEEE RO-MAN 2005, pp. 371–377 (2005)

43. Nielsen, C.W., Goodrich, M.A., Ricks, R.W.: Ecological interfaces for improving mobile robot teleoperation. IEEE Trans. Rob. **23**(5), 927–941 (2007)

44. Norman, D.: Stages and levels in human-machine interaction. Int. J. Man-Mach. Stud. **21**(4), 365–375 (1984)

45. Norman, D.: Cognitive artifacts. Des. Interact.: Psychol. Hum.-Comput. Interface **1**(1), 17–38 (1991)

46. Norman, D.A., Draper, S.W.: User Centered System Design: New Perspectives on Human-Computer Interaction. L. Erlbaum Associates Inc., Mahwah (1986)

47. Omidshafiei, S., et al.: MAR-CPS: measurable augmented reality for prototyping cyber-physical systems. In: AIAA Infotech Aerospace Conference (2015)

48. Perzanowski, D., Schultz, A.C., Adams, W., Marsh, E., Bugajska, M.: Building a multimodal human-robot interface. IEEE Intell. Syst. **16**(1), 16–21 (2001)

49. Prendergast, D., Szafir, D.: Improving object disambiguation from natural language using empirical models. In: Proceedings of the ACM International Conference on Multimodal Interaction (ICMI 2018), pp. 477–485 (2018)

50. Rastogi, A., Milgram, P., Drascic, D., Grodski, J.J.: Telerobotic control with stereoscopic augmented reality. In: Stereoscopic Displays and Virtual Reality Systems III, vol. 2653, pp. 115–123. International Society for Optics and Photonics (1996)

51. Sanghvi, J., Castellano, G., Leite, I., Pereira, A., McOwan, P.W., Paiva, A.: Automatic analysis of affective postures and body motion to detect engagement with a game companion. In: ACM/IEEE International Conference on Human-Robot Interaction (HRI 2011), pp. 305–311 (2011)
52. Sato, S., Sakane, S.: A human-robot interface using an interactive hand pointer that projects a mark in the real work space. In: IEEE International Conference on Robotics and Automation (ICRA 2000), vol. 1, pp. 589–595 (2000)
53. Sauppé, A., Mutlu, B.: Robot deictics: how gesture and context shape referential communication. In: Proceedings of the ACM/IEEE International Conference on Human-Robot Interaction, pp. 342–349 (2014)
54. Schuemie, M.J., Van Der Straaten, P., Krijn, M., Van Der Mast, C.A.: Research on presence in virtual reality: a survey. CyberPsychol. Behav. **4**(2), 183–201 (2001)
55. Shen, J., Jin, J., Gans, N.: A multi-view camera-projector system for object detection and robot-human feedback. In: IEEE International Conference on Robotics and Automation (ICRA 2013), pp. 3382–3388 (2013)
56. Spofford, J.R., Garcia, K.D., Gatrell, L.B.: Machine vision augmented displays for teleoperation. In: Proceedings of the IEEE International Conference on Systems, Man, and Cybernetics, pp. 19–23 (1991)
57. Stiefelhagen, R., Fugen, C., Gieselmann, R., Holzapfel, H., Nickel, K., Waibel, A.: Natural human-robot interaction using speech, head pose and gestures. In: Proceedings of the IEEE/RSJ International Conference on Intelligent Robots and Systems (IROS 2004), vol. 3, pp. 2422–2427 (2004)
58. Stone, R.: Advanced human-system interfaces for telerobotics using virtual reality and telepresence technologies. In: IEEE International Conference on Advanced Robotics, pp. 168–173 (1991)
59. Sutherland, I.E.: The ultimate display. In: Proceedings of IFIP Congress, pp. 506–508 (1965)
60. Sutherland, I.E.: A head-mounted three dimensional display. In: Proceedings of the ACM AFIPS Fall Joint Computer Conference, pp. 757–764 (1968)
61. Szafir, D., Mutlu, B., Fong, T.: Communication of intent in assistive free flyers. In: Proceedings of the HRI 2014, pp. 358–365 (2014)
62. Szafir, D., Mutlu, B., Fong, T.: Communicating directionality in flying robots. In: Proceedings of the ACM/IEEE International Conference on Human-Robot Interaction (HRI 2015), pp. 19–26. ACM (2015)
63. Takahashi, T., Sakai, T.: Teaching robot's movement in virtual reality. In: IEEE/RSJ International Workshop on Intelligent Robots and Systems (IROS 1991), pp. 1583–1588 (1991)
64. Tellex, S., Knepper, R.A., Li, A., Rus, D., Roy, N.: Asking for help using inverse semantics. In: Robotics: Science and Systems (RSS 2014), vol. 2 (2014)
65. Trafton, J.G., Cassimatis, N.L., Bugajska, M.D., Brock, D.P., Mintz, F.E., Schultz, A.C.: Enabling effective human-robot interaction using perspective-taking in robots. IEEE Trans. Syst. Man Cybern. **35**(4), 460–470 (2005)
66. de Vries, S.C., Padmos, P.: Steering a simulated unmanned aerial vehicle using a head-slaved camera and HMD. In: Head-Mounted Displays II, vol. 3058, pp. 24–34. International Society for Optics and Photonics (1997)
67. Walker, M., Hedayati, H., Lee, J., Szafir, D.: Communicating robot motion intent with augmented reality. In: ACM/IEEE International Conference on Human-Robot Interaction (HRI 2018), pp. 316–324 (2018)
68. Walker, M., Hedayati, H., Szafir, D.: Robot teleoperation with augmented reality virtual surrogates. In: ACM/IEEE International Conference on Human-Robot Interaction (HRI 2019) (2019, in press)

69. Watanabe, A., Ikeda, T., Morales, Y., Shinozawa, K., Miyashita, T., Hagita, N.: Communicating robotic navigational intentions. In: IEEE/RSJ International Conference on Intelligent Robots and Systems (IROS 2015), pp. 5763–5769 (2015)
70. Whitney, D., Rosen, E., Ullman, D., Phillips, E., Tellex, S.: ROS reality: a virtual reality framework using consumer-grade hardware for ROS-enabled robots. In: IEEE/RSJ International Conference on Intelligent Robots and Systems (IROS 2018), pp. 1–9 (2018)
71. Williams, T., Núñez, R.C., Briggs, G., Scheutz, M., Premaratne, K., Murthi, M.N.: A Dempster-Shafer theoretic approach to understanding indirect speech acts. In: Bazzan, A.L.C., Pichara, K. (eds.) IBERAMIA 2014. LNCS (LNAI), vol. 8864, pp. 141–153. Springer, Cham (2014). https://doi.org/10.1007/978-3-319-12027-0_12
72. Xiao, Y., Zhang, Z., Beck, A., Yuan, J., Thalmann, D.: Human-robot interaction by understanding upper body gestures. Presence: Teleoperators Virtual Environ. **23**(2), 133–154 (2014)
73. Zhai, S., Milgram, P.: Telerobotic virtual control system. In: Cooperative Intelligent Robotics in Space II, vol. 1612, pp. 311–323. International Society for Optics and Photonics (1992)

# Brain eRacing: An Exploratory Study on Virtual Brain-Controlled Drones

Dante Tezza$^{(\boxtimes)}$, Sarah Garcia, Tamjid Hossain, and Marvin Andujar

University of South Florida, Tampa, FL 33620, USA
{dtezza, sarahgarcia, tamjidh}@mail.usf.edu,
andujar1@usf.edu

**Abstract.** As Brain-Computer Interface (BCI) technology become more ubiquitous, lower cost and expands from research laboratories to user's home, there is an emerging field and application on brain-controlled games. The use of BCI for gaming does not only allows an extra channel of communication between player and game systems, but it also extends its use to users with physical disabilities. This paper presents a brain-controlled drone game, where users can control a drone avatar with their brain-waves through motor imagery. To control the game, players wear a non-invasive BCI device, which measures and decodes the brain activity into game commands. Furthermore, this paper presents the results of a exploratory study performed to evaluate the gameplay experience, how the game changes participants affective state, and evaluate the user's perception towards brain-controlled games. Our findings show that players had a statistically significant increase in their positive affect score during the gameplay, as well as an increase in alertness, attentiveness, and inspiration.

**Keywords:** Brain-computer interfaces · User experience · Video games · e-sports · Virtual reality · Accessibility

## 1 Introduction

The video game industry is fast growing, and new technologies are being developed to provide realistic, immersive, and enjoyable experiences to users. Video games have been traditionally played using joysticks, keyboards, mouse, and gaming controllers, but this approach is not well suited for people with physical disabilities. Recently, there has been a shift in gaming devices to include more natural control modalities such as body gestures (i.e. Microsoft Kinect), but these controllers also present limitations for users with physical disabilities (i.e. upper limb differences or those on a wheelchair). A novel approach is to use Brain-Computer Interface (BCI) devices as a gaming controller, which can be used by both able-bodied participants and with disabilities [1]. As BCI technologies become more ubiquitous, lower cost, and its usage expands from research laboratories to user's homes, BCI devices will be widely adapted for brain-controlled activities. Technology advancements in the past two decades allow the use of BCIs for decoding brain signals into control commands for both videogames [1] and drones [2]. In this paper, we present a brain-controlled drone racing game built with the Unity engine. In addition, we present the results of a user study performed to evaluate

© Springer Nature Switzerland AG 2019
J. Y. C. Chen and G. Fragomeni (Eds.): HCII 2019, LNCS 11575, pp. 150–162, 2019.
https://doi.org/10.1007/978-3-030-21565-1_10

how the game affects participants affective state, participant's performance, game usability, and to receive qualitative feedback towards the concept of brain-controlled games.

Drones are used for a wide range of applications, such as photography, power and pipeline inspection, search and rescue, and environmental monitoring. Furthermore, they are also widely used for racing and entertainment. As drone racing grows as a sport, we expect that drone racing videogames will also grow in popularity. Analogous to popular car racing games, a drone racing game can be used to overcome potential hassles of racing physical drones. For example, a game/simulation would allow players to practice at a lower cost, without the danger of crashes, and does not require special authorizations for flying what physical drones do (i.e. FAA regulations in USA).

The game allows users to control the movement of a virtual drone using an electroencephalography (EEG) headset while performing motor imagery, Fig. 1 shows a player wearing the BCI headset while playing the game. Motor imagery in this context is defined as the imagination of muscle movement, resulting in signals in the motor cortex area of the brain allowing the use of BCI devices to infer user's intent [1]. The game allows selection of different drones to be used as the racing avatar, type of race (i.e. lap-based vs. drag), and customization of distractions (i.e. sound and visual). As the game requires the user to focus to perform motor imagery, customized distractions can be used to increase the difficulty and improve players ability. The current prototype of the gaming simulation is played using the Emotiv Insight BCI, a non-invasive 5-channel EEG headset that reads electrical signal from the scalp through semi-dry electrodes.

**Fig. 1.** Player controlling a virtual drone using a non-invasive brain-computer interface.

This paper's contributions include an analysis of the change in players affective state, analysis of player performance due to different backgrounds (i.e. gaming experience), evaluation of the system, and user's perception towards brain-controlled drone racing games. The standard PANAS survey [3] was used to score the players positive and negative affect scores, the GEQ questionnaire [4] was used to evaluate the gameplay experience, furthermore, open-ended questions allowed participants to provide their insights about the experiment and the concept of controlling games with BCI devices.

The remaining of this paper is organized as the following: Sect. 2 presents previous work done in the fields of brain-controlled games and brain-controlled drones. Following, Sect. 3 describes the developed system, including technical details and gameplay characteristics. Section 4 presents the methodology of the user study and Sect. 5 contains the analysis and results. Concluding this paper, Sect. 6 summarizes our findings and discusses future work possibilities.

## 2 Related Work

Previous research has explored the use of BCI for gaming purposes, which can benefit both able-bodied and users with disabilities by creating a new communication channel between the player and the game [5]. Among different BCI technologies, non-invasive EEG headsets are the most suitable for gaming due to high temporal resolution, low cost (compared to other BCI's), safety, and portability [1]. BCI have been used for action, simulation, puzzle, strategy and role-playing games [1]. For instance, a modified version of the popular World of Warcraft game changes the player's avatar form accordingly to his/her affective state measured with a BCI [6]. Other examples include a brain-controlled Pacman and Pong game [7].

Previous research has also explored passive use of these devices for gaming. In the latter case, they can be used to measure the players cognitive activity and detect what they are experiencing during gameplay [8]. Such information could serve as an extra information channel and allow the game to adapt its track or even difficulty level to provide a better user experience. Previous work found that adapting the game to the user's affective state allows adjustment of the information flow, providing an effective and pleasant experience [9].

The concept of controlling unmanned aerial vehicles using brain computer interfaces has existed for almost a decade, studies in this field date back to 2010 [10]. As drone-racing emerges as a sport, brain-drone racing has the ability to become a universal sport, allowing all participants to compete fairly independently of body type, gender or disabilities; the first brain-drone race was held at University of Florida in 2016 [11]. Although brain-control of physical drones already exists, there are many advantages for a videogame version, analogous to racing games that simulates real car racing. A videogame allows players to train controlling drones with BCI without the constraint of physical drones (i.e. cost, legislation, danger of accidents).

This paper presents the first brain-controlled drone racing simulation to be used as a game, including gamification characteristics such as score keeping and competition among players. Furthermore, this work differs from previous as it approaches the topic of brain-controlled videogames and drones from a human-computer interaction perspective. Lastly, this paper presents the results of an exploratory study containing both quantitative data about the participants affective state change during gameplay and qualitative data on the system.

## 3   System Description

The created prototype is a racing game where players can control a virtual drone around different racing tracks. The current iteration, the drone avatar is programmed to follow a pre-programmed path, while the user can control the speed of the drone using a BCI device. The player performs motor imagery to accelerate the drone and relax his/her mind to de-accelerate. The system was developed using the Unity Game Engine and integrated with the Emotiv Insight EEG headset.

The brain-controlled drone transverses through the environment by following a series of pre-determined waypoints. In order to ensure smooth turns through the track, a series of cubic Bezier curves with four control points were used to create a parametric curve. Since each turn would contain a copious number of points to transverse, a smooth turn is achieved as these points are always in close proximity to each other. An example can be seen in Fig. 2, which demonstrates the race track and the drone's pre-programmed path in pink.

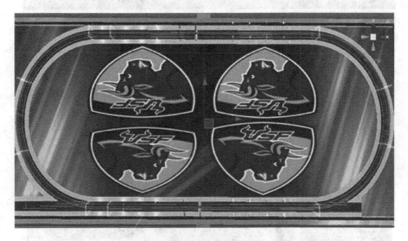

**Fig. 2.** Race track with drone pre-programmed race track demonstrated in pink. (Color figure online)

Upon starting the game, the user is prompted to create or log in to their account. When the user logs in using appropriate credentials, they will have the option to view the leaderboard, play the game or access the game tutorial. If the user proceeds to play the game, they will be redirected to a drone selection menu (see Fig. 3) where they will be able to choose the drone that they wish to use. After selecting a drone, the player must select the desired track as shown in Fig. 4. An example of a race track is show in Fig. 5, on the top right corner the lap time is displayed allowing the player to keep track of his/her performance. At completion of each lap, the lap time is recorded and saved along with the user name and ID. The game data was stored into Firebase Realtime Database cloud-hosted database service.

**Fig. 3.** Drone selection menu.

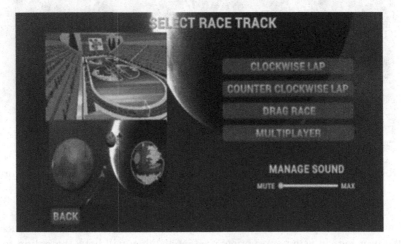

**Fig. 4.** Track selection menu.

**Fig. 5.** Brain-controlled drone game stadium race track.

## 4 Methodology

This study explored the use a BCI device as a control modality for videogames, more specifically drone racing games. A user study was performed to evaluate players performance accordingly to their different backgrounds, changes in their affective state while playing the game, and evaluate their experience of using a BCI device as a gaming controller.

### 4.1 Design

The experiment consisted of an exploratory user study where participants controlled a virtual racing drone around the track using a non-invasive 5-channel EEG headset. Study sessions were conducted individually with each user. Participants completed four laps around the track, and their performance (lap-time) was recorded for post-analysis. A pre/post questionnaire was used to elicit participants positive and negative affective state before and after the experiment through PANAS questionnaire to analyze how their affect state changed. A standard questionnaire was also administered after the experiment to assess the gameplay experience. Lastly, participants were asked to provide feedback about the experiment and concept of brain-controlled games through open-ended questions.

Two standardized questionnaires were used in this user study. The "Positive Affect and Negative Affect Scale" (PANAS) [3] was used as a pre/post questionnaire to calculate the affective state changes during gameplay. The "Game Experience Questionnaire" (GEQ) was used to receive feedback and evaluate the participants gameplay experience during the study [4].

**PANAS.** This standard questionnaire is designed to calculate the user's positive and negative affect state. In this study it was administered as a pre/post questionnaire, as participants answered the questions immediately before and after the gaming experience. This approach allows the comparison of pre/post PANAS scores, and analysis of how the game influenced the participants affect state. The PANAS consists of a 20 items scale, 10 items are related to positive affect (enthusiastic, interested, determined, excited, inspired, alert, active, strong, proud, and attentive) and 10 items for negative affect (scared, afraid, upset, distressed, jittery, nervous, ashamed, guilty, irritable, and hostile). Each item is scored on a 5-point Likert scale (1- not at all, a little, moderately, quite a bit, 5- extremely).

**GEQ.** This standard questionnaire aims to assess game experience, scoring it in seven categories: competence, sensory & imaginative immersion, flow, tension/annoyance, challenge, negative affect and positive affect. The questionnaire was administered through a Qualtrics link immediately after participants ended the game. The core module of GEQ used in this study consists of 33 statements which the participant must score using a 1-5 Likert scale (1- not at all, slightly, moderately, fairly, and 5- extremely).

### 4.2   Participants

A total of 30 participants were recruited to participate in the experiment, all of them were students at the University of South Florida, Tampa, Florida, USA. Eighteen of them were male, 12 females; 24 participant's age were between 18 and 24, and 6 participants were between 25 and 34 years old. Eighteen participants reported that they play videogames in a weekly basis.

### 4.3   Equipment

The experiment was performed using the Emotiv Insight headset, a non-invasive 5 channel EEG headset (Fig. 6). The headset is used to read the electrical activity on the participant's scalp through the use of semi-dry electrodes. The Emotiv ControlPanel software was used to interface with the hardware device, reading and decoding the brain activity into either a neutral or action state. Furthermore, the Emotiv Emokey software is connected to the ControlPanel and it emulates keyboard strokes to control the game based on the current brain activity state (neutral vs action).

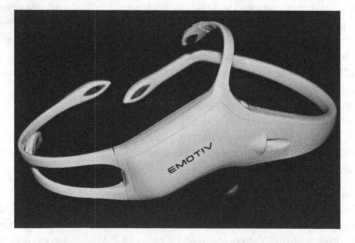

**Fig. 6.** Emotiv Insight, the BCI headset used to control the game.

## 4.4   Procedure

Each participant attended one session that lasted approximately 30 min, and it was comprised of four phases: (1) introduction; (2) pre-survey; (3) game; and (4) post-survey. During the introduction, the procedures were explained, and informed consent was acquired in order to proceed with the experiment. During the pre-survey phase, participants were asked to answer a series of questions using a Qualtrics survey on a provided computer. Questions were designed to elicit demographic data, handedness, gaming background, coffee and energy drink consumption, and how many hours participants slept during the prior night. During this phase, participants also answered the PANAS standard survey.

During the third phase participants were instructed on how to perform motor imagery to control the game and were assisted in wearing the BCI headset, ensuring good electrode-skin contact and signal quality. A research team member aided each participant to create and train a profile using the Emotiv ControlPanel software. This training phase consisted of capturing and recording brain activity during a neutral phase (baseline) and then again during the execution of motor imagery, such data was used to train the Emotiv software algorithms and allow it to decode the brain activity into game commands. Following this, the participant controlled the drone to perform 4 laps around the race track, with sounds disabled and visual distractions (i.e. fireworks, flags) enabled, each lap completion time was recorded.

Lastly, the participant was asked to complete the post-ex-experiment Qualtrics. Feedback about the experience was acquired through the Game Experience Questionnaire (GEQ) [4]. The participant also completed the PANAS survey [3] once more, allowing for comparison of positive and negative affects prior and after the game. Finally, open ended questions were presented to acquire qualitative feedback about the experience, and the concept of using BCI devices for gaming.

## 5   Results and Discussion

### 5.1   PANAS: Affective State Change

The responses to the PANAS survey can be seen in Fig. 7, which demonstrates the individual items mean score across participants for before and after the experiment. The average positive and negative affect scores were calculated by adding its respective PANAS items and are displayed in Table 1. A paired T-test demonstrated a significant increase in the average positive affect from 34.7 to 37.43 with a p value of 0.0039, there was no significant change in the decrease of negative affect score (Table 1). Furthermore, as shown in Table 2 there was also significant increases in positive items (alert, inspired, attentive, proud) and decreases in negative items (distress, scared, afraid).

Our analysis of participant's affective state changes demonstrated interesting results. The statistically significant increase in the average positive score indicates a positive experience to participants. We believe that this result is related to participants enthusiasm to be able to control a video-game solely through their brain-waves, and due to the novelty of our system. Our data also demonstrates an increase in alertness and attention, suggesting that our simulation can potentially be used for ADHD

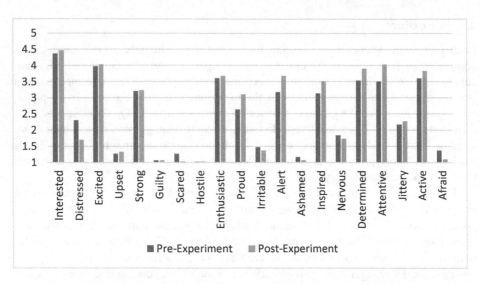

**Fig. 7.** PANAS scores prior and after experiment.

**Table 1.** PANAS analysis results. Positive and negative score prior and after experiment.

|  | Mean positive score | Mean negative score |
|---|---|---|
| Pre-experiment | 34.7 | 14.93 |
| Post-experiment | 37.43 | 13.7 |
| Δ score | 2.73 | −1.23 |
| p value | 0.0039 | 0.1616 |

**Table 2.** Paired T-Test result in PANAS items. Items not displayed were not statistically significant. Positive affective items displayed in white, negative items displayed in red.

| PANAS Item | Pre-experiment | Post-Experiment | Δ score | p value |
|---|---|---|---|---|
| Distressed | 2.3 | 1.7 | -0.6 | 0.0036 |
| Scared | 1.27 | 1.03 | -0.23 | 0.0169 |
| Proud | 2.63 | 3.4 | 0.47 | 0.0504 |
| Alert | 3.17 | 3.67 | 0.5 | 0.0014 |
| Inspired | 3.13 | 3.5 | 0.37 | 0.0091 |
| Attentive | 3.5 | 4.03 | 0.53 | 0.0109 |
| Afraid | 1.37 | 1.1 | -0.27 | 0.0434 |

therapy. Additionally, participants also benefited from a decrease in negative items; we believe that the game immersion lead to a decrease in distress. Moreover, a decrease in two fear-related items (scared, afraid) suggests that participants were apprehensive prior to trying the BCI device and got more comfortable during the experiment.

## 5.2  GEQ: Gameplay Experience

Results from the Game Experience Questionnaire can be seen in Table 3, which displays the mean, and the standard deviation across all participant responses. The GEQ score guidelines described in [4] were used to calculate category scores for competence, sensory & imaginative immersion, flow, tension & annoyance, challenge, negative affect, and positive affect; which are shown in Fig. 8. The highest scores (above

**Table 3.**  GEQ results (mean, std deviation and variance) for each questionnaire item

|  | Mean | Std deviation |
|---|---|---|
| I felt content | 3.13 | 1.15 |
| I felt skillful | 3.1 | 1.19 |
| I was interested in the game's story | 3.47 | 1.48 |
| I thought it was fun | 4.33 | 0.94 |
| I was fully occupied with the game | 4.13 | 1.02 |
| I felt happy | 3.67 | 1.16 |
| It gave me a bad mood | 1.3 | 0.64 |
| I thought about other things | 2.23 | 1.26 |
| I found it tiresome | 2 | 1.15 |
| I felt competent | 3.23 | 1.12 |
| I thought it was right | 3.5 | 1.12 |
| It was aesthetically pleasing | 3.73 | 1.18 |
| I forgot everything around me | 3.13 | 1.38 |
| I felt good | 3.67 | 1.14 |
| I was good at it | 2.77 | 1.28 |
| I felt bored | 1.2 | 0.48 |
| I felt successful | 3.33 | 1.22 |
| I felt imaginative | 3.37 | 1.28 |
| I felt that I could explore things | 3.5 | 1.28 |
| I enjoyed it | 4.3 | 1.04 |
| I was fast at reaching the game's target | 2.6 | 1.17 |
| I felt annoyed | 1.6 | 1.02 |
| I felt pressured | 1.93 | 1.12 |
| I felt irritable | 1.3 | 0.69 |
| I lost track of time | 2.6 | 1.36 |
| I felt challenged | 4.03 | 1.14 |
| I found it impressive | 4.33 | 1.01 |
| I was deeply concentrated in the game | 3.8 | 0.98 |
| I felt frustrated | 1.73 | 0.93 |
| I felt like a rich experience | 3.73 | 1.09 |
| I lost connection with the outside world | 3.13 | 1.33 |
| I felt time pressure | 2.8 | 1.56 |
| I had to put a lot of effort into it | 3.43 | 1.12 |

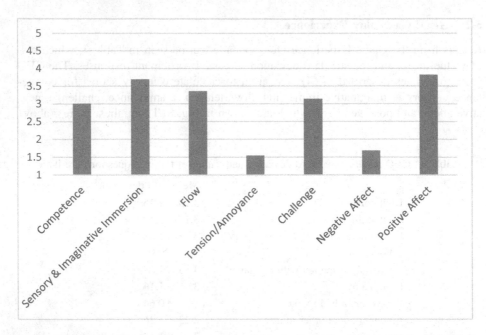

**Fig. 8.** GEQ categories average score across participants. Scale: 1 = "not at all", 2 = "slightly", 3 = "moderately", 4 = "fairly", 5 = "extremely".

4.0) were all positive items: impressiveness, challenge, fun, and fully occupation with the game; while the lowest scores (below 2.0) were negative items: annoyance, boredom, and irritation.

### 5.3  Performance

During the experiment, each participant completed four laps around the race track with the respective lap times being recorded. The average time for lap completion can be seen on Table 4. A paired T-test was executed to compare the average times of male and female, as well as participants with gaming experience versus participants without. Although, average results were different across populations, our results were not statistically significant ($P > 0.05$).

**Table 4.**  Average time to complete lap around race track.

| Population | N | Time (s) |
|---|---|---|
| All participants | 30 | 54.88 |
| Male | 18 | 45.07 |
| Female | 12 | 69.6 |
| Gamers | 18 | 47.5 |
| Non-gamer | 12 | 65.9 |

## 5.4   Qualitative Feedback

In addition, participants also provided feedback about the experiment and the concept of using BCI for gaming. Majority of the feedback was positive, for instance, when asked if they had any extra comments about the experiment 12 out of 30 participants described the experience enthusiastically (i.e. "It was a lot of fun!", "Very exciting!", "The game was impressive"). Furthermore, participants stated that BCI for gaming is a very promising concept, and that they expect it to become popular in the future. Such feedback with our expectation that BCI devices can be used as a gaming controller for drone racing games, proving a positive experience to gamers. Additionally, three players described that the game allowed them to improve their focus, which is aligned with the results presented in Sect. 5.1. This data enforces our belief that this simulation can potentially be used as a therapy tool to help users diagnosed with ADHD improve their attention. The open-ended questions were also useful to acquire improvement suggestions for our system. Participants suggested the development of a "free flight" mode to allow controlling the drone in three dimensions, improvements of graphics, and improvements in the flight dynamics (i.e. drone acceleration could be more realistic). It was also suggested by three participants that BCIs should be integrated with virtual reality games.

## 6   Conclusion

In this study we presented a brain-controlled drone racing game and the results of a user study where participants had to control the virtual drone around the race track 4 times. Our results demonstrate a statistically significant increase in the positive affect of participants after the experiment, indicating that the game was a pleasant experience for its users. Furthermore, our analysis also discovered significant increases in pride, alertness, inspiration and attention scores for participants, while decreasing distress, scariness and fear. Our analysis did not show any statistical significance in performance based on the comparison of gender and previous gaming experience. Positive feedback was received from users, both through a standard game experience questionnaire and open-ended questions. Additionally, 29 out of 30 participants stated that they would purchase a brain-computer interface device for gaming purposes. These data suggest that BCI's have potential as the next generation game controllers.

In future iterations of this project we plan to improve the game based on participants suggestions. Moreover, we propose further research to understand what factors influence players performance, as we did not find significant results in this matter.

## References

1. Marshall, D., Coyle, D., Wilson, S., Callaghan, M.: Games, gameplay, and BCI: the state of the art. IEEE Trans. Comput. Intell. AI Games 5(2), 82–99 (2013)
2. Nourmohammadi, A., Jafari, M., Zander, T.O.: A survey on unmanned aerial vehicle remote control using brain–computer interface. IEEE Trans. Hum.- Mach. Syst. 48, 337–348 (2018)

3. Watson, D., Clark, L.A., Tellegen, A.: Development and validation of brief measures of positive and negative affect: the PANAS scales. J. Pers. Soc. Psychol. **54**(6), 1063 (1988)
4. IJsselsteijn, W.A., de Kort, Y.A.W., Poels, K.: The Game Experience Questionnaire. Technische Universiteit Eindhoven, Eindhoven (2013)
5. Nijholt, A., Bos, D.P.O., Reuderink, B.: Turning shortcomings into challenges: brain–computer interfaces for games. Entertain. Comput. **1**(2), 85–94 (2009)
6. van de Laar, B., Gürkök, H., Bos, D.P.O., Poel, M., Nijholt, A.: Experiencing BCI control in a popular computer game. IEEE Trans. Comput. Intell. AI Games **5**(2), 176–184 (2013)
7. Krepki, R., Blankertz, B., Curio, G., Müller, K.R.: The Berlin Brain-Computer Interface (BBCI)–towards a new communication channel for online control in gaming applications. Multimed. Tools Appl. **33**(1), 73–90 (2007)
8. Nijholt, A.: BCI for games: a 'State of the Art' survey. In: Stevens, S.M., Saldamarco, S. J. (eds.) ICEC 2008. LNCS, vol. 5309, pp. 225–228. Springer, Heidelberg (2008). https://doi.org/10.1007/978-3-540-89222-9_29
9. Gilleade, K., Dix, A., Allanson, J.: Affective videogames and modes of affective gaming: assist me, challenge me, emote me. In: DiGRA 2005: Changing Views–Worlds in Play (2005)
10. Akce, A., Johnson, M., Bretl, T.: Remote teleoperation of an unmanned aircraft with a brain-machine interface: Theory and preliminary results. In: 2010 IEEE International Conference on Robotics and Automation (ICRA), pp. 5322–5327. IEEE, May 2010
11. World's First Brain Drone Race. http://braindronerace.com/. Accessed 15 Jan 2019

# Human-Robot Interaction During Virtual Reality Mediated Teleoperation: How Environment Information Affects Spatial Task Performance and Operator Situation Awareness

David B. Van de Merwe[1]([⊠]), Leendert Van Maanen[1],
Frank B. Ter Haar[2], Roelof J. E. Van Dijk[2], Nirul Hoeba[2,3],
and Nanda Van der Stap[2]

[1] UvA Amsterdam, 1001 NK Amsterdam, The Netherlands
davidvandemerwe@gmail.com
[2] TNO The Hague, 2597 AK The Hague, The Netherlands
[3] TU Delft, 2628 CD Delft, The Netherlands

**Abstract.** Virtual Reality (VR) mediated teleoperation is a relatively new field in robotics which means little is known about the Human-Robot Interaction (HRI). The objective of this study was to investigate the effects of environmental information presentation on Human-Robot Team (HRT) task performance and operator Situation Awareness (oSA).

**Method.** The study consisted of two components. First, we developed a VR mediated teleoperation framework approachable for non-professional operators. Second, we performed an experiment to assess the effects of environment information presentation on HRT task performance and oSA. Under a within-subject design and pseudorandom sequence, twenty participants performed the experiment and answered an oSA questionnaire.

**Results.** The results for the HRT task performance indicated that participants were significantly faster during the full information context. The accuracy results did not differ between information contexts. The study could not establish a significant difference of subjective oSA between contexts.

**Discussion.** The results suggest better performance during full information contexts. For future VR mediated teleoperation design, we suggest incorporating context cues, either directly from the natural environment or artificial ones. This paper concludes that providing environmental context information can lead to better performance during VR mediated teleoperation and that it does not lead to different levels of oSA.

**Keywords:** Human-Robot Interaction · Virtual Reality · Teleoperation · Task performance · Situation Awareness

© Springer Nature Switzerland AG 2019
J. Y. C. Chen and G. Fragomeni (Eds.): HCII 2019, LNCS 11575, pp. 163–177, 2019.
https://doi.org/10.1007/978-3-030-21565-1_11

# 1  Introduction

## 1.1  Teleoperation and Virtual Reality

Imagine you are performing a choreography on a crowded dance floor. After grabbing a full drink from the bar, you need to get back to your initial position. You side step, slide, make a double turn, all the while avoiding both dynamic and static objects. You finish at the empty bar table you had seen earlier, where you place your drink after looking around in preparation for your next move. These steps are deliberated as to resolve the problem of "dancing from point a to point b without spilling your drink". Standard motor-programs for 'grabbing' and 'moving around', flow seamlessly from one into the other in congruence with cognitive monitoring of the action plan (Leisman, Mostafa and Shafir 2016). Now imagine performing a similar task without this motor-automaticity, whilst you yourself aren't even physically performing the task. You are not in the same room but are replaced by a robot you are controlling. The dance floor and drink have been replaced by a hazardous environment like a nuclear plant and radioactive material. This is the perspective of a human operator teleoperating a robot (DeJong, Colgate and Peshkin 2004).

Teleoperation represents any technical implementation that via a communication medium extends the human operator's capacity to manipulate objects to a manipulator positioned within a remote environment (Hokayem and Spong 2006). Adequate interpretation and accuracy in manipulation of the remote environment is essential, as the human operator typically referred to as 'master' holds the executive position over the manipulator or 'slave'.

Increased telepresence through properly implemented Virtual Reality (VR) technology is believed to improve the interpretability of and control over remote environments (Kot and Novak 2018; Freund and Rossmann 1999). During teleoperation, the human operator is believed to build an affordance based mental model (i.e. a mental model of functional opportunities of a given context) of the remote environment (DeJong, Colgate and Peshkin 2004). VR can diminish the amount of translations on visual input necessary to adequately build such mental models as it presents spatial information of the remote environment in higher dimensionality compared to two-dimensional displays. On the command end, current VR technology offers the possibility to send tracker-based commands ("About The Vive" 2018), increasing the ease of end-effector based control. At the same time, the application of VR technology for teleoperation poses perceptual and cognitive questions and limitations (Rubio-Tamayo, Barrio and Garcia Garcia 2017). Signal instability, noise and limited bandwidth can be countered by selecting and transforming environmental data before transmission (Turkoglu et al. 2018). Such technologically beneficial measures may deplete the immersive nature of VR implementation (Bowman 2007). However, selecting the proper information as a processing step might prove to be beneficial in countering perceptual problems such as information overload and misinterpretation of signal and noise in VR based environment representations.

Immersion and presence express the quality of the perceptual experience of the human operator in VR (Bowman and McMahan 2007; Slater et al. 1999). Coarsely defined, presence is the sensory identification with the Virtual Environment (VE) or being "there" (being part of the virtual or mediated environment) whilst physically being present in another environment (Nowak and Biocca 2003; Witmer and Singer 1998; Sheridan (1992a). Presence is often equated to the ecological validity of VR devices or the nature of their implementation (Mestre et al. 2006). Whilst immersion can be summarized as the technological sophistication of a particular VR system, presence can be seen as its perceptual counterpart. More immersive technologies typically elicit a greater sense of presence (Mestre et al. 2006). Implementation manipulations which make a VE more 'natural' can also increase presence dramatically (such as realistic lighting, photo realism, shadowing) (Slater et al. 2009; Yu, Mortensen, Khanna, Spanlang and Slater 2012). However, this increase in presence does not always equate to improved task performance (Lok et al. 2003; Slater et al. 1999). It has been suggested that effects on task performance relate to both the nature of the task and sense of agency within a given Virtual Environment (VE) (Kilteni, Groten and Slater 2012).

For the current research, human-robot interaction (HRI) is defined as follows: the process of a human and a robot working together to perform a specific task. Goodrich and Schultz (2008) make a distinction between 'Remote' and 'Proximate' HRI, where remote HRI may be more restricted due to indirect communication through technical interfaces and time lag. Remote interaction applied in the real world suffers from multiple factors which interfere with the Human Robot Team (HRT) operation. Whereas teleoperation can formally be considered remote interaction, VR as an interface can provide the interaction during teleoperation akin to proximate teleoperation such as an increased experience of proximity.

Within the current study, the aim is to better understand how information presentation influences HRT task performance and oSA during VR mediated teleoperation. This aim calls for two objectives: (i) Construct a technical framework within which a robot with limited autonomy can be controlled through VR mediated teleoperation by nonprofessional robot operators. (ii) Create and perform an experiment the technical framework is applied, and HRT task performance and oSA can be assessed.

## 1.2  Theoretical Framework

To investigate the influence of information presentation on HRI a controlled experiment has been performed, mimicking real world teleoperation. Two informational contexts were provided within which the HRT performed a representative task, the informational contexts being: *full information* or *preprocessed*. The full information context shows all contextual and task-related information of the robot's environment to the operator. The preprocessed context depicts a minimized version of the environment, showing merely task-related information (see also the Methods section). Reducing informational resolution, either by compressing the 3D-video stream or by computationally preprocessing a scene, improves technical efficiency of information transmission.

Within the framework as studied, the human operator holds the executive position, therefore it is important that operator Situation Awareness (oSA) is guarded. The experience of oSA is often affected by a trade-off between attention and informational load. Informational clutter can restrict the information attended to, whilst too little information can limit sufficient situational understanding (Salmon et al. 2009;

Taylor 1990). Concerning attention, overly extensive automation and information processing has been known to limit oSA, but reducing situational information can extend the scope of information attended to (Salmon et al. 2009; Endsley 1995). One of the latent factors within the Situation-Awareness-Rating-Test (SART) as developed by Taylor (1990) is the attentional demand of a given situation. In the current framework we equate attentional demand to the amount of information which draws attention to it as discussed by Endsley (1995).

Immersion, presence and task performance are a mixed bag. Whilst some studies show that immersion and presence hardly affect task performance (Slater et al. 1999), others have found strong effects (Bowman and McMahan 2007; Slater 1999). A distinction can be made based on the origin of the immersive level of a set-up being highly informative (i.e. depth cues during a spatial task) or less informative (i.e. depth cues during a math's challenge). Other research suggests that for spatial tasks, adding context can cause presence-related performance increases (Chamizo 2002).

In the current research, we hypothesize that HRT task performance is better within a full information context than within a preprocessed context, since both depth cues and contextual information are informative. We furthermore hypothesize that oSA is higher within a full information context than within a preprocessed context, because of higher levels of situational understanding and attentional supply. Last, we hypothesize that attentional demand is better (i.e., lower) during a preprocessed context than within a full information context.

## 2 Methods

### 2.1 Technical Implementation

**Interface.** To emulate true teleoperation, a VR interface and a robotic arm were booted on two computers which were connected through custom-made software RDA (Fig. 1). The experimental setup consisted of a simulated robotic arm (KUKA IIWA LBR 7, Kuka, Augsburg, Germany) and a generic table, which were dynamically simulated using the Gazebo platform (Gazebo, OSRF, San Jose, USA), booted on an Ubuntu pc. The arm was controlled using the ROS platform (Robotic Operating System, OSRF, San Jose, USA). The operator viewed and interacted in VR with an HTC ViveTM HMD (HTC, New Taipei, Taiwan), programmed using Unity$^{TM}$ (Unity Technologies, San Francisco, USA), booted on a Microsoft Windows 8.1 laptop pc with a Nvidia GTX980 M graphics card and a 2.50 GHz x64 processor.

**Robot.** The simulated robot was a KUKA LBR IIWA 7, henceforth referred to as 'the robot'. This robot is 7 DOF robotic arm with 7 joints, 7 movable links and 1 base. It was controlled using ROS, version Kinetic 1.12.12. The motor planning of the robot was based on a Jacobian solver for Euclidian position control. The motor planner received the desired position and orientation from the human operator through RDA and continuously published to ROS in order to move the robot correspondingly. The positions of the individual robot links were continuously published to RDA to visualize the live state of the robot in VR. The robot was rated between level 2 or 3 of Sheridan's scale of autonomy (Sheridan and Verplank 1978).

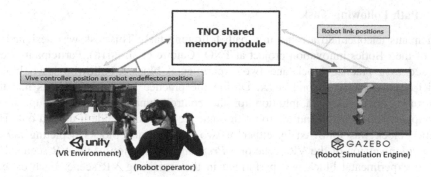

**Fig. 1.** The *interface between the simulated robotic arm and the VR environment.*

**VR Hardware.** The VR setup was developed using Unity™ (2017.3.1f1). The Microsoft Windows 8.1 laptop pc had an Nvidia GTX980 M graphics card and a 2.50 GHz x64 processor. STEAM-VR, a unity package, enabled the usage of HTC Vive™ VR gear 1. The HTC Vive™ VR gear 1 consisted of a head mounted display (HMD), two controllers of which one was used, and two lightboxes which were mounted on tripods. The HMD was used as the immersive device displaying the experiment scenes as run in Unity. The controller was used by the operator to control the robot arm based on a combination of button presses and movement in three-dimensional Euclidian space.

**VR Scene.** The VR scene consisted of a blue void, a table, a model of the robot, and the Vive controller. The robot model was composed of several links which mimicked the states of the corresponding links in Gazebo as published in RDA.

In the 'practice'-block (Sect. 2.4), the participant stood in front of a white table with the robot positioned on the other side. In the 'preprocessed'-block, the table was replaced by a rectangular white sheet containing a black path. A translucent magenta box represented the start of the path and a translucent magenta sphere represented the end of the path. In the 'full information'-block, the sheet was projected on a table. This block also included a three-dimensional mesh rendering of our laboratory. This mesh was created with RTAB-map Tango version 0.11.14 booted on a Lenovo Phab 2 Pro (Fig. 2).

*Full Information*                                    *Preprocessed*

**Fig. 2.** Two screenshots from participant perspective during both experimental contexts.

## 2.2    Path Following Task

Participants teleoperated a robot in a path following task. This task was designed as part of the i-Botics innovation project at TNO (Catoire et al. 2018). Participants were exposed to a practice block and two experimental blocks. Following each block, participants had a 30 second-break. During the practice block, participants had the opportunity to develop an intuition for the control dynamics of the set-up. Next, participants had to command the robot through the table and guide it up and out. The practice block was followed by either of two experimental blocks depicting a *Full information* version of the VR scene or a *Preprocessed* version of the VR scene. The second experimental block was performed in the remaining VR scene. Each experimental block consisted of 10 trials. Part of the ISO-9283 path was used in differing orientations during the experiment. The robot always started at the translucent magenta box (start box, Fig. 3) and finished at the translucent magenta sphere (finish sphere, Fig. 3). An audio signal indicated the start and successful completion of a trial.

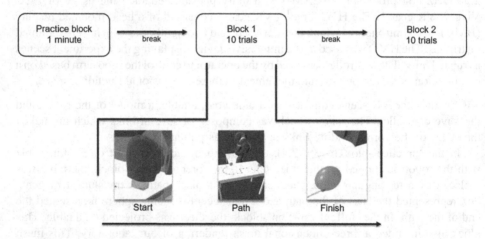

**Fig. 3.** A depiction of the experimental blocks and a representation of a single trial.

## 2.3    Operator Situation Awareness Questionnaire

Following each experimental block, participants answered a questionnaire concerning oSA, the Situational Awareness Rating Technique (SART; Taylor 1990). (For further information concerning the SART – see Taylor 1990).

## 2.4    Procedure

After signing an informed consent form, participants received a leaflet with information and instructions concerning robot control and the tasks they were about to perform. Next, the experimental supervisor explained the process during the experiment. Thereafter, the supervisor showed the HMD and controller; and measured and calibrated the participants' inter-pupillary distance (IPD). Next the participants were positioned on a white cross and both the HMD and controller were fitted. In case a participant was lefthanded they were positioned with their left foot just to the right of this white mark on the floor. The participant was positioned between the lightboxes, to have enough room to move around (Fig. 4).

After checking if the participant was ready the supervisor verbally prepared participants for the following visuals. The experiment followed the sequences as depicted in Fig. 3, booting each VR scene accordingly. After a minute of practice, participants were asked if they had enough experience. If anything was unclear, the supervisor provided clarification limited to the content of the information leaflet. After each break the supervisor again fitted the HMD and controller. Before each trial the participant had to position the head of the robot arm within the start box (Fig. 3). For each trial the supervisor verified that the participant was ready, after which the starting sound triggered the participant to perform the task. Between trials the supervisor switched the trial path as necessary. Following each experimental block, the supervisor helped to remove the HMD and controller after which the participant had to answer the oSA questionnaire followed.

**Fig. 4.** The picture to the left shows the room as seen when entered by the participant. The picture to the right shows the participant as positioned when the experiment commences.

## 2.5  Participants

A total of 20 participants between the ages of 23 and 42 were recruited based on screening criteria. To ensure group homogeneity, participants had to be healthy and be between 20 and 42 years of age, read and write the English language and have some video gaming experience. Exclusion criteria were deemed as follows: general contraindications for VR usage (such as epilepsy) or extensive experience with teleoperation.

The experimental group (N = 20) consisted of 17 males and 3 females. Two participants were excluded due to interruptions during the experiment. Statistical analyses concerning time and oSA were performed based on the results of 18 participants Two participants could not be included due to faulty measurement. Statistical analyses on accuracy were therefore executed based on the results of the 16 remaining participants.

## 2.6  Data Analysis

The primary independent parameter was the experiment block type, either Full Information or Preprocessed. The primary dependent parameters were oSA and HRT task performance during the pattern separation task. An oSA score and Attentional Demand score were calculated based on answers to the SART questionnaire (Taylor 1990) following each experimental block. HRT Task performance was assessed based on time and accuracy. Time reflected the number of seconds to finish a trial. Accuracy reflected by the mean distance between the performed trajectory and the ideal path within Euclidian space and in 2D. The reason to include both Euclidian space and 2D accuracy was to ensure that accuracy both in general space and in the horizontal plane, which was the orientation of the track, could be regarded separately All time and accuracy values were subject to paired t-test analyses. Both oSA and attentional demand were subject to paired t-test analyses.

# 3  Results

## 3.1  HRT Task Performance

The paired t-test on time between *Full information* ($M$ = 14.58, SD = 1.43) and *Preprocessed* ($M$ = 15.16, SD = 1.49) showed a significant difference ($t(17)$ = −2.19, $p$ = .043) (Fig. 5).

The paired t-test on two-dimensional accuracy between *Full information* ($M$ = 0.033, SD = 0.01) and *Preprocessed* ($M$ = 0.034, SD = 0.01) showed no significant difference ($t(15)$ = 0.7223, $p$ = 0.72). The paired t-test on Euclidian accuracy between *Full information* ($M$ = 0.0324, SD = 0.012) and *Preprocessed* ($M$ = 0.0336, SD = 0.009) showed no significant difference ($t(15)$ = 0.445, $p$ = 0.66).

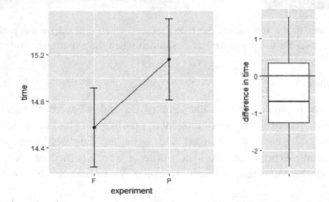

**Fig. 5.** Effect of experiment type on average trial performance time in seconds. The figure to the left shows the average time for *full information* (F) and *preprocessed* (P) including standard-error bars. The figure to the right shows a boxplot of the paired difference F-P for time.

## 3.2   oSA

The paired t-test on oSA between Full information (M = 18.78, SD = 6.85) and Pre-processed (M = 19.89, SD = 5.92) showed no significant difference (t(17) = −1.035, p = .32). The paired t-test on attentional demand between Full information (M = 9.28, SD = 4.00) and Preprocessed (M = 7.56, SD = 2.83) showed a significant difference (t(17) = 2.5139, p = .02) (Fig. 6).

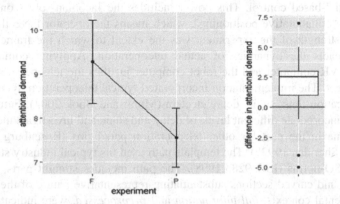

**Fig. 6.** Effect of *experiment* type on subjective *attentional demand*. The figure to the left shows attentional demand for *Full information* (F) and *Preprocessed* (P) including standard-error bars. The figure to the right shows a boxplot of the paired difference F-P for attentional demand.

## 4   Discussion

In the current study we aimed to investigate the influence of information presentation on operator Situational Awareness (oSA) and Human-Robot Team (HRT) task performance during VR mediated teleoperation. To solve this problem two tasks were conducted: First, a technical framework within which oSA and HRT task performance could be tested within a teleoperation context was designed and created. Second, within this context was examined how oSA and HRT task performance were affected. We have demonstrated a novel framework which extensively re-enacts a VR mediated teleoperation setting.

The integral way in which VR mediated teleoperation has been implemented and examined, particularly for the effects of information presentation on task performance and oSA, can be deemed both novel and effective. Previous research on VR implementation for teleoperation has often been performed within the context of extremely high predictability. For instance, factory contexts where the robot system performance was highly stable, freedom of operation was limited and the task environment provided no dynamics (Burdea 1999). Although the task environment in the current framework was static as well, participants had extensive freedom in operating the system and were confronted with some robot control and robot environment dynamics. Research and development with a higher focus on situation and system dynamics have done this primarily for systems with the highest level of human control (Kot and Novak 2018). Such research has often disregarded the effects of different sensory transferal modes from the robotic end to the operator end - a central notion for the current study. Typical research on high control teleoperation also demands extremely high operator skill levels, for which training time is extensive (DeJong, Colgate and Peshkin 2004). The framework in our study has drastically diminished operator training time to the reading of one page on robot control and one minute of practice. Though the current study was not a comparative one, the previous sentence is indicative of the power of combining VR and spatial-based control. This power includes the Jacobian-solver on the robot end, and the "collaborative positioning", which means the operator faces the robot.

Another strength of the experiment was the extent to which the framework adequately re-enacts the dynamics of actual teleoperation. Applying communication between the VR computer and the robot computer justifies the teleoperation claim in this experiment. The implementation incorporated typical teleoperation dynamics such as communication time, static, delay etcetera (Munir and Book 2003). Future experiments could incorporate different levels of delay and static and investigate the effects as has been done in the past for other teleoperation paradigms (Rosenburg 1993a, b; Kaber 2000; Sheridan 1992b). The template path used fits typical industry standards as it is based ISO-norms (ISO 9283:1998). The path includes straight parts, sharp and wide angles, and curved sections substantiating representative nature of the path. The two experimental contexts, *full information* and *preprocessed,* were indicative of two ways that environmental information can be communicated to an operator. *Full information* representing an interface which incorporates more of the typical surroundings in which tasks would be performed, and *preprocessed* representing a context where merely information directly related to the task was provided. Importantly, the surroundings within the *full information* context were constructed from 3D footage of an actual robot laboratory.

Lacking in the experiment are extensive dynamics (e.g. falling objects, mission changes, obstructions, limited signal), reducing ecological validity. This caveat increases the difficulty of relating performance and perceptual experience in this experiment, and other experiments, to real world teleoperation settings (Paljic 2017; Deniaud and Mestre 2015; Walsh, Sherlock, Ling and Carnahan 2012).

The acquired results indicate better HRT task performance during a *full information* context. While HRT task performance accuracy is equal between the full information and preprocessed contexts, task performance time is significantly lower for the *full information* context. Concerning oSA, the results suggest that overall oSA does not differ between informational contexts, however, *attentional demand* was significantly higher during the *full information* context. The HRT performed tasks significantly faster during the *full information* context than during the *preprocessed* context. All accuracy measures showed no significant difference between experimental contexts. If the speed-accuracy trade-off (SAT) is considered, performance can be viewed as a function of the speed and accuracy with which a task is performed (Heitz 2014; Bogacz et al. 2010; van Maanen 2016). This perspective indicates that performance was better during the *full information* context. The expectation of superior performance during *full information* contexts was ascribed to the heightened levels of presence and immersion due to increased contextual information (Slater, Linakis, Usoh and Kooper 1996; Barfield et al. 1995) which also fits implicit importance of context for task performance propagated within radical embodied cognition (Kiverstein and Miller 2015) and ecological psychology (Heft 2001).

The results could not support the hypothesized higher oSA for the *full information* context. On a whole, the plethora of situation awareness measures is both extensively varied and broadly scrutinized (Wickens 2008; Salmon et al. 2006). It is important to note that the performance results portray 'objective' measurements during task execution. In contradiction the SART, a self-rating score, asks participants to reflect on their experience after task execution (Taylor 1990). The SART has been further scrutinized for its limited sensitivity (Salmon et al. 2006). It therefore might be hard to find strong differences. This can specifically be the case for experimental contexts which are highly similar concerning the nature and amount of situation dynamics as the SART was largely developed to assess situation dynamics' cognitive derivatives (Taylor 1990). A possible alternative would be to apply performance-related measures inspired by the SAGAT in future experiments (Endsley et al. 1998).

Attentional demand was significantly higher during the *full information* context. This corroborates with the expectation that increased amounts of task non-specific information demands more attention as there is more information to attend to (Taylor 1990; Endsley 1995). The attentional demand results shed more light on the general SART scores and their equivalence across experimental contexts. As the SART score is calculated by adding *situation understanding* and *attentional supply* and subtracting *attentional demand*, the significantly differing *demand* results suggest that for the *full information context*, higher *situation understanding* and *supply* scores might balance the general SART scores. Particularly *situation understanding* which resembles the flow of situation understanding to levels 2 and 3 - *comprehension* and *projection* respectively - in the Endsley SA model (for a full reading - Endsley, 1995) or general *epistemic actions* in active inference theory (see Friston et al. 2015). This may indicate relevance to the nature of oSA – i.e. the interaction or combination of *understanding*, *supply*, and *demand* – rather than general oSA alone.

The simultaneity of significantly better task performance and higher *attentional demand* results for the *full information* context may seem confusing at first. Attention demanding contexts, such as those with increased environmental complexity, have shown to diminish performance (Horberry 2006; Graydon 1989). The lack of significant oSA differences between experimental contexts may help to further explain this phenomenon. As discussed before, while the level of subjective oSA may be similar, the nature of oSA may differ between information contexts. Combining this insight with the increased performance results during a *full information* context suggest that not only is the calculated level of oSA indicative of performance, the nature of oSA may be so, too. Though limited research touches upon this specific explanation, the explanation fits with both the SA model by Endsley (1995) and active inference theory (see Friston 2015). Both theories are founded upon a balance of cognitive resource division and complexity, environmental understanding or future state prediction, and error or surprise minimization (Engström 2018). The *full information* context provides more task non-specific information. However, in doing so it also provides a context within which a participant may expect to perform robot operation. This may already increase both the specificity and accuracy of perceptual expectations (Engström 2018).

With respect to VR presence and teleoperation performance, future research is advised to disentangle depth cues from context cues. In the current study, non-specific information may be deemed 'constructive' information, for instance the additional walls and familiar objects within the room may increase depth perception (Hanna et al. 2002; Rosenburg 1993a, b). To disentangle the effects of expected context from improved depth information on performance, future research may investigate a stripped version of the *full information* context, providing the same depth cues without providing contextual information such as recognizable objects and extensive color features. In doing so, depth perception effects can be regarded separate from general presence effects.

## 4.1    Recommendations for Teleoperation Design

Based on the current study and previous research, suggestions concerning VR mediated robot teleoperation design can be made, particularly related to information context and relative operator positioning during end-effector based robot control. With respect to VR presence and teleoperation performance, future research is advised to disentangle depth cues from context cues. In the current study, non-specific information may be deemed 'constructive' information, for instance the additional walls and familiar objects within the room may increase depth perception (Hanna et al. 2002; Rosenburg 1993a, b). To disentangle the effects of expected context from improved depth information on performance, future research may investigate a stripped version of the *full information* context, providing the same depth cues without providing contextual information such as recognizable objects and extensive color features. In doing so, depth perception effects can be regarded separate from general presence effects.

Artificial realistic contextual information (such as a floor, recognizable objects walls etcetera.) may be provided to add presence and depth cues so long as indispensable information from the robot scene is not replaced. Particularly for situations with limited bandwidth or dodgy signal, such an artificial context layer may serve as both a contextual and spatial anchor (Rosenberg 1993a, b). With respect to relative positioning of an operator for end-effector based control, the collaborative position seems to bear fruit. All participants were non-professionals concerning teleoperation and were able to perform smoothly with limited training. Two mechanisms could explain the success of the framework: one being the diminished amount of mental rotations an operator needs to make (DeJong, Colgate and Peshkin 2004); the other may lay in the possibility of the collaborative perspective, facing the robot, extending the scope of perception of the task environment. The robotic arm simply is not obstructing the field of view (FoV) of the operator. Additionally, operators may be inclined to move around more during collaborative positioning, increasing the possibility of improved depth perception and observation of task performance compared to traditional third person robot control.

# 5   Conclusion

The current study has provided a novel and promising technical framework for VR-mediated teleoperation research and development. This framework was applied to assess the influences of the informational context of the operator on Human-Robot team (HRT) task performance and operator Situation Awareness (oSA) during a path following task. Performance was better during a *full information* context, for which task performance time was significantly faster than during a *preprocessed* context and accuracy was equivalent in both informational contexts. Significant differences in general oSA levels were not found, however, attentional demand scores showed to be significantly higher for the *full information* context. Based on these results we provided recommendations for design, most importantly the incorporation of either natural or artificial context characteristics in VR presentation to the operator.

# References

About the Vive Controller. https://www.vive.com/nz/support/vive/category_howto/about-the-controllers.html. Accessed 2 July 2018

Barfield, W., Zeltzer, D., Sheridan, T., Slater, M.: Presence and performance within virtual environments. Virtual Environ. Adv. Interface Design (2), 473–513 (1995)

Bogacz, R., Wagenmakers, E.J., Forstmann, B.U., Nieuwenhuis, S.: The neural basis of the speed–accuracy tradeoff. Trends Neurosci. **33**(1), 10–16 (2010)

Bowman, D.A., McMahan, R.P.: Virtual reality: how much immersion is enough? Computer **40**(7), 36–43 (2007). https://doi.org/10.1109/MC.2007.257

Burdea, G.C.: Invited review: the synergy between virtual reality and robotics. IEEE Trans. Roboti. Autom. **15**(3), 400–410 (1999)

Catoire, M., Krom, B.N., van Erp, J.B.F.: Towards a test battery to benchmark dexterous performance in teleoperated systems. In: Prattichizzo, D., Shinoda, H., Tan, H.Z., Ruffaldi, E., Frisoli, A. (eds.) EuroHaptics 2018. LNCS, vol. 10894, pp. 440–451. Springer, Cham (2018). https://doi.org/10.1007/978-3-319-93399-3_38

Chamizo, V.D.: Spatial learning: conditions and basic effects. Psicologica **23**(1), 33–57 (2002)

DeJong, B.P., Colgate, J.E., Peshkin, M.A.: Improving teleoperation: reducing mental rotations and translations. In: IEEE International Conference on Robotics and Automation. Proceedings of ICRA 2004, vol. 4, pp. 3708–3714. IEEE (2004)

Deniaud, C., Mestre, D.: La sensation de présence comme condition nécessaire de la validité comportementale des simulateurs de conduite. Le travail humain **78**(4), 285–306 (2015)

Endsley, M.R.: Toward a theory of situation awareness in dynamic systems. Hum. Factors: J. Hum. Factors Ergon. Soc. **37**(1), 32–64 (1995). https://doi.org/10.1518/001872095779049543

Endsley, M.R., Selcon, S.J., Hardiman, T.D., Croft, D.G.: A comparative analysis of SAGAT and SART for evaluations of situation awareness. In: Proceedings of the Human Factors and Ergonomics Society Annual Meeting, vol. 42, no. 1, pp. 82–86. SAGE Publications, Sage, Los Angeles (1998)

Engström, J., et al.: Great expectations: a predictive processing account of automobile driving. Theor. Issues ergon. Sci. **19**(2), 156–194 (2018)

Freund, E., Rossmann, J.: Projective virtual reality: bridging the gap between virtual reality and robotics. IEEE Trans. Robot. Autom. **15**(3), 411–422 (1999)

Friston, K., Rigoli, F., Ognibene, D., Mathys, C., Fitzgerald, T., Pezzulo, G.: Active inference and epistemic value. Cogn. Neurosci. **6**(4), 187–214 (2015)

Goodell, K.H., Cao, C.G., Schwaitzberg, S.D.: Effects of cognitive distraction on performance of laparoscopic surgical tasks. J. Laparoendosc. Adv. Surg. Tech. **16**(2), 94–98 (2006)

Goodrich, M.A., Schultz, A.C.: Human–robot interaction: a survey. Found. Trends® Hum.–Comput. Interact. **1**(3), 203–275 (2008). https://doi.org/10.1561/1100000005

Graydon, J., Eysenck, M.W.: Distraction and cognitive performance. Eur. J. Cogn. Psychol. **1**(2), 161–179 (1989)

Hanna, G.B., Cresswell, A.B., Cuschieri, A.: Shadow depth cues and endoscopic task performance. Arch. Surg. **137**(10), 1166–1169 (2002)

Heft, H.: Ecological Psychology in Context: James Gibson, Roger Barker, and the Legacy of William James's Radical Empiricism. Psychology Press, Hove (2001)

Heitz, R.P.: The speed-accuracy tradeoff: history, physiology, methodology, and behavior. Front. Neurosci. **8**, 150 (2014)

Hokayem, P.F., Spong, M.W.: Bilateral teleoperation: an historical survey. Automatica **42**(12), 2035–2057 (2006)

Horberry, T., Anderson, J., Regan, M.A., Triggs, T.J., Brown, J.: Driver distraction: the effects of concurrent in-vehicle tasks, road environment complexity and age on driving performance. Accid. Anal. Prev. **38**(1), 185–191 (2006)

ISO norms authority. Industriële robots - Prestatie-eisen en bijbehorende beproevingsmethoden (ISO 9283:1998)

Kaber, D.B., Riley, J.M., Zhou, R., Draper, J.: Effects of visual interface design, and control mode and latency on performance, telepresence and workload in a teleoperation task. In: Proceedings of the Human Factors and Ergonomics Society Annual Meeting, vol. 44, no. 5, pp. 503–506. SAGE Publications, Los Angeles, July 2000

Kilteni, K., Groten, R., Slater, M.: The sense of embodiment in virtual reality. Presence: Teleoperators Virtual Environ. **21**(4), 373–387 (2012)

Kiverstein, J., Miller, M.: The embodied brain: towards a radical embodied cognitive neuroscience. Front. Hum. Neurosci. **9**, 237 (2015)

Kot, T., Novák, P.: Application of virtual reality in teleoperation of the military mobile robotic system TAROS. Int. J. Adv. Robot. Syst. **15**(1), 1729881417751545 (2018)

Leisman, G., Moustafa, A.A., Shafir, T.: Thinking, walking, talking: integratory motor and cognitive brain function. Front. Public Health **4**, 94 (2016). https://doi.org/10.3389/fpubh. 2016.00094

Lok, B., Naik, S., Whitton, M., Brooks, F.P.: Effects of handling real objects and self-avatar fidelity on cognitive task performance and sense of presence in virtual environments. Presence: Teleoper. Virtual Environ. **12**(6), 615–628 (2003)

Mestre, D., Fuchs, P., Berthoz, A., Vercher, J.L.: Immersion et présence. Le traité de la réalité virtuelle. Paris: Ecole des Mines de Paris, 309–38 (2006)

Munir, S., Book, W.J.: Control techniques and programming issues for time delayed internet based teleoperation. J. Dyn. Syst. Meas. Contr. **125**(2), 205–214 (2003)

Nowak, K.L., Biocca, F.: The effect of the agency and anthropomorphism on users' sense of telepresence, copresence, and social presence in virtual environments. Presence: Teleoperators Virtual Environ. **12**(5), 481–494 (2003)

Paljic, A.: Ecological validity of virtual reality: three use cases. In: Battiato, S., Farinella, G., Leo, M., Gallo, G. (eds.) ICIAP 2017 International Workshops. LNCS, vol. 10590, pp. 301–310. Springer, Cham (2017). https://doi.org/10.1007/978-3-319-70742-6_28

Rosenberg, L.B.: The use of virtual fixtures to enhance operator performance in time delayed teleoperation (No. AL/CF-TR-1994–0139). Armstrong Lab Wright-Patterson Afb Oh Crew Systems Directorate (1993a)

Rosenberg, L.B.: Virtual fixtures: perceptual tools for telerobotic manipulation. In 1993 IEEE Virtual Reality Annual International Symposium, pp. 76–82. IEEE (1993b)

Rubio-Tamayo, J., Gertrudix Barrio, M., García García, F.: Immersive environments and virtual reality: systematic review and advances in communication, interaction and simulation. Multimodal Technol. Interact. 1(4), 21 (2017)

Salmon, P., Stanton, N., Walker, G., Green, D.: Situation awareness measurement: a review of applicability for C4i environments. Appl. Ergon. 37(2), 225–238 (2006)

Salmon, P.M., et al.: Measuring situation awareness in complex systems: comparison of measures study. Int. J. Ind. Ergon. 39(3), 490–500 (2009)

Sheridan, T.B., Verplank, W.L.: Human and computer control of undersea teleoperators. Massachusetts Inst Of Tech Cambridge Man-Machine Systems Lab (1978)

Sheridan, T.B.: Telerobotics, Automation, and Human Supervisory Control. MIT Press, Cambridge (1992a)

Sheridan, T.B.: Musings on telepresence and virtual presence. Presence: Teleoper. Virtual Environ. 1(1), 120–126 (1992b)

Slater, M., Khanna, P., Mortensen, J., Yu, I.: Visual realism enhances realistic response in an immersive virtual environment. IEEE Comput. Graph. Appl. 29(3), 76–84 (2009)

Slater, M., Linakis, V., Usoh, M., Kooper, R.: Immersion, presence and performance in virtual environments: an experiment with tri-dimensional chess. In: Proceedings of the ACM Symposium on Virtual Reality Software and Technology, pp. 163–172. ACM, July 1996

Slater, M., Linakis, V., Usoh, M., Kooper, R.: Immersion, presence, and performance in virtual environments: an experiment with tri-dimensional chess. In: ACM Virtual Reality Software and Technology (VRST) (1999)

Taylor, R.M.: Situation awareness rating technique (SART): the development of a tool for aircrew systems design. In: Situational Awareness. Aerospace Operations, vol. 3. Neuilly sur-Seine, NATO-AGARD-CP-478, France (1990)

Turkoglu, M.O., ter Haar, F.B., van der Stap, N.: Incremental learning-based adaptive object recognition for mobile robots. Manuscript submitted for publication (2018)

van Maanen, L.: Is there evidence for a mixture of processes in speed-accuracy trade-off behavior? Top. Cogn. Sci. 8(1), 279–290 (2016)

Walsh, C.M., Sherlock, M.E., Ling, S.C., Carnahan, H.: Virtual reality simulation training for health professions trainees in gastrointestinal endoscopy. Cochrane Database Syst. Rev. (6) (2012)

Wickens, C.D.: Situation awareness: review of Mica Endsley's 1995 articles on situation awareness theory and measurement. Hum. Factors 50(3), 397–403 (2008)

Witmer, B.G., Singer, M.J.: Measuring presence in virtual environments: a presence questionnaire. Presence 7(3), 225–240 (1998)

Yu, I., Mortensen, J., Khanna, P., Spanlang, B., Slater, M.: Visual realism enhances realistic response in an immersive virtual environment-part 2. IEEE Comput. Graph. Appl. 32(6), 36–45 (2012)

# Investigating the Potential Effectiveness of Allocentric Mixed Reality Deictic Gesture

Tom Williams$^{(\boxtimes)}$, Matthew Bussing, Sebastian Cabrol, Ian Lau, Elizabeth Boyle, and Nhan Tran

Colorado School of Mines, Golden, CO, USA
twilliams@mines.edu

**Abstract.** Mixed reality technologies offer interactive robots many new ways to communicate their beliefs, desires, and intentions to human teammates. In previous work, we identified several categories of visualizations that when displayed to users through mixed reality technologies serve the same role as traditional deictic gestures (e.g., pointing). In this work, we experimentally investigate the potential utility of one of these categories, allocentric gestures, in which circles or arrows are rendered to enable human teammates to pick out the robot's target referents. Specifically, through two human subject experiments, we examine the objective and subjective performance of such gestures alone as compared to language alone and the combination of language and allocentric gesture. Our results suggest that allocentric gestures are more effective than language alone, but to maintain high robot likability allocentric gestures should be used to complement rather than replace complex referring expressions.

**Keywords:** Mixed reality · Augmented reality · Deixis · Natural language generation · Human-robot interaction

## 1 Introduction

Robots designed to interact with humans must be able to do so in a way that is natural, efficient, and human-like. This is especially important for many of the domains that the field of Human-Robot Interaction (HRI) is interested in, such as search-and-rescue, in which users (e.g., search-and-rescue victims) may never have interacted with a robot before, may be physically unable to control it through some other means, and may not have the time or willingness to undergo training to learn to operate the robot; or in which other users (e.g., search-and-rescue operators) may not have the cognitive bandwidth to dedicate to direct operation. Accordingly, researchers are increasingly turning to *natural language* as an intuitive and flexible modality for controlling and interacting with robots.

All authors are with the MIRRORLab (mirrorlab.mines.edu).

© Springer Nature Switzerland AG 2019
J. Y. C. Chen and G. Fragomeni (Eds.): HCII 2019, LNCS 11575, pp. 178–198, 2019.
https://doi.org/10.1007/978-3-030-21565-1_12

When humans verbally communicate, they typically accompany their utterances with various physical gestures. When picking out objects, people, and locations in the environment, humans typically use deictic gestures, such as pointing, to quickly draw their interlocutors' attention to their intended target without the use of overly complex description. Indeed, deictic gesture in particular is one of the most important communicative faculties available to humans, and one of the earliest arising communicative strategies in human development. Deictic gestures not only allow speakers to speak more concisely, but they lighten speakers' cognitive load [1] and working memory load [2]. Moreover, deictic gestures facilitate listeners' comprehension by amplifying semantic content [3] and shifting their attention [4], which in turn facilitates reference resolution [5] and helps to establish joint attention [6]. Indeed, in many situated contexts, it is difficult to effectively communicate *without* the use of deictic gesture.

Accordingly, HRI researchers have explored how robots might generate deictic gestures to allow robots to reap these same benefits. And while this previous work has largely been focused on pointing, HRI researcher shave also studied how robots might generate many other forms of deictic gesture, such as presenting, exhibiting, touching, grouping, and sweeping, and have studied how these different forms of gesture are differentially perceived by humans [7].

In our work, we are exploring robots' use of deictic gesture beyond even this wide variety of forms, to examine entirely new classes of deictic gestures enabled by recent technological developments. Specifically, we are interested in how new Augmented and mixed reality technologies can be used to enable mixed reality Deictic Gestures: new types of deictic gestures visualized in mixed reality environments. These new forms of gesture may replace or complement traditional (physical) deictic gestures in contexts where those gestures are impossible, e.g., when a robot lacks arms with which to gesture; or in contexts in which physical gestures are possible but suboptimal, e.g., when a robot is not colocated with their human interlocutor, or in environments in which traditional gestures would be difficult to see, such as dark and dusty subterranean environments.

In Sect. 2, we briefly survey previous work on human and robot use of deictic gesture, as well as of recent work at the intersection of augmented and mixed reality and HRI, including the limited set of work previously exploring mixed reality deictic gesture for HRI. In Sects. 3 and 4, we then describe two human subject experiments designed to provide a preliminary investigation of the effectiveness and human perception of mixed reality deictic gesture, in which we assess human perceptions of videos simulating the display of one category of mixed reality deictic gestures, *allocentric gestures*. In Sect. 4.3, we then introduce preliminary work we have performed towards enabling robot generation of allocentric gestures. Finally, in Sect. 6, we conclude with several possible directions for future work.

# 2  Related Work

## 2.1  Human Deictic Gesture

Deixis is one of the most crucial forms of human-human communications [8,9], as well as one of the oldest, both anthropologically and developmentally. Humans point while speaking even from infancy, with deictic gesture beginning around 9–12 months [10], and general deictic reference mastered around age 4 [11]. Deictic gestures have been shown to be a powerful technique for language learners, as they allow speakers to communicate intended referents before being able to do so in language, just as other types of gestures help speakers to communicate their intended sense or meaning when they otherwise lack the words to do so. Indeed, developmental changes in deictic gestural capabilities in humans are a strong predictor of changes in language development [12].

In addition, long past infancy, humans continue to rely on deictic gesture as a core communicative capability, as its attention-direction presents an efficient and workload-reducing referential strategy in complex environments, far beyond that of purely verbal reference [13–17], and as deictic gesture allows for communication in environments in which verbal communication would be difficult or impossible, such as in noisy factory environments [18]. Accordingly, it is no surprise that Human-Robot Interaction researchers have sought to enable this effective and natural communication strategy in robots.

## 2.2  Robot Deictic Gesture

There is widespread evidence for the effectiveness of robots' use of physical deictic gesture: studies have shown that robots' use of deictic gesture is effective at shifting attention in the same way as is humans' use of deictic gesture [19], and that robots' use of deictic gesture improves both subsequent human recall and human-robot rapport [20]. This effectiveness has been demonstrated across different contextual scales as well, including gestures to nearby objects on a table-top [21], gestures to larger regions of space between the robot and its interlocutor [22], and gesture to large-scale spatial locations during direction-giving [23]. Furthermore, this effectiveness has shown to be especially true when gestures are generated in socially appropriate ways [24].

Research has also shown that robots' use of deictic gesture is especially effective when paired with other nonverbal signaling mechanisms [25], such as *deictic gaze*, in which a robot (actually or ostensibly) shifts its gaze towards its intended referent [22,26,27], and that this is especially effective when gaze and gesture are appropriately coordinated [28]. These findings have motivated a variety of technical approaches to deictic gesture generation [29–31], as well as a number of approaches for integrating gesture generation with natural language generation [32] (see also [33–35]).

Of particular interest is the work of Sauppé and Mutlu [7]. Building off the work of Clark, who showed that humans use many deictic gestures beyond pointing [36], Sauppé and Mutlu explored a selection of robotic deictic gestures: pointing, presenting, exhibiting, touching, grouping, and sweeping. Sauppé and Mutlu were especially interested in how these categories differed in both effectiveness and perceived naturality, and how different contextual factors, such as the density of candidate referents, the number of fully ambiguous distractors for the referent, and the distance of the referent from the referrer. As we will describe, the set of questions we are interested in investigating both in this work and in future work has a number of parallels with those of interest to Sauppé and Mutlu, and accordingly, as we will also describe, the experiment presented in this paper was designed with careful attention to Sauppé and Mutlu's design.

## 2.3   Augmented Reality for HRI

Research on augmented and mixed reality have been steadily progressing over the past several decades [37–39], and there have been a number of papers over the past twenty-five years highlighting the advantages of leveraging augmented reality (AR) technologies to facilitate human-robot interactions [40,41]. Augmented and mixed reality technologies lies primarily in two areas: (1) their potential to increase the flexibility of users' control over robots through visualizations of robot-controlling interface elements, and (2) their potential to increase the expressivity of users' view into those robots' internal states through visualizations that reflect information from the robot's internal state [42]. Historically, however, there has been surprisingly little research on this topic.

Recently, this has changed, with research at the intersection of these fields beginning to dramatically increase [43,44], with approaches being presented that use AR for robot design [45], calibration [46], and training [47], and for communicating robots' perspectives [48], intentions [49,50] and trajectories [51–53]. Most relevant to this paper are recent works on aligning human and robot perspective to facilitate communication. Amor et al. project instructions and highlight task-relevant objects, but with no language generation, and with visualizations cast as part of the environment, rather than as the robot's communication [54]. Sibirtseva et al. present an approach in which, as a human describes a referent, the robot's distribution over intended referents is visualized by circling remaining reference candidates in the user's AR Head-Mounted Display (HMD) [55] (cp. [56]). The visualizations used in this work are cast as being from the robot's perspective, but this is passive backchannel communication rather than active communication of the robot's intentions. Also of interest is recent work from Reardon et al., in which a robot draws the trajectory a human should take into their HMD, highlighting the intended target [57]. This work takes a more active communication approach than the work of Sibirtseva et al., but does not involve robot language generation.

To explore the use of AR in active, linguistic, robotic communication, we have presented a framework for categorizing deictic gestures available in mixed reality human-robot interactions, including both traditional physical gestures and virtual deictic annotations (categorized into allocentric gestures (e.g., circling a target referent in a user's AR HMD), perspective-free gestures (e.g., projecting a circle around a target referent on the floor of the shared environment), ego-sensitive allocentric gestures (e.g., pointing to a target referent using a simulated arm rendered in a user's AR HMD), and ego-sensitive perspective-free gestures (e.g., projecting a line from the robot to its target on the floor of the shared environment)), as well as combinations of different forms of mixed reality deictic gesture [58,59]. Crucially, we argue that not only do tradeoffs exist between different forms of mixed reality deictic gestures (including differences in privacy, cost, and legibility), but moreover, that there are a number of contextual factors that dictate the circumstances in which mixed reality deictic gestures become especially valuable, including teammate workload, auditory and visual perceptual load, and so forth [60].

This framework is especially valuable for our research as, in conjunction with the work of Sauppé and Mutlu [7], it suggests concrete hypotheses regarding the effectiveness and perception of mixed reality deictic gestures in different contexts, allowing us to empirically investigate whether mixed reality deictic gestures have the same communicative benefits as physical gestures, and how those benefits differ according to context. In this paper, we present a set of such hypotheses, and describe two human subject experiments designed to investigate them [61,62].

## 3    Experiment 1

Our first experiment [61] investigated the combination of language and mixed reality deictic gesture for robot communication. Here, participants viewed videos of a robot referring to 12 objects within a visual scene. This IRB-approved experiment was designed so as to follow the within-subjects paradigm used in the seminal evaluation of physical robot gesture presented by Sauppé and Mutlu [7].

### 3.1    Experimental Design

**Interaction Design:** Our first independent variable was *communication style*. For one-third of the objects, the robot used *complex reference* alone, generating an expression of the form "Look at that {color} {shape}" (e.g. "Look at that red cube"). These utterances followed a common fixed-length form even if it was not fully disambiguating, in hopes of better studying reaction time. For another third of the objects, the robot used a mixed reality deictic gesture, drawing a circle around the target and stating "Look at that" (cp. the gestural conditions used by Sauppé and Mutlu). For the remaining objects, the robot used both complex reference *and* mixed reality deictic gesture, circling the target and then generating a complex reference as described above (cp. the gestural and fully articulated conditions used by Sauppé and Mutlu).

**Environment Design:** The experimental environment contained a Kobuki robot positioned behind an array of eighteen blocks, of four shapes (cubes, triangles, cylinders, towers) and four colors (red, yellow, green, blue), evenly spaced in four rows. Specifically, there were six unique blocks and six pairs of non-unique blocks (a difference of *inherent ambiguity*), evenly split between the front and rear rows (a difference of *distance*), and distributed as uniformly as possible according to color and shape (as shown in Fig. 1). This sought to simultaneously capture multiple environmental dimensions previously determined by Sauppé and Mutlu to affect the accuracy and perceived effectiveness of reference: *ambiguity* and *distance from referrer* while controlling for the other dimensions previously investigated by Sauppé and Mutlu (object clustering, visibility, and noise). Our second and third independent variables were thus referent ambiguity and referent distance[1], yielding a total of twelve ($3 \times 2 \times 2$) experimental conditions.

**Fig. 1.** Task environment, with simulated AR visualization (Color figure online)

## 3.2  Procedure

Participants were recruited online using Amazon's Mechanical Turk platform, and directed towards a psiTurk experimental environment [63]. After providing informed consent and providing demographic information, participants were instructed that they would watch a series of videos in which a robot described and/or visually gestured towards a target object by drawing a circle around it. They were told that they should click on the object that was being described as soon as they had identified it. Participants were then assigned to one of twelve conditions each corresponding to a different video order determined through a counterbalanced Latin Square array. Participants then watched twelve videos, each corresponding with a different experimental condition. When mixed reality deictic gesture was used in a video, gesture onset began 660 ms before speech onset, based on the gestural timing model presented by Huang and Mutlu [64] and leveraged by Sauppé and Mutlu [7]. Clicking on any object within a video sent the participant to a survey page in which they were asked to assess the effectiveness of the robot's speech and gesture and the likability of the robot, using the measures described below. Upon answering these survey questions, participants were allowed to proceed to the next video in the series. All videos were six seconds in length, including padding before and after the robot's utterance.

---

[1] We did not expect to see effects of distance, but included distance as an independent variable so that we can use an identical experimental design in future experiments in which we will use other types of gestures, e.g., pointing gestures generated with real or simulated arms, for which we *would* expect to see a potential difference.

## 3.3  Hypotheses

In this experiment, we examined four core hypotheses:

**H1.** We hypothesized that participants would have worse accuracy in identifying the robot's target referent only when ambiguous complex noun phrases were used without an associated mixed reality deictic gesture (i.e., in the complex reference condition for targets with inherent ambiguity).

**H2.** We hypothesized **(H2.1)** that the speed at which participants would be able to identify the robot's target referent would be better when mixed reality deictic gesture was used, as it would allow target referents to be disambiguated even before speech began, and **(H2.2)** that this reaction time would increase when a reference was ambiguous.

**H3.** We hypothesized **(H3.1)** that participants would perceive the robot to be more effective when mixed reality deictic gesture was used, especially **(H3.2)** when used in combination with complex reference, and **(H3.3)** when the target referent was ambiguous.

**H4.** We hypothesized that the robot's likability would correlate with its effectiveness, and accordingly, that **(H4.1)** perceived likability would be higher when mixed reality deictic gesture was used, **(H4.2)** especially in combination with complex reference, and **(H4.3)** for ambiguous targets.

## 3.4  Measures

To assess these hypotheses, objective and subjective measures were used.

**Accuracy:** An objective measure of *accuracy* was gathered by recording which item in each scene participants clicked on, and determining whether or not this was in fact the object intended by the robot.

**Reaction Time:** An objective measure of *reaction time* was gathered by recording time stamps at the moment each video phase began (i.e., when the page loaded) and ended (i.e., when an object was clicked on).

**Effectiveness:** A subjective measure of robot *effectiveness* was gathered using a version of the Gesture Perception Scale [7] modified to make reference to mixed reality deictic gesture rather than simply gesture [61]. Each participants' scores for each video were then transformed to a range of 0–100 and averaged. A reliability analysis indicated that the internal reliability of this scale was very high for our experiment, with Cronbach's $\alpha = 0.955$.

**Likability:** A subjective measure of robot *likability* was gathered using the Godspeed II Likability scale [65]. Our modified version asked participants to rate their perception of the robot along each dimension by clicking a point anywhere along a five-point Likert-type scale. Each participants' scores for each video were transformed to a range of 0–100 and averaged. A reliability analysis indicated very high internal reliability (Cronbach's $\alpha = 0.963$).

## 3.5   Participants

50 participants were recruited from Amazon Mechanical Turk (19 F, 31 M). Participants ranged in age from 19 to 69 (M = 39.07, SD = 11.35). None had participated in any previous studies from our laboratory under the account used.

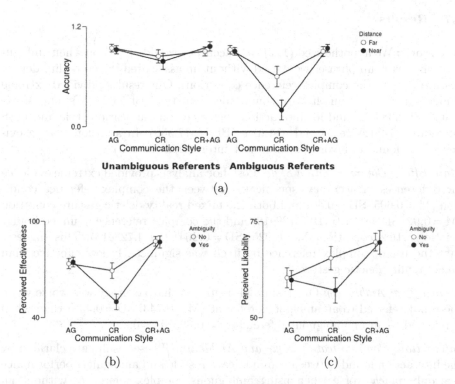

**Fig. 2.** (a) Effect of communication style (augmented gesture (AG), vs complex reference (CR) vs both (CR+AG)), referent ambiguity and referent distance on participant accuracy. (b) Effect of communication style (augmented gesture (AG), vs complex reference (CR) vs both (CR+AG)) and referent ambiguity on perceived effectiveness. (c) Effect of communication style (augmented gesture (AG), vs complex reference (CR) vs both (CR+AG)) and referent ambiguity on likability

## 3.6   Analysis

Data analysis was performed within a Bayesian analysis framework using the JASP 0.8.5.1 [66] software package, using the default settings as justified by Wagenmakers et al. [67]. All data files are available at tinyurl.com/hri19data. For each measure, a repeated measures analysis of variance (RM-ANOVA) [68–70] was performed, using communication style, ambiguity, and distance as random factors. Baws factors [71] were then computed for each candidate main effect and interaction, indicating (in the form of a Bayes Factor) for that effect the evidence weight of all candidate models including that effect compared to the evidence weight of all candidate models not including that effect. When sufficient evidence was found in favor of a main effect of communication style (a three-level factor), the results were further analyzed using a post-hoc Bayesian t-test [72,73] with a default Cauchy prior (center $= 0$, $r = \frac{\sqrt{2}}{2} = 0.707$).

## 3.7  Results

**Accuracy:** We hypothesized (**H1**) that accuracy would only drop when ambiguous complex noun phrases were used without an associated mixed reality deictic gesture (i.e., in the complex reference condition). Our results provided extreme evidence in favor of an effect of communication style (Bf 5.626e28)[2] and ambiguity (Bf 2.380e7), and for interactions between communication style and both ambiguity (Bf 1.521e13) and distance (Bf 44577.358). In addition, strong evidence was found in favor of a three-way interaction (22.183).

*Main Effect: Communication Style:* Post-hoc analysis provided extreme evidence for differences in accuracy, specifically between the complex reference condition (M $= 0.605$, SD $= 0.49$) and both the mixed reality deictic gesture condition (M $= 0.92$, SD $= 0.272$) (Bf 1.129e15) and the complex reference + mixed reality deictic gesture condition (M $= 0.925$, SD $= 0.264$) (Bf 4.728e13). This suggests that the use of complex reference by itself was significantly less effective than mixed reality deictic gesture.

*Main Effect: Ambiguity:* Our results also suggest that accuracy was worse when the robot referred to an ambiguous referent (M $= 0.743$, SD $= 0.438$) than when it referred to an unambiguous referent (M $= 0.89$, SD $= 0.313$).

*Interaction: Communication Style and Ambiguity:* These results are clarified by the interaction found between communication style and ambiguity: performance was only *much* worse when using ambiguous complex references without an associated gesture. This confirms hypothesis **H1**.

*Interaction: Communication Style and Distance:* Our results demonstrate that when a target referent was close to the robot, using a complex reference alone significantly harmed performance more than when the referent was far away.

*Interaction: Communication Style, Ambiguity, and Distance:* This effect is further clarified through the three-way interaction, which shows that performance drops only occurred when the reference was ambiguous, as shown in Fig. 2a.

*Reaction Time:* We hypothesized (**H2.1**) that reaction time would drop when mixed reality deictic gesture was used, as it would allow target referents to be disambiguated even before speech began, and (**H2.2**) that reaction time would increase when a reference was ambiguous. No results were found in favor of our

---

[2] Bayes Factors above 100 indicate extreme evidence in favor of a hypothesis [74]. Here, for example, our Baws Factor Bf of 5.626e28 suggests that our data were 5.626e28 times more likely to be generated under models in which communication style is included than under those in which it is not.

hypotheses: in fact, our analysis provided strong evidence against a main effect of ambiguity or any interaction effect. Median reaction time was 7.7 s.

**Effectiveness:** We hypothesized (**H3.1**) that perceived effectiveness would be higher when mixed reality deictic gesture was used, especially (**H3.2**) when used in combination with complex reference, and (**H3.3**) when the target referent was ambiguous. Our results provided extreme evidence in favor of main effects of communication style (Bf 1.601e36) and ambiguity (Bf 216.516), and for an interaction between communication style and ambiguity (Bf 1.04e6).

*Main Effect: Communication Style:* Post-hoc analysis provided extreme evidence in favor of a difference in perceived effectiveness between communication styles (mixed reality deictic gesture (M = 74.17, SD = 23.59) vs. complex reference (M = 59.67, SD = 27.30) (Bf 2.038e7); mixed reality deictic gesture vs. complex reference + mixed reality deictic gesture (M = 87.50, SD = 17.08) (Bf 1.462e10); complex reference vs complex reference + mixed reality deictic gesture (Bf 1.581e23)). Specifically, our results show a strong perceived ordering in effectiveness: complex reference < mixed reality deictic gesture < complex reference + mixed reality deictic gesture. This confirms hypotheses **H3.1** and **H3.2**.

*Main Effect: Ambiguity:* In addition, our results showed that robots were perceived as less effective when describing ambiguous referents (M = 70.63, SD = 26.98) than when describing unambiguous referents (M = 76.93, SD = 23.92).

*Interaction: Communication Style and Ambiguity:* These results are clarified by examining the observed interaction between communication style and ambiguity, which suggests that while the robot was perceived as less effective when using complex reference alone even when the referent was unambiguous, the robot was perceived as *much* less effective when using complex reference alone to describe ambiguous targets, as seen in Fig. 2b. This confirms hypothesis **H3.3**.

**Likability:** We hypothesized that robots' perceived likability would correlate with their perceived effectiveness, and that (**H4.1**) perceived likability would be higher when mixed reality deictic gesture was used, (**H4.2**) especially in combination with complex reference, and (**H4.3**) when the target referent was ambiguous. Our results provided extreme evidence in favor of a main effect of communication (Bf 5.986e9), and moderate evidence in favor of an effect of ambiguity (Bf 3.088) or its interaction with communication (Bf 7.985).

*Main Effect: Communication Style:* Post-hoc analysis provided extreme evidence in favor of a difference in likability between the use of complex reference *and* mixed reality deictic gesture (M = 69.68, SD = 19.27) and the use of *either* complex reference (M = 61.35, SD = 22.40) (Bf 81289.052) *or* mixed reality deictic gesture (M = 60.11, SD = 19.64) (Bf 9.940e7). This suggests that participants much more strongly liked the robot when it used both communication styles in combination, confirming hypothesis **H4.1**.

*Main Effect: Ambiguity:* Our results suggested that participants liked the robot less when it referred to ambiguous referents.

*Interaction: Communication Style and Ambiguity:* This interaction effect suggested that when the robot's target referent was unambiguous, participants exhibited a likability ordering: mixed reality deictic gesture < complex reference < mixed reality deictic gesture + complex reference; but when the robot's target referent ambiguous, participants particularly disliked the use of complex reference alone (which is unsurprising given that in such cases complex reference alone did not allow the target to be properly disambiguated). These findings, as seen in Fig. 2c, confirming hypotheses **H4.3** and partially supporting **H4.2**.

### 3.8   Discussion

Our results suggest that mixed reality deictic gestures may be an accurate, likable, and effective communication strategy for human-robot interaction, much the same as traditional physical deictic gestures. In this section, we will discuss these results in detail, and leverage them to produce design guidelines for enabling mixed reality deictic gestures.

**Objective Effectiveness of Mixed Reality Deictic Gesture:** Our first and second hypotheses considered the objective effectiveness of mixed reality deictic gestures. Specifically, we hypothesized (**H2.1**) that mixed reality deictic gestures would facilitate faster human reference resolution, especially in the case of ambiguous referents (**H2.2**) – for which referents we also hypothesized that mixed reality deictic gesture would enable increased accuracy (**H1**). Our results did indeed suggest that participants had better accuracy in selecting ambiguous referents when mixed reality deictic gestures were used, and especially when referents were ambiguous (supporting **H1**). This is not particularly surprising, as when complex reference alone was used to refer to otherwise ambiguous referents, the specific descriptions we used were not themselves sufficient to disambiguate those referents. Specifically, to appropriately control language complexity, all instances of complex reference took the form "Look at that {color} {shape}". When a referent was ambiguous (i.e., there were more than one object of that color and shape), clearly this expression itself was still ambiguous. As we will describe below, in our second experiment we sought to instead use a complex reference condition that more fully aligned with the "fully articulated" baseline used by Sauppé and Mutlu [7], which sacrifices control over linguistic complexity for assurance of complete disambiguation. This draws an interesting contrast with Sauppé and Mutlu's experiment, in which the fully articulated baseline was fully disambiguating, but the majority of the deictic gestures examined were *not*; the opposite pattern as observed in our own experimental design.

But while our first hypothesis was supported, no effects on reaction time were observed, thus failing to support **H2**. As median reaction time was 7.7 s for videos that were around 5–6 s in length, this suggests that participants nearly uniformly waited until videos completed before selecting their targets, and were not hindered by ambiguity. We expected that despite our instructions to click on target referents as soon as they were identified, participants may simply not have been aware of the ability or benefit of doing so. As we will describe below, we sought to address this concern in our second experiment. In future work, it could also be interesting to gain an even more fine-grained measure of how mixed reality deictic reference affects reaction time in complex, multi-entity reference, using eye-tracking techniques such as those employed in Visual World-paradigmatic experiments [75].

In addition, we found a surprising interaction between communication style and distance. We believe that this finding may best be explained by imagining an attentional cone extending in front of the robot. Several theories of qualitative spatial reference (e.g., Ternary Point Configuration Calculus [76]) consider one entity to be "in front" of another if it falls within just such a cone. Our results suggest that when participants had to choose between options that had not been fully disambiguated, they were biased towards options that could be considered to be "in front" of the robot because they fell within that cone. Because of the conic nature of this region, all objects far from the robot may have been considered "in front" of the robot, yielding no bias for any particular distant object, whereas only some of the objects close to the robot would have been considered "in front" of it, yielding a bias towards those objects. This led to poor accuracy in cases of ambiguity where the "true" target referent did not fall within that attentional cone. We would also note that our experimental design uniquely enabled us to identify this interaction; no such interaction was observed by Sauppé and Mutlu because their experimental design did not allow distance and ambiguity to be simultaneously investigated. That being said, as we will describe below, in our second experiment, we sought to remove the need for participants to occasionally select between not-fully-disambiguated referents, trading ability to investigate this effect for the ability to better capture the overall potential for impact for mixed reality deictic gesture.

**Subjective Perceptions of Mixed Reality Deictic Gesture:** Our final hypotheses considered the subjective perception of mixed reality deictic gestures. Specifically, we hypothesized (**H3.1/H4.1**) that participants would perceive the robot to be more effective and likable when mixed reality deictic gesture was used, especially when used in combination with complex reference (**H3.2/4.2**), and when used to refer to an otherwise ambiguous referent (**H3.3/4.3**).

Our results supported all of these hypotheses, with the possible exception of **H4.2**: when the target referent would *not* have been otherwise ambiguous, participants actually reported liking the robot more when complex reference alone was used than for mixed reality deictic gesture alone (accompanied only by a minimally articulated verbal reference). This serves to emphasize that, like physical gesture, mixed reality deictic gesture should be used to supplement rather than replace natural language (excepting extreme circumstances). However, clearly these differences may be exaggerated by the same features of our complex references that potentially exaggerated the accuracy effects.

# 4    Experiment 2

To clarify the results of Experiment 1, we designed a second human subject experiment [62], which slightly modified the design of our initial experiment. First, while in Experiment 1 complex references all followed a uniform pattern ("Look at that {color} {shape}"), in this experiment we deviated from that pattern when there were multiple objects of the same color and shape, "Look at the {color} {shape} on your {direction relative to the person}" (e.g. "Look at the red tower on your right").

Second, to encourage faster reaction times, we implemented a reaction time based point system. At the top of each survey page, participants were shown the number of points gained in the previous trial. For each video the participant would receive $15 - t$ points if correct, where t is the time in seconds taken to click on the object from when the video began. All videos were six seconds in length, including padding before and after the robot's communicative act.

In this experiment we again examined four core hypotheses:

**H1.** Counter to Experiment 1, in this experiment we hypothesized that participants would have equal accuracy regardless of what communication style was used, as all communication styles that were used allowed for full disambiguation.

**H2–4.** We hypothesized the same expected effects of reaction time and perceived effectiveness and likability that we hypothesized in Experiment 1.

## 4.1    Measures and Participants

The same measures used in Experiment 1 were used in this Experiment. In this experiment, internal reliability scores for Effectiveness were still high (Effectiveness $\alpha = 0.975$, Likability $\alpha = 0.963$). 48 participants were recruited from Amazon Mechanical Turk (25 M, 17 F, 6 NA; ages 18 to 66, M $= 33.95$, SD $= 9.67$). None had participated in any previous studies from our laboratory.

## 4.2    Results

**Accuracy:** We hypothesized **(H1)** that participants would have equal accuracy regardless of what communication style was used, as all communication styles that were used allowed for full disambiguation. In fact, in refutation of H1, our results provided extreme evidence *in favor* of an effect of communication style (Bf 5.157e13), as seen in Fig. 3a.

Post-hoc analysis provided extreme evidence for differences in accuracy, between the complex reference condition (M $= 0.73$, SD $= 0.45$) and both the mixed reality condition (M $= 0.927$, SD $= 0.261$) (Bf 3.774e6) and the complex reference + mixed reality condition (M $= 0.938$, SD $= 0.242$) (Bf 3.160e7). This suggests that the use of complex reference by itself was significantly less effective than mixed reality deictic gesture. This effect was also seen in Experiment 1; the other effects seen in Experiment 1 did not appear in this experiment.

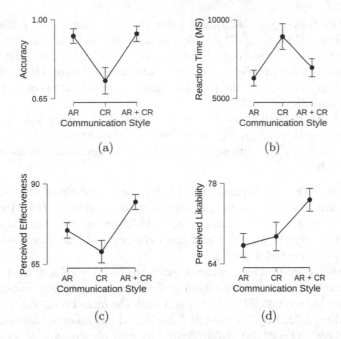

**Fig. 3.** (a) Effect of communication style (augmented reality (AR) vs complex reference (CR) vs both (AR+CR)) on participant accuracy. (b) Effect of communication style (augmented reality (AR) vs complex reference (CR) vs both (AR+CR)) on participant reaction time. (c) Effect of communication style (augmented reality (AR) vs complex reference (CR) vs both (AR+CR)) on perceived effectiveness (d) Effect of communication style (augmented reality (AR) vs complex reference (CR) vs both (AR+CR)) on perceived likability

**Reaction Time:** We hypothesized **(H2.1)** that reaction time would drop when mixed reality deictic gesture was used, as it would allow target referents to be disambiguated even before speech began, and **(H2.2)** that this difference in reaction time would be greater when a reference was ambiguous. While initial analysis provided strong evidence against an interaction between communication style and ambiguity (Bf 0.073, refuting **(H2.2)**), the evidence against a main effect of communication style was only anecdotal (Bf 0.665), prompting further exploration. Post-Hoc analysis provided moderate evidence in favor of a differences in reaction time between the complex reference condition (M = 12.42 s, SD = 13.19) and the mixed reality deictic gesture condition (M = 9.69, SD = 10.78) (Bf 4.204).

The extremely large standard deviations seen here led us to inspect our data, which showed a small number (about 5%) of our reaction time data points were very long, over 30 s. Removing all reaction time datapoints for any participant with at least one outlier reaction time left 29 data points. Re-analyzing this subset of the data provided extreme evidence in favor of an effect of communication style (Bf 1.074e8), as seen in Fig. 3b. Post-hoc analysis provided extreme in favor of an effect of communication style specifically between the complex reference condition (M = 9.25 s, SD = 4.59) and both the both the mixed reality deictic gesture condition (M = 6.78, SD = 3.39) (Bf 5.705e6) and the complex reference + mixed reality deictic gesture condition (M = 7.25, SD = 3.40) (Bf 1081.64). Figure 3b also appears to reflect a potential advantage of pure AR vs. AR paired with complex reference, but the post-hoc analysis provided anecdotal evidence against such an effect (Bf 0.705).

This suggests that the use of complex reference by itself may have taken longer to process than when augmented reality visualizations were used. This effect was not seen in Experiment 1, which failed to find evidence for or against the first hypothesis.

**Effectiveness:** We hypothesized (**H3.1**) that perceived effectiveness would be higher when mixed reality deictic gesture was used, especially (**H3.2**) when used in combination with complex reference, and (**H3.3**) when the target referent was ambiguous. Our results provided extreme evidence in favor of a main effect of communication style (Bf 3.42e14).

Post-hoc analysis provided extreme evidence in favor of a difference in perceived effectiveness between the mixed reality deictic gesture + complex reference condition (M = 84.33, SD = 17.86) and both the mixed reality deictic gesture condition (M = 75.52, SD = 22.25) (Bf 2.49e7) and the complex reference condition (M = 68.89, SD = 22.98) (Bf 1.65e10), as well as strong evidence in favor of a difference between the mixed reality deictic gesture and complex reference conditions (Bf 13.97). Specifically, our results show the same strong perceived ordering in effectiveness seen in Experiment 1: complex reference < mixed reality deictic gesture < complex reference + mixed reality deictic gesture, as seen in Fig. 3c. This confirms hypotheses **H3.1** and **H3.2**.

This specific ordering effect was also seen in Experiment 1; the other effects seen in Experiment 1 did not appear in this experiment.

**Likability:** We hypothesized that robots' perceived likability would correlate with their perceived effectiveness, and accordingly, that (**H4.1**) perceived likability would be higher when mixed reality deictic gesture was used, (**H4.2**) especially in combination with complex reference, and (**H4.3**) when the target referent was ambiguous. Our results provided extreme evidence in favor of a main effect of communication (Bf 1.64e6).

Post-hoc analysis provided extreme evidence in favor of a difference in likability between the mixed reality deictic gesture + complex reference condition (M = 75.14, SD = 19.10) and both the mixed reality deictic gesture condition (M = 67.20, SD = 21.73) (Bf 1.64e6) and the complex reference condition (M = 68.75, SD = 20.25) (Bf 632.99), as shown in Fig. 3d. This suggests that participants much more strongly liked the robot when it used both communication styles in combination, confirming hypothesis **H4.1**. This effect was also seen in Experiment 1; the other effects seen in Experiment 1 did not appear in this experiment.

## 4.3   Discussion

Our results suggest that mixed reality deictic gestures may be an accurate, efficient, likable, and effective communication strategy for human-robot interaction, much the same as traditional physical deictic gestures. In this section, we will discuss these results in detail, and leverage them to produce design guidelines for enabling mixed reality deictic gestures.

**Objective Effectiveness of Mixed Reality Deictic Gesture:** Our first and second hypotheses considered the objective effectiveness of mixed reality deictic gestures. Specifically, we hypothesized that while we did not expect there to be significant advantages in accuracy (**H1**), we did expect (**H2.1**) that the speed at which participants would be able to identify the robot's target referent would be better when mixed reality deictic gesture was used, as it would allow target referents to be disambiguated even before speech began, and (**H2.2**) that this advantage in reaction time would be greater when a reference was ambiguous.

 With respect to accuracy, our results suggest that the use of AR significantly increased accuracy over the use of bare complex reference, and that when complex reference was used by itself, participants incurred significant penalty to accuracy, *even though complex references were uniquely disambiguating and explicitly framed from participants' point of view.* This surprising result refutes (**H1**), painting an even stronger picture of the benefits of mixed reality gesture.

 With respect to reaction time, our results suggest that the use of AR significantly decreased reaction time over the use of bare complex reference, regardless of whether or not the target referent was ambiguous. This result supports (**H2.1**) and refutes (**H2.2**), again strengthening the overall utility of mixed reality deictic gesture, and demonstrating that the modifications made in this experiment over our previous work were an effective means to assess reaction time. However, additional study will be needed on this point, for two reasons. First, we suspect that advantages in the case of ambiguous referents will emerge as the number of distractors increases. Second, the number of temporal outliers that needed to be removed serves as a strong motivator for the need for the replication of this experiment in a live laboratory environment with realistic AR hardware, where such outliers would not be likely.

**Subjective Perceptions of Mixed Reality Deictic Gesture:** As in Experiment 1, our final hypotheses considered the subjective perception of mixed reality deictic gestures, hypothesizing (**H3.1/4.1**) that participants would perceive the robot to be more effective and likable when mixed reality deictic gesture was used, especially in combination with complex reference (**H3.2/4.2**), and for ambiguous referents (**H3.3/4.3**).

 Our results suggest, as in Experiment 1, that the use of mixed reality deictic gesture improved perceived effectiveness *especially* when paired with complex reference (supporting (**H3.1**) and (**H3.2**) but refuting (**H3.3**)), and improved perceived likability *only* when paired with complex reference (supporting (**H4.2**) and partially supporting (**H4.1**) but refuting (**H4.3**)). These results emphasize that, like physical gesture, mixed reality deictic gesture should be used to supplement rather than replace verbally expressive natural language. That being said, we would expect for very complex utterances that AR paired with referring expressions of reduced complexity would be preferred. Future work will be needed to determine if this is the case, and if so, how the tradeoff between referential complexity and positive perceptions of verbal expressivity should be quantified.

## 5    Current Implementation

In recent work, we have been working to enable generation of mixed reality deictic gestures on the Microsoft Hololens. As described in recent work [60], we propose to decide when to generate mixed reality deictic gestures based on a variety of neurophysiological factors. This decision will be made by new components that will communicate with the Referring Expression Generation capabilities [77] of the Distributed, Integrated, Affect, Reflection, Cognition architecture [78, 79]. When it is decided to generate a gesture, this must be communicated to the Hololens. We have established a bidirectional server-Hololens connection using websockets, which we can use to send commands to show/hide visualizations over particular targets. When the Hololens receives such a command, we render mixed reality deictic gestures through Unity over the appropriate location (Fig. 4). While we currently are mainly using ARTags to define object positions, in the future we hope to leverage object and pose recognition techniques to achieve these results without ARTags.

**Fig. 4.** Hololens-projected arrow

## 6    Conclusion

We have explored the actual and perceived effectiveness of allocentric mixed reality deictic gestures in multi-modal robot communication. Our results suggest that these allocentric gestures may well be beneficial for human-robot communication in mixed reality environments, but highlight the importance of using them to complement complex referring expressions rather than purely as a replacement. Future work should seek to examine the tipping point at which referential overcomplexity overwhelms the subjective benefits of verbal expressivity. Second, it will be important to investigate a wider variety of mixed reality deictic gestures, with respect to both Sauppé and Mutlu [7] and our own [58] frameworks, and to investigate that wider array of gestures and evaluation criteria. We also hope to investigate the effect of different classes of mixed reality deictic gesture when used by robots of differing morphologies, e.g., robots that lack arms vs. robots that have arms they could use instead of (or in combination with) allocentric gestures. Finally, after completing our integration on the Microsoft Hololens, we will attempt to replicate our experimental results on that system for increased external validity.

# References

1. Ping, R., Goldin-Meadow, S.: Gesturing saves cognitive resources when talking about nonpresent objects. Cogn. Sci. **34**(4), 602–619 (2010)
2. Cook, S., Yip, T., Goldin-Meadow, S.: Gestures, but not meaningless movements, lighten working memory load when explaining math. Lang. Cogn. Process. **27**(4), 594–610 (2012)
3. Tfouni, L.V., Klatzky, R.L.: A discourse analysis of deixis: pragmatic, cognitive and semantic factors in the comprehension of 'this', 'that', 'here' and 'there'. J. Child Lang. **10**(1), 123–133 (1983)
4. Marslen-Wilson, W., Levy, E., Tyler, L.K.: Producing interpretable discourse: the establishment and maintenance of reference. In: Speech, Place, and Action (1982)
5. Hanna, J.E., Tanenhaus, M.K.: Pragmatic effects on reference resolution in a collaborative task: evidence from eye movements. Cogn. Sci. **28**(1), 105–115 (2004)
6. Bangerter, A., Louwerse, M.M.: Focusing attention with deictic gestures and linguistic expressions. In: Proceedings of the Annual Meeting of the Cognitive Science Society (2005)
7. Sauppé, A., Mutlu, B.: Robot deictics: How gesture and context shape referential communication. In: Proceedings of the International Conference on Human-Robot Interaction (2014)
8. Levinson, S.C.: Deixis. In: The Handbook of Pragmatics, pp. 97–121. Blackwell (2004)
9. Norris, S.: Three hierarchical positions of deictic gesture in relation to spoken language: a multimodal interaction analysis. Vis. Commun. **10**(2), 1–19 (2011)
10. Bates, E.: Language and Context: The Acquisition of Pragmatics. Academic Press, Cambridge (1976)
11. Clark, E., Sengul, C.: Strategies in the acquisition of deixis. J. Child Lang. **5**(3), 457–475 (1978)
12. Iverson, J.M., Goldin-Meadow, S.: Gesture paves the way for language development. Psychol. Sci. **16**(5), 367–371 (2005)
13. Glenberg, A.M., McDaniel, M.A.: Mental models, pictures, and text: integration of spatial and verbal information. Memory Cogn. **20**(5), 458–460 (1992)
14. Gullberg, M.: Deictic gesture and strategy in second language narrative. In: Workshop on the Integration of Gesture in Language and Speech (1996)
15. De Angeli, A., Gerbino, W., Cassano, G., Petrelli, D.: Visual display, pointing, and natural language: the power of multimodal interaction. In: AVI (1998)
16. Goldin-Meadow, S.: The role of gesture in communication and thinking. Trends Cogn. Sci. (TiCS) **3**(11), 419–429 (1999)
17. Jancovic, M., Devoe, S., Wiener, M.: Age-related changes in hand and arm movements as nonverbal communication: some conceptualizations and an empirical exploration. Child Dev. **46**(4), 922–928 (1975)
18. Harrison, S.: The creation and implementation of a gesture code for factory communication. In: Proceedings of the International Conference on Gesture in Speech and Interaction (2011)

19. Brooks, A.G., Breazeal, C.: Working with robots and objects: revisiting deictic reference for achieving spatial common ground. In: Proceedings of the International Conference on HRI (2006)

20. Breazeal, C., Kidd, C., Thomaz, A.L., et al.: Effects of nonverbal communication on efficiency and robustness in human-robot teamwork. In: IROS (2005)

21. Salem, M., Kopp, S., Wachsmuth, I., Rohlfing, K., Joublin, F.: Generation and evaluation of communicative robot gesture. Int. J. Soc. Robot. **4**(2), 201–217 (2012)

22. Clair, A.S., Mead, R., Matarić, M.J.: Investigating the effects of visual saliency on deictic gesture production by a humanoid robot. In: RO-MAN (2011)

23. Okuno, Y., Kanda, T., Imai, M., Ishiguro, H., Hagita, N.: Providing route directions: design of robot's utterance, gesture, and timing. In: HRI (2009)

24. Liu, P., Glas, D., Kanda, T., Ishiguro, H., Hagita, N.: It's not polite to point: generating socially-appropriate deictic behaviors towards people. In: HRI (2013)

25. Cha, E., Kim, Y., Fong, T., Mataric, M.J.: A survey of nonverbal signaling methods for non-humanoid robots. Found. Trends Robot. **6**(4), 211–323 (2018)

26. Admoni, H., Weng, T., Scassellati, B.: Modeling communicative behaviors for object references in human-robot interaction. In: ICRA (2016)

27. Admoni, H., Weng, T., Hayes, B., Scassellati, B.: Robot nonverbal behavior improves task performance in difficult collaborations. In: HRI (2016)

28. Salem, M., Eyssel, F., Rohlfing, K., Kopp, S., Joublin, F.: Effects of gesture on the perception of psychological anthropomorphism: a case study with a humanoid robot. In: Mutlu, B., Bartneck, C., Ham, J., Evers, V., Kanda, T. (eds.) ICSR 2011. LNCS (LNAI), vol. 7072, pp. 31–41. Springer, Heidelberg (2011). https://doi.org/10.1007/978-3-642-25504-5_4

29. Salem, M., Kopp, S., et al.: Towards an integrated model of speech and gesture production for multi-modal robot behavior. In: RO-MAN (2010)

30. Holladay, R.M., Srinivasa, S.S.: RoGuE: robot gesture engine. In: Proceedings of the AAAI Spring Symposium Series (2016)

31. Whitney, D., Rosen, E., MacGlashan, J., Wong, L.L., Tellex, S.: Reducing errors in object-fetching interactions through social feedback. In: ICRA (2017)

32. Fang, R., Doering, M., Chai, J.Y.: Embodied collaborative referring expression generation in situated human-robot interaction. In: HRI (2015)

33. Piwek, P.: Salience in the generation of multimodal referring acts. In: Proceedings of the International Conference on Multimodal Interfaces, pp. 207–210. ACM (2009)

34. Gatt, A., Paggio, P.: Learning when to point: a data-driven approach. In: Proceedings of International Conference on Computational Linguistics (COLING), pp. 2007–2017 (2014)

35. Van Der Sluis, I.F.: Multimodal reference, studies in automatic generation of multimodal referring expressions. Ph.D. thesis, University of Tilburg (2005)

36. Clark, H.: Coordinating with each other in a material world. Discourse Stud. **7**(4), 507–525 (2005)

37. Zhou, F., Duh, H.B.L., Billinghurst, M.: Trends in augmented reality tracking, interaction and display: a review of ten years of ISMAR. In: ISMAR (2008)

38. Van Krevelen, D., Poelman, R.: A survey of augmented reality technologies, applications and limitations. Int. J. Virtual Reality **9**(2), 1–20 (2010)

39. Billinghurst, M., Clark, A., Lee, G.: A survey of augmented reality. Found. Trends Hum.-Comput. Interact. **8**(2–3), 73–272 (2015)

40. Milgram, P., Zhai, S., Drascic, D., Grodski, J.: Applications of augmented reality for human-robot communication. In: Proceedings of IROS (1993)

41. Green, S., Billinghurst, M., Chen, X., et al.: Human-robot collaboration: a literature review and augmented reality approach in design. Int. J. Adv. Robot. Syst.
**5**(1), 1–18 (2008)
42. Williams, T., Szafir, D., Chakraborti, T.: The reality-virtuality interaction cube.
In: VAM-HRI (2019)
43. Williams, T., Szafir, D., Chakraborti, T., Ben Amor, H.: Virtual, augmented, and
mixed reality for human-robot interaction. In: Companion of the HRI (2018)
44. Williams, T., Szafir, D., Chakraborti, T., Amor, H.B.: Report on the 1st international workshop on virtual, augmented, and mixed reality for human-robot interaction (VAM-HRI). AI Mag. **39**(4), 64 (2018)
45. Peters, C., Yang, F., Saikia, H., Li, C., Skantze, G.: Towards the use of mixed
reality for HRI design via virtual robots. In: VAM-HRI (2018)
46. Schönheits, M., Krebs, F.: Embedding AR in industrial HRI applications. In: VAM-
HRI (2018)
47. Sportillo, D., Paljic, A., Ojeda, L., Partipilo, G., Fuchs, P., Roussarie, V.: Training
semi-autonomous vehicle drivers with extended reality. In: VAM-HRI (2018)
48. Hedayati, H., Walker, M., Szafir, D.: Improving collocated robot teleoperation with
augmented reality. In: International Conference on HRI, pp. 78–86. ACM (2018)
49. Ganesan, R.K., Rathore, Y.K., Ross, H.M., Amor, H.B.: Better teaming through
visual cues. IEEE Robot. Autom. Mag. **25**(2), 59–71 (2018)
50. Chakraborti, T., Sreedharan, S., Kulkarni, A., Kambhampati, S.: Alternative
modes of interaction in proximal human-in-the-loop operation of robots. arXiv
preprint arXiv:1703.08930 (2017)
51. Zu Borgsen, S., Renner, P., Lier, F., et al.: Improving human-robot handover
research by mixed reality techniques. In: VAM-HRI (2018)
52. Walker, M., Hedayati, H., Lee, J., Szafir, D.: Communicating robot motion intent
with augmented reality. In: Proceedings of HRI, pp. 316–324. ACM (2018)
53. Rosen, E., et al.: Communicating robot arm motion intent through mixed reality
head-mounted displays. arXiv preprint arXiv:1708.03655 (2017)
54. Amor, H.B., Ganesan, R.K., Rathore, Y., Ross, H.: Intention projection for human-
robot collaboration with mixed reality cues. In: VAM-HRI (2018)
55. Sibirtseva, E., et al.: A comparison of visualisation methods for disambiguating
verbal requests in human-robot interaction. In: Proceedings of RO-MAN (2018)
56. Perlmutter, L., Kernfeld, E., Cakmak, M.: Situated language understanding with
human-like and visualization-based transparency. In: RSS (2016)
57. Reardon, C., Lee, K., Fink, J.: Come see this! augmented reality to enable human-
robot cooperative search. In: International Symposium on Safety, Security, and
Rescue Robotics (2018)
58. Williams, T., Tran, N., Rands, J., Dantam, N.T.: Augmented, mixed, and virtual
reality enabling of robot deixis. In: Chen, J.Y.C., Fragomeni, G. (eds.) VAMR
2018. LNCS, vol. 10909, pp. 257–275. Springer, Cham (2018). https://doi.org/10.
1007/978-3-319-91581-4_19
59. Williams, T.: A framework for robot-generated mixed-reality deixis. In: VAM-HRI
(2018)
60. Hirshfield, L., Williams, T., Sommer, N., Grant, T., Gursoy, S.V.: Workload-driven
modulation of mixed-reality robot-human communication. In: ICMI Workshop on
Modeling Cognitive Processes from Multimodal Data (2018)
61. Williams, T., Bussing, M., Cabrol, S., Boyle, E., Tran, N.: Mixed reality deictic
gesture for multi-modal robot communication. In: HRI (2019)
62. Williams, T., Bussing, M., Cabrol, S., Lau, I.: Toward allocentric mixed-reality
deictic gesture. In: VAM-HRI (2019)

63. Gureckis, T.M., et al.: psiTurk: an open-source framework for conducting replicable behavioral experiments online. Behav. Res. Methods **48**(3), 829–842 (2016)
64. Huang, C.M., Mutlu, B.: Modeling and evaluating narrative gestures for humanlike robots. In: Robotics: Science and Systems (RSS), pp. 57–64 (2013)
65. Bartneck, C., Kulić, D., Croft, E., Zoghbi, S.: Measurement instruments for the anthropomorphism, animacy, likeability, perceived intelligence, and perceived safety of robots. Int. J. Soc. Robot. (IJSR) **1**(1), 71–81 (2009)
66. JASP Team: JASP (version 0.8.5.1) [computer software] (2018)
67. Wagenmakers, E., Love, J., Marsman, M., Jamil, T., Ly, A., Verhagen, J.: Bayesian inference for psychology, part II. Psychon. Bull. Rev. **25**(1), 58–76 (2018)
68. Crowder, M.J.: Analysis of Repeated Measures. Routledge, New York (2017)
69. Morey, R., Rouder, J.: Bayesfactor (version 0.9. 9) (2014)
70. Rouder, J.N., Morey, R.D., Speckman, P.L., Province, J.M.: Default Bayes factors for ANOVA designs. J. Math. Psychol. **56**(5), 356–374 (2012)
71. Mathôt, S.: Bayes like a Baws: interpreting Bayesian repeated measures in JASP [blog post], May 2017
72. Jeffreys, H.: Significance tests when several degrees of freedom arise simultaneously. Proc. Roy. Soc. London Ser. A Math. Phys. Sci. **165**(921), 161–198 (1938)
73. Westfall, P.H., Johnson, W.O., Utts, J.M.: A Bayesian perspective on the bonferroni adjustment. Biometrika **84**(2), 419–427 (1997)
74. Berger, J.O., Pericchi, L.R.: The intrinsic Bayes factor for model selection and prediction. J. Am. Stat. Assoc. **91**(433), 109–122 (1996)
75. Huettig, F., Rommers, J., Meyer, A.S.: Using the visual world paradigm to study language processing: a review and critical evaluation. Acta Psychol. **137**(2), 151–171 (2011)
76. Moratz, R., Ragni, M.: Qualitative spatial reasoning about relative point position. J. Vis. Lang. Comput. **19**(1), 75–98 (2008)
77. Williams, T., Scheutz, M.: Referring expression generation under uncertainty: algorithm and evaluation framework. In: INLG (2017)
78. Scheutz, M., Williams, T., Krause, E., Oosterveld, B., Sarathy, V., Frasca, T.: An overview of the distributed integrated cognition affect and reflection DIARC architecture. In: Aldinhas Ferreira, M.I., Silva Sequeira, J., Ventura, R. (eds.) Cognitive Architectures. ISCASE, vol. 94, pp. 165–193. Springer, Cham (2019). https://doi.org/10.1007/978-3-319-97550-4_11
79. Scheutz, M., Briggs, G., Cantrell, R., Krause, E., Williams, T., Veale, R.: Novel mechanisms for natural human-robot interactions in the DIARC architecture. In: Proceedings of the 2013 AAAI Workshop on Intelligent Robot Systems (2013)

# Autonomous Agent Teammate-Likeness: Scale Development and Validation

Kevin T. Wynne[1]([⊠]) and Joseph B. Lyons[2]

[1] University of Baltimore, Baltimore, USA
kwynne@ubalt.edu
[2] Air Force Research Laboratory, Wright-Patterson AFB, Dayton, USA
joseph.lyons.6@us.af.mil

**Abstract.** The current paper examined the construct of Autonomy Agent Teammate Likeness (AAT). Advanced technologies have the potential to serve as teammates versus as mere tools during tasks involving human partners, yet little research has been done to quantify the factors that shape teaming perceptions in a human-machine domain. The current study used a large online sample to test a set of candidate measures related to the AAT model. Psychometric analyses were used to gauge their utility. The results demonstrate initial support for the validity of the AAT model.

**Keywords:** Autonomous agent · Autonomy · Teams · Teammate · Human-machine teaming · Human-robot interaction

## 1 Introduction

Advancements in autonomy are beginning to allow humans to partner with machines in order to accomplish work tasks in various settings. These technological advances necessitate novel approaches toward human-machine interaction. Machines are believed to help enable efficiency and in some cases decision superiority and adaptability, yet in dynamic environments such as those that exemplify the real-world, communication and understanding of intent and maintaining shared awareness are critical for collaboration [1]. As human-agent teaming (HAT) becomes more prevalent in the field and as a research topic [1, 2], the need to understand humans' psychological perceptions of the intelligent agent (technological work partner) is increasingly important, especially in terms of the agent's perceived role, which may impact trust processes and, ultimately, HAT effectiveness. Specifically, it remains unclear how humans actually perceive intelligent agents and how consistent these perceptions are with existing taxonomies found in the psychology of teams. In particular, *as autonomous technology becomes more sophisticated, do human operators come to see their intelligent partners more as teammates than as tools,* and *what are the key factors leading to such perceptions?* These global research questions are the focal topics of interest that we begin to address in the present study.

The present research builds on nascent theoretical foundations on the construct of autonomous agent teammate-likeness (AAT) and initiates a direct test of a recently published novel conceptual model of AAT [3], which defines the AAT construct and

© Springer Nature Switzerland AG 2019
J. Y. C. Chen and G. Fragomeni (Eds.): HCII 2019, LNCS 11575, pp. 199–213, 2019.
https://doi.org/10.1007/978-3-030-21565-1_13

presents a comprehensive model of its proposed antecedents and outcomes (see Fig. 1 below). The overarching goal is to contribute to the extant literature on HAT by conducting the first known empirical tests of the AAT construct with the explicit goal of developing a valid measure of AAT, an important advancement from which researchers can further progress research on HAT.

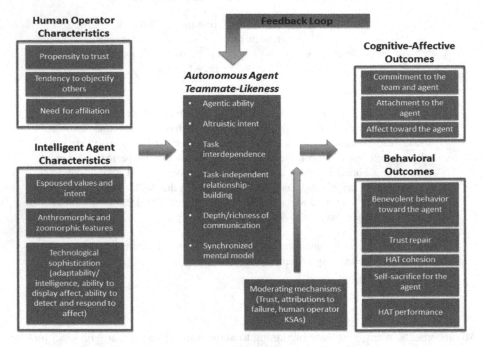

**Fig. 1.** Autonomous Agent Teammate-Likeness (AAT) conceptual model.

## 2 Theoretical Background and Current Research

### 2.1 Human-Machine Teaming

HMT is a relatively recent phenomenon, and research on the process of HAT is relatively nascent. According to Chen and Barnes [4], an *agent* refers to an entity that has some level of autonomy, the ability to sense and act on the surrounding environment, and the ability and authority to direct activities toward goals. While teaming and research on teams of people has been an omnipresent topic of inquiry within the management literature for decades, the concept of human-agent teams is novel [1–4].

Nass et al. [5–7] were among the first to systematically theorize and empirically study perceptions of intelligent agents as potential teammates. Around the time personal computing was gaining popularity, Nass et al. [7] conducted five studies demonstrating that interactions with non-humans (computers) are indeed fundamentally social. Interestingly, a recent study had a similar finding, discovering that people felt uncomfortable giving a robot a response that would be potentially upsetting or distressing to the robot [8].

Nass, Fogg and Moon [6] conducted a study focusing on people's perceptions of personal computers (PCs) specifically as teammates, with the understanding that PCs have become more than merely tools (e.g., dialogue partners, secretaries). These authors attempted to trigger team perceptions with manipulations built around team formation (as evidenced in social psychology literature). Overall, the study demonstrated that at least some human-computer teaming processes mirror human-human teaming processes.

Groom and Nass [5] argued that, according to universal definitions of what constitutes a successful team (e.g., sharing mental models, subjugating individual needs for group needs, trusting one another), human-robot partners based on current technology lacked "humanness" and thus cannot yet be considered as teammates. When implementing human-agent teams, Groom and Nass recommend a complementary model or approach in which intelligent agents and human partners compensate for one another's weaknesses, rather than forcibly substituting an intelligent agent for a human partner. However, an important caveat to note about the Groom and Nass research paper is that these authors focused on objective features of teams—based on common definitions of teams—rather than humans' *perceptions* of their partners. While intelligent agents may not yet have the full capabilities of a human partner, Wynne and Lyons [3] contend that humans may very well come to perceive "teammate-likeness" in their counterparts, as suggested by Nass et al.'s [6] earlier work. In fact, interestingly, "humanness" was the #1 most cited requirement for an extant *instrumental* relationship to be viewed as a *teammate-based* relationship, based on recent analyses of qualitative data [9]. Additionally, a recent article found that humans may have different attitudes toward their human teammates versus their robot teammates in heterogeneous teams [10].

The aforementioned early research on HMT sets the stage for human-machine interaction in future applications. Yet, human perception of machine teammates is still relatively unexplored and thus unknown. The present research builds on emergent theory on AAT (Wynne and Lyons [3]) in the quest to understand psychological perceptions of machine teammates and the consequences of these perceptions.

## 2.2 Autonomous Agent Teammate-Likeness

*Autonomous agent teammate-likeness* (AAT) is defined as, "the extent to which a human operator perceives and identifies an autonomous, intelligent agent partner as a highly altruistic, benevolent, interdependent, emotive, communicative, and synchronized agentic teammate, rather than simply an instrumental tool" [3; p. 3]. Wynne and Lyons [3] conceptualized the AAT construct to have six distinct dimensions (reflecting each aspect of the definition above), two general clusters of antecedents, and two general clusters of outcomes (as well as boundary conditions, contextual factors, and a feedback loop), as illustrated in Fig. 1. Antecedents can be grouped into characteristics of each of the partners in the human-agent team (i.e., human operator characteristics and intelligent agent characteristics). Outcomes that theoretically may manifest from human operators' psychological perceptions of AAT can be grouped into cognitive-affective outcomes and behavioral outcomes.

The AAT construct is predicated on the notion that shared awareness among teammates is central to effective teamwork. Collaboration is driven by shared awareness of intent between team members [11], while this is often noted in the domain of collaborating human partners, this is also very relevant in the domain of collaboration between humans and intelligent agents [2]. The AAT construct helps to align team process factors to the domain of human-machine teaming.

The AAT taxonomy has support from a recent qualitative study. Lyons et al. [9] asked an online sample to describe the reasons why they view an intelligent technology (one that they have experience with) as a teammate versus as a tool. These open-ended responses were then coded based on a set of trained coders. The overall results of the study showed that the six dimensions of the AAT model played prominently in participants' rationale for teammates versus tools explanations. Humanness was also heavily mentioned, yet it is plausible that this dimension represents a higher-order combination of the other 6 dimensions. In sum, it appears that these six factors— perceived agentic capability, perceived benevolence/altruistic intent, perceived task interdependence, task-independent relationship-building, richness of communication, synchronized mental model (see Table 1 for construct definitions)—might, in theory, explain the variance in human operators' perceptions of AAT, or the perception that the intelligent agent is more like a teammate than like a tool. The current research begins the process of answering Wynne and Lyons' (3) call to advance the AAT model with empirical examination of the various proximal and distal outcomes likely to emanate from perceptions of AAT. Specifically, we attempt to extend research in this line of inquiry by (1) developing and (2) validating appropriate methods to measure and confirm these dimensions. After a robust instrument is created and tested, it can be used in the future to empirically examine the relationships proposed in Wynne and Lyons [3].

## 2.3   Current Research: Purpose

In sum, despite the proliferation of autonomous technology with which humans partner to accomplish tasks in the field (in military, industrial, and civilian/consumer contexts), to date there is not yet an existing validated instrument that measures perceptions of HMT. Until recently, the concept of AAT has been noticeably absent in the research literature. The purpose of the current paper, therefore, is to begin to establish the validity of a novel measure of teammate perceptions (AAT scale, or AATS) to be used to measure humans' perceptions of their technological work partners.

The immediate next step in this stream of research, thus, was to conduct a set of empirical studies as an initial test of the AAT model. The present paper is the first of such studies. Specifically, activities in the present research involves building a psychological instrument with which AAT can be measured. The current paper describes research that involves data collection and findings across an online sample. We expect the measure to demonstrate strong psychometric properties. Specifically, we expect results to demonstrate initial support for the proposed factor structure.

**Table 1.** Description of the six AAT dimensions and their construct definitions (as cited in Wynne Lyons [3]).

| Dimension | Dimension construct definition |
|---|---|
| Perceived agentic capability | The perception that the intelligent agent as an autonomous agent, has some degree of decision-making latitude and an affordance, ability, and authority for self-control |
| Perceived benevolent/altruistic intent | The perception that the intelligent agent fundamentally has good intentions toward the operator and is generally oriented toward being helpful |
| Perceived task interdependence | The perception that the human and the intelligent agent are mutually dependent, that the human's and intelligent agent's respective tasks are mutually dependent, and that goals and consequences are shared |
| Task-independent relationship-building | The perception that behavior from the intelligent agent is relationship-oriented, with communication focused in team-building rather than focused on task accomplishment |
| Richness of communication | The perception that the intelligent agent communicates in a way that is relatively complex, sophisticated, clear, highly informative, and interactive |
| Synchronized mental model | The perception that the intelligent agent behaves in a predictable manner and responds as expected such that respective actions and reactions are synchronized, seamless, and natural |

# 3 Method

## 3.1 Analytical Approach

The methodology in the present research is based on a well-established process of psychological scale development [12]. This process, which represents professional best practices and guidelines on scale development, involves six primary steps or stages: (1) Item Generation, (2) Questionnaire Administration, (3) Initial Item Reduction, (4) Confirmatory Factor Analysis, (5) Convergent/Discriminant Validity, and (6) Replication. According to Hinkin [12], first, a large number of items are written by researchers based on prior theory and/or empirical findings (e.g., quantitative or qualitative results from pilot studies, etc.), such that the breadth of the construct of interest is exhaustively represented. These items are then put into a questionnaire (survey)—along with measures of constructs that are purported to be related and unrelated to the construct of interest (see step 5)—and administered to a sample of respondents in order to gather data on the items and test them. Next, the performance/quality of the items is tested using various item analyses (e.g., inspection of means, item-total correlations) and scale analyses (exploratory factor analysis, or EFA); the pool of items is reduced based on the removal of poorly performing items that demonstrate poor psychometric properties. At this point, the researchers may choose to re-test the revised pool of items with another data collection from a new sample of respondents. The performance of the resulting scale is tested using scale analyses, and a confirmatory factor analysis (CFA) is conducted to confirm the proposed factor structure of the developing scale. Then, researchers attempt to demonstrate construct validity by examining relationships between constructs that are purported to be related (convergent validity) and unrelated (discriminant validity) to the construct of interest. Finally, the items and scale may be refined further and then the process is replicated with data collected from a new sample of respondents to confirm the results.

As a first step in the AAT scale development process, grounded in theory [3] and informed by preliminary empirical findings [(focus group data and qualitative data collection results) 9], item content was written by the present authors in order to develop a first draft of the AATS. Specifically, we had generated an exhaustive list of potential scale items through a process of writing, reviewing, revising, and refining a large number of items.

The next major step in this process involved a quantitative data collection (i.e., survey with closed-ended questions administered to individuals online) to develop the AATS, whereby the theoretically derived initial AAT measure was tested with scale and item analyses, to be followed by an iterative series of revision, additional data collection, re-testing, and refinement until the scale shows adequate psychometric properties. The present paper (Study 1) describes the quantitative data collection (i.e., Step 2 in Hinkin's guidelines); notably, a follow-up study (Study 2) is currently in progress to validate the final, developed version of the scale and replicate prior results (i.e., Steps 3–6 in Hinkin's guidelines).

## 3.2  Participants and Procedure

To collect data for Study 1, a participant recruitment advertisement was placed on Amazon Mechanical Turk (MTurk) using a third-party web-based application called TurkPrime, which is a data collection platform designed by and for behavioral science researchers [13]. MTurk is an online system that connects researchers—and others seeking participants to engage in certain tasks ("requesters")—with individuals ("workers") who wish to participate in various activities for remuneration ("Human Intelligence Tasks" or HITs), such as filling out survey-based questionnaires for research purposes. The recruitment advertisement solicited individuals who had some type of experience with a sophisticated technology (autonomous system, smart technology, technological partner, etc.). In order to be eligible to participate, respondents were required to be at least 18 years of age and a U.S. citizen.

The survey questionnaire was created using Qualtrics, a web-based surveying platform, and then it was administered to workers via a web link to the Qualtrics survey within the MTurk HIT. The survey had been previously pilot-tested with internal subject matter experts to ensure it was error-free and functioned as designed upon launch. Two-hundred and thirty-two participants responded to all items and completed the study.

## 3.3    Measures

**Autonomous Agent Teammate-Likeness.** AAT was measured with a comprehensive initial list of items created by the current authors, based on the AAT theoretical framework [3]. Participants were first asked to think of and describe the single most technologically advanced equipment that he or she works with "as part of your job or one that you use regularly in your life." Then they were asked to rate their agreement with a series of statements (each item representing one of the six AAT dimensions) using a 5-point Likert-type scale ranging from "Strongly Disagree" to "Strongly Agree." The Agency scale had 10 items ($\alpha = .75$), benevolence had 10 items ($\alpha = .91$), communication ($\alpha = .71$) and interdependence ($\alpha = .83$) each started with 12 items, synchrony used 8 items ($\alpha = .80$), and relationship-building started with 13 items ($\alpha = .89$). The content of the actual items used in the study are listed in the tables below (Tables 3, 4, 5, 6, 7 and 8).

# 4    Results

Item analyses (e.g., means) and scale analyses (e.g., EFA) were conducted to assess the psychometric quality of the initial AATS instrument. Means, reliabilities, and inter-correlations across each of the six AAT dimensions are shown in Table 2. All dimension subscales demonstrated adequate internal consistency. Means tended to be near the mid-point of each scale, indicating that respondents perceived a moderate level of AAT in their interactions with their respective technological partners. Thus, a fairly high base rate of AAT perceptions was evidenced.

**Table 2.** Means, reliabilities, and intercorrelations of the six AAT factors.

|            | M     | Agent | Benev | Comm  | Inter | Sync  | Team  |
|------------|-------|-------|-------|-------|-------|-------|-------|
| 1. Agent   | 3.309 | (.75) | .42   | .28   | .16   | .51   | .42   |
| 2. Benev   | 3.272 |       | (.91) | .57   | .58   | .63   | .71   |
| 3. Comm    | 3.569 |       |       | (.71) | .34   | .51   | .53   |
| 4. Inter   | 3.159 |       |       |       | (.83) | .52   | .48   |
| 5. Sync    | 3.382 |       |       |       |       | (.80) | .70   |
| 6. Team    | 3.088 |       |       |       |       |       | (.89) |

*Note:* Agent = perceived agentic capability. Benev. = perceived benevolent/altruistic intent. Comm = richness of communication. Inter = perceived task interdependence. Sync = synchronized mental model. Team = task-independent relationship-building (teaming). Cronbach's alpha is reported along the diagonal in parentheses.

Additionally, the six AAT dimensions were fairly strongly and positively correlated within one another, indicating that the six dimensions were related. Notably, multi-collinearity, which represents redundancy among variables, was not present, suggesting the six dimensions were indeed distinct constructs [14].

Results from the EFAs for each AAT dimension (shown in Tables 3, 4, 5, 6, 7 and 8) were used to identify and eliminate poorly performing items. First, principle components analysis (PCA) plots were produced and interpreted, which suggest how many "factors" are present in a particular scale for each dimension. Then, EFAs were conducted; factor loadings were inspected to determine how each item tended to fit in the factor(s). Generally, items that did not fit neatly into a factor (e.g., weak loadings, cross-loading) were flagged to be dropped from the scales, after their content was reviewed for fit with the construct in light of the empirical results. In theory, items that do not load well onto a factor—and thus do not fit well into the factor—express and represent something different than the other items in the factor [12]. These types of items are essentially interpreted by respondents as distinct from the other items in the scale. Refer to Tables 3 through 8 for EFA results (factor loadings) and item content for each of the six AAT dimensions.

**Table 3.** EFA results (factor loadings) for each original item, for the perceived agentic capability AAT dimension.

### AAT Dimension 1: Agent

| Variable/Item Content | Factor1 |
|---|---|
| AAT_Agent_1 | 0.710 |
| Has the ability to make some decisions on its own. | |
| AAT_Agent_4 | 0.690 |
| Has the authority to make decisions. | |
| AAT_Agent_5 | 0.714 |
| Has the capability to control its actions. | |
| *AAT_Agent_6 | |
| Always seems to need my help. | |
| AAT_Agent_7 | 0.714 |
| Does not require me to control it 100% of the time. | |
| AAT_Agent_8 | 0.727 |
| Can perform its tasks autonomously. | |
| AAT_Agent_9 | 0.713 |
| Is in control of its own actions. | |
| *AAT_Agent_10 | 0.480 |
| Executes the best course of action. | |
| *AAT_Agent_11 | |
| Requires me to monitor it. | |
| AAT_Agent_12 | 0.664 |
| Can operate with little to no oversight. | |

*Note:* *Items to be dropped denoted with an asterisk.

**Table 4.** EFA results (factor loadings) for each original item, for the perceived benevolent/altruistic intent AAT dimension.

|  |  |
|---|---|
| **AAT Dimension 2: Benev** | |

| Variable/Item Content | Factor1 |
|---|---|
| AAT_Benev_1 | 0.834 |
| Is truly focused on helping me. | |
| AAT_Benev_12 | 0.854 |
| Wants to help me. | |
| *AAT_Benev_13 | 0.538 |
| Cares about me. | |
| AAT_Benev_14 | 0.684 |
| Seems to be concerned about my well-being. | |
| AAT_Benev_15 | 0.848 |
| Has my best interests built in. | |
| *AAT_Benev_16 | |
| Treats me like an object. | |
| AAT_Benev_17 | 0.843 |
| Appears to be motivated to help me. | |
| AAT_Benev_18 | 0.773 |
| Intends to support me. | |
| AAT_Benev_19 | 0.761 |
| Would put my needs ahead of its own. | |
| AAT_Benev_20 | 0.823 |
| Would help me if I needed help. | |

*Note:* *Items to be dropped denoted with an asterisk.

Upon inspection of analysis results, three of the original 10 items were dropped from the *agency* dimension; two of the original 10 items were dropped from the *benevolence* dimension; six of the original 12 items were dropped from the *communication* dimension; none of the original 12 items were dropped (all retained for further testing) from the *interdependence* dimension; three of the original 8 items were dropped from the *synchrony* dimension; and two of the original 13 items were dropped from the *relationship-building* (teaming) dimension.

In sum, results from the current study (Study 1) demonstrated initial support for the proposed factor structure of the AATS. Furthermore, item elimination from these data analyses resulted in a revised, shortened AAT scale to be further tested and validated in subsequent studies.

**Table 5.**  EFA results (factor loadings) for each original item, for the richness of communication AAT dimension.

AAT Dimension 3: Comm

| Variable/Item Content | Factor1 | Factor2 |
|---|---|---|
| AAT_Comm_1 | 0.543 | |
| I don't get useful information from [my technology]. | | |
| *AAT_Comm_12 | | |
| I wish I could get better information from [my technology]. | | |
| AAT_Comm_13 | 0.733 | |
| [my technology] and I exchange information well. | | |
| AAT_Comm_14 | 0.800 | |
| When I get information from [my technology] I know exactly what it means. | | |
| *AAT_Comm_15 | 0.421 | 0.430 |
| [my technology] adapts its communication to changing circumstances. | | |
| *AAT_Comm_16 | | 0.524 |
| [my technology] knows when I'm frustrated. | | |
| *AAT_Comm_17 | | 0.796 |
| [my technology] shows that it understands when I'm having difficulty. | | |
| AAT_Comm_18 | 0.529 | 0.366 |
| [my technology] provides effective feedback. | | |
| AAT_Comm_19 | 0.551 | |
| [my technology] is highly interactive. | | |
| *AAT_Comm_20 | 0.326 | 0.541 |
| [my technology] engages in a continuous feedback loop with me. | | |
| AAT_Comm_21 | 0.494 | |
| [my technology] understands my commands. | | |
| *AAT_Comm_22 | 0.425 | 0.380 |
| I feel like [my technology] and I exchange information freely. | | |

*Note:* *Items to be dropped denoted with an asterisk.

**Table 6.** EFA results (factor loadings) for each original item, for the perceived task interdependence AAT dimension.

AAT Dimension 4: Interdep

| Variable/Item Content | Factor1 |
|---|---|
| AAT_Interdep_1 | 0.318 |
| Cannot do its job without me. | |
| AAT_Interdep _12 | 0.646 |
| ...and I depend on each other to get the job done. | |
| AAT_Interdep_13 | 0.770 |
| ...and I share responsibility for our actions. | |
| AAT_Interdep_14 | |
| Acts on its own regardless of what I think. | |
| AAT_Interdep_15 | 0.333 |
| Will fail without me. | |
| AAT_Interdep_16 | 0.493 |
| Is required in order to do my own job. | |
| AAT_Interdep_17 | 0.499 |
| Relies on me for survival. | |
| AAT_Interdep_18 | 0.723 |
| Shares my goals. | |
| AAT_Interdep_19 | 0.624 |
| Has tasks that are intertwined with mine. | |
| AAT_Interdep_20 | 0.722 |
| Has goals that are intertwined with mine. | |
| AAT_Interdep_21 | 0.334 |
| Is highly dependent on me for it to perform successfully. | |
| AAT_Interdep_22 | 0.482 |
| Is necessary for me to be effective. | |

## 5 Discussion

Despite the proliferation of autonomous technology with which humans partner to accomplish tasks in the field (in military, industrial, and civilian/consumer contexts), to date there is not yet an existing validated instrument that measures perceptions of human-machine teaming (HMT). Until recently, the concept of AAT has been noticeably absent in the research literature. The purpose of the present research was to begin to establish the validity of a novel measure of teammate perceptions (AAT scale, or AATS) to be used to measure humans' perceptions of their technological work partners.

**Table 7.** EFA results (factor loadings) for each original item, for the synchronized mental model AAT dimension.

| AAT Dimension 5: Sync | | | |
| --- | --- | --- | --- |
| Variable/Item Content | Factor1 | Factor2 | Factor3 |
| AAT_Sync_1 | 0.571 | 0.415 | 0.705 |
| Is generally on the "same page" as me. | | | |
| AAT_Sync_12 | 0.686 | | |
| Gets me what I need before I ask for it. | | | |
| *AAT_Sync_13 | | | |
| ...and I feel out of step with one another. | | | |
| *AAT_Sync_14 | 0.784 | | |
| Is engaged with me throughout the entire task. | | | |
| *AAT_Sync_15 | 0.430 | | |
| Reacts in expected ways. | | | |
| AAT_Sync_16 | 0.564 | 0.514 | |
| Adapts to new situations when I do. | | | |
| AAT_Sync_17 | 0.785 | | |
| Anticipates my actions. | | | |
| AAT_Sync_18 | 0.855 | 0.333 | |
| Anticipates my needs. | | | |

*Note:* *Items to be dropped denoted with an asterisk.

In the current study, we conducted an initial test of the AAT model with the development of a psychometrically sound measure of AAT perceptions. Early results suggest that, not only do humans have fairly strong perceptions of AAT in regards to their technological partners, but also that the AAT model appears to have some empirical support. Our results provide an early indication that the AATS generally is a strong reflection of the AAT theoretical model and offers promise that it is a good measure of what it is purported to measure (i.e., AAT perceptions).

A theoretical review paper advanced the new AAT theory by introducing and defining the AAT construct, presenting a conceptual framework, and proffering a number of testable propositions to guide future research [3]. The purpose of the present research is to follow up on the seminal Wynne and Lyons [3] paper; specifically, the goal was to conduct a set of empirical studies as an initial test of the AAT model. Data are still being collected, but the eventual contributions will be: (1) building a psychological instrument with which AAT can be measured, and (2) validating the instrument by examining relationships with various germane constructs using a "vignette" or narrative-based study that presented different AAT scenarios to participants (low-teaming vs. high-teaming manipulations) though the latter is an ongoing activity (i.e., Study 2). Human-machine teaming (HMT) is a relatively recent phenomenon, but it will continue to garner significant interest in the coming years, and the AATS will contribute to our knowledge of how people will come to trust and appropriately use increasingly human-like autonomous agent teammates.

**Table 8.** EFA results (factor loadings) for each original item, for the task-independent relationship-building AAT dimension.

| AAT Dimension 6: Team | | |
|---|---|---|
| Variable/Item Content | Factor1 | Factor2 |
| AAT_Team_1 | 0.714 | |
| Communicates in a warm way. | | |
| AAT_Team_12 | 0.644 | |
| Understands me. | | |
| AAT_Team_13 | 0.805 | |
| Has a connection with me. | | |
| AAT_Team_14 | 0.784 | |
| ...and I have a unique connection. | | |
| AAT_Team_15 | 0.832 | |
| Makes me feel appreciated. | | |
| AAT_Team_16 | 0.767 | |
| Expresses genuine interest in its communication with me. | | |
| AAT_Team_17 | 0.516 | |
| Responds to me with appropriate etiquette. | | |
| AAT_Team_18 | 0.830 | |
| Has a rapport (close bond) with me. | | |
| *AAT_Team_19 | 0.321 | 0.766 |
| Is cold and distant. | | |
| *AAT_Team_20 | | -0.508 |
| Treats me like an object. | | |
| AAT_Team_21 | 0.770 | |
| Treats me like a teammate would. | | |
| AAT_Team_22 | 0.708 | |
| Interacts with me in social ways. | | |
| AAT_Team_23 | 0.764 | |
| ...and I "feel" connected. | | |

*Note:* *Items to be dropped denoted with an asterisk.

## 5.1 Practical Implications: Applications and Future Directions

HMT is a priority topic for human factors psychology research, yet there does not exist a valid measure for evaluating the psychological manifestation of teammate perceptions. Thus, while many researchers tout "teaming" as the objectives, few will truly understand if "teaming" was accomplished unless measures related to teaming are employed in research designs. The AATS will be a highly useful tool to measure perceptions of technological work partners and how they may change over the course of the coming decades as autonomy evolves and becomes increasingly prevalent and relevant in military and other contexts. In the future, we hope that scientist-practitioners will (1) use the (soon-to-be) validated AATS to measure perceptions of AAT and (2) continue to test the elements of the AAT model [3] and implement the findings in applications of HMT.

Ultimately, we expect the final, refined version of the AATS to demonstrate adequate psychometric properties—as defined by gold standards outlined in the scale development literature [12] —as well as strong construct validity. Once data collection and analysis for Study 2 are complete, we expect findings will be of great interest to researchers focused on trust, teams, and/or HMT. We expect that the outcome of this research will have great potential in spurring additional research on trust in autonomy. In particular, we exhort researchers in this space to build off of these studies and test one (or more) of the many theoretical propositions in the Wynne and Lyons AAT conceptual model [3]. Future research should aim to further empirically test the model and investigate AAT relationships with affect, trust behaviors, commitment, team performance, and other phenomena relevant to HMT.

## 5.2 Conclusion

In conclusion, autonomous technologies—and human interaction with those technologies—are rapidly proliferating in both military and non-military environments. Despite the continuing growth of HMT and the emergence of HAT specifically, an understanding of how human operators perceive their machine partners is lacking. In particular, it remains unknown how humans perceive the AAT of their machine partners, or the extent to which the autonomous technology is more like a tool versus like a teammate. The overarching goal of this line of research is to understand how people perceive their machine partners over time, what affects synchrony and trust within human-agent teams, and what factors may influence HAT effectiveness. The AAT model is intended to motivate dialogue and future research in this expanding literature to support more effective HAT research and applications.

**Funding.** This research was supported an AFRL Summer Faculty Fellowship award to Dr. Kevin Wynne and by Air Force Research Laboratory contracts FA8650-16-D-6616-0001.

# References

1. Chen, J.Y.C., Lakhmani, S.G., Stowers, K., Selkowitz, A., Wright. J., Barnes, M.: Situation awareness-based agent transparency and human-autonomy teaming effectiveness. Theoret. Issues Ergon. Sci. **19**, 259–282 (2018)
2. Barnes, M.J., Lakhmani, S., Holder, E., Chen, J.Y.C.: Issues in human-agent communication. Aberdeen Proving Ground (MD): Army Research Laboratory, Report No: ARL-TR-8336 (2019)
3. Wynne, K.T., Lyons, J.B.: An integrative model of autonomous agent teammate-likeness. Theoret. Issues Ergon. Sci. **19**, 353–374 (2018)
4. Chen, J.Y.C., Barnes, M.J.: Human-agent teaming for multirobot control: a review of the human factors issues. IEEE Trans. Hum.-Mach. Syst. **44**, 13–29 (2014)
5. Groom, V., Nass, C.: Can robots be teammates? Benchmarks human-robot teams. Interact. Stud. **8**, 493–500 (2007)

6. Nass, C., Fogg, B.J., Moon, Y.: Can computers be teammates? Int. J. Hum.-Comput. Stud. **45**, 669–678 (1996)
7. Nass, C., Steuer, J., Tauber, E.R.: Computers are social actors. In: Proceedings of Human Factors in Computing Systems, pp. 72–78 (1994)
8. Hamacher, A., Bianchi-Berthouze, N., Pipe, A.G., Eder, K.: Believing in BERT: using expressive communication to enhance trust and counteract operational error in physical human-robot interaction. In: Proceedings of IEEE International Symposium on Robot and Human Interaction Communication (RO-MAN). IEEE, New York (2016)
9. Lyons, J.B., Wynne, K.T., Mahoney, S., Roebke, M.A.: Trust and human-machine teaming: a qualitative study. In: Lawless, W., Mittu, R., Sofge, D., Moskowitz, I., Russell, S. (eds.) Artificial Intelligence for the Internet of Everything. Elsevier (in press)
10. Perelman, B.S., Evans, A.W., Schaefer, K.E., Hill, S.G.: Attitudes toward risk and effort tradeoffs in human-robot heterogeneous team operations. In: Proceedings of the Human Factors and Ergonomics Society Annual Meeting (2018)
11. Salas, E., Cooke, N.J., Rosen, M.A.: On teams, teamwork, and team performance: discoveries and developments. Hum. Factors **50**, 540–547 (2008)
12. Hinkin, T.R.: A brief tutorial on the development of measures for use in survey questionnaires. Organ. Res. Methods **1**, 104–121 (1998)
13. Litman, L., Robinson, J., Abberbock, T.: TurkPrime.com: a versatile crowdsourcing data acquisition platform for the behavioral sciences. Behav. Res. Methods **45**, 1–10 (2016)
14. Tabachnick, B.G., Fidell, L.S.: Using Multivariate Statistics. Pearson Education, Boston (2007)

# VAMR in Learning, Training and Entertainment

# Augmented Reality in Education: A Study on Preschool Children, Parents, and Teachers in Bangladesh

Mohammad Fahim Abrar[1], Md. Rakibul Islam[1], Md. Sabir Hossain[1],
Mohammad Mainul Islam[2(✉)], and Muhammad Ashad Kabir[3]

[1] Chittagong University of Engineering and Technology, Chittagong, Bangladesh
`fahimabrar02@gmail.com`, `rakibcuet16@gmail.com`, `sabir.cse@cuet.ac.bd`
[2] Extend View Inc., Irvine, CA, USA
`sujan.cse.cuet@gmail.com`
[3] School of Computing and Mathematics, Charles Sturt University,
Bathurst, NSW, Australia
`akabir@csu.edu.au`

**Abstract.** Augmented reality (AR) is a technology that is being used in various aspects of life, including education. Many studies have been performed to investigate the effectiveness of using AR in educational settings. The purpose of this study is to investigate the effectiveness of AR in teaching preschool children in a developing country such as Bangladesh. To conduct the study, we have developed two AR-based apps for Android using marker-based tracking techniques. We have run our study in a classroom of a school in Bangladesh where 25 students, 13 parents, and three teachers voluntarily participated. We taught students using our AR apps and evaluated their learning improvements through pre- and post-test results. The results show at least 30% learning improvement. We have observed children's reaction and engagement, and surveyed parents and teachers for acceptance of such technology and suggestions for improvement. Our preliminary study finds that AR can be useful for preschool students learning in a developing country such as Bangladesh. Through our study, we also identify a list of requirements for designing and developing an AR app for education.

**Keywords:** Augmented reality · Preschool teaching ·
Early childhood education · Learning technology · AR in education ·
Bangladesh

## 1 Introduction

Augmented reality (AR) can be defined as a technology that integrates virtual 3D objects into a real 3D environment in real time [2]. It has been widely used in various disciplines, including defense, medicine, manufacturing, training, and tourism [1]. Lee [11] reports how people can be educated and trained using AR

© Springer Nature Switzerland AG 2019
J. Y. C. Chen and G. Fragomeni (Eds.): HCII 2019, LNCS 11575, pp. 217–229, 2019.
https://doi.org/10.1007/978-3-030-21565-1_14

technology. In particular, the paper presents how AR is being used in various sectors, such as education, business, astronomy, and different sectors of science. With such a technology, doctors can see the internal organs of a patient interactively in 3D without performing surgery [9,13], and customers can see a 3D model of a product from home before they buy it online [4].

In recent years, AR has gained much research attention for its potential use in education [18]. Researchers are mainly focused on demonstrating the various advantages of AR in education, such as enhancing learning achievements, increasing motivation, raising the level of engagement, decreasing the cognitive load, and so on [1]. Research in this domain is usually conducted in a specific setting – for example, in a specific country, with a specific age group of children, with a specific subject (children, parents, or teachers), and focusing on a specific teaching topic (e.g., the alphabet, animals, geometry, etc.).

In a developing South Asian country such as Bangladesh, the education system is mostly outdated and does not contain digital resources. Therefore, student engagement with textbooks is low, and the lack of motivation eventually increases the dropout rate. Given that a smartphone is available to almost every family and, thus, to the children, AR-based mobile apps could attract the attention of children and enhance their learning experience. To the best of our knowledge, no such research has studied the impact of AR in education for preschool children in Bangladesh.

In this research, we have studied the effectiveness of AR in teaching preschool children in Bangladesh. In particular, we have developed two AR-based mobile apps to teach children the alphabet and about animals. The key distinctive feature of our apps compared to other research apps is that ours feature learning tests. We have studied both the usability of the apps and the effectiveness of AR in education (in terms of degree of satisfaction, impact, knowledge, and creativity) from the perspective of the students, their teachers, and their parents.

Some design requirements should be considered to create a successful AR app for the classroom, including flexible and customizable content for the needs of the children and a focus on institutional and curricular requirements [10]. Considering these requirements, we have developed one of our AR apps based on a government-provided textbook that is easily available to preschool children for free. Our other app is developed to teach animals that are not generally visible in residential areas and that children are not familiar with.

The contributions of this research are summarized below:

- We have developed two AR-based apps with testing features to teach the Bangla alphabet and about common animals.
- We have investigated the effectiveness (in particular, the learning improvement) of using AR apps as a teaching and learning tool for preschool children.
- We have consolidated our study from the perspective of the students, their parents, and their teachers in a South Asian developing country, Bangladesh.

The rest of the paper is organized as follows. Section 2 describes the two AR apps we have developed in this research. The methodology and empirical study of our research are presented in Sect. 3. Section 4 reports our results and findings followed by a discussion in Sect. 5. Section 6 reviews related work. Finally, Sect. 7 concludes this paper and highlights future work.

## 2  Augmented Reality Apps

We have developed two mobile apps, AR Zoo and Bangla AR Book, to teach animals and the Bangla alphabets, respectively. These apps were developed for Android using a game engine called Unity3D [17] and a marker-based AR technology called Vuforia [15]. A marker is an image that is recognized by the app to visualize a corresponding 3D model in a real-time video. Vuforia uses advanced computer vision techniques to detect and track markers in a video and super impose the virtual content accordingly so that virtual objects appear as real in the video.

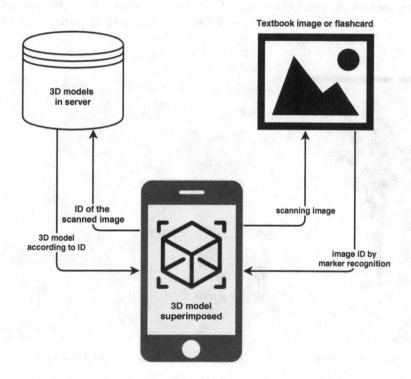

**Fig. 1.** Working procedure of developed AR apps.

The working procedure for both apps is visualized in Fig. 1. We have created unique IDs for all the pictures in the book. When a picture from the book is scanned using the app, the app obtains the unique ID of the corresponding picture. After the scan is completed, the obtained ID is used to find the respective 3D model from a server. Then the respective 3D model is downloaded and stored in the app directory of the mobile phone so that the model can be used later from the directory without downloading it again. The 3D contents used in both apps were either purchased online or custom developed using 3D modeling tools such as Maya [8].

## 2.1  AR Zoo App

The AR Zoo app (Fig. 2 shows some screenshots) includes 3D models of 24 animals with animations and their sounds. For each animal a printed flashcard is used as a marker. During learning, the user holds the phone over the marker, and the corresponding 3D model of that animal appears on the screen, and the sound of the animal is played (Fig. 2a). The user could see the presented 3D model from any direction. In the test, the app randomly shows three images of different animals and plays the sound of the target animal as a hint (Fig. 2b), and the user has to select the image of the correct animal. After the completion of the test, a summary of the test results with the number of correct and wrong answers is displayed (Fig. 2c).

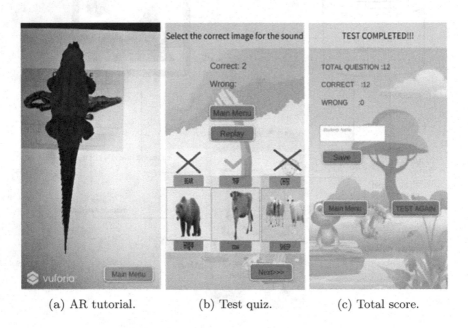

(a) AR tutorial.          (b) Test quiz.          (c) Total score.

Fig. 2. Screenshots of the AR Zoo app.

## 2.2  Bangla AR Book App

The Bangla AR Book app (Fig. 3 shows some screenshots) is based on a national curriculum textbook for preschool students in Bangladesh entitled "Amar Boi". Like the AR Zoo app, Bangla AR Book uses images from that textbook as markers, and custom-designed 3D models that are superimposed when the user holds the phone over the pages of the book (Fig. 3a). Two types of test sessions are implemented to assess how much children could learn from AR contents. In the first test, the children are given a letter and three images and are required to choose the one image whose name is starting with that letter (Fig. 3b). The other test is reversed – that is, the children are required to choose the one letter from a list of three that corresponds to the image (Fig. 3c). Each of the testing session contains ten matching tests. At the end of each test session, the app presents a summary of the entire test, which is also saved in a text file for further analysis.

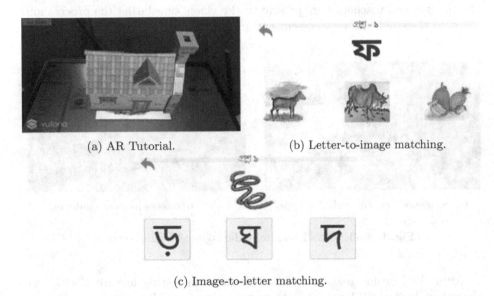

(a) AR Tutorial.                    (b) Letter-to-image matching.

(c) Image-to-letter matching.

**Fig. 3.** Screenshots of the Bangla AR Book app.

## 3   Methodology and Empirical Study

We ran our empirical study in a primary school in Bangladesh. Twenty five preschool children ages five to six years old (8 male, 17 female), 13 parents, and 3 teachers participated. None of the participating subjects had knowledge of AR. We conducted a pre-test to determine what the children knew about the letters and animals before teaching them using our app. We printed flashcards of animals to be used as markers for AR Zoo app. Students had their textbook of which we made the Bangla AR Book app. We started the pre-test with the textbook by asking students to identify letters randomly. Then we asked students to name the animals by showing them the flashcards randomly. Students answered some of the questions correctly but were mostly incorrect. We took their answers as pre-test results so that we could compare them with the post-test results.

After a short presentation on AR and how to use our apps, we divided the students into five groups and assigned two volunteers to each group. The volunteers taught the students the letters and animals using our apps (Fig. 4 shows some pictures of our study session in the classroom). Students were shown both apps in groups. Each group had only one mobile phone, and children used it by taking turns. They were given enough time to play with the apps and were very engaged. While using apps, a student was so excited that he said, "I can't believe what I'm seeing! Is this magic?" The students were learning through the mobile apps. Overall, we found the students to be very engaged and highly motivated. The students were so keen that they kept asking how they could get the apps. The parents and teachers were present in the classroom during the process and observed the children's engagement and performance.

(a) Students learning with AR apps.        (b) Volunteers helping students.

**Fig. 4.** Students and volunteers during the learning session.

After the learning session, we used the built-in testing feature of our apps (described in Sects. 2.1 and 2.2) to test the students' learning improvement. Students found the test feature of our apps interesting, and they completed it with enjoyment. Test results were automatically saved to the mobile phones. After completing the test session, we conducted a survey consisting of eight questions (answers ranging from 1 for *strongly disagree* to 5 for *strongly agree*) with each of the subjects (i.e., the children, their parents, and the teachers) to identify the effectiveness of AR in education. Table 2 presents the questions for the students, and Table 4 presents the questions for teachers and parents (these tables can be found in Sect. 4). These questions covered various aspects such as usability, degree of satisfaction, impact, motivation and vividness.

We asked the parents for their opinions about the apps and student engagement. Because the parents observed the entire learning session, we asked them what they thought about AR apps, what could be improved, and what type of content should be taught using this type of technology. We also asked how their children passed the time at home and what they do when they have a mobile phone. We received very good responses and ideas from the parents. Some of them told us that they were concerned that their children were becoming addicted to the mobile phone for games and cartoons. They were happy to see that their children could now learn through mobile apps as well. Many of them installed our apps on their mobile phones after the learning session. They also suggested adding more animations to the apps.

We also surveyed the teachers who had observed the entire process as well, and they completed the survey we designed for them. One of the teachers suggested that we shall add a reward system to our apps for answering test questions correctly and that the app cheer students with a voice saying phrases such as "That's good", and "Very good".

## 4    Survey Results and Findings

In this section we present our findings from both quantitative and qualitative analysis.

### 4.1    Quantitative Analysis

Table 1 presents the average scores of the pre-test and post-test with the learning improvement of the 25 students. On average, 6 out of 12 questions were answered correctly before learning through the AR Zoo app. After using the app, students could answer 10 out of 12 questions correctly, which is a 33% improvement. Similarly, the learning improvement for the Bangla AR Book app was 30%.

**Table 1.** Average test scores and learning improvement of 25 students

| App name | Pre-test score | Post-test score | Learning improvement |
|---|---|---|---|
| AR Zoo | 6 out of 12 (50%) | 10 out of 12 (83%) | 33% |
| AR Book | 8 out of 20 (40%) | 14 out of 20 (70%) | 30% |

Students were asked to answer eight questions from five categories (two questions in each category) by rating their agreement on a scale 1 to 5, where 1 means strongly disagree, 2 means disagree, 3 means neutral, 4 means agree and 5 means strongly agree. Our interview results with students are presented in Table 2, and Table 3 shows the average and standard deviation in the question categories. The results show that the average score is around 4.61 out of 5 with a standard deviation of around 0.18 for all categories. This score indicates that students feel very positively about AR apps in general.

Similarly, we conducted surveys of the parents and teachers with another set of eight questions in four categories: impact, satisfaction, motivation and creativity. Table 4 presents our interview results with 13 parents and 3 teachers, and Table 5 shows the average and standard deviation in the question categories. The results show that the average score is around 4.73 out of 5 with a standard deviation of around 0.11 for all categories. This score indicates that both parents and teachers feel very positively about AR apps in general.

**Table 2.** Students' interview results

| Category | Question | 5 | 4 | 3 | 2 | 1 | Avg |
|---|---|---|---|---|---|---|---|
| Usability | The apps are very easy to use | 15 | 8 | 0 | 2 | 0 | 4.44 |
| | The 3D models used the app are fine | 22 | 3 | 0 | 0 | 0 | 4.88 |
| Satisfaction | Study with AR apps is easy | 18 | 7 | 0 | 0 | 0 | 4.72 |
| | I am pleased to study using the AR apps | 19 | 6 | 0 | 0 | 0 | 4.76 |
| Impact | It would be good if we were taught using AR apps | 18 | 6 | 1 | 0 | 0 | 4.68 |
| | I will use AR apps for my study | 12 | 11 | 2 | 0 | 0 | 4.40 |
| Vividness | Sounds and animations have made these apps very attractive | 18 | 5 | 0 | 2 | 0 | 4.56 |
| | The 3D models look real | 13 | 10 | 1 | 1 | 0 | 4.40 |

**Table 3.** Summary of students' interview results

| Category | Average | Std. deviation |
|---|---|---|
| Usability | 4.66 | 0.31 |
| Satisfaction | 4.74 | 0.02 |
| Impact | 4.54 | 0.20 |
| Vididness | 4.48 | 0.11 |
| All | 4.61 | 0.18 |

**Table 4.** Parents' and teachers' interview results

| Category | Question | 5 | 4 | 3 | 2 | 1 | Avg |
|---|---|---|---|---|---|---|---|
| Impact | AR app is very potential for teaching | 10 | 6 | 0 | 0 | 0 | 4.63 |
| | I will use AR apps for teaching | 11 | 5 | 0 | 0 | 0 | 4.69 |
| Satisfaction | Students enjoyed using AR apps | 14 | 2 | 0 | 0 | 0 | 4.88 |
| | By AR apps students have learned very quickly | 11 | 5 | 0 | 0 | 0 | 4.69 |
| Motivation | AR apps are very helpful for teaching | 12 | 4 | 0 | 0 | 0 | 4.75 |
| | Students will be benefited if AR apps are used in a classroom | 13 | 3 | 0 | 0 | 0 | 4.81 |
| | AR apps build child enthusiasm to study | 14 | 2 | 0 | 0 | 0 | 4.88 |
| Creativity | AR increases the imagination power of students | 9 | 7 | 0 | 0 | 0 | 4.56 |

**Table 5.** Summary of parents' and teachers' interview results

| Category | Average | Std. deviation |
|----------|---------|----------------|
| Impact | 4.66 | 0.04 |
| Satisfaction | 4.78 | 0.13 |
| Motivation | 4.81 | 0.04 |
| Creativity | 4.56 | - |
| All | 4.73 | 0.11 |

## 4.2 Qualitative Analysis

In this section we present our research findings from a qualitative analysis using three perspectives.

**Children's Experience Using AR Apps.** Most of the children who participated in the research study were familiar with smartphones and used them every day to play games or watch videos. However, none of them were familiar with augmented reality. They were very excited when they saw a 3D model appeared in the book. They were also very excited to learn through a mobile phone or tablet rather than through regular class lectures, which are conducted on a blackboard. When they saw virtual content superimposed onto the real world, they were amazed. They never thought that mobile technology could help them learn. Many of them use mobile phone to watch cartoons, but their experience with AR was exceptional and very positive.

This study makes us believe that AR should be officially integrated into digital education materials. This technology can draw the attention of the students. One child who participated in the study commented, "I use my parents' mobile phone to play video games, but this is really amazing". The students reacted positively to our apps, and some of them amazed to see that the model appeared on the mobile screen. They were checking the book to see whether there was really something on the book. It was like magic to them.

**Learning Through AR Apps.** First, we guided the teachers on how to use our AR apps and how to teach the students through them. Then a teacher used the apps to teach a group of students. Another teacher taught another group of students traditionally. After that, both groups of students took the tests in our apps. The results show that the group of students who used the AR apps was more successful in both tests than the group of students who was taught using the traditional teaching style. Moreover, the students were happy to use the AR apps. They preferred learning through the AR apps rather than through traditional classroom learning. Thus, we argue that the interactive learning session offered with AR can help preschool children enjoy the classes and, most importantly, learn faster.

**Taking Classes Through AR Apps.** Traditionally, teachers teach the students by using a blackboard. They write different letters on the board and teach the alphabet. Using AR apps, the teachers do not have to use the board. They can easily teach the students by using a smartphone or tablet. The teachers found it easy to teach using AR. The students were also quiet and cheerful while learning through it. Therefore, managing the classes could become easier for teachers with the use of AR technology. The teachers in this study were comfortable using the AR apps. They stated that if AR were available in the classroom, they would definitely use it to teach their students.

## 5   Discussion

In our research, we tried to determine whether AR could be used in early childhood education in Bangladesh, and the survey results were very exciting. The motivation level of the students was amazing. The findings from the survey prove that the children learned better through AR technology and were very much interested in it. This technology enhanced the children's motivational level so much that they did not want to stop using the apps, as observed during the survey. Additionally, looking at the moving content on top of the printed material helped them understand and memorize the content of the topic easily.

Parents were surprised when they found their children busy with AR apps and learning through them. One of the ways children learn is through imagination by reading books. However, textbooks and the low-quality 2D images in these books alone are limited in their ability to improve the imagination power of children. AR can be a great tool to help students imagine a real object that they have never seen in real life.

This study has been successful in supporting the potential of AR to teach preschool children. Our comparison between teachers use of AR and their use of traditional teaching materials has illustrated that AR can be used to help preschool students learn the Bengali alphabet. The teachers in this study recognized the potential of AR technology and also said that it would be much more helpful if the app were flexible to use. Their feedback suggests that these features would enable them to involve children more in their studies.

Through our study, we have identified the following requirements for designing and developing a good AR app for education to provide a better learning experience:

- Augmented Reality apps should be flexible for the teachers so that they can adapt them to the needs of individual children.
- The user interface of such apps should be customizable and easy to use.
- The 3D models of the apps should have animations and sounds to engage children better.
- The apps should have test features for children to evaluate their learning outcomes.
- Gamification can be incorporated into the apps to engage students more in learning as suggested by both students and their parents.

# 6 Related Work

The most traditional way of teaching children in Bangladesh is through the classroom and by the parents at home. Digital content and mobile app based learning opportunities are not yet widely available, but some initiatives have been taken. An Android app called Bino [12] presents 3D educational content using augmented reality. It has its own designed textbook, and the app superimposes related 3D models on top of the book. However, here in Bangladesh, parents are not very aware of teaching and learning through technology. Additionally, parents are reluctant to choose a different textbook than the one that is taught in the classroom and provided by the government. Therefore, Bino is not very popular, especially in rural areas.

In recent years, a number of research studies have been conducted on using AR in learning and education. A comparison of the existing research in connection to our research is shown in Table 6.

**Table 6.** Literature review summary and comparison

| Literature | Alphabets | Animals | Knowledge test | Age Group (yrs) | Country of study | Subjects studied |
|---|---|---|---|---|---|---|
| Parhizkar et al. [14] | No | No | No | 4–12 | Malaysia | Students |
| Rasslenda et al. [16] | Yes | Yes | No | 6 | Malaysia | Students |
| Dong and Si [6] | No | Dinosaur only | No | – | No study | None |
| Cheng and Tasi [5] | No | Yes | No | 4–5 | Spain | Students and parents |
| Barreira et al. [3] | No | Yes | Yes | 7–9 | Portugal | Students and teachers |
| He et al. [7] | No | Yes | Yes | 4–6 | China | Students |
| Our | Yes | Yes | Yes | 5–6 | Bangladesh | Students, parents and teachers |

Parhizkar et al. [14] proposed an AR app called Augmented Reality Children Storybook (ARCS) to encourage reading habits among children. ARCS is a storybook for young learners aged from 4 to 12 with different categories of stories for different learning skills and levels. However, there is no evaluation performed to measure how much it can improve children's reading habits. Rasslenda et al. [16] conducted a study on Malaysian preschool children to observe the usability of AR in the classroom. They found that students respond to AR more than traditional teaching styles. Their study indicates that AR apps increase children's engagement in learning, which is also confirmed by our findings. Chunxia and Zhanjun [6] proposed an AR app combined with a paper book called Dinosaur ABC to teach different types of dinosaurs. The 3D models of dinosaurs used in the app had animation, sounds, and different types of interactive actions. The authors concluded that AR could help expand the scope of the traditional book to 3D interaction, which could help regain the attention of readers to read traditional paper books. Cheng and Tasi [5] analyzed the behavioral patterns and cognitive attainment of children and their parents when they read an AR picture book. They ran their research on 33 parent-child pairs and concluded that shared reading of AR books could be beneficial for children. A game called MOW Augmented Reality [3] was proposed to teach students words in different languages. When a student matches the word with a picture, the related 3D model appears. However, the app taught the name of only a few animals. Finally, He et al. [7] proposed an app to help English as a Foreign Language (EFL) students learn new words. However, the app was developed to teach only eight words.

## 7　Conclusion

Augmented reality could add a new dimension to our education system if we utilize its potential. Preschool children can acquire much more knowledge and enjoy learning by using this technology in the classroom than by using traditional methods of learning. Our study confirms the previous study outcomes from other researchers and further clarifies that AR can be useful for preschool students learning in a developing country such as Bangladesh. Our study shows that, although the children were not initially familiar with AR technology, they responded well to it. They completed the sessions quite easily with interest and enjoyment. We also found that AR technology increased their motivational levels and engagement in learning, helping them grasp and recall the letters and corresponding pictures. Traditional books combined with an AR app could not only improve children's reading habits of classroom materials but also expand the books' scope to three-dimensional interaction. Our experimental results show that AR technology provides a fun and engaging environment for children. Therefore, using AR technology as an educational tool could be very useful for teaching students. However, the design of the AR app should be very user-friendly and customizable to be used by parents and teachers easily. These design requirements should be considered to develop better AR apps to be used by teachers in preschool education to enhance the learning experience.

In future work, we plan to consider those design requirements, include new features such as interactive gaming and math lessons, and develop better UI and graphics to enhance the user experience.

**Acknowledgement.** We would like to thank the CUET Primary School authority, especially the head teacher, for allowing us to conduct the study on students, parents and teachers.

## References

1. Akçayır, M., Akçayır, G.: Advantages and challenges associated with augmented reality for education: a systematic review of the literature. Educ. Res. Rev. **20**, 1–11 (2017). https://doi.org/10.1016/j.edurev.2016.11.002
2. Azuma, R.T.: A survey of augmented reality. Presence: Teleoper. Virtual Environ. **6**(4), 355–385 (1997)

3. Barreira, J., Bessa, M., Pereira, L.C., Adão, T., Peres, E., Magalhães, L.: MOW: augmented reality game to learn words in different languages: case study: learning english names of animals in elementary school. In: 2012 7th Iberian Conference on Information Systems and Technologies (CISTI), pp. 1–6. IEEE (2012)
4. Inter IKEA Systems B.V.: IKEA place (2019). https://highlights.ikea.com/2017/ikea-place/. Accessed 17 Jan 2019
5. Cheng, K.H., Tsai, C.C.: Children and parents' reading of an augmented reality picture book: analyses of behavioral patterns and cognitive attainment. Comput. Educ. **72**, 302–312 (2014)
6. Dong, C., Si, Z.: The research and application of augmented reality in 3D interactive books for children. In: Zhao, P., Ouyang, Y., Xu, M., Yang, L., Ren, Y. (eds.) Applied Sciences in Graphic Communication and Packaging. LNEE, vol. 477, pp. 293–299. Springer, Singapore (2018). https://doi.org/10.1007/978-981-10-7629-9_35
7. He, J., Ren, J., Zhu, G., Cai, S., Chen, G.: Mobile-based AR application helps to promote EFL children's vocabulary study. In: 2014 IEEE 14th International Conference on Advanced Learning Technologies (ICALT), pp. 431–433. IEEE (2014)
8. Autodesk Inc.: Autodesk Maya (2019). https://www.autodesk.com/products/maya/overview. Accessed 12 Feb 2019
9. Kakadiaris, I.A., Islam, M.M., Xie, T., Nikou, C., Lumsden, A.B.: iRay: mobile AR using structure sensor. In: 2016 IEEE International Symposium on Mixed and Augmented Reality (ISMAR-Adjunct), pp. 127–128. IEEE (2016)
10. Kerawalla, L., Luckin, R., Seljeflot, S., Woolard, A.: "Making it real": exploring the potential of augmented reality for teaching primary school science. Virtual Reality **10**(3–4), 163–174 (2006)
11. Lee, K.: Augmented reality in education and training. TechTrends **56**(2), 13–21 (2012). https://doi.org/10.1007/s11528-012-0559-3
12. Microtech Interactive LTD: Bino (2018). http://ilovebino.com/. Accessed 18 Jan 2019
13. Navab, N., Blum, T., Wang, L., Okur, A., Wendler, T.: First deployments of augmented reality in operating rooms. Computer **45**(7), 48–55 (2012)
14. Parhizkar, B., Shin, T., Lashkari, A.H., Nian, Y.: Augmented Reality Children Storybook (ARCS). In: 2011 International Conference on Future Information Technology (2011)
15. PTC Inc.: Vuforia, SDK (2018). https://www.vuforia.com/. Accessed 18 Jan 2019
16. Rasalingam, R.R., Muniandy, B., Rass, R.: Exploring the application of Augmented Reality technology in early childhood classroom in Malaysia. J. Res. Method Educ. (IOSR-JRME) **4**(5), 33–40 (2014)
17. Unity Technologies: Unity (2019). https://unity3d.com/. Accessed 22 Jan 2019
18. Wu, H.K., Lee, S.W.Y., Chang, H.Y., Liang, J.C.: Current status, opportunities and challenges of augmented reality in education. Comput. Educ. **62**, 41–49 (2013)

# Physically Extended Virtual Reality (PEVR) as a New Concept in Railway Driver Training

Małgorzata Ćwil[1(✉)] and Witold Bartnik[2]

[1] Kozminski University, 57/59 Jagiellonska St, Warsaw, Poland
cwil.malgorzata@gmail.com
[2] Faculty of Transport, Warsaw University of Technology, 75 Koszykowa
Street, 00-662 Warsaw, Poland
bartnikw@gmail.com

**Abstract.** The objective of this article is to describe a new concept of using Physically Extended Virtual Reality (PEVR) for simulation-based railway driver training. The concept is based on an initial, pilot version presented at the InnoTrans railway fair in 2016. Since that time the device has been developed further which resulted in the addition of new significant functionalities. This has been driven in part by the results of surveys performed during the fairs, which measured user experience and where one of the most common complaints concerned the lack of immersion. The new version has been presented at the InnoTrans 2018 and another similar survey was performed in order to obtain comparable data for both versions of the device. The comparative results of those surveys are described and analysed in order to obtain better understanding about the quality of the proposed solution and possible improvements. An additional User Experience Questionnaire (UEQ) was used to determine the participants' perception of the PEVR railway simulator. Possible improvements and extensions of this research are proposed that could further the understanding of how to develop better and more immersive training solutions for railway drivers.

**Keywords:** Virtual reality · VR · Railway driver · Simulator

## 1 Simulators in Railway Driver Training

Using simulators for vehicle operator training is a well-established procedure among transportation providers. They are employed for educational purposes by airplane pilots [1–3], train drivers [4, 5] and road vehicle drivers (i.e. trucks, buses and cars) [6, 7]. The air transportation industry in particular requires pilots to go through numerous rounds of simulator training before they start flying actual planes and to keep retraining during their career. Some countries have also introduced mandatory simulator training for railway drivers (e.g. Poland) [8]. The popularity of these schemes stems from two distinct factors. One of them is the high financial and social cost of a potential mistake made while steering a large passenger airship or railway vehicle. The other one concerns the difficulty of recreating potentially useful training settings in the real world. Both pilots and railway drivers need to practice their actions in emergency situations in order to ensure the safety of their passengers and their own.

© Springer Nature Switzerland AG 2019
J. Y. C. Chen and G. Fragomeni (Eds.): HCII 2019, LNCS 11575, pp. 230–242, 2019.
https://doi.org/10.1007/978-3-030-21565-1_15

Several companies have developed simulators for railway purposes in the last few decades, the most notable among them are CORYS (France) and Lander (Spain). Most devices delivered during this period were the so-called full-scale simulators which means a complete recreation of the driver's cab of the simulated train with one or multiple TV screens or projection mats mounted outside of the cab in the place of the windshield (and sometimes rearview mirrors). In order to achieve additional immersion many customers order these simulators to be mounted on moving platforms with six degrees of freedom enabling them to simulate the jerks and forces related to acceleration, braking and other events that may happen during training.

These solutions, while reliable and realistic, are, however, quite costly, which has limited their proliferation. In order to increase their market appeal producers have developed desktop simulators, which usually consist of a simplified desk panel with some controllers and a TV screen. These devices come at a vastly reduced cost but suffer from significantly reduced realism.

The concept described in this paper of a VR-based railway simulator has been developed primarily in order to support energy efficient driving. The set of techniques used for that purpose is called eco-driving and is a well-researched concept in the context of both rail and road transportation [9–11]. Industry experience and scientific papers both show that implementing these energy-efficient driving techniques can significantly reduce the energy consumption of a railway operator. Results that were published point to savings of up to 10% [12, 13]. These savings are achievable through the efficient usage of a time reserve called schedule padding, which is added into timetables to avoid delay propagation between trains [14, 15]. Eco-driving projects vary in implementation and may be simply based on providing drivers with feedback about their energy consumption (this information is actually available only to a limited group of railway drivers at this time). It has been decided that a multi-faceted approach might prove to be a better way to convey information to drivers which is the main reason why the VR-based eco-driving simulator was created. This enables instructors and their trainees to try out differing driving strategies in a realistic environment while obtaining information about the current and total energy consumption. This helps develop and propagate efficient driving techniques leading to potential energy savings.

The use of virtual reality for railway training purposes has already been proposed by several companies and organizations [16–18]. Most uses suggested and offered so far were, however, not concerned with the steering and control of the train, but rather revolved around supplementary training for railway workers other than drivers. Trainees using these devices learned how to repair, switch or exchange certain railway elements and how to move safely in railway environments, which differ strongly from the use proposed for the device described in this paper.

## 2  Virtual Reality

### 2.1  History

The concept of virtual reality was born in the 1950s when Morton Heilig proposed to simulate the whole environment of the simulation participant in a manner indiscernible from reality. Heilig built such a device in 1962 and named it Sensorama [19]. Due to technological constraints Sensorama was completely mechanical. Within the next decade the first digital VR projects were born, pioneered by Thomas Furness, whose main achievement was the creation of the first flight simulator for airplane pilots, named Visually-Coupled Airborne Systems Simulator (VCASS) [20]. The main problem of these early VR approaches was caused by technological constraints: both the computational and graphical capabilities available during that time were insufficient to create real immersion. This delayed the true onset of VR devices until the 21st century. In the last few years the pace of technological progress has finally reached the stage where realistic immersion became feasible. At first this was achieved through the use of completely surrounding TV screens. This technique was, however, quickly overtaken by VR-capable goggles displaying simulation computed by personal computers (Oculus Rift, HTC Vice) or mobile phones (Samsung Gear). At this time virtual reality devices are quickly gaining in popularity with some sources claiming that their growth is similar to that observed for mobile phones, personal computers and color TVs before reaching market saturation. That would suggest that within the next decade VR devices could be as widespread as these other everyday use devices are right now.

Virtual reality has been particularly popular since its inception in industries, where providing real-life training is very expensive or even impossible. One of the best examples of that is the space industry [21]. Astronauts require extensive training before leaving the Earth. This training should be provided in conditions as close to reality as possible. Although weightlessness on Earth may only be achieved by using special diving airplanes, all the other space flight conditions may be recreated using immersive simulators. A similar reasoning has led to the immense popularity of simulators in military and medical training allowing future and current doctors and soldiers to practice their skills without endangering lives. Additionally, industries using costly and complicated machines (e.g. mining) which are not easily available for training purposes also use simulators in order to train their personnel [21]. In 2017, 63% of surveyed business personnel answered that the main purpose they were planning to use VR in their company was training, which was by far the most popular response among other uses of VR such as product design, data visualization or marketing [22]. This suggests an increasingly attractive future for VR in the professional and educational aspect. At the same time Mixed Reality (MR) and Augmented Reality (AR) devices are also gaining popularity in a manner that might make them serious competitors to standard VR within the next few years [23, 24].

## 2.2  Reality-Virtuality Continuum

The concept of a reality-virtuality continuum was introduced by Milgram and Kishino [25] in 1994. The idea is based on the premise that all technologies which involve some joining of the real and virtual worlds belong to a continuum between a completely virtual reality where immersion is total and a completely real environment, where there are no virtual elements whatsoever and all the elements exist objectively. All the intermediate solutions fall within the realm of Mixed Reality as shown in Fig. 1. Mixed reality is therefore defined as an environment where real world and virtual world objects are presented together using one method of display. Millgram also proposed an additional partition between Augmented Reality (AR) and Augmented Virtuality (AV). Augmented reality is, within the scope of this framework, information technology and media nested in real-world environments whereas augmented virtuality is the realtime representation of the current state of the real world and its elements in media and information technology environments.

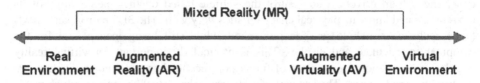

Fig. 1.  Reality-virtuality continuum [25].

A somewhat different definition of Augmented Reality was given by Azuma in 1997 [26], who distinguishes it from Virtual Reality through the access to the real world- in VR computer generated content replaces all other experience, whereas in AR it is rather added onto the real-world experience.

In the described version of physically extended virtual reality simulator for train drivers, there are some elements of virtual environment as well as parts from real environment used so the simulator falls between the two edges of the presented continuum.

## 3   User Experience in Railway Simulators

### 3.1   Definition of User Experience

User experience is defined in the literature as an evaluation of the qualitative experience that a user has during his interaction with a product [27]. The most up-to-date International Organization for Standardization definition of user experience is concentrated on the perceptions and responses of people using a product, system or service [28]. According to this definition, user experience includes all the emotions, beliefs, preferences, perceptions, physical and psychological responses, behaviors and accomplishments that occur before, during and after the use.

### 3.2   First Version of the PEVR Simulator

The first pilot version of the VR simulator was designed for Innotrans 2016 - the world's largest trade fair focused on the rail transport industry. The concept of a physically extended virtual reality railway simulator was based on two main components: hardware and software.

The hardware component consisted of virtual reality goggles, computer and the driver's desk and chair. In order to increase immersion an additional LeapMotion hands detector was mounted on the table to enable users to see their hands and help them correctly use the train cab devices. One of the most important parts of the simulator is the driver's desk which had a few real controls added in order to make the haptic part of simulation more realistic (for acceleration, electrodynamical and electropneumatic braking, the deadman's switch).

The software component consisted of three main parts: simulation logic and physics, 3D environment and driver cab visualization. The first part is needed to provide training scenarios and realistic train behaviour. This is particularly important for experienced train drivers, who control the vehicle based on their perceptions of its movements and know its physical characteristics very well. The 3D environment needs to be realistic enough to provide immersion while still being manageable for the computer to calculate and display. This is particularly important for virtual reality goggles, where much higher rates of frame per second than for regular displays are required to avoid nausea. The last part of software is the virtual driver cab, which needs to correspond well to its physical extensions in order to provide immersion. This has forced the developers to modify the location of the components that are available also in the real world in order to avoid confusion for users. That is caused by the physical limitations of a desktop simulator, which was somewhat smaller that the real driver's desk.

In order to measure user experience of the described simulator each person taking part in the simulation during Innotrans was asked to fill a survey about their experience and attitude towards virtual reality in the railway context. In 2016 the questionnaire consisted of 4 closed questions and 1 open one assessing: overall user experience, the quality of simulation, similarity to real world and the idea to supplement train driver training with a VR simulator.

### 3.3   New Version of the PEVR Simulator

In 2016, generally the proposed VR-based simulator solution was very well received. Most visitors accepted it and even those who pointed out certain limitations to its current design and technology usually supported the idea of using it as a training tool for train drivers. Many of them pointed, however, to the main obstacle - lack of enough immersion, which was lowering the user experience. In order to answer this complaint the new version for Innotrans 2018 had significant new physical controllers added. In addition to the already present main train controller and deadman's switch, a separate pneumatic brake lever as well as sanding, horn, reverser, pantograph and door controls were included. The LeapMotion detector, which was formerly located directly above the trainee's hands on the driver's desk has been mounted directly on the goggles increasing the quality of hand detection. The comparison between two versions of the simulator is the main subject of this analysis.

This simulator in its new, enhanced version was presented at the 2018 edition of the InnoTrans railway transportation fairs. User experience was measured using questionnaires – the same questions as in 2016 as well as added question from User Experience Questionnaire [29] - and has been analysed quantitatively, as well as comparatively using the results from the 2016 survey. The results are presented in the following paragraphs.

## 4  Methods

In order to measure user experience in both versions of the PEVR simulator (in 2016 and 2018) a short questionnaire was used. It started with 4 closed-ended questions:

Q1: How would you rate your experience on the PEVR train simulator?
Q2: How would you rate the quality of simulation?
Q3: How similar is this simulation to the real world in your opinion?
Q4: How would you rate the idea to supplement train driver training with PEVR simulation?

The answers to these questions were marked on a symmetrical five-point Likert scale. In 2018 additionally a short version (due to the time constraints of the fairs) of User Experience Questionnaire [29] was performed enabling the authors to compare UX between simulator versions and the UEQ of the new version with similar products. At the end of each questionnaire there was an open-ended question in which people could give more detailed information about their opinions and reactions.

## 5  Results

Firstly the summary results from both editions were analysed. This is presented in Table 1.

**Table 1.** Number of people included in both parts of the research (2016 and 2018).

|       |       | Frequency | Percent |
|-------|-------|-----------|---------|
| Valid | 1     | 144       | 75.4    |
|       | 2     | 47        | 24.6    |
|       | Total | 191       | 100.0   |

A significantly lower number of surveys was collected during the second edition (2018). This was caused partially by technical issues with the new version of the simulator which limited the hours of availability for Innotrans participants, and partially by the fact, that only one fully functional device was available in 2018, whereas in 2016 two identical simulators have been presented. Table 2 presents the statistical information regarding the age of survey participants.

**Table 2.** Age of the participants.

|  |  | Frequency | Percent | Valid percent | Cumulative percent |
|---|---|---|---|---|---|
| Valid | <20 | 9 | 4.7 | 5.0 | 5.0 |
|  | 20–29 | 45 | 23.6 | 25.1 | 30.2 |
|  | 30–39 | 59 | 30.9 | 33.0 | 63.1 |
|  | 40–49 | 43 | 22.5 | 24.0 | 87.2 |
|  | 50–59 | 18 | 9.4 | 10.1 | 97.2 |
|  | 60–69 | 4 | 2.1 | 2.2 | 99.4 |
|  | >70 | 1 | .5 | .6 | 100.0 |
|  | Total | 179 | 93.7 | 100.0 |  |
| Missing System |  | 12 | 6.3 |  |  |
| Total |  | 191 | 100.0 |  |  |

Within the 93.7% of surveys which contained information about age, the dominant age groups are distinguishable - over 80% of participants were 20–49 years old which is standard in a usual fair public. If the survey was extended for the open public days, they would have probably contained a lot more responses from people under 20.

The geographical dispersion was significantly different for both surveys, probably due to the sample sizes. In the 2016 edition 32 different countries from 6 continents were named by users, whereas in 2018 people from only 18 countries and 3 continents took part in the survey. In both of the cases the dominant nations were Germany and Poland, which is explained by the fairs' location (Berlin) and the nationality of the company presenting the devices (Poland). Professionally participants were very diverse – although most of them worked in the railway business, they ranged from train drivers, through mid- and high-level managers to CEOs.

Table 3 presents the general descriptive results of the four questions from the closed part of the questionnaire.

**Table 3.** Descriptive statistics for closed-ended questions

|  | N | Min. | Max. | Mean | SD |
|---|---|---|---|---|---|
| Q1 | 190 | 2 | 5 | 4.61 | .551 |
| Q2 | 190 | 2 | 5 | 4.33 | .667 |
| Q3 | 186 | 3 | 5 | 4.16 | .643 |
| Q4 | 189 | 3 | 5 | 4.71 | .529 |
| Valid N (listwise) | 185 |  |  |  |  |

Generally positive answers may be observed, particularly for questions Q1 and Q4. There were no completely negative answers (i.e. ones) recorded. A larger standard deviation has been observed for questions Q2 and Q3, where the average answer was worse than for the others. Altogether 185 valid surveys were collected.

In order to compare the responses to different versions of the proposed PEVR simulator the responses were analysed for both editions separately as well. Table 4 presents the results of this analysis.

**Table 4.** Descriptive statistics for closed-ended questions separately for both editions

| Edition | | N | Min. | Max. | Mean | SD |
|---|---|---|---|---|---|---|
| 1 | Q1 | 143 | 2 | 5 | 4.59 | .573 |
| | Q2 | 143 | 2 | 5 | 4.41 | .654 |
| | Q3 | 140 | 3 | 5 | 4.18 | .626 |
| | Q4 | 142 | 3 | 5 | 4.73 | .493 |
| | Valid N | 139 | | | | |
| 2 | Q1 | 47 | 4 | 5 | 4.66 | .479 |
| | Q2 | 47 | 3 | 5 | 4.09 | .654 |
| | Q3 | 46 | 3 | 5 | 4.09 | .694 |
| | Q4 | 47 | 3 | 5 | 4.68 | .629 |
| | Valid N | 46 | | | | |

As can be observed in Table 4, the mean for the question 1 (concerning overall user experience) is higher for the second edition of the research, while for all of the other questions (concerning quality of simulation, similarity to real world or the idea to supplement training with PEVR simulator) the average obtained score was higher in 2016 in comparison to 2018.

In order to determine whether any other significant differences were found between these two groups a non-parametric U-Mann-Whitney test has been performed. The results are presented in Table 5.

**Table 5.** Results of U-Mann-Whitney test comparing both editions

| | Q1 | Q2 | Q3 | Q4 |
|---|---|---|---|---|
| Mann-Whitney U | 3203.500 | 2458.500 | 3003.500 | 3327.500 |
| Wilcoxon W | 13499.500 | 3586.500 | 4084.500 | 13480.500 |
| Z | −.571 | −3.052 | −.768 | −.039 |
| Asymp. sig. (2-tailed) | .568 | **.002** | .442 | .969 |

a. Grouping Variable: Edition

According to the results presented in Table 5, the only significant difference was observed for question Q2, which concerns the quality of simulation. It was judged worse in the newer version, which may have been caused by the technical problems during the first days of the fairs.

In order to determine whether any significant correlations exist between answers obtained in the survey, an analysis was performed on the data, separately for 2016 and 2018. The results of Spearman's rho correlation tests are presented in Table 6.

**Table 6.** Results of Spearman's rho test for both editions

| Edition | | | Q1 | Q2 | Q3 | Q4 |
|---|---|---|---|---|---|---|
| 1 | Q1 | Correlation coefficient | 1,000 | .468** | .404** | .272** |
| | | Sig. (2-tailed) | . | .000 | .000 | .001 |
| | | N | 143 | 143 | 140 | 142 |
| | Q2 | Correlation coefficient | .468** | 1.000 | .528** | .203* |
| | | Sig. (2-tailed) | .000 | . | .000 | .015 |
| | | N | 143 | 143 | 140 | 142 |
| | Q3 | Correlation coefficient | .404** | .528** | 1.000 | .054 |
| | | Sig. (2-tailed) | .000 | .000 | . | .528 |
| | | N | 140 | 140 | 140 | 139 |
| | Q4 | Correlation coefficient | .272** | .203* | .054 | 1.000 |
| | | Sig. (2-tailed) | .001 | .015 | .528 | . |
| | | N | 142 | 142 | 139 | 142 |
| 2 | Q1 | Correlation coefficient | 1.000 | .307* | .416** | .425** |
| | | Sig. (2-tailed) | . | .036 | .004 | .003 |
| | | N | 47 | 47 | 46 | 47 |
| | Q2 | Correlation coefficient | .307* | 1.000 | .665** | .176 |
| | | Sig. (2-tailed) | .036 | . | .000 | .237 |
| | | N | 47 | 47 | 46 | 47 |
| | Q3 | Correlation coefficient | .416** | .665** | 1.000 | .361* |
| | | Sig. (2-tailed) | .004 | .000 | . | .014 |
| | | N | 46 | 46 | 46 | 46 |
| | Q4 | Correlation coefficient | .425** | .176 | .361* | 1.000 |
| | | Sig. (2-tailed) | .003 | .237 | .014 | . |
| | | N | 47 | 47 | 46 | 47 |

**Correlation is significant at the level 0.01
*Correlation is significant at the level 0.05

Almost all of the questions in the survey were observed to be positively correlated to each other, with especially high correlation between Q2 and Q3 in both of the editions of the research. The correlations can be interpreted in the following manner:

- Correlation between Q1 and Q2: the higher people rate the quality of simulation, the better their experience on the simulator is
- Correlation between Q1 and Q3: the more similar the simulation is to the real world, the higher people rate their experience on the simulator
- Correlation between Q1 and Q4: the higher people rate their experience on the simulator, the more likely they are to support the idea to supplement train driver training with VR simulation
- Correlation between Q2 and Q3: the more similar the simulation is to the real world, the higher people rate the quality of simulation
- Correlation between Q2 and Q4 (only in 1st edition): the higher people rate the quality of simulation, the more likely they are to support the idea to supplement train driver training with VR simulation

- Correlation between Q3 and Q4 (only in 2nd edition): the more similar the experience is to the real world, the more likely people are to support the idea to supplement train driver training with VR simulation

The lack of correlation observed for questions 3 and 4 in the research conducted in 2016 and for questions 2 and 4 in 2018 means that even when the quality of the simulation is not perfect and the experience is quite different from real world, people still think that it can be useful in train driver training. Meanwhile the particularly strong correlation between questions 2 and 3 can be explained by the fact that most people judge the quality of a simulation by comparing it to the real world.

Table 7 presents the results of the analysis of the correlation between the survey participants' age and their answers.

**Table 7.** Correlation between the age and answers given to closed-ended questions

|  |  | Q1 | Q2 | Q3 | Q4 |
|---|---|---|---|---|---|
| Age | Correlation coefficient | 0.052 | .173* | 0.109 | 0.061 |
|  | Sig. (2-tailed) | 0.489 | 0.021 | 0.150 | 0.421 |
|  | N | 178 | 178 | 174 | 177 |

*Correlation is significant at the level 0.05

A significant correlation may only be observed for question 2 - the older the participant, the more positive his or her view of the simulation quality. This may be partially explained by the relative lack of experience with computer simulation technology of the older participants compared to their younger counterparts.

Table 8 presents the descriptive results of the second part of the survey (User Experience Questionnarie), which was performed in 2018 only. In order to compare the results to other research papers they have been scaled to the range of -3 (horribly bad) to +3 (extremely good).

**Table 8.** Results of User Experience Questionnaire

| Item | Mean | SD | N | Negative | Positive | Scale |
|---|---|---|---|---|---|---|
| 1 | 2.1 | 0.8 | 46 | Obstructive | Supportive | Pragmatic quality |
| 2 | 1.9 | 1.1 | 47 | Complicated | Easy | Pragmatic quality |
| 3 | 1.8 | 1.0 | 45 | Inefficient | Efficient | Pragmatic quality |
| 4 | 1.9 | 1.1 | 46 | Confusing | Clear | Pragmatic quality |
| 5 | 2.2 | 1.0 | 47 | Boring | Exciting | Hedonic quality |
| 6 | 2.5 | 0.7 | 47 | Not interesting | Interesting | Hedonic quality |
| 7 | 2.1 | 0.8 | 46 | Conventional | Inventive | Hedonic quality |
| 8 | 1.8 | 0.9 | 45 | Usual | Leading edge | Hedonic quality |

Items belonging to the same scale (pragmatic or hedonic quality) should show a high correlation. The consistence of a scale is measured by the Cronbach Alpha Coefficient which equals 0.75 for pragmatic quality and 0.76 for hedonic quality and that means both scales are consistent.

The results from the UEQ questionnaire have also been compared to other systems evaluated using this method. The total sample in this comparison consisted of 14056 people across 280 studies concerning different products, including business software, web pages, web shops and social networks. Figure 2 shows the results of this comparison. Both the pragmatic and hedonic qualities were judged as excellent by the participants.

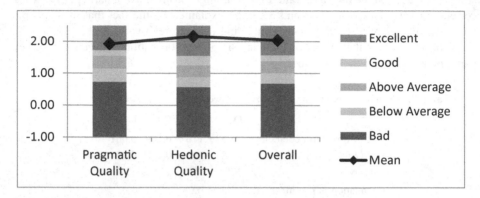

**Fig. 2.**  Scores of UEQ.

In order to obtain more qualitative feedback on the proposed PEVR simulator solution an open-ended question was added to the questionnaire in both its editions. In 2016, 32 people out of 144 decided to leave supplementary comments. The negative ones concerned mainly the resolution of the Oculus goggles, which may be problematic when simulating some of the conditions that train drivers meet. Train drivers complained about the lack of some of the real controls, which was one of the main reasons for their addition in the 2018 version. Positive feedback was usually an enthusiastic addition the evaluation in the close-ended part of the survey. In 2018, 13 people out of 47 decided to add some comments. They were once again related to the resolution, but also to the LeapMotion solution for hand detection, which was not working perfectly at the fairs. For example on of the PEVR simulator users observed that "Tracking sensors for hand tracking could be better", whereas another suggested "maybe higher resolution". The positive feedback was related to the quality of the immersion and the whole experience and included opinions like "I had a feeling that the chair was moving!", "Need one at home!" or "I love it, thank you for the experience!".

## 6   Limitations and Future Research

The main limitations of this research are related to its specific location and target group. Firstly, the number of participants in the second edition was considerably smaller than in the first one making it harder to compare the results. Secondly, the participants of the survey represented a wide array of professionals in the railway industry. It might be beneficial to perform a similar survey on train drivers only, with the possible inclusion of people related to railway safety and training. An additional interesting path of research could concern the comparison of training using a full-scale simulator with motion simulation with the use of PEVR solutions like the one described in this article.

# 7  Conclusions

The surveys from 2016 and 2018 analysed in this paper show that the new concept of a Physically Extended Virtual Reality railway simulator is a very attractive solution that could potentially be used for train driver training. The feedback during the 2016 and 2018 editions of Innotrans railway fairs has been positive and the UEQ questionnaire from the second edition has shown clearly that the PEVR perception by the general railway business public is excellent. According to the survey participants, amongst the things needing improvement the foremost are the goggles' resolution and hand detection software, as these two factors affect immersion very strongly. Interestingly, the second, improved version on the PEVR simulator was actually evaluated as worse than its predecessor. This might have been caused by the fact, that the significant increase in the number of simulator physical controllers has made the task of driving the train more difficult. That would be in line with the comments made by the train drivers using the first version, who insisted on adding more physical controllers in order to make the PEVR simulator more realistic. In the near future PEVR simulators may become very widespread in railway training processes due to their comparatively low price and high immersion levels.

# References

1. Longridge, T., Bürki-Cohen, J., Go, T.H., Kendra, A.J.: Simulator fidelity considerations for training and evaluation of today's airline pilots (2001)
2. Page, R.L.: Brief history of flight simulation. In: SimTecT 2000 Proceedings, pp. 11–17 (2000)
3. Caro, P.W.: Aircraft simulators and pilot training. Hum. Factors 15(6), 502–509 (1973)
4. Naweed, A., Balakrishnan, G.: Simulators in the rail industry: touching the third rail of driver training. Simulation, Australia (2018). http://www.simulationaustralasia.com/files/upload/pdf/research/Simulators_In_The_Rail_Industry_Touching_the_Third_Rail_of_Driver_Training_-_A_Naweed.Pdf
5. Bartnik, W., Ćwil, M.: Koncepcja zastosowania symulatora opartego o technologię wirtualnej rzeczywistości do szkolenia maszynistów w zakresie efektywnego energetycznie prowadzenia pociągu. Innowacje w polskiej nauce w obszarze matematyki i informatyki., vol. 95 (2017)
6. Strayer, D.L., Drews, F.A.: Simulator training improves driver efficiency: transfer from the simulator to the real world (2003)
7. Roenker, D.L., Cissell, G.M., Ball, K.K., Wadley, V.G., Edwards, J.D.: Speed-of-processing and driving simulator training result in improved driving performance. Hum. Factors 45(2), 218–233 (2003)

8. Regulation of the Polish Minister of Infrastructure and Development dated February 10th 2014 on the train driver's license, Journal of Laws of the Republic of Poland position 212, Chapter 3

9. González-Gil, A., Palacin, R., Batty, P., Powell, J.P.: A systems approach to reduce urban rail energy consumption. Energy Convers. Manag. **80**, 509–524 (2014)

10. Alam, M.S., McNabola, A.: A critical review and assessment of eco-driving policy & technology: benefits & limitations. Transp. Policy **35**, 42–49 (2014)

11. Zhou, M., Jin, H., Wang, W.: A review of vehicle fuel consumption models to evaluate eco-driving and eco-routing. Transp. Res. Part D: Transp. Environ. **49**, 203–218 (2016)

12. PKP SA Annual Report 2016 (2016). http://pkpsa.pl/grupapkp/raporty/Annual-Report-PKP-Group2016_ENG.pdf. Accessed 11 Feb 2019

13. Przewozy Regionalne (Regional Transport) Annual Report 2014, https://polregio.pl/media/1696/raport2014.pdf. Accessed 11 Feb 2019

14. Scheepmaker, G.M., Goverde, R.M., Kroon, L.G.: Review of energy-efficient train control and timetabling. Eur. J. Oper. Res. **257**(2), 355–376 (2017)

15. Urbaniak, M., Jacyna, M.: Wybrane zagadnienia wielokryterialnej optymalizacji ruchu kolejowego w aspekcie minimalizacji kosztów. Probl. Kolejnictwa **169**, 61–67 (2015)

16. Tichon, J., Wallis, G., Mildred, T.: Virtual training environments to improve train driver's crisis decision making. In: Proceedings of SimTecT, Melbourne, Australia, May (2006)

17. David, P., Lourdeaux, D.: A simulator using virtual reality techniques for training driver to manual interventions on the tracks. In: Poster presented at the WCRR'01 World Conference on Railway Research, Cologne (2001)

18. Qumak website. http://www.qumak.pl/en/polish-locomotive-simulator-will-train-drivers-in-a-virtual-reality/. Accessed 11 Feb 2019

19. Heiling, M.: US Patent #3,050,870, Sensorama Simulator Patent (1962). http://www.mortonheilig.com/SensoramaPatent.pdf. Accessed 11 Feb 2019

20. Sutherland, I.E.: The ultimate display. Multimedia: from wagner to virtual reality, pp. 506–508 (1965)

21. Aoki, H., Oman, C.M., Natapoff, A.: Virtual-reality-based 3D navigation training for emergency egress from spacecraft. Aviat. Space Environ. Med. **78**(8), 774–783 (2007)

22. Seidel, R.J., Chatelier, P.R. (eds.): Virtual Reality, Training's Future? Perspectives on Virtual Reality and Related Emerging Technologies, vol. 6. Springer, Heidelberg (2013)

23. Opportunities in XR: Where are the Real Opportunities in the Immersive Tech Market? SuperData Research Holdings, USA (2017)

24. State of the XR Market, SuperData Research Holdings, USA (2018)

25. Milgram, P., Kishino, F.: A taxonomy of mixed reality visual displays. IEICE Trans. Inf. Syst. **77**(12), 1321–1329 (1994)

26. Azuma, R.T.: A survey of augmented reality. Presence: Teleoper. Virtual Environ. **6**(4), 355–385 (1997)

27. McCarthy, J., Wright, P.: Technology as experience. Interactions **11**(5), 42–43 (2004)

28. International Organization for Standardization: Ergonomics of human system interaction - Part 210: Human-centered design for interactive systems (formerly known as 13407). ISO F ± DIS 9241–210:2009

29. Schrepp, M., Hinderks, A., Thomaschewski, J.: Design and evaluation of a short version of the user experience questionnaire (UEQ-S). Int. J. Interactive Multimed. Artif. Intell. **4**(6), 12 (2017)

# Developing a VR Training Program for Geriatric Patients with Chronic Back Pain

## A Process Analysis

Rebecca Dahms$^{(\boxtimes)}$, Oskar Stamm, and Ursula Müller-Werdan

Geriatric Research Group, Charité – Universitätsmedizin Berlin,
Reinickendorfer Strasse 61, 13347 Berlin, Germany
`rebecca.dahms@charite.de`

**Abstract.** Back pain is increasing with age. Current studies have shown positive effects of virtual reality (VR) interventions for patients with neuropsychiatric diseases such as anxiety and chronic pain. However, little is known about the use of VR by geriatric patients with chronic back pain. This study was conducted as part of the research project "ViRST" (virtual reality for pain therapy). This approach intends to provide a new non-pharmacological therapy concept. The aim of this study was to learn more about the administrative efforts and business goals of physiotherapeutic and psychotherapeutic institutions. Additionally, we wanted to identify daily strategies of geriatric patients for dealing with their back pain to identify current therapies and possible training programs for VR. A process analysis with two physiotherapists and two psychotherapists in an executive position of a hospital and rehabilitation center was conducted. All interviews were performed according to a semi-structured guideline. The data were analyzed to the principles of systematic structured content analysis by Mayring using a data analysis program. Regarding multimorbidity and in contrast to the psychotherapists, the physiotherapists recommended an individual therapy for back pain at patients' homes. Regardless, the VR system should support geriatric users by complementing long-term postural correction and muscular strengthening to prevent fear-avoidance behavior. In terms of everyday practice, interventions for the VR treatment of back pain problems in geriatric patients are rarely implemented. Nevertheless, for most of the interviewees the back pain training via VR under the instruction of competent therapists was conceivable at patients' homes.

**Keywords:** Virtual reality · Chronic back pain patients · Training program · Process analysis

## 1 Current Research

### 1.1 Physiotherapists and Psychotherapists in Germany

According to statistics from 2015, 231,000 people were employed in the field of *physiotherapy* [1]. After the three-year qualification has been completed, in Germany it is possible for physiotherapists to work in clinics, nursing homes, rehabilitation centers

© Springer Nature Switzerland AG 2019
J. Y. C. Chen and G. Fragomeni (Eds.): HCII 2019, LNCS 11575, pp. 243–255, 2019.
https://doi.org/10.1007/978-3-030-21565-1_16

and fitness-oriented institutions, but also in physiotherapeutic or medical (mostly orthopedic) practices. However, it is also possible to set up your own practice as an independent physiotherapist [2]. In addition, it is possible to study physiotherapy at a few universities in Germany. After physiotherapeutic treatment has been ordered by the doctor, treatment plans are drawn up and carried out with the patient [2]. This includes so-called passive therapy - guided by the therapist (e.g., massage or manual therapy) after injuries, postural defects, paralysis, etc., and active therapy [3] - movement therapy and independent movement carried out by the patient (e.g., physical therapy) through strengthening exercises to improve posture and coordination [4].

*Psychotherapists*, on the other hand, diagnose, advise and treat people with psychosomatic and mental diseases using psychotherapeutic procedures [5]. The training as a psychotherapist, however, provides for an obligatory university degree, which leads to at least three years' psychotherapeutic qualification with the aim of obtaining a license of approbation at the specialist level [6]. In addition, the training is very cost-intensive and can take up to five years, depending on full or part-time employment. The number of psychotherapists working in Germany has risen by 20% in recent years [7]. According to current figures, in 2015 a total of 40,000 psychotherapists were employed [1] in various care settings: outpatient (practices), inpatient (clinics, clinical palliative wards) and self-employed [5].

## 1.2 Use of Physiotherapeutic or Psychotherapeutic Services for Chronic Back Pain

One of the most common reasons patients seek physiotherapeutic care is back pain (ICD-10: M54), which accounted for one third of patients in 2015 [8–10]. However, the prevalence rates of mental disorders show the highest rate in major depression, followed by phobias and somatoform disorders. However, in mental disorders the comorbidity of physical impairments is to be considered [11]. A study by Wittchen [12] shows the highest co-morbidity rate besides depression of 34.1% in musculoskeletal disorders compared to other physical disorders such as endocrine disorders. This means that back pain does not always have a medical cause, but can also be attributed to psychological complaints. However, there are many reasons patients with progressive chronification make less use of psychotherapeutic help. These include no lasting improvement and with increasing age, a lack of knowledge and motivation as well as reservations and fears with regard to treatment among people aged over 65 [13]. As a result, body-medicated patients incur significantly higher costs and inadequate treatment remains ineffective. Chronic back pain is therefore one of the most cost-intensive [8, 14] and common diseases in older adults [9]. Chronic back pain is increasing with age. The results of a European study show that the prevalence of chronic pain is increasing strongly, especially in people aged over 75. More than 50% of Europeans in this age group suffer from moderate to severe pain every day [15]. The Robert Koch Institute conducted a health survey which shows the prevalence of back pain for the German population, with the finding that while 11.3% of those aged under 30 had an episode of chronic back pain in the last 12 months, the occurrence rate increases to 30.4% in people aged 65 and over [16]. Compared to acute pain, chronic pain is characterized by a duration of at least 3–6 months, a trigger that is no longer clearly recognizable and a reduced quality of life. In addition, chronic pain is associated with physical, mental and social impairments (see Fig. 1).

### 1.3 Interventions with Virtual Reality

Although Virtual Reality (VR) has been researched for years, it is still largely untested beyond the gaming industry in the fields of physiotherapy, psychotherapy, physical medicine and medical technology, and is therefore in the early stages. Current study results show effective treatment successes with VR in psychotherapeutic therapy for fear of heights [17], fear of flying [18] and social phobia [19], as well as depression [20]. In the majority of the therapeutic medicine applications already implemented in case studies, however, it is a question of patients learning certain skills with the help of VR. In contrast, therapies that use VR primarily to distract from symptoms can be identified [21] (for an overview of usage by cancer patients).

Within the therapy the use of VR allows amputated limbs, for example, to be experienced and treats phantom pain [22]. The patient thus experiences an ability which has been lost through an amputation. In another study, burn victims were distracted from pain by using the play instinct [23, 24].

There is already a good evidence base on the effect of virtual therapy in pain patients. However, little is known about the training and use of VR by geriatric patients with chronic back pain.

## 2 Development of a VR Training Program for Geriatric Patients with Chronic Back Pain

### 2.1 Multimodal Pain Therapy as a Treatment for Geriatric Patients with Chronic Back Pain

Pain is a very complex phenomenon that always involves an unpleasant sensory or emotional experience [25]. Pain always goes hand in hand with an emotional experience (e.g., anger, anxiety), a cognitive rating (e.g., dangerous, unpleasant) and a behavioral impulse (e.g., save oneself). As such, psychological factors play an important role and can only be adequately understood and treated within the bio-psycho-social disease model that has been in use since first conceptualized by Engel in 1977 [26]. This model describes the complex network of pain factors that leads to pain intensity and impairment. Persistent pain not only leads to physical changes, such as posture, changes in physical structures (e.g., muscle loss, muscular tension), but also has an effect on the psychological and social level. Due to increasing duration, pain has a negative effect on the psyche, but also on family, peers/friends and professional contexts [27]. For example, over-cautious actions, e.g., due to an accident or injury, often lead to anxiety and excessive protection. Through retreat and protection, the affected person focuses more on the pain and usually perceives it strongly. At the same time, excessive protection leads to increased negative consequences and an endless cycle (e.g., absences from work, conflicts within the family) [28].

With the changed understanding of pain, which goes beyond the biomedical understanding and integrates psychological and social aspects, therapeutic approaches have also expanded. Interdisciplinary multimodal pain therapy is also based on a bio-psycho-social approach. In contrast to the usual purely medical diagnostics, chronic back pain patients must be treated by a broad spectrum of medical, physiotherapeutic, ergotherapeutic (also known as occupational therapeutic) and psychotherapeutic specialists as well as occasionally also including social pedagogues and music and art therapists, by means of the multimodal pain therapy concept in order to grasp all dimensions of the symptoms [29]. In order to achieve the greatest possible effect against back pain, the pain therapeutic assessment is regularly carried out by the interdisciplinary team in a close temporal and spatial context. The aim of multimodal pain therapy is to achieve the best possible pain relief and to improve quality of life. Since patients with chronic pain, for example, exhibit passive or gentle behavior and movement is associated with anxiety and pain, multimodal treatment is intended to show patients that movement and stress do not cause harm, but are useful and necessary for maintaining physical functionality [30].

## 2.2    The Joint Project ViRST

*Physiotherapeutic and psychotherapeutic therapy* represent an important contribution to multimodal pain therapy for this large group of patients. This type of therapy requires a high degree of patients' initiative. By using VR, the possibilities and motivation for physiotherapeutic and psychotherapeutic therapies should be significantly increased both in inpatient care institutions and at home. Therefore, a joint project called ViRST was initiated to develop a concept for multimodal pain treatments for chronic, geriatric back pain patients using an immersive VR exergame and sensor technology. The research project is financed by the German Federal Ministry of Education and Research (BMBF). This project is an ongoing project, which lasts two years and began in April 2018. The purpose is not to replace the conventional, medical therapy but to complete and combine the physiotherapeutic and psychotherapeutic approach within a multimodal pain therapy concept. The objective of the research project is also to explore and implement a concept for the therapeutic use of innovations as demonstrations in the field of VR from both a medical and commercial perspective, based on existing basic research.

## 2.3    Concept of ViRST

This approach intends to create a new non-pharmacological therapy concept. The following innovations should provide this new therapy concept:

- The use of personalized and adaptive VR based on immersive interaction sequences and gamification
- The sensor-based presentation of content with dynamic, adaptive and personalized storytelling for therapeutic recommendations through multimodal interaction with the content

The conventional multimodal pain therapy concept envisages a therapy of approximately four to six weeks initially in an inpatient context. The concept requires not only a high degree of personal initiative on the part of the patient, but also a certain motivation for sustainable use, which does however tend to decrease considerably towards the transition to the inpatient context, because the patients usually feel overwhelmed. With the virtual therapy by ViRST an improved therapeutic supply, lower waiting times, as well as more acceptance and compliance is intended. Accordingly, the system is planned to be designed so that it is not environment dependent, so that back pain patients can perform their exercises in the virtual room, e.g., in nature, as well as in a sports hall.

In addition, the system can first be trained in the inpatient setting and the multimodal concept can be continued within the outpatient setting. According to the different disciplines, different learning and exercise content can also be integrated, e.g., to avoid coping strategies.

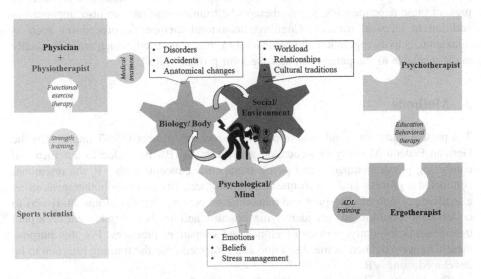

**Fig. 1.** The complement of the VR therapy program within the different disciplines of the multimodal pain therapy concept and the bio-psycho-social influencing factors on a back pain patient.

The figure (Fig. 1) summarizes the complex interaction of different disciplines for the diagnosis and treatment of geriatric patients with chronic back pain via a VR training program and vital sensors with regard to the bio-psycho-social pain model described in Sect. 1. These innovations described above are applied in the following two therapies.

**Physiotherapeutic Pain Therapy**
Due to the positive effects of regular physical activity on pain patients, an interactive, customizable training program for patients with chronic back pain will be developed. The therapist has a pool of exercises in one training plan, which can be made available to the patient according to the patient's individual needs. The patient can independently perform the recommended exercises in an inpatient care institution or in the patient's home environment. Various motivational feedback and gamification elements are integrated to strengthen long-term use. After a training session, the patient is asked about the current degree of pain through standardized assessments (e.g., Short Form 8-Health Survey [SF 8]) and satisfaction with the training. The therapist also receives this feedback in order to enable any necessary adjustments to the training plan.

**Psychotherapeutic Pain Therapy**
Somatic complaints always have a psychological component. On the one hand, psychological stress (e.g. overload, conflicts) can cause pain. On the other hand, physical pain causes psychological symptoms (e.g. sleep disorders, depression). In order to prevent these dependencies, psychotherapeutic training sessions are also important in addition to physical training. Cognitive-behavioral therapeutic procedures such as relaxation, activity regulation and behavioral exercises are used, which are individually made available to the patient through the joint project ViRST.

## 3 Methods

The present study was conducted as part of the research project ViRST financed by the German Federal Ministry of Education and Research (BMBF). Due to our focus on combining physiotherapeutic and psychotherapeutic concepts with VR, the researcher conducted a process analysis to question physiotherapists and psychotherapists in an executive position of a hospital and rehabilitation center. The aim of this study was to collect data about the process-identifying structure and needs within current back pain treatments in the daily practice of clinics and outpatient practices. For this purpose these data were defined as the status quo and projected onto the training program to be developed using VR.

The Charité - Universitätsmedizin Berlin was the study center and recruited all participants for the present study. Before interviews started, experts were informed about the study contents and inclusion and exclusion criteria were reviewed.

These included:

- Experience in the treatment of chronic back pain patients
- At least three years' professional experience with back pain patients
- Currently working as a physiotherapist or psychotherapist

In addition, care was taken to ensure that experts were recruited from both the outpatient and inpatient sectors. After that, participants had 24 h to give their final decision with regard to the agreement of the study. Before interviews started, all participants gave written informed consent. Furthermore, the participants received a questionnaire with questions regarding their socio-demographic status, e.g., age, gender, professional position, etc. In addition, physiotherapists and psychotherapists were asked to watch a film sequence that gives a brief insight into the therapy with VR.

All interviews were conducted by telephone, took approximately 30 min and were performed according to a semi-structured guideline, developed by the researchers. The guideline contained several subjects and questions related to training concepts, training setting, therapy and training units (e.g., activity regulation) in order to enable reliable assessments to which implementation in the VR system can lead to significant time savings. Consequently, changes in the therapy process and existing training barriers were identified. At the end of the telephone interview, quantifiable decision questions were asked, e.g., regarding the offer of individual or group therapy in VR as well as documentation in the conventional way or documentation in the system. The system to be developed is expected to improve therapy adherence by supporting virtual self-training with the help of a therapist.

## 4   Data Analysis

Each of the four semi-structured interviews was recorded and partially transcribed using a result protocol to summarize the most important contents of the interviews. After completion, two trained scientists analyzed the interviews according to the principles of Mayring's systematic structured content analysis [31] using the data analysis program ATLAS.ti 8. This involved certain techniques for code-taking, paraphrasing, generalization and reduction of the codes. The following figure shows the process of Mayring's systematic content analysis (Fig. 2). The process of coding required continuous reworking, changes and the adding of new codes, which were not included in the semi-structured manual. After the final paraphrasing, generalization and reduction, the codes were categorized to generate the requirements. With a view to avoiding errors and ensuring the statistical reliability of the collected data, the two scientists worked on the "four-eyes" principle, and the coding and analysis were controlled reciprocally. For example, the following codes were collected: duration, length of pause, frequency of the therapy, documentation, accounting procedures, safety factors, etc. Since the final requirements for the conception and the further progress of the project play an important role, these requirements were prioritized within a workshop with all project partners. Moreover, quantitative socio-demographic data were also collected, e.g., the profession of the therapists or position within the institution.

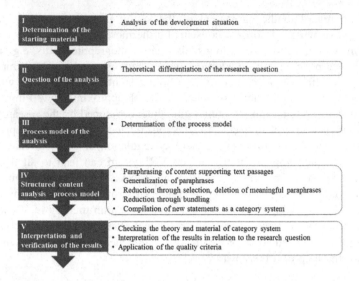

| I<br>Determination of the<br>starting material | • Analysis of the development situation |
| II<br>Question of the analysis | • Theoretical differentiation of the research question |
| III<br>Process model of the<br>analysis | • Determination of the process model |
| IV<br>Structured content<br>analysis – process model | • Paraphrasing of content supporting text passages<br>• Generalization of paraphrases<br>• Reduction through selection, deletion of meaningful paraphrases<br>• Reduction through bundling<br>• Compilation of new statements as a category system |
| V<br>Interpretation and<br>verification of the results | • Checking the theory and material of category system<br>• Interpretation of the results in relation to the research question<br>• Application of the quality criteria |

**Fig. 2.** Process of Mayring's systematic content analysis

# 5  Results

## 5.1  Sample

A total of four experts who care for and have daily contact with geriatric, chronic back pain patients were interviewed. Two of these interviewees were engaged in the profession of physiotherapy ($\male = 1$; $\female = 1$) in an expert position, while two other interviewees had a current employment relationship as psychotherapists/psychologists ($\female = 2$) in a managerial position. Furthermore, they were experts from the outpatient ($n = 2$) and inpatient ($n = 2$) care sector. Two of the respondents stated that they were more likely to be in contact with patients with age-related diseases, such as dementia, fractures caused by falls or pain syndromes caused by degenerative diseases. These respondents also had a thematic expertise in the treatment of geriatric patients. In the decision questions, the interviewees stated that they could imagine both individual and group therapy for pain therapy using VR. Three participants indicated that the system should be applied to patients' homes, while one respondent felt that it should be used in the equipment room under general supervision (Fig. 3). All respondents agreed that written documentation should be maintained in the system. Moreover, all respondents had no experience with current technologies in the field of VR in everyday professional life and did not use VR for diagnostics or therapy with chronic RS patients. Since the ViRST project aims to create a physiotherapeutic as well as a psychotherapeutic pain therapy concept, the different types of expertise are separated in the following.

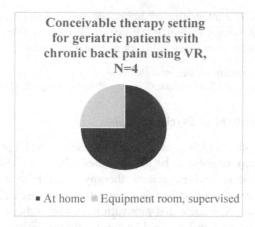

**Fig. 3.** Conceivable therapy setting for back pain patients using VR

## 5.2    Process Perspectives of Physiotherapists

In order to implement a VR *therapy concept* for geriatric patients with chronic back pain, the physiotherapists could imagine both mobility and relaxation training as well as cardiovascular warm-up and cool-down phases during breaks, in addition to conventional therapy. Additionally, it would be conceivable to adjust the sensorimotor system of the central nervous system within long-term of use of VR therapy through spinal stabilization training.

> *"Since we exclusively treat pain patients (...) and therefore the recognition and observation of movements and exercises [is important], I can imagine very well to implement work-hardening (...) also referred as every day training (...) with exercises for everyday life such as bending, lifting, turning into the system." (♂)*                                                                    (1)

For the *duration and frequency of therapy*, the interviewees found therapy units ranging from daily use to at least two or three times a week to be recommended. The VR therapy should either be part of a holistic, therapeutic treatment or offered as part of an outpatient multimodal pain therapy. The participants agreed that an average therapy duration of 30 min should not be exceeded with the VR system.

Regarding the *therapeutic environment*, the physiotherapists recommended individual therapy units for home training considering the multimorbidity of geriatric patients.

> *"It would be better to have 1:1 contact and then take it home, that's very important. Because it's definitely a stimulus that needs to be used frequently to really change the nervous system, to adapt [to] the [ViRST system]." (♂)*                                                                    (2)

In order to *implement the therapy the therapy program*, it is recommended that patients first learn how to use the system in the practice or clinic in order to be able to handle the VR system after discharge from the hospital to their homes. Employees in the inpatient care sector should be given the opportunity by technical instructors to try out the functionality of the VR system themselves with a loan device. The integration of a documentation tool should facilitate the obligatory documentation of physiotherapists and psychotherapists. The integration of diagnostic assessments would be conceivable. In order to use the VR therapy system, it is necessary to receive a detailed safety briefing in advance, for example, to prevent fall risks as much as possible.

> *"There is surely such a safety briefing, so in the sense of, "if you can't do more, then close your eyes or open your eyes and lift your glasses" is actually quite sufficient." (♂)*        (3)

## 5.3  Process Perspectives of Psychotherapists

The interviewed psychotherapists considered an educational approach to be very suitable for the ***therapy concept*** to be implemented. Concepts and exercises that are based on communication and behavioral therapy (e.g., relaxation exercises) and therefore require patients to reflect and deal with their own disease, have a supportive and positive effect on compliance and motivation. Among other things, showing the movements as a biofeedback in VR could be helpful for the patient, e.g., to avoid pain-induced incorrect postures and movements in the future.

> *"Psychotherapeutically, the educational part would be that there might be some kind of introduction or an avatar to accompany the [training]." (♀)*        (4)

For the ***duration and frequency of therapy***, it is important to offer long-term regular therapy units in VR pain therapy, with the aim of using the system at least three times a week up to daily use during the inpatient stay. Accordingly, it can be assumed that the frequency of use of the system in outpatient care or by patients with chronic back pain living at home will decrease. Nevertheless, back pain patients should aim for and the system should support training once a day. The duration of a unit should not exceed 30 min.

The interviewees could imagine the inpatient as well as the outpatient care sector as the ***therapy environment***. In an inpatient context, it is important to train and instruct the use of the system with the help of physiotherapists or professional instructors to intervene in the case of incorrectly performed exercises, in order to avoid protective and avoidance postures in long-term use. In the ambulatory context, it is important that the system automatically has a corrective and stimulating effect.

> *"I imagine that would be a bit strange if all eight people had glasses on. (...) In the education units, they could wear it more easily and talk about it. (...) I think in the group you have to make sure that everyone has these [glasses] on (...)." (♀)*        (5)
> *"In any case, it must first have been tested with the patient, in the presence of a therapist. The therapist must introduce him, explain it to him, try it out with him and finally show the patient how to use it. Only then, if the patient is either able to deal with it, or if relatives are there, that is also another variant (...), only then it would come into question for independent practicing at all." (♀)*        (6)

For the ***implementation of the therapy concept into a therapy program***, the interviewees could imagine digital documentation of the therapy units, e.g., via tablet or similar devices. The interviewees could also explicitly imagine that psychological test procedures could be illustrated and evaluated. Before back pain patients learn the system, professionals such as physiotherapists and psychotherapists should learn how to use the system and there should be given the opportunity to test the VR system themselves.

*"We experience with all electronic or digital [systems] that a lot of lead time is required as well as the training of staff. And I would definitely let the employees try it out for themselves."* (9) (7)

With regard to safety precautions, care should be taken that the therapy room offers sufficient freedom of movement to keep the risk of falls as low as possible. In addition, as a safety precaution (e.g., in case of dizziness), it should be made possible for the VR system to switch itself off immediately.

*"During standing exercises, there should be a way for the patient to hold on securely."* (9) (8)

# 6 Discussion and Conclusion

The aim of the study was to determine the process-identifying needs of a VR training program for geriatric patients with chronic back pain. While the majority of studies concerning VR therapies have so far been more evidenced with fears, such as fear of flying [18, 32], depression [20], phobias [19], there are however also controlled case studies dealing with the effect on pain patients [22–24], the study situation for VR-treated, geriatric back pain patients is efficient. While some studies are more concerned with how patients with VR (re)learn certain skills [17, 33], case studies show how VR is used to primarily distract from symptoms [21]. The ViRST project is less about distracting from symptoms through VR and more about providing drug-based, conventional therapy to supplement chronic, geriatric back pain patients. Therefore the holistic, interdisciplinary approach of multimodal pain therapy [30] is applied, which is generally recommended in Germany according to the national care guideline [34]. Within the underlying process analysis of this project, experts in physiotherapy and psychotherapy filtered out the contents of the therapy program that are important for conceptualization. General exercises in physiotherapy and psychotherapy, the duration and frequency of therapy, the therapeutic environment and the implementation in the therapy program were discussed.

This paper highlighted the difference between the conventional pain therapy concept and the ViRST therapy program. While the conventional pain therapy concept ends after four to a maximum of six weeks [34] in the inpatient setting and compliance decreases strongly at the transition into outpatient setting, the ViRST therapy program also serves the holistic, multimodal approach, but with the possibility to continue the therapy in the outpatient environment long-term and regularly with all learned exercises. This aims for better therapeutic care, less waiting time for therapy units and more acceptance. Since the multimodal concept provides for a therapist to instruct in the exercises and to advise and correct incorrect postures, the experts for the VR therapy program initially recommend a therapist to provide guidance and instruction. This therapist can be replaced in the home setting by integrating educational learning content and motion sensors in order to provide corrective support.

In the future, it may be possible that VR therapy could also be used for employees with back pain as well as for other target groups. This is because back pain is a most-common disease for which immense costs could be saved by the health insurance funds [8, 14]. In addition, it would be conceivable to offer the VR therapy program within other inpatient settings such as rehabilitation facilities. The ViRST therapy program will initially be implemented on the basis of physiotherapeutic and psychotherapeutic content. However, it may also be feasible to implement sports science, music or occupational therapy content in order to complete the holistic multimodal pain therapy approach.

# References

1. Statistisches Bundesamt: Gesundheitspersonal - Fachserie 12 Reihe 7.3.1. 48 (2017)
2. Physiotherapie in Deutschland - Berufliche Tätigkeit Physiotherapeut/in. https://www. physio.de/physio/taetigkeit.php
3. Deutscher Verband für Physiotherapie (ZVK) - Definition Physiotherapie. https://www. physio-deutschland.de/patienten-interessierte/physiotherapie/definition.html
4. Deutscher Verband für Physiotherapie (ZVK) – Krankengymnastik. https://www.physio-deutschland.de/patienten-interessierte/wichtige-therapien-auf-einen-blick/krankengymnastik. html
5. Berufsverband Deutscher Psychologinnen und Psychologen (BDP) - Berufsbild Psychologischer Psychotherapeut. https://www.bdp-verband.de/binaries/content/assets/beruf/berufsbild/psychologische-psychotherapie.pdf
6. Deutsche Psychotherapeuten Vereinigung (DPtV). https://www.deutschepsychotherapeuten vereinigung.de/der-verband/lg/hessen/angestellte-psychotherapeuten/
7. Verband Psychologischer Psychotherapeutinnen und Psychotherapeuten (VPP) - Die Psychotherapeutenausbildung. https://www.vpp.org/politik/ausbildung/
8. Robert Koch-Institut: Inanspruchnahme physiotherapeutischer Leistungen in Deutschland. RKI-Bib1 Robert Koch-Inst. (2017). https://doi.org/10.17886/rki-gbe-2017-118
9. Wong, A.Y., Karppinen, J., Samartzis, D.: Low back pain in older adults: risk factors, management options and future directions. Scoliosis Spinal Disord. **12** (2017). https://doi. org/10.1186/s13013-017-0121-3
10. Statista - TOP 10 Diagnosen für Verordnungen von Krankengymnastik im Jahr 2016. https:// de.statista.com/statistik/daten/studie/701816/umfrage/top-10-diagnosen-fuer-verordnungen-von-krankengymnastik/
11. Senf, W., Broda, M.: Praxis der Psychotherapie - Ein integratives Lehrbuch. Thieme Verlag KG, Stuttgart, New York, Delhi, Rio (2012)
12. Wittchen, H.-U., Hoyer, J. (eds.): Klinische Psychologie & Psychotherapie. Springer, Berlin Heidelberg (2011). https://doi.org/10.1007/978-3-642-13018-2
13. Peters, M.: Psychosoziale Beratung und Psychotherapie im Alter. Vandenhoeck & Ruprecht (2006)
14. Robert-Koch-Institut: Gesundheitsberichterstattung des Bundes. Heft 53. Rückenschmerzen. 36
15. König, H.-H.: Health status of the advanced elderly in six european countries: results from a representative survey using EQ-5D and SF-12. 11 (2010)
16. Gesundheitsberichterstattung des Bundes, Gesundheit in Deutschland - Prävalenz ausgewählter Muskel-Skelett-Erkrankungen. http://www.gbe-bund.de/gbe10/abrechnung.prc_abr_test_logon?p_uid=gast&p_aid=0&p_knoten=FID&p_sprache=D&p_suchstring=24192
17. Emmelkamp, P.M., Krijn, M., Hulsbosch, A., de Vries, S., Schuemie, M., van der Mast, C. A.P.: Virtual reality treatment versus exposure in vivo: a comparative evaluation in acrophobia. Behav. Res. Ther. **40**, 509–516 (2002). https://doi.org/10.1016/S0005-7967(01) 00023-7

18. Wiederhold, B.K., Gevirtz, R.N., Spira, J.L.: 14 Virtual Reality Exposure Therapy vs. Imagery Desensitization Therapy in the Treatment of Flying Phobia. 21
19. Klinger, E., et al.: Virtual reality therapy versus cognitive behavior therapy for social phobia: a preliminary controlled study. Cyberpsychol. Behav. **8**, 76–88 (2005). https://doi.org/10.1089/cpb.2005.8.76
20. Falconer, C.J., et al.: Embodying self-compassion within virtual reality and its effects on patients with depression. BJPsych Open. **2**, 74–80 (2016). https://doi.org/10.1192/bjpo.bp.115.002147
21. Chirico, A., Lucidi, F., Laurentiis, M.D., Milanese, C., Napoli, A., Giordano, A.: Virtual reality in health system: beyond entertainment. a mini-review on the efficacy of VR during cancer treatment. J. Cell. Physiol. **231**, 275–287 (2016). https://doi.org/10.1002/jcp.25117
22. Lewis, T., Writer, S.: Virtual Reality Treatment Relieves Amputee's Phantom Pain. https://www.livescience.com/43665-virtual-reality-treatment-for-phantom-limb-pain.html
23. Maani, C., Hoffman, H.G., Magula, J., Maiers, A., Gaylord, K.: Pain control during wound care for combat-related burn injuries using custom articulated arm mounted virtual reality goggles. 6 (2008)
24. Ambron, E., Miller, A., Kuchenbecker, K.J., Buxbaum, L.J., Coslett, H.B.: Immersive low-cost virtual reality treatment for phantom limb pain: evidence from two cases. Front. Neurol. **9** (2018). https://doi.org/10.3389/fneur.2018.00067
25. Merskey, H., International Association for the Study of Pain (eds.): Classification of Chronic Pain: Descriptions of Chronic Pain Syndromes and Definitions of Pain Terms. IASP Press, Seattle (1994)
26. Engel, G.L.: The need for a new medical model: a challenge for biomedicine. Science **196**, 129–136 (1977). https://doi.org/10.1126/science.847460
27. Kröner-Herwig, B.: Schmerz als biopsychosoziales Phänomen – eine Einführung. In: Kröner-Herwig, B., Frettlöh, J., Klinger, R., Nilges, P. (eds.) Schmerzpsychotherapie, pp. 3–16. Springer, Heidelberg (2017). https://doi.org/10.1007/978-3-642-12783-0_1
28. Neustadt, K., Kaiser, U., Sabatowski, R.: Das biopsychosoziale Schmerzmodell: Entwicklung, Definition und Implikationen. In: Langenmayr, A., Radbruch, L. (eds.) Was hält Leib und Seele zusammen? pp. 49–54. Vandenhoeck & Ruprecht, Göttingen (2017)
29. Casser, H.-R., et al.: Interdisziplinäres Assessment zur multimodalen Schmerztherapie: Indikation und Leistungsumfang. Schmerz. **27**, 363–370 (2013). https://doi.org/10.1007/s00482-013-1337-7
30. Hildebrandt, J., Pfingsten, M., Franz, C., Saur, P., Seeger, D.: Das Göttinger Rücken Intensiv Programm (GRIP)—ein multimodales Behandlungsprogramm für Patienten mit chronischen Rückenschmerzen, Teil 1. Schmerz. **10**, 190–203 (1996). https://doi.org/10.1007/s004820050040
31. Mayring, P.: Qualitative Inhaltsanalyse: Grundlagen und Techniken. Beltz (2010)
32. Schubert, T., Regenbrecht, H.: Wer hat Angst vor virtueller Realität? 35
33. Emmelkamp, P.M.G., Bruynzeel, M., Drost, L., van der Mast, C.A.P.G.: Virtual reality treatment in acrophobia: a comparison with exposure in vivo. Cyberpsychol. Behav. **4**, 335–339 (2001). https://doi.org/10.1089/109493101300210222
34. Nationale VersorgungsLeitlinie Nicht-spezifischer Kreuzschmerz – Kurzfassung, 2. Auflage. Version 1. 43 (2017)

# A Multi-procedural Virtual Reality Simulator for Orthopaedic Training

Gino De Luca[✉], Nusrat Choudhury, Catherine Pagiatakis,
and Denis Laroche

National Research Council Canada, Boucherville, Canada
Gino.DeLuca@nrc.ca

**Abstract.** Interactive simulation based on virtual reality (VR) offers a valuable complement to the conventional apprenticeship for surgical skills training. Orthopaedic VR surgical training is relatively new but has been quickly evolving over the last decade. A few simulators are commercially available to train the high volume arthroscopic procedures. However, open orthopaedic interventions are thus far inadequately covered. This paper presents a prototype of a multi-procedural VR platform accommodating three different anatomical sites. An iterative development process was employed to develop the interactive simulator. This stems from the fact that the overall quality, accuracy and realism of a medical task simulation requires an optimal balance between several interdependent factors and that surgical cues are often automated in the expert. The VR prototype targets open orthopaedic surgery training. It integrates the use of tactile and visual feedback for bimanual interactive practice of technical and procedural skills in three different specialties: transforaminal lumbar interbody fusion in spine surgery, antegrade femoral nailing in traumatology and orbital floor reconstruction in craniomaxillofacial surgery. The working prototype meets the requirements established with the subject matter experts (SMEs). The next step targets the validation by residents and surgeons for surgical skills training.

**Keywords:** Education and training · Medical and healthcare ·
Surgical skill training · Interactive simulation · Virtual reality ·
Psychomotor skills · Orthopaedic surgery · NeuroTouch · NeuroVR · Haptics

## 1 Introduction

Surgery requires a high level of knowledge, cognitive decision-making and communication skills as well as a high level of dexterity [1]. Dexterity typically refers to the ability to precisely coordinate the movements of small muscles in one's wrists, hands and fingers with one's eyes in order to perform a given task. This psychomotor skill is not necessarily innate or hereditary and can be acquired and reinforced by experience and practice [1–3].

The worldwide, long-standing, gold standard for surgical training is the Halstedian apprenticeship model in which the operating room and patient are used as the forum for teaching and learning [4, 5]. Although effective, this model is not optimal because it

J. Y. C. Chen and G. Fragomeni (Eds.): HCII 2019, LNCS 11575, pp. 256–271, 2019.
https://doi.org/10.1007/978-3-030-21565-1_17

requires the apprentice to be exposed to a large number of surgeries that can only be taught by a limited number of faculty mentors. This is problematic in modern medical practice where working hour restrictions, institutional financial pressure as well as ethical and medico-legal issues further reduces training opportunities and hands-on experience for apprentices [4–6]. In addition, this method only offers a subjective evaluation of skill acquisition. For these reasons, surgical education has been undergoing an important paradigm shift in recent years wherein simulation-based training (SBT) has grown in importance and is used to effectively and efficiently complement traditional patient-based training [3, 5, 7–9].

SBT has several advantages. First, is that it is safe for the patient. Usually occurring in dedicated laboratories, it offers the apprentice the possibility to develop their skills in a standardized environment, without the pressure of the operating room, thus permitting consequence-free mistakes to be made. Immediate objective performance measures can also be obtained, permitting measures-based evaluation criteria compared to the traditional subjective evaluation [5, 7]. Today, several important medical organizations and associations recognize the potential benefits of SBT and are advocating its use, such as the Food and Drug Administration (FDA) who has endorsed its role for a decade. In the specific field of orthopaedics, the American Board of Orthoapedic Surgery (ABOS) and American Academy of Orthopaedic Surgeons (AAOS) have also clearly expressed their support [5, 10, 11].

As in other surgical specialties, SBT in orthopaedics is performed with physical (cadaveric, live animal and synthetic) and computer-based models [3, 7–9]. Computer-based models are relatively new compared to their physical counterparts but have been quickly evolving over the last decade due to technological advancements and increased clinician involvement [3]. They can potentially circumvent some of the limitations presented by physical models such as ethical and regulatory restrictions, expensive procurement and maintenance, risk for disease transmission as well as reduced realism with respect to anatomy, tactile feedback and physiological dynamics and the need for supervised training and assessment [3, 7–9].

Computer-based models typically teach and/or train the key steps of a given surgery using various input and output modalities and levels of immersion. In its simplest form, a training simulator can consist of a smartphone- or tablet-based application, such as the one developed by TouchSurgery [12]. Although this mobile application does not offer an immersive or natural hand-based psychomotor interaction, it permits apprentices to cognitively simulate the key steps of several standard surgical procedures [9, 11]. In its more sophisticated form, a training simulator can consist of a medical cart workstation using 3D glasses or a VR headset for immersion and haptic devices to manipulate a computer-generated surgical scene. While most forms of computer-based simulation offer opportunities for self-paced and self-directed learning, those that incorporate hand-based interactions with haptics can potentially offer a more realistic learning experience and more advanced metrics with regards to manual skills [3, 8, 9]. Finally interactive systems can provide immediate objective performance measures and feedback favoring optimal learning which not only helps to assess trainee competency and progress but also builds confidence and an understanding of the corresponding technique [3, 4, 7, 9]. Despite their potential, there are few commercially-available computer-based orthopaedic training simulators.

This paper describes the development of a new VR orthopaedic simulator by the National Research Council of Canada (NRC). NRC has previously developed interactive simulation platforms for various surgical specialties including endoscopy, otolaryngology, cardiothoracic surgery [13–16] and most notably for neurosurgery with NeuroTouch (now distributed as NeuroVR by CAE Healthcare, Montreal, Canada) [17–21]. The simulator developed in this work is haptic-based, multi-procedural and allows for task-based bimanual skills training. The prototype targets three different specialties of orthopaedic surgery: transforaminal lumbar interbody fusion (TLIF) in spine surgery, antegrade femoral nailing in traumatology and orbital floor reconstruction in craniomaxillofacial (CMF) surgery. This paper is organized as follows: Sect. 2 consists of a brief overview of existing commercial haptic-based orthopaedic simulators; Sect. 3 describes the development process employed to create the simulator; Sect. 4 presents the resulting design; Sects. 5 and 6 respectively present a discussion and future work.

## 2 Background

Virtual reality simulation training has been well established in high-risk industries and pioneering works in laparoscopic surgery have shown evidence of shortened learning curves and improved patient outcomes [5]. Recent reviews have gathered, classified and presented the different simulators that have been developed and reported for skills and surgical procedure training in orthopaedics [3, 8, 22]. From these reviews, it appears that, while a number of research initiatives seem to have led to interesting VR training platforms, only a few have become commercially available. To the best of the authors' knowledge, this short list includes: Sim-Ortho by OSSimTech (Montreal, Canada), TraumaVision and ArthroVision by Sewmac (Linköping, Sweden), Arthro-Sim by ToLTech (Aurora, USA), ArthroMentor by 3D Systems (formerly Simbionix, Littleton, USA) and ArthroS by VirtaMed (Zurich, Switzerland), summarized in Table 1.

**Table 1.** Features of commercially available simulators for orthopaedic training

| Simulator name | Anatomical region targeted | Simultaneous instruments | Haptics | Handles | View |
|---|---|---|---|---|---|
| Sim-Ortho | Spine, femur, knee | 1 | 5DOF | Generic | Patient 3D, fluoroscopic |
| TraumaVision | Spine, hip | 1 | 3DOF | Stylus | Patient 2D, fluoroscopic |
| ArthroVision | None | 2 | 3DOF | Stylus | Arthroscopic |
| ArthroSim | Shoulder, knee | 2 | 3DOF | Realistic | Arthroscopic |
| ArthroMentor | Shoulder, hip, knee | 2 | 3DOF | Generic | Arthroscopic |
| ArthroS | Shoulder, hip, knee | 2 | None | Realistic | Arthroscopic, fluoroscopic |

All of the commercial simulators that permit the simultaneous use of two instruments (i.e. bimanual) target arthroscopic training. These simulators allow for surgical techniques and skills training by using 3 degree-of-freedom (DOF) haptic systems for force feedback. In addition, they provide 2D graphics rendering for simulated arthroscopic view and, in some cases, offer an additional 2D patient and/or fluoroscopic view. One simulator outside of the arthroscopic domain uses a single 5DOF haptic system. A 5DOF device allows for torque feedback in addition to force. Thus, bimanual skills training is currently not well covered for open orthopaedic procedures involving the anatomical region of the spine, femur, knee and hip; only training exercises involving one instrument are available. Each of the simulator platforms provide to the user either the original stylus of the haptic device at the hand or have modified end-effectors to connect generic or realistic surgical instrument handles.

# 3  Method

## 3.1  General Requirements

The key requirements, defined in conjunction with the SMEs, were to (1) develop a multi-procedural prototype accommodating three different anatomical sites on a single platform. This includes permitting 3D, fluoroscopic and endoscopic views as well as surgical instrument interaction with both non-deformable, hard bone and soft tissue (examples: nerve, dura and muscle). Consequently, a haptic system being able to reproduce the appropriate workspace and tactile feedback for a wide range of tissue stiffness was required. As well, this entails the additional requirement to (2) provide multiple instruments with the possibility for bimanual haptic feedback and single-handed dynamic tool exchange as well as to (3) implement the corresponding virtual surgical instrument models. An additional requirement was to (4) create 3D computational models from anatomical segmentations provided by the SMEs. A final requirement was to (5) conceptualize pedagogical exercises targeting the essential skills navigable with a basic user interface.

## 3.2  Instrument Interaction Requirements

There were requirements specific to the procedure to be simulated. They focused on representing the functionalities and interactions of a given surgical instrument. For each procedure, the key surgical instruments were identified and are described below. Note that the suction and bipolar instruments are available and used for multiple procedures. More specifically, the suction aspirates blood to clear the operative view and retract tissue. The bipolar is used for grasping and to manage bleeding by cauterizing tissue.

**Transforaminal Lumbar Interbody Fusion.** Five different surgical instruments were required for this procedure namely the microdrill, Kerrison punch, bone curette, rongeur and implant applicator. The microdrill erodes bone to thin away the planned resection area. The Kerrison punch cuts out soft and hard tissue while protecting underlying delicate structures. The bone curette strips tissues (softer than bone) and is used to scoop away disc nucleus and scrape cartilaginous endplates. The rongeur grasps and bluntly tears away the disc nucleus. The implant applicator is used to manipulate and position the implant. When bound to the instrument, blunt force applied to the applicator allows the implant to be advanced into the disc opening. The implant can interact with surrounding structures and is geometrically constrained by the disc corridor such that if a proper angle is maintained, it will advance into the proper position.

**Lateral Femoral Nailing.** Four instruments were to be made available in this simulated procedure namely an awl, guidewire, reamer and drill. The awl, when forced against the bone and simultaneously rotated, pierces through cortical bone to create a canal. The guidewire then enters this canal and penetrates spongy bone to create the pilot path for the reamer. The guidewire is flexible and therefore bends when any part of its length is constrained by the femoral shaft. The reamer erodes the medullary canal in order to accommodate the femoral nail. Finally, the drill erodes through cortical bone to allow for screws to be inserted for distal locking of the nail. Several reamer head and drill bit sizes should be made available.

**Orbital Floor Reconstruction.** Five surgical instruments were required for the procedure, namely the malleable retractor, periosteal freer elevator, plate-holding forceps, screwdriver and endoscope. The malleable retractor holds back (retracts) the contents of the orbit to expose the surgical site. The periosteal freer elevator strips away tissue adhesions to expose bone. The plate holding forceps are used to grasp, displace and position the orbital plate (implant used to cover the orbital floor fracture). The screwdriver manipulates (binds to, displaces and inserts) screws into bone in order to fix the orbital plate into place. The endoscope provides a magnified 2D view to inspect the surgical bed.

### 3.3   Analysis and Mock-Ups

Meetings were held for each of the targeted procedures with the corresponding SME to establish key steps and essential skills to learn. The required surgical instruments functionalities, their interactions with tissues as well as the anatomical structure/tissue representation and behaviour were elaborated. The emerging conclusions from the analysis stage were conceptualized as mock-ups detailing task definition and simulation scene content. The procedures were broken down with start and end points/conditions, including identification of the surgical view. The simulation scenarios were conceptualized with pedagogical content including: training goals, learning activities, surgical landmarks and cues as well as performance measures. A similar process was previously used by the team for neurosurgical simulation [18].

### 3.4   Iterative Development Process

The overall quality, accuracy and realism of a medical task simulation is contingent upon an optimal balance between several interdependent factors. These factors are related to both surgical task analysis and technical (software and hardware) development and implementation. A strategy is to obtain guidance and expert feedback at the start of the development cycle to assure that what is being developed will be valid and useful for the end user. Their input is not only necessary at the start of development, but also throughout the process because surgical cues are often automated in the expert; as successively more comprehensive and refined simulations are tested, details regarding surgical cues and intervention/simulation features that were not previously discussed can come to surface. In addition, an optimal level of detail in the models that meet the surgical task objectives and real-time simulation constraints must be validated by the SMEs. For example, the level of detail of the mesh and mechanical models should preserve a realistic perception for the user, both on the visual and haptic level. Due to the nature of the task as well as the extensive number of requirements, an iterative design process consisting of several cycles of implementation, internal testing and external demonstration to end users was used.

**Implementation.** The implementation consisted of translating the requirements, as well as the results from the analysis phase into their respective hardware and software components: (1) a hardware design to accommodate the various ergonomics constraints imposed by several anatomical sites and procedures was targeted. In order to adequately capture the different workspaces for the three interventions as well as to represent the required hard and soft tactile feedback, it was determined that custom haptics would be required; (2) physical handles with custom connectors to permit dynamic tool exchange were fabricated; (3) virtual models of the instruments were implemented within an in-house simulation software. Visual rendering was based on CAD files provided by the SMEs. Collision detection of instruments was primitive-based: cylindrical, spherical and box primitives were used to represent their geometry. New instrument mechanisms (for example flexible and bending wires) and interaction models (for example tissue punching) were implemented, as well as the functionalities to manipulate rigid bodies (surgical objects). New software features were also developed and integrated, in particular, rigid body dynamics and their interaction with tissues and other manipulated rigid bodies; (4) for the development of 3D models, the basic segmented anatomical models provided by the SMEs were systematically refined via sculpting using Blender [23], capturing the relevant tissues/structures as well as their state (for example: whether the tissue is retracted). The computational tissue models were subsequently generated using in-house software; (5) key skills training in orthopaedics were identified for each of the interventions. Generally, in orthopaedics, a positive outcome depends on the surgeon's proficiency in using appropriate, albeit high, force to perform specific manipulations while aiming to protect surrounding soft tissue [3]. Accordingly, the exercises were designed with an emphasis on performing force-based tasks while capturing errors involving injury to critical structures.

**Internal Testing.** Successive iterations of individual software and hardware developments were tested together. Specifically, the visual and haptic realism was evaluated while verifying that real-time performance was met (i.e. simulation's clock runs at the same speed or faster as a real clock). This involved iterating on the computational mesh resolution while still capturing key anatomical structures as well as adapting the models representing surgical instrument interaction with tissues. It was also verified that hard bone and soft tissue could be distinguished. Mechanical properties from literature were used as a starting point, and subsequently adjusted to achieve realistic behaviour with optimal simulation performance. The usability of the cart by the end-user, as related to ergonomics, was also tested.

**External Demonstration.** Several hands-on and interactive demonstrations were scheduled with the SMEs during the developmental process. These demonstrations served to highlight the advancements and validate the simulations from a clinical perspective. More specifically, the anatomical structures and their representation in terms of visual and tactile feedback, instrument behavior and ergonomics of the recreated surgery were discussed and corroborated. The targeted training goals and performance measures were also validated. Feedback and comments from SMEs were collected and subsequently used to guide the next round of developments.

# 4   Results

A working VR prototype for interactive training in orthopaedic surgery has been developed. The prototype simulator supports three surgical sites (lumbar spine, right femur and the left eye). The sites correspond to three surgical procedures namely, transforaminal lumbar interbody fusion (TLIF) in spine surgery, antegrade femoral nailing in traumatology and orbital floor reconstruction in craniomaxillofacial (CMF) surgery. The simulated procedures are decomposed into nine scenarios using a total of 16 surgical instruments.

## 4.1   Cart Hardware

The proposed platform is a customized, transportable cart with adjustable height for user comfort while respecting the various ergonomic requirements (Fig. 1a). The workstation uses a 3.7 GHz Intel Core i7-5930K processor with 6 cores and 16 GB of RAM as well as a GeForce GTX 1080 GPU for computing and graphics. It includes two screens, one for 3D vision and one for 2D display and user-interface (UI) navigation. The lower screen supports NVidia 3D vision with glasses and is used to display the surgical workspace. The upper screen is a touchscreen to facilitate UI navigation and serves as a view for an observer. When required, the upper screen can display 2D fluoroscopic and endoscopic views parallel to the surgical workspace.

The haptics are 3DOF devices from Entact Robotics (Toronto, Canada) designed to have a customized level of force (1.5N continuous, 6.0N instantaneous) and negligible friction for high resolution bimanual interactions. In terms of workspace, the two haptic devices are separated by approximately 50 cm while the respective reach of each of their arms is about 35 cm.

The handle of each haptic device was removed to accommodate a customized surgical instrument connector permitting quick-release, automatic instrument recognition and signal transmission for articulating instruments. The developed connector also permits one-handed surgical instrument exchange during the simulation. The dynamic, single-handed tool exchange not only enhances user experience, but also accommodates constraints related to the execution of the selected surgical procedures (Fig. 1b and c). The instrument handles that accompany the customized connectors are shown in Fig. 2. The handles include, when required, an activation mechanism (ex: keyhole at fingertip) or a sensor to detect whether articulating instruments are open or closed.

(a)                                                        (b)

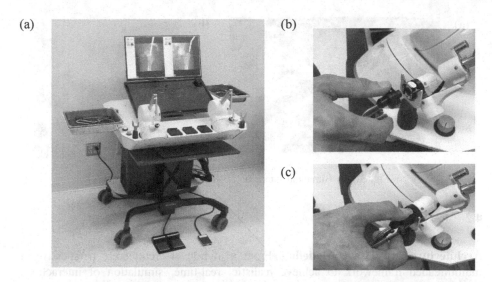

(c)

**Fig. 1.** (a) Orthopaedic VR simulation cart with lower display enabling NVidia 3D vision; upper display for 2D patient view and fluoroscopy; Haptic devices; VR ready PC; (b), (c): Customized connector for rapid one-handed instrument exchange and automatic recognition;

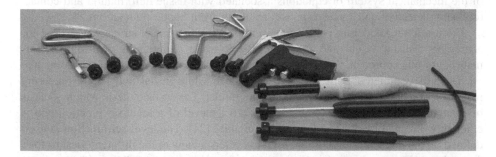

**Fig. 2.** Instrument handles replicating the ergonomics of the surgical procedure.

The required peripherals for surgical instrument activation or intensity control include foot pedals, control knobs and push buttons. The foot pedals are used to activate certain surgical instruments such as the microdrill and to take fluoroscopic images of the surgical scene. The control knobs are used to adjust the intensity of certain surgical instrument functionalities such as the power of aspiration of the suction tool. Push buttons permit instrument selection without changing the tool handle, used for example, when changing the size of a drill bit. Various accessories can be conveniently attached to the simulation cart between the two haptic devices. For example an armrest can be used for bimanual instrument manipulations or tasks requiring stability (Fig. 3).

(a)                                                        (b)

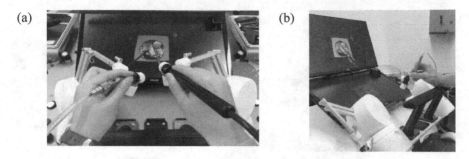

**Fig. 3.** (a) Bimanual interactions; (b) Armrest accessory

## 4.2 Real-Time Software

**Architecture and Tissue Modeling.** From a high-level architecture perspective, a multithreaded framework to achieve realistic, real-time, simulation of interactions between surgical instruments and tissue has been developed. The framework divides the computational work into graphic, haptic, physics and simulation (manager for exchange of information) threads, at 60 Hz, 1000 Hz, 1500–3000 Hz and 100–300 Hz respectively (Fig. 4a). Parallel computing on CPU and GPU is used for the resolution of the mechanical system of equations associated with tissue deformation and contact (collision detection and force response) resulting from haptic interactions.

From a tissue modeling perspective, a multiresolution mesh strategy was used for achieving realistic visual and haptic feedback while maintaining real-time performances. In this approach, the mechanical behavior of a fine tissue model is computed on a coarse volumetric finite element (FE) mesh while visual and haptic rendering make use of a fine surface attached to the fine model. The surface mesh, which consists of triangular elements, corresponds to the zero isolevel of a level-set function and is efficiently obtained by the Marching Cube method [24]. The level-set function is itself defined on the fine volumetric mesh. Figure 4 offers a view of the different meshes for a femur head. The mechanical behaviour of deformable tissues follows a hyperelastic model and is computed using the Total Lagrangian Explicit Dynamics (TLED) algorithm on a structured mesh [25]. Topology changes associated with soft and hard tissue removal (erosion) are supported through sculpting of the level-set surface. Contact between surgical instruments and deformable tissues uses penalty-based forces and virtual coupling models [26].

**Instrument Models.** The simulation framework supports manipulations (contact and/or topology change) of deformable tissue and rigid bodies with surgical instruments. It also permits to control (aspiration and cauterization) bleeding and to render different visualisations of the operating field (stereoscopic, endoscopic and fluoroscopic).

The surgical instruments that were developed for this simulation platform can be classified according to four basic functions: dissection, retraction, grasping and blood management. As such, interaction models corresponding to these functions were implemented. These models were further adapted and/or combined to represent the specific behaviour required for each instrument. For example, tissue dissection is achieved using a cutting primitive wherein the volume of tissue cut is determined by that of the cutting primitive on the instrument. The mechanism by which tissue is removed by a specific instrument can be customized by modifying the number, position, and size of the sphere(s). In addition, combinations of the basic interaction models can be implemented in order to achieve advanced behaviour leading to progressive or blunt tissue removal. The manipulation of rigid objects using surgical instruments allows their interaction with other rigid objects and tissues. More specifically, the current framework supports the handling of implants (grasping, binding with and release from articulating instruments such as forceps, displacement within the surgical scene and their insertion and positioning near soft and hard tissues). The simulation can additionally handle screw insertion and removal from hard tissues using a screwdriver, so as to secure simulated plate placement.

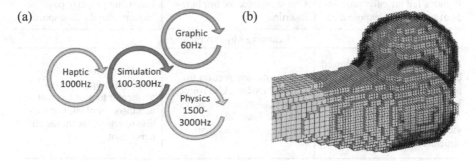

**Fig. 4.** (a) Schematic of the framework with the simulation thread acting as the manager of information exchanged between threads; (b) Femur head multiresolution mesh representation.

### 4.3   Simulation Exercises

Three orthopaedic procedures are simulated: (1) TLIF in spine surgery, (2) lateral femoral nailing in traumatology and (3) orbital floor reconstruction in CMF. Tables 2, 3 and 4 provide details for the procedures respectively. Based on the surgical goals and key learning objectives identified in the analysis and mock-up stages with the SMEs, each of the procedures have been divided into simulation exercises with specific start and end points. Each of the exercises recreate the surgical view, simulation scenario concept, essential surgical cues and performance measures with the notation (+) for outcome measures and (−) for errors.

**Table 2.** Key steps of the TLIF spine surgery. The intervention is performed on lower spine to remove intervertebral disc and join two or more vertebrae. It is generally done to decompress and stabilize the spine. The simulation involves the anatomy of L4 and L5 vertebrae.

| Disc Exposure | Discectomy | Implant Insertion |
|---|---|---|
| | | |
| **Goals** | | |
| Remove left articular processes of vertebrae to expose disc | Create corridor for implant insertion | Insert and properly position implant into the disc space |
| **Learning objectives** | | |
| Use drill to thin bone followed by Kerrison punch for complete removal; Use curette and Kerrison punch to resect ligamentum; Use suction to keep view clear of blood and retract structures | Use bipolar and suction to control bleeding; Use rongeur and curette to remove accessible disc material; Use suction to retract structures | Use Kerrison to remove cartilage endplates; Use applicator to grasp, orient and insert implant; use suction to retract thecal sac and nerve root |
| **Surgical cues** | | |
| Bleeding visually discriminates between cancellous and cortical bone, ligamentum flavum has a yellow hue, ligamentum flavum is softer to the touch than bone | Adequate disc removal is achieved when material is no longer accessible, tissue stiffness discrimination between nucleus, endplates and annulus | Sufficient retraction of dura and nerve branch is achieved when cartilage endplates can be visualized |
| **Performance measures** | | |
| (+) Area of bone removed corresponds to that defined by expert, disc is adequately exposed<br>(-) Injury to nerve tissue and/or thecal sac due to high forces | (+) % disc removed corresponds to that defined by expert<br>(-) Piercing anterior region of disc, injury to nerve tissue and/or thecal sac due to high forces | (+) Disc in position defined by expert;<br>(-) Piercing anterior region of disc, injury to nerve tissue and/or thecal sac due to high forces |

**Table 3.** Key steps of lateral femoral nailing. The intervention is performed under fluoroscopy to repair a femoral fracture. The simulation involves the left femur with a reduced shaft fracture.

| Medullary Canal Entry | Canal Reaming | Distal Locking |
|---|---|---|
| | | |
| **Goals** | | |
| Identify proper trochanteric entry point and open canal using the awl | Enlarge medullary canal to accommodate nail | Drill through locking holes to prepare for distal locking |
| **Learning objectives** | | |
| Place awl at tip of trochanter; Use awl to enter medullary canal; Use fluoroscopic guidance | Use guidewire to create reaming path; Gradually enlarge canal with reamer; Use fluoroscopic guidance | Align drill bit using fluoroscopy |
| **Surgical cues** | | |
| Haptic discrimination between cortex and canal | Audio and tactile "chatter" of reamer when cortex is reached | Locking hole becomes opaque under fluoroscopy when drill is centered |
| **Performance measures** | | |
| (+) Entry point and angle, volume of bone removed, canal opening and path, no. of fluoroscopy shots (-) Entry point outside of expert defined region, piercing through cortical bone | (+) Reamer size selected, canal enlarged to physeal scar, no. of fluoroscopy shots (-) Piercing through cortical bone | (+) Drilling aligned with locking hole, no. of fluoroscopy shots (-) Screw has encountered nail, injury to soft tissue |

**Table 4.** Key steps of orbital floor reconstruction. The intervention serves to repair a fracture in the orbital floor and restore ocular movement and orbital integrity. The simulated anatomy involves a fracture in the left eye, extending up to the wall of the nose.

| Fracture Exposure | Plate Insertion | Forced Duction Test |
|---|---|---|
| | | |
| **Goals** | | |
| Expose fracture site | Insert plate over fracture below orbital rim | Verify eye mobility has been preserved |
| **Learning objectives** | | |
| Retract tissue with malleable retractor; Use a freer elevator to strip periosteum from bone | Use forceps to position plate; Use screwdriver to fix plate; Use endoscope and bipolar forceps to manage bleeding | Use toothed forceps to grasp and move the eye; Perform and understand forced duction test |
| **Surgical cues** | | |
| Detection of posterior ledge indicates sufficient exposure | Improper screw angle causes plate kick-up | Loss of mobility indicates entrapment of tissue |
| **Performance measures** | | |
| (+) Bone fracture is exposed (-) Injury to eye due to high retraction force | (+) Plate covers defect, in contact with floor and on posterior ledge; (-) Injury to structures due to high force; plate not in position; hemostasis not reached | (+) Understand forced duction test; (-) Injury to eye or periorbital tissue due to high forces |

# 5 Discussion

The working prototype has been evaluated by the SMEs. It was concluded that the simulator can adequately reproduce the ergonomics of the three different interventions on a single platform. The anatomical representations of tissues and structures have achieved an appropriate level of detail.

The step requiring the most iterations in the process was the one encompassing the development of the anatomical structures and surgical instrument interaction models as it required the most extensive feedback from the SME. The implementation consisted of successive tuning of tissue mechanical properties with SMEs as the reference to what felt acceptably realistic. At the same time, when the anatomical level of detail was insufficient for realistic haptic and/or visual representation, adjustments of the mesh models were required on the developmental side with possible workarounds to meet real-time constraints. The adjustments were then re-evaluated for realistic perception by the SMEs.

An acceptable level of realism has been achieved for the surgical instrument interaction models. Certain improvements could further enhance realism. Particular to this work, and as already previously noted in similar studies [8], it was determined that the simulation of contact with bone can sometimes give the sensation of a slippery surface. This occurs when an instrument tip contacts a convex hard bone surface. A non-slip contact is often difficult to reproduce because it requires a high resolution mesh capturing bone surface rugosity, not easily amenable to real-time simulation with current computational capabilities. Similarly, the ability to discern between the different types of soft tissue based on their texture could further enhance the learning experience. A potential improvement could lie in the implementation of tissue-specific friction models.

Custom haptics with specialized connectors were designed to permit a more realistic experience. In particular, the inclusion of quick-release connectors allows for dynamic tool exchange to more realistically capture the various configurations of instruments-in-hand that a surgeon may use during the intervention. When hard bone is involved, the surgeon may choose to place both hands on one surgical instrument or one hand on an instrument while the other is stabilized on an arm rest or patient back, for example. With soft tissue, the surgeon may be required to perform bimanual manipulations involving the simultaneous use of two instruments, such as retracting critical structures out of the way with the non-dominant hand while performing the task with the other. In addition, the choice was made to provide realistic surgical instrument handles to more closely replicate the ergonomics of the surgical manipulations. As such, the handles were reproduced 3D printing or other machining techniques based on designs from real instrument CAD files when available or fabricated from repurposed surgical instruments.

3DOF haptic devices were chosen for this platform due to their relative affordability and their capacity to provide force feedback while respecting ergonomic constraints of the three surgeries. This set-up was well received by the SMEs. The realism of certain interactions such as medullary canal opening or implant insertion into a disc could potentially benefit from having an additional torque feedback and higher force feedback. Torque could be made possible by upgrading the platform with 5DOF haptic devices for each hand. A haptic system capable of generating higher continuous force (for example, 10N rather than the current 1.5N) could be used, however concerns for user safety and affordability arise.

# 6 Conclusions and Future Work

There is little doubt that SBT has an important role to play in the current and future of orthopaedic surgery training. There will be continued advances in technology to improve realism and increased availability of simulators which may help to compensate for the reduced hours of experience in the operating room (OR) of surgeons in training.

A prototype of a VR orthopedic training simulator meeting the requirements of the SMEs has been developed. The efforts have resulted in a platform targeting three orthopaedic procedures at three different anatomical sites with a total of 16 surgical instrument-mimicking handles. Each procedure has been split into a total of three exercises highlighting key tasks, according to SME input and technical feasibility, resulting in a total of nine simulation exercises. The exercises include pedagogical content, complete with training goals, instructions and performance measures within a user interface. The simulator prototype allows bimanual haptic feedback and single-handed dynamic tool exchange. Visual feedback includes a 3D vision-enabled screen also permitting endoscopic view. Additionally, a second screen is available for observer display or fluoroscopic view. The next step includes technical evaluation and initial validation by residents and surgeons for formal skills training. Future work could focus on further increasing the realism of the instrument interaction models as well as increasing haptic forces. The eventual goal for this simulator is to achieve transfer-ability evidence of simulation skills to OR surgical practice, thereby demonstrating a clear benefit of VR for training.

# References

1. Information NC for B., Pike USNL of M 8600 R., MD B., USA 20894: Surgical simulation for training: skills transfer to the operating room. Centre for Reviews and Dissemination (UK) (2012)
2. Sadideen, H., Alvand, A., Saadeddin, M., Kneebone, R.: Surgical experts: born or made? Int. J. Surg. **11**, 773–778 (2013). https://doi.org/10.1016/j.ijsu.2013.07.001
3. Ruikar, D.D., Hegadi, R.S., Santosh, K.C.: A systematic review on orthopaedic simulators for psycho-motor skill and surgical procedure training. J. Med. Syst. **42**, 168 (2018). https://doi.org/10.1007/s10916-018-1019-1
4. de Montbrun, S.L., MacRae, H.: Simulation in surgical education. Clin. Colon. Rectal. Surg. **25**, 156–165 (2012). https://doi.org/10.1055/s-0032-1322553
5. Akhtar, K.S.N., Chen, A., Standfield, N.J., Gupte, C.M.: The role of simulation in developing surgical skills. Curr. Rev. Musculoskelet. Med. **7**, 155–160 (2014). https://doi.org/10.1007/s12178-014-9209-z
6. Singh, H., Kalani, M., Acosta-Torres, S., El Ahmadieh, T.Y., Loya, J., Ganju, A.: History of simulation in medicine: from Resusci Annie to the Ann Myers Medical Center. Neurosurgery **73**(Suppl. 1), 9–14 (2013). https://doi.org/10.1227/NEU.0000000000000093
7. Madan, S.S., Pai, D.R.: Role of simulation in arthroscopy training. Simul. Healthc. J. Soc. Simul. Healthc. **9**, 127–135 (2014). https://doi.org/10.1097/SIH.0b013e3182a86165
8. Vaughan, N., Dubey, V.N., Wainwright, T.W., Middleton, R.G.: A review of virtual reality based training simulators for orthopaedic surgery. Med. Eng. Phys. **38**, 59–71 (2016). https://doi.org/10.1016/j.medengphy.2015.11.021

9. Stirling, E.R.B., Lewis, T.L., Ferran, N.A.: Surgical skills simulation in trauma and orthopaedic training. J. Orthop. Surg. **9**, 126 (2014). https://doi.org/10.1186/s13018-014-0126-z
10. Cecil, J., Gupta, A., Pirela-Cruz, M.: An advanced simulator for Orthopaedic surgical training. Int. J. Comput. Assist. Radiol. Surg. **13**, 305–319 (2018). https://doi.org/10.1007/s11548-017-1688-0
11. Gardner, A.K., et al.: Best practices across surgical specialties relating to simulation-based training. Surgery **158**, 1395–1402 (2015). https://doi.org/10.1016/j.surg.2015.03.041
12. Touch Surgery - Prepare for Surgery. https://www.touchsurgery.com/
13. Rosseau, G., et al.: The development of a virtual simulator for training neurosurgeons to perform and perfect endoscopic endonasal transsphenoidal surgery. Neurosurgery **73** (Suppl. 1), 85–93 (2013). https://doi.org/10.1227/NEU.0000000000000112
14. Varshney, R., et al.: The McGill simulator for endoscopic sinus surgery (MSESS): a validation study. J. Otolaryngol. - Head Neck Surg. J. Oto-Rhino-Laryngol. Chir. Cervico-Faciale **43**, 40 (2014). https://doi.org/10.1186/s40463-014-0040-8
15. Varshney, R., et al.: National Research Council Canada: development of the McGill simulator for endoscopic sinus surgery: a new high-fidelity virtual reality simulator for endoscopic sinus surgery. Am. J. Rhinol. Allergy. **28**, 330–334 (2014). https://doi.org/10.2500/ajra.2014.28.4046
16. World's first simulator for pulmonary endarterectomy will bring life-saving skill to more thoracic surgeons. https://www.uhn.ca/corporate/News/Pages/world_first_simulator_pulmonary_endarterectomy_bring_life_saving_skill.aspx
17. Delorme, S., Laroche, D., DiRaddo, R., Del Maestro, R.F.: NeuroTouch: a physics-based virtual simulator for cranial microneurosurgery training. Neurosurgery **71**, 32–42 (2012). https://doi.org/10.1227/NEU.0b013e318249c744
18. Choudhury, N., Gélinas-Phaneuf, N., Delorme, S., Del Maestro, R.: Fundamentals of neurosurgery: virtual reality tasks for training and evaluation of technical skills. World Neurosurg. **80**, e9–e19 (2013). https://doi.org/10.1016/j.wneu.2012.08.022
19. Gélinas-Phaneuf, N., Del Maestro, R.F.: Surgical expertise in neurosurgery: integrating theory into practice. Neurosurgery **73**, S30–S38 (2013). https://doi.org/10.1227/NEU.0000000000000115
20. Gélinas-Phaneuf, N., et al.: Assessing performance in brain tumor resection using a novel virtual reality simulator. Int. J. Comput. Assist. Radiol. Surg. **9**, 1–9 (2014). https://doi.org/10.1007/s11548-013-0905-8
21. Winkler-Schwartz, A., et al.: Bimanual psychomotor performance in neurosurgical resident applicants assessed using NeuroTouch, a virtual reality simulator. J. Surg. Educ. **73**, 942–953 (2016). https://doi.org/10.1016/j.jsurg.2016.04.013
22. Morgan, M., Aydin, A., Salih, A., Robati, S., Ahmed, K.: Current status of simulation-based training tools in orthopaedic surgery: a systematic review. J. Surg. Educ. **74**, 698–716 (2017). https://doi.org/10.1016/j.jsurg.2017.01.005
23. Blender Foundation: Home of the Blender project. Free and Open 3D Creation. Software. https://www.blender.org/
24. Lorensen, W.E., Cline, H.E.: Marching cubes: a high resolution 3D surface construction algorithm. In: Proceedings of the 14th Annual Conference on Computer Graphics and Interactive Techniques, pp. 163–169. ACM, New York (1987)
25. Miller, K., Joldes, G., Lance, D., Wittek, A.: Total Lagrangian explicit dynamics finite element algorithm for computing soft tissue deformation. Commun. Numer. Methods Eng. **23**, 121–134 (2007). https://doi.org/10.1002/cnm.887
26. Neubauer, A.: Haptic collision handling for simulation of transnasal surgery. In: Computer Animation and Virtual Worlds. Wiley Online Library (2013). https://onlinelibrary.wiley.com/doi/abs/10.1002/cav.1489

# Exploring Extended Reality as a Simulation Training Tool Through Naturalistic Interactions and Enhanced Immersion

Daniel Duggan[1], Caroline Kingsley[1(✉)], Mark Mazzeo[2],
and Michael Jenkins[1]

[1] Charles River Analytics Inc., Cambridge, MA, USA
{dduggan, ckingsley, mjenkins}@cra.com
[2] Combat Capabilities Development Command Soldier Center, Simulation
and Training Technology Center (CCDC SC STTC), Orlando, FL, USA
mark.v.mazzeo.civ@mail.mil

**Abstract.** Augmented reality (AR), mixed reality (MR), and virtual reality (VR) technologies – collectively extended reality (XR) – have been discussed in the context of training applications since their introduction to the market. While this discussion was initially founded on potential benefit, the rapid pace and advancements within the XR industry allow the technology to fulfill initial expectations in terms of training utility. As XR becomes an effective training tool, two open areas of research, among many, include integrating experiences between VR and AR/MR simulations, as XR training often obscures the trainer from the trainee's environment, and determining the optimal level of fidelity and overall usability of interaction within XR simulations for the training of fine- and gross-motor control tasks, as new peripherals and technologies enter the market supporting a variety of interaction fidelities, such as data glove controllers, skeletal motion capture suits, tracking systems, and haptic devices. XR may show more promise as a training platform the closer it can replicate real world and naturalistic training interactions and immersion. This paper discusses efforts in these two research areas, including a planned usability study on the impact of the fidelity of interactions on training of fine- and gross-motor control tasks in virtual environments.

**Keywords:** Extended reality · Naturalistic interaction · Training transfer · Virtual reality · Augmented reality · Mixed reality · Interaction fidelity

## 1 Introduction

This paper presents an overview of our ongoing work across the Extended Reality (XR) Head-Mounted Displays (HMDs) and Simulation domain, with a focus on two areas; integrating experiences between Augmented and Mixed Reality HMDs and Virtual Reality HMDs; and a planned usability study on the impact of the fidelity of interactions on training of fine- and gross-motor control tasks in virtual environments. While seemingly disparate, this work is being done under a larger, existing research and development program exploring ways to increase users' naturalistic interactions

© Springer Nature Switzerland AG 2019
J. Y. C. Chen and G. Fragomeni (Eds.): HCII 2019, LNCS 11575, pp. 272–282, 2019.
https://doi.org/10.1007/978-3-030-21565-1_18

(through the support of a variety of devices including AR/MR HMDs, VR HMDs, data glove controllers, skeletal motion capture suits, tracking systems, and haptic devices) and immersion (through time- and event-based scripting for dynamic environments, voice-based interactions, etc.) in extended reality environments, with the goal of improving XR's utility as a training tool [1, 2]. The projected outcome of this larger effort is an open-source XR software development kit, designed to enable more rapid and consistent development of XR-based simulations with a focus on supporting natural human interactions to foster more realistic virtual simulations and training.

## 2 Networked Training

While the augmented reality (AR), mixed reality (MR), and virtual reality (VR) in-dustries rapidly progress—especially in the healthcare training domain [3]—there remains a gap in how these extended realities can interface with one another. In an effort to advance the greater XR field in the spirit of its core principles, we are exploring how users wearing AR/MR HMDs and VR HMDs can observe each other's virtual environments and interactions. Our motivation to investigate this area is driven by the limitations of XR in the training domain [4]; specifically, while existing, non-XR computer-based training fits well into the traditional trainer-trainee model, whereas the nature of HMDs makes instruction more difficult as the trainer cannot directly see what actions the trainee is performing in their environment. Currently, the primary approach for observing a trainee's actions in XR is to watch from a computer screen that is mirroring the trainee's HMD screen. The mirrored screen approach is insufficient because it does not convey the spatial nature of manipulation in XR, particularly VR. Furthermore numerous VR and AR HMDs, especially the lower-cost models appealing to large scale training needs, are trending towards standalone models that do not interface with desktop computers. For example, the Oculus Go used in Walmart's experimental VR training is a standalone model. Microsoft's Hololens and the Magic Leap One are the current front-runners in the AR domain and operate without a desktop computer.

We recently explored a solution to this problem in the training domain, allowing a "trainer" wearing an MR HMD (Magic Leap One) to observe a "trainee" in a virtual environment wearing a VR HMD (HTC Vive). In our prototype interface, focused on a medic training scenario based on Tactical Combat Casualty Care (TCCC) [5], we synchronized key data between the VR simulation and the trainer's MR HMD over a local network connection: the key data including the position and rotation of critical objects and the medical state of simulated patients. By initializing the origin point for both the MR and VR HMDs to the same point, we enabled the trainer to observe the trainee's environment overlaid on the same locations. The trainer was additionally allowed to view simulated patient data unavailable to the trainee such as heart rate, blood volume, and blood pressure. We believe that this asymmetrical multi-user approach will be valuable for creating training systems in the future; it lends itself to a classic trainer-trainee and/or teacher-student relationship where the trainer/teacher withholds information and the trainee/student is provided the tools or framework to perform an action or produce an answer in relation to that information, for the trainer/teacher to then evaluate.

## 2.1 VR Training Simulation

Our VR training simulation was built in Unity using VSDK, an XR development kit we developed under an Army-funded project called VIRTUOSO, for rapid prototyping of XR scenarios. VSDK will be released as Open Source in 2019 and enables developers to create immersive simulations by providing interoperability between COTS XR hardware devices—including HMDs, controllers, tracking systems, hand trackers, skeletal trackers, and haptic devices—as well as systems supporting naturalistic XR interactions, including a high-level gesture recognition system, and an XR-focused event handling system. Our training simulation was focused on combat medic training and consisted of a narrative component followed by an active component where the trainee must treat several casualties following a blast.

For the VR training simulation, we constructed a virtual environment consisting of a city street with an adjacent alley and park in a fictional megacity. The virtual environment had three distinct zones: (1) a military checkpoint on the side of the street; (2) an alleyway adjacent to the roadblock; and (3) an open field or park where a medical helicopter could land. The trainee was able to freely teleport between the three areas. For this scenario, we created four simulated patients—three squad members and a squad leader. During the narrative component, the trainee is instructed to guard the alleyway. Once in the alleyway, they are instructed to participate in a "radio test" which is used to calibrate a voice recognition system for later portions of the medical training scenario. Once calibration is completed, an enemy vehicle arrives at the roadblock location and detonates, injuring the three squad members (the squad leader is uninjured and issues orders to the trainee). At this point, the trainee can proceed with treatment as they see fit. Each patient has unique injuries backed by a real-time patient simulation. The patient simulator is driven by a set of finite state machines with associated physiological variables. States correspond to different wounds, and trainee interventions transition state machines between states. For example, a wound might have the states bleeding and not bleeding. By applying a bandage to the wound, the state can transition to not bleeding which would affect the blood loss per tick.

**Unscripted Training.** Although combat medic training [5] specifies how treatment should be prioritized based on established triage principles (e.g. treat massive hemorrhage first, treat airway obstruction next, treat respiratory distress next, treat circulation-related issues next, treat head injury/hypothermia next, etc.) [5, 6], the trainee is free to treat the patients in any order in the simulation just as they are in the real world (applying trained triage principles accordingly). In the simulation, the trainee can use both voice commands and hand-based interactions to treat the patients, to mimic a real world situation as much as possible. For voice commands, the trainee has the option of asking the squad leader to perform a security sweep, asking patients if they can treat themselves, or calling for an evacuation helicopter on the radio. In terms of physical interaction fidelity, we mounted a Leap Motion hand tracker on the VR HMD to allow the user to interact with the tools using their hands rather than a controller. This naturalistic interaction is supported with the goal of improving immersion and training transfer. Further enabling freedom of trainee decision and hopefully promoting prior triage training and retention, the virtual environment has several tools that the trainee can choose from and use to perform treatments, including bandages, scissors, a needle chest decompression, a tourniquet, and a Nasopharyngeal airway (NPA) tube, just as they may in their pack. In our simulation scenario, the first patient's injuries are an amputated leg and a small shrapnel wound on the chest. The trainee must apply a tourniquet to the patient's leg, remove his shirt with the scissors, and apply a bandage to the chest wound. The second patient has a significant chest wound that is causing blood to enter the lungs. Again the user must use the scissors to remove the shirt and apply a bandage to the wound, but a needle chest decompression is also required to prevent the patient's lungs from filling with blood. The third patient is unconscious and having trouble breathing, so an NPA tube is used to open the Nasopharyngeal airway. However, the only way a user can diagnose these injuries and decide how to treat them is through visual cues (i.e. visible wounds, casualty vitals, casualty skin pallor), existing knowledge, and the equipment they have available, as it would be in the field. Once all of the patients have been treated and the helicopter has been called, the trainee must load the patients (using a menu item) and then board the helicopter to finish the scenario.

## 2.2   MR Training Simulation

We built the MR trainer's application using VSDK as well, starting with the same environment as the trainee application. We removed the city environment because MR works best when only key elements of the scene are shown. We then built a networking component to enable us to send data to the MR application from the VR training simulation. In order to minimize network traffic and latency, we narrowed the shared data down to position and rotation of the trainee and patients as well as the state data of the patients (see Fig. 1). When configured correctly, the trainer would be able to see a helmet hovering over the trainee's HMD and would be able to see the trainee perform treatments. However, tool position was not synchronized so the current version only allowed the trainer to see the result of a treatment after it occurred. For example, after a tourniquet is applied to the first patient's leg, the trainer would see a tourniquet appear on the first patient's representation.

The trainer also receives additional information hidden from the trainee from the simulated patients. This information, such as blood pressure, heart rate, and hydration, would not be immediately measureable by the trainee without the proper tools but would be valuable to a trainer instructing a trainee on which patient or wound to address next. We displayed this information to the trainer via information cards floating above each patient (Fig. 1). The trainer can grab and move the information cards using the 6-degrees-of-freedom (6dof) controller provided with the Magic Leap One MR HMD in order to rearrange the information to see it better.

Another novel networked feature we implemented between our VR and AR simulation, is a mini-map feature. While the two environments are networked, if the AR user flips over the controller in their hand (in this case, the 6dof controller provided with the Magic Leap One), a mini-map spawns above and locks to the backside of the controller, allowing the user in AR to see a map of the full simulation environment. Within that mini-map, the user in VR is represented by a colored icon within the map, as well as the user in AR. We believe this functionality can greatly enhance situational awareness between the user in AR and the user in VR, as it provides a snapshot of the full VR environment as well as the two users' respective locations in the context of that environment.

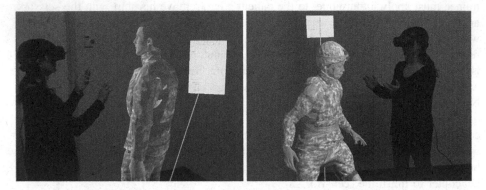

**Fig. 1.** These images demonstrate networking between our VR environment (worn by user pictured) and AR environment (worn by photographer), from the AR point of view (Magic Leap One). This simulation shows the presence of a non-player character (NPC) which is present in both VR and AR environments, as well as dynamic TCCC card [5] depicting NPC health state metrics, only viewable by the user in AR.

## 2.3 Recommendations

We believe this approach helps to address one of the key limitations in XR training, which is the reduced ability of trainers to observe trainee behavior and provide recommendations. However, our current implementation has a few drawbacks that could be improved on. The main drawback is that communication is only in one direction: from the trainee's VR simulation to the trainer's MR HMD. While this gives the trainer the ability to observe the trainee, it does not provide them any opportunities for providing additional information or assistance to the trainee (unless the trainee removes their headphones, reducing immersion). We are currently exploring approaches for meaningful bidirectional collaboration, including reversed visualizations, remote observation, and trainer tools for manipulation of the environment and the simulation.

**Reversed Visualizations.** Reversed visualizations are an important next step, not only for educational benefits but also for trainee safety. When operating in a VR environment, a trainee cannot see the real environment and is at risk of colliding with a trainer. While most trainers can stay out of the way, any collisions are likely to reduce user trust in virtual reality technology. We are exploring two avenues for supplying trainer positional data to the trainee: skeletal motion capture suits and networked transmission of AR/MR HMD position. Skeletal motion capture suits (such as Xsens or Synertial), frequently used by animation studios to capture actor performance, are seeing increased interest in the XR domain because they enable applications to track the user's entire body [7, 8]. We have explored using real time motion capture to pose a 3D model of a human in real time, allowing one user in VR to see another who is wearing the motion capture suit. Full body capture requires a desktop computer, which limits the usage for trainers with standalone HMDs. The alternative option is to transmit the position and rotation of the trainer's HMD to the trainee's application. This seems like an option that is more likely to gain traction due to the high cost of tracking suits. Both options enable the trainer to direct the trainee; even without additional features, the trainer can point and gesture to patients and injuries for non-verbal instruction.

**Remote Observation.** The current solution is only configured to work on a local network. Future versions could be configured to work over distance to enable remote observation. Remote observation could benefit trainees working in distant locations far from training centers without missing out on the experience of expert trainers. Adopting a more robust networking protocol could also enable multiple team members to train together. This would likely decrease existing barriers to training and improve overall training adherence.

**Real Time Manipulation.** The next step beyond allowing the trainer to see the trainee's environment is to enable the trainer to modify it in real time to create a more collaborative training environment. Depending on the task and training context, trainees are likely to be challenged by different types and aspects of scenarios. Trainers are ideally positioned to provide augmentations to training programs that account for specific trainee needs. Future developments of the extended reality integration should enable trainers to make meaningful augmentations. In the medic training example, a trainer may notice that the trainee has difficulty applying tourniquets in the default scenario; the trainer could augment the scenario by introducing additional casualties with injuries that require a tourniquet for treatment. Alternatively, the trainer my want to remove other casualties to encourage the trainee to focus or even step in and demonstrate the appropriate procedure. We can also see these first steps develop into full XR scenario customization systems to allow for even more specially tailored training scenarios unique to each trainer or trainee.

## 3    Training and Interaction Fidelity

While the coexistence of MR and VR HMDs strives to improve the trainee-trainer relationship within virtual simulation training, we are also exploring improved training transfer from virtual to real-world environments through fidelity of interactions. Specifically, we have designed and will be conducting a usability study designed to answer this research question: does the fidelity of fine- and gross-motor control interactions impact training of fine- and gross-motor control tasks in virtual environments? Our study will consist of three phases: a training phase, a usability phase, and finally an evaluation phase. The usability phase is dual purpose and strives to both distract the subjects from their initial training and to collect meaningful data on which levels of fidelity are appropriate for different tasks. During the training phase, the subjects will be trained in a particular task using both a real world device and a virtual reproduction of that task, restricted to a level of fidelity. During the evaluation phase, the subjects will be instructed to perform the real world task a second time.

This planned study will elicit a mix of quantitative (i.e. task execution, reaction time, accuracy, errors) and qualitative data (i.e. usability questionnaire, simulator sickness questionnaire, NASA-TLX workload assessment). To balance this need with other constraints (i.e. time, recruiting), our goal is to run at least 30 participants for the planned study, 10 participants for each of our three study tasks.

## 3.1    Study Tasks

We have selected three tasks for study, based on difficulty, trainability, and ease of reproduction in virtual environments. We also selected these tasks to include a mixture of fine- and gross-motor control skills. Tasks must be difficult enough that some subjects could struggle with the task and yet trainable so that subjects can improve with virtual training. Our three tasks for the planned study are: (1) wire-tracing, fine-motor; (2) mirrored writing, fine-motor, cognitive; and (3) drum rhythms, gross-motor (Fig. 2). We will vary both the task and the level of fidelity on a per-subject basis.

**Fig. 2.**  These images depict the real world materials that will be used for our three planned study tasks. From left to right; mirrored writing apparatus, electronic drum kit, and wire tracing game.

**Fine Motor Wire Tracing Task.**  For the wire-tracing task (available off the shelf as an 'electronic wire game') subjects will need to move a small, wand-like object around a rigid wire. The wand is conductive and if it touches the wire a buzzer sounds. This seemingly simple task requires both hand-eye coordination and fine-motor skills to complete without error. We will be tracking both time to complete the task and the number of errors to determine a task completion score. Once the user has tried the real world version of the task, they will be able to train with an XR recreation of the real world object. The virtual version of the wire-tracing task will be an exact replica; our goal is to have the user training model the real world as closely as possible. Since this is a primarily hand-based task, we will be varying the fidelity of hand-based interactions by changing devices between users while trying to configure each device to work as close to the real task as possible. We will be using controllers, vision-based hand tracking, and data gloves. For controllers, such as the Vive "wand" controller, we will have the controller act as the wand rather than as the user's hand. For vision-based hand tracking (e.g. the Leap Motion) and the data gloves (e.g. ManusVR gloves) we will have a virtual wand that users will be able to pick up and manipulate.

**Cognitive Mirrored Writing Task.** During the mirrored writing task, subjects will need to trace letters or shapes with a pen but will only be able to see a mirrored version of their writing hand. This task has been demonstrated to be difficult but trainable [9]. In the real version of the task, this will be accomplished through a mirrored writing apparatus designed specifically for research studies. Performance will be measured based on how many letters or shapes are backwards in the final version. For the virtual recreation, we will use a rendering effect to mirror the subject's hand and writing. For this task we will also be using controllers, vision-based hand tracking, and data gloves. Similarly to the first task, we will treat the controllers as pens to mirror the real world task as closely as possible. For the other input methods, the user will be able to pick up a virtual pen to attempt the task.

**Fig. 3.** Early iteration of VR drum model based on real world drum kit. These images depict a user holding the drum sticks via HTC VIVE controllers, which is one of the several interaction fidelities we plan to test. The image on the right shows a highlighted drum pad, indicating a pattern for the user to follow, learn, and rehearse.

**Gross Motor Drumming Task.** The third task will require the subject to memorize a drum rhythm. For the real version of the task, we will be using an electronic drum set with 7 drum pads to allow for complicated patterns. The user will be shown an animation indicating the order the pads must be activated in and will be able to listen to the pattern. The subject will be judged based on whether they hit the correct pads in the correct order and how long it took to complete the rhythmic pattern. For the virtual training session, we will recreate the drum pad and sounds, and the animation will play directly on the drum pads (Fig. 3). On top of the previous interaction methods mentioned, we will also secure trackers to both the drum sticks and the drum pad to allow for mixed reality training.

**Usability Sub-tasks.** In addition to the primary tasks, we will have a series of smaller XR usability tests to run each subject through; these usability tasks will function to both distract participants from the original task training and to collect data on the usability of XR interactions. This will include subjective questionnaires (i.e. likert scales) aimed at discovering whether the subject found an interaction easy to use. We have prototyped several interactions from medical and mechanical domains covering both gross and fine motor skills across a variety of XR devices. Table 1 lists some of the tasks we will use during the usability portion of the test.

**Table 1.** Example usability sub-tasks for interaction fidelity study.

| Domain | Fine- or Gross-motor | Task | Devices |
|---|---|---|---|
| Medical | Fine | Scalpel incision | Controller, hand tracker, glove with force feedback, MR tool |
| Medical | Fine | Chest tube insertion | Controller, hand tracker, glove with force feedback |
| Medical | Gross | Check pulse | Controller, hand tracker, haptic feedback gauntlet, glove with force feedback |
| Medical | Gross | Tourniquet application | Controller, hand tracker, glove with force feedback |
| Mechanical | Fine | Bolt tightening/ loosening | Controller, hand tracker, glove with force feedback |
| Mechanical | Fine | Insert wire through small hole | Controller, hand tracker, glove with force feedback |
| Mechanical | Fine | Soldering component | Controller, hand tracker, glove with force feedback, MR device |
| Mechanical | Gross | Fitting large component (e.g. oil filter) | Controller, hand tracker, glove with force feedback |
| Mechanical | Gross | Welding | Controller, hand tracker, glove with force feedback |
| Mechanical | Gross | Hammering | Controller, hand tracker, glove with force feedback |
| Generic | Mixed | Firing a weapon | Controller, hand tracker, MR device |

## 3.2   Impacts

We anticipate that our results will have several impacts that will influence the design of XR. First, we believe that both portions of our study will contribute insights into device selection for XR training simulations. Currently, devices are selected by either qualitative assessment by resident scientists and developers or out of convenience. Clearer evidence for which devices provide the most training impact will help demystify the process of device selection at the start of development. Second, we believe that both the insights into fidelity and the usability studies will highlight which approaches to XR interaction and scenario design create more effective training scenarios.

# 4    Conclusion

While our larger program addresses numerous aspects of XR in an effort to increase the realism and immersion of XR simulation and requisite training capabilities, this paper focused on two areas within this larger effort; real-time networking of different XR environments (VR and AR/MR), and a planned study on the impact of the fidelity of interactions on training of fine- and gross-motor control tasks in virtual environments as well as the usability of specific XR interactions.

We see promise in our concept for networking different XR environments, such as VR and MR (Magic Leap One), for a variety of training applications, as it can help solve the issue of VR training obscuring the trainer from the trainees' environment and interactions, and allows for specific objects and information to be kept separate between two environments. We believe we have barely scratched the surface in the space of networked multi-reality simulations and see numerous areas for future research and exploration, including reversed visualizations, remote observation, and trainer tools for manipulation of the environment and the simulation.

Additionally, we described the design of a planned study on interaction fidelity and usability of XR interactions. This study is designed to evaluate the effect of VR interaction fidelity (e.g. controller vs. data glove vs. camera-based hand tracking) on the training transfer of fine- and gross-motor tasks. This planned study will evaluate three distinct tasks; a fine-motor wire tracing task, a fine-motor and cognitive mirrored writing task, and a gross-motor drumming sequence task. Participants will complete the real world task, train on the task in VR (at varying levels of fidelity across participants), complete a series of tasks designed to evaluate the usability of XR tool-based inter-actions and act as distractors from the training task, then finally complete the real world task again. This study has the potential to provide interesting insights for XR devel-opers and researchers, potentially on the optimal level of fidelity of XR interaction, selection of XR peripherals and devices, and the overall design of HCI/XR interactions.

The XR field will likely continue to grow and training applications will increase in both quantity and quality [2, 4]. Our intention is to aid the advancement of the XR field; thus our aforementioned VSDK will become open-source in 2019, supporting our networked XR capabilities and naturalistic interactions, and we will disseminate our findings from our usability study once we finalize data collection and analysis, later in 2019 as well.

**Acknowledgements.** Research was sponsored by the Combat Capabilities Development Command and was accomplished under Contract No. W911NF-16-C-0011. The views and conclusions contained in this document are those of the authors and should not be interpreted as representing the official policies, either expressed or implied, of the Combat Capabilities Development Command or the US Government. The US Government is authorized to reproduce and distribute reprints for Government purposes notwithstanding any copyright notation herein. Any opinion, findings, and conclusions or recommendations expressed in this material are those of the authors and do not necessarily reflect the views of the Combat Capabilities Development Command.

# References

1. McMahan, R.P., Lai, C., Pal, S.K.: Interaction fidelity: the uncanny valley of virtual reality interactions. In: Lackey, S., Shumaker, R. (eds.) VAMR 2016. LNCS, vol. 9740, pp. 59–70. Springer, Cham (2016). https://doi.org/10.1007/978-3-319-39907-2_6
2. Champney, R., Salcedo, J.N., Lackey, S.J., Serge, S., Sinagra, M.: Mixed reality training of military tasks: comparison of two approaches through reactions from subject matter experts. In: Lackey, S., Shumaker, R. (eds.) VAMR 2016. LNCS, vol. 9740, pp. 363–374. Springer, Cham (2016). https://doi.org/10.1007/978-3-319-39907-2_35
3. de Ribaupierre, S., Kapralos, B., Haji, F., Stroulia, E., Dubrowski, A., Eagleson, R.: Healthcare training enhancement through virtual reality and serious games. In: Ma, M., Jain, L.C., Anderson, P. (eds.) Virtual, Augmented Reality and Serious Games for Healthcare 1. ISRL, vol. 68, pp. 9–27. Springer, Heidelberg (2014). https://doi.org/10.1007/978-3-642-54816-1_2
4. Cohn, J., et al.: Training evaluation of virtual environments. In: Baker, E., Dickieson, J., Wulfeck, W., O'Neil, H. (eds.) Assessment of Problem Solving Using Simulations, pp. 81–106. Routledge, New York (2011)
5. Tactical Combat Casualty Care Handbook. 5th edn. Center for Army Lessons Learned, Fort Leavenworth (2017)
6. Montgomery, H.: Tactical Combat Casualty Care Quick Reference Guide. 1st edn (2017)
7. Xsens Customer Cases. http://www.xsens.com/customer-cases. Accessed 15 Mar 2019
8. Chan, J., Leung, H., Tang, K., Komura, T.: Immersive performance training tool using motion capture technology. In: Proceedings of the First International Conference on Immersive Telecommunications, p. 7. ICST, Brussels (2007)
9. Latash, M.: Mirror writing; learning, transfer, and implications for internal inverse models. J. Mot. Behav. **31**(2), 107–111 (1999)

# A Study on the Development of a Mixed Reality System Applied to the Practice of Socially Interactive Behaviors of Children with Autism Spectrum Disorder

Yu-Chen Huang and I-Jui Lee[(✉)]

Department of Industrial Design, National Taipei University of Technology,
Taipei, Taiwan
audrey50629@gmail.com, ericlee@ntut.edu.tw

**Abstract.** Before entering the adult world, typically developing (TD) children tend to learn how to socialize with others in the process of getting along and interacting with their peers at school. However, children with autism spectrum disorder (ASD) have difficulty understanding others' emotions and discerning non-verbal social clues due to their innately impaired social interaction and lack of theory of mind (ToM). Therefore, while socializing with others, children with ASD might not understand the facial expressions or the body movements of others. This causes great difficulty in discerning other people's emotions and recognizing the relationships between themselves and others when interacting with different people in different situations, and as a consequence, to perform the appropriate social reciprocal acts. Therapists or special education teachers usually conduct role-playing strategies to train children with ASD to practice their social reciprocity behavior, after which these children with ASD can practice socializing with others. In reality, however, such a method is generally limited to a single classroom environment and specific situations. For unimaginative children with ASD, such intervention situations and teaching methods are typically limited with low effectiveness. In response, this study adopted mixed-reality (MR) technology to establish a semi-immersive social-interactive situated teaching platform for training emotional representations and non-verbal social cues. The system allows children with ASD to socialize with 3D virtual characters who have different relationships in different virtual situations, enabling them to practice performing the appropriate social reciprocal acts.

**Keywords:** Nonverbal social cues · Mixed reality · Autism spectrum disorder · Interactive learning environments · Social reciprocal acts · Social reciprocity skills

## 1 Introduction

Children with ASD commonly have difficulties with social interaction and communication; hallmarks of impaired social skills (American Psychiatric Association 2013; World Health Organization 2018). Furthermore, a lack both imagination and abstract thinking, coupled with repeated behaviors, constitute the core disability of children

© Springer Nature Switzerland AG 2019
J. Y. C. Chen and G. Fragomeni (Eds.): HCII 2019, LNCS 11575, pp. 283–296, 2019.
https://doi.org/10.1007/978-3-030-21565-1_19

with ASD (Boelte and Hallmayer 2013). Typical social deficiencies consist of failures to properly respond to greetings, incapability of understanding non-verbal social cues, and inability to gaze into other people's eyes for emotional communication (Lee et al. 2018). Such social deficiencies make it difficult for children with ASD to socialize with others and integrate themselves into social activities involving their peers (Fodstad et al. 2009). Bauminger and Kasari (2000) suggested that compared with TD children, children with ASD are less able to socialize with others and involve themselves in group activities; nevertheless, these children still desire interactions with others. However, because of their innate social deficiencies, children with ASD are prone to fear and anxiety in the face of social interactions in life (White et al. 2009). Consequently, children with ASD are also more likely to suffer from social isolation and loneliness (White and Roberson-Nay 2009). However, even as children with ASD grow older, such deficiencies in their social skills fail to improve. This fact brought them setbacks in social interactions, and then may allow children with ASD to be afraid or reluctant to come into contact with others (White et al. 2009). Or even the fact may cause their avoiding social interaction with others (Bellini et al. 2007). Finally, such influences may give rise to some inappropriate behaviors, such as impolite behaviors due to their failure in correctly judge others' social body movements (Lee et al. 2018). As such, enhancing social skills is one of the most important improvement goals for children with ASD (DiGennaro Reed et al. 2011).

## 1.1  Current Training Methods for Teaching Social Reciprocity Skills

Recent studies have found that if children with ASD did not train their social skills at an early age, it would be more challenging for them to socialize with others in the face of more complex social situations in the future (Mundy and Crowson 1997). Or, these children might not be able to establish profound and positive social contacts and friendships with others (Williams White et al. 2007). Therefore, one direct way of helping children with ASD improve their social skills is to develop strategies of social skills training which offers more frequent practice and presents authentic events and situations (Jarrold et al. 2013). Such training will contribute to increasing opportunities for children with ASD to more extensively interact with others in different social situations. In addition, the training can allow children with ASD to make judgments and make appropriate social responses when encountering different social situations. Therefore, in order to improve social reciprocal behaviors of children with ASD, therapists or special education experts tend to use the social story method, or adopt teaching strategies such as role-playing so that children with ASD can imitate and understand social interactions in different situations (Parsons and Mitchell 2002).

## 1.2  Primary Problem with Current Training

However, previous studies have proposed different views. Bellini et al. (2007) argued that the traditional role-playing strategy difficult to interest children with ASD, which meant that these children tended to feel bored and lose patience. Compared with the traditional role playing method, training in a real-world environment with interactive games would enhance the learning motivation of children with ASD and generate a superior training effect. Therefore, related studies have suggested that educators should conduct more extensive and diversified social skills intervention training through games and other interactive modes in various authentic environments (Jarrold et al. 2013). This recommendation is important for children with ASD, because such children may have severe difficulty in transferring their application of social skills from one situation to another one. When confronting a new situation and new social objects, children with ASD often feel overwhelmed. Therefore, social training for children with ASD must be conducted in a more natural and straight state (Jarrold et al. 2013), which was more effective than treatments in statically defined and rigid classroom environments (Bellini et al. 2007). As a result, this study is aimed at decomposing complex social behaviors into visual clues, specific rules of games, and steps of interaction conducted under visual, tangible and structured social interaction scenarios. Thus, it is indispensable to translate abstract social concepts into practical social operational tasks and social interaction processes (Krasny et al. 2003). Meanwhile, this study also intends to employ a social training environment produced by MR and enable children with ASD to experience many different contextual interactions in such a training environment.

## 2  Related Work

### 2.1  Benefits of AR and VR

With the advancement of technology, more researchers have begun to apply technology to the social skills training of children with ASD in terms of social interaction and emotional perception. According to a study by Parsons and Mitchell (2002), the application of assistive technology to the social training of children with ASD can boost their learning interest and provide opportunities of repeated social exercises. In contrast to traditional single role-playing and static graphic storytelling book, the rigid and inflexible classroom learning method has been unable to interest children with ASD. In this case, the application of assistive technology such as augmented reality (AR) or virtual reality (VR) is quite beneficial for children with ASD in social interaction learning (Mesa-Gresa et al. 2018), because applications of technology media can provide repeated exercises and visual pictures with a better sound-light effect, which is also more attractive for children with ASD.

Previous studies (Lee et al. 2018; Syahputra et al. 2018) have also pointed out that AR can enhance the concentration of children with ASD, and provide visual clues to focus their attention on observing non-verbal social cues. Thus, AR can facilitate the enhancement of their ability to recognize other people's emotions and social body movements, thereby increasing their chances of successfully interacting with people and responding properly to greetings (Lee et al. 2018). Therefore, more and more studies have begun to suggest that AR can provide different social training options for children with ASD.

Compared to AR, other research has also put forward a positive view on the application of technology such as VR. The research pointed out that VR has realized social interaction and on-the-spot experience that cannot be achieved by traditional

Video Modeling (VM) and the role-playing method (Parsons and Mitchell 2002). Compared with AR, VR has an advantage in assisting role-playing and in understanding abstract social concepts, because it can provide social training, training for emotional skills and daily life, and communication skills and attention training of children with ASD (Didehbani et al. 2016; Herrera et al. 2008; Ip et al. 2018; Kandalaft et al. 2013). VR is most frequently used in social skills training, because VR can not only simulate situations in daily life, but can also increase the chances of training in different contextual scripts under the control of therapists as well as in safe simulated environments (Mesa-Gresa et al. 2018). Besides, VR can simulate a variety of situations so as to allow participants to socialize with virtual characters, and can reduce the pressure of participants in case of face-to-face communication with others (Bai et al. 2015), thereby easing the concern of being rejected due to making mistakes or even conflicting with people (Didehbani et al. 2016; Maskey et al. 2014). In addition, participants are more willing to express their real ideas or reveal their emotions and behaviors to virtual characters than to real people. And further, virtual characters have the same social characteristics as real people, and can better convey social cues than pictures or videos. Moreover, VR stimuli can be used to imitate complex social situations, and social interaction with virtual characters can not only possibly influence the social behaviors of children with ASD, but also improve the bottleneck of children with ASD in social greeting training (Lee et al. 2018). In terms of instructing children with ASD how to recognize and understand other people's social greetings and then make appropriate social responses, the application of VR can create quite intuitive status of social reciprocity which approximates real life. Therefore, related research has also found that VR technology can allow children with ASD to interact directly with characters in virtual scenes as if they were in real world, which is of great assistance for children with ASD who require real social contextual exercises (Didehbani et al. 2016).

## 2.2 Shortcomings and Deficiencies of AR & VR in Existing Social Training

Although AR offers different forms for children with ASD to interact with others in a more authentic environment in new ways, under the AR training platform, children with ASD can only socialize with interactive objects via a 2D screen and are also limited by the frame of the picture. However, the inability to directly interact with social objects constitutes a serious deficiency for using AR in social training. In addition, and in contrast to AR, although VR can enable users to be immersed in a virtual world and to socialize with virtual characters through a head-mounted display, users can not see the real environment and therefore fail to establish a connection to the real environment. Such a failure has an impact on the perception of children with ASD because people tend to upgrade their understanding and mastery of situations through experiencing the real environment so as to establish emotional connections and perform social interactions.

### 2.3 Advantages of Mixed Reality Applied to Social Reciprocity Training of Children with ASD

As a result, MR, which combines the advantages of both AR and VR technologies, constitutes a new opportunity for training children with ASD. Accurate computer calculations and image operations of MR allow virtual objects to be accurately superimposed on real objects, enabling 3D virtual characters or objects to be combined with the real environment. In this way, it can create a new MR environment that is generally visually recognized. In addition, according to studies by Cheok et al. (2002); Pan et al. (2006), MR can provide a realistic but controlled learning environment where "virtuality" coexists with reality, and at the same time, MR can produce instant interactions. Kors et al. (2016) adopted MR to allow users to play other roles and feel what such characters can feel from a first-person perspective. Dasgupta et al. (2018) believed that via MR, in which virtual structures are embedded in the physical world and interactions with virtual characters in MR can use real objects to perform social reciprocal interactions, users can feel as if situated in the new environment created by the combination of MR and real environment. The generated feelings facilitate their understanding of situations, and slowly increase their social mastering of and emotional attachment to interactive characters. Therefore, MR might be a powerful technology to help children with ASD since it allows fun and direct interactions between children with ASD and virtual characters. Additionally, it also allows children with ASD to be able to participate in role playing and interact with virtual characters from a first-person perspective, as if they were socializing with real people. Also, it can protect children from the fear of facing real people in real social environments. Such training can reduce the cognitive load on children with ASD, and the training is definitely suitable for the repeated learning of children with ASD.

## 3 Method

This study developed an MR system for the social-interaction training of children aged 7–9 with ASD, and is aimed at constructing a social interactive situated teaching platform. The purpose of this training platform is for instructing children with ASD to perform proper social reciprocal behaviors while interacting with others. This system design is based on discussions between a designer, therapist, and parent. And further, a therapist, an engineer and two designers were invited to participate in the development of an MR social-training system. The study also included observations and interactions with individual children with ASD in the occupational therapy center to have a better understanding of ASD cases. Based on discussions with the therapist regarding the observations, the designers and therapist of the study jointly determined the optimal system form and structure, which was then applied to develop the platform for the social training of children with ASD.

### 3.1    Instruments

**Development of MR-Based Social Interaction Training System.** The MR-based Social Interaction Training System (MR-SITS) in this study was focused on training children with ASD to identify others' social body movements that correspond to emotional representations (Fig. 1). In addition, this study also targeted the recognition of related social reciprocal behaviors. In addition to facial expressions, the content for training on the MR-SITS also includes understanding others' emotional manifestations by means of body movements, and then conducting social reciprocal behaviors in response to those body movements. Therefore, the MR-SITS differs from previous training systems primarily via the use of the MR system. Indeed, MR can better strengthen the relationship between body movements and the environment, and focus on situations such as saying hello to neighbors near home, shaking hands with an old friend in the park, or waving goodbye to friends at school, instead of facial expressions or other non-verbal social cues. The MR-SITS consists of three parts: (1) design of interactive context; (2) social story scripts; and, (3) social task scheduling and social body movement identification. During training, the therapist employed the MR-SITS to conduct social training of the children and scenario simulation. Moreover, the therapist strived to familiarize the children with different social situations through the platform, thereby gradually allowing children with ASD to not only have more chances of interacting with others, but also the ability to perform appropriate social reciprocal behaviors and actions in daily life.

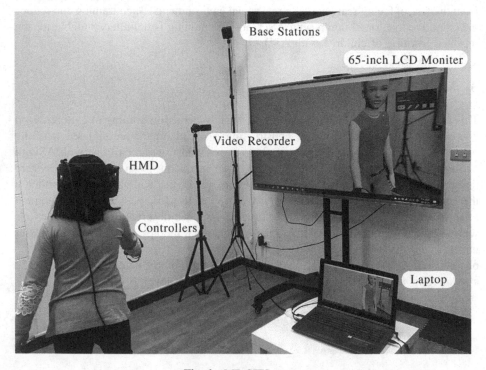

**Fig. 1.** MR-SITS set up

**System Development.** This study applied Unity3D for system construction and development of the MR-SITS. Unity3D is an engine supporting game development, the software of which is widely used for the production of interactive games and the construction of MR systems. In addition, the platform can construct contextual scenes and animated characters required by intervention training in interactive games. Developers mainly employ C# programming to achieve interactive presentations. The MR system uses a head-mounted display (HTC VIVE Pro) for spatial positioning and character tracking, which allows the participants to more naturally integrate themselves into the scenes and then socialize with virtual characters (Fig. 1). To create the virtual characters, this study used Iclone7, which can employ the front and lateral views of real people to create characters around training objects, such as students, teachers and unfamiliar social roles. In addition, the social body movements such as handshaking, hugging or handholding were defined based on discussions with the therapist and relevant experts, and then applied to the design of characters who will establish social reciprocal relationships with children with ASD.

**Setting.** The MR environments constructed in this study consisted of homes, schools, parks, stations, and other places, which contained related furnishings or furniture. These locations were chosen because such places are often visited by school age children where they would likely need to engage in social behaviors, and so were designed as interactive contextual fields. Using the MR-SITS, children with ASD encounter virtual characters, who establish various social relationships with the children in different situations, for example their families, classmates, teachers, neighbors and grocery-store clerks, or anyone with whom they may encounter often. As for visual manifestation, based on discussions with the therapist and special education experts, the scripts set by this study deleted interference factors not related to social reciprocal behavior, and the manifested content of each event simply included: (1) contextual scenes; (2) virtual characters; (3) text script and, (4) spoken dialogue.

**Design of Training Materials.** After discussing the desired scripts and scenarios with the therapist and individual parents, the study used the social-story strategy to create 15 situational story scripts. These scripts were generally inspired by children's daily life and social experiences or inspired by social situations where children often make judgement mistakes. Then, the scripts were reviewed by two experts with experience in implementing intervening teaching of social story scripts. This study created the design of the social contextual story scripts based on the severity of ASD cases as well as the learning content. The researchers constructed different social story scripts to emphasize different learning goals, such as making new friends, integrating into groups, not interrupting others, caring for others, dealing with others' anger, and so on. For example, in the story scripts, there may be the following circumstances: after school, my father is waving at me at the school gate; or when I arrive home, my mother is waiting for me with open arms. We simulated current contextual scripts through the MR environment, and asked the children with ASD to fulfill tasks of social judgement while interacting with virtual characters. In order to allow children with ASD to have a better understanding of relationships between emotions and social body movements, this study focused on six emotions proposed by Ekman and Friesen (1971): (1) happy; (2) sad; (3) angry; (4) fear; (5) disgust; and, (6) surprise. Interactions with people in different social relationships were also included. Simultaneously, this study also targeted the training of children with ASD for making appropriate social responses. In terms of social greetings, the study also defined ten different social greetings through discussions, including: (1) waving; (2) nodding and smiling; (3) handshaking; (4) handholding; (5) hugging; (6) head shaking; (7) bowing; (8) patting on shoulder; (9) clapping; and, (10) putting a hand on shoulders. Usually, such greetings are common in daily life in Taiwan.

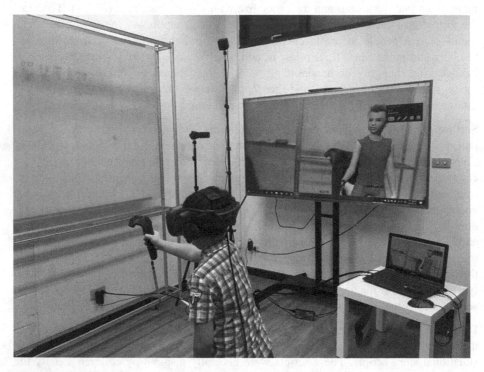

**Fig. 2.** Therapist teaching children how to use the MR-SITS and how to interact with the 3D role-play avatar

*System Operation and Interactive Program.* Upon using the MR-SITS (Fig. 2), (a) the user initially enters a virtual field, after which the children with ASD can choose to visit different contextual fields (such as a home, school, a store, and a parketc.). The system switches scenes based on the chosen location and displays different contextual scripts and scenarios corresponding to the background environment of different events. (b) Regarding operation, the platform encourages children with ASD to first explore their environment by walking around the permitted space ($3 * 3 \text{ m}^2$) and then searching the environment to detect clues embedded in the surroundings. (c) When the children with ASD walk into a specific space, they trigger the corresponding social story content and virtual characters to be encountered in that space. (d) These virtual characters then perform social behaviors in response to the predefined situation of the story script, (e) and prompt the children with ASD to respond by body movements and make social judgments (Fig. 3). (f) When the children with ASD perform the correct body movements and social judgments, the system immediately responds with clear visual pictures and auditory feedback, alerting the children with ASD that they gave the appropriate social reciprocity response. The system adopts different text scripts and 3D contextual character animations to provide more non-verbal visual cues for children with ASD. These visual cues are mainly aimed at helping children with ASD observe and understand the environment and situation within which they are located, as well as the causal relationship between social events. In this process, in addition to visual information such as the virtual scenes and the behaviors of the virtual characters, the platform also provides information such as event descriptions, background sounds in different occasions, character dialogues and facial expressions. It should be noted that such information does not suggest answers, but supports children in making judge-ments. In addition, the therapist or individual parent was asked to help the children understand and use the MR-SITS.

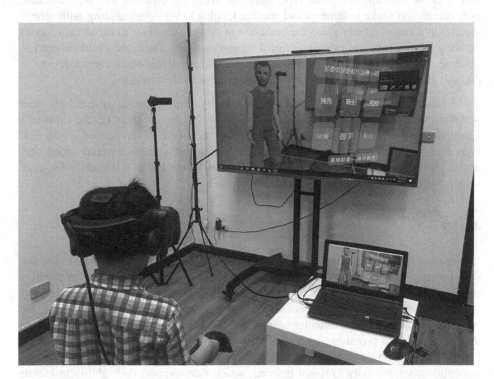

**Fig. 3.** The children with ASD to respond by body movements and make social reciprocity behavior judgments

**Social Reciprocity Behavior Judgment and Social Response.** In the MR-SITS, there are different social reciprocal tasks and judgements of emotions suggested by body movements and meanings of social behaviors. With regard to tasks, the therapist applied the platform to train children with ASD to better understand others' social body movements and emotional representations behind the body movements. Each contextual story script involved two phases of tasks. The first phase task required answers to test questions: (1) body emotions, and (2) responding to social greetings (social reciprocal behaviors). There are six options for each question, and these options were randomly selected from the aforementioned six emotions and ten social greeting behaviors defined by the researchers. The children were required to answer test questions in accordance with the system instructions before they could start the second phase, namely, role playing. The system asked the children with ASD to perform the social actions and actual social reciprocal behaviors to fulfill the role-playing tasks. As mentioned, these training situations and socially interactive behaviors were embedded within the contextual scripting of the system so as to help children with ASD improve their social interaction skills. Therefore, in each test question, the children were required to recognize emotions suggested in body movements and respond to social actions in terms of specific events. Test questions appeared during the process of social reciprocal actions and are given repeatedly, allowing the children to have numerous opportunities to make judgments and receive feedback. While socializing with others, the children must first recognize the emotions of others according to facial expressions or body movements and other emotional representations. Then, the children need to observe the body movements of others to determine what the other person desires to do, and finally, make social responses to the received information.

*Field Observations and Assessments.* In the study, the items the researchers were watching for included: (1) the social body movements of the children; (2) the children's judgments of emotions suggested in the social reciprocal behaviors of others and responses to such behaviors; and, (3) the children's ability to understand social situations. Additionally, the observed results and status could act as a reference for more in-depth contextual design and system development.

# 4   Results

In order to evaluate the impact of the MR-SITS on the physical and emotional state and social reciprocal behaviors of the children with ASD, we invited researchers engaged in special education to observe and evaluate the system. Also, we had in-depth interviews with three therapists and seven special education experts. Interviews were held after the expert observations and evaluations, in which they stated that the system appeared attractive and was promising as a tool for the social training of children with ASD. They further proposed that the teaching strategies associated with MR could enhance the children's receptivity to social training, which may support their ability to handle more complicated social situations and interactions with others. Moreover, the MR-SITS allowed children with ASD to receive training more often as well as have more opportunities to interact with different characters under different contextual scripts. And, the process of playing games on the MR-SITS platform along with the performance of children with ASD in contextual training could serve as a reference for therapists when making decisions on strengthening the training of children with ASD and determining the social interaction disorders of such children under certain circumstances. This system can provide appropriate social training courses for children with ASD at the ages of 7 to 9, since script content, personas and virtual situations were created to be of interest to them. Furthermore, with respect to the implementation of the MR-SITS, the special education experts reported that the operation process of the platform was smooth and intuitive. This platform integrates the real environment and virtual characters, thus assisting children with ASD in forming partial connections with certain circumstances and then reducing their cognitive load due to their lack of imagination.

In addition, it is noteworthy that according to the interviews and field observations, the therapist stated that the operating system design was remarkably intuitive. And she also reported that the system had the function of quickly switching the scenes and options, the functionality of which was aimed at helping the therapist control the training process and reduces the system failures caused by improper operation by the children. In addition, seven special education experts agreed that the MR-SITS was interesting and interactive. Feeling a similar interest, many children with ASD were willing to take the initiative to interact with 3D virtual characters; some children would approach and observe the virtual characters, and even reached out and tried to touch them. Accordingly, they also believed that such a system could indeed attract children's attention and boost their enthusiasm to learn. However, two experts mentioned that if a head-mounted display were worn for a long period of time, it may cause dizziness and discomfort for the children. Further, the therapist proposed that the manual controllers could be improved because the existing Vive controllers could not be used for performing certain gestures, such as waving hands, clapping out and patting on the back. Indeed, such gestures were not intuitive with the current operators. In addition, the special education experts reported that children with ASD are generally sensitive to light and sound, and therefore suggested adding a few optional buttons to control the brightness, hue, and audio volume so that the training conditions could be quickly adjusted to better accommodate the needs of each child with ASD. The special education experts also advised that the images of the virtual characters should conform to the background of the event, because the repeated training would make the children associate the story script with the corresponding role and retain such associations in mind. Put another way, such associations may affect the child's first impression of anyone they meet in the future. Such factors must be considered carefully in future research to avoid negative impacts.

## 5 Discussion

The MR-SITS is a tool developed for assisting therapists in conducting social training of children with ASD, not replacing therapy. In addition, the MR-SITS is expected to enhance the ability of children with ASD to understand the emotions reflected in others' social body movements, recognize social interaction behaviors, and improve social skills. The advantages of MR in social training are listed as follows.

## 5.1   Realistic Situations and Flexible Teaching Strategies

The semi-immersive MR-SITS reinterprets previous socializing teaching strategies in certain innovative ways, such as social stories, role playing while reading story books, and VM. It allows the training of children with ASD to occur in any space, and the sensors, head-mounted display and handle can be used to easily simulate and reproduce any situation and character so as to enable children with ASD to interact with others. The MR environment can connect the virtual environment with the real environment, allowing children with ASD feel immersed and in direct interaction with virtual characters. Differing from previous rigid learning methods and monotonous training, with such rewards and game feedback, the MR-SITS may become a visual media and training platform that attracts children with ASD to participate in the training.

## 5.2   Assisting the Children with ASD in Dealing with Diversified Social Situations and Making Immediate Responses

The MR-SITS focuses on social relationships and social interactive events, and the children are prompted to complete different social tasks within different social relationships. In the MR environment, the children were encouraged to repeatedly interact with a wide variety of virtual characters created for the MR-SITS and establish simple social relationships with them. When a child wears the head-mounted display, he or she sees virtual situations, virtual objects, virtual characters, and text of the situation scripts. What he or she sees can jointly simulate authentic situations, so that the child can observe body movements and facial expressions of virtual characters from different perspectives. Also, the MR-SITS gives children an opportunity to correct their mistakes. Moreover, a child need not worry about being hurt in a virtual simulation; as such, he or she will likely be more willing to approach that which they are reluctant to touch and have reduced fear of socializing with people.

## 5.3   MR Can Quickly and Easily Restore Social Contextual Events and Selectively Strengthen the Social Training Required in Each Case

The MR-SITS permits quick and easy changes of scenes and characters, and such a training environment can satisfy various contextual needs of therapists in social training. Simultaneously, children with ASD can see the actual therapist in the MR, which allows the therapist to assist the children in training for social skills. This enhances the sense of safety of children with ASD, and also allows therapists to provide assistance and instruction any time. In addition, the easy implementation of the system can make it easy for special education experts, therapist, and individual parents to conduct such training for children with ASD to simply and intuitively perform physical and emotional representations, recognitions of non-verbal clues and other social skills. The MR-SITS identifies completed levels and tracks scoring, which can be provided to the therapist and individual families as evaluation data. In addition, the scores could be used to better understand what needs strengthening in each case, and then for the intensification of social training of weak parts.

# 6 Conclusions

This study concerned only the preliminary design of the MR-SITS, which is set to be more focused on social skills training. The system created virtual characters with which children with ASD can interact. Such a design, namely that the MR system integrates virtual characters into different situations, is an innovative approach used in the social training of children with ASD. In the future, we will exploit the visual advantages of MR and combine these advantages with multi-sensory experiences to create more complete and attractive training content. Finally, we hoped that this study can inspire other studies and bring a new research area and opportunity to studies concerning ASD.

**Acknowledgments.** We are grateful to the Executive Yuan and Ministry of Science and Technology for funding under project. No. MOST 107-2218-E-027-013-MY2.

# References

American Psychiatric Association: Diagnostic and Statistical Manual of Mental Disorders, 5th edn. American Psychiatric Association, Washington, DC (2013)

Bauminger, N., Kasari, C.: Loneliness and friendship in high-functioning children with autism. Child Dev. **71**(2), 447–456 (2000)

Bai, Z., Blackwell, A., Coulouris, G.: Using augmented reality to elicit pretend play for children with autism. IEEE Trans. Vis. Comput. Graph. **21**(5), 598–610 (2015)

Bellini, S., Peters, J.K., Benner, L., Hopf, A.: A meta-analysis of school-based social skills interventions for children with autism spectrum disorders. Remedial Spec. Educ. **28**(3), 153–162 (2007)

Boelte, S., Hallmayer, J.: Autism Spectrum Conditions: FAQs on Autism, Asperger Syndrome, and Atypical Autism Answered by International Experts. Hogrefe Publishing, Ashland (2013)

Cheok, A.D., Yang, X., Ying, Z.Z., Billinghurst, M., Kato, H.: Touch-space: mixed reality game space based on ubiquitous, tangible, and social computing. Pers. Ubiquit. Comput. **6**(5), 430–442 (2002)

Dasgupta, A., Buckingham, N., Gračanin, D., Handosa, M., Tasooji, R.: A mixed reality based social interactions testbed: a game theory approach. In: Chen, J.Y.C., Fragomeni, G. (eds.) VAMR 2018. LNCS, vol. 10910, pp. 40–56. Springer, Cham (2018). https://doi.org/10.1007/978-3-319-91584-5_4

Didehbani, N., Allen, T., Kandalaft, M., Krawczyk, D., Chapman, S.: Virtual Reality Social Cognition Training for children with high functioning autism. Comput. Hum. Behav. **62**, 703–711 (2016)

DiGennaro Reed, F.D., Hyman, S.R., Hirst, J.M.: Applications of technology to teach social skills to children with autism. Res. Autism Spectr. Disord. **5**(3), 1003–1010 (2011)

Ekman, P., Friesen, W.V.: Constants across cultures in the face and emotion. J. Pers. Soc. Psychol. **17**(2), 124 (1971)

Fodstad, J.C., Matson, J.L., Hess, J., Neal, D.: Social and communication behaviours in infants and toddlers with autism and pervasive developmental disorder-not otherwise specified. Dev. Neurorehabil. **12**(3), 152–157 (2009)

Herrera, G., Alcantud, F., Jordan, R., Blanquer, A., Labajo, G., De Pablo, C.: Development of symbolic play through the use of virtual reality tools in children with autistic spectrum disorders: two case studies. Autism **12**(2), 143–157 (2008)

Ip, H.H.S., et al.: Enhance emotional and social adaptation skills for children with autism spectrum disorder: a virtual reality enabled approach. Comput. Educ. **117**, 1–15 (2018)

Jarrold, W., et al.: Social attention in a virtual public speaking task in higher functioning children with autism. Autism Res. **6**, 393–410 (2013)

Kandalaft, M.R., Didehbani, N., Krawczyk, D.C., Allen, T.T., Chapman, S.B.: Virtual reality social cognition training for young adults with high-functioning autism. J. Autism Dev. Disord. **43**(1), 34–44 (2013)

Kors, M.J.L., Ferri, G., van der Spek, E.D., Ketel, C., Schouten, B.A.M.: A breathtaking journey. On the design of an empathy-arousing mixed-reality game. In: Paper Presented at the Proceedings of the 2016 Annual Symposium on Computer-Human Interaction in Play, Austin, Texas, USA (2016)

Krasny, L., Williams, B.J., Provencal, S., Ozonoff, S.: Social skills interventions for the autism spectrum: essential ingredients and a model curriculum. Child Adolesc. Psychiatr. Clin. North Am. **12**(1), 107–122 (2003)

Lee, I.-J., Lin, L.-Y., Chen, C.-H., Chung, C.-H.: How to create suitable augmented reality application to teach social skills for children with ASD. In: State of the Art Virtual Reality and Augmented Reality Knowhow, vol. 8, pp. 119–138. IntechOpen (2018)

Lee, I.J., Chen, C.H., Wang, C.P., Chung, C.H.: Augmented reality plus concept map technique to teach children with ASD to use social cues when meeting and greeting. Asia-Pac. Educ. Res. **27**(3), 227–243 (2018)

Maskey, M., Lowry, J., Rodgers, J., McConachie, H., Parr, J.R.: Reducing specific phobia/fear in young people with autism spectrum disorders (ASDs) through a virtual reality environment intervention. PLoS One **9**(7), e100374 (2014)

Mesa-Gresa, P., Gil-Gómez, H., Lozano-Quilis, J.-A., Gil-Gómez, J.-A.: Effectiveness of virtual reality for children and adolescents with autism spectrum disorder: an evidence-based systematic review. Sensors **18**(8), 2486 (2018)

Mundy, P., Crowson, M.: Joint attention and early social communication: implications for research on intervention with autism. J. Autism Dev. Disord. **27**(6), 653–676 (1997)

Pan, Z., Cheok, A.D., Yang, H., Zhu, J., Shi, J.: Virtual reality and mixed reality for virtual learning environments. Comput. Graph. **30**(1), 20–28 (2006)

Parsons, S., Mitchell, P.: The potential of virtual reality in social skills training for people with autistic spectrum disorders. J. Intellect. Disabil. Res. **46**(5), 430–443 (2002)

Syahputra, M., Arisandi, D., Lumbanbatu, A., Kemit, L., Nababan, E., Sheta, O.: Augmented reality social story for autism spectrum disorder. J. Phys.: Conf. Ser. **978**(1), 012–040 (2018)

White, S.W., Oswald, D., Ollendick, T., Scahill, L.: Anxiety in children and adolescents with autism spectrum disorders. Clin. Psychol. Rev. **29**(3), 216–229 (2009)

White, S.W., Roberson-Nay, R.: Anxiety, social deficits, and loneliness in youth with autism spectrum disorders. J. Autism Dev. Disord. **39**(7), 1006–1013 (2009)

Williams White, S., Keonig, K., Scahill, L.: Social skills development in children with autism spectrum disorders: a review of the intervention research. J. Autism Dev. Disord. **37**(10), 1858–1868 (2007)

World Health Organization (2018). http://www.who.int/en/news-room/fact-sheets/detail/autism-spectrum-disorders

# Cicero VR - Public Speaking Training Tool and an Attempt to Create Positive Social VR Experience

Michał Jakubowski[✉], Marcin Wardaszko, Anna Winniczuk,
Błażej Podgórski, and Małgorzata Ćwil

Kozminski University, Warsaw, Poland
{mjakubowski, wardaszko, awinniczuk, bpodgorski,
mcwil}@kozminski.edu.pl

**Abstract.** Cicero VR game is a simulation gaming tool for public speaking skills training. The game system is measuring user efforts regarding the volume and speed of speech, gesticulation and eye contact with in-game models. There are two modes of play: practice (where you can train how to speak with use of benchmark presentation) and challenge (where you can upload your presentation that pitches new product or service).

Presentation in practice mode features a scenario of a yearly report submission in front of a board about a new brand in the company. We have created a fictional car-sharing service, and the user has to present all valuable data standing in a conference room in one of the downtown skyscrapers. The virtual audience varies regarding demographic representation (race, gender and age). They will also react to users performance quality. If the talk is performed with right volume, gesticulation, and maintaining the eye contact – then board avatars will act as more engaged and vice versa.

The following paper will describe outcomes of the testing phase of such gaming artifact with analysis of overall VR experience reception. The simulation game was tested by business university students in fall of 2018.

**Keywords:** Virtual reality · Digital game-based learning ·
Serious game design · Immersion · Public speaking skills ·
User experience research

## 1 Introduction

Advancement in IT technologies creates disturbances to the business and scientific world but also create many opportunities. One of such technologies is Virtual reality (henceforth VR). VR can create and simulate a three-dimensional (3D) interactive environments. Such technology can create immersive learning experiences in a new and unique way (Sun, Wu and Cai 2018). The aim of this article is to show the conclusions from the design, production and testing the serious VR game for teaching soft-skills in public teaching through a simulated scenario of a board meeting. We would also like to discuss the various learning contexts, in which such games can be used and implemented.

© Springer Nature Switzerland AG 2019
J. Y. C. Chen and G. Fragomeni (Eds.): HCII 2019, LNCS 11575, pp. 297–311, 2019.
https://doi.org/10.1007/978-3-030-21565-1_20

The capabilities of the VR technology for learning and education is potentially very broad (Hockey et al. 2010), from creating simulators and showcasing functioning of almost any environment possible to imagine, through supporting 3D driven design and development, up to the full function interactive virtual worlds and supporting telepresence. The VR environments, in todays form, present both intrinsic and extrinsic value to the learners (Shukla and Conrad 2011). Although, VR technologies for learning show their true learning capabilities when are linked in interactions with the physical world (Christopoulos et al. 2018; Bower et al. 2010; Hoshi et al. 2009). Looking for synergies between serious VR game design and learner choices in the interactive environment can create a very high level of engagement and increase the learning effectiveness with the educational content that is present in the virtual and physical environment.

When considering using VR tools in classroom environment one needs to challenge the problem of group participation. As the VR headsets are rather expensive to have more than one at once in use, the VR experience designers are trying to overcome that with engaging the whole audience in the experience. It would be extremely difficult to maintain everyone's attention while doing the same exercise with only one participant at once. The idea of including course participants who don't wear the HMD at the moment into whole learning experience was a design goal throughout the project.

VR technology also faces a range of limitations. One of the major limitations is simulator sickness (Maraj et al. 2017) or as many researchers relate it to the VR implantation through HMD as cybersickness. Rebenitsch and Owen (2016:102) define cybersickness as "the onset of nausea, oculomotor and/disorientation while experiencing virtual environments in head-mounted displays, large screens, and curved screen systems." The growing number of research is concentrated around the topic of sources of cybersickness, and the results are mixed. Some of the research results reported that HMD usage in VR environments could cause cybersickness (Yörük et al. 2018; Treleaven et al. 2015) and it has a negative effect on the presentence in the VR environments. However, other earlier studies indicated that walking and movements, which are in line with the natural body movement can prevent simulator sickness (Chance et al. 1998) or that presence in the VR environment is not related to the cybersickness but other external effects are causing it (Nichols et al. 2000). The topic of cybersickness is still underdeveloped and more research on this topic is still needed for a better understanding of this phenomena.

The following paper describes design concept of positive social VR and presents results of a pilot study of VR user experience perspective. That data was a valuable input for the next iterations of the simulation development and can be treated as a benchmarking measure for similar projects.

## 2   Game Design

One of the most challenging tasks in the VR application for learning is designing the environment that is both natural and immersive. The VR games are good at recreating existing or fictional environments with a high grade of physical fidelity. However, in simulation gaming, we use abstraction for showing high-level theoretical concepts or when dealing with complex systems. VR games present on the market so far for educational purposes are struggling in using abstraction without being perceived as silly or unprecise. Thus designing a serious VR game for management filed in the soft skills area was a very challenging and uneasy task.

The serious VR game "CICERO" has been designed with learners of beginner or entry level of knowledge and skills in public speaking for business. The basic aim of the game is to create a realistic environment and game scenarios that will incorporate the most typical business environments and situations that require public speaking skills.

The whole idea for creating a VR presentation training tool was ignited during a brainstorming session of the core team. As a starting point of generating ideas the team got the concept proper use of VR medium with a focus on building an immersive simulation of a situation that can be helpful for business school students. The final choice was made after an internal discussion about the most valuable scenario to simulate. What is interesting is that forms of interactions were present in most of the ideas, which were using voice and gesture recognition.

Design goals set at first were as follows:

1. Training of public speaking in a realistic environment and context: the user will have the possibility to try her skills in a situation that can occur in the future.
2. Focus on creating a feeling of presence inside VR: real-time reactions of virtual models, background sounds, questions from the audience.
3. Measurement of users performance: development of the scoring system that can be used throughout different scenarios and will enhance engagement.

Since the simulation was aimed to be used in a classroom setting there was an additional design goal of extending the experience beyond just one user wearing a VR headset. Including a broader audience was definitely an interesting challenge that could result in the increased attention span of the whole group and not only the person that is in the training process at the moment. One of the main objectives of the game system design was to fully use the potential of VR hardware and create an immersing virtual reality environment, which will help with public speaking training. Cicero can be used as a solo experience or in a classroom environment, with the live audience. In making the experience more attractive for all people present in the room we have designed asynchronous and asymmetric participation experience for the audience. We provide a simple voting mobile tool, which they can collectively choose questions based on the majority rule. The chosen questions will be asked by virtual models inside the simulation. That corresponds to Jagnow (2017) talk during VRDC Fall 2017 about building positive social VR. He mentions three attributes of VR and AR experiences that are not getting much attention yet during design: asymmetric, asynchronous and abuse. Asymmetric is about joining the same experience from different devices. Asynchronous enables participation of a group of users at different time intervals. Abuse aspect treats negative interactions that can be present within the virtual group experience between its participants. In Cicero we designed an asymmetric and asynchronous experience, if the training takes part in the classroom. The first version of the voting tool aimed to research on how that positive social experience of VR will work in a learning context.

By design the voting will happen after the user finishes her presentation and the real audience will vote on one out of four questions randomly chosen from the whole set of twenty (Fig. 1).

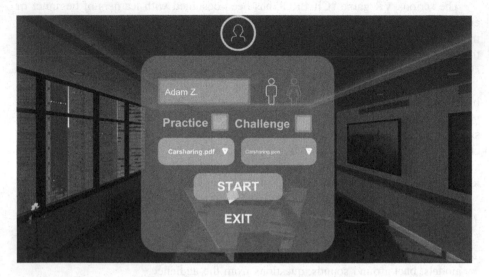

**Fig. 1.** The starting screen of Cicero VR

The game has been designed and build in the Unity3D engine with HTC Vive head-mounted displays in mind. The type of the HMD is important as they feature very different screen resolution and thus have implication for the depth of the field of vision presented to the player. The field of vision depth is important for the design of the CICERO VR game as we present periodically the information on the effectiveness of the player on the edge of the field of vision in the form of a HUD (heads-up display).

One of the other concerns was cybersickness. Although, it is impossible to fully get rid of the cybersickness in VR, we can decrease the probability of the cybersickness occurrence with the game design (Yörük et al. 2018; Treleaven et al. 2015; Chance et al. 1998). In the case of CICERO, the player is positioned in the natural way of a presenter standing in the brightly lighted room. The movement in the game is natural (walking) and limited to the 2–3 steps in every direction and this is in-line with the role of the presenter in the game.

## 3   Game Scenario

In the process of the scenario design for the first version of the game, we have decided to use the two most common scenarios with different game modes in mind.

Scenario no 1. The first scenario is a typical boardroom setup. The story follows the situation when you are the project manager of the growing carsharing company (CarMa), and you present two variants of the project execution options to the board of directors. In this case, you will receive a prepared presentation from your "team", and your task is to present it in front of the board in a professional way.

In this scenario, the game works in the mastery mode. In this mode, the task of the learner is to be as close as possible to the perfect presentation pattern, i.e. master. The mastery, in this case, is established by two public speaking professionals – male and female, who present the same presentation in an instructional video. Also, the learner has a virtual card in one of the hands with useful hints and tips, which can work as a form of a virtual teleprompter. In the master mode, the internal scoring system counts the deportations of the learner from the "perfect" master presentation and displays the positive and negative scores in the form of the visual aids every time the learner switches the slide in the game. The presentation has 18 slides (with starting and the closing one) the whole scenario has been designed to be played around 15 min to minimalize cybersickness occurrence probability (Yörük et al. 2018; Kolasinski 1995). In this scenario, there are also around 20 questions with a different level of complexity. In the classroom setting live audience can vote with a specially designed companion web app on the up to 4 questions that can be assigned to be asked by one of the avatars anytime in the game.

Scenario no 2. The second scenario describes a situation of the business idea pitch to potential investors. In this case, the learner can provide their presentation in PDF form, and it will be implemented into the game by the instructor. Thus the learner can see and interact with own presentation. In this, scenario game works in the challenge mode. In the challenge mode, the game does not show any scores on the player's performance but records the presentation and all designated parameters.

Both scenarios feature some elements and measures for gameplay and learning effectiveness. The first and one of the mechanics of the most important game is the four dimension measure system. The game measures and in the mastery mode scores following four elements:

- Sight direction – where the players look during the gameplay, measured in seconds by object or avatar;
- Speaking speed – how fast is the player speaking, measured by the number of words per minute;
- Speaking sound volume - how loud is the player speaking and if she modulates the voice, measured by decibels per millisecond – approx. Ten times per second.
- Gestures – how often a player is gesticulating, measured by the distance between HMD and haptic virtual controllers in the player's hands.

The virtual room setup and interactive avatars are the common features of both scenarios. The room setup, table placements, and avatar positioning pattern are the key factors in this design area (Fig. 2).

The key features of this room setup are the professional office setting for better immersion, the boardroom is in the high floor of downtown's skyscraper, and from the windows, you can see other buildings. In the room, you find v-shaped table of the furniture and decoration, the position of the table and other elements in the room is

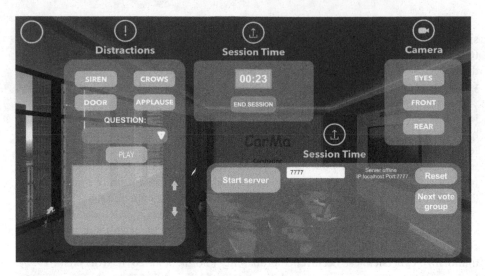

**Fig. 2.** Control panel view with real time preview of users actions in the background

designed with gaze positioning in mind, so no other object comes in the way. In this way, we achieve the ability to monitor the position of the players gaze without disturbing the game flow and immersion.

Second common design elements are interactive avatars. In total, up to 5 avatars spawn at the beginning of every each around the V-shaped table. The basic rule to the spawning point is an only non-obstructive view to each avatar so it can be seen clearly and the gaze mechanic measurement system can work seamlessly. The avatar models have both male and female versions (Fig. 3).

The avatars can have different skin tones, hairstyles, eye color, and ethnic resemblance. The algorithm spawning the avatars randomizes the gender and ethnic origin with diversity in mind. It creates up to 5 avatars and places them at the table. Their clothes are always business casual, but cloth colors and details can vary. The avatars have assigned a fixed set of animations that can be applied both indecently (player independent reactions) and as visual feedback to the presenter (player dependent reactions) (Slater, Pertaub, Steed 1999). Each one of them also can ask the question, female and male versions of the questions audio has been recorded for this purpose.

The last common design mechanic in the game for both scenarios are distraction mechanic. Distractions are a series of audio-visual incidents that can be administered to the virtual environment by the instructor at random. There are two types of incidents. The first group is incidents based only on sound, e.g. a sudden fire alarm or police sirens. The second group is audio-visual incidents, e.g. a flock of loud birds is flying outside the window or someone opens the door and looks inside the room quickly etc. The role of the incidents is twofold. The first role is to create a distraction. The second is to create stronger immersion by stepping up the environment fidelity and prepare a player for such distractions in the real public speaking environment.

**Fig. 3.** Avatar models sitting at the conference table.

## 4   Learning Modules and Strategy

The VR technology has significant potential for learning, but it is critical how the game is positioned within the learning experience and how it mixes with physical reality for better learning effectiveness (Christopoulos et al. 2018; Bower et al. 2010; Hoshi et al. 2009).

Four different combinations of technology and learning can be pieced together: learning about technology, learning from technology, learning with technology and learning in technology (Schrader 2008). This approach is very similar to the traditional placement of simulation gaming placement within the learning space represented by Klabbers (2006) or Duke and Geurts (2004). In case of the VR game in this particular scope is critical how player communicates with the game. Players can move and move within the virtual space (Herbet et al. 2012; Hockey et al. 2010) they can speak, gaze and use hand gestures (Carter 2012; Hockey et al. 2010).

The optimal setting for the course has been designed with people who are beginners in public speaking or have little experience. The basic aim of the game-based learning program is to give the students basic knowledge of the public speaking and the necessary skills. The whole course is organized in the experiential learning methodology (Kolb and Kolb 2005). Before the beginning of the course, students receive two pages of instructions with information about the course and the game. In the instruction, they also find a link to the closed YouTube channel with video material. The video material contains seven video materials. First, two contain the presentation from the scenario no 1 performed by two professional public speaking experts (male and female). In the third and fourth video, they explain the presentation techniques they have used in the presentation. The fifth and sixth video material is devoted to the most important aspect of public speaking and their view on the presenter's style and charisma. The last material is a short tutorial on how to play the CICERO VR game. Altogether, it is around 1 h of video material divided in the short videos of 7 to 15 min long. The students are asked to review this material before the game with special care to the presentation itself and the VR game tutorial. The instruction also contains the link to the copy of the presentation so they can train it before the game session.

In scenario no 1, players learn by example and by repeating the masters. In a scenario no 2 the players learn from feedback analysis of their performance. The game measures four player actions and gives visual feedback in the game and also presents all data in the performance report produced in the PDF file on the end of the gaming session. The sessions should be separated in time so the simulator fatigue will not increase the chance of cybersickness.

The icons presented in Table 1 appear in a HUD style with color code in the bottom of the HMD field of vision depth every time the player changes to the next slide, as the players control the pace of the presentation. The color-coded icons are the primary feedback system, which informs the player how he or she performed in the previous slide; they glow red or green for a few seconds. This secondary feedback system is

**Table 1.** Visual feedback icons in CICERO VR game.

| Player actions | Visual feedback icon | Measurement unit | Scoring in the mastery mode |
|---|---|---|---|
| Sight direction | | Seconds per object or avatar; | The player scores the points by looking at the different avatars and presentation and not on objects, windows, etc. |
| Speaking speed | | Number of words, words per minute, average words per minute; | Scoring is made by the departure from the optimal value corridor. |
| Speaking sound volume | | Voice loudness in decibels per millisecond; | Players need to talk loud enough to be heard (in decibels) but should modulate the voice; |
| Gestures | | A number of hand gestures measured by the distance between HMD and haptic virtual controllers in the player's hands. | There are a set number of specific gestures that the player should perform during each slide; |

avatar behavior. As mention in the game design section, each avatar comes with two sets of behavior manifested by the animations. First avatar behavior set is player independent and represents the basic set of human behavior. The purpose of this mechanic is to increase immersion and bring the avatars more to live, e.g. following the player with eyesight, looking at the phone or out the window, etc. The second set of avatar behavior is player performance dependent. Basically, the avatars will pay less attention and will be distracted more often if the performance is poor and more focused and engaged if the performance is high.

After the game session finishes, the system automatically creates a PDF file with generated data from the measurement and scoring system, and it can be sent to the player's email (see Appendix 1).

Each playthrough should be accompanied by a debriefing session with the instructor. In the classroom setup player, group and instructor can analyze the data and talk about the performance of the players. After the gameplay analysis instructor assigns the players with reading, other exercises activities and lectures but in this setup can individualize the learning program based on the gathered data and gameplay video.

## 5 Research Methodology

Research of the created VR simulation was an important step not only because of improving user experience of our tool but also to generate data that could be later used as a benchmark for other simulations. Three research questions were stated:

1. How students perceive the current usability of the VR presentation training tool?
2. What are the design elements that can be improved?
3. What are the design elements that are missing?

Participants were chosen among university students, aged 19–24. We involved 36 people (15 female, 21 male), most of them (20 people) had experienced some form of VR before with PlayStation VR as a leading brand.

Each of the students had to prepare before the test by watching instructional videos and get familiar with presentation slides. Although there were some students that were just observers as the participation in the research was voluntary. After finishing the presentation in VR users were asked to complete a questionnaire. We have used modified version Game Experience Questionnaire (GEQ) which was created to examine UX of games and similar software (IJsselsteijn et al. 2013), which our VR presentation training seemed to fit better than into other tools (i.e. UEQ). GEQ is based on 3 modules: core questionnaire, social presence module, and post-game module. We have given up the social presence module due to no vivid interactions with in-game models at the moment. That will be needed in our regard in the next iteration of the simulation. Other modules were used in the original form of the questionnaire. In our case there were additional open questions regards better recognition of which elements are working good and which are missing.

The experience of asymmetric and asynchronous experience was not in the scope of this research. To make more reliable we decided to improve the VR experience first.

## 6 The Results

We used a modified version Game Experience Questionnaire (GEQ) for this research and thus the first analysis is focused on the reliability of the questionnaire and gathered data. Statistical analysis was based on Cronbach's alpha test to assure the reliability of answers for each component (Table 2).

**Table 2.** The questionnaire reliability analysis.

| Component | Cronbach's alpha* | Statistical significance |
|---|---|---|
| Competence | ,843 | Yes |
| Sensory and Imaginative Immersion | ,34 | No |
| Flow | ,246 | No |
| Tension | ,805 | Yes |
| Challenge | ,295 | No |
| Tiredness | ,745 | Yes |
| Positive affect | ,654 | Yes |
| Negative affect | ,481 | Limited |
| Returning to reality | ,799 | Yes |

*all calculations with the $p < 0.05$

Reliability of answers for most components resulted as significant, which means that those components can be analyzed in the whole population of the study. The results show that we were able to reliably measure the Competence, Tension, Tiredness, Positive affect and Returning to reality also Negative affect with borderline significance (Fig. 4).

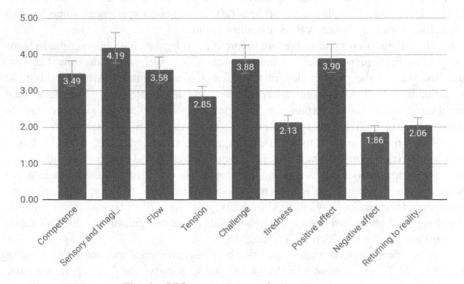

**Fig. 4.** GEQ components and average means

Majority of the students felt competent while playing the game, which is a design intent logic. Moreover, from the internal correlation matrix (Pearson's at $p < 0,05$) they were statistically significant correlated with Positive affect (Pearson's 0,4703) and negatively correlated with Tension (Pearson's −0,3582). Tension was also statistically significant correlated with the Returning to reality (Pearson's 0,4510). Tiredness is statistically significant correlated to the Returning to reality (Pearson's 0,3353), which is logical and points at the fact that cybersickness is an important and always present issue. We were not able to reliably measure the perception of the Sensory and Imaginative Immersion, Flow and Challenge. Thus our conclusions about these elements for the design have to be limited. The reasons being lack of reliability can be relatively low number of data or more refined questionnaire data, as we had to adapt the research tool that was not designed with VR serious games in mind.

For those components that were statistical significant, it is possible to conclude about components and answers for its questions among the investigated population. In Competence component, about 50% of users felt successful while doing the task and using their skills. Responses for Tension component questions have shown that 80% didn't feel frustration and 77% were not irritated during the experience. From the post-game components, about 70% of users were satisfied of the experience (Positive affect) and about 60% felt tired or unsatisfied (Negative affect). Relatively high results in the last significant component – Returning to reality – where about 66% stated that they had disorientation and tiredness problems.

Three open questions stated at the end of the questionnaire has helped to understand better user experience and needs for making it better in future iterations of the tool. During the process of coding four categories emerged from the answers which are described as follows:

1. Visuals (positive/negative): This category contains how users were satisfied or unsatisfied about the visual side of the simulation. On the positive side, they have stated that they like the conference room and models or the view from the window. On the negatives – blurry image, problems with readability of the slides. That was something that may be hard to improve without changing headset technology into higher resolution in HMD.
2. Novelty (positive/negative): This category contains how users perceived novelty of the simulation and how they feel about it. On the positive side, they liked that new experience and possibilities that it has to offer. On the negatives, we found answers about the inconvenience of the device or unfamiliarity of the training process.
3. Immersion (positive/negative): This category contains how users feel a presence inside the simulation. Positive aspects they perceived were connected to audio cutout from the rest of the room (via headphones and ambient noise) or realistic set and setting of the scene. Negative aspects that influenced immersion were distractions played by the instructor and dissonance between VR scene and real room – some were afraid that they will hit something while moving in virtual space.
4. Stress (positive/negative): This category contains perceived feelings about stress level of users during the simulation. On the positives, the students stated such opinions like the ability to challenge own presentation skills, less embarrassment when presenting in VR, less stress in the virtual room. Negative stress factors of the

experience were on the contrary – some of the users were stressed because of the awareness that there are other people in the real room watching them during the simulation (Fig. 5).

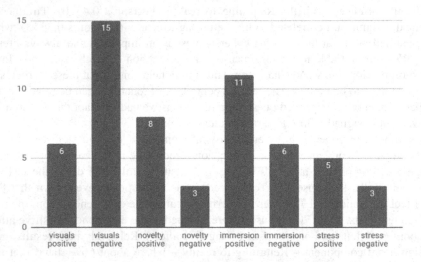

**Fig. 5.** Open questions coding and frequency distribution

Additional question about missing features resulted in a couple of interesting remarks about the quality of current models of the audience in VR. It was hard to read their reactions or body language and treat it as quick feedback for the presentation. Some students stated that adding more ways for interaction with between real audience and simulation user would enhance both experiences. That is another lead to explore during the next iterations that will be taken into consideration.

## 7 Limitations

Authors are aware of the limitations of described research. It was already stated that it is a pilot study of a rather novel use of VR in educational purposes and the knowledge about the proper way of conducting such study is still not grounded. The GEQ that we have used was created with entertainment games in mind, although it rather well worked with this case then some tweaks of this tools can be made to consider other factors of experience that are VR specific.

## 8 Conclusions

The VR game design process and implantation into learning experience produced a large number of interesting insights into the specific aspects of the VR technology, as well as, questions about effective implantation of the VR gaming technology in the curriculum (Shen et al. 2018).

VR technology allows game designers to create an environment they desire or need for the particular setup. In serious game design, we want to use this feature with the player and purpose in mind (Duke 1972). In this particular setup, the author chose to use VR technology in the way of mimicking the reality with additional gaming layer and by creating a safe space environment for users to play with (Kriz 2003).

Every technology comes with some limitations. The VR technology comes with limitations to hardware nature in the form of cybersickness when using HMD, while designing the serious game we have to keep in mind safety of the players and incorporate safety design and procedures while testing and playing. Instructors have to undergo safety training and follow the procedure of decreasing the potential for cybersickness. The soft limitation is the ability of the game to immerse the players and deliver a meaningful experience. This limitation works with the notion, that so far the VR technology is rather weak in transferring highly theoretical or complex knowledge and systems. However, we expect this to change in the coming years, as much more good quality games and solutions will appear on the market and in the research.

In the end, authors support the statement that serious VR games work in a most effective way in connection with the physical world (Christopoulos et al. 2018; Bower et al. 2010; Hoshi et al. 2009) through interactions and meaning. Giving the ability to include the player's own presentation into the virtual environment was designed with that statement in mind.

## Appendix 1. Smaple Exert from the Players Perfromance Report

### VR Presentation Skills Training
Student: MR X

#### Your results:

| | | |
|---|---|---|
| | Volume points | 7 |
| | Word speed points | 10 |
| | Look points: | 5 |
| | Sign points: | 2 |
| | OVERALL: | 24 |

Detailed report

Session's time was: 10 min 12 s

Student had observed following objects:
1. Shelves had been observed for: 5.9 s
2. ludekF had been observed for: 6.7 s
3. Screen had been observed for: 49.5 s
4. ludekA had been observed for: 4.7 s
5. ludekC had been observed for: 6.1 s
6. Door had been observed for: 1.5 s
7. Boss had been observed for: 9.7 s
8. Picture (right) had been observed for: 0.6 s
9. ludekD had been observed for: 0 s
10. Picture (left) had been observed for: 0.1 s
Student's average volume was: 0.2 s

Student said 148 words in total.
Average words per minute: 52.38164.

# References

Bower, M., Cram, A., Groom, D.: Blended reality: issues and potentials in combining virtual worlds and face-to-face classes. In: Proceedings of the Australasian Society for Computers in Learning in Tertiary Education (Ascilite), Sydney, pp. 129–140 (2010)

Bracken, C.C., Skalski, P.: Immersed in media: telepresence in everyday life. Routledge, London (2010)

Carter, B.: Virtual Harlem: an innovative past, an evolving present and an exciting future. In: Gardner, M., Garnier, F., Kloos, C.D. (eds.) Proceedings of the 2nd European Immersive Initiative Summit, Paris, France, pp. 24–37 (2012)

Chance, S.S., Gaunet, F., Beall, A.C., Loomis, J.M.: Locomotion mode affects the updating of objects encountered during travel: the contribution of vestibular and proprioceptive inputs to path integration. Presence 7(2), 168–178 (1998)

Christopoulos, A., Conrad, M., Shukla, M.: Increasing student engagement through virtual interactions: how. Virtual Reality 22, 1–17 (2018)

Duke, R., Geurts, J.L.: Policy Games for Strategic Management. Dutch University Press, Amsterdam (2004)

Heiling, M.: Sensorama simulator (1962). http://www.mortonheilig.com/. Accessed 19 Oct 2018

Herbet, A., Thompson, F., Garnier, F.: Immaterial art stock: preserve, document and disseminate the pioneering works of art created inside online immersive platforms. In: Gardner, M., Garnier, F., Kloos, C.D. (eds.) Proceedings of the 2nd European Immersive Education Summit, Paris, France, pp. 101–113 (2012)

Hockey, A., Esmail, F., Jimenez-Bescos, C., Freer, P.: Built environment education in the era of virtual learning. In: W089— Special Track 18th CIB World Building Congress, Salford, pp. 200–217 (2010)

Hoshi, K., Pesola, U.M., Waterworth, E.L., Waterworth, J.A.: Tools, perspectives and avatars in blended reality space. Ann. Rev. Cyberther. Telemed. 7, 91–95 (2009)

Lorenz, M., Busch, M., Rentzos, L., Tscheligi, M., Klimant, P., Fröhlich, P.: I'm there! The influence of virtual reality and mixed reality environments combined with two different navigation methods on presence. In: 2015 IEEE Virtual Reality (VR), pp. 223–224. IEEE, March 2015

IJsselsteijn, W.A., de Kort, Y.A.W., Poels, K.: The game experience questionnaire. Technische Universiteit Eindhoven, Eindhoven (2013)

Jagnow, R.: Building VR communities: asymmetry, asynchrony, and abuse. In: Talk at VRDC Fall 2017 Conference (2018)

Klabbers, J.: The Magic Circle: Principles of Gaming & Simulation. Sense Publishers, Rotterdam (2006)

Kolasinski, E.M.: Simulator sickness in virtual environments (ARI Technical report 1027). Army Research Institute for the Behavioral and Social Sciences, Alexandria (1995)

Kolb, A.Y., Kolb, D.A.: Learning styles and learning spaces: enhancing experiential learning in higher education. Acad. Manag. Learn. Educ. 4(2), 193–212 (2005)

Maraj, C.S., Badillo-Urquiola, K.A., Martinez, S.G., Stevens, J.A., Maxwell, D.B.: Exploring the impact of simulator sickness on the virtual world experience. In: Kantola, J.I., Barath, T., Nazir, S., Andre, T. (eds.) Advances in human factors, business management, training and education, pp. 635–643. Springer, Cham (2017). https://doi.org/10.1007/978-3-319-42070-7_59

North, M.M., North, S.M., Coble, J.R.: Virtual reality therapy: an effective treatment for the fear of public speaking. Int. J. Virtual Reality (IJVR) 03(3), 1–6 (2015)

Nichols, S., Haldane, C., Wilson, J.R.: Measurement of presence and its consequences in virtual environments. Int. J. Hum Comput Stud. 52(3), 471–491 (2000)

Rebenitsch, L., Owen, C.: Review on cybersickness in applications and visual displays. Virtual Reality 20(2), 101–125 (2016). https://doi.org/10.1007/s10055-016-0285-9

Shen, C.W., Ho, J.T., Ly, P.T.M., Kuo, T.C.: Behavioural intentions of using virtual reality in learning: perspectives of acceptance of information technology and learning style. Virtual Reality 23, 1–12 (2018)

Schrader, P.G.: Learning in technology: reconceptualizing immersive environments. AACE J. 16 (4), 457–475 (2008)

Sun, R., Wu, Y.J., Cai, Q.: The effect of a virtual reality learning environment on learners' spatial ability. Virtual Reality 1–14 (2018). https://doi.org/10.1007/s10055-018-0355-2

Treleaven, J., et al.: Simulator sickness incidence and susceptibility during neck motion-controlled virtual reality tasks. Virtual Reality 19(3–4), 267–275 (2015)

Yörük Açıkel, B., Turhan, U., Akbulut, Y.: Effect of multitasking on simulator sickness and performance in 3D aerodrome control training. Simul. Gam. 49(1), 27–49 (2018)

Sagayam, K.M., Hemanth, D.J.: Hand posture and gesture recognition techniques for virtual reality applications: a survey. Virtual Reality 21(2), 91–107 (2017)

Slater, M., Pertaub, D., Steed, A.: Public speaking in virtual reality: facing an audience of avatars. IEEE Comput. Grap. Appl. 19(2), 6–9 (1999)

# Virtual Dome System Using HMDs: An Alternative to the Expensive and Less Accessible Physical Domes

Yun Liu[1], Zhejun Liu[2(✉)], and Yunshui Jin[1]

[1] College of Arts and Media, Tongji University, Shanghai, China
{liu.yun, jinyunshui}@tongji.edu.cn
[2] College of Design and Innovation, Tongji University, Shanghai, China
wingeddreamer@tongji.edu.cn

**Abstract.** It is known that the dome display, as one of the Immersive Virtual Environments (IVEs), has its prominent advantages that viewers can experience highly immersive sensation thanks to the frameless image with a wide Field of View (FOV). However, fulldome projection systems have limited accessibility because of the technical complexity and high construction cost. Recently, the development and popularization of Head-Mounted Displays (HMDs) have changed the ways of inquiry and production in many media industries. In this research, the authors developed a virtual dome system using HMDs and assessed it quantitatively from the perspective of user immersion. An experiment was conducted to compare the difference of users' immersion between a physical dome and a virtual one using modified Immersive Tendency Questionnaire (ITQ) and the Virtual Reality Immersion (VRI) Questionnaire. 44 participants took part in this research. In conclusion, as far as user immersion is concerned, the virtual dome system is capable of bringing a similar, if not better, experience when compared with the physical one. Although the defects intrinsic to a virtual dome system, such as the limited resolution, uncomfortableness to wear and the lack of shared experience should not be overlooked, this paper proved that the virtual dome system can be a relatively low-cost and more accessible alternative for one to experience a fulldome movie, and thus worth further study and application.

**Keywords:** Immersive Virtual Environment · Dome display ·
Virtual dome system · Head-Mounted Display (HMD) · Immersion

## 1 Introduction

It is known that domes, as one type of the IVEs, have prominent advantages of providing highly immersive experience thanks to the seemingly frameless images made possible with wide FOVs [1]. Therefore, domes are favored by the education and entertainment industries. However, fulldome projection systems have limited accessibility due to the technical complexity and high cost to build a dome theater [2]. As a result, to watch or to produce a fulldome movie is not common. Recently, the development and popularization of HMDs have changed the ways of inquiry and production

© Springer Nature Switzerland AG 2019
J. Y. C. Chen and G. Fragomeni (Eds.): HCII 2019, LNCS 11575, pp. 312–328, 2019.
https://doi.org/10.1007/978-3-030-21565-1_21

in many media industries. According to the literature review, some researchers have already suggested to use HMD-based software to preview a fulldome movie, but nobody has yet actualized this concept or tested its validity [3–5].

Different researchers hold different opinion towards fulldome experience, but most of them agree that it is the immersion experience that makes fulldome unique and attractive [6–8]. In order to consider an HMD-based virtual dome as a possible alternative to a physical one, the proof that a viewer can obtain a similar experience, especially a similar level of immersion, is necessary. Therefore, a virtual dome system was developed using HMDs and user immersion it provided was assessed quantitatively in this research.

## 2 Related Works

### 2.1 Overview of Dome Display and HMD

**Dome Display.** A dome display refers to immersive projections on the inside of a dome. The hemisphere, horizontal or tilted, is filled with real-time or pre-rendered CG animations, live-capture footages or any other kinds of visual content, possibly with surrounding sound. Integrating technologies from fields like domed architecture, planetariums, multi-projector film environments, flight simulation, and Virtual Reality (VR), the dome display environments have many applications in education and entertainment across a wide range of disciplines.

A dome display typically uses single or multiple projector to display a seamless wrap-around image on the inside of a dome structure, with the intention of completely filling its viewer's FOV. Following the definition of IVEs as environments that perceptually surround users [9], dome displays qualify as an innovative medium through which to present content for a multitude of potential applications [10].

In 2012, Schnall et al. provided a theoretical framework to examine the properties of fulldome environments. The representation of space has featured prominently in IVE research in the past, because the visual elements of the display environment are typically the most prominent difference in regards to the elements of immersion, and this is also a critical element to explore within dome displays [10].

**Head-Mounted Display (HMD).** A head-mounted display, abbreviated as HMD, is a display device, worn on the head or as a part of a helmet, that has a small optic display in front of one (monocular HMD) or each eye (binocular HMD). HMDs have great potential in many fields, including gaming, aviation, engineering, and medicine. A head-mounted display is the primary component of VR headsets that is effectively used in simulation systems for virtual experience to improve users' concentration on images [11].

Aside from much lower prices, the new generation of HMDs also offered better-quality User eXperience (UX). One of the most significant factors affecting the UX of HMDs is FOV. Wearing an HMD, the natural human FOV of 180° is limited both horizontally and vertically and this influences the perceived realism of the VR experience. The new generation of HMDs have FOVs above 100° [12], which greatly enhance the UX they offer.

## 2.2   Measuring Immersion in Virtual Reality

According to the literature review, immersion has been mentioned and defined many times, but in different fields the definitions of immersion are not exactly the same. In the field of virtual environments, immersion is defined as "a psychological state characterized by perceiving oneself to be enveloped by, included in, and interacting with an environment that provides a continuous stream of stimuli and experiences" [13]. And another more vivid description defined immersion as the "illusion" that "the virtual environment technology replaces the user's sensory stimuli by the virtual sensory stimuli" [14].

There are numerous studies on measuring immersion in games or Augmented Reality (AR), presence in VR and UX in VR. However, studies focusing on immersion in VR are much less.

According to the literature review, immersion was often conceptualized as a three-level construct composed of: engagement, engrossment and total immersion [15], which was the theoretical model for most of the subsequent questionnaires developed to measure immersion in the field of games [16, 17] and AR applications [18]. In 2017, Georgiou et al. employed totally seven scales of immersion based on Cheng et al.'s assumption of multi-dimensionality within each one of the three immersion levels. The seven hypothetical scales consisted of interest, time investment, usability, emotional attachment, focus of attention, presence and flow [18].

In 2016, Tcha-Tokey et al. reviewed the scales of UX questionnaires and developed the questionnaires with 82 items which can be used in most of the fields of VR [14]. Then they compared the UX effects in a CAVE and with an HMD, and drew the conclusion that CAVEs induced a greater user experience than HMDs with significant difference in presence, engagement, flow, skill, judgement and experience consequence. The results also shew that there was no significant difference in immersion, usability, emotion and technology adoption between CAVEs and HMDs [19]. In 2018, they furtherly developed a model of UX in IVEs [20].

## 3   Experiments: Measuring Immersion in a Physical and a Virtual Dome

### 3.1   Environment and Test Material

**Physical Dome.** The physical dome used in this research was inclined, 5.5 m in diameter, 45° in tilted angle. It had a 2048 × 2048 resolution achieved by blending 6 XGA projections together (see Fig. 1). Third-party hardware was used for geometric correction and edge blending to achieve seamless rendering on the dome screen. In this research, audiences were seated on a sofa facing the center of the dome screen. The environment was equipped with 5.1 channel speakers.

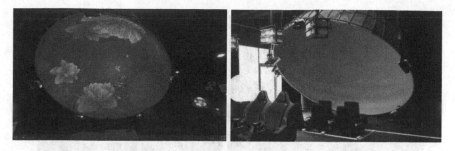

**Fig. 1.** Inclined dome display used in the experiment. Left: front view with projection; Right: side view.

**Virtual Dome.** The virtual dome system was developed using the Unity3D game engine and the Oculus Rift CV1, one of the most popular models on the market. The device comprises a lightweight (0.38 kg) headset with separate displays for both eyes, each with a 1080 × 1200 resolution, yielding a 110° horizontal field of view (FOV) and a framerate of 90 Hz. As shown in Fig. 2, the virtual dome software supported both 360-degree panoramic movies and 180-degree fulldome movies. Figure 3 shows the most significant parameters with which a user may set the diameter, tilt angle of the virtual dome, and the relative position of the virtual viewer by X, Y, Z offsets. With these settings, it is possible to mimic a specific physical dome environment more closely. Finally, a movie file in the dome master format can be loaded and played back (see Fig. 4).

As for this research, this virtual dome system was driven by one single GeForce GTX 1070 card running on a workstation. The 180-degree dome was selected and the parameters were modified to match the real dome mentioned above, that is to say, the diameter was set to 5.5 m, tilted angle 45°. The virtual viewer was placed 1 m away from the center of the sphere (Offset Y) and 1.2 m above the ground (Offset Z), which matched the physical world closely.

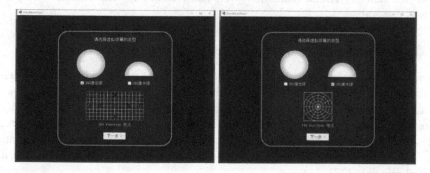

**Fig. 2.** Choice of movie type. Left: 360-degree panorama movie; Right: 180-degree fulldome movie.

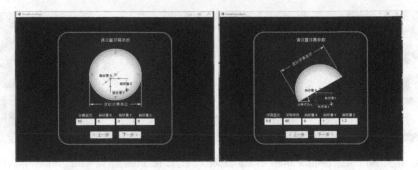

**Fig. 3.** Parameters. Left: parameters for 360-degree dome; Right: parameters for 180-degree dome.

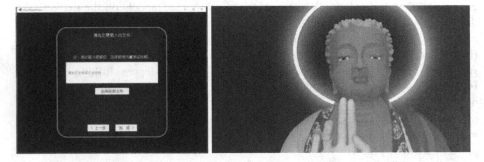

**Fig. 4.** Left: file loading interface; Right: a frame displayed in the virtual dome.

**Contents.** The author prepared five fulldome short movies produced in the College of Arts and Media. Two of them were abstract movies that used the dome only as a curved screen; two were feature movies created for the dome display; the last one was a 3D animation of high presence that aimed to provide a virtual experience of space navigation (see Table 1). All the animations were rendered in 3ds Max with the V-Ray fisheye lens camera.

## 3.2 Immersive Tendency Questionnaire (ITQ)

ITQ was used to measure the differences in the tendencies of individuals to experience presence [13]. The questionnaire began with a participant identification survey asking about personal information (name, gender, age, occupation and major). The following 18 items were derived from Witmer and Singer's immersive tendency questionnaire [13]. All the questions were in Chinese according to Yu Tian's Chinese translation [21]. The ITQ used a seven-point scale format that was based on the semantic differential principle [22].

**Table 1.** Types of fulldome short movies.

| Type of movie | Thumbnail & Title | |
|---|---|---|
| Abstract movie | Samsara | Nightmare |
| Feature movie | Blue | Dun Huang |
| Space navigation | Indoor Navigation | |

## 3.3 Tailoring the VRI Questionnaire to the Experiment

This research focused on the comparison of users' immersion between a physical dome and a virtual one. The first step to build a VRI questionnaire was to identify the scales of immersion. According to the literature review, a three-level construct [15] and seven scales [18] of immersion were used in the VRI questionnaire. Almost all the scales in UX questionnaires [14] can be correspondingly merged into the seven immersion scales, except "simulator sickness" for the evaluation of negative symptoms experienced by users in IVEs. These negative symptoms have been associated prominently with HMD displays, and no systematic study on large scale domes has examined the incidence of these symptoms [10]. However, considering the fact that simulator sickness directly affects a user's basic experience, it was investigated in this study.

After determining the scales of immersion, items were developed to compile the VRI questionnaire. In this research, all the participants are Chinese, so all the items were developed in Chinese to avoid ambiguity in language translation and comprehension. Items were rearranged to better measure user immersion in VR (see Table 2).

**Table 2.** Items selected from the existing questionnaires for VRI questionnaire.

| Scales | Subscales | Original questionnaire | Item ID in the original questionnaire |
|---|---|---|---|
| Engagement | Interest | PQ | 20 |
| | | Immersion questionnaire | 3, 9 |
| | | ARI questionnaire | A1, A2 |
| | Time investment | | A8, A9, A10 |
| | Usability | | A13, A18 |
| Engrossment | Emotional attachment | | B3 |
| | | AEQ | 1, 8 |
| | | Immersion questionnaire | 17 |
| | Focus of attention | | 21, 23, 25, 26 |
| | | ARI questionnaire | B6, B8 |
| Total immersion | Presence | Immersion questionnaire | 19, 29 |
| | | ARI questionnaire | C4, C7 |
| | Flow | | C9, C10, C11, C12 |
| Immersion | Immersion scores | Immersion questionnaire | 33 |
| Simulator sickness | Nausea | SSQ | 6, 7, 8 |
| | Oculomotor | | 2, 3, 4 |
| | Disorientation | | 10, 12, 14 |

- From the Augmented Reality Immersion (ARI) Questionnaire [18], 16 items representing seven immersion scales were selected and adjusted to fit our context (e.g. "The AR application we employed captured my attention" became: "The physical/virtual dome we employed captured my attention").
- From the Immersion Questionnaire developed by Jennett et al. [16], 10 items were selected and modified to fit our context. For most of the questions, the words "game" was changed to "physical/virtual dome". The last question: "How immersed did you feel?" aimed to know a participant' s subjective judgement of immersion.
- From the Presence Questionnaire (PQ), item 20 was picked as a reference. It's known that one advantage of physical dome displays was that the users in it could look at the projected image in an arbitrary direction freely [6]. Meanwhile, in an HMD display, users could also look at the image from multiple angles by rotating their heads. Therefore, question 5 was changed to "I'm interested in watching movies in an arbitrary direction in physical/virtual dome".
- From the Achievement Emotions Questionnaire (AEQ) [23], 2 items representing the scale of emotional attachment were picked. One item was positive and activating: enjoyment, the other one was negative and deactivating: boredom.
- From the Simulator Sickness Questionnaire (SSQ) [24], 9 SSQ symptoms were selected. All these 9 symptoms were combined as a matrix scale in question 29: When you were watching films in the physical/virtual dome, how did you feel about

the following symptoms? A seven-point scale (where 1 represented "completely no feeling" and 7 represented "completely feeling") was employed to evaluate simulator sickness.

Finally, the VRI questionnaire contained 2 items to collect personal information ("What's your name?" and "Have you ever experienced a physical dome/an HMD?").

The 30 items to measure immersion were numbered. A seven-point scale (where 1 represented "completely disagree" and 7 represented "completely agree") was employed for each item. The majority of questions were positive, where a higher score reflected a higher level of perceived immersion (component); only 3 gave negative marks (Q13, Q18 and Q30).

The VRI questionnaire was used to measure user immersion both in the physical dome and the virtual one, so there were two different versions labeled with either "VRIQPD" (VRI questionnaire for the physical dome) or "VRIQVD" (VRI questionnaire for the virtual dome).

### 3.4 Experiment Design

Firstly, ITQ was used to measure the tendency of an individual to experience presence. Then he/she watched a film (or 2 films) in the physical dome and then with the oculus rift CV1, or in the contrary sequence, according to the random group assignment. After each experience, a VRI questionnaire was employed to measure his/her immersion obtained from it. Finally, data was collected and analyzed to understand the differences.

**Participants.** 44 participants (25 females and 19 males) took part in the experiment aging from 19 to 30. The main age group was 19 to 22 (70.45%). 41 participants were university students and the other three were teachers. 16 participants majored in animation; 13 participants worked or studied in other field of arts or communication (e.g., MA, MFA, advertising, journalism, radio and TV director); 15 participants worked or studied in the fields of science and technology (e.g., material science and engineering, vehicle engineering, computer science, energy engineering). They were randomly assigned to four groups to watch different test movies, as shown in Table 3.

**Table 3.** Arrangement and procedure of experiment.

| Group | Movie(s) | Arrangement | Number |
|---|---|---|---|
| Group A | Samsara | The same abstract movie tested in two environments | 10 |
| Group B | Indoor Navigation | The same space navigation movie tested in two environments | 10 |
| Group C | Samsara & Nightmare | Two different abstract movies tested in two environments | 12 |
| Group D | Blue & Dun Huang | Two different feature movies tested in two environments | 12 |

**Arrangement.** The experiment took place in the Non-planar Screen Lab in the College of Arts and Media, Tongji University. Movies for group A and B, an abstract animation and a space navigation movie, represented two typical and most common types of dome films. They were analyzed to verify whether a virtual dome system can possibly perform as well as a physical one in common scenarios. Group A and C were compared to see whether different content exerted an influence on user immersion. Finally, group D were designed to see whether two environments gave user the same experience of immersion when showing feature movies.

**Procedure.** In the experiment, each participant went solo through the following steps:

Firstly, an ITQ was used to measure the tendency of an individual to experience presence. It has been verified that a higher ITQ score reflect a greater tendency to become involved or immersed [13] so that an individual with high ITQ scores tend to report more immersion on a VRI questionnaire. In order to compare the experimental results between groups, it is necessary to avoid big difference in ITQ mean value of each group. As a result, participants with abnormally low ITQ scores shall be excluded from this study.

Secondly, participants watched the same movie(s) once in each environment. In each group, half of the participants experienced the physical dome first, and the other half, virtual dome first in order to avoid the sequential effect.

Thirdly, an VRI questionnaire was required to be filled in by a participant immediately after the experience was over. (There were 2 versions of VRIQs, namely VRIQPD and VRIQVD. The choice was based on the type of the dome the participant just experienced).

Finally, some of the participants were interviewed to know more about which environment they preferred and why. The answers to these questions were collected to extract insights for future studies.

### 3.5 Collected Data and Analysis

Each of the 44 participants experienced two immersive environments and filled in two VRI questionnaires respectively. Therefore, 44 ITQs and 88 VRI questionnaires were collected. They were all validated and the data analysis was done using SPSS v21.

## 4 Results

### 4.1 Overview

The resultant alpha of the 44 ITQs was 0.751, showing a good reliability (alpha > 0.7). After the test for equality of variances ($p = 0.283 > 0.05$), 44 valid ITQs were examined with one-way ANOVA and multiple comparison to see whether immersion tendencies varied too much among groups. The result indicated no significant difference between each group ($p = 0.56 > 0.05$) (see Table 4), making it reasonable to compare immersion with data from the VRI questionnaires.

**Table 4.** The effects of different groups on immersion by method of one-way ANOVA.

| Experiment group | N | Mean ± SD | F | p |
|---|---|---|---|---|
| Group A | 10 | 85.70 ± 14.50 | 0.696 | 0.560 |
| Group B | 10 | 78.80 ± 10.96 | | |
| Group C | 12 | 83.33 ± 11.68 | | |
| Group D | 12 | 81.33 ± 7.062 | | |

The VRI questionnaires had a resultant alpha of 0.947 (N = 88), which also suggested a high reliability. Paired-sample test was used to compare the virtual dome with the physical one in each scale of the VRI questionnaires. In order to further understand the influences of other factors, ANOVA was used to analyze variables including visual content, exposure order, prior experience and so forth. Finally, a small random sample from the participants was interviewed to obtain more insights into the actual cause of the differences.

## 4.2  User Immersion Between the Physical and Virtual Dome in Each Group

Data for the paired-sample tests were analyzed in 5 scales and the results are presented below:

In group A (see Fig. 5), there was no significant difference found in the means of all the scales. However, the data variance from the virtual dome was obviously greater, especially in the scales of engagement and immersion score, which meant that participants' experience in virtual dome brought different levels of immersion. Two of the participants thought that the immersion experience in the virtual dome was significantly worse. By analyzing the interview results, the reasons were found out to be the low resolution of the HMD and the uncomfortableness of wearing it.

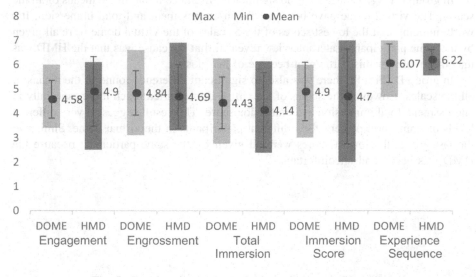

**Fig. 5.** Results of paired-sample tests of group A (N = 10).

In group B (Fig. 6), it's obviously that all the virtual dome gave better results of immersion. According the paired-sample tests, the user engrossment was higher in the virtual dome (M = 5.07, SD = 0.99) than the physical one (M = 4.19, SD = 1.05), t (10) = −2.612, p = 0.028; the immersion score user rated was also higher in the virtual dome (M = 5.3, SD = 0.67) than the physical one (M = 4.3, SD = 1.06), t (10) = −3, p = 0.015. It's not difficult to draw a conclusion that user immersion was better in a virtual dome than a physical one when watching space navigation movies.

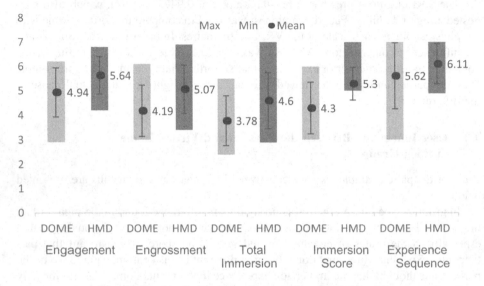

**Fig. 6.** Results of paired-sample tests of group B (N = 10).

In group C (Fig. 7), there was no significant difference found in the means of all the scales. The virtual dome gave better results in engrossment and total immersion. It's worth noticing that the lowest scores of the 5 scales of the virtual dome were all given by the same participant. Later interview revealed that the cause was that the HMD was uncomfortable for this participant because of his glasses.

In group D (Fig. 8), there was also no significant difference found in the means of all the scales. However, the scores of the virtual dome varied much more especially in engrossment, total immersion and immersion score. This result suggested very different levels of immersion perceived by different participants in the virtual dome. Similar to the last group, the lowest scores were all given by the same participant because the HMD was heavy and uncomfortable.

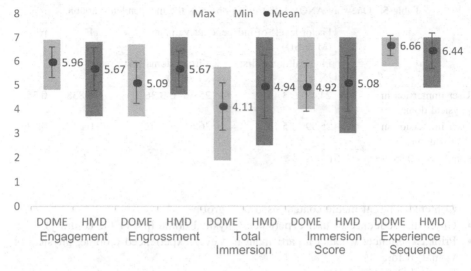

**Fig. 7.** Results of paired-sample tests of group C (N = 12).

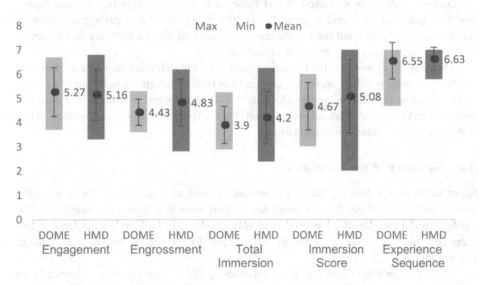

**Fig. 8.** Results of paired-sample tests of group D (N = 10).

## 4.3    Other Possible Influential Factors

In addition to the difference between a physical dome and a virtual one, other factors might also influence user immersion. These possible influential factors were also analyzed in this study. In this part, user immersion, the dependent variable was the sum of 5 scales' mean values, and the independent variables include:

**Table 5.** One-way ANOVA test using order as the independent variable

|  | Factor levels of independent variable (M ± SD) | | F | p |
|  | Physical dome first (N = 22) | Virtual dome first (N = 22) | | |
| --- | --- | --- | --- | --- |
| User immersion in physical dome | 24.42 ± 3.45 | 25.36 ± 3.36 | 0.838 | 0.365 |
| User immersion in virtual dome | 25.99 ± 5.13 | 26.65 ± 4.02 | 0.227 | 0.636 |

Note. * $p < 0.05$; ** $p < 0.01$.

- Content: different media content used in 4 groups
- Order: the sequence of user experience (physical dome first or the contrary)
- Prior Experience: whether a participant had ever experienced a dome, physical or virtual, before
- Personal Data: gender, age, occupation, major and immersive tendency.

One-way ANOVA was used to test these factors, but no significance was found. For example, Tables 5 and 6 shew the results using order and prior experience as independent variables, but the results are similar and all the p values are much greater than 0.05, suggesting no significant difference.

The only exception was the test using content as the independent value as shown in Table 7. Though p values were also greater than 0.5, but the p value of the test for the physical dome was 0.058, pretty close to 0.5. It is possible to conclude with some confidence that in a physical dome, one may experience lower immersion when watching a space navigation animation.

### 4.4    Summary of the Interviews

Short interviews following the questionnaires aimed to know more about what the participants subjectively thought about their experiences in different environments. The survey used a sample of 22 people randomly chosen from all the participants. There were only two questions in the survey: Q1. Which do you prefer, the physical dome or the virtual one? Q2. Why?

Table 8 shows the summary of the interviews. The factors directly influenced user immersion are marked with asterisks.

## 5    Discussion

This research analyzed and compared two IVEs (Dome and HMD) in terms of user immersion with an adjusted VRI questionnaire covering three components of immersion. By inspecting user immersion, which is the most significant feature of a dome experience, in physical and virtual domes, this research tried to prove that a virtual dome system based on HMDs could provide immersion to a remarkable extent.

**Table 6.** One-way ANOVA test using prior experience as the independent variable

| | Factor levels of independent variable (M ± SD) | | F | p |
|---|---|---|---|---|
| | With prior experience | Without prior experience | | |
| User immersion in physical dome | 24.23 ± 3.26 (N = 25) | 25.77 ± 3.46 (N = 19) | 2.299 | 0.137 |
| User immersion in virtual dome | 25.89 ± 5.50 (N = 16) | 26.57 ± 4.03 (N = 28) | 0.227 | 0.636 |

Note. * $p < 0.05$; ** $p < 0.01$.

**Table 7.** One-way ANOVA test using content as the independent variable

| | Factor levels of independent variable (M ± SD) | | | | F | p |
|---|---|---|---|---|---|---|
| | Group A (N = 10) | Group B (N = 10) | Group C (N = 12) | Group D (N = 12) | | |
| User immersion in physical dome | 24.81 ± 3.00 | 22.83 ± 3.95 | 26.74 ± 2.83 | 24.83 ± 3.06 | 2.705 | 0.058 |
| User immersion in virtual dome | 24.65 ± 5.84 | 26.72 ± 3.53 | 27.79 ± 4.36 | 25.91 ± 4.39 | 0.913 | 0.443 |

Note. * $p < 0.05$; ** $p < 0.01$.

**Table 8.** The summary of interviews.

| | Answer to Q1 | Answer to Q2 | |
|---|---|---|---|
| | | Positive factors | Negative factors |
| Physical dome | 11 | Wide FOV High resolution Comfortable environment* Easier looking-around * | Easy to get disturbed* Insecurity caused by large space* Dizzy (Group B)* |
| Virtual dome | 11 | High immersion* Better sound environment Isolation from the outside world* Interactivity* | Narrow FOV Need to find the pictures of movie* Heavy and uncomfortable Not friendly to people wearing glasses Low resolution |

Note. * Factors directly influential to immersion.

The results of paired-sample analysis from each group shew that subjective user immersion was almost the same in the physical dome and the virtual one. Group A (tested with an abstract movie), group C (tested with two different abstract movies) and group D (tested with two feature movies), almost reported the same levels of user immersion. As for group B (tested with a space navigation movie), greater user immersion was reported by virtual dome experiences with significant difference found in engrossment and immersion. Overall, the user immersion brought by a virtual dome is as good as, if not better than a physical one.

The results of the one-way ANOVA across groups shew that the group tested with a space navigation movie reported lower user immersion in the physical dome experience. And other different types of content caused no significant difference in user immersion. Moreover, no significant difference was found to be caused by the other factors either. The participants with no prior dome and VR experience reported a bit higher level of immersion when they experienced the virtual dome first, but the difference was minor.

The results from the random sampling interview shew that half of the subjects preferred the experience in the physical dome, and other half prefer the virtual one. Most of the reasons why participants disliked the virtual dome was caused by the intrinsic problems of HMDs, such as a narrow FOV, a lower resolution and etc. Most of the positive comments about immersion were given to the virtual dome and many interviewees thought that it brought a more immersive experience because it isolated the outside world much better.

## 6  Conclusion

In this research, experiments were carried out to prove the hypothesis that a virtual dome system built with HMDs could bring a similar subjective user immersion when compared to a physical dome. According to the outcomes from the experiments, the hypothesis was successfully proved. Although the defects intrinsic to a virtual dome system, such as the problems of limited resolution, narrow FOV, uncomfortableness to wear and the ack of shared experience should not be overlooked, a virtual dome system could be used as a low-cost and more accessible alternative to a physical dome to offer an immersive experience of fulldome movie.

**Acknowledgments.** This work was supported by the National Key Research and Development Program of China (\#2018YFB1004903). Meanwhile, we would like to thank the Non-planar Screen Lab of the College of Arts and Media, Tongji University and the participants who took time to engage in this research.

## References

1. Ogi, T., Tateyama, Y., Lee, H., Furuyama, D., Seno, T., Kayahara, T.: Creation of three dimensional dome contents using layered images. In: 2011 IEEE International Symposium on VR Innovation (ISVRI), 19–20 March 2011, pp. 255–260. IEEE, Piscataway (2011)
2. Tredinnick, J., Richens, P.: A fulldome interactive visitor experience: a novel approach to delivering interactive virtual heritage experiences to group audiences in fulldome projection spaces, evaluated through spatial awareness and emotional response. In: 2015 Digital Heritage, 28 September–2 October 2015, pp. 413–414. IEEE, Piscataway (2015)

3. Luciani, D.T., Lundberg, J.: Enabling designers to sketch immersive fulldome presentations. In: 34th Annual CHI Conference on Human Factors in Computing Systems, CHI EA 2016, 7–12 May 2016, pp. 1490–1496. Association for Computing Machinery, San Jose (2016)
4. Li, S., et al.: Interactive theater-sized dome design for edutainment and immersive training. In: 2014 Virtual Reality International Conference, VRIC 2014, 9–11 April 2014. Association for Computing Machinery, Laval, France (2014)
5. Hirose, M., Yokoyama, K., Sato, S.I.: Transmission of realistic sensation: development of a virtual dome. In: Proceedings of IEEE Virtual Reality Annual International Symposium, 18–22 September 1993, pp. 125–131. IEEE, New York (1993)
6. Ogi, T., Yokota, T.: Effect of visual attention guidance by camera work in visualization using dome display. Int. J. Model. Simul. Sci. Comput. **9**(3) (2018)
7. Ka Chun, Y., Saham, K., Sahami, V., Sessions, L., Denn, G.: Group immersive education with digital fulldome planetariums. In: 2017 IEEE Virtual Reality (VR), 18–22 March 2017, pp. 237–238. IEEE, Piscataway (2017)
8. Goddard, W., Muscat, A., Manning, J., Holopainen, J.: Interactive dome experiences: designing AstroSurf. In: 20th International Academic Mindtrek Conference, AcademicMindtrek 2016, 17–18 October 2016, pp. 393–402. Association for Computing Machinery, Inc., Tampere (2016)
9. Bailenson, J.N., Yee, N., Blascovich, J., Beall, A.C., Lundblad, N., Jin, M.: The use of immersive virtual reality in the learning sciences: digital transformations of teachers, students, and social context. J. Learn. Sci. **17**(1), 102–141 (2008)
10. Schnall, S., Hedge, C., Weaver, R.: The immersive virtual environment of the digital fulldome: considerations of relevant psychological processes. Int. J. Hum.-Comput. Stud. **70**(8), 561–575 (2012)
11. Shibata, T.: Head mounted display. Displays **23**(1–2), 8 (2002)
12. Jensen, L., Konradsen, F.: A review of the use of virtual reality head-mounted displays in education and training. Educ. Inf. Technol. **23**(4), 1515–1529 (2017)
13. Witmer, B.G., Singer, M.J.: Measuring presence in virtual environments: a presence questionnaire. Presence **7**(3), 225–240 (1998)
14. Tcha-Tokey, K., Loup-Escande, E., Christmann, O., Richir, S.: A questionnaire to measure the user experience in immersive virtual environments. In: 2016 Virtual Reality International Conference, VRIC 2016, 23–25 March 2016. Association for Computing Machinery, Laval, France (2016)
15. Brown, E., Cairns, P.: A grounded investigation of game immersion. Paper Presented at the CHI 2004 Extended Abstracts on Human Factors in Computing Systems, pp. 1297–1300. ACM Press (2004)
16. Jennett, C., et al.: Measuring and defining the experience of immersion in games. Int. J. Hum.-Comput. Stud. **66**(9), 641–661 (2008)
17. Cheng, M.T., She, H.C., Annetta, L.A.: Game immersion experience: its hierarchical structure and impact on game-based science learning. J. Comput. Assist. Learn. **31**(3), 232–253 (2015)
18. Georgiou, Y., Kyza, E.A.: The development and validation of the ARI questionnaire: an instrument for measuring immersion in location-based augmented reality settings. Int. J. Hum Comput Stud. **98**, 24–37 (2017)
19. Tcha-Tokey, K., Loup-Escande, E., Christmann, O., Richir, S.: Effects on user experience in an edutainment virtual environment: comparison between CAVE and HMD. In: Proceedings of the European Conference on Cognitive Ergonomics, pp. 1–8. Association for Computing Machinery, NY, USA (2017)

20. Tcha-Tokey, K., Christmann, O., Loup-Escande, E., Loup, G., Richir, S.: Towards a model of user experience in immersive virtual environments. Adv. Hum.-Comput. Interact. **2018**, 1–10 (2018)
21. Yu, T., Yulong, B., Peiguo, H., Xiaoyue, L., Peng, W., Fengqiang, G.: Validation and reliability of the chinese version of immersed tendency questionnaire. Adv. Psychol. **05**(06), 386–392 (2015)
22. Dyer, R., U.S. Army Research Institute for the Behavioral and Social Sciences: Questionnaire Construction Manual. Annex: Literature Survey and Bibliography (1976)
23. Pekrun, R., Goetz, T., Frenzel, A.C., Barchfeld, P., Perry, R.P.: Measuring emotions in students' learning and performance: the Achievement Emotions Questionnaire (AEQ). Contemp. Educ. Psychol. **36**(1), 36–48 (2011)
24. Kennedy, R.S., Lane, N.E., Berbaum, K.S., Lilienthal, M.G.: Simulator sickness questionnaire: an enhanced method for quantifying simulator sickness. Int. J. Aviat. Psychol. **3**(3), 203–220 (1993)

# GVRf and Blender: A Path for Android Apps and Games Development

Bruno Oliveira$^{(\boxtimes)}$, Diego Azulay$^{(\boxtimes)}$, and Paulo Carvalho$^{(\boxtimes)}$

SIDIA (Samsung R&D Institute Brazil), Manaus, Brazil
{b.araujo, diego.a, p.alexandre}@samsung.com

**Abstract.** Virtual reality on mobile devices has been used in many areas such as entertainment, health care, training and simulations, although it still has limitations in terms of graphics quality and application performance. The ease of portable devices that can be used for virtual experiences in other "worlds" provides its fascinations, however, this technology can not match the virtual reality for personal computers, with high levels of quality in its graphics, with multiple features and high superior processing power while offering simplicity in use and being cheaper than its competitors on other platforms, such as personal computers and video game consoles. Thus, the purpose of this essay is to present a solution that GVRf, together with Blender, the GVRf Exporter, that makes the process of developing applications for VR technologies more optimized.

**Keywords:** Virtual reality · Gear VR · GVRf · Blender · Exporter · 3D

## 1 Introduction

In recent years, the improvement of new technologies such as Virtual Reality (VR) and its capabilities to transport users to immersive environments has been fascinating, researches to explore the potential of these technologies have allowed the creation of innovative experiences that have excited the interest of emerging technology enthusiasts [1]. The combination of these factors stimulates the search for efficient alternatives on the part of the developers for the optimization of resources, and for the process of development of VR systems, Gear VR framework (GVRf) with Blender present as an effective possibility.

The process of developing an application for VR systems basically consists of organizing the assets created by artists (concept, modeling, texturing, animation, etc.) into a set of libraries in the game engines where the application will be generated by adding the logical part of the game, in that all of these objects receive programming, as well as creating artificial intelligence and all the functionality for each application element. However the environment of these artistic tools like Blender [13] and Z-Brush [14] etc., are different from the engine used in the rendering and execution of the application. As they render materials, shaders and other elements show discrepancies from one platform to another. When artists are creating assets for an application, although they finish their work, in Blender, for example, needs to see how this feature behaves on the final platform and make adjustments to leave the scene as intended. In

© Springer Nature Switzerland AG 2019
J. Y. C. Chen and G. Fragomeni (Eds.): HCII 2019, LNCS 11575, pp. 329–337, 2019.
https://doi.org/10.1007/978-3-030-21565-1_22

addition, they need to see how the scene is on the device and how the end user will experience it. It is quite important to have this validation of the built scene to make sure that the user will have the best experience possible with the use of the application. However, one of the unwelcome problems in the development for VR mobile devices it's the necessity to always build an application (APK) to have a correct perception of how the application will perform, that is, create a new version of the app, this having a very significant impact on software development and art pipeline, making them both slow down because of this additional step. Generating a new APK build for any changes, even for small changes, can impact the pipeline as a whole, whether for use by an artist asset or a change in the code line, those small changes can make the workflow more difficult and tedious. As often as there are changes, such as 3D assets that can happen all the time, but this testing process is not ideal and even optimized built scenes creates one more step to be taken into consideration.

This was the problem that motivated the creation of a Blender add-on called GVRf Exporter, a Blender add-on that exports 3D scene components from Blender to a GVRf client application running on a mobile device. GVRf exporter, export the objects of a Blender scene to a mobile device so that the artist can preview the scene and see exactly what the user of the application will see. Thus, the 3D artist can view and validate animations, sharing animatics - a visual resource widely used for the preview of scenes with narrative structure, visual effects and other elements that after a previous analysis, will be produced later [17] - to other android devices connected to a VR and scenes where the application of physics to objects occurs and make adjusts as well as see in real-time the modifications done, making the creation process much faster, mainly for developers and artists who are looking for a VR mobile software solution and more flexibility to their pipeline. Also for who want to have an open platform that allows people to make any kind of change in their source code, to create some application for your own company without the need to purchase licenses from other development platforms, such as Unity or Unreal. Artists that use Blender and want to test a scene in VR, by doing in the cheapest way possible, using only Gear VR and their mobile device, that way anyone can create VR content only using Blender and GVRf.

## 2    Gear VR as an Alternative to Resource Optimization

Project development processes use Unity 3D – a cross-platform game engine designed to support and develops 2D and 3D video games, simulations for computers, virtual reality, consoles and mobile devices platform [2] - and GVRf - a lightweight and powerful open source rendering engine with a Java interface for developing mobile VR games and applications for Gear VR and Google Daydream View [3]. These development platforms require certain protocols for their operation, be it a game or a simple application. These protocols, in turn, have as their starting point the development recommendations of VR device manufacturers, such as Oculus [4], suitable for developers and content creators.

## 3   Realistic vs. Stylized

3D graphics have certain complexities that involve in certain artistic choices with regard to the visual of the applications/games. These choices often direct artistic style to a realistic look or stylized look, but portable virtual reality on mobile devices does not yet have the capabilities to support highly realistic graphics such as PCs can handle. This carries a simpler approach in artistic terms that translates into products or applications that largely use the low poly style, such as Look to the Sky [5] - an app developed with GVRF that gives to users a view of the night sky, the user can look at the stars according to his location - (Fig. 1) as a choice for a solution that blends artistic refinement with the optimized application/gaming capability.

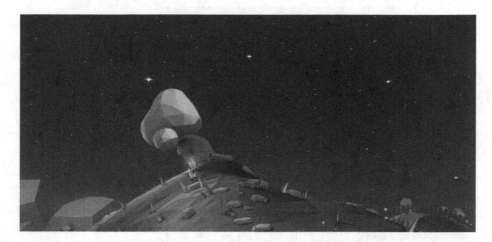

**Fig. 1.**  Look into the sky [5]

## 4   GVRf

The Gear VR framework (GVRf) is a lightweight and powerful open source rendering engine with a Java interface for developing mobile VR games and applications for Gear VR and Google Daydream View [3].

The project GVRf is driven by Samsung Research America (SRA) [18] e SIDIA [19] collaborate creating news features and giving support to improvements other features.

## 5   Blender

Blender is an open source software that performs 3D computing tasks such as modeling, animation, texturing, composing, rendering using different techniques, such as raytracing, radiosity, ambient occlusion, or scanline rendering, video editing and creation of interactive 3D applications such as games through Blender Game Engine, an integrated game engine. Blender is available for all major operating systems under the GNU General Public License and is being actively developed under the supervision of the Blender Foundation [7].

## 5.1   General Application/Game Production Pipeline

A application/game production pipeline is basically a concept of workflow management for use in the game development process. The phases of this pipeline are certain tasks need to be fulfilled until the release of an application/video game [15]. The tasks are well defined for each phase, as The tasks are well defined for each phase (Fig. 2):

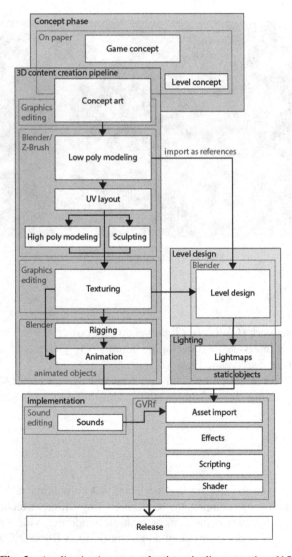

**Fig. 2.** Application/game production pipeline overview [15].

# 6   Blender Add-on

GVRf Exporter [6] is a Blender add-on that exports 3D scene components from Blender to a GVRf client application running on a mobile device.

GVRf exporter was created based on the necessity of accelerate the creation and exportation pipeline of assets for VR applications. There are some tools that makes a job similar to the GVRf exporter, like the Blender2Ogre [10] and Godot [11] blender exporter. But these tools are limited to export the scene from a 3D software, in this specific case, from Blender, in a way that the render engine will be able to import and render the content exported from the Digital Content Creation (DCC) Tool [12]. GVRf Exporter gives a step ahead because, not only it can export the content from DCC Tool, but shows immediately after the export the result on the final platform.

The idea for the creation of the add-on arose from a request of SRA for the development of a tool of creation of content with physics for GVRf, because until then, the only way to have a simulation of physics in a GVRf application was program-matically. That way Blender came into the scene, which, because it is open source, does not require the need to get a software license.

During the resolution of this case, a question arose was whether it was possible to perform the combination of work between Blender and Gear VR: how to simplify certain procedures for generating deploys of scenes created in the graphical environ-ments of development platforms, such as Unity 3D [2] - where the pipeline consists of creating the scene with the assets in Blender and then exporting the set of assets to Unity 3D?

Based on this issue, several features were created so that you could export multiple objects between different Blender files, as well as scenes directly to an Android application installed on some device, so that you could benefit from the flexibility of a wireless device without the need to connect to another platform, such as a PC. One of the references on the market was Blinking Dalai Plug-In for Blender VR: That Con-cerning a preview of VR for the viewport in Blender 2.77 [16], only changed the fact that, instead of being rendered inside the computer was rendered on a mobile device via file transfer.

The GVRf Exporter is composed of three parts: remote scripting application, a http file server and the Blender add-on.

## 6.1   Components

**Remote Scripting**
It's a GVRf application capable of executing JavaScript commands (which are con-verted to Java) sent from a remote source. This is the application that shows the scene exported from Blender (Fig. 3).

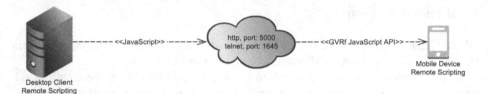

**Fig. 3.** Remote scripting.

**Http File Server**

The remote scripting application uses the file server to get the objects (.fbx) and textures exported.

**Blender Add-on**

The add-on provides a interface from Blender to the http server and the remote scripting client. The user can configure and export through its UI.

The Blender add-on is responsible for exporting files, sending JavaScript commands to the remote scripting application and maintain the http file server (Fig. 4).

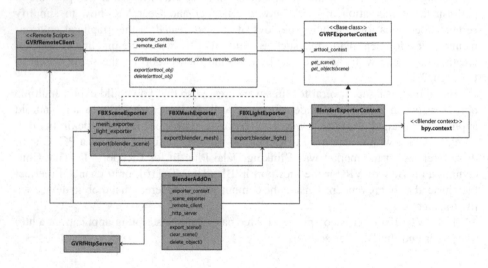

**Fig. 4.** Blender add-on.

The GVRf exporter can export the following objects:

- Meshes (with textures and armature);
- Lights (all the types supported by GVRf, which are Direct, Point, and Spot);
- Camera (GVRf supports only one camera per scene).

The available configurations are:

- Choose to export all objects or just selected objects of a scene;
- Choose the directory where to export the files;
- Set the scale of exported objects.

## 6.2    How to Use

Working with GVRf Exporter requires a number of steps. First, run the GVRf-remove-scripting client application on a device. Then, enable the GVRf-exporter add-on on Blender through user preferences menu (Fig. 5) and click on Import-Export tab of toolshelf (Fig. 6). Choose the directory to export (default dir is GvrfExportWorkspace located on user's home). Set Client's IP field to reflect the client's device IP address (Fig. 7), then click on Export button, then it will be possible to view the scene created in the Blender viewport directly on the mobile device.

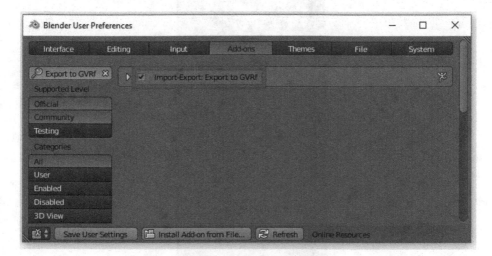

**Fig. 5.**  Export to GVRf menu.

**Fig. 6.**  Export to GVRf menu.

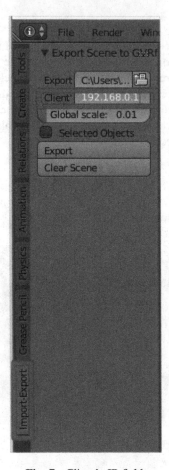

**Fig. 7.** Client's IP field.

## 7 Conclusion

The research made possible the understanding of the content creation process for GearVR, as well as its development process in the Android environment, using GVRf as a flexible tool that optimizes the development time in the experimental stage of experiments with the help of Blender and GVRf Exporter. At the same time it became practical for modeling artists during the artist validation process, where they could observe how the assets would be in the scenes created by them, without necessarily having to send all the assets to the programmers to set the scene in development environment to be validated.

GVRf Exporter has some room for improvements. As future works, its UI can show more informations, including draw calls and the FPS (frame per second) of the running scene on the mobile device. Another function that will be befit its user is to export physics using the .bullet file format. This file is used both by Blender and the Bullet physics engine, which is the physics engine of GVRf. With this feature, it will possible to create physics for the objects inside the DCC tool and the device will run the scene with physics simulation without any additional code. Another issue to be solved is to maintain its stable performance after exporting and cleaning the scene successively. Finally, GVRf can be ported to another DCC tools, like Maya [8] and 3DSMax [9].

**Acknowledgments.** This essay was the result of the combined efforts of the SIDIA Solutions Team and SRA (Samsung Research America). It is also important to highlight the company's performance in supporting and promoting the research and development of systems that are present in the main technology products in the domestic market. We thank Samsung Electronics da Amazonia Ltda., as part of the results presented in this study were obtained from Project SXR SDK (Gear VR Framework), financed by the company under the Law 8387 (art.2)/91. For all the people involved in this project, our sincere thanks.

# References

1. Psotka, J.: Educational games and virtual reality as disruptive technologies. Educ. Technol. Soc. **16**(2), 69–80 (2013)
2. Unity 2018. Unity Documentation – 3D projects. https://docs.unity3d.com/. Accessed 30 Jan 2019
3. Gear VR Framework. http://www.gearvrf.org
4. Oculus Developer Center. https://developer.oculus.com/documentation/
5. Look to the Sky VR App on Oculus Store. https://www.oculus.com/experiences/gear-vr/1236186189841229/
6. Blender Add-on for GVRF. http://www.gearvrf.org/blog/blender_plugin_guide
7. Hatka, M., Haindl, M.: Advanced material rendering in blender. Int. J. Virtual Reality **11**(2), 15–23 (2011)
8. Maya - Computer Animation & Modeling Software – Autodesk. https://www.autodesk.com/products/maya/overview
9. 3DSMax - 3D Modeling, Animation & Rendering Software – Autodesk. https://www.autodesk.com/products/3ds-max/overview
10. blender2ogre: Blender exporter for the OGRE 3D engine. https://github.com/OGRECave/blender2ogre
11. Godot-Blender-Exporter: Add-on for Blender to directly export to a Godot Scene. https://github.com/godotengine/godot-blender-exporter
12. Importing 3D Scenes - Godot Engine latest documentation. http://docs.godotengine.org/en/3.0/getting_started/workflow/assets/importing_scenes.html
13. Blender - Free and Open 3D Creation Software. https://www.blender.org
14. Pixologic: ZBrush - The all-in-one-digital sculpting solution. http://pixologic.com/
15. Aquino, M., Grashäftl, F., Kohl, S., Labschütz, M., Krösl, K.: Content Creation for a 3D Game with Maya and Unity 3D. CESCG (2011)
16. Felinto, D.: Virtual Reality Viewport in Blender 2.77 (2015). https://github.com/dfelinto/virtual_reality_viewport
17. Negrete-Yankelevich, S., Morales-Zaragoza, N.: e-Motion: a system for the development of creative animatics. In: Proceedings of the Fourth International Conference of Computational Creativity (2013)
18. Samsung Research America. https://www.sra.samsung.com/
19. SIDIA. http://www.sidia.org.br/

# Designing Educational Virtual Environments for Construction Safety: A Case Study in Contextualizing Incident Reports and Engaging Learners

Alyssa M. Peña[1]([✉]), Eric D. Ragan[1,2], and Julian Kang[1,2]

[1] Texas A&M University, College Station, USA
alyspena@gmail.com, juliankang@tamu.edu
[2] University of Florida, Gainesville, USA
eragan@ufl.edu

**Abstract.** Safety education is important in the construction industry, with many onsite injuries and fatalities. Reviewing incident reports can be valuable in preventing the same mistakes from reoccurring and in reinforcing the concept of designing for construction safety. However, the required information can be difficult for students and non-experts to understand in a meaningful way without instructor facilitation. Recently research has shifted into using 3D virtual environments for safety education, with applications teaching learners how to identify hazards and operating procedures. While there are exploratory results on student engagement and overall learning, there is less focus on how the design influences the learning outcomes. For these reasons we conducted a case study in system design to understand how to effectively contextualize raw incident reports into a meaningful 3D educational experience. From our case study, we present a single-learner educational application with both a desktop computer and VR version. The desktop version was used in development of the application's design framework and in a controlled study testing how interaction techniques influence learning and behavioral outcomes. The results showed that interaction technique did significantly affect total time spent using the application, but did not affect remembering and understanding. We discuss how lessons learned from the user study were applied to the VR version, what designs revisions needed to be made, and overall usability. Lastly, we summarize the experiences and evaluations from the case study by listing design guidelines for creating educational virtual environments from existing 2D information records.

**Keywords:** Virtual environments · Virtual reality · Educational technology · Construction safety

© Springer Nature Switzerland AG 2019
J. Y. C. Chen and G. Fragomeni (Eds.): HCII 2019, LNCS 11575, pp. 338–354, 2019.
https://doi.org/10.1007/978-3-030-21565-1_23

# 1   Introduction

Construction site accidents can result in human injury or fatalities, and even in the most benign cases, are costly for companies. On average, it has been estimated that construction companies could save $42,000 for each prevented injury or illness resulting in lost time, or $1,450,000 for each avoided occupational fatality [15]. While identifying hazards is an important aspect of reducing on site accidents, emphasis should also be placed on the design for construction safety concept. The concept has been linked to prior fatality investigation reports, suggesting that incidents can be avoided by considering construction site safety in the design of the project [3]. Similarly, Saleh et al. argue that teaching accident causation to engineering students may prevent recurrences of failures in engineering systems by both reinforcing safety requirements and empowering students to advocate system safety at a multidisciplinary level [24].

While construction incident reports can be reviewed and presented for educational use, their primary purpose is to record any details associated to the accident. They are thus highly descriptive, overly detailed, and lack a useful narrative for understanding the entirety of the accident. For this reason how and why the incidents happened aren't always intuitive, often resulting in instructors assigning a report to be read and later conducting a discussion. This approach engages students in the understanding of incident factors, but to be effective, requires a teacher or collaborators to participate. Even still, students might have difficulty conceptualizing the accidents without sufficient on site experience [23,27].

As a highly interactive medium, educational virtual environments offer opportunities to engage students in memorable experiences that represent concepts in unique and meaningful ways [14,29,31]. Many researchers have suggested that virtual reality (VR) could have educational value for conveying spatial concepts that are difficult to comprehend (e.g., [6,8,31]). VR can also provide the ability to simulate scenarios that could not practically be experienced in normal life. Prior research in construction education have implemented these techniques to teach construction safety education concepts—such as safety protocols and hazard recognition—supporting the value of disseminating content via a digital application [9,16,22]. However, it is not clear what level of interactive control should be used to keep participants engaged without having to spend too much time familiarizing themselves with the nuances of the application [4,9].

Our research addresses the need for long-term incident prevention, by introducing a single-learner VR educational application to contextualize accident causation and safety procedures (see Fig. 5). The application is grounded in the results of a case study in system design, wherein we question how to effectively translate raw incident reports into a meaningful 3D educational experience. We developed a system framework leveraging educational modules that integrate relevant information from two Occupational Safety and Health Administration incident reports into a contextualized virtual construction space. The modules provide visual unification of the essential report details in various formats (text, numerical tables, static images, and spatial diagrams). We used the framework to develop a desktop version of the application and conducted a user study testing the effects of interactive control on learning behaviors and outcomes. The results of the study established a baseline understanding of the usability of our application. Lessons learned were then applied to the final VR version.

Through our educational application, we aim to allow students to be able to better understand the fundamental elements of construction safety by reviewing real examples in an engaging format. By presenting our advancements and development of an VR application for construction education our work contributes the following: (1) design guidelines from our case study of integrating incident report information in an educational 3D environment, (2) empirical results from a controlled experiment studying the implications of interaction techniques in a desktop application, and (3) usability studies with both VR and desktop versions of the application.

**Fig. 1.** The desktop application (left) and VR version (right) used different presentation formats for data annotations.

## 2   Related Research

Many researchers have discussed the potential benefits of 3D virtual environments for educational purposes (e.g., [30,31]). VR can increase the level of realism by surrounding the user with a multitude of sensory information, thus replicating conditions similar to the real world. Additionally, stories or scenarios can also be added for users to take part in [28]. Taking advantage of these interactions in educational applications may lead to increased user engagement.

Researchers have explored how to design educational applications in many different disciplines. One well known example is *ScienceSpace* [6], which uses VR to teach science concepts such as Newtonian physics and electromagnetism. In work focusing on mathematics education, Roussos et al. used a virtual playground to teach numerical fractions through interactions with 3D animated characters [21]. Focusing on history education, Singh et al. [26] demonstrated the use of mobile augmented reality to contextualize evidence of historic events into real-world sites through an interactive detective experience. Furthering interactive engagement, Bowman et al. [4] conducted a study suggesting virtual environments (VE)s can be useful for better understanding the relationship between spatial and abstract information. Their study emphasized the importance of enabling interactive control that allows users to move freely and efficiently around the environment but without disorientation.

Researchers have also studied whether advanced display and interaction technology of VR might provide benefits for cognitive tasks. For instance, Ragan et al. [17] found improved recall when abstract information was presented at different locations around participants in a VE rather than only at the same place. This study showed evidence that participants were using spatial strategies with the VE to assist in memorization. In other work, a study by Ragan et al. [19] found significant improvements for a VR system using higher-fidelity features (higher field of view; better fidelity of visual view; and more surrounding screen space) for a memory task, demonstrating potential benefits of using immersive VR technology for certain types of learning scenarios. In later research comparing an immersive VR system to a similar system with limited display functionality enabled, researchers found evidence of improved memory of information locations in a VR environment with data annotations distributed throughout a virtual cave system [20]. However, this study also found participants experiencing worse sickness when using more interactive control techniques for 3D travel.

Challenges with 3D travel and control is especially important given that a high level of interactivity is one of the common claims for the educational benefits of VR [31]. If too much focus is given to interacting with the environment and how to operate the controls, the learner might be distracted from the learning content, which could negatively affect learning outcomes [18]. Determining the ideal level of interactive control for any educational application can be challenging and largely depends on the specifics of the application and the learning objectives. This becomes especially important for 3D applications due to the wide variety of possible ways to interact within it [31].

Virtual simulations can also be beneficial for safety. Real on-the-job hazards of construction safety training can be avoided by utilizing VEs to simulate the construction environment for off-site training. For example, Perlman et al. [16] developed a virtual construction environment that could be toured in a preset order using a VR CAVE system. They tested how well superintendents could identify hazards and how well they perceived the risk level. Often, emphasis is placed on learning how to identify hazards because it can be taught as a game to increase engagement, and scores can be used to assess participants' progress [1, 10,13]. Alternatively some have taught operation procedures [7,11]. Research by Le et al. covered both hazard identification and operation procedures in separate VEs by first having a discussion over incident report contents between students and teacher in a virtual classroom [9]. Results from their preliminary evaluation showed that instructors were required to provide more input and that it took time for students to adjust to the controls. Overall, the findings of prior research supports studying how to contextualize incident reports in VEs and how interactive control affects learning outcomes.

# 3  Application Design Framework

In this section, we present the resulting application design framework as part of the case study in system design.

## 3.1  Incident Reports

The framework we used to design our educational application consisted of incident reports by the Occupational Safety and Health Administration (OSHA). These were used because they had public accessibility and similar objectives in trying to help people working in the construction industry identify problems in construction design. For our case study, we chose to review two reports to understand how we would represent different types of information consistently.

From our review, we found that incidents did not occur as a result of one person's actions, rather an accumulation of design flaws and not following safety operations. In the first report, a wall collapsed in 2013, killing two workers and injuring one. This was a result of structural support rods in the wall not being properly placed, no actions to remedy the situation, and inadequate design and quantity of braces used to support the wall. The second report also occurred in 2013, when an overhead crane collapsed. One worker was killed and eight were injured. The accident was the result of poor structural design, failure to conduct a load test, and key participants not properly reviewing the design. We chose to describe accident causation by noting key participants, incident factors [27], and dates.

## 3.2  Learning Objectives

Our educational objectives were to have the users learn (1) the factors leading up to the accident, (2) proper procedures, and (3) details of the construction site and project. Following the construct of cognitive processes from the revised version of Bloom's taxonomy [2], the application's format was designed for the user to remember and understand these objectives. By contextualizing information using spatial locations of 3D objects, text, and the objects themselves we encouraged exploration, which in turn could increase engagement. This design choice also introduced spatial information, an automatic form of information processing [12]. We spread the information out into key areas when possible and grouped related information as lessons that had a beginning and end.

## 3.3  Application Development

We first began developing a desktop prototype of the educational application. The hope was that by easing usability and accessibility for students in common educational settings, flaws in the design could be more apparent. The software was implemented using Unity's game engine with assets modeled in Autodesk Maya. The setup consisted of a screen/monitor and a standard keyboard and mouse for input. Annotations, menus, documents, or images in the desktop application were displayed as a 2D overlay. We discuss the necessary revisions in information display and input control for the VR version in Sect. 5.

Development followed an iterative process that involved continuous updates between the virtual environment and presentation of the learning content. Frequent informal evaluations of the system framework on prototype applications were conducted to help identify issues for improvement. Testers had few comments regarding the visual aesthetics or how the information was conveyed, but made it clear that how they explored and interacted with the environment to access information influenced their willingness to learn. These preliminary findings demonstrated how basic choices in information accessibility and control could influence the educational experience. Based on this work, we later refined the application to a working state by focusing only on the virtual environment contextualizing the masonry wall collapse.

## 3.4  Data Contextualization

The data in the reports consisted of text, on-site images, construction drawings, documents, and data tables. Our goal was to include as much of the source information as possible with the intention of observing which types of information were of most interest and value to learners. To contextualize the report, we designed virtual environments to reflect the construction site in appearance and layout, changes in time, and the inclusion of embedded images and text. We discuss our findings and design outcomes after the iterative development and testing process.

To give the user a sense of being on the site, it was important to show the entirety of the site despite lack of detail for areas not related to the incident. We modeled the environment to scale when information was provided, and we used construction standards to approximate dimensions when they were not specified. To address the problem of the environment feeling empty, relevant assets were placed throughout the site to aid in the creation of a more meaningful setting.

In both incidents, the actual accident occurred in a matter of seconds. Yet, when looking at the dates provided in the reports, the factors leading up to it often happened weeks to months prior. This provided a major challenge for application design—it was necessary to represent facts, spatial content and changes over a large period of time. Our solution was to create time steps for periods of time where key events or problems occurred. The application included the ability to switch between time steps and observe the corresponding changes in the environment and its structures. Figure 2 shows images demonstrating the key time steps and environmental changes of the incidents. For example, the masonry wall collapse is visually represented in three steps: improper installation, inadequate brace placement and design, and then the collapsed wall.

The system showed sequential events within a time step through the designed lessons. In the same example of the masonry wall, the lesson for the first timestep began with the environment showing misplaced straight support rods and a

## Masonry Wall Collapse

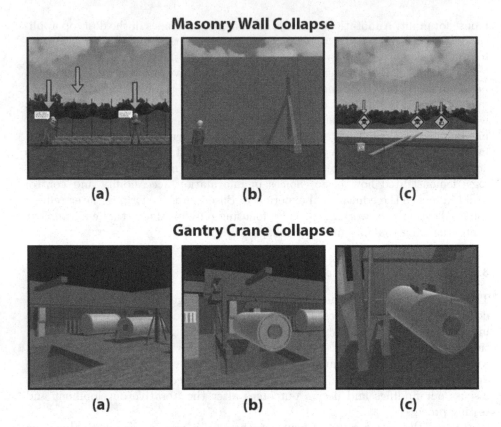

## Gantry Crane Collapse

**Fig. 2.** Screenshots from the two accident scenarios showing key time steps.

virtual character of the masonry contractor who first noticed the mistake. Upon the user interacting with both assets, a new lesson would start. The environment would change to then show the bent support rods with the general contractor proceeding with construction despite warnings. Lastly, the inspector was shown making no note of the mistake. Each asset or event within a lesson was explained via textual annotations.

All reports included certain pieces of information (e.g., sample documentation and images of construction drawings) that could not easily be shown through 3D representations in the environment. Such information was presented using annotations, through a menu, or as virtual 2D documents. To provide context while presenting the disparate collection of documents and images, relevant items were grouped together at locations to help provide memorable access. Photographs of the construction site were also integrated into the 3D space by placing them in the locations corresponding to where they would have been taken in the virtual environment (Fig. 3, left).

**Fig. 3.** Image cubes that open when interacted with (left) and a table showcasing 2D virtual documents (right).

The virtual environments were designed to facilitate gathering information about the incident and proper (or improper) construction procedures. Interacting with assets within the environment revealed associated information in a contextualized presentation. To promote interest in key areas, large oscillating arrows appeared over items that could be interacted with. We included a mini-map with a top-down view of the site to assist in understanding location and orientation. The locations of key areas, and embedded photographs were also shown on the mini-map. Additionally, a menu was made available to select a timestep and initiate a lesson. Items not related to the lessons were used to display additional information from the report such as images of the construction drawings or photographs of the site.

## 4   Study on Learning Behaviors and Outcomes

It is important to understand the implications of different degrees of interactivity and techniques supported for interactive control when using interactive media, as unnecessary or difficult interactions can have negative implications [18,31]. For this reason, we conducted a user study to test how different interactive techniques influence learning behaviors and outcomes. The goal of the study was to investigate the appropriate level of interactive control for information access in the educational prototype. For experimental control and simplification of the procedure, the study used the desktop version of the application with only the virtual environment contextualizing the incident involving the partial collapse of a masonry wall. This was done to avoid possible distractions that often comes with the novelty of VR and the head-tracked experience. By only including one virtual environment, we were able to test user's understanding and memory of the content. The results of the study were used as baseline understanding that was later compared against the VR version.

### 4.1   Study Design

The study focused on interactive control for travel and information access, which determines the method of exploring the environment and the limits on where participants could go at any given point in time. The study followed a between-subjects design to compare three versions of interactive control, which we refer to as *active, directed,* and *guided.* The *active* mode allowed for full navigational control, which permitted users to move freely to any location within the environment. The application used the mouse for orientation view control and the keyboard (WASD) for positional movement. Similar to the preset tour of a construction environment by Perlman et al. [16], the *directed* mode was a semi-automated tour of the environment's key locations. In this mode the user was placed in positions aligning with content or lessons within the environment in a predefined order. While the user had no control of their position, they could change the orientation of the camera and choose when to proceed to the next position via a button click.

The *guided* mode was a hybrid of the *directed* and *active* modes. Participants had control of movement in the environment but were limited to contained areas at predetermined sites. The sites were chosen as areas containing groups of information for the application, and participants could not travel outside of these areas before all groups of information were discovered. We hypothesized that the *guided* mode would yield better results because we expected the limited freedom would ease cognitive load of navigational decision making while still allowing some freedom of interactive viewing.

## 4.2 Procedure

The study was approved by our organization's Institutional Review Board (IRB) and took no more than 90 min from start to finish. We recruited 30 participants, limited to university students over the age of 18. Almost a third of the students were from the construction science department. Each participant used the desktop version of the application with one of the three types of interactive control. Participant's first completed a short background questionnaire. They then were then asked to spend at least five minutes in a tutorial VE to increase their understanding of how to navigate the VE and interact with its content. Before beginning the main educational activity, participants were told that they would be tested on the information found in the environment and asked to read a short summary of the incident. Participants were given 20 min to explore the environment with the option to finish early or to restart the exploration at any time. Verbal assistance about the controls or interface were given if requested.

Immediately after participants finished using the application, they took a thirty-eight question quiz on paper. The quiz covered information found within the environment and tested the cognitive processes of understanding and remembering, following the Anderson et al. [2] revision of Bloom's Taxonomy. There were 38 questions in total: 29 multiple choice questions on details and procedures to assess how much participants remembered and 9 short answer questions to assess their understanding of the incident events and factors. Examples of questions include: "Who designed the brace installation?", "Where should the rebar be located in the CMU brick?", "What was wrong with the braces?".

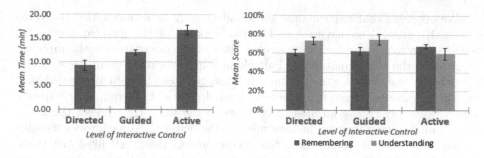

**Fig. 4.** A summary of study results: mean completion times (left), scores for remembering and understanding questions (right).

Participants then proceeded to fill out the industry standard systems usability scale (SUS) questionnaire [5]. A closing questionnaire was also administered, allowing them to provide additional comments about their experience and usability of the application. Finally, a brief interview was conducted should the participant want to elaborate on their comments.

## 4.3 Results and Discussions

In our study we tested behavior and learning outcomes from participants using our application by gathering both quantitative and qualitative evidence. We hypothesized that an intermediate level of interactive control (in this case, the *guided* condition) would produce the best learning results by balancing freedom of exploration with ease of use. In conjunction, we wanted to get a baseline understanding on the usability of the desktop application to compare against the VR version. We present our findings, analyzing quantitative results using Analysis of variance (ANOVA) tests and summarizing qualitative results.

Overall we found no evidence towards our hypothesis because there was no statistical difference in post-study scores for either *remembering* or *understanding* question types (see Table 1). However, it is interesting to note, that there was a significant statistical difference for the average time participants spent using the application (see Fig. 4). Further analysis using a post-hoc Tukey HSD test found the time for the *active* condition to be significantly higher than both the *directed* and *guided* conditions. We speculate that while it may appear that the *directed* condition is the best choice given higher scores for less time, further research should be done to understand long-term recall. These results are also intuitive; given the freedom to continue viewing the virtual environment within the 20-min time limit, participants chose to explore.

The mean SUS scores ranged from 75.50 to 81.25. Since these were above what is considered an average usability score of 68 (see [25]), we consider the application to be reasonably well-designed for its purposes. We found no statistical difference in the mean SUS scores across the three conditions.

We observed that participants' goals and viewing behaviors varied based on interactive control on navigation. The participants of the *directed* group did not seem to rotate the camera, choosing the default orientation with emphasis on reading the text annotations. Participants in the *guided* group treated the application more like a game to find all interactive assets, sometimes verbalizing their desire to move on to the next area. In the *active* group, participants would randomly choose an area to visit, go to the next, then revisit the areas to find information they might have missed. Participant feedback was generally positive towards the application. Some commented that they liked the story telling aspect of the visual information mixed with textual annotations. Some critiques of the application included concerns distinguishing which elements of the environment were interactive and wanting a clearer role or purpose in the construction scenario.

**Table 1.** Effects of interactive control on learning outcomes and usability, statistical analysis results.

| | | Mean Score | | | | |
|---|---|---|---|---|---|---|
| | Metric Range | Directed | Guided | Active | F(2,27) | p |
| Understanding | 0-100% | 73 | 75 | 60 | 2.207 | 0.130 |
| Remembering | 0-100% | 61 | 63 | 68 | 1.165 | 0.327 |
| Time (min) | 0-20 | 9.20 | 12.00 | 16.70 | 16.315 | < 0.001 * |
| Usability (SUS) | 0-100 | 81.25 | 80.25 | 75.50 | 0.530 | 0.595 |

## 5  Extending to Virtual Reality

For the last stage of the case study in designing an educational 3D application for construction safety, we developed a VR version of the application. For our goals of supporting information contextualization, the immersive format offered the benefits of being a highly engaging and appealing medium. However, VR is also generally expected to utilize a degree of interactivity. Thus, we followed our design framework for contextualizing incident reports and used the results from the study on learning behaviors and outcomes to guide the necessary design revisions for a VR version of the application.

### 5.1  VR Design Updates

The VR application was developed for use in an HTC Vive system with a head-mounted display and one wand controller. Since the desktop application relied on mouse and keyboard interaction, the VR application required support for the new tracked input devices. It was also necessary to make design revisions towards

**Fig. 5.** Screenshots from the educational virtual environment show the map interface (left) and menu design (right) in the VR version of the application, while the virtual construction site is in the background.

relaying textual information because head-based rendering was enabled for viewing. To promote exploration, we decided to prioritize engagement and interest. Referring to the usability results of the user study (see Sect. 4), we decided to lean more towards highly interactive travel. Though this choice might have led to increased complexity of interaction, we felt the activity and contextualized content would be more meaningful if learners felt more willing to continue to explore the 3D space. Therefore, learners were not limited in travel area and could move wherever they wanted.

We limited the number of wands to one to reduce the cognitive load on the learner. Raycasting with the wand was used to select interactive items for further detail in the VR version rather than mouse selection. Users had the option to physically walk within the tracked area of the real world room to be more precise when trying to investigate particular objects. The tracked area was represented in the VE as a semi-transparent boundary that would display when the user approached a corner or edge. The virtual tracked area could be moved by using the directional buttons on the wand or trigger clicking the mini-map to warp to a desired location (Fig. 5, left).

In desktop version of the application, textual information from lessons were 2D annotations overlaid on the screen. Since this was no longer feasible in the immersive format, the VR version used hand-anchored text displays attached to a pivot point just above the controller and billboarded to always face the user's view. The menu was accessed by clicking the top button the wand and was presented on a 2D surface at a predefined distance from the user (Fig. 5, right). While viewing it, the virtual tracked area was constrained. We opted against using the prior two techniques for the mini-map because we wanted to user to have the ability to trigger click it and warp. We instead used a heads up display that could be toggled on or off by pressing the grip buttons on the controller. Figure 1 shows an example of interface differences for presenting annotations.

## 5.2  Usability Observations and Feedback

To get a better idea of the usability of the VR application, we conducted a small informal usability study of five participants. The procedure was similar to the study on learning outcomes and behaviors. Participants were asked to use a tutorial application to familiarize themselves with the controls, then asked to explore the environment however they wanted. For this informal study, we did not ask participants to do a post-study questionnaire on the content. We did however, ask for feedback on the application, particularly what stood out. We also observed how they used the application, navigated the environment, and their ability to find the learning content. Overall, the participants spent more time using the application, had difficulties with interactions, but enjoyed using the VR application to explore the environment.

Observations regarding the order participants chose to view the lessons using the active level of navigation control for the desktop application carried over to the VR system, but with one difference. Instead of searching for assets to interact with, participants were more interested in just looking at the environment. One participant in particular, used the touchpad to move the virtual tracked area forward while looking down at bricks. Many users appreciated trigger clicking the mini-map to warp to specific locations, but wanted more precise control. They tried to get closer to the targeted location by using the touchpad to move the virtual tracked area, but often overshot. A few times we observed participants moving the virtual tracked area back and forth to get into the correct position. It is interesting to note that participants rarely physically moved around to get a better look at objects in the environment which would have solved precision issues. We suspect they were uncomfortable moving around without knowing the exact layout of their real world surroundings. In the tested application participants could trigger click interactive assets to initiate lessons, but many preferred using the menu.

We also noted that the display fidelity and ease of participant location and orientation influenced what assets were looked at. For example, photographs of the environment were interacted with less frequently due to the trouble of precisely positioning the virtual tracked area and participants unwillingness to physically position themselves in a way that allowed them to align the photograph with the environment. We also found that virtual documents with high amounts of text and details (Fig. 3, right) were far less useful in VR due to (a) the lower resolution of the display system, and (b) difficulty in aligning the virtual 2D documents for reading.

We identified several pitfalls in the newly designed user interface. Many participants physically and verbally expressed confusion in using the buttons on the controller to bring up the menu and mini-map. For example, one button was assigned to opening the menu. Later, when a lesson was started, the same button was reassigned to acknowledge that the information had been read. We also observed that the user would open the mini-map and forget to turn it off, leaving it to block the center view of the HMD. The textual information placed just above the location of the controller, always aiming toward the participant was used, but not in the way we expected. We designed the interface so the participant could lift an arm to select the interactive asset and then keep it there to read the information, allowing them to read the text while preserving their view of the asset for context. However, such use was not commonly observed; due to comfort and fatigue of arm movements, participants would often lower their arm and look down at the text, taking attention away from the asset.

## 6    Discussion and Conclusion

We presented a novel VR application for construction safety education. Our research followed a case study in the design and development of an educational 3D application with both desktop and VR versions. By using information from real OSHA incident reports, we developed a design framework for contextualizing raw report data into a meaningful 3D space. Our framework demonstrated techniques for integrating different forms of incident report information into a virtual environment.

We used iterative application development in our case study with both formal and informal user testing to improve design decisions and functionality. A summary of the key study findings are shown in Table 2. Through an experiment with varying levels of interactive control for travel and information access, we found participants were more likely to spend an increased amount of time in the application and be engaged when adopting a higher degree of control. While this effect is likely related to technique effectiveness for information access, the finding also demonstrates that control methods may also influence total time and attention given to content in an educational application. Follow-up research would be needed to further investigate the reasons for the outcomes.

**Table 2.** Properties of interactive control levels

|  | Directed | Guided | Active |
|---|---|---|---|
| Learning | linear | linear | non-linear |
| Controls | semi-automated tour with control of the camera rotation and pacing | blend of directed and active, limited to an area | full navigational control |
| Qualitative Results | Pressed button, read information, repeat | Finished area by area, like completing levels | Participants not sure where to go, more exploratory |
| Explore Time | Least | Middle | Most |

The results of the evaluations and case studies helped to motivate the decisions for taking advantage of VR's interactivity for an engaging educational experience. Overall, our approach resulted in the development of a new educational application, and the usability results from our studies provide evidence of general usability and design success. Based on the design process and the results of our evaluations with participants, we provide a summary of design recommendations for developing educational 3D applications for the purposes of contextualizing a construction incident report. Our guidelines cover data preparation, learning objectives and storyboarding, choosing a system device, visual aesthetic, representing temporal change, data representation, and interaction techniques within a VE. An overview of the guidelines are shown in Table 3. While not a definitive set of rules, others may use our results to help in the development of educational applications.

**Table 3.** Summary of design guidelines

| Data Preperation | Understand the data within the construction incident report. What events led up to the incident? What are the types of data? |
|---|---|
| Learning Objectives and Storyboarding | To design how the application will work the learning objective should be defined. Consider if they will be learning new knowledge, comprehending, analyzing, or creating. The learning objective should shape how the application will work. |
| Choosing a System Device | The system device you choose will influence the interactions within the environment. Types of devices can include a desktop computer or head-mounted displays for virtual reality. Some may increase engagement, but at the cost of familiarity of controls. |
| Visual Aesthetic | Consider using a simplistic, stylized, or realistic style as it determines the level of detail. The design may deviate, if it maintains a consistent look. |
| Representing Temporal Change | Contextualizing time in a static virtual environment is difficult and there are many ways to approach it. Make the changes in time clear for the learner to understand the progression of events. |
| Data Representation | The data can be represented through visual, textual, spatial, or audio representation. Deciding which one to use or how depends on the amount of data and resources. |
| Interaction Techniques | To access the information the user must interact with the environment. This could include selecting objects, an intuitive user interface, and/or navigation. |

Although our results support a successful design and development process, our research is not without its limitations. Following iterative development, we conducted a formal user study with the desktop evaluation to help study approaches for interaction, but we did not conduct formal user study on the VR application. Future work will also require testing with construction students to better understand suitability for educational contexts.

Similarly, our experiment only assessed short-term recall with simple memory and understanding learning outcomes. Participants completed the knowledge assessment immediately after using the application. We are interested in extending our research by also testing longer-term recall (i.e., after several days or weeks). We suspect longer-term retention might provide more meaningful results as it could validate the correlation of increased engagement to recall and perhaps show whether or not a certain type of information (spatial, textual, visual) is better retained.

Another possible limitation is that although our approach focuses on the presentation of construction incident reports, this is only one method used to teach construction safety. Future advancement in this direction of research could also consider alternative design schemes for educational VR to present safety concepts in a meaningful way.

# References

1. Albert, A., Hallowell, M.R., Kleiner, B., Chen, A., Golparvar-Fard, M.: Enhancing construction hazard recognition with high-fidelity augmented virtuality. J. Constr. Eng. Manag. **140**(7), 04014024 (2014)
2. Anderson, L.W., et al.: A taxonomy for learning, teaching and assessing: a revision of bloom's taxonomy. In: Artz, A.F., Armour-Thomas, E. Longman Publishing, New York (1992). Development of a cognitive-metacognitive framework for protocol analysis of mathematical problem solving in small groups. Cogn. Instruct. **9**(2), 137–175 (2001)
3. Behm, M.: Linking construction fatalities to the design for construction safety concept. Saf. Sci. **43**(8), 589–611 (2005)
4. Bowman, D.A., Hodges, L.F., Allison, D., Wineman, J.: The educational value of an information-rich virtual environment. Presence: Teleoper. Virtual Environ. **8**(3), 317–331 (1999)
5. Brooke, J., et al.: SUS-a quick and dirty usability scale. Usabil. Eval. Ind. **189**(194), 4–7 (1996)
6. Dede, C., Salzman, M.C., Loftin, R.B.: ScienceSpace: virtual realities for learning complex and abstract scientific concepts. In: Proceedings of the IEEE Virtual Reality Annual International Symposium 1996, pp. 246–252. IEEE (1996)
7. Guo, H., Li, H., Chan, G., Skitmore, M.: Using game technologies to improve the safety of construction plant operations. Accid. Anal. Prevent. **48**, 204–213 (2012)
8. Kaufmann, H., Schmalstieg, D., Wagner, M.: Construct3D: a virtual reality application for mathematics and geometry education. Educ. Inf. Technol. **5**(4), 263–276 (2000)
9. Le, Q.T., Pedro, A., Park, C.S.: A social virtual reality based construction safety education system for experiential learning. J. Intell. Robot. Syst. **79**(3–4), 487–506 (2015)
10. Lin, K.Y., Son, J.W., Rojas, E.M.: A pilot study of a 3D game environment for construction safety education. J. Inf. Technol. Constr. **16**(5), 69–83 (2011)
11. Lucas, J., Thabet, W.: Implementation and evaluation of a VR task-based training tool for conveyor belt safety training. J. Inf. Technol. Constr. (ITcon) **13**(40), 637–659 (2008)

12. Mandler, J.M., Seegmiller, D., Day, J.: On the coding of spatial information. Mem. Cogn. **5**(1), 10–16 (1977)
13. Mayer, I., Wolff, A., Wenzler, I.: Learning efficacy of the 'hazard recognition' serious game. In: Ma, M., Oliveira, M.F., Petersen, S., Hauge, J.B. (eds.) SGDA 2013. LNCS, vol. 8101, pp. 118–129. Springer, Heidelberg (2013). https://doi.org/10.1007/978-3-642-40790-1_12
14. Moreno, R., Mayer, R.E.: Learning science in virtual reality multimedia environments: role of methods and media. J. Educ. Psychol. **94**(3), 598 (2002)
15. National Safety Council: National safety council injury facts, 2015 edition (2015)
16. Perlman, A., Sacks, R., Barak, R.: Hazard recognition and risk perception in construction. Saf. Sci. **64**, 22–31 (2014)
17. Ragan, E.D., Bowman, D.A., Huber, K.J.: Supporting cognitive processing with spatial information presentations in virtual environments. Virtual Reality **16**(4), 301–314 (2012)
18. Ragan, E.D., Huber, K.J., Laha, B., Bowman, D.A.: The effects of navigational control and environmental detail on learning in 3D virtual environments. In: 2012 IEEE Virtual Reality Short Papers and Posters (VRW), pp. 11–14. IEEE (2012)
19. Ragan, E.D., Sowndararajan, A., Kopper, R., Bowman, D.A.: The effects of higher levels of immersion on procedure memorization performance and implications for educational virtual environments. Presence: Teleoper. Virtual Environ. **19**(6), 527–543 (2010)
20. Ragan, E.D., Wood, A., McMahan, R.P., Bowman, D.A.: Trade-offs related to travel techniques and level of display fidelity in virtual data-analysis environments. In: ICAT/EGVE/EuroVR, pp. 81–84 (2012)
21. Roussou, M., Oliver, M., Slater, M.: The virtual playground: an educational virtual reality environment for evaluating interactivity and conceptual learning. Virtual Reality **10**(3–4), 227–240 (2006)
22. Sacks, R., Perlman, A., Barak, R.: Construction safety training using immersive virtual reality. Constr. Manag. Econ. **31**(9), 1005–1017 (2013)
23. Occupational Safety and Health Administration: Outreach training program. https://www.osha.gov/dte/outreach/construction/index.html
24. Saleh, J.H., Pendley, C.C.: From learning from accidents to teaching about accident causation and prevention: multidisciplinary education and safety literacy for all engineering students. Reliab. Eng. Syst. Saf. **99**, 105–113 (2012)
25. Sauro, J.: A practical guide to the system usability scale: background, benchmarks & best practices. Measuring Usability LLC (2011)
26. Singh, G., et al.: CI-Spy: designing a mobile augmented reality system for scaffolding historical inquiry learning. In: 2015 IEEE International Symposium on Mixed and Augmented Reality-Media, Art, Social Science, Humanities and Design (ISMAR-MASH'D), pp. 9–14. IEEE (2015)
27. Suraji, A., Duff, A.R., Peckitt, S.J.: Development of causal model of construction accident causation. J. Constr. Eng. Manag. **127**(4), 337–344 (2001)
28. Tennyson, R.D., Breuer, K.: Improving problem solving and creativity through use of complex-dynamic simulations. Comput. Hum. Behav. **18**(6), 650–668 (2002)
29. Virvou, M., Katsionis, G.: On the usability and likeability of virtual reality games for education: the case of VR-ENGAGE. Comput. Educ. **50**(1), 154–178 (2008)
30. Wickens, C.D.: Virtual reality and education. In: 1992 IEEE International Conference on Systems, Man and Cybernetics, pp. 842–847. IEEE (1992)
31. Winn, W., Jackson, R.: Fourteen propositions about educational uses of virtual reality. Educ. Technol. **39**, 5–14 (1999)

# Augmented Reality (AR) Assisted Laryngoscopy for Endotracheal Intubation Training

Ming Qian[1], John Nicholson[1(✉)], David Tanaka[2], Patricia Dias[2], Erin Wang[1], and Litao Qiu[1]

[1] Lenovo Research, 7001 Development Dr, Morrisville, NC, USA
{mqian, jnichol, ewang}@lenovo.com, lqiu@motorola.com
[2] Department of Pediatrics, Duke University Medical Center, Durham, NC, USA
{david.tanaka, tricia.dias}@duke.edu

**Abstract.** Medical trainees require sufficient practice to gain the experience and confidence needed to safely and reliably perform endotracheal intubations. While video laryngoscopy has been used to provide an advanced glottic view that can reduce intubation failure, prevent prolonged intubation time, and reduce repeated intubation attempts, most current devices require visualization on external monitors, disrupting the direct line-of-sight view. These devices also present a deep intra-oral view of the airway that may not be visible during a typical unassisted intubation attempt. As a result, these differences create new challenges to gaining competency in the standard, direct laryngoscopy technique when using video laryngoscopy as a learning tool.

To address these challenges, Lenovo Research and the Duke Neonatal Intensive Care Unit jointly developed an Augmented Reality-Assisted Laryngoscopy (ARAL) system using a head-mounted device (HMD). Healthcare providers with minimal intubation experience wore an HMD while performing intubations on an infant manikin with a camera attached to the laryngoscope blade. An enhanced image of the patient's airway was projected onto the visual field of the HMD, giving the intubators improved oral and glottic visualization while still maintaining focus on the direct line-of-sight view. Our user survey evaluates the effectiveness of the ARAL system, the configuration of the AR view, and the users' behaviors and preferences when switching their attention between the AR view and the direct line-of-sight view.

The approach of using an AR HMD to provide live camera feeds to assist health care providers in performing medical procedures is novel and can be expanded to many other areas of medicine. The advantages of maintaining the direct line-of-sight view during a procedure, in addition to improved supervisory capabilities, have the potential to improve efficacy and efficiency of a wide range of medical and surgical procedures.

**Keywords:** Augmented Reality · AR · Head-mounted device · HMD · Smart glasses · Line of sight · Augmented Reality Assisted Laryngoscopy · ARAL · Intubation · Assisted Laryngoscopy · Training · Instruction

J. Y. C. Chen and G. Fragomeni (Eds.): HCII 2019, LNCS 11575, pp. 355–371, 2019.
https://doi.org/10.1007/978-3-030-21565-1_24

# 1  Introduction

## 1.1  Medical Application Background

Current trainees in pediatric residency programs are often unable to achieve competency in many necessary procedures before completing their medical education [1–5]. One such procedure is neonatal intubation (the placement of a flexible plastic tube through the mouth down into the trachea in order to maintain an open airway), which remains a critical skill for any general pediatrician responsible for delivering babies or nursery coverage. In the pediatric medical literature, intubation proficiency is defined as the ability for a provider to successfully intubate more than 80% of the time [6]. A recent study [7] found that an average of 8 to 10 intubation opportunities may be required to achieve this competency level. This same study also demonstrated that medical trainees' intubation opportunities have been reduced from more than 30 over a 3 year training period per trainee to less than 3.

Thus, it can be argued that the decrease in intubation proficiency may be directly attributed to the decrease in exposure of pediatric residents to neonatal intubation. There are multiple factors contributing to this decrease in intubation opportunities, including the recent restriction of resident duty hours, the increased use of non-invasive mechanical ventilation for neonates [8, 9], the new recommendations of the Neonatal Resuscitation Program regarding management of non-vigorous infants with meconium-stained fluid, and the expansion of non-physician providers (such as neonatal nurse practitioners) in many academic medical institutions [10].

Given these current limitations on intubation opportunities, there is a significant need for the development of new techniques to teach novice providers the skill of neonatal intubation. Many programs are relying on learners' experiences in simulation labs to compensate for the decreased opportunities to intubate real patients. However, the learning process is heavily dependent upon the provider's understanding of the intraoral anatomy as seen in real life (as opposed to the views obtained with current simulation manikins) [11].

It is well known that although every intubation attempt performed by a learner is supervised by a competent intubator, the actual process of learning this skill is constrained by the fact that the supervisor cannot actually see what the novice intubator is viewing. To overcome this handicap, several teaching medical centers have begun to utilize video laryngoscopy systems wherein the supervisor may have access to the same view as the learner. Currently available video laryngoscope systems, such as the Glidescope (Verathon Medical, Bothell, WA) and Storz C-MAC D-blade (Karl Storz, Tuttlingen, Germany), are prohibitively expensive ($22,000–$55,000), contain fragile fiber optic components, and require the operator to learn the skill using non-standard equipment and techniques. It is uncertain whether the learning process using these costly non-standard systems will translate to clinical environments that do not have access to these highly specialized intubation tools.

Another concern with using traditional video laryngoscopy is that it requires the intubator to turn his or her head towards the video monitor, thus interrupting direct line-of-sight visualization. Video laryngoscopy also presents a deep intra-oral view of the airway that bears little resemblance to the typical unassisted view. These two differences create a new challenge to gaining competency in direct laryngoscopy (with the focus being on a direct line-of-sight view) while using video laryngoscopy as a learning tool (with the focus being on an enhanced glottic view without a direct line-of-sight view).

## 1.2   Proposed Solution and Contribution

In this research project, Lenovo Research and the Duke NICU (a member of the National Institute of Child Health and Human Development [NICHD] Neonatal Research Network) jointly developed an Augmented Reality-Assisted Laryngoscopy (ARAL) system using a head-mounted device (HMD) also known as "smart glasses". Medical providers with limited intubation experience wore these smart glasses while performing intubations on an infant manikin with a high-resolution camera attached to the laryngoscope blade. An enhanced image of the patient's airway was projected onto the glasses' visual field, giving the intubator improved glottic visualization while still maintaining focus on the direct line-of-sight view of the larynx.

It has been previously demonstrated that coaching by a supervisor viewing the video images, either on the same screen or on a different device, increases the likelihood of successful intubations and shortens intubation times for novice providers on intubation manikins [12]. By making both the enhanced glottic view and the direct line-of-sight view continuously available to trainees, the ARAL system combines the benefits of both direct and video laryngoscopy and may help enhance trainees' ability to subsequently perform direct laryngoscopy successfully without the use of AR.

The approach of using an AR HMD to provide views of live camera feeds in order to assist health care providers in performing medical procedures is novel and can be expanded to many other areas of medicine. The advantages of maintaining the direct line-of-sight view along with the enhanced glottic visualization, as well as the shared supervisor view, have the potential to improve efficacy (rate of successful intubation) and efficiency (time to intubate) for both trainees as well as experienced providers.

The objectives of this paper are to explore the design issues and tradeoffs associated with the ARAL system. The results of a recently completed pilot study exploring the use of the described ARAL system is currently being prepared for publication. We will discuss the effectiveness of the improved glottic visualization, mechanisms for improved supervisor experience in order to facilitate coaching, flexibilities displaying the glottic visualization window in the AR HMD, and the users' behavior and preferences when switching their visual focus between the glottic visualization window and the direct line-of-sight view while performing the intubation.

## 1.3   Paper Organization

This paper has six sections: Introduction; System Design and User Experience; Pilot Survey and User Survey; Pilot Study Results; User Survey Results, and Conclusion.

## 2  System Design and User Experience

In this section, we describe the system design and user experience of the ARAL system.

### 2.1  Application Scenario and Hardware Arrangements

Figure 1 graphically depicts the application scenario. A standard neonatal intubation manikin and disposable laryngoscope (BritePro Solo, FlexiCare, UK) are used in the teaching program today and are carried forward in the ARAL system. Onto the laryngoscope we add an HD resolution (1280 × 720) camera through the means of a clip-on adapter, described in detail below. The camera used in this paper is a TD-B20903-76 (Misumi Electronics Corp., Taiwan). This device is a small (3.5 mm diameter, 13 mm long) camera designed for the medical industry. The camera is connected to a Capture PC/laptop through a cabled USB connection. The capture PC performs some video processing and encoding, and the real-time video streaming content is then transmitted from the capture PC to the client devices (AR HMD and/or tablet) with a Wi-Fi link using the real-time protocol (RTP). Consequently, the live video stream can be displayed on the AR HMD headset with minimal latency. A supervisor can use the display on the laptop, or connect with another device such as a tablet, to also see the intubation camera video stream and provide verbal coaching to the intubator.

We developed an adapter (Fig. 2) to hold the camera and attach it to the laryngoscope. The adapter is small and lightweight, and supports the Miller-type BritePro Solo laryngoscope blades (sizes 00 through 2). To support other Miller-type blades minor adjustments may be required. Impact on the intubator is minimal, as the camera/adapter unit weighs less than 10 grams, permits direct line-of-sight visualization, and allows for quick attachment to the laryngoscope blade. In preliminary studies, we observed that the camera-adapter unit created a view similar to that of commercially available video intubation systems. More importantly, unlike these latter systems, neither the adapter nor the camera will enter the oral cavity given that the camera does not extend past the intubation handle.

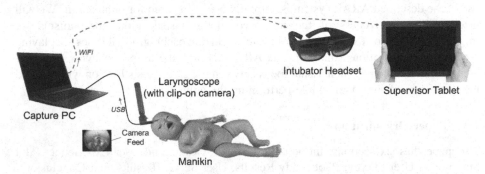

**Fig. 1.** Pilot scenario of AR-Assisted Laryngoscopy

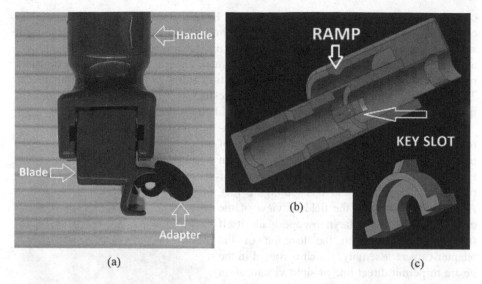

**Fig. 2.** Adapter to hold the camera in the laryngoscope blade (a) photograph of the adapter in place on an assembled laryngoscope (b) a CAD model of the adapter; the ramp enables support for a range of blade sizes; the key slot ensures proper camera orientation (c) a detailed view of the key, which is attached to the camera tube

In this paper, the AR HMD that we used were the ODG R-7 Smartglasses (Osterhout Design Group, USA). These glasses have two HD resolution (1280 × 720) displays, one for each eye. During development and when working with early test users, we found that the buttons on the underside of the temples of the smart glasses were accidentally pressed frequently, typically as the user would put the glasses on or take them off. To provide a better user experience, we disabled or limited the functionality of these buttons. Additionally, in a medical setting the health care provider frequently has their hands occupied by the medical procedure and cannot operate controls such as these. As such, settings for the display of the camera stream in the AR HMD were provided on the Capture PC and could be operated by an assistant at the verbal instruction of the intubator.

## 2.2 Software Arrangements and User Experience

A key user experience requirement for this solution is an easy and seamless connection mechanism. In a medical environment, having the equipment turn on and *just work* is an expected behavior. In our solution, there are several challenges: the battery life of the smart glasses is short, the boot time is long, and Wi-Fi networks can be difficult and finicky to set up. At this early stage of our work, we have implemented a limited number of features to address these issues. First, we have addressed the Wi-Fi client-server connection discovery problem through the use of a quick response (QR) code. The Capture PC, which also acts as an RTP server, generates a QR code with the necessary information to connect, including the network name and the IP address. The camera integrated in the smart glasses is used to read the QR code, and initiate the connection. We also include the network name and IP address in human-readable form with the QR code, which can help the user in diagnosing any problems. Second, we automatically launch our application on the smart glasses when they have finished booting the operating system, and the application starts in the QR scanning mode. These two components helped make the early testing and pilot study possible, but are insufficient as a final solution to resolve the challenges listed above.

Our solution includes a pan-and-zoom feature that enables us to focus on a region of interest in the camera field of view. As shown in Fig. 3, the camera will see some of the exterior of the manikin's face and lips (subfigure (a)). Additionally, much of the field of view of the camera will be of the laryngoscope blade itself (subfigure (b)), due to the location of the adapter-camera assembly, which is rooted in the desire to permit direct line-of-sight visualization and prevent the adapter/camera from entering the oral cavity. The pan-and-zoom feature enables our solution to primarily display the enhanced glottic view, without showing much of the patient's face or the laryngoscope blade, but still showing enough of these visual features to provide a frame of reference to the intubator.

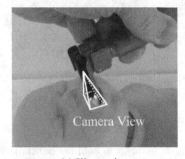

(a) Illustration

(b) Capture

**Fig. 3.** Camera field of view

Another feature of our solution that was found to be profoundly important during early testing was a manual camera settings interface, particular a setting for exposure. In the intubation scenario, the camera view captures a large range of brightness. Additionally, the camera view inside the oral cavity includes reflective surfaces (either plastic in the manikin or oral secretions in a patient). In our experience, the auto-exposure algorithm available in many cameras did not properly adjust to the conditions seen during intubation, and the manual exposure setting was an important inclusion. Eventually, an auto-exposure algorithm dedicated to this scenario would be a necessary improvement.

We also have two features that are speculative in nature. First, we support the ability to resize and reposition the glottic visualization window in the display field of the smart glasses. The hypothesized benefit of our ARAL system is that the wearer of the headset can see both the patient and the environment with their direct line-of-sight as well as the camera view in the headset display. If the glottic visualization window showing the camera view takes up too much of the visual field, the direct line-of-sight view may be compromised. Similarly, the second feature would support the use of both of the displays (binocular, one in each eye), or only one (monocular, in either the left or the right eye). Rather than reducing the size of the glottic visualization window, the window can be shown only in one eye. This would introduce a binocular rivalry to the wearer, allowing them to choose to focus their visual attention on the glottic visualization window in one eye, or the direct line-of-sight view available to the other eye. In the case of intubation, where a direct binocular view into the oral cavity is partially obstructed, we hypothesize that this monocular approach may be a productive one. However, in the case of the ODG R-7 glasses that are used in this paper, the optics support only a 30° field of view of the wearer, so the resize and reposition feature was not found to be useful. In the future as AR HMD optics improve in resolution and field of view, we suspect the feature may become useful.

One additional pedagogical feature implemented in this solution is an instructor telestrator function. As described in Sect. 1.2, the camera video stream is shown on a display separate from the HMD, such as the Supervisor Tablet in Fig. 1. This allows the experienced intubator to see what the learner is seeing and provide specific verbal coaching. The instructor can also use their finger or a stylus to draw on top of the video stream, which the trainee will see on the HMD display in real-time. This visual instruction thus supplements the verbal feedback being given to the trainee during the actual intubation attempt.

# 3  Pilot Study and User Survey

## 3.1  Selection of Subjects

Duke NICU nurses were selected as the subjects for this study. The selection of these subjects was based on the assumption that although these individuals have theoretical knowledge of the intubation process and an understanding of intraoral anatomy, they do not have hands-on experience (with either a manikin or a real patient). This approach allows us to study this technology as it is designed to be used, as an educational tool for novice providers.

## 3.2  Subject Recruitment and Compensation

Subjects were recruited during their nursing shifts in the hospital. If they volunteered to participate, the study would take place at their convenience (usually during one of their scheduled breaks in the unit's conference room). There was no compensation for participation in this study.

## 3.3  Pilot Study

45 test subjects were randomly assigned to one of three groups (with 15 providers in each group). The first group intubated an infant manikin using direct laryngoscopy (DL), which is the standard intubation technique. The camera and adapter were left attached to the laryngoscope so that the same obstruction was in place, but the camera was not powered on. The second group intubated an infant manikin using indirect video laryngoscopy (IL) – these providers relied solely on a video stream of the mouth and airway that was projected onto the Capture PC laptop placed beside the manikin, but without the use of the AR HMD. The third group intubated an infant manikin using AR-assisted video laryngoscopy – these providers were able to view the manikin

directly (by peering beneath the smart glasses frame) while simultaneously using the video stream projected onto the glasses to supplement their view. All three groups were given verbal coaching during their attempts by an expert intubator, who was able to view the video stream in real time while assisting those in the second and third groups.

Each participant attempted intubation five times. The outcome of each attempt was documented as either successful (endotracheal tube placed in the airway in less than 30 s), unsuccessful due to time (endotracheal tube placed in the airway within 30 to 60 s), unsuccessful due to attempt being aborted at 60 s, or unsuccessful due to esophageal intubation (endotracheal tube placed in the esophagus instead of the airway). The time required to acquire (or visually identify) the airway as well as the time required to intubate were also recorded.

The preliminary results of this pilot study are described in Sect. 4 with a more detailed analysis being readied for publication in the near future.

### 3.4    User Survey

The following nine questions were listed on a survey generated through SurveyMonkey and the nurses who joined the pilot study were asked to provide answers anonymously. Eight questions offer 5-point Likert-scale answer options: strongly agree, agree, neutral, disagree, and strongly disagree, and an additional comment box was provided in case respondents wanted to provide any other opinions. Question 8 was in the form of an open-ended question.

Q1. It is easier to identify the magnified airway with the smart glasses compared to just using my eyes.

Q2. It is advantageous that the supervisor can see the same view that I see on the smart glasses so that she can give me better verbal guidance and instructions.

Q3. It is advantageous that the instructor can mark on the view of the smart glasses so she can circle the airway location for me.

Q4. I would like to have the ability to turn off the smart glasses display if necessary so that I can focus on the direct view of the manikin.

Q5. I would like to have the flexibility of changing the size and position of the view in the smart glasses.

Q6. I would like the ability to change the zoom factor of the camera and make the airway even larger.

Q7. It would be nice if the smart glasses had a bigger field of view (display size) as the technology continues to improve.

Q8. While performing intubation using the smart glasses, did you use the see-through capability of the glasses to look directly at the manikin for any purpose (e.g., to insert the tube into the mouth)? Or was everything done by looking at the smart glasses display of the camera stream? Feel free to elaborate.

Q9. (Assuming you did look at the manikin directly) It is easy to switch my attention between looking at the smart glasses display and directly at the manikin.

Questions 1, 2 and 3 solicit opinions on the general utility and effectiveness of the enhanced glottic view, the shared view between trainee and instructor, and telestrator function. Questions 5, 6, and 7 solicit opinions on AR view configurations. Questions

4, 8 and 9 solicit opinions on users' visual focus behavior and preference when they swap between the two available views (the direct line-of-sight view and the camera view). Note that following the collection of the data from the pilot study described in the previous section, all participants were allowed to experience the AR solution regardless of assigned group. This allowed the test subjects in the DL and IL groups to also answer questions about AR-assisted view. The results of the survey are described in Sect. 5.

# 4  Pilot Study Results

The overall outcomes for the three groups (DL, IL and AR-assisted) are reflected in Table 1 and Fig. 4. As illustrated, the success rate for participants in the DL group was significantly lower than the success rate of participants in the IL and AR groups. The largest contributor to this disparity was the number of esophageal intubations – over a quarter of the providers in the DL group intubated the manikin's esophagus, while there were no esophageal intubations in the IL or AR groups. This can be attributed to the specific verbal coaching that is afforded by the live video stream – the expert intubator was able to identify the esophagus and the airway for the novice provider, thus preventing malposition of the endotracheal tube.

The time required to intubate was also improved with the use of video laryngoscopy (both indirect and AR-assisted). The average time to complete one intubation (successful or otherwise) in the DL group was 36.59 s, compared to 26.17 s in the IL group and 26.31 s in the AR group. This improvement in speed is directly related to the intubator's ability to visually identify the airway – participants in the DL group acquired the airway in 18.00 s (on average), compared to 5.06 s and 4.65 s in the IL and AR groups respectively.

Table 1. Overall outcomes for the three groups (DL, IL and AR)

|  | Success (%) | Failure due to time (%) | Attempt aborted (%) | Esophageal intubation (%) |
| --- | --- | --- | --- | --- |
| DL Group | 32 | 20 | 21.33 | 26.67 |
| IL Group | 72 | 21.33 | 6.67 | 0 |
| AR Group | 70.67 | 18.67 | 10.66 | 0 |

In summary, the pilot study illustrates the utility of video laryngoscopy in improving intubation proficiency in a simulation environment. We hypothesize that the ARAL system will prove to be both more efficacious and efficient in teaching new providers than indirect video laryngoscopy when this technology is used in real

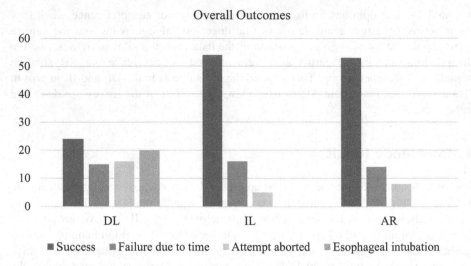

**Fig. 4.** Overall outcomes for the three groups (DL, IL and AR)

patients. In an effort to assess cross-transference of intubation skills acquired through the use of the ARAL system, we plan to conduct additional studies examining the success rates of providers trained with the use of the ARAL system and subsequent attempts with direct laryngoscopy.

## 5 User Survey Results

A user survey was distributed to the test subjects several weeks after the pilot study and each test subject filled them out on a voluntary basis. Altogether, 26 subjects filled out the survey: 7 from the DL group, 7 from the IL group, and 12 from the AR group. Table 2 lists the survey responses for the Likert-scale questions in tabular form.

### 5.1 General Utility of Solution

In this section we focus on the questions having to do with the general utility or effectiveness of the AR-assisted solution. Question 1 (Fig. 5), question 2 (Fig. 6), and question 3 (Fig. 7) show that the majority of the respondents agreed that the improved glottic view, shared glottic view, and telestration feature did make learning and performing the intubation easier, demonstrating that the ARAL system is an effective teaching tool.

**Table 2.** User survey responses

| Question | Strongly agree | Agree | Neutral | Disagree | Strongly disagree | Other |
|---|---|---|---|---|---|---|
| Q1. It is easier to identify the magnified airway with the smart glasses compared to just using my eyes | 14 | 7 | 3 | 2 | 0 | 0 |
| Q2. It is advantageous that the supervisor can see the same view that I see on the smart glasses so that she can give me better verbal guidance and instructions | 18 | 6 | 2 | 0 | 0 | 0 |
| Q3. It is advantageous that the instructor can mark on the view of the smart glasses so she can circle the airway location for me | 14 | 8 | 4 | 0 | 0 | 0 |
| Q4. I would like to have the ability to turn off the smart glasses display if necessary so that I can focus on the direct view of the manikin | 10 | 8 | 5 | 3 | 0 | 0 |
| Q5. I would like to have the flexibility of changing the size and position of the view in the smart glasses | 4 | 11 | 10 | 1 | 0 | 0 |
| Q6. I would like the ability to change the zoom factor of the camera and make the airway even larger | 4 | 10 | 9 | 3 | 0 | 0 |
| Q7. It would be nice if the smart glasses had a bigger field of view (display size) as the technology continues to improve | 0 | 14 | 10 | 1 | 1 | 0 |
| Q9. (Assuming you did look at the manikin directly) It is easy to switch my attention between looking at the smart glasses display and directly at the manikin | 3 | 13 | 4 | 3 | 0 | 3 |

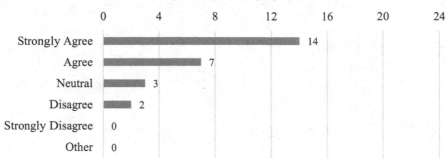

Fig. 5. Effectiveness of magnified airway (improved glottic view) with the AR smart glasses

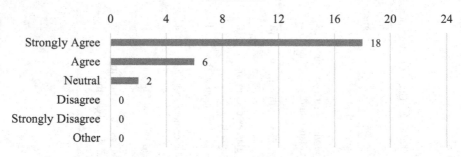

Fig. 6. Effectiveness of shared glottic view

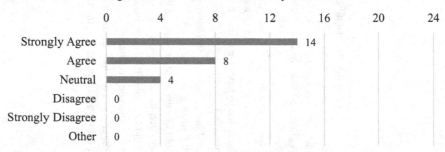

Fig. 7. Effectiveness of telestration feature

## 5.2   View Configuration

We also asked a series of questions about potential desire for user configuration of the display of the camera stream in the smart glasses. Question 5 (Fig. 8), question 6 (Fig. 9), and question 7 (Fig. 10) show the results of the survey in this view config-uration category. The majority of the respondents liked the idea of having flexibility to configure the size, position, and zoom factors of the AR view, and they expressed a desire to have a larger field of view once more advanced technology becomes available, though the preferences were not as strong as those regarding the general utility questions.

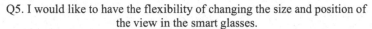

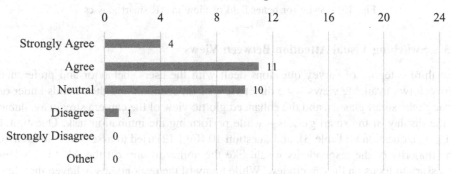

**Fig. 8.** AR display size and position configuration

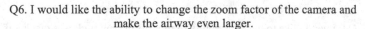

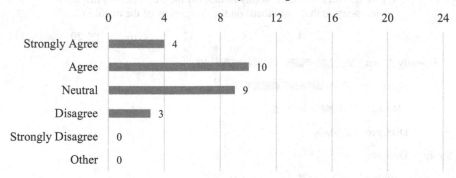

**Fig. 9.** AR display zoom factor configuration

Q7. It would be nice if the smart glasses had a bigger field of view (display size) as the technology continues to improve.

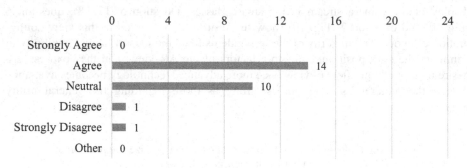

Fig. 10. Desire for better field of view in AR smart glasses

## 5.3 Switching Visual Attention Between Views

The third category of survey questions dealt with the users' behavior and preference between two available views – the direct view of the manikin and their hands under or through the smart glasses, and the enhanced glottic view of the camera stream available in the display of the smart glasses – while performing the intubation task. Question 4 (Fig. 11), question 9 (Table 3), and question 10 (Fig. 12) tried to assess this difference. The majority of the respondents would like the ability to turn off the AR view when necessary to focus on the direct view. While many of the respondents believed that they could easily switch between the two views, a sizable number of the respondents were not so sure (or, as was provided in the comments, at least wanted more practice before considering it as being "easy"), and several believed that switching views was hard.

Q4. I would like to have the ability to turn off the smart glasses display if necessary so that I can focus on the direct view of the manikin.

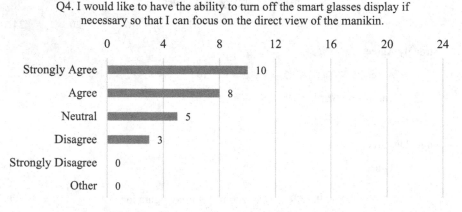

Fig. 11. The capability to turn off the AR view

*Q8. While performing intubation using the smart glasses, did you use the see-through capability of the glasses to look directly at the manikin for any purpose (e.g., to insert the tube into the mouth)? Or was everything done by looking at the smart glasses display of the camera stream? Feel free to elaborate.*

**Table 3.** Open-ended responses about the use of see-through AR display technology

| # | Response |
|---|---|
| 1 | I looked through the glasses to insert the ETT in the mouth. I actually tried to look underneath the frame of the glasses when inserting the ETT into the airway (after visualizing with the glasses) so that I could see where I'm going with my own eyes. I struggled with the back and forth between smart view and see through. That's why I looked underneath |
| 2 | I used both the see-through capability and the Smart Glasses display. I primarily used the see-through for the intubation process and the Smart Glasses for any direction provided externally |
| 3 | A little bit of one…a little bit of the other…used in combination like the perfect pb&j (peanut butter and jelly sandwich fyi…) |
| 4 | I looked the Smart glasses screen AND through the lens to directly look at the manikin |
| 5 | I briefly looked at the manikin to check my hand placement but mostly looked through camera stream |
| 6 | I used both |
| 7 | I used the see-through capability |
| 8 | I used the see through capability |
| 9 | Looking through the smart glasses |
| 10 | Yes, to visualize the mouth when inserting the ETT |
| 11 | I did use the see-through to initially get in place |
| 12 | When first putting tube in mouth |
| 13 | I looked at the manikin to double check |
| 14 | I used the Smart Glasses exclusively |
| 15 | Everything was done by looking at smart glasses |
| 16 | Everything done by looking at the smart glasses display of the camera stream |
| 17 | Everything was done looking through the glasses only |
| 18 | No |
| 19 | Unsure |

Table 3 lists all the answers to Question 9 (the use of direct view). We collected 19 responses, while 7 respondents chose not to comment. One respondent said he or she did not know, 5 respondents (26%) claimed that they only used the AR view, and 13 respondents (68%) claimed that they used both the AR view and the direct view. Among them: four respondents used the direct view to insert the intubation tube into the mouth at the beginning; one respondent used the direct view for intubation and only looked at the AR view when the instructor delivered verbal advice; two respondents only looked at the direct view to double check what they saw in the AR view; and six respondents claimed that they used the direct view without specifying more details.

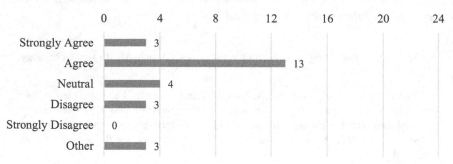

Q9. (Assuming you did look at the manikin directly) It is easy to switch my attention between looking at the smart glasses display and directly at the manikin.

**Fig. 12.** Ease of switching visual focus between direct and enhanced views.

## 6 Conclusion

This pilot study illustrates the utility of both indirect and AR-assisted video laryngoscopy in improving intubation proficiency in a simulation environment. We hypothesize that AR-assisted video laryngoscopy will prove to be more efficacious than indirect video laryngoscopy when this technology is used in real patients. A manikin provides a static environment to practice intubations without the challenges of patient movement, oral secretions, differing anatomies of individual infants, and other challenges during intubation that are unique to live patients. Future projects are planned to study this theory.

The user survey supports the effectiveness of the magnified airway with the AR smart glasses, shared video stream view between trainees and the expert instructor, and telestrator capability. Users of this technology also like the flexibility of configuring the size, position, and zoom factor of the AR view, and they would like to have an even larger field of view once technology advances further. For the static manikin simulation, the majority of medical participants used both the AR view and the direct view. Most users also found it feasible to switch their attention between the two views. Once again, when facing the challenges during intubation that are unique to live patients, we hypothesize that the direct line-of-sight view will be needed more so than when intubating a manikin.

The approach of using an AR HMD to provide live camera feeds to assist health care providers in performing medical procedures is novel and can be expanded to many other areas of medicine. The advantages of maintaining the direct line-of-sight view in addition to the telestrator capabilities have the potential to improve efficacy and efficiency in many medical fields.

# References

1. Downes, K.J., Narendran, V., Meinzen-Derr, J., McClanahan, S., Akinbi, H.T.: The lost art of intubation: assessing opportunities for residents to perform neonatal intubation. J. Perinatol. **32**(12), 927–932 (2012)
2. Bismilla, Z., Finan, E., McNamara, P.J., LeBlanc, V., Jefferies, A., Whyte, H.: Failure of pediatric and neonatal trainees to meet Canadian Neonatal Resuscitation Program standards for neonatal intubation. J. Perinatol. **30**(3), 182–187 (2010)
3. Haubner, L.Y., Barry, J.S., Johnston, L.C., et al.: Neonatal intubation performance: room for improvement in tertiary neonatal intensive care units. Resuscitation **84**(10), 1359–1364 (2013)
4. Kamlin, C.O., O'Connell, L.A., Morley, C.J., et al.: A randomized trial of stylets for intubating newborn infants. Pediatrics **131**(1), 198–205 (2013)
5. Sanders Jr., R.C., Giuliano Jr., J.S., Sullivan, J.E., et al.: Level of trainee and tracheal intubation outcomes. Pediatrics **131**(3), 821–828 (2013)
6. Falck, A.J., Escobedo, M.B., Baillargeon, J.G., Villard, L.G., Gunkel, J.H.: Proficiency of pediatric residents in performing neonatal endotracheal intubation. Pediatrics **112**(6 Pt 1), 1242–1247 (2003)
7. DeMeo, S.D., Katakam, L., Goldberg, R.N., Tanaka, D.: Predicting neonatal intubation competency in trainees. Pediatrics **135**(5), 1229–1236 (2015)
8. Finer, N.N., Carlo, W.A., Duara, S., et al.: Delivery room continuous positive airway pressure/positive end-expiratory pressure in extremely low birth weight infants: a feasibility trial. Pediatrics **114**(3), 651–657 (2010)
9. Lindner, W., Vossbeck, S., Hummler, H., Pohlandt, F.: Delivery room management of extremely low birth weight infants: spontaneous breathing or intubation? Pediatrics **103**(5 Pt 1), 961–967 (1999)
10. Smith, S.L., Hall, M.A.: Advanced neonatal nurse practitioners in the workforce: a review of the evidence to date. Arch. Dis. Child. Fetal Neonatal Ed. **96**(2), 151–155 (2011)
11. Katakam, L.I., Goldberg, R.N., Tanaka, D.T.: Developing intubation skills: incremental learning or an epiphany? In: Pediatric Academic Society Meeting, Honolulu, HI (2008)
12. Witt, S.A., Lenfestey, R.W., Tanaka, D.T., Smith, P.B.: Preliminary data on video laryngoscopy assisted coaching improves simulated infant intubation success. In: Pediatric Academic Society Meeting, Baltimore, MD (2009)

# TurtleGO: Application with Cubes for Children's Spatial Ability Based on AR Technology

Yoonji Song[1], Jaedong Kim[2], and Hanhyuk Cho[1(✉)]

[1] Department of Mathematics Education, Seoul National University,
Seoul, Republic of Korea
{songyj,hancho}@snu.ac.kr
[2] Graduate School of Culture Technology, KAIST, Daejeon, Republic of Korea
jaedong27@kaist.ac.kr

**Abstract.** In this paper, we introduce a new application called TurtleGO that uses augmented reality (AR) technology, with which K-2 children can experience a geometric sense of the egocentric perspective. This application was developed with the concept of Logo-MicroWorlds, which allows children to examine and simulate their geometric ideas in a virtual world with a turtle agent. TurtleGO provides children with real-time feedback in a monitor representing the augmented turtle image on blocks based on AR technology while children are playing with actual blocks. Our application is flexible and inexpensive as it makes possible the use of various sized cubes already in possession. All the children between grades 2 through 5 improved in their ability to distinguish pair of stimuli as identical or mirror images when they used TurtleGO. However, we found that our application provides an effective and intuitive AR learning environment to lower grade elementary students, improving their spatial transformation skills since upper graders could solve the tasks easily without it.

**Keywords:** Augmented reality (AR) · Tangible interaction · Body syntonic · Spatial ability · Egocentric perspective · Spatial transformation

## 1 Introduction

The Common Core State Standards for Mathematics (CCSSM) suggests that children from kindergarten to grade 2 should learn to identify, describe, analyze, compare, and reason various shapes and the attributes of those shapes in geometry [1]. Also, it is recommended that students take lessons to create, draw or analyze two- and three-dimensional shapes in order to learn about the characteristics of the shapes and describe the relative positions of these objects using terms such as 'above, 'below', 'beside', 'in front of', 'behind' and 'next to' in later grades. Therefore, it becomes necessary to provide a variety of opportunities for students to experience their geometric senses with not only "flat" shapes but also "solid" objects.

Spatial ability defined as a fundamental cognitive ability that includes retrieving, retaining, and manipulating visuo-spatial information [2, 3] is an important factor in the Science, Technology, Engineering, and Mathematics (STEM) fields including

© Springer Nature Switzerland AG 2019
J. Y. C. Chen and G. Fragomeni (Eds.): HCII 2019, LNCS 11575, pp. 372–383, 2019.
https://doi.org/10.1007/978-3-030-21565-1_25

geometry [4, 5]. Although there had been prejudice that spatial ability was fixed, Uttal [6] concluded that it can be improved through training because of its malleability. Activities with manipulative materials such as blocks, puzzles, shape games [7, 8] or utilization of relational language regarding space [9] would improve spatial abilities of children including preschoolers.

Among the several spatial abilities, spatial transformation is classified into object-based transformation, which is the imaginary movement of an object on an axis, and egocentric perspective transformation, which is the imaginary movement of one's perspective in relation to other objects [10]. From the view of an egocentric perspective, students can describe other objects around them using terms such as "front," "back," "left," and "right" [11].

Papert [12], who have developed constructionism, believed children could learn the concept of geometry by using "body syntonic." He claimed that children think of the turtle's motion by imagining themselves as the turtle, moving under two commands—rotate and forward—in the virtual world. As these two commands have already been embodied in humans, Papert suggested children could gain geometric sense easily when they simulate, explore, and develop their thoughts in the logo-MicroWorld with 2D figures by using these commands. In other words, even if children cannot study geometry through rigorous definition, they can learn it through tools that are appropriate for their level.

We propose a new application "TurtleGO," based on Augmented Reality (AR) technology and expect that it would be a helpful tool for children to learn and experience the sense of the spatial transformation. They would acquire a strategy of the view of the egocentric perspective transformation through the application, regarding the augmented turtle agent as themselves. Also, they would be able to express the movement of the turtle using "body syntonic" for recognizing three dimensional objects.

## 2 Related Work

Radu [13] conducted a meta-analysis of 26 studies about augmented reality in education. The research identified positive effects of AR based learning compared to non-AR based learning in regard to enhanced understanding of spatial structure contents or language associations, long-term memory retention, and student motivation. Also, the disadvantages of AR based learning were described as a difficulty in use, an ineffective integration in classroom, and displaying little to no effect depending on the person or contents. The author suggested in the conclusion that AR based learning may be utilized as an effective tool for teaching 3D spatial but may not be effective for text or 2D content.

In education, AR technology were used with tangible objects such as cards, cubes or blocks, and has provided the opportunity to acquire abstract knowledge including programming and mathematics for children. [14]. Zhu et al. [15] introduced an educational game based on AR technology teaching abstract concepts such as color mixing, mathematics, and two- and three- dimensional shape recognition for preschool children. It allowed children to use physical cards and blocks to construct buildings in the virtual world. Jin [16] developed a tangible programming tool named AR-Maze, which consisted of games on mobile devices, location map and three kinds of programming blocks to connect the game. Children were provided with an intuitive and exciting environment paired with audio, textual or image feedbacks when they were coding. However, most of the research used their own tangible materials to connect physical to digital devices. This made them expensive to use or hard to get. They were used many times for a specific-purpose rather than for a general-purpose. Therefore, we have made our application utilizing cubes of various sizes available for everyone's use.

Bujak et al. [17] established a framework of three perspectives, including physical, cognitive, and contextual perspectives in order to understand the AR use in mathematics classroom. First, through physical manipulations, younger students become easily involved in educational content and they could interact naturally with objects. In other words, their cognitive load which is not directly related to learning goals since the physical object has an affordance the children already know. Second, in the case of cognitive dimension, children have to learn abstract concepts in mathematics, thus information aligned spatiotemporal properly used by AR can assist student's symbolic understanding by scaffolding, or connecting the physical and the abstract. Third, on the contextual perspective, AR experience could make children construct personally meaningful experience of learning as it lets them easily access the virtual world, contextually relevant content and engage with personally-relevant content.

From the perspective of Bujak et al., our application TurtleGO has educational benefits in three dimensions: physical, cognitive and contextual. Since our application TurtleGO is used based on the children's block activity, it could be said that the affordance of the object, that is, the play with blocks, causes a natural interaction in the physical dimension. In the case of cognitive dimension, it displays the augmented turtle on the block where the children put it down, so it is possible to identify the movement of the turtle directly. Children can explore a three-dimensional object by considering themselves as moving the turtle, which reduces their cognitive load by properly placing information. Finally, in contextual dimension, children can have their own meaningful experiences as they can manipulate the blocks in their own way.

## 3  TurtleGO

### 3.1  Design Inspiration

**Turtle Geometry and JavaMAL MicroWorld.** In the perspective of Constructionism coined by Seymour Papert, learning is most effective when learners experience an activity by constructing meaningful knowledge [18]. Therefore, Papert proposed that geometry could be educated to elementary students by using a turtle metaphor, a "tool for thought," in the Logo MicroWorld, which can construct figures by two commands —forward and rotate—movements children already embodied.

According to this idea, Cho et al. [19] suggested a 3D representation system— JavaMAL—by which learners can write executable expressions to generate 3D polycubes in the Web 2.0 environment. For instance, if the learner imagines the path of the imaginary turtle and writes down an executable expression "s" into JavaMAL Micro-World, then a unit cube would be added to the previous form as the imaginary turtle is moving one step forward from the previous position. Thus, to create their favored shape, learners only have to imagine the turtle's path where it goes forward or rotates and write down executable expressions: "s" (to go forward), "r" (to go right), "l" (to go left), "u" (to go upward), "d" (to go downward), "R" (to turn right), and "L" (to turn left) (Fig. 1). Since the cubes were made according to the executable expression students write down, it could trace student's thinking process as they use JavaMAL MicroWorld. Being involved in the activity would construct and deepen the mathematical knowledge for users through the process of generating, constructing, sharing patterns, and producing outcomes using the cubes in the JavaMAL MicroWorld [19–22].

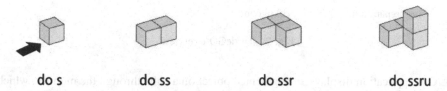

**do s**          **do ss**          **do ssr**          **do ssru**

**Fig. 1.** Example of polycube formations and executable expressions. The arrow indicates the direction of the imaginary turtle.

Unfortunately, this activity is not suitable for younger children since their cognitions are not developed enough to understand the concepts. Therefore, we wanted to provide an environment for younger children with tangible cubes and show the augmented turtle rather than flat objects on the monitor or the turtle children had to imagine. We expected that they could imagine a turtle's path without a turtle after experiencing a hands-on activity with real cubes with our TurtleGO.

## 3.2 TurtleGO

TurtleGO using augmented reality (AR) technology needs a camera and a monitor to provide students with an experience of a tangible interaction. It allows the student to see the virtual turtle in real-time feedback. While they play with tangible cubes, children can see the turtle on a cube in the monitor, as shown in Fig. 2(b). Children can recognize the movement of the turtle, which depends on the placement of cubes. They are expected to distinguish mirror images of the turtle's path they imagine in 3D stimuli.

As TurtleGO is a user-friendly system, teachers may find it easy to use. This becomes an important issue as the turtle is controlled by teachers while the children are playing with the blocks. Therefore, teachers should be able to easily teach their children according to their intentions by determining the turtle's direction at the starting point.

TurtleGO is both economical and flexible in that this application does not require further purchase of tools and equipment but can be run in the classroom with no difficulty. During the activity using the application, children were able to reach the desired level of understanding and performance, which includes designing a turtle's path in 3D shapes to recognize three-dimensional objects or distinguish mirror images.

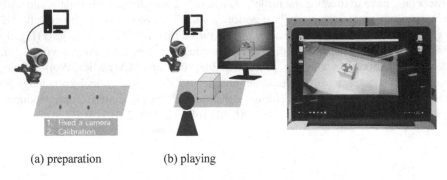

(a) preparation          (b) playing

**Fig. 2.** TurtleGO overview

Our application displays an augmented object on a cube through the monitor, which requires two steps. First, the camera has to be fixed so that the camera can picture the whole scene of the hands-on activity. Second, to visualize the turtle on a cube, the four vertices of the position of the initial block's bottom face has to be input into the program for calibration as shown in Fig. 2(a). Then, the teacher moves the augmented turtle using letters on the keyboard: "w" (to go straight), "a" (to go left), "s" (to go back), "d" (to go right), "u" (to go up), and "j" (to go down); the teacher can also change the direction of an augmented turtle with the "e" key, based on cube arrangement.

## 4  Pilot Study

In order to find the most effective grade for using TurtleGO, we conducted a pilot test on volunteers from second to fifth grade and compared the results of a group who were engaged in TurtleGO with the group who were not (Fig. 3(a) and (b)).

a) A child playing with blocks.    b) Children could recognize where the turtle moves from.

**Fig. 3.** Pilot study

### 4.1    The Tasks

Although TurtleGO used by 'body syntonic' might be available to improve geometric sense or spatial ability, we chose the spatial transformation tasks by providing mirror images in Soma cube easily accessible to the children (Fig. 4). This strategy will aid with imaging the turtle's path and analyzing turtle's perspective to identify if children will think the tasks are too difficult to perform.

**Fig. 4.** Mirror images in Soma cube

To confirm that they had the ability to imagine and analyze the path of the turtle, the children were asked to take another test called perspective-taking test, testing for whether they could identify the left or right of an agent—the turtle—before the tasks.

### 4.2    Procedures

We divided the students into two groups—one with TurtleGO hands-on activity included in the session, the other without the activity. As the control group, 19 children (12 girls and 7 boys from grade 2 to 5 and aged 9 to 12, (M = 10.05, SD = 1.08)), were asked to take a paper-and-pencil test. After being provided with an explanation about mirror images and the turtle geometry, they took another paper-and-pencil test on spatial transformation consisting of pieces in the SOMA cube (Fig. 5). A week later, the other group of 14 children (8 girls and 6 boys from grade 2 to 4 and aged 9 to 11, (M = 9.64,  SD = 0.63)), went through the same process with the control group. However, students in this group were instructed to participate in the block-building activity and shaped pieces in the SOMA cube with TurtleGO before taking the same paper-and-pencil test. Both sessions took about 30 min.

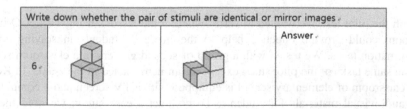

**Fig. 5.** Example of the spatial transformation task

We asked the children to mark and write the path they imagined the augmented turtle would take on the test sheet expecting that they could distinguish the stimuli based on the virtual turtle's path they have written down.

## 4.3  Results

We compared the results of spatial transformation tasks between the control group and the experimental group. Although the number of children who participated in the session of the control group was 19 and that in the experimental group was 14, we analyzed only 13 children's answers (3 in grade 2, 4 in grade 3, 3 in grade 4, 3 in grade 5) in the control group and 11 children's answers (3 in grade 2, 6 in grade 3, 2 in grade 4) in the experimental group since the others did not take the test seriously or had already learned a mental rotation skill. Children could take part in only one session, but we made three children (3 in grade 3) participate in both sessions to compare the paired data according to the use of TurtleGO. Our findings have three aspects.

First, in general, the children in the experimental group could better distinguish whether the stimulus was identical or mirror images. Even though all children were asked to distinguish the mirror image and to justify their answers, some children in the control group answered "they are the same" for all the questions of the test or the others replied "I don't know." When requested why they thought it was the same, they answered "it looks the same" or "they are the same if one stimulus would rotate." Even though it was not the same. On the other hand, the children of the experimental group imagined the path of the turtle agent and provided a rationale for themselves whether they thought the two stimuli were the same or different from each other.

Second, only one of the three participants who participated in both sessions performed worse after using TurtleGO. He scored 10 out of 10 questions first, but only 9 out of 10 same questions after using TurtleGO. When imagining the path of the turtle, he was somewhat confused to decide whether the stimuli were the same, one of which was rotated in the z-axis. As all children in both groups could not distinguish the pair of the stimuli rotated in the z-axis, this gives us a clue that TurtleGO might not be useful when the stimulus is rotated in the z-axis.

Third, although we found tendency supporting the fact that higher the grade, the better performance in the experimental group, it was confirmed that it would be used more meaningfully as an educational tool for second graders since upper graders can solve the tasks easily without TurtleGO.

## 5  Case Study

Through the pilot test, we wanted to verify whether the lessons using TurtleGO in the classroom could provide effective help to the grade 2 students in solving spatial transformation tasks. We tested with a group of second graders in a classroom setting with the same tasks of the pilot study except for an item rotated in the z-axis. In Korea, every classroom of elementary school is equipped with a TV screen and a computer to show audiovisual materials for students. To conduct a case study, we used the TV screen and physical cubes, which were already in the classroom. We also used cameras and laptops because of the installation issues of the application. If teachers wanted to use our application, they could install it on their computer.

### 5.1 Procedures

Three lessons were held for 40 min at a time during the span of two weeks with 27 students (13 boys, 14 girls), a researcher and a teacher. The teacher confirmed that there were no problems in contents and operations before the experiment.

In the first lesson, children were presented with an explanation of mirror images and the rotation tasks and they took a perspective-taking test as same as the pilot test. After the end of the first lesson, TurtleGO was introduced.

In the second lesson, after given a brief review of the first lesson, students observed the two stimuli by touching pieces of SOMA cube. The paper-and-pencil test on spatial transformation tasks was performed. Although the strategy of egocentric perspectives was introduced, no strategies for solving the tasks were suggested. The test was the same as the one used in the pilot test, but the item with a z-axis transformation task was removed.

In the final lesson, seven children had the opportunity to manipulate the cube with our application and all students could see the augmented turtle on the large display in front of the classroom (Fig. 6). The teacher could explain the path of the augmented turtle and change the direction of it as needed, and the students shouted together the path of the virtual turtle watching the display. The same test on spatial transformation tasks was conducted at the end of the lesson after experiencing TurtleGO. The whole lesson was video recorded.

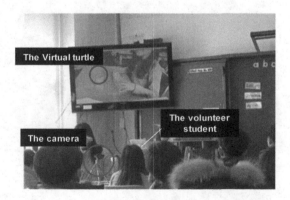

**Fig. 6.** A screenshot of recorded video from the case study

### 5.2 Results

As in the study of Radu [13], the children were highly motivated when the lesson was given with TutleGO based on AR technology and actively volunteered for a role in manipulating the cube. They were in a situation where they were learning, but they seemed to be experiencing play rather than study.

We analyzed the perspective-taking test, pre- and post-tests on spatial transformation tasks of 27 students with 1 point per item. The perspective-taking test had 16 items and the test on spatial transformation tasks had 9 items. First, the result of the perspective-taking test presented that 7 children (Group A) were found to have difficulty in distinguishing between the left and the right side of the agent. Their average score was only 5.33 out of 16 while the average score of the others (Group B) was 14.8 and the median score was 15 (Table 1).

**Table 1.** Comparison between Group A and Group B.

|  | Group A | Group B |
|---|---|---|
| The number of children | 7 | 20 |
| The average score | 5.33 | 14.8 |

The data of pre- and post-test on spatial transformation tasks was classified with four groups. The first group was 8 students who performed better after using TurtleGO. The second group was 6 students who maintained high scores in both pre- and post-test on spatial transformation with little difference in performance. The third group was 11 students who received low scores both before and after the use of TurtleGO. The fourth group consisted of 2 students who performed lower after using TurtleGO. The average scores for each group can be seen in Fig. 7 and the distribution of two groups classified by the results of the perspective-taking test in each group categorized by the results of the spatial transformation tasks is presented in Fig. 8.

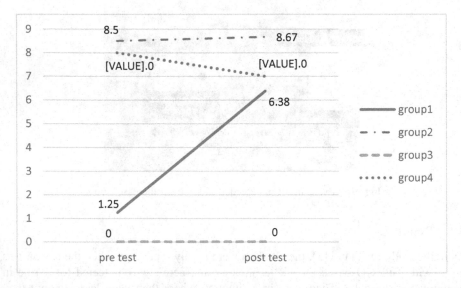

**Fig. 7.** The average scores of the pre- and post-tests on spatial transformation tasks in categorized groups

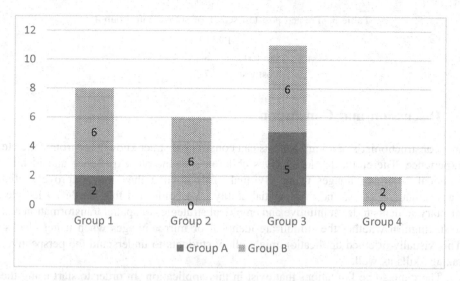

**Fig. 8.** The distribution of the two groups classified into the lower (Group A) and upper (Group B) groups of the perspective-taking test in categorized groups

We concluded TurtleGO was an effective tool for group 1 while it was a useless tool for group 3 as they showed no improvement. Group 2 presented little improvement from the average score but they had already gotten a high score. Contrary to our expectation, group 4 showed a drop in the score after using TurtleGO while they were good at the perspective-taking test.

The results of group 1's pre-and post-test scores can be seen in Table 2. The scores of the students in group 1 were dramatically enhanced after hands-on activity with our application. The majority of them received a zero score in the pre-test, but their post-test score increased by as little as 4 and as much as 7. Participant 7 and Participant 8 was in group A which meant they had a poor skill for perspective-taking test. We could assume that not only skills for spatial-transformation tasks but skills of perspective-taking were improved through using TurtleGO.

**Table 2.** Pre- and post-test scores of students in group 1

|           | P1 | P2 | P3 | P4 | P5 | P6 | P7 | P8 |
|-----------|----|----|----|----|----|----|----|----|
| Pre-test  | 0  | 0  | 0  | 0  | 6  | 0  | 0  | 4  |
| Post-test | 6  | 7  | 4  | 5  | 9  | 6  | 5  | 9  |

In the case of group 4, the detailed results of their scores are presented in Table 3. Although two students in group 4 got 8 points in the pre-test they lost one score after using our application. When determining whether the stimuli were identical or mirror images they used the strategy of the mental rotation in the pre-test rather than the strategy of imaging virtual turtle's path used in the post-test. And both of them was in group A of perspective-taking test.

**Table 3.** Pre and post-test scores of students in group 4

|           | P9 | P10 |
|-----------|----|-----|
| Pre-test  | 8  | 8   |
| Post-test | 7  | 7   |

## 6  Discussion and Conclusion

In a constructionist's opinion, students can construct abstract knowledge from concrete experience. Therefore, TurtleGO gives children a chance to experience and identify identical or mirror images using a virtual turtle so that they may improve spatial transformations skills, and thus, spatial ability. We confirmed that TurtleGO led elementary students to learn intuitive and empirical strategies of spatial transformation and to distinguish whether the stimuli are identical or mirror images when using blocks. This visually oriented application might allow students to understand the perspective-taking skills as well.

There are some limitations that exist in this application. In order to start using the application, teachers are required to input four points of the bottom of the initial block, and this process may become tricky. Therefore, we suggest to utilize our application with AR markers to overcome this difficulty by finding the exact coordinates of the first cube. Using AR marker can further simplify the preparation phase. Second, teaching with TurtleGO was not beneficial to everyone. As shown in the Freitas and Campos [23] study, AR-based learning was useful for students with low or average achievements but not for high-performing students on spatial transformation tasks. For students with high achievement, we suggest further research that show the effectiveness after adjusting the difficulty of task performance.

**Acknowledgments.** We would like to thank all the participants of the study and thanks to Jisun Kim, Balgeum Song and Jimin Rhim who provided insights and improvement for this paper.

## References

1. Common Core State Standards Initiative: Common Core State Standards for Mathematics (CCSSM). National Governors Association Center for Best Practices and the Council of Chief State School Officers, Washington, DC (2010)
2. Linn, M.C., Petersen, A.C.: Emergence and characterization of sex differences in spatial ability: a meta-analysis. Child Dev. **56**(6), 1479–1498 (1985). https://doi.org/10.1111/j.1467-8624.1985.tb00213.x
3. Lohman, D.F.: Spatial ability and g. Hum. Abil. Nat. Measur. **97**, 116 (1996)
4. Uttal, D.H., Cohen, C.A.: Spatial thinking and STEM education: when, why, and how? Psychol. Learn. Motiv.-Adv. Res. Theory 147–181 (2012). https://doi.org/10.1016/b978-0-12-394293-7.00004-2
5. Wai, J., Lubinski, D., Benbow, C.P.: Spatial ability for STEM domains: aligning over 50 years of cumulative psychological knowledge solidifies its importance. J. Educ. Psychol. **101**(4), 817–835 (2009). https://doi.org/10.1037/a0016127
6. Uttal, D.H., et al.: The malleability of spatial skills: a meta-analysis of training studies. Psychol. Bull. **139**(2), 352–402 (2013). https://doi.org/10.1037/a0028446

7. Verdine, B.N., Golinkoff, R.M., Hirsh-Pasek, K., Newcombe, N.S., Filipowicz, A.T., Chang, A.: Deconstructing building blocks: preschoolers' spatial assembly performance relates to early mathematical skills. Child Dev. **85**(3), 1062–1076 (2014). https://doi.org/10.1111/cdev.12165

8. Casey, B.M., Andrews, N., Schindler, H., Kersh, J.E., Samper, A., Copley, J.: The development of spatial skills through interventions involving block building activities. Cogn. Instruct. **26**(3), 269–309 (2008). https://doi.org/10.1080/07370000802177177

9. Pruden, S.M., Levine, S.C., Huttenlocher, J.: Children's spatial thinking: does talk about the spatial world matter? Dev. Sci. **14**(6), 1417–1430 (2011). https://doi.org/10.1111/j.1467-7687.2011.01088.x

10. Kozhevnikov, M., Motes, M.A., Rasch, B., Blajenkova, O.: Perspective-taking vs mental rotation transformations and how they predict spatial navigation performance. Appl. Cogn. Psychol. Off. J. Soc. Appl. Res. Memory Cogn. **20**(3), 397–417 (2006). https://doi.org/10.1002/acp.1192

11. Tversky, B., Hard, B.M.: Embodied and disembodied cognition: Spatial perspective-taking. Cognition **110**(1), 124–129 (2009). https://doi.org/10.1016/j.cognition.2008.10.008

12. Papert, S.: Mindstorms: Children, Computers, and Powerful Ideas. Basic Books Inc., New York (1980)

13. Radu, I.: Augmented reality in education: a meta-review and cross-media analysis. Pers. Ubiquit. Comput. **18**(6), 1533–1543 (2014). https://doi.org/10.1007/s00779-013-0747-y

14. Mateu, J., Lasala, M.J., Alamán, X.: Tangible interfaces and virtual worlds: a new environment for inclusive education. In: Urzaiz, G., Ochoa, S.F., Bravo, J., Chen, L.L., Oliveira, J. (eds.) Ubiquitous Computing and Ambient Intelligence. Context-Awareness and Context-Driven Interaction. LNCS, vol. 8276, pp. 119–126. Springer, Cham (2013). https://doi.org/10.1007/978-3-319-03176-7_16

15. Zhu, Y.J., Yang, X.Y., Wang, S.J.: Augmented reality meets tangibility: a new approach for early childhood education. EAI Endorsed Trans. Creat. Technol. **4**(11), 1–8 (2017). https://doi.org/10.4108/eai.5-9-2017.153059

16. Jin, Q., Wang, D., Deng, X., Zheng, N., Chiu, S.: AR-Maze: a tangible programming tool for children based on AR technology. In: Proceedings of the 17th ACM Conference on Interaction Design and Children, pp. 611–616. ACM (2018). https://doi.org/10.1145/3202185.3210784

17. Bujak, K.R., Radu, I., Catrambone, R., Macintyre, B., Zheng, R., Golubski, G.: A psychological perspective on augmented reality in the mathematics classroom. Comput. Educ. **68**, 536–544 (2013). https://doi.org/10.1016/j.compedu.2013.02.017

18. Sabelli, N.: Constructionism: a new opportunity for elementary science education. DRL Division of research on learning in formal and informal settings, pp. 193–206 (2008)

19. Cho, H.H., Song, M.H., Lee, J.Y., Kim, H.K.: On the design of logo-based educational microworld environment. Res. Math. Educ. **15**(1), 15–30 (2011)

20. Cho, H.-H., Lee, J.-Y., Shin, D.-J., Woo, A.-S.: MCY-mentoring activities by creating and communicating mathematical objects. Res. Math. Educ. **15**(2), 141–158 (2011)

21. Kim, H, Cho, H.H., Shin, D.J., Lee, J.: Exploring pattern generalization in the logo-based microworld. In: Proceedings of the Seventeenth Asian Technology Conference in Mathematics, pp. 16–20 (2012)

22. Lee, J.Y., Cho, H.H., Song, M.H., Kim, H.K.: Representation systems of building blocks in logo-based microworld. Res. Math. Educ. **15**(1), 1–14 (2011)

23. Freitas, R., Campos, P.: SMART: a system of augmented reality for teaching 2nd grade students. In: Proceedings of the 22nd British HCI Group Annual Conference on People and Computers: Culture, Creativity, Interaction, vol. 2, pp. 27–30. BCS Learning & Development Ltd. (2008)

# LumaPath: An Immersive Virtual Reality Game for Encouraging Physical Activity for Senior Arthritis Patients

Xin Tong[✉], Diane Gromala, and Federico Machuca

Simon Fraser University, 13450 102 Avenue, Surrey, Canada
{tongxint, gromala, fmachuca}@sfu.ca

**Abstract.** Arthritis occurs typically in the senior populations which involves stiff and painful joints. The prevalence of arthritis in the U.S. is 20% and in Canada is 15.8% for 4.3 million, and it decreases the patients' joint movement and physical activity to a severe degree. Even worse, more than half of the patients do not receive any treatment at all. Studies have shown that physical exercise or movement of the affected joint can noticeably improve long-term pain relief. In general, studies have shown that arthritis patients' movement of the affected joint implies physical activity. However, very few commercial games or research prototypes have been specially designed for arthritis population for promoting activities and their Range of Motion (RoM). Therefore, we created an immersive VR game named *LumaPath*. Meanwhile, we conducted a pilot study with five senior arthritis patients to evaluate their experience and assess *LumaPath*, and twenty-three healthy participants among which there are three senior participants. Overall, the study results showed that *LumaPath* had great potential as a gamified tool to motivate senior adults to stay physically active. Furthermore, we discovered that patients' limited physical movement and RoM, and the age were significant factors affecting their gaming experience, interactions and how to execute certain physical movements.

**Keywords:** Virtual reality · Arthritis patients · Range of Motion ·
Physical activity · Game design · Senior adults

## 1 Introduction

Arthritis is a term often used to describe a disorder that involves stiff and painful joints and decreases the Range of Motion (RoM) of the joints. There are many kinds of arthritis and the two most common forms are osteoarthritis arthritis (OA) and rheumatoid arthritis (RA). Osteoarthritis (OA) usually happens in the senior population, and can affect fingers, knees, and hips. Rheumatoid arthritis (RA) is an autoimmune disorder in about 0.24% of the population and often affects the hands and feet [1, 2]. In the U.S., 20% of senior adults have some kind of doctor-diagnosed arthritis [3]. In Canada, over 4.6 million Canadian adults (one in six Canadians aged 15 years and older) report having arthritis, and most of those patients (67%) are over 55 years old. In China, more than one billion people are arthritis patients and less than half get treatment [4]. Arthritis becomes a severe health condition that affects the senior population's Quality of Life (QoL).

© Springer Nature Switzerland AG 2019
J. Y. C. Chen and G. Fragomeni (Eds.): HCII 2019, LNCS 11575, pp. 384–397, 2019.
https://doi.org/10.1007/978-3-030-21565-1_26

In general, studies have shown that physical exercise or movement of the affected joint can noticeably improve long-term pain relief [5]. Furthermore, performing exercises of the arthritic joint are encouraged to maintain the health of the particular joint, the overall body of the person, and delay the need for surgical intervention in advanced cases [5]. Regular and moderate activity is one of the best ways to ease the pain, increase mobility, and overcome the limitations of arthritis [4, 5]. That said, it is possible to damage affected joints by overuse. Taking exercise of the arthritic joint is encouraged to maintain the health of the particular joint and the overall body of the arthritic person. However, their hurt arthritic joints and painful experience become obstacles for them to maintain a healthy physical activity level, let alone to keep a sustainable exercise. Many approaches are recommended to elderly patients for promoting their physical activity, such as general physical exercise, Yoga, Pilates, tai-chi, therapeutic rehab with physiotherapists, playing sports or digital games, etc.

Immersive VR is a computer technology and 3-dimensional (3D) environment of high immersion and interactivity, presence, and sense of body ownership. VR is a quickly emerging technology that has been shown to help motivate physical activity, especially forms of rehabilitation or chronic disease and pain management. Through the VR environment, a user can live, act or interact in a virtual world which simulates the reality. Interaction with the environment and presentation of the world is achieved using assistive devices of a Head-Mounted Display (HMD), biosensors, controllers and other devices. From previous studies that had done with pain patients for pain management and rehab exercise purposes, VR approach showed a significantly higher level of impact at patients' pain levels compared to both of the traditional management approach and game approach [6, 7].

Moreover, scientific experiments found that the sensorimotor experiences and tasks created in VR games enhanced participants' sense of agency and task performances compared to doing the same tasks with PC display control group. Therefore, VR leads to great promise in creating systematic human testing and treatment environments compared to traditional management, where virtual representations of real environments can be precisely controlled and guided according to therapy needs. Furthermore, game mechanics have been demonstrated to generate greater motivation for adults when using VR environment. For instance, the ease of use and external motivations created by its game design made Wii Sports quite popular with older adults. Retirement community members in Lincolnshire, England, for example, with an average age of 77, were actively using Wii Sports not only to have fun, but to be physically active while socially engaged with their peers [8].

Therefore, the goals of this research were to investigate elderly arthritis patients' experience and feedback on *LumaPath*, especially how they felt about the difficulty of the game interactions and the ease of control. Furthermore, we would like to study how effective *LumaPath* is for promoting arthritis patients' physical activity and RoM in VR and explore what are the potential factors that can affect one's movement. Here, we designed and created an immersive VR game named *LumaPath* to promote arthritis patients' physical activity and RoM. Meanwhile, we conducted a pilot study with 5 senior arthritis patients to evaluate their experience and assess *LumaPath*, and 23 healthy participants among which there were three senior participants (here, senior participants meant adults who are older than 50 years old). Overall, the study results showed that *LumaPath* had great potential as a gamified tool to motivate senior adults to stay physically active. During the design and testing processes, the limitations of senior adults emerged as a significant factor since it can fundamentally affect the way these senior patients interact with the VR environment. In this paper, we introduce the background of this research, the VR game tasks, study methodologies and results, as well as our discussions.

## 2 Related Work

Keeping the body physically and mentally active is important for a healthier Quality of Life (QoL). As a person ages, this may become more challenging, let alone for arthritis patients. For instance, changes in motor, cognitive and psychological skills will affect a person's perception and visual abilities, which are the common aspects of the aging process [3, 10]. Moreover, activities that need physical dexterity – like quickly pressing buttons on a controller or reacting to fast visual cues – might become more difficult to perform by the senior populations [17]. Memory, especially short-term memory, and attention are also profoundly affected. Aging changes not only affect how an individual uses VR controllers, but also affects how they learn the conventions inside a game. Such limitations must be considered when designing virtual environments, since they can completely change how this demographic will interact with the digital systems compared to a younger or healthier population. Therefore, in this section, we review literature which discusses how the senior population or patient groups would interact with Virtual Environments (VE) or play games and how it can benefit the elderly group of people or how the games motivate them to have more physical activities, so their findings could shed lights on our research.

### 2.1 Games, Virtual Environments and the Senior Population

Many studies have shown the positive effects of interacting with VE or playing games for older adults' health, not only physically, but also mentally. As mentioned in a study [9], the repetitiveness of games that has players quickly reacting to visual and auditory cues for long periods of time while mastering a particular skill in the virtual environment can, for example, improve the motor coordination of older adults. These VEs can be fun and provide mental stimuli for older adults, heightening their self-esteem through game rewards, providing constant positive feedback and a sense of mastery. Researchers [6] found that participants who played Super Tetris 5 h a week for 5 weeks demonstrated a significant improvement in study tasks' reaction. Furthermore, the participants also reported higher self-esteem and emotional well-being ratings. Benefits such as these can happen even in situations where players have moderate physical and mental limitations.

To counter the aging-related speech processing ability decline, Miller et al. developed *HiFi* [12] – a game to boost the functions of the aging brain. In their study, they recruited ninety-five healthy participants whose average age was 80 were split into the gaming group, the PC lecture group, and the control group. In the game group, participants played the game for an hour each day for 8 weeks, while the second group spent the same time watching lectures on their computers. The third group didn't change their routines. The group that played games increased their scores on a standardized test of memory and attention by an average of 50% more points compared to the other two groups. According to the researchers, this improvement could be compared to the performance of people who are 10 years younger than them.

Some studies have also shown that VE or VR can be more entertaining than the traditional therapy approach. For instance, in a feasibility study [14], the researchers aimed at testing a low-cost system using Kinect for rehabilitation of the stroke survivors who had an impaired upper limb. The authors developed the game in conjunction with a physical therapist team. In this case study, a forty-six years old stroke survivor played the game for ten days, in which she was required to move her impaired arm by sliding it on top of a transparent screen. In the post-test survey, the participant acknowledges interest in using a similar system at home every day.

Muñoz et al. developed a *Microsoft Kinect* game prototype called *Exerpong* for senior adults, which requires the player to use a paddle to hit the ball using their body. They implemented real-time adaptations to the game task according to the player's HR level [9], so that the game difficulty and exertion level are changed accordingly. Results showed that the seniors increased 40% the time they spent in the recommended levels of exertion compared with conventional training. However, this was a full body movement and it was not customized for arthritis patients.

## 2.2 Gaming for More Physical Activity

Wii Sports is a Nintendo game that was released in 2006 [20]. Players use motion controllers to interact with a collection of games based on 5 different sports: tennis, bowling, golf, boxing and baseball. The ease of use and the external motivations provided by the game rewards made Wii Sports quite popular among older adult players. For instance, as mentioned in IJsselsteijn's research [9], the retirement community members in Lincolnshire, England, whose average age were 77, were actively using Wii Sports not only to have fun, but also to engage in the physical activities and social interactions with their peers.

In 2007, Nintendo released the next iteration of "games to play by moving" with the Wii Fit [19]. Wii Fit's game experience was very different compared to Wii Sports, because it included the new Wii Balance Board besides the controllers. This new input method allowed the players to use their weight to balance, and their feet positions to control the game world. Exercise using the Wii Fit was proved to be feasible, safe and efficacious according to a few studies. In a study with 36 women aged 56 and above [15], Wii Fit was tested in the experimental group as an alternative to traditional balance exercises to decrease the risk and fear of fall. Participants in the experimental group ended up requiring less supervision from their therapists or assistants initially and later were also able to perform their exercises more independently compared with the control group. The positive result happened possibly because the game system could provide real-time feedback regarding the players' performance. In another study conducted by a therapist [4], they recruited 32 participants aged between 65 and 80 using Wii Fit three times a week for eight weeks. Results showed that the participants' balance ability improved considerably compared to the control group which did not have exercise at all for eight weeks. In Tsuda's research [16] with 16 hospitalized senior patients (aged 60 years and above) who had hematologic malignancies, the participants were asked to exercise for 20 min a day from the start of their chemotherapy until hospital discharge using the Wii Fit, five times a week. The adherence rate was 66.5% and most of them reported enjoy playing the game.

Nintendo Wii's Big Brain Academy had also been investigated by a group of researchers [1]. They recruited 78 adults between 50 and 71 years old, and asked them to complete 20 sessions of one-hour training game over one month. In the following month, the participants completed the same amount of time playing the game, but this time they were asked to read articles on 4 different topics. Cognitive and perceptual speed were tested before and after each month of training, along with a knowledge test. Results showed a clear increase in performance with the group who had Wii games, but less improvement on the knowledge tests, and practice-related improvements. Participants said they enjoyed the game activities more than the reading sessions, and 40% of the participants reported a potential interest in continuing to play after the study was over.

In a recent study, the researchers evaluated the actual and perceived exertion of various commercial games through measuring the ten participants' Max HR, Self-reported Borg score, enjoyment and time spent in each game [10]. The VR games included *Fruit Ninja, Holopoint, Hot Squat*, and *Portal Stories*. Results found that different games brought participants various levels of actual and perceived exertion. For instance, *Hot Squat* had a heavy perceived exertion and *Holopoint* had a moderate level of exertion, while *Fruit Ninja* had a light exercise level and *Portal Stories* brought the lowest exertion. Furthermore, no correlation was found between participants' enjoyment level of the games and their exertion levels. The authors draw the conclusion that these VR games could provide exertion. But the result suggested that an engaging game can have a lower level of perceived exertion compared to the actual exertion. This result indicates that VR games have the potential to motivate players' physical activity.

However, none of the games tested in Yoo et al.'s research designed specifically for increasing arthritis patients' exertion. Neither did these game considered the concerns of how the senior population would interact with the game control or inputs. Therefore, we designed an immersive VR game combining specific motor tasks for senior upper limb arthritis patients and evaluated its effectiveness and patients' feedback.

# 3  Methodology

## 3.1  Study Goals

The goals of this study were threefold. Firstly, we'd like to understand if the VR game and two movement interventions/tasks designed in *LumaPath* would affect participants' physical activities and exertion. Secondly, we'd like to understand what are the player's thoughts and experience on this VR game from various aspects, and how they would interact with the VE. Lastly, how arthritis patients and healthy subjects would perform differently and what might be the possible differences between young participants versus seniors.

## 3.2   Procedures

**Participants.** The inclusion criteria are either (1) healthy adults who are older than 19 years old for the control group; or (2) arthritis patients who have arthritis and are older than 19 years old for the experimental group. Twenty-eight people participated in this study (Female = 15, Male = 13, M = 37.63, SD = 18.89), and their age ranging from 20 to 79. Eight of the twenty-eight were senior adults (>50 years old), and five were arthritis participants out of these senior adults with limitations in physical movement (3 females, mean = 61.5, SD = 11.01). The participants were recruited via the convenient sampling approach.

**The Game.** *Lumapath* is a VR system that uses HTC VIVE VR Head-Mounted Display (HMD) [11], a stereoscopic VR headset that comes with handheld controllers, to track the user's position in space, including their arm and hand gestures. The HMD is 1080 × 1200 pixels per eye (2160 × 1200 pixels combined), 90 Hz refresh rate and 110 degrees field of view, and its weight is 470 grams. The system is designed to create a safe virtual environment for users to be immersed in and work on their RoM. "Safe" is defined here as a VE that takes the target player's physical limitations in consideration to create an experience that will not motivate players to perform possible dangerous physical movements. *Lumapath* was created to motivate people with arthritis to physically move as much as possible and focused on providing the player with motion gestures which allow the upper limb joints movement (wrists, elbows, and shoulders) to have a larger RoM. In *Lumapath*, the player can drive a ship and can travel to different planets in search of rare plants and life forms using the motion controllers. Figure 1 shows the screen grab of the Cactus Planet and the look inside the player's ship, and Fig. 2 was a picture of one participant playing the game.

**Fig. 1.** Screenshots of *LumaPath* game scene: the cactus world (left) and the living room inside the ship (right)

In *LumaPath*, two different types of motion tasks were included as the interventions for promoting the patients' activities, as demonstrated in Fig. 3. The left one is originated from Tai-chi, to draw lines with different shapes, which requires the participants to use both controllers to match the VR task, move at a slow speed according to the performances. While the second task (the right image in Fig. 3) is "connecting the dots" in 3D space as inspired by Yoga and Pilates movement – reaching and holding positions. The images in Fig. 4 illustrates the controllers' visual look in *LumaPath*, and how the players can teleport from one location to another using the controller in VR beside physical movement.

**Fig. 2.** The study setup, one patient with the HTC VIVE HMD and the handheld motion controllers.

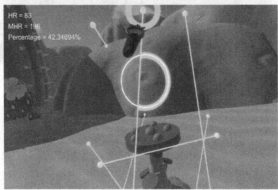

**Fig. 3.** The two intervention tasks in *LumaPath*: (left) following the tracks and drawing circles or irregular shapes (i.e. taichi gesture); (right) connecting different pairs of dots into lines (i.e. stretching gesture).

**Fig. 4.** Left, the two controllers used in *LumaPath* to perform physical activities (game actions) in VR; Right, participants use teleporting to move among all teleport spots to move in a larger range (they normally walk to reach objects in shorter distances).

**Procedures.** This was a mixed-method study design with both quantitative measurement and a qualitative semi-structured interview which was audiotaped after obtaining consent from the participant. First, the participants were given 20 min to free-explore in this game after a 10-min tutorial, during which period their real-time Heart Rate Variation (HRV) data were collected. After the test, the participants were asked to fill in the Rating of Perceived Exertion (RPE) Scale questionnaire. At the end of the study, the participants had a short semi-structured interview with the researchers about their thoughts, experience and feelings in playing *LumaPath*. The entire study takes 40–50 min for each participant.

### 3.3 Instrument

HTC VIVE VR headset was used to provide the immersive experience and motion tracking, and Scosche's Rhythm + Heart Rate Monitor Armband [12] that participants wore on their forearm during the VR study.

### 3.4 Measurement

The measurements include capturing real-time Heart Rate (HR) and Heart Rate Variability (HRV) data. As shown in Table 1, participants' perceived physical exertion was documented using The Borg Rating of Perceived Exertion (RPE) questionnaire [13] and we adopted Yoo et al.'s [10] mapping to compare HR to Borg Score in the result session. The RPE is a subjective way of measuring one's physical activity intensity level. The results from the RPE questionnaire were compared to the Heart Rate data collected afterward. In addition, a semi-structured interview was conducted with each participant after the intervention regarding their gaming experience, ease of control, the interactions with the game, and their feelings about their activity level. During the interview, participants took notes of the conversation and the transcribed the interviews after the study. The researchers coded the interview transcription according to the question categories (game exploration and aesthetics, instructions, motion sickness of VR environment, input and interactions, and the session length - 'dosage') and then summarized the results to different themes.

**Table 1.** Mapping of intensity: borg rating of perceived exertion scale and its mapping to as %-age of max HR.

| Intensity | Max HR % | Borg score |
|-----------|----------|------------|
| No exertion | 20–39 | 6–7 |
| Very light | 40–59 | 8–10 |
| Light | 60–69 | 11–12 |
| Moderate | 70–79 | 13–14 |
| Heavy | 80–89 | 15–16 |
| Very heavy | 90–99 | 17–18 |
| Maximal | 100 | 19–20 |

## 4   Result and Discussion

### 4.1   Physical Activity and Exertion

Four out of the healthy subjects' HR data was lost because of the hardware malfunction. For the HR and HRV data, we found there was an increase in HRV as participant's age increases. Patients reported perceived physical exertion rated by from the Borg Rating of Perceived Exertion Scale is lower than their real exertion collected from the wearable HR watch (M = 82.25, SD = 7.05). This indicated that our VR game was able to immerse and distract the patients from the amount of physical activity without noticing that they were already in an aerobic state. Overall, all participants had their average HR of above or close to their 50% HR thresholds value (threshold values are the maximum HR they experienced). Ten of the twenty-four participants had an average HR above their 50% threshold of max HR. This means that on average they were in a light aerobic state while playing *Lumapath*. Six participants had their HR go above their 60% threshold at least once during the game. One participant had their HR go above their 70% threshold once during gameplay. It's also important to note that all senior participants above 40 years of age had their average HR above or very close to their 50% threshold (also shown in Fig. 5).

As for the RPE data, nine participants had a perceived exertion lower than their actual average HR. Four participants had a perceived exertion of only 1 or 2 BPM higher than their average HR. The other eleven participants had a perceived exertion of 5 or more BPM compared to their average HR. If comparing the perceived exertion to the lowest and highest HR (Fig. 5 Blue area) of participants, only 6 participants had a perceived HR above that area. Ten participants were above their 50% of max HR threshold. They reported that *Lumapath* was able to immerse players enough so that they were distracted from the amount of physical activity they were performing. No patterns were found regarding participants' gender, experience with digital games or physical exercises.

## 4.2 Qualitative Interview Analysis

From the qualitative interview, in general, we found out patients liked the immersion side of our VR game and the overall gameplay design. The interview results were coded by the researchers and then categorized into below themes:

**Game Exploration and Aesthetics.** Overall, the environments were interesting and participants wanted to look around and see new things. Participants reported that they "loved" exploring the environments and were visibly enthusiastic. Exploring the environment was the most mentioned aspect of the experience that participants said they liked most. Based on participants' reports, aesthetic immersion was important to complement gameplay mechanism, and to give it more meaning and context. As mentioned by the participants, "... I really liked the environments. I wish I could have walked a bit further cause at some point there was a wall." (09) "... the space is quite hard to see in real life, the desert and the cactus." (13).

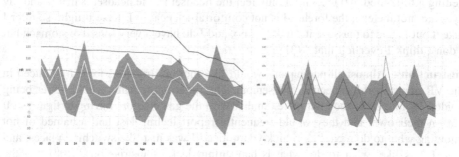

**Fig. 5.** Left: participant's HR vs. max HR thresholds (50% yellow line, 60% orange line and 70% red line. Right: perceived exertion (pink line) vs. average HR (blue line) vs. lowest and highest HR (blue area) of 24 participants. (Color figure online)

Exploration also appeared to be a crucial aspect that kept some of the participants from feeling embarrassed or apologetic when they didn't know how something worked since they felt they were discovering interactions just like they were discovering new areas while they played. "I have control issues so not having any direction of what the task was or not knowing what I was supposed to be doing, but, like, I didn't mind like, trying to figure it out so much, just exploring the environment, yeah." (14).

One of the main "aha" moments of the experience was when participants were in the cacti planet and then they saw the ship for the first time. Players would instantly start either mentioning how cool it was or questioning themselves if that was the ship they came from. It motivated most of the participants to teleport closer, or to explore more of the environment. For instance, "I liked how you are in the ship and it is up in the air and then you teleport down and you can see the whole thing." (06) "I like the exploring part, just like looking around, like looking up and seeing the ship, 'ok I guess this is my ship'. I liked that a lot." (09) "... the environments were really cool. I think my favorite part was I like looking at all the environment like, 360 looking around. And then I didn't even notice the ship was up in the air at one point and that was really cool too." (12).

**Discomfort or Motion Sickness.** No one reported motion sickness during the study, even participants who initially reported that they might be sensitive to the issue. From the participants' replies, having static, clear geometric shapes around the player helped them feel grounded. They have also suggested that the environment animations should be kept to a minimum amount since it can trick the brain into thinking the body is moving, even though the player might be physically still. Furthermore, having enough contrast in color values and hue provided the players with a clear visual reference of the space around them. Any avatar related movement that happens in the VE should be controlled or at least expected by the player.

However, over half of the participants did mention that the HMD was heavy and it was a possible cause for not seeing themselves playing the game for a longer period of time. Below are some participants' quotes. "Only towards the end. It was not motion sickness, but my head felt a little heavy, I felt something in the back of the head, I was getting a little tired. (01) "... no, I only feel the headset is, the headset is heavy and my eyes are, not the eye, the forehead is not comfortable because I make it tight, so after I take it out I have to massage it." (04) "... no, and I do have a very sensitive stomach but I don't think I ever felt that." (21).

**Instructions.** Almost all participants would like more instructions to be introduced in the VR game world, especially the seniors. The older participants would prefer being guided for longer, so they felt more familiar with the game before having to figure stuff out on their own, and they would frequently report feeling lost and ashamed of not knowing what to do next. "... I think you noticed I was just like switching places, and then I was like, what to do, what is happening, lack of instructions." (08) "... the tutorials are fine, but when I start to walk on my, own I don't know where I'm going to." (11) "... there were only a few things that were harder to understand like what to do in some areas, where to go when there were so many options like in the house." (15) "... It took a little while to discover that there were little hints to do things. I probably never got the feel of which buttons did what, although I expect that eventually that would have occurred to me." (21) It also seemed that some participants didn't mind feeling lost because of the sense of exploration that the environment created. Discovering how the game worked seemed to players like it was part of their exploration.

**Input Simplicity.** A lot of participants mentioned they would prefer if the inputs required to interact with the game world were simpler somehow. Memorizing the actions to the buttons sometimes was a problem for the older participants and patients comparing to non-patients.

Moreover, the tactile feedback of the controllers also helped players with immersion and functioned as cues for some of the interactions. For example, P5 said that "... it's really cool... I'm holding something that I can create, like Iron Man like I don't know, virtual stuff... that was really cool." P11 mentioned that "... I think I really like the vibration because it feels like touching something, holding something... the only thing I feel is real because it's in my hand."

**The "Dosage": Session Length.** Overall, the participants stayed in the virtual environment for approximately 20 min. In the end, many would mention that the HMD was heavy, but wouldn't mention standing for the last 20 min as a problem. Based on the perceived exertion, participants felt it was, on average, light activity. This shows that the game managed to keep participants immersed enough to not notice the fatigue of standing and moving their arms around for at least 20 min. Participant 14 had a sore hand before the gameplay session started, but still managed to play the game for 31 min without mentioning her hand once. Like P14 reported, "... my hand was hurting a bit at the beginning but the experience did not make it worse. It didn't make it worse, it's just tingling, so I don't know if it's from vibrating... it's not unpleasant I can feel I did something. The responsiveness and the light touch on the controllers wasn't a challenge for me."

In general, most of the participants enjoyed playing the game. The mechanics seemed to be rewarding, also challenging enough to make players feel a sense of achievement and progress. Using the participants' feedback as references, "... I liked realizing I learned something. It was an accomplishment." (07) "In the past, I actually only experienced very simple things like when you are under the sea or flying in the sky. You can change your direction and see different things. But this time I actually can control more. It's cool to change the mode and do something I want to, and when I succeed, I feel a sense of achievement." (11) We have voiced participants' interests in seeing more of the game world and experience more tasks, which would result in longer play time. This is particularly important since the physical benefits or behavior changes of interacting with the game could only be seen in more frequent and long-term use.

# 5   Conclusion

VR shows great promise in creating testing and treatment environments where virtual representations can be precisely controlled and guided according to therapy needs. Therefore, the goal of this pilot study was to explore how arthritis pain patients and normal senior adults might like or dislike our VR environment and how effective it was at promoting physical activity. The HRV and RPE results confirmed that the initial difficulty presented by the tasks was enough to get senior adults into an aerobic state. One of the main objectives of *LumaPath* was to motivate the participants to work on their joint RoM movement. Based on the way participants interact with the game, it was clear that they were not only stretching their upper body, but also working on their balance to compensate for the upper body movements. No participant reported any problems during their gameplay session, and none were observed. Even when they mentioned some kind of physical limitation, the system never put them in actual danger of hurting themselves. Therefore, the objective of creating a safe VE appears to have succeeded in this test so far. However, the main question is if the system would be able to adjust its difficulty to increase the average HR of not only senior adults, but also of younger arthritis patients' activity level.

To conclude, participants not only enjoyed the VR experience and being immersed in *Lumapath*'s game world, no matter of their age, but most of them were also in an aerobic state according to their HRV data. This supports the idea that designing a VR system that motivates physical movement and increases players QoL is possible, particularly when care is taken to address all possible needs of the target player group. However, it's important to consider some of the possible limitations of this study. On average, participants played *Lumapath* for 20–30 min, including the tutorial. This can be a problem since participants need to learn many new things to better interact and explore this game, such as how to use the hardware to interact with more objects, and several other different rules and mechanics – all before even starting to freely experience the game. Because of the time limitation and the participants spent a majority of the testing time in the tutorial, the experience of the participants in the first 10 min could greatly vary, compared to the experience they could have in the last 10 min of the gameplay session. Therefore, in the future, a longitudinal test would be important to measure the efficiency of all the implemented mechanics. Patients should ideally interact with the game in their own home, so that the game's ability to keep players interested could be really tested over time. We understand that there is room for the game to be improved from participants' semi-structured interviews, so constant iterations are needed and the design process would be beneficial in the longitudinal study too.

**Acknowledgement.** We thank the Natural Sciences and Engineering Research Council of Canada (NSERC) #371783 for funding this study.

# References

1. March, L., et al.: Burden of disability due to musculoskeletal (MSK) disorders. Best Pract. Res. Clin. Rheumatol. **28**(3), 353–366 (2014)
2. Nancy Garrick, D.D.: Arthritis and rheumatic diseases. National Institute of Arthritis and Musculoskeletal and Skin Diseases 20 April 2017. https://www.niams.nih.gov/health-topics/arthritis-and-rheumatic-diseases. Accessed 15 Jan 2019
3. Arthritis-Related Statistics: Data and Statistics: Arthritis: CDC. https://www.cdc.gov/arthritis/data_statistics/arthritis-related-stats.htm. Accessed 15 Jan 2019
4. Bhatia, D., Bejarano, T., Novo, M.: Current interventions in the management of knee osteoarthritis. J. Pharm. Bioallied Sci. **5**(1), 30–38 (2013)

5. Fransen, M., Crosbie, J., Edmonds, J.: Physical therapy is effective for patients with osteoarthritis of the knee: a randomized controlled clinical trial. J. Rheumatol. **28**(1), 156–164 (2001)

6. Gromala, D., Tong, X., Choo, A., Karamnejad, M., Shaw, C.D.: The virtual meditative walk: virtual reality therapy for chronic pain management. In: Proceedings of the 33rd Annual ACM Conference on Human Factors in Computing Systems, New York, NY, USA, pp. 521–524 (2015)

7. Gromala, D., Tong, X., Shaw, C., Amin, A., Ulas, S., Ramsay, G.: Mobius Floe: an immersive virtual reality game for pain distraction. Electron. Imaging **2016**(4), 1–5 (2016)

8. Ijsselsteijn, W., Nap, H.H., de Kort, Y., Poels, K.: Digital game design for elderly users. In: Proceedings of the 2007 Conference on Future Play, New York, NY, USA, pp. 17–22 (2007)

9. Muñoz, J.E., Cameirão, M., Bermúdez i Badia, S., Gouveia, E.R.: Closing the loop in exergaming - health benefits of biocybernetic adaptation in senior adults. In: Proceedings of the 2018 Annual Symposium on Computer-Human Interaction in Play, New York, NY, USA, pp. 329–339 (2018)

10. Yoo, S., Ackad, C., Heywood, T., Kay, J.: Evaluating the actual and perceived exertion provided by virtual reality games. In: Proceedings of the 2017 CHI Conference Extended Abstracts on Human Factors in Computing Systems, New York, NY, USA, pp. 3050–3057 (2017)

11. VIVE$^{TM}$: Discover Virtual Reality Beyond Imagination. https://www.vive.com/us/. Accessed 15 Jan 2019

12. Heart Rate Monitor Armband: Rhythm+ $^{TM}$. https://www.scosche.com/rhythm-plus-heart-rate-monitor-armband. Accessed 15 Jan 2019

13. Williams, N.: The Borg Rating of Perceived Exertion (RPE) scale. Occup. Med. **67**(5), 404–405 (2017)

# A New Practice Method Based on KNN Model to Improve User Experience for an AR Piano Learning System

Hong Zeng, Xingxi He$^{(\boxtimes)}$, and Honghu Pan

Department of Mechatronics, College of Mechanical Engineering,
Chongqing University, Chongqing 400044, China
xingxi@cqu.edu.cn

**Abstract.** To improve the novices' short-term piano learning performances, we presented an AR piano learning system with a new practice method proposed. Initially, an Android AR app was developed for the smart glasses Moverio BT-300. The system with the user-friendly graphical augmentations on the real piano and the multi-marker design reduces the cognitive load and supports faster learning of a novice without prior sight-reading skills. In addition, a new practice method with this AR system was studied, which not only considered the practice of a song at slower speed, but also included the repeated practice of some difficult measures selected by a k-Nearest Neighbor classifier. Finally, an evaluation was implemented to compare the new practice method with the normal practice, which treats all the measures in a song equally as important. And we found that this new practice method is more useful for novices to improve their performances during short-term learning.

**Keywords:** Augmented reality · K-nearest neighbor model · Piano learning

## 1 Introduction

Augment Reality (AR) [1] has become a hot research topic in recent years and is widely used in medical, education, manufacturing, entertainment, military and other fields [2]. Especially, AR has been proved to be efficient for piano-aided learning as it could set the virtual scene on the screen and interact with the real world [3]. Therefore, AR can help the piano learners, such as novices, reduce the difficulty of learning sheet music notation and its mapping to the piano keys.

There has been quite a few Augment Reality systems or applications designed for novices to skip the sheet music reading and play the piano for either training or entertainment purposes [3, 4]. Huang et al. [5] proposed a piano teaching system, Piano AR, based on a markerless augmented reality method. By detecting and calculating the transformation matrix from keyboard coordinate to camera coordinate, the system can track the real keyboard of piano naturally. Sun et al. [6] developed a portable piano tutoring system, which can give instructions and feedbacks to help novices on fundamental piano skills. Augmented songbook [7], a mobile augmented

© Springer Nature Switzerland AG 2019
J. Y. C. Chen and G. Fragomeni (Eds.): HCII 2019, LNCS 11575, pp. 398–409, 2019.
https://doi.org/10.1007/978-3-030-21565-1_27

reality educational system for young children, which can raise their awareness of musical notation and inspire their interest in music.

Although these AR systems give hints of the notes that need to be played, due to the rapid position changes of virtual keys and the requirement to reach far keys in some pieces of music, the average percentage of correctly pressed notes remains as low as around 50% for a learner's short-term learning performances. Therefore, in order to improve a novice's short-term performance, we designed a new practice method for an AR system with an added practice session in which some selected measures considered "difficult" will be practiced at slower speed. Those measures, i.e. the segments between the bars in a musical notation, labelled "difficult" are where a novice most likely would make mistakes based on a machine learning classifier. In this experiment, more than 50 but less than 1k labelled samples are collected, no text data is involved and therefore either k-Nearest Neighbor (kNN) method or Naïve Bayesian method are suitable. In this paper, the KNN classifier is chosen.

Li et al. [8] improved the kNN algorithm by making use of the mean value's thought of the Baseline algorithm and by adding to the standard deviation of the rating, and presented a music personalized recommendation system, which can recommend music more accurately for users. In this article, each measure is considered as a sample labelled by the difficulty of playing, either "difficult" or "easy". In this two-class problem, the simple non-weight kNN algorithm will be implemented to choose the measures labelled "difficult" for practice session.

In addition, the AR system to display augmentation superimposed on the piano key can also greatly affect the user experience [9], and a well-designed AR displaying method can reduce cognitive load, ease the learning process and foster the user's interest to learn the piano. The paper developed an application to display augmentation with multi-markers for the AR smart glasses to help the novices learn to play a real piano.

## 2 Methods

In this section, the app design is firstly described. Then the kNN classification algorithm and the implementation of the KNN are introduced in detail.

### 2.1 The Design of the Application

To improve the user's experience, an android application was developed by using Java and artoolkitX, an open source augmented reality SDK, and installed on the AR smart glasses, Epson Moverio BT300. The Epson Moverio BT300, illustrated in the Fig. 1, weighs 69 g with binocular see-through viewing and runs Android 5.1. The user needs to sit in the front of the real piano and wear the smart glasses, and they can see the video stream with augmentations through the smart glasses.

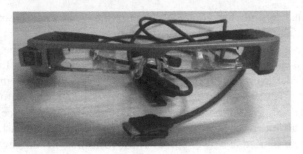

**Fig. 1.** The Epson Moverio BT300

In order to improve one of the optical limitations of the smart glasses, i.e. the limited field of view, this application adopts a multi-maker tracking method. We divide the piano keyboard into four zones, each with a marker for tracking and registration, shown in Fig. 2. Zone B and C include one octave of 12 notes or 7 white keys and 5 black keys. Though Zone A or D include a larger range, only one octave in each zone will be used in most musical pieces.

**Fig. 2.** A piano keyboard divided into four zones and each zone with a marker. Marker A is on the note f, marker B on f1, marker C on f2, and the marker D on f3.

As far as the graphic augmentations, Hackl et al. [9] compared the differences between two ways to display the augmentation, i.e. the instant way and the Beatmania way. The instant way provides no hints for the next note to be played and the display interface is clear and simple. However, when there is no prompt message for the next note, the user might experience some discomfort due to the limited time to react and press the next key and the error rate would rise for the short-term performance. The Beatmania way has some hints for the coming notes to be played which is better than the instant way. However, the Beatmania way might increase the cognitive load or add unnecessary confusion to the user.

The article designed a novel app that draws three kinds of virtual objects in the augmentation layer shown in the Fig. 3. A green solid cube indicates the notes that need to be pressed at the current moment. The user is supposed to press and hold the key until the virtual key disappears. The set period of time of holding a key corresponds to the duration of a note. When the black keys on the piano needs to be pressed, the color of the solid cube will turn red. The second type, a green hollow box or frame whose location means that the notes to be pressed at the next moment. Another virtual object, the arrow is supposed to remind the user of switching the view.

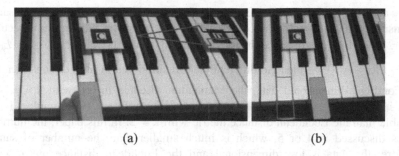

(a)                                    (b)

**Fig. 3.** The video stream with augmentations (Color figure online)

For example, Fig. 3 shows the video stream with augmentations and Fig. 3(a) displays a green solid cube superimposed on the note e2, and a red arrow pointing to the left. This means that the player needs to press the piano key e2 at the current time until the cube disappears or appears in another position. And the virtual red arrow on the marker D indicates that the player should shift the sight to the left, leaving zone D for the key to be pressed is in the zone C. Figure 3(b) shows a cube superimposed on the note g2 and a hollow green box on the note e2 which refers that the player is supposed to press the note g2 until the cube superimposed on the note e2.

## 2.2  Algorithm of KNN to Select the Measures in a Musical Staff for Practice

In order to select the difficult measures in a song where the novices most likely would make some mistakes, the kNN classification algorithm is used as one of the simplest and the most used machine learning algorithms. By using the kNN classifier, no prior knowledge about or the assumptions on the data distribution is needed. Due to the feature similarity, the majority vote of the class label of the k nearest neighboring samples in a feature space will be assigned to a test sample.

The general steps of the kNN classification include (1) calculate the distance from all the training samples against the test sample in the feature space, (2) sort the training samples by the value of distance in ascending order, (3) select the value of k and (4) the test sample will be assigned to the class most common among its k nearest neighbors.

The proximity or similarity between two samples is represented by calculating their distance in the feature space. Either the Euclidean distance or the Manhattan distance can be used, which are expressed as follows:

$$d_E(\mathbf{x}, \mathbf{y}) = \sqrt{\sum_{i=1}^{n} (x_i - y_i)^2} \tag{1}$$

$$d_M(\mathbf{x}, \mathbf{y}) = \sum_{i=1}^{n} |x_i - y_i| \tag{2}$$

where n represents the number of features, $d_E$ refers to the Euclidean distance, $d_M$ is the Manhattan distance, x and y are a test sample and a training sample respectively. The smaller the distance between two samples in the feature space, the more alike their features and so the more similar the two samples will be. That is why k nearest samples are considered and the right choice of k value can avoid the bias in one direction or another. The different distance metrics using $L_k$ norm ($x$, $y \in R^d$, $k \in Z$, $L_k(x,y)$ $= \sum_{i=1}^{d} \left( ||x^i - y^i||^k \right)^{1/k}$) lead to different classification rate in high dimensional space [10]. For high dimensional data, the Manhattan distance metric with k = 1, which results in the more meaningful notion of proximity between two samples, is more preferable than the Euclidean distance metric with k = 2. In this paper, the number of features discussed is 4 or 5, which is much smaller than the number of samples. Therefore, the data is low dimensional and the Euclidean distance metric can be applied.

## 2.3    Training Data Acquisition and Features in the Learning Model

To obtain the training data, 5 volunteers with no previous piano experience in learning were invited to play 13 sections from 7 songs which are either elementary songs or the easy version of pop songs. 7 sections are taken from the right-hand melody of a song with a dominant melody and the rest of 6 sections from the left-hand harmony. Those sections have various difficulty levels for novices and their lengths range from 16 bars to 32 bars, resulting in a total of 232 bars or measures. Each bar or measure is considered as one sample in the learning model and the difficult measures are supposed to be selected for the practice purpose. The age of five volunteers are between 21 to 24. In the experiment, each person first spent some time to get used to wearing the smart glasses and practiced a small song to be familiar with the augmentations while playing. Each session ranged from one hour and a half to two hours for a participant to finish playing 13 songs. The volunteers are supposed to play each song only once and their initial performances are recorded and evaluated for labelling. When the player hit the wrong note, the measure where that note is located would be marked. However, the duration of each note were not considered or counted. If the number of people who made mistakes at a certain measure is greater than a threshold (equal to 2 in this article), then this measure is labelled "difficult". In this way, the paper simplify the problem to a two-category task. More precisely speaking, in the model, the label of the difficult measures are set to 1, the others set to 0, and no text data is involved.

In the learning model, we extracted five features and processed the labels of the samples according to certain rules. Considering that if the distance between two notes is too far, the player has a high probability of making mistakes at this measure, the paper sums up the distances between all the pairs of neighboring notes inside one measure, $D_I$, as one of the features. Sometimes the distance between the two notes before and after a vertical bar is large and influential to the player. Therefore, the distance between two adjacent measures, $D_W$, is also considered as a feature. Intuitively, in one measure if there are quite a few notes with short durations such as 1 or 2 described in the app, the player would also easily make mistakes. Therefore, we count the number of notes with the first and the second shortest duration, 1 or 2 in one measure, $n_s$, as a feature. Similarly the number of notes in a sequence where each note has duration of 1 or 2 consecutively in one bar, $n_c$, is also chosen as a feature. At last, it is found that the difficulty levels of the left-hand and right-hand part of a song are different in general, and it will affect the classification results to some extent. So, whether it is the left- or right-hand part of a song is also considered as a feature, h. In summary, the data for each sample contains 5 features and a corresponding label.

## 2.4 Training Results

The paper divided the 232 samples into training set and development set in the ratio 7:3, and calculated the accuracy rate for the model validation. For the accuracy rate, only the false negative classification is counted as an error, which means the positive measure (1 or labelled "difficult") is classified as negative (0 or labelled "easy"). However, the false positive classification is not considered as an error. False positive means originally a negative measure (0 or labelled "easy") is classified as positive (1 or labelled "difficult"). It is believed that the practice of those false positive measures labeled "easy" would not affect the performance of players or at least it would not lead to a decline in performance. The classification accuracy rate for the development set is calculated as follows:

$$\text{accu} = \frac{1}{n}\sum\nolimits_{i=1}^{n}(n - k_i), \; k_i = \begin{cases} 1, & if \; y_i = 1, \; \bar{y}_i = 0 \\ 0, & else. \end{cases} \tag{3}$$

where n is the number of development set samples, $y_i$ is the original label of the ith test sample, and $\bar{y}_i$ is the classification result.

In the kNN algorithm, choosing the right value of k is important for better accuracy. Higher value of k has lesser chance of error. However, if k is too large, the computing time should be of concern because for each new test sample, all the training data stored has to be used. In addition, the quality of feature extraction will also affect the classification results. Therefore, we analyzed the impact of different features and different k values on model predictions. This model is developed based on Python and implemented in an library (sklearn). Table 1 displays the accuracy rate for the development set with different features and k values. The feature h, the left- or right-hand part of a song, has a greater influence on the accuracy when k value is smaller. When any one of $D_I$ and $D_W$ is missing, different k values have little effect on the prediction results, and the prediction accuracy is relatively low. The effects of features $n_s$ and $n_c$ on the prediction rate are similar because the values of the two features in the same sample are close to each other. Finally four features $D_I$, $D_W$, $n_c$ and h are chosen as the features of the samples, the k value is set to 11 in the model and the accuracy rate is 0.8805. The chosen k value also satisfy the following two conditions: (1) an odd number to avoid a tied result of voting; (2) $k = \sqrt{n}$ where n is the total number of training samples and equal to 162 in the model validation.

**Table 1.** Accuracy rate on development set of different features and k values

| Features | k values | | | | |
|---|---|---|---|---|---|
| | 3 | 5 | 7 | 9 | 11 |
| | The accuracy rate on development set | | | | |
| $D_I D_W n_s n_c h$ | 0.8642 | 0.8647 | 0.8667 | 0.8638 | 0.8722 |
| $D_I D_W n_s n_c$ | 0.8448 | 0.8549 | 0.8638 | 0.8664 | 0.8716 |
| $D_I D_W n_s h$ | 0.8670 | 0.8705 | 0.8740 | 0.8741 | 0.8795 |
| $D_I D_W n_c h$ | 0.8635 | 0.8699 | 0.8769 | 0.8775 | 0.8805 |
| $D_I n_s n_c h$ | 0.8651 | 0.8583 | 0.8463 | 0.8555 | 0.8603 |
| $D_W n_s n_c h$ | 0.8552 | 0.8527 | 0.8511 | 0.8533 | 0.8641 |

## 3  Evaluation and Experiment

An evaluation experiment was implemented to examine the impact of the new practice method on the learning. We invited 6 volunteers different from those who participated in the training data acquisition and divided them into two groups, the experimental group and the control group, each of which has 3 members. All the volunteers are novices in playing piano and have no knowledge of the five-line staff based sheet music notation. The age of six volunteers are between 21 to 24. The experimental group was asked to use the new practice method for piano practice with the help of the developed AR system. The shortened easy-to-play versions of two songs, a pop song "I do" with 33 measures and "swan lake" with 24 measures, were selected for the evaluation. Only the right-hand melody was played and the difficulty level of the two songs is similar to or a little harder than those used in the training data. After applying the KNN classifier to the 57 new test samples each of which has 4 features, 11 measures from "I do" and 4 measures from "swan lake" were chosen for practice. Those measures labelled "difficult" were repeated multiple times (3 times for "I do" and 6 times for "swan lake") so that both groups received the equivalent amount of practice. During the practice, the augmentations were displayed more slowly than usual while during the performance evaluation displayed at normal speed. For practice, the control group was supposed to play the original songs twice and the experimental group needed play the original songs once and the chosen measures once. Every participant devoted 40 min on average at their evaluation session.

### 3.1  Flowchart of Evaluation

The evaluation flowchart is depicted in Fig. 4. Initially for the evaluation, every volunteer was asked to use the practice programmed in the app to be accustomed to wearing the smart glasses and the way of virtual keys display on the piano. The volunteers were supposed to hit a few notes which do not form any certain melody. However, in this evaluation preparation, all the virtual objects in the augmentation design are involved and all the four markers are used. Afterwards, the following steps were repeated for the two test songs, first the "swan lake" and then followed by the "I do". Every participant from both groups started with playing the song at normal speed

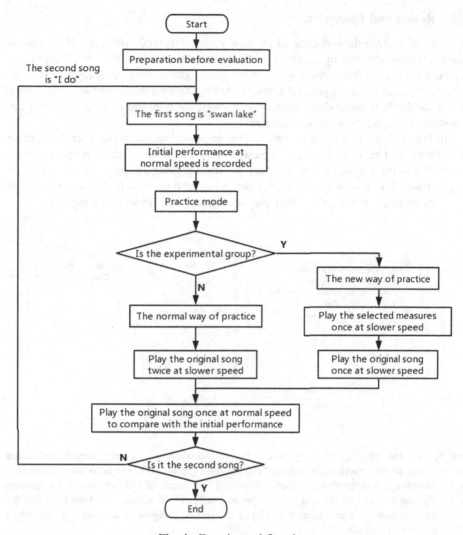

**Fig. 4.** Experimental flowchart

and this initial performance would be recorded for later analysis. Next, the volunteers entered into the different practice mode. The participants in the control group practiced the original song twice at slower speed while those in the experimental group played the selected measures from KNN once and the original song once also at slower speed. Finally, after the practice, everyone played the original song again at normal speed and the performance was recorded for comparison.

## 3.2  Results and Discussion

In order to analyze the influence of the new practice method with the AR system on piano learning, the playing accuracy rate was calculated before and after the practice for both the experimental group and control group. The playing accuracy rate is equal to the number of correctly pressed notes divided by the total number of notes in a song. As in the KNN training data acquisition process, the duration of each note was not considered for playing accuracy calculation.

In Fig. 5 the playing accuracy rate and the improved accuracy rate after the practice are illustrated. The x values of 1–3 represent the 3 volunteers in each group (6 persons in total) and the corresponding y values are their playing accuracy of the first song "swan lake". The x values of 4–6 represent the same 6 persons in the two groups and the corresponding y values are their playing accuracy of the second song "I do".

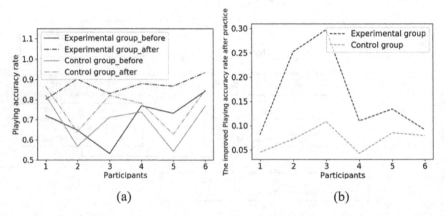

**Fig. 5.** (a) The playing accuracy rates. "experimental group_before" means the initial performance of the experimental group, "experimental group_after" refers to the performance of the experimental group after the practice session. The x values of 1–3 indicate the 3 volunteers in each group who played the first song of "swan lake", and the x values of 4–6d represent the same three persons in each group who played the second song of "I do". (b) The improved playing accuracy rate after practice.

In Fig. 5(a), after the practice session, the participants in both groups showed improvement in playing accuracy rate compared with the initial performance. Another thing to note is that the average values of the initial playing accuracy rate of both groups are close to each other, i.e. 0.6336 for the experimental group and 0.6997 for the control group. Therefore it can be assumed that all the novices in both groups are on the same level of playing the piano at the beginning, which ensures that the experimental results are not disturbed by the previous learning experiences of participants.

Figure 5(b) shows that the improved accuracy rate of the experimental group at each point is greater than that of the control group. The average increase of the experimental group is 0.1610 (SD = 0.08316), and greater than that of the control group 0.07208 (SD = 0.02279). The results indicate that the practice involving the new method, which chooses some difficult measures based on the KNN classifier and arranges the repeated practice of those measures, is more helpful than the method that treats all the measures in a song equally as important.

For the first song "swan lake", the average value of the improved accuracy rate for the experimental group is 0.2102 (SD = 0.09314) and for the control group is 0.0751 (SD = 0.02581). For the second song "I do", the average value of the improved accuracy rate for the experimental group is 0.1118 (SD = 0.01753) and for the control group is 0.0691 (SD = 0.01882). The improvement of playing the first song is greater than that of playing the second one. It is because the second song is harder to play that the improvement is limited after a short-term practice.

In Fig. 5(b), the improved rates of the experimental group at two points are much larger than others. To explain those two points, it is found that in Fig. 5(a), those two participants have comparatively low rates for the initial performance, i.e. 0.6486 and 0.5315, lower than the average value 0.6997. It can be explained that at the beginning, those learners are not familiar with the AR system, and after a period of practice, they become accustomed to the AR display and can perform better.

### 3.3   Test Data Acquisition and Evaluation

In order to evaluate the generalization ability of the model in the test set, the measures labelled "difficult" in the test samples based on the KNN model are compared with the measures labelled "difficult" by experiment. Five out of six volunteers for evaluation were randomly selected and their initial performance data before the practice was used for labelling. According to the same criteria as applied to the KNN training data labelling, if the number of people who made mistakes at a measure is greater than 2, this measure is labelled "difficult".

Finally, 57 new test samples in the evaluation were labelled, and Table 2 showed the prediction results. The measure numbers of true positive, true negative, false positive and false negative are listed respectively for both songs to evaluate the performance of the KNN classifier. According to the Eq. (3), the prediction accuracy for the test samples is illustrated by Eq. (4). Only the false negative classification is counted as an error, which means the positive measure (1 or labelled "difficult") is classified as negative (0 or labelled "easy"), which is the same as before. As is shown in Eq. (4), the accuracy rate for the test set is 85.965%, close to the accuracy rate for the development set. Therefore, the developed KNN classifier based on the training set is verified by the new test samples.

**Table 2.** The prediction results for the 57 measures

| Songs | TP | TN | FP | FN |
|---|---|---|---|---|
| I do | 13 | 18 | 0 | 2 |
| swan lake | 11 | 7 | 0 | 6 |
| sum | 24 | 25 | 0 | 8 |

TP = True Positive, TN = True Negative, FP = False Positive, FN = False Negative.

$$accu_{test} = 1 - \frac{TN}{TP + TN + FP + FN} = 1 - \frac{8}{57} = 85.965\% \qquad (4)$$

## 4 Conclusion and Future Work

In this article, to foster the interests of novices to learn the piano and to improve the performance of a short-term learner, we presented a new practice method with an AR system. It turned out that this new practice method is more helpful than the normal practice method for novices to improve their short-term learning performance. The increase in the average correctness rate of the experimental group is 0.1610 (SD = 0.08316), and greater than that of the control group 0.07208 (SD = 0.02279).

Further studies will include more volunteers so that the obtained data is more statistically significant. In the future, our research interest will adopt other more advanced machine learning methods, for example deep neural networks, to improve user experience of the AR aided piano learning system.

**Acknowledgments.** The authors would like to thank all the volunteers in the study. All of them are students at Chongqing University.

## References

1. Azuma, R.T.: A survey of augmented reality. Presence Teleoperators Virtual Environ. **6**(4), 355–385 (1997)
2. Billinghurst, M., Clark, A., Lee, G.: A survey of augmented reality. Found. Trends® Hum.– Comput. Interact. **8**(2–3), 73–272 (2015)
3. Rogers, K., et al.: PIANO: faster piano learning with interactive projection. In: Proceedings of the Ninth ACM International Conference on Interactive Tabletops and Surfaces, pp. 149– 158. ACM, November 2014
4. Das, S., Glickman, S., Hsiao, F.Y., Lee, B.: Music everywhere–augmented reality piano improvisation learning system
5. Huang, F., Zhou, Y., Yu, Y., Wang, Z., Du, S.: Piano AR: a markerless augmented reality based piano teaching system. In: 2011 International Conference on Intelligent Human- Machine Systems and Cybernetics (IHMSC), vol. 2, pp. 47–52. IEEE, August 2011
6. Sun, C.H., Chiang, P.Y.: Mr. Piano: a portable piano tutoring system. In: 2018 IEEE XXV International Conference on Electronics, Electrical Engineering and Computing (INTER- CON), pp. 1–4. IEEE, August 2018
7. Rusiñol, M., Chazalon, J., Diaz-Chito, K.: Augmented songbook: an augmented reality educational application for raising music awareness. Multimed. Tools Appl. **77**(11), 13773– 13798 (2018)

8. Li, G., Zhang, J.: Music personalized recommendation system based on improved KNN algorithm. In: 2018 IEEE 3rd Advanced Information Technology, Electronic and Automation Control Conference (IAEAC), pp. 777–781. IEEE, October 2018
9. Hackl, D., Anthes, C.: HoloKeys-an augmented reality application for learning the piano
10. Beyer, K., Goldstein, J., Ramakrishnan, R., Shaft, U.: When is nearest neighbors meaningful? In: ICDT Conference Proceedings (1999)

# Enabling Immunology Learning in Virtual Reality Through Storytelling and Interactivity

Lei Zhang[⊠], Doug A. Bowman, and Caroline N. Jones

Virginia Tech, Blacksburg, VA 24060, USA
{leiz,dbowman,jonescn}@vt.edu

**Abstract.** Immunology concepts typically taught at the college level involve both factual and process-based knowledge and present learning barriers to college students. Immunology knowledge can be difficult for students to visualize and relate to. To help students better understand specific immunology concepts and increase their learning motivation and engagement, we designed the Immunology virtual reality (VR) application. Immunology VR leverages the rich interactivity and immersion offered by virtual reality systems to create a highly interactive and narrative-driven immersive VR experience that takes students on an exciting journey inside the human body. In this paper, we describe the design of the Immunology VR experience, focusing on our use of an interactive digital storytelling approach to enable learning.

**Keywords:** Immersive virtual reality · Storytelling · Interactivity · Immunology · Learning · Education · Instructional design

## 1 Introduction

Immunology concepts typically taught at the college level are inherently complex, abstract, and process-based, involving difficult factual knowledge and jargon of the field (Raimondi 2016) and may present learning barriers to college students. Immunology knowledge can be difficult for students to visualize and relate to. Current methods of teaching immunology, usually in large-size didactic lecture classes plus lab exercises, do not promote learning in an active way for most students (Freeman et al. 2014).

Research on STEM (science, technology, engineering, and mathematics) education has shown that to improve students' understanding of the concepts and increase their course performance, active learning is an effective teaching practice that supports learning (Freeman et al. 2014). Experiments that focus on different variations of active learning in biology and immunology education have shown that digital games (Cheng et al. 2014, Raimondi 2016), card games (Su et al. 2014), and role playing (Elliott 2010), are all effective instructional tools to improve students' learning of immunology concepts to some degree.

However, limitations of using games were also found in those studies. First, game designers and educators tried to embed all concepts into the game and let students learn the concepts completely from gameplay, which made the game simply a substitute for classroom lectures. Students felt frustrated with the complexity of the game and did not

J. Y. C. Chen and G. Fragomeni (Eds.): HCII 2019, LNCS 11575, pp. 410–425, 2019.
https://doi.org/10.1007/978-3-030-21565-1_28

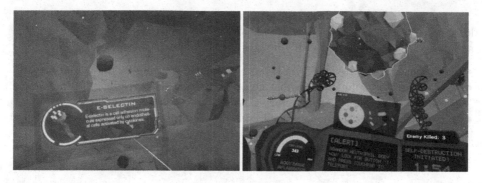

**Fig. 1.** Screenshots from the experience (left: selecting a virtual object to see its information, right: using the NETS weapon to kill bacteria in body tissues)

ultimately have fun playing it (Raimondi 2016). Second, in a study of using card game for immunology learning, students were so absorbed in the competition of the game that they tended to neglect reviewing the embedded concepts and therefore learned little (Su et al. 2014). These limitations suggest that current game design for immunology learning doesn't do an optimal job helping students understand complex immunology concepts, even though they are more embraced by students than traditional lectures and show some effectiveness in promoting learning.

Emerging technologies provide new opportunities as instructional tools to promote active learning in STEM education. In particular, virtual reality (VR) has many strengths that can be used to create engaging learning experiences (Freina and Ott 2015; Slater and Sanchez-Vives 2016). Unique affordances of VR include rich interactivity, immersion, embodiment, multisensory stimuli, and a first-person point of view (POV). In the case of immunology learning, a VR experience could allow a learner to embody an immune cell with a first-person POV and travel inside the human body to search for invading bacteria, a scenario that would be difficult to visualize in other instructional media and tools. Existing studies on using VR for science education suggest that VR can help students learn abstract concepts with custom designed virtual environments (VEs) for learning (Dede et al. 1996). A meta-analysis on the effectiveness of VR-based instruction on learning outcomes also suggests that VR is effective for teaching students in both K12 and higher education settings (Merchant et al. 2014).

To make abstract science concepts accessible to students, many educators have been using storytelling techniques in instructional practices. Studies show that storytelling is an effective tool to communicate complex science concepts. In one study, researchers created short stories and used them in teaching science subjects like astronomy, biology, chemistry, geology, and physics. They found students had more accurate understanding of the subject concepts after reading relevant stories, as well as increased interest in the subjects (Clough 2010). More recently, storytelling has been embedded into VR experiences by filmmakers to create a novel, immersive cinematic experience for general audiences (Dooley 2017; Mateer 2017), which brings a lot of new possibilities for instructional design.

In this paper, we present the design of a novel tool for college-level immunology learning, based on immersive interactive storytelling in VR. We hypothesize that this new tool, called Immunology VR (Fig. 1), has the following strengths:

- Rich interactivity provided by VR promotes active learning by doing and playing.
- Embedded storytelling and virtual guide features in the experience help learners work through complex immunology concepts and scaffold learning.
- First-person POV and immune cell embodiment create an immersive experience that engages students in contextual and situated learning.

## 2    Related Work

### 2.1    Definitions of Interactivity

Throughout the literature, definitions of interactivity vary from one to another due to different contexts and fields in which it has been used, and there is little agreement on a consistent definition (Sims 1997; Domagk et al. 2010).

In the area of instructional multimedia, interactivity is considered an important characteristic of media and is believed to contribute greatly to learning (Sims 1997). Barker (1994) argues that interactivity is "a necessary and fundamental mechanism for knowledge acquisition and the development of both cognitive and physical skills." From a human-computer interface view, Sims (1997) defines interactivity as the function of input given to the user by the system and the action provided by the system in response to those inputs in a meaningful way. Researchers also attempted to identify levels of interactivity in instructional media design. One definition by Rhodes and Azbell (1985) proposes three levels of interactivity, ranging from the lowest level, reactive, where the learner has little control of content and structure; to coactive, where the learner is provided with controls for sequence, pace, and style; to proactive, the highest level, where the learner controls both structure and content. With this definition, level of interactivity is directly connected to the amount of user control over content and structure within the media.

In the context of VR applications, a widely cited definition of interactivity regards interactivity as the degree "to which users can participate in modifying the form and content of a mediated environment in real time" (Steuer 1992). Roussou et al. (2007) specifies a three-level definition of interactivity in the context of VR learning based on an original definition by Pares and Pares (Pares and Pares 2001). It states that the interactivity in a virtual learning environment should promote the learner's physical and cognitive activities through one or more of the three forms: to explore the virtual environment by way of navigation (explorative), to manipulate virtual objects or elements (manipulative), and to construct or modify the environment as a whole (contributive).

Based on Steuer's definition of general VR interactivity and Roussou's definition of interactivity in a virtual learning environment setting, we identified types of interactivity that would be useful in our project by considering how interactive features of the

VR experience could support the learning concepts through the user's actions. Specifically, interactivity provided by the virtual experience supports a user's freedom in navigation, the ability to select virtual objects and apply intended effects, and the ability to access specific learning information in the VE.

## 2.2  Interactivity and Learning

How does interactivity affect learning outcomes? Many studies have addressed that question in the context of instructional multimedia design. In an early study, Schaffer and Hannafin (1986) evaluated effectiveness of interactivity in a multimedia-based interactive video on learning. They compared the learning outcomes of 98 high schoolers with four treatment conditions with gradually increased interactivity levels in interactive video lessons. Their results concluded that students' learning recall was significantly affected by the amount and type of interactivity provided, and the most interactive version of the video lessons yielded the greatest recall. Khalifa and Lam (2002) investigated level of interactivity in web-based learning applications by comparing a distributed passive web-learning environment with a distributed interactive learning environment. Their results suggest that the interactive condition was superior to the passive condition in terms of both the learning process and learning outcome.

In the area of VR learning, there are fewer studies on the level of interactivity and its effect on learning. However, positive results were also found in a study by Bailenson et al. (2008), which examined the effect of interactivity on learning physical actions in VR. In the study, they found that the learners in an interactive VR condition perform better than those in a video learning condition.

To sum up, empirical evidence from past studies has shown that level of interactivity can sometimes be positively linked to learning outcomes.

## 2.3  Virtual Reality's Potential to Support Learning

VR has been embraced by educators and researchers as a powerful and promising tool for educational purposes because of its unique features that distinguish it from other instructional media (Mikropoulos and Natsis 2011). Mikropoulos and Bellou (2006) list some VR features that pedagogically support learning, including creation of 3D spatial representations, multisensory channels for user interaction, immersion, and intuitive interaction through natural manipulations in real time.

Many studies have been conducted on the effectiveness of using VR for learning. A ten-year (1999–2009) review of empirical research on educational VR by Mikropoulos and Natsis (2011) indicates that the learning outcomes in almost all of the studies being reviewed (53 in total) are shown to be positive when mediated by educational virtual environments. In another study specifically addressing desktop-based VR technologies, Merchant et al. (2014) did a meta-analysis to examine instructional effectiveness of three major categories of desktop-based VR applications (games, simulations, and virtual worlds) on students' learning outcomes in K-12 and higher education settings. Their analysis suggests that games, simulations, and virtual worlds are effective in improving learning outcome gains, and that games show higher learning gains than simulations and virtual worlds.

Compared to research on desktop VR, there are fewer studies on effectiveness of immersive VR for learning. However, several studies conducted in immersive VR settings have also achieved some positive results. Kaufmann et al. (Kaufmann et al. 2000) built an immersive VR application, Construct3D, to support mathematics and geometry education. Their results indicate that the tool promotes learning by doing and training of spatial ability. It is useful to solve simple problems in mathematics and geometry education. Roussou and Oliver (2006) investigated the effects of interactivity in an immersive VR application, the virtual playground, on conceptual learning with primary school students. Their results suggest that immersive passive VR guided by a virtual robot works best in terms of student reflection, knowledge recall, and conceptual change. Dede et al. (1997) developed ScienceSpace, an immersive VR application to support learning of complex and abstract scientific concepts. Results show that students developed an in-depth understanding of the subject matter, and that students enjoyed the learning experience and appeared to be more engaged in activities. However, no significant difference was found in students' change of mental models with only a single session usage of the application.

It is noteworthy that development of many of these educational VR applications was driven by constructivist teaching and learning theory and followed a "learning by doing" approach (Dede et al. 1997; Kaufmann et al. 2000; Roussou and Oliver 2006) in accordance with the core principle of constructivism that knowledge is actively constructed through learners' interaction with the environment around them, and with other people in social and cultural settings (Sjøberg 2007). However, our approach is to rely on storytelling as the main vehicle to convey necessary information to the learners. In doing so, we hypothesize that with interactive storytelling, new information will be more accessible to the learners, and it will be easier for them to process the information from stories than from self-exploration and discovery, given the complexity of the learning concept and the short exposure time in the VE.

## 2.4    Using Storytelling for Learning

Science has uncovered many amazing facts about the world, but it can be hard to explain. Science textbooks are mostly written with expository facts and are full of terminology, which creates learning barriers for many people. Thus, educators have used stories in science teaching to make subjects relatable to novice learners. Studies have shown that storytelling in science education promotes students' understanding of complex science concepts. Helstrand and Ott (1995) used a science fiction novel, The Time and Space of Uncle Albert, to teach the theory of relativity in four classes. Their results indicate that using novels to teach scientific theories is an efficient way to help students acquire basic science concepts. In another study, Banister and Ryan (2001) developed a science-teaching pedagogy using storytelling to help children develop science concepts about the water cycle. Their outcomes showed that, in the long run, the children remembered more abstract science concepts when taught with a storytelling-based pedagogy. Evidence from these studies suggests the possibility of using custom designed stories in immunology education to break down the complexity of abstract concepts and communicate them in an easy way to students.

The way a story is told and transmitted has also been influenced by rapidly changing technologies and evolving digital media. Digital storytelling is a recent form of creating interesting stories in combination with computers and multimedia such as computer graphics, audio, and video clips (Robin 2008). Digital storytelling can also be interactive and custom designed for educational purposes. For example, RiverCity (Clarke et al. 2006) is a research project that aims to train middle-school students in scientific inquiry skills in a multi-user virtual environment. The project is backed by a strong storyline in which a student travels back in time, bringing 21st century technology and skills to investigate and solve 19th century health problems in a small town. Results suggest that interactive storytelling in a multi-user virtual environment effectively encourages authentic scientific inquiry in middle school science education.

Storytelling in VR is not a new practice. However, studies that are specifically dedicated to the topic are scarce in the literature. One of the earliest examples of storytelling in VR was a Disney attraction based on the film "Aladdin" (Pausch et al. 1996). In the experience, the user follows a narrative storyline and flies a magic carpet through a virtual world. This project was an early VR storytelling attempt designed for a completely computer-generated virtual environment. After that, very few experiments with similar designs were found in the literature. However, in recent years, storytelling in VR, or cinematic VR, has been embraced by filmmakers in the form of 360-degree videos (Mateer 2017). One example of such a VR storytelling experience is an award-winning animated music video, *Pearl*, in which the user acts as a ghost viewer who sits in the passenger seat of a 1970 hatchback and watches how a single father tries to raise his young daughter from a child to a teenager, and experiences joys and sorrows in life with them. Although storytelling in 360-degree video has the potential for teaching and learning, one major downside is that most of them lack the interactivity that supports the process of knowledge construction (e.g., allowing users to change viewpoints or interact with characters in the scene). We hypothesize that passive 360-degree video learning experiences might lead to a loss of engagement if a user is exposed to the medium very often or for a long time. Thus, we aim to provide immersive storytelling that is also highly interactive.

## 3 Designing Immunology VR

### 3.1 Design Approach

At the beginning of our design, we tried to define the scope of the virtual learning experience to be designed in terms of the amount of storytelling and the amount of interactivity. We developed the following major principles to be realized in the Immunology VR experience:

- The storytelling experience should be interactive, and learners should be able to influence the story by selecting among options.
- The virtual experience may include some gameplay elements (such as missions, goals, scores, and number of lives) to motivate learners to interact with virtual objects in the environment and to see a cause and effect relationship related to the embedded concepts.

- The experience should be guided so that learners can make better sense of the complex learning concepts embedded in a relatively short-duration experience.
- The tool should allow learners to make sense of new information through trial and error and provide necessary and immediate feedback to the learners' actions.

With these principles in place, we wanted to achieve a balance between storytelling and interactivity in our designs in terms of the influences they may have on concept learning. On the one hand, we did not want to create a passive storytelling experience in VR like many 360-degree videos. On the other hand, we did not want to make the experience as highly interactive as a computer game, since pure games may reduce learners' attention to the embedded learning concepts. Therefore, our design solution can be described as an immersive learning experience built on non-linear digital storytelling and gameplay connected through unique affordances in VR.

## 3.2   Design Process

VR experience design by its nature requires interdisciplinary teamwork, and our project is no exception. The project team includes members and expert advisors from different domains, including art and design, computer science, biological sciences, instructional design, education, and cinema. Within an interdisciplinary design context, there are no standard design processes for us to follow, so we had to explore and experiment with a design process that worked best with our design goals. We decided to focus our design process on providing an engaging and immersive user experience intended to help users learn immunology concepts. We chose an iterative human-centered design (HCD) approach to meet these goals.

An iterative design process was important for us, because in VR design it is unlikely to get the experience right on the first attempt. Rather, we needed to test our designs with end users frequently, identify major issues that hinder the user experience, make quick changes, and then test the new designs again. VR user experience consultant Jerald (2016) states that, "VR design must be iteratively created based off of continual redesign, prototyping, and feedback from real users," which suggests that the iterative design approach is critically important for VR applications. He also proposed an iterative design process, the define-make-learn cycle, which is applicable to many common VR applications (Jerald 2014). In the define stage, designers attempt to get a clear picture of what to make and list requirements of design goals. The make stage includes any assets needed to create the experience and the way to put them together. In the learn stage, designers find out what works and what does not, and the answers are fed back into the define stage to help refine the design. Such an iterative design cycle was repeated several times during the ideation, prototyping, and implementation process of our project.

Our particular design process for this VR experience included the following major stages, which we describe in detail in the sections below:

1. Get to know the problem by communicating with an immunology professor and her students to identify learning barriers and determine learning goals
2. Based on chosen immunology concepts, create a story-based user scenario
3. Create visualizations of learning concepts and the user scenario

4. Design 3D interactions that help users carry out learning tasks in the experience
5. Create interactive experience prototypes in VR
6. Test the prototype with immunology students and make necessary refinements.

### 3.3  Immunology Concept

We spoke with professors and graduate students in the Biological Sciences Department to identify learning barriers in immunology education. From these discussions, we identified one specific concept area in immunology that many undergraduate students had problems with in regular classroom learning and lab exercises. The concept is about a specific type of white blood cells called neutrophils. Neutrophils are the most abundant white blood cells in the human immune system and serve as the first responders to any infections in the human body. Their major functions in the immune defense process involve fast transmigration from blood vessels to an infection site in body tissue and the use of several different mechanisms (degranulation, phagocytosis, and neutrophil extracellular traps) to kill bacteria there.

This learning concept involves factual, conceptual, and process-based knowledge and presents learning difficulties to students in classroom instruction. Specifically, students need to learn a complex process with many steps to understand the actions of neutrophils. In addition, our interviews with students suggested that extensive and unfamiliar terminology is another issue preventing them from fully understanding the concept. Finally, limited images in textbooks do little to help them understand and contextualize the ways that neutrophils work.

Based on the concept, we developed the following learning objectives for the VR experience:

- Students need to understand the role of neutrophils in the human immune system and how they complement other white blood cells.
- Students need to understand the steps and process of neutrophil transmigration, including selectin binding and neutrophil rolling.
- Students need to understand the differences between three major mechanisms used by neutrophils to kill bacteria: degranulation, phagocytosis, and neutrophil extracellular traps (NETS).

### 3.4  VR Story Design

After deciding on the immunology concept to be embedded into the virtual learning experience, we went further to create a story-based user scenario with specifications of user tasks and missions to be performed in the experience.

In the experience, the user/learner plays the role of a neutrophil "pilot" in the innate immune system's "armed forces" in the human body. The user's routine mission is to patrol inside the blood vessel and to be on call for infection alerts from the immune system headquarters. The user's mission starts when he is told that there is a serious infection happening inside his host's body tissues and he has limited time to go to the site of infection to prevent it from getting worse. However, the user first needs to look for a portal so that he can transmigrate into the infected body tissue. After finding the portal and transmigrating, the user is faced with different types of bacteria and needs to use the appropriate weapons to eliminate them, controlling both inflammation and infection.

The experience includes two scenes and follows a common three-act narrative structure. In the first scene, the user travels in the blood vessel and gets the infection alert, which starts Act 1 as an inciting incident. In the second scene, the user is faced with different bacteria and needs to find a way to eliminate them within a limited time. However, the weapons are not all available initially, and the user needs to kill enough bacteria in order to use the weapon of choice. This is Act 2, where the main character is unable to solve the problem initially due to lack of skills and power. The user finally is able to access each weapon and figures out how to utilize their killing power to control the infection. This completes Act 3, in which the main character is able to find a resolution to the problem. However, in order to make the story interactive, the experience doesn't always conclude with a happy ending. The actual ending of the story, as in a video game, depends on the user's choice of weapons, the types of bacteria targeted by the chosen weapons, and the activation of a second life. The failure or success of the mission is ultimately up to the user and depends on rapid learning of the concepts.

## 3.5    Visual Design

### 2D Conceptual Illustrations

We started the visual designs of the experience with 2D conceptual sketches and illustrations and created several versions of storyboards. In the 2D visual design process, we were able to visualize key interactions the learners need to perform during the experience and get an idea of the 3D environment complexity for the next step. Figure 2 shows a storyboard that visualizes a neutrophil's transmigration process.

### 3D Asset Creation

The 3D asset creation was based on 2D conceptual sketches, illustrations, and many microbiology image references provided by immunology experts. We chose a low-polygon style instead of a photorealistic style for the 3D environment, immune cells, and bacteria due to several considerations. First, low-poly 3D models take less time to create, so they shorten prototyping time. Second, low-poly geometries do not need a complex texture and shader setup in a game engine like Unity3D, thus consuming less computing power and ensuring a high frame rate in VR. Third, the low-poly graphic style is popular in many mainstream games and will look familiar to learners.

For the creation process, we used multiple 3D authoring tools in our modeling pipeline by utilizing different features of each tool. For example, we used a 3D sculpting tool, Zbrush from Pixologic, to speed sculpt a rough shape of a 3D asset and imported it into Maxon Cinema4D to reduce its polygon count and create a stylized low-poly look.

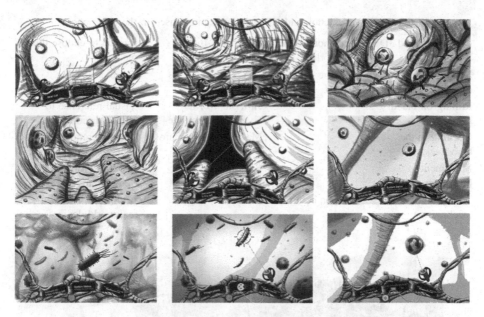

**Fig. 2.** Storyboard illustrating a neutrophil transmigrating from a blood vessel into body tissues.

## 3.6   3D Interaction and UI Design

3D interactions are a key component of our VR experience design. To create a smooth and intuitive 3D interaction experience in VR that helps facilitate the learning process, we adopted design strategies based on findings from previous studies on 3D interaction design. LaViola et al. (2017) suggest several strategies for designing and developing 3D interactions:

1. Borrowing from the real world. This strategy simulates and adapts interactions from the real world. Its major advantage is that users are already familiar with real-world interactions, reducing learning time.
2. Adapting from 2D user interfaces. This design strategy is based on the fact that most users are quite familiar with 2D UIs in their life through interactions with smartphones and computers. In addition, 2D UIs are much easier to use than 3D UIs for some 3D interaction tasks.
3. Magic and aesthetics. This strategy utilizes magic interaction techniques that overcome many human limitations in the real world and enhance users' capabilities to interact with virtual objects in the VE.

We developed our 3D UIs with references to real-world metaphors and magic interactions from popular culture such as adventure and sci-fi movies. We describe some design examples in Table 1.

**Table 1.** 3D interaction and UI design metaphors used in the experience

| Interactions and 3D UIs | Metaphors from real world | Metaphors from popular culture | Reason to choose the metaphor |
|---|---|---|---|
| Neutrophil control center | Airplane cockpit | | Familiarity with dashboards |
| Rolling on blood vessel surface | | *Jurassic World* Gyrosphere vehicle | Visual reference to reduce discomfort |
| Opening in the blood vessel | | Magic portal in many sci-fi movies | Transmigration is like using a portal |
| Movement in the body tissues | | Spiderman web slinging movement | Popularity of Spiderman |
| Multiple killing mechanisms | Weapon control panel | | Button selections in real-world devices |

**Fig. 3.** A user playing the project prototype with an HTC Vive Pro VR system.

### 3.7   VR Implementation

The VR experience was designed and developed to be used with an HTC Vive Pro VR system, which includes a headset, two controllers, two lighthouse trackers, and a high-end desktop computer to run the application. We chose the Vive system due to its higher headset resolution for sharper graphics, easily available development tools, and better headset ergonomic design that allows users with glasses to use it comfortably. Although the Vive system provides room-scale tracking, we designed our virtual experience as a seated experience with slow virtual movement, which fits best into our design scenario of a user piloting a neutrophil and moving inside the human body. We developed the application in the Unity3D game engine, a game engine that is popular among VR/AR game developers because of its simple development pipeline and abundant online development resources. Figure 3 shows an image of system implementation with a user in the experience.

### 3.8 Design Iterations

An iterative design cycle was a major part of our VR experience design, which allowed us to continuously refine our user experience based on user test feedback. We share some examples of our iterative design practice in this section.

Our first example of iterative design was during the development of the story-based user scenario. We originally wrote the script to focus primarily on documentation and visualization of user interactions with the system, instead of telling a story involving the user. The scenario was also short of some key elements of a story, such as development of the conflicts and rising tensions that could help engage users. Having discovered the problem, we reworked the scenario with an addition of a virtual guide, Lexie, who talks to the user, gives instructions, and helps the story progress.

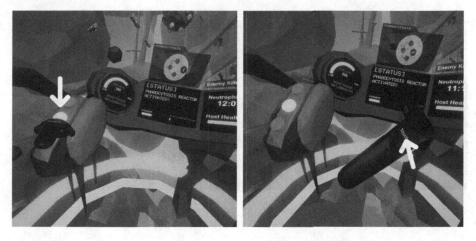

**Fig. 4.** Old and new weapon switching designs. (Left: using a virtual controller to touch virtual buttons. Right: pressing controller touchpad repeatedly to toggle among virtual buttons)

A second design iteration example relates to a usability design issue for the weapon switching mechanism. We originally used a button push metaphor in which users had to physically move their controllers in space to touch virtual buttons on the console. However, our user tests revealed that some users were confused about the relationship between virtual buttons and the physical buttons on the VR controller, because both were used in the experience. Our redesign of the weapon switching mechanism improved consistency by using the touchpad on the controller to toggle through the available weapons. Our user retest results showed that the new interaction design is more intuitive to the users and works much better than the original design. Figure 4 shows a comparison between the two designs.

## 4  User Feedback

We have demonstrated and tested our working prototype of the VR storytelling experience with nearly 90 people from diverse backgrounds, including secondary school students (Fig. 5), science and art exhibition visitors, teachers and students from Biological Sciences, and visiting scholars of the University. Overall, we received very positive feedback from people who tried the experience. Many users felt that the experience was "fun," "interesting," "engaging," "interactive," and "helpful for learning immunology concepts." Nearly one-fourth of the users mentioned (without prompting) that the experience made them "more focused" than they were in the classroom. Many users said that the visualization of a microscopic world inside the human body in the experience "connected the concept with visual representations" and "helped with learning." Some users also mentioned that the experience provided them with a "hands-on practice of immunology concepts through learning by doing" and worked better than lab exercises. Finally, several users indicated that the experience could serve as a good "add-on or supplement for classroom learning."

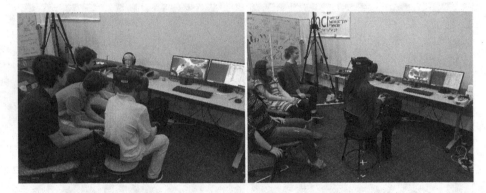

**Fig. 5.** Middle schoolers playing the Immunology VR experience.

## 5  Conclusions and Future Work

Motivated by existing instructional design tools and media in science education and emerging practices in VR storytelling, we proposed interactive VR storytelling as a novel instructional medium for immunology learning and have designed a working prototype of it. We explored a human-centered design process and discovered some design strategies that worked well in our design workflow. Our major takeaways from this interdisciplinary VR experience design practice can be summarized here:

- Communication is key
  It is very important to get to know the needs of the target audience thoroughly and create a VR experience specifically tailored to them. To achieve that, in our case, we communicated with our collaborators in Biological Sciences as often as possible in order to get the learning problems identified and learning goals correctly defined.

We also frequently invited expert advisors from other fields to try the experience and give us feedback. Without effective communication between each party in the design team, we could not make things right in our designs.

- Iterative design pays off
  We have gone through several iterations during our design process, with changes made in storyline, learning concepts and gameplay mechanism integration, and 3D UI usability. The result is a more smooth, engaging, and simple learning experience in VR. The time spent on those refinements and redesigns paid off.
- Co-design with learning concept providers is critical
  Since the developers on our team are not experts in immunology, we had to meet our collaborators in Biological Sciences frequently in order to make sure we visualized the concepts correctly. When in doubt, we provided them with several design solutions and asked for their preferences. With those practices, we were able to make sure that the learning messages conveyed from our VR experience truly respect the original concepts.

This working prototype of immunology VR storytelling will serve as a testbed for evaluating the validity of several research hypotheses in the future. Specifically, we hypothesize that the level of interactivity in a VR experience affects students' learning outcomes and are planning a study comparing three levels of interactivity. We are also interested in how different storytelling designs affect the students' learning experiences and will continue to develop different versions of Immunology VR for comparison.

# References

Bailenson, J., Patel, K., Nielsen, A., Bajscy, R., Jung, S.-H., Kurillo, G.: The effect of interactivity on learning physical actions in virtual reality. Media Psychol. 11(3), 354–376 (2008)

Banister, F., Ryan, C.: Developing science concepts through storytelling. Sch. Sci. Rev. 83(302), 75–83 (2001)

Barker, P.: Designing interactive learning. In: de Jong, T., Sarti, L. (eds.) Design and Production of Multimedia and Simulation-Based Learning Material, pp. 1–30. Kluwer Academic, Dordrecht (1994)

Bucher, J.: Storytelling for Virtual Reality, 1st edn. Routledge, Abingdon (2017)

Chen, C.J.: Theoretical bases for using virtual reality in education. Themes Sci. Technol. Educ. 29, 71–90 (2009). Special issue. Klidarithmos Computer Books

Cheng, M.-T., Su, T.F., Huang, W.-Y., Chen, J.-H.: An educational game for learning human immunology: what do students learn and how do they perceive? Br. J. Educ. Technol. 45(5), 820 (2014)

Clarke, J., Dede, C., Ketelhut, D.J., Nelson, B.: A design-based research strategy to promote scalability for educational innovations. Educ. Technol. 46, 27–36 (2006)

Clough, M.P.: The story behind the science: bringing science and scientists to life in post-secondary science education. Sci. Educ. 20, 701–717 (2010)

Da Rosa, A.C.M., Osowski, L.F., Tocchetto, A.G., Niederauer, C.E., Andrade, C.M.B., Scroferneker, M.L.: An alternative teaching method for the regulation of the immune response. J. Furth. High. Educ. 27, 105–109 (2003)

Domagk, S., Schwartz, R.N., Plass, J.L.: Interactivity in multimedia learning: an integrated model. Comput. Hum. Behav. **26**, 1024–1033 (2010)

Dooley, K.: Storytelling with virtual reality in 360-degrees: a new screen grammar. Stud. Aust. Cine. **11**(3), 161–171 (2017)

Dede, C., Salzman, M.C., Loftin, R.B.: ScienceSpace: virtual realities for learning complex and abstract scientific concepts. In: Proceedings of IEEE VRAIS 1996, Santa Clara, CA, USA, 30 March–3 April 1996, p. 246 (1996)

Dede, C., Salzman, M.C., Loftin, R.B., Ash, K.: Using virtual reality technology to convey abstract scientific concepts. In: Learning the Sciences of the 21st Century: Research, Design, and Implementing Advanced Technology Learning Environments. Lawrence Erlbaum, London (1997)

Elliott, S.L.: Efficacy of role play in concert with lecture to enhance student learning of immunology. J. Microbiol. Biol. Educ. **11**(2), 113–118 (2010)

Evans, C., Gibbons, J.N.: The interactivity effect in multimedia learning. Comput. Educ. **49**(4), 1147–1160 (2007)

Freeman, S., et al.: Active learning increases student performance in science, engineering, and mathematics. Proc. Natl. Acad. Sci. **111**(23), 8410–8415 (2014)

Helstrand, A., Ott, A.: The utilization of fiction when teaching the theory of relativity. Phys. Educ. **30**(5), 284–286 (1995)

Jerald, J.: The VR Book: Human-Centered Design for Virtual Reality, p. 2016. Association for Computing Machinery and Morgan and Claypool, New York (2016)

Kaufmann, H., Schmalstieg, D., Wagner, M.: Construct3D: a virtual reality application for mathematics and geometry education. Education and Information Technologies **5**(4), 263–276 (2000)

Khalifa, M., Lam, R.: Web-based learning: effects on learning process and outcome. IEEE Trans. Educ. **45**(4), 350–356 (2002)

LaViola Jr., J.J., Kruijff, E., McMahan, R., Bowman, D.A., Poupyrev, I.: 3D User Interfaces: Theory and Practice, 2nd edn. Addison-Wesley Professional, Redwood City (2017)

Mateer, J.: Directing for cinematic virtual reality: how the traditional film director's craft applies to immersive environments and notions of presence. J. Media Pract. **18**(1), 14–25 (2017). Practice Symposium

Merchant, Z., Goetz, E.T., Cifuentes, L., Keeney-Kennicutt, W., Davis, T.J.: Effectiveness of virtual reality-based instruction on students' learning outcomes in K-12 and higher education: a meta-analysis. Comput. Educ. **70**, 29–40 (2014)

Mikropoulos, T.A., Natsis, A.: Educational virtual environments: a ten-year review of empirical research (1999–2009). Comput. Educ. **56**, 769–780 (2011)

Pares, N., Pares, R.: Interaction-driven virtual reality application design (a particular case: El ball del fanalet or lightpools). PRESENCE: Teleoperators Virtual Environ. **10**(2), 236–245 (2001)

Pausch, R., Snoddy, J., Taylor, R., Watson, S., Haseltine, E.: Disney's Aladdin: first steps toward storytelling in virtual reality. In: Proceeding SIGGRAPH 1996, pp. 193–203 (1996)

Rhodes, D.M., Azbell, J.W.: Designing interactive video instruction professionally. Train. Dev. J. **39**(12), 31–33 (1985)

Roussou, M.: Learning by doing and learning through play: an exploration of interactivity in virtual environments for children. ACM Comput. Entertain. **2**(1), Article no. 1 (2004)

Roussou, M.: Can interactivity in virtual environments enable conceptual learning? In: Proceedings of the 7th Virtual Reality International Conference (VRIC), First International VR-Learning Seminar, Laval, France, pp. 57–64 (2005)

Roussou, M., Oliver, M., Slater, M.: The virtual playground: an educational virtual reality environment for evaluating interactivity and conceptual learning. Virtual Reality **10**, 227–240 (2006)

Raimondi, S.L.: ImmuneQuest: assessment of a video game as a supplement to an undergraduate immunology course. J. Microbiol. Biol. Educ. **17**, 237–245 (2016)

Robin, B.: Digital storytelling: a powerful technology tool for the 21st-century classroom. Theory Pract. **47**(3), 220–228 (2008)

Schaffer, L.C., Hannafin, M.J.: The effects of progressive interactivity on learning from interactive video. Educ. Commun. Technol. J. **34**(2), 89–96 (1986)

Sims, R.: Interactivity: a forgotten art? Comput. Hum. Behav. **13**(2), 157–180 (1997)

Sjøberg, S.: Constructivism and learning. In: International Encyclopaedia of Education, 3rd edn. Elsevier, Oxford (2007)

Slater, M., Sanchez-Vives, M.V.: Enhancing our lives with immersive virtual reality. Front. Robot. AI **3**, 2016 (2016)

Steuer, J.: Defining virtual reality: dimensions determining telepresence. J. Commun. **42**(4), 73–93 (1992)

Su, T.F., Cheng, M.-T., Lin, S.-H.: Investigating the effectiveness of an educational card game for learning how human immunology is regulated. CBE-Life Sci. Educ. **13**, 504–515 (2014). Fall 2014

# VAMR in Aviation, Industry and the Military

# Augmented Reality for Product Validation: Supporting the Configuration of AR-Based Validation Environments

Albert Albers, Jonas Reinemann[✉], Joshua Fahl,
and Tobias Hirschter

IPEK – Institute of Product Engineering,
Karlsruhe Institute of Technology (KIT), Karlsruhe, Germany
jonas.reinemann@kit.edu

**Abstract.** Organizations are increasingly recognizing the importance of early and continuous validation activities as a means of addressing customer requirements in product development in a better way. At the same time, early validation activities come with additional challenges resulting from a high degree of uncertainty and a lack of resources at this stage. The use of Augmented Reality technology offers a promising approach for addressing these challenges and allows different product variants to be experienced early in the development process, thus generating meaningful customer feedback. However, in many cases, the use of AR technology in product development practice is not target-oriented as it lacks methodological support. Building on this observation, this paper presents a method for supporting the configuration of AR-based validation environments as one of the central preparatory activities for product validation using AR technology. It also introduces a descriptive model for AR-based validation environments laying the theoretical foundations for the method.

**Keywords:** Augmented Reality · Product validation ·
Early development stage · Customer centricity

## 1 Introduction

In the face of increasing global competition and constantly shortening development cycles, the companies' ability to react more precisely and quickly to customer requirements is becoming more and more critical to success. With this in mind, new forms of direct customer integration in product development processes are being developed. With these processes, customer requirements are taken into account through continuous, accompanying validation activities [1, 2].

A prerequisite for generating meaningful customer feedback during validation is the availability of representations of the future product [3, 4]. Physical prototypes, which could be considered for this, can usually only be realized later in the development process or are associated with high financial and time expenditure. Instead, Virtual Reality and Augmented Reality applications (VR and AR) allow an early integration of the customers into the development process, enabling them to experience different variants of a product at an early stage [5, 6].

© Springer Nature Switzerland AG 2019
J. Y. C. Chen and G. Fragomeni (Eds.): HCII 2019, LNCS 11575, pp. 429–448, 2019.
https://doi.org/10.1007/978-3-030-21565-1_29

AR technology offers particular potential here, as it makes it possible to combine existing physical reference products with virtual projections. The use of AR-based prototypes is therefore not limited to the validation of visual product features. AR-based prototypes can also represent product features whose exploration requires physical interaction by the user. Thus, the use of AR technology in the context of product validation offers a good compromise between the use of resources and a realistic product experience in the early development phase in many applications [5, 6].

This paper presents a method for supporting the configuration of AR-based validation environments as one of the central preparatory activities for product validation using AR technology. It also introduces a descriptive model for AR-based validation environments laying out the theoretical foundations for the method.

## 2   Background

### 2.1   The System Triple of Product Engineering

According to Ropohl's theory of system engineering, an initially vague system of objectives is transformed into a system of objects by means of an operation system in the course of product development [7]. The system of objectives contains all relevant objectives for the product to be developed, as well as their interactions and boundary conditions.

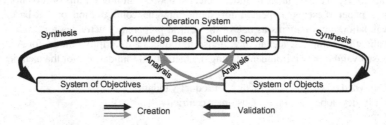

**Fig. 1.** Extended system triple of product engineering according to Albers et al. [8]

In order to emphasize the iterative character of product development and the central role of the developer, Albers et al. add the basic activities of analysis and synthesis to the model. At the same time, they further specify the operation system by introducing the knowledge base and the solution space (see Fig. 1). According to the model obtained in this way, product development can be described as a repetitive sequence of many creation and validation steps. Creation consists of the basic activities of target analysis and object synthesis, while validation can be understood as object analysis and subsequent target synthesis [8].

### 2.2   Customer Centric Product Development

A customer will only buy a product if its features and functions promise a perceived customer benefit that exceeds the customer's perceived costs [9]. For this reason, it is essential to consider the requirements of customers and users as early as possible during product development. This is particularly true given the increasingly competitive market environment in many industries, which is reflected in more and more differentiated market segments and products that are becoming increasingly customized [10].

Developing successful products in such a demanding competitive environment is a complex decision making process [11]. On the one hand, companies must anticipate customer and user benefits in the system of objectives early on [12]. On the other hand, it is essential to also reflect the provider's benefits in the system of objectives, not least in order to ensure profitability of an innovation project. This understanding is reflected in the definition of innovation, laid out by Albers et al. in reference to Schumpeter. According to this definition, a product can only be regarded an innovation if it has been successfully introduced to the market [13, 14].

In practice, there are many methods and technologies aiming to support product developers in various different ways in identifying, understanding and considering customer and user requirements in the product development process (e.g., Quality Function Deployment, Conjoint Analysis, Lean Management, Design Thinking, Eye Tracking) [15]. Due to the leverage effect of early development phases, considering customer and user requirements when defining the initial system of objectives is of particular importance. To support the definition of the initial system of objectives while taking into account customer, user and provider requirements, Albers et al. introduce the so-called product profile. Being a solution-open product model, the product profile does not anticipate the technical realization of a product, but rather provides a solution-open description of the set of customer, user and provider benefits to be addressed by a product. The product profile serves as a starting point for the development of a product and ensures early and subsequent development activities to be consistently aligned towards future product success. At the same time, the product profile serves as a basis for early and continuous validation activities aiming at securing the intended customer, user and provider benefits [12, 16].

## 2.3   Validation of Technical Systems

According to Albers, validation is the central knowledge-generating activity in the product development process. Through validation, new knowledge is generated which is used to detail, expand or, if necessary, reduce the system of objectives. During the validation, the system of objects (represented by prototypes demonstrating selected aspects of the future product) as well as the system of objectives are compared and aligned with the requirements of various stakeholders. Validation goes thus beyond verification, which only covers the comparison of the system of objects with the system of objectives. Validation consequently attempts to find an answer to the question "Are we doing the right thing?", while verification is guided by the question "Are we doing it right?". The integration of stakeholder views, in particular of customers and users, therefore plays a key role in product validation [8].

There is a variety of approaches for integrating validation activities into the product development process (see e.g., [17]). Due to their leverage effect, many of them emphasize the importance of early validation activities [18]. This goes back to the so-called "Rule of Ten", according to which the costs for eliminating conceptual errors increase tenfold with each phase in the advancing product development process [19].

In many process models, validation is regarded as a self-contained phase (see e.g., [17]). As agile product development processes are becoming increasingly popular, however, the need for continuous, accompanying validation activities is being stressed more and more frequently [20]. In the agile *Scrum* framework for example, which originates from software development and is successively being used in mechatronic system development, the role of the validation engineer does not exist anymore, since every member of the development team must take on the role of a tester and ensure the validity of his development results [21]. The creative problem-solving technique *Design Thinking* also provides a repetitive test phase after prototype construction [22]. Another agile development approach, *ASD - Agile Systems Design*, is based explicitly on the principle of early and continuous validation [23].

With the IPEK-X-in-the-Loop-Approach (IPEK-XiL-Approach), Albers et al. present a continuous validation concept that operationalizes this principle and makes it usable for mechatronic development [8]. In the underlying modelling approach, the sum of all developed systems, methods and processes for the validation of a system is called a validation system. The selection of the elements of the validation system that enable the achievement of one or more specific validation objectives in one or more specific test cases constitutes a validation environment. Validation environments in turn have at least one validation configuration, a specific combination of methods, test cases, resources and parameterizations (e.g., degree of virtualization), which is derived from the validation environment [24].

A mandatory element of every validation configuration is the developed system itself (System-in-Development), which can be available in physical, virtual or mixed physical-virtual form and on different system levels (from the complete system to a single working surface pair). For the validation, the system to be investigated is integrated into the overall system, the environment and, if necessary, other interacting sub-systems (Connected Systems), which can also be physically, virtually or mixed physically-virtually. Sub-systems not capable of establishing a direct connection are connected via Koppelfunctions (Coupling Functions) which are implemented via Koppelsystems (Coupling Systems). These usually consist of pairs of sensors and actuators [24–26].

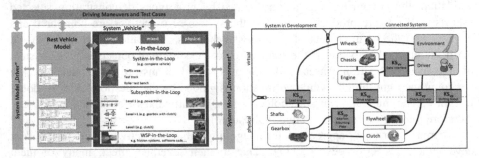

**Fig. 2.** Left: IPEK-XiL-Framework, right: model of the IPEK-XiL-Architecture using the example of the validation of a powertrain [8, 24]

With the IPEK-XiL-Framework and the Model of the IPEK-XiL-Architecture (see Fig. 2), the IPEK-XiL-Approach provides suitable descriptive models for generic validation environments (IPEK-XiL-Framework) and validation configurations (IPEK-XiL-Architecture) [24].

## 2.4  Augmented Reality (AR)

Milgram et al. describe the concept of Augmented Reality in distinction to other forms of visualization and perception along the so-called Reality-Virtuality Continuum as a mixed form between the real environment and the completely virtual environment (Virtual Reality) [27]. According to Burdea and Coiffet, a virtual environment is characterized by the three qualities of immersion, interaction and imagination [28]. Immersion plays a special role. It describes the integration of the user into the virtual environment. Once the virtual environment reaches a high degree of immersion, the user is in extreme cases no longer able to distinguish between the real and the virtual environment. However, the degree of immersion depends in particular on the ability of the virtual environment to stimulate different sensorial modalities (in particular visual, auditive, haptic) [29]. Through the possibility of combining virtual and real elements, AR environments tend to achieve higher levels of immersion than a purely virtual environment. This can be attributed, among other things, to the haptic sensory stimuli emanating from the real elements in the AR environment [30].

Generally speaking, AR environments are realized by means of an AR system. According to Azuma, AR systems on the functional level can be described by the combination of reality and virtuality, real-time interaction and 3D position detection [31]. These three functions can be mapped to the different technical sub-systems of an AR system. These sub-systems include a tracking system, a scene generator, a display system and a database system [31, 32]. For modern AR systems, all these sub-systems are combined in one device, the so-called AR interface. Damgrave distinguishes between window-bound (e.g., via a tablet or smartphone screen), immersive (via a head-mounted display) and spatial (via projections) AR interfaces [33].

Although the first research work on Augmented Reality dates back to the early 1980s, it is only the availability of increasingly powerful and more compact hardware components at reasonable prices in recent years that has initiated the further spread of the technology. A study by the technology company PTC estimates the global market for AR applications in 2018 at $7 billion ($1.3 billion in 2016). The study forecasts a growth up to 63 billion dollars by 2021 [34]. The Gartner Hype Cycle for Emerging Technologies 2018 sees AR technology almost passing the Trough of Disillusionment approaching the Slope of Enlightenment. In contrast, VR technology is for the first time not listed in the 2018 issue of the Hype Cycles, being now classified as a mature technology [35, 36].

The commercial development of AR interfaces for a broader market (e.g., the Microsoft® HoloLens™) has enabled the productive and widespread use of Augmented Reality in recent years. As a result, companies from various industries are now beginning to make use of AR technology in their business processes [35]. In practice, there are various applications of AR technology in the fields of architecture, industry, military, medicine, entertainment and leisure [5]. Some first applications in the context of product development in general and product validation in particular are also described, for example by Katicic, Schilling or Bordegoni et al. [5, 29, 37]. The use of Augmented Reality technology offers a promising approach for addressing the specific challenges associated with early validation activities, allowing different product variants to be experienced early in the development process and thus consequently generating meaningful customer feedback.

**Fig. 3.** Reference process model for early product validation in AR-based validation environments [38]

With the increasing spread of AR technology in product development and validation processes, there is a growing need for methodical support for product developers. In order to address this need, the authors of this paper have published a reference process model that describes the approach to early product validation in AR-based validation environments in five steps (see Fig. 3). The process model serves as a framework for the methodological support developed in this paper for the configuration of AR-based validation environments (step 2 in the process model) [38].

## 3 Motivation

The potential of AR technology for the use in early validation activities has been recognized in recent years both in practice and in science. First applications of AR technology in the context of product development in general and product validation in particular are described by Katicic, Schilling or Bordegoni et al. for example [5, 29, 37].

Due to the accelerated technological development of AR interfaces in recent years, they are known to an increasing number of developers and are available in more and more companies. In a customer survey conducted by software manufacturer PTC in 2017 with 107 participants, manufacturing companies for industrial products and companies in the automotive industry were among the ones with the highest average usage rate of AR-based solutions with 21% and 11%, respectively [34]. A survey with 66 participants conducted in the course of this research project among German industrial companies from the automotive and supplier industries also confirms the increasing spread of AR technology in industrial practice. The survey showed that 88% of the respondents indicated that they were familiar with AR technology while 55% said that AR technology is used in their company (see Fig. 4).

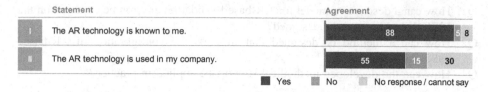

**Fig. 4.** Selected results of the questionnaire study on challenges associated with the use of AR technology in practice (n = 66)

However, the same survey also shows that the use of AR technology for product validation in practice is in many cases not target-oriented. 77% of the respondents fully or rather agree with this statement (see Fig. 5).

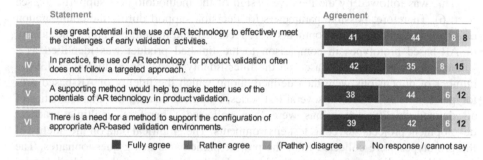

**Fig. 5.** Selected results of the questionnaire study on challenges associated with the use of AR technology in practice (n = 66)

One of the central preparatory activities for product validation using AR technology is the configuration of the AR-based validation environment [38]. During the configuration, the degree of virtualization is determined for each sub-system, i.e. the decision is made as to which product characteristics are to be mapped physically and which ones virtually in the AR environment. Given the lack of experience with the AR technology, product developers are often overwhelmed with this decision. 81% of the respondents therefore fully or rather agree to the need for a method to support the configuration of AR-based validation environments (see Fig. 5). Within the scope of this research project, a method was developed that supports decision-making in the configuration of AR-based validation environments.

## 4  Research Approach

Three research questions were defined as a basis for the development of the methodological support for the configuration of AR-based validation environments:

Q1. How can a descriptive model for AR-based validation environments based on the IPEK-XiL-Approach be designed?

Q2. How can a method be designed that supports the configuration of AR-based validation environments?

Q3. How can the developed methodical support be applied in practice?

The development of a methodical support for the configuration of AR-based validation environments requires the availability of a uniform approach for their description and specification. For this purpose, a descriptive model is needed. In Sect. 2.3, existing descriptive models for generic validation environments and configurations were presented in the form of the IPEK-XiL-Framework and the IPEK-XiL-Architecture. In the course of this research project, both were used to describe AR-based validation environments and configurations. To do this, they were first adapted to the requirements of an AR-specific use case (Q1, see Sect. 5).

This was followed by the iterative design of the methodological support (Q2, see Sect. 6). Therefore, possible parameters for decision support during the configuration of AR-based validation environments were recorded in a literature search. The fidelity of AR-based prototypes in comparison to the finished product was identified as a suitable decision criterion. Based on the filter fidelity model by Kohler et al. [39], a number of dimensions were then defined, along which the fidelity of AR-based prototypes can be evaluated. In several test series, empirical data on the characteristics of all defined fidelity dimensions were then collected. Therefore, multiple practical development projects served as test environments. The empirical data on the fidelity of the prototypes were collected from the project participants using questionnaires. The data collected then served as the basis for the development of the methodological support.

Finally, the developed support was evaluated in a first case study (Q3, see Sect. 7). A so-called Live-Lab served as the evaluation environment in which student teams worked on a real development task over a period of several months in cooperation with an industrial company.

## 5 Describing AR-Based Validation Environments

The IPEK-XiL-Approach according to Albers et al. provides descriptive models for generic validation environments and configurations in the form of the IPEK-XiL-Framework and the IPEK-XiL-Architecture (see Sect. 2.3). These were used in this work to describe AR-based validation environments and configurations. In order to meet the requirements of the special use case, a selective concretization of the generic descriptive models of the IPEK-XiL-Approach was necessary. The scope of the specific descriptive model for AR-based validation environments and configurations resulting from this concretization represents a subsection of the scope of the original, generic descriptive models of the IPEK-XiL-Approach (see Fig. 6).

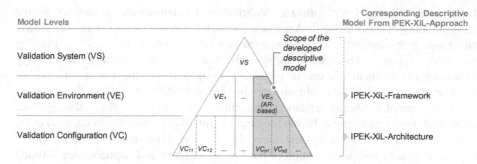

**Fig. 6.** Targeted model levels and scope of the specific descriptive model for AR-based validation environments and configurations

To adapt the generic descriptive models of the IPEK-XiL-Approach to the requirements of AR-specific validation environments, there were made concretizations in three areas. These concern the integration of the user into the validation environment, the modeling of AR interfaces as part of the validation environment as well as the modeling of mixed physical-virtual sub-systems. Table 1 provides an overview of the concretizations of the generic descriptive models of the IPEK-XiL-Approach for the specific use case of AR-based validation environments.

**Table 1.** Overview of AR-specific concretizations of the generic descriptive models of the IPEK-XiL-Approach

| | IPEK-XiL-Approach [8, 24–26] | AR-specific concretizations |
|---|---|---|
| Integration of the user into the validation environment | Users can be physically integrated or represented by virtual real-time simulation models | The real user must be physically integrated |
| Modeling AR interfaces | Sub-systems not capable of establishing a direct connection are connected via Koppelfunctions (Coupling Functions) which are implemented via Koppelsystems (Coupling Systems) | An AR interface provides the Koppelfunction of connecting all virtual and physical sub-systems of the validation environment. The AR interface is modeled as a Koppelsystem |
| Modeling of mixed physical-virtual sub-systems | Individual sub-systems can be part of either the physical or the virtual domain of the validation environment. The validation configuration makes a clear assignment | AR technology enables individual sub-systems to exist as mixed physical-virtual systems in two domains simultaneously. There is a functional relationship via the AR interface between them. The affiliation of the physical and virtual instances of one and the same sub-system is indicated by a special symbol in the descriptive model |

**Integration of the User into the Validation Environment.** According to the understanding of the IPEK-XiL-Approach, the validation of a sub-system will always take place in the context of its super-system as well as the connected systems [8]. The user also belongs to those interacting systems. The user is a mandatory part of every validation environment. He can be physically integrated into the validation environment or represented by a virtual real-time simulation model that replaces the real user.

In the case of AR-based validation environments, however, the physical integration of the real user is mandatory. This is because AR interfaces available on the market are designed for the operation by real users. In addition, there are no suitable virtual substitute models for the evaluation of the visual, auditory and haptic sensory stimuli addressed in the AR environment.

**Modeling AR Interfaces.** AR interfaces such as AR glasses or tablets play a central role in AR-based validation environments. Following the terminology of the IPEK-XiL-Approach, their function can be described as a so-called Koppelfunction, which is implemented by a Koppelsystem, namely the AR interface. AR-based validation environments therefore have at least one Koppelsystem. Its Koppelfunction serves for connecting all virtual and physical sub-systems of the validation environment (i.e. the System-in-Development, the user and all other connected systems). An example for this is the overlay of a physical prototype with a virtual texture realized by using AR glasses.

The modeling of AR interfaces as Koppelsystems is, in accordance with the definition given in the IPEK-XiL-Approach, only allowed if they have no influence on the system behavior [24, 25]. For AR interfaces, this is a simplified assumption. In reality, existing technical deficits of AR interfaces available on the market lead to the fact that such an influence cannot be ruled out. The user's perception of the AR environment is to a certain extent influenced not only by the surrounding physical and virtual sub-systems but also by the characteristics of the AR interface as a Koppelsystem. These perception-influencing properties of AR interfaces include wearing comfort, render quality of the virtual content, color effect and opacity of the screen technology used, or the accuracy of the Simultaneous Localization and Mapping (SLAM) method used [40]. With the progressive development of AR technology, however, an increasingly smaller influence of the AR interface on the system behavior is to be expected. With this in mind, the modeling of the AR interface as a Koppelsystem in the sense of the IPEK-XiL-Approach appears to be justified.

**Modeling of Mixed Physical-Virtual Sub-systems.** The use of AR interfaces in AR-based validation environments makes it possible to display individual sub-systems of the validation environment not either physically or virtually but rather mixed physically-virtually. In the example of a physical prototype overlaid with a virtual texture, for example, the surface roughness is physically represented, while the color effect of the same sub-system is represented virtually. In the IPEK-XiL-Architecture, the descriptive model of the IPEK-XiL-Approach for validation configurations, individual sub-systems can be either part of the physical or virtual domain of the validation environment [8, 24]. The validation configuration therefore makes a clear assignment. In the concretized descriptive model for configurations of AR-based validation environments, this restriction is lifted. This means that instances of the same sub-system can exist simultaneously in the physical and virtual domain of the validation environment. There is a functional relationship via the AR interface between them. The affiliation of the physical and virtual instances of one and the same sub-system to each other is marked by a special symbol in the concretized descriptive model.

In the concretized descriptive model, analogous to the IPEK-XiL-Approach, the description and set-up of an AR-based validation environment and its configuration follow a top-down approach, which is based on the three relevant super-systems User, Product and Environment. While Product and Environment can be physical, virtual or mixed physical-virtual, the real user is always physically integrated into the AR-based validation environment. A distinction is made between the System-in-Development and the Residual Product System as sub-systems of the Product System. The selection of sub-systems included in an AR-based validation environment serves to fulfill one or more specific validation objectives in one or more specific test cases. Figure 7 shows the selected modeling approach for the description of AR-based validation environments based on the IPEK-XiL-Framework [8, 24, 41].

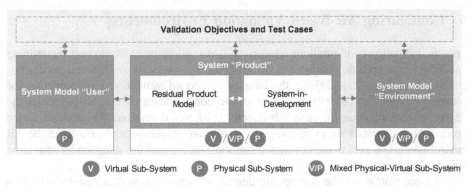

**Fig. 7.** Concretized description model for AR-based validation environments based on the IPEK-XiL-Framework

The sub-systems of a validation environment can be further subdivided into Systems-in-Development and Connected Systems. Between the sub-systems of a validation environment there are (mutual) functional relationships. The functional and structural elements of a validation environment provide the basis for the modelling approach used to describe the configuration of AR-based validation environments based on the model of the IPEK-XiL-Architecture (see Fig. 8). [8, 24]

The descriptive model also indicates the selected representation domain (physical vs. virtual) for each of the sub-systems by classifying them into one of the four quadrants. As described above, instances of mixed physical-virtual sub-systems exist simultaneously in the physical and virtual domains of the validation environment. There is a functional relationship via the AR interface between them. The affiliation of the physical and virtual instances of one and the same sub-system to each other is marked by a special symbol.

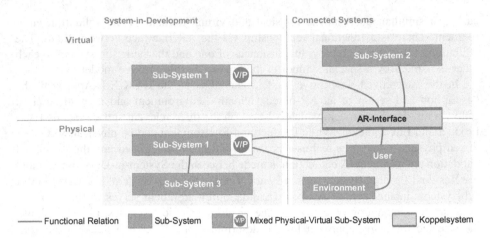

**Fig. 8.** Concretized descriptive model for the configuration of AR-based validation environments based on the model of IPEK-XiL-Architecture

# 6 Configuring AR-Based Validation Environments

Specific validation configurations are derived from validation environments by defining and selecting a specific combination of methods, test cases, resources and parameterizations (see Sect. 2.3) [24]. In the case of AR-based validation environments, the parameterizations to be defined as part of the configuration include in particular the degree of virtualization for each sub-system. With this definition, it is decided which product characteristics are to be mapped virtually and which ones physically in the AR environment. The goal of the developed method is to support this decision by providing suitable decision criteria.

The decision about the appropriate degree of virtualization of a sub-system in an AR-based validation environment is a trade-off decision that is influenced by various parameters. These parameters include the implications of the selected degree of virtualization for the effort involved in setting up the AR-based validation environment. In addition, it must be considered whether the desired validation results can be achieved in the desired quality using the respective degree of virtualization [38].

The so-called fidelity is proposed in literature as a criterion for deciding on the suitability of a given prototype for a particular validation task. Such approaches can be found in Rudd et al. or McCurdy et al. for example [42, 43]. The term fidelity refers to the similarity of a prototype to the finished product. High-fidelity prototypes, whose fidelity is very close to the finished product, can be distinguished from low-fidelity prototypes whose fidelity is far from the finished product. McCurdy et al. emphasize that a prototype cannot usually be described by a single fidelity value; instead, its fidelity can be higher in some aspects and lower in others. They refer to this phenomenon as Mixed Fidelity [43]. Following McCurdy et al., Lim et al. develop a list of different fidelity dimensions of prototypes [44]. This list is used by Kohler et al. to develop the so-called filter fidelity profile [39].

In the course of this research project, the fidelity dimensions from Lim et al. and Kohler et al. were picked up and complemented by selected dimensions in order to meet the special requirements of AR-based prototypes. The 22 fidelity dimensions compiled in this way can be divided into five dimensions: Appearance (visual), Appearance (non-visual), Functionality, Interactivity and Meta-Functionality. They can be used to evaluate the fidelity of virtual features of AR-based validation environments. To allow further differentiation, the developed method does not assess fidelity at the level of sub-systems but rather at the level of individual product characteristics of sub-systems.

To support the decision of determining the degree of virtualization based on fidelity, it should not be evaluated in absolute terms but in relation to the requirements posed to it, which in turn depend on the respective validation objective. The method developed therefore consists of two steps: the definition of the fidelity requirements and the determination of the degree of virtualization by means of comparing the Requirement and Reference Profiles. In the course of the requirement definition, the requirements for the product characteristics to be considered are first evaluated along all defined fidelity dimensions on a scale of 0–5 (see Fig. 9). A value of 0 indicates that the particular fidelity dimension is not relevant for the respective characteristic.

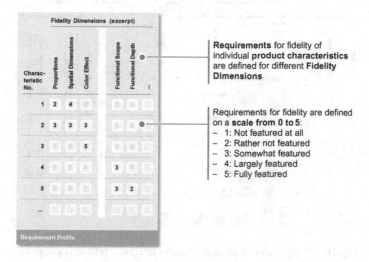

**Fig. 9.** Approach for defining the fidelity requirements for individual characteristics

Following the requirements definition, the Requirements and Reference Profiles are compared to each other. In order to create the Reference Profile, empirical data on the extent of fidelity along all dimensions was collected in a series of test studies. For this, a development project at a German automobile manufacturer served as a test environment. In the course of the development project, regular validation activities took place at intervals of four weeks and over a period of five months during which AR-based prototypes were used which were experienced using Microsoft® HoloLens™.

At the same time, additional empirical data was obtained from test studies with students in which the fidelity of various representative AR-based prototypes was evaluated which could be experienced using a tablet (Samsung® Galaxy™ Tab S4). The AR environment was developed using the Unity runtime and development platform or, in some cases, the PTC® Vuforia™ Studio software. In all cases, the empirical data was collected from the test persons using questionnaires.

The data from the reference profile express in what percentage of all documented cases from the conducted test series a certain level of fidelity was achieved in a fidelity dimension. By comparing the Requirement and Reference Profiles for each product characteristic under consideration, the scope of virtual display can be defined.

This is done by using a decision heuristic, stating that only those product characteristics are to be displayed virtually in the AR environment whose specified fidelity requirements have been met in more than 70% of all documented cases. This value marks the boundary of the upper two quartiles of the sample collected in the course of the research project. Figure 10 shows an example of the approach used to determine the degree of virtualization of individual product characteristics by comparing Requirement and Reference Profiles.

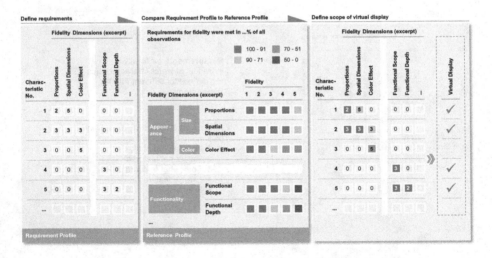

**Fig. 10.** Comparison of requirement and reference profile (exemplary)

From the mapping of the considered product characteristics to the sub-systems of the validation environment, the degree of virtualization can be determined at sub-system level. Mixed physical-virtual sub-systems are characterized by both virtual and physical product characteristics. The approach for aggregating product characteristics back to the level of individual sub-systems is shown in Fig. 11.

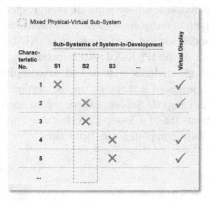

**Fig. 11.** Aggregation of product characteristics to the level of individual sub-systems

## 7   Evaluation

The developed methodological support was evaluated in a case study. For this, a so-called Live-Lab was used as the application environment. According to Albers et al. Live-Labs are "validation environments which enable a design researcher to investigate design processes, methods and tools under realistic conditions and with a high controllability of the boundary conditions at the same time" [45]. This way, Live-Labs offer a good trade-off between traditional laboratory studies and field tests.

In this case, the methodological support developed was applied in an innovation project carried out by a group of students in cooperation with an industrial partner at the IPEK – Institute of Product Engineering at the Karlsruhe Institute of Technology (KIT) in the period from October 2018 to February 2019. The industrial partner in the project was a diversified German industrial group with a focus on steel processing. The task of the students was to develop various product concepts in the field of mining equipment. A total of 41 Master students in mechanical engineering, distributed among 7 teams, took part in the project.

The developed methodological support was used in a workshop attended by all students. During the workshop, each team had a concept idea that was developed by the team itself and had previously been selected at a milestone by the industry partner. The aim of the workshop was to prepare an early validation study for the individual concept ideas in an AR-based validation environment with the participation of representatives of the industry partner. In preparation for the workshop, each team defined a validation objective in addition to concretizing the concept idea, which had originally been formulated in a solution-open way, with regard to the sub-systems and product characteristics, which should be considered in the validation environment.

The application of the developed method took place in each team individually with the help of templates that were made available. In accordance with the methodological approach developed, the students first defined the requirements for the fidelity of the product characteristics to be investigated for their respective concepts. By comparing the requirements with the provided Reference Profile, they then determined the degree of virtualization of the individual sub-systems of their respective validation environment. The resulting validation configuration was then modelled by each team using the developed descriptive model for the configuration of AR-based validation environments based on the Model of the IPEK-XiL-Architecture.

Following the workshop, students were asked to complete a questionnaire. The questionnaire contained a series of statements on the applicability and success of the methodological support developed. Students were asked to indicate their agreement with each of these statements using a 5-step Likert scale. The survey results shown in Fig. 12 are based on 33 fully completed questionnaires.

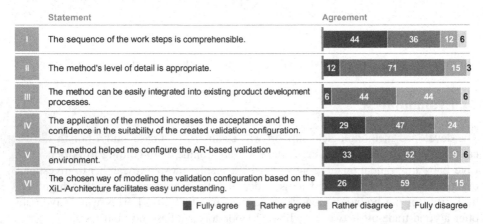

**Fig. 12.** Selected results of the survey for the evaluation of the developed methodological support (n = 33)

The evaluation results show a generally positive picture with regard to both the applicability (I–III) and the success contribution (IV–VI). For every statement examined, except for statement III, the share of students who fully or rather agree is at least 68%. Accordingly, a majority of the students surveyed rated the sequence of the work steps of the developed method as comprehensible (I) and its degree of detail as appropriate (II). The majority of students surveyed also agree with the statement that the developed method helped with the configuration of AR-based validation environments (V) and that the descriptive model used contributes to a better understanding of the modeled validation configuration (VI). Only half of the students surveyed agreed with the ease of integration into existing product development processes (III). This indicates that the formal requirements for the application of the method will have to be made more flexible in the future in order to enable application in different process contexts.

## 8   Summary and Future Work

Given the potential of AR technology for use in product validation and the growing spread of AR interfaces in industry, the need for supporting methods is increasing. This paper contributes to supporting product developers with product validation in

AR-based validation environments. Therefore, a descriptive model for AR-based validation environments and configurations based on the IPEK-XiL-Approach was derived. In addition, a method was presented that supports decision-making in the course of configuring AR-based validation environments.

The methodological support was applied and evaluated in a first case study in a Live-Lab at the IPEK – Institute of Product Engineering with 41 participants in a practical innovation project. The evaluation results generally confirm the applicability and the success contribution of the developed methodical support. Building on the knowledge gained, further research will be carried out. A starting point for further development of the methodological support is the flexibilization of the formal requirements for the application of the method in order to enable its application in various contexts. In addition, a tool support should be considered in the future. Especially in the modelling of the AR-based validation configuration, which was done paper-based in the application example, potentials for automation may be utilized.

The reference profile, which was compiled from empirical data, constitutes another area for further research. The empirical data represent the current state of the art for AR interfaces. In order to take into account future technical developments, further empirical data on the achievable fidelity of AR-based mixed physical-virtual prototypes must be collected at regular intervals. It is to be expected that the fidelity which can be achieved through a virtual representation of sub-systems will improve in the future as a result of technical advances in AR technology.

In addition to improving the method developed to support the configuration of AR-based validation environments, the development of methods to support other steps in the process of early product validation in AR-based development environments is also to be targeted in the future. In addition, it should be investigated how AR-based validation environments can be integrated with existing validation environments (e.g., test benches in engine and automotive development) in order to combine the potentials of both approaches. Finally, further evaluation runs beyond the initial application study will also have to be carried out.

# References

1. Ponn, J., Lindemann, U.: Konzeptentwicklung und Gestaltung technischer Produkte. Systematisch von Anforderungen zu Konzepten und Gestaltlösungen, 2nd edn. VDI-Buch. Springer, Heidelberg (2011). https://doi.org/10.1007/978-3-642-20580-4
2. Enkel, E., Perez-Freije, J., Gassmann, O.: Minimizing market risks through customer integration in new product development. Learning from bad practice. Creat. Innov. Manag. (2005). https://doi.org/10.1111/j.1467-8691.2005.00362.x
3. Stolper, M.: Market driving-Konzept. Diss., Universität Dortmund (2007)
4. Rix, J., Haas, S., Teixeira, J.: Virtual Prototyping. Springer, Boston (1995). https://doi.org/10.1007/978-0-387-34904-6
5. Schilling, T.: Augmented reality in der Produktentstehung. Diss., TU Ilmenau (2008)
6. Peddie, J.: Augmented Reality. Where We Will All Live. Springer, Cham (2017). https://doi.org/10.1007/978-3-319-54502-8
7. Ropohl, G.: Einleitung in die Systemtechnik. In: Ropohl, G. (ed.) Systemtechnik. Grundlagen und Anwendung, pp. 1–77. Hanser, München (1975)

8. Albers, A., Behrendt, M., Klingler, S., Matros, K.: Verifikation und Validierung im Produktentstehungsprozess. In: Lindemann, U. (ed.) Handbuch Produktentwicklung, pp. 541–569. Carl Hanser Verlag, München (2016)
9. Day, G.S.: Market Driven Strategy. Processes for Creating Value. Free Press, New York (1990)
10. Kumar, S., Phrommathed, P.: New Product Development. An Empirical Approach to Study of the Effects of Innovation Strategy, Organization Learning and Market Conditions, 1st edn. Springer, Heidelberg (2005). https://doi.org/10.1007/b101081
11. Albers, A., Lohmeyer, Q., Ebel, B.: Dimensions of objectives in interdisciplinary product development projects. In: Proceedings of the 18th International Conference on Engineering Design, Kopenhagen, 15–19 August 2011 (2011)
12. Albers, A., et al.: Product profiles. Modelling customer benefits as a foundation to bring inventions to innovations. In: Proceedings of 28th CIRP Design Conference, Nantes, 23–25 Mai 2018 (2018)
13. Schumpeter, J.A.: Business Cycles. A Theoretical, Historical, and Statistical Analysis of the Capitalist Process. McGraw-Hill, New York (1939)
14. Albers, A., et al.: Managing Systems of objectives in the agile development of mechatronic systems by ASD - agile systems design. In: Proceedings of NordDesign 2018, Linköping, 14–17 August 2018 (2018)
15. Matthiesen, S., Meboldt, M., Ruckpaul, A., Mussgnug, M.: Eye tracking, a method for engineering design research on engineers' behavior while analyzing technical systems. In: Proceedings of the 19th International Conference on Engineering Design, Seoul, 19–22 August 2013 (2013)
16. Albers, A., Heitger, N., Haug, F., Fahl, J., Hirschter, T., Bursac, N.: Supporting potential innovation in the early phase of PGE – product generation engineering. Structuring the development of the initial system of objectives. In: Proceedings of The R&D Management Conference 2018, Mailand, 30 Juni–4 Juli 2018 (2018)
17. Eigner, M., Roubanov, D., Zafirov, R.: Modellbasierte virtuelle Produktentwicklung. Springer, Heidelberg (2014). https://doi.org/10.1007/978-3-662-43816-9
18. Paulweber, M., Lebert, K., List, A.V.L., Kiel, F.H.: Mess- und Prüfstandstechnik. Springer, Heidelberg (2014). https://doi.org/10.1007/978-3-658-04453-4
19. Ehrlenspiel, K., Meerkamm, H.: Integrierte Produktentwicklung. Denkabläufe, Methodeneinsatz, Zusammenarbeit, 5th edn. Hanser, München (2013)
20. Schmidt, T.S., Chahin, A., Kößler, J., Paetzold, K.: Agile development and the constraints of physicality. A network theory-based cause-and-effect analysis. In: Proceedings of the 21st International Conference on Engineering Design (2017)
21. Gloger, B.: Scrum Produkte zuverlässig und schnell entwickeln. Hanser, München (2008)
22. Thoring, K., Müller, R.M.: Understanding design thinking: a process model based on method engineering. In: Kovacevic, A., Ion, W., McMahon, C., Buck, L., Hogarth, P. (eds.) DS 69. Proceedings of E&PDE 2011. 13th International Conference on Engineering and Product Design Education, London, 8–9 September 2011, pp. 493–498 (2011)
23. Albers, A., Bursac, N., Heimicke, J., Walter, B., Reiß, N.: 20 years of co-creation using case based learning. An integrated approach for teaching innovation and research in product generation engineering. In: Auer, M.E., Guralnick, D., Uhomoibhi, J. (eds.) Proceedings of the 20th ICL Conference (2017)
24. Albers, A., Mandel, C., Yan, S., Behrendt, M.: System of systems approach for the description and characterization of validation environments. In: Marjanović, D., Cetić, N., Pavković, N. (eds.) Proceedings of the DESIGN 2018 15th International Design Conference, pp. 2799–2810 (2018)

25. Albers, A., Pinner, T., Yan, S., Hettel, R., Behrendt, M.: Koppelsystems. Obligatory elements within validation setups. In: Marjanović, D., Štorga, M., Pavković, N., Bojčetić, N., Škec, S. (eds.) Proceedings of the DESIGN 2016 14th International Design Conference, DESIGN 2016, Dubrovnik, 16–19 Mai 2016, pp. 109–118 (2016)
26. Pinner, T.: Ein Beitrag zur Entwicklung von Koppelsystemen für die Validierung im Kontext des X-in-the-Loop-Frameworks am Beispiel eines Schaltroboters. Diss., Karlsruher Institut für Technologie (2017)
27. Milgram, P., Takemura H., Utsumi A., Kishino, F.: Augmented reality. A class of displays on the reality-virtuality continuum. In: Das, H. (ed.) Proceedings of Telemanipulator and Telepresence Technologies. Telemanipulator and Telepresence Technologies (1994)
28. Burdea, G., Coiffet, P.: Virtual reality technology (2003)
29. Katicic, J.: Methodik für Erfassung und Bewertung von emotionalem Kundenfeedback für variantenreiche virtuelle Produkte in immersiver Umgebung. Diss., Karlsruher Institut für Technologie (2012)
30. van Krevelen, D.W.F., Poelman, R.: A survey of augmented reality technologies, applications and limitations. Int. J. Virtual Reality 9(2), 1–20 (2010)
31. Azuma, R.T.: A survey of augmented reality. Presence: Teleoperators Virtual Environ. (1997). https://doi.org/10.1162/pres.1997.6.4.355
32. Alt, T.: Augmented Reality in der Produktion. Maschinenwesen. Utz Verlag, München (2003)
33. Damgrave, R.: Augmented reality. In: Laperrière, L., Reinhart, G. (eds.) CIRP Encyclopedia of Production Engineering, pp. 66–67 (2014)
34. PTC Inc.: The State of Industrial Augmented Reality 2017 (2017)
35. Gartner Inc.: Top Trends in the Gartner Hype Cycle for Emerging Technologies (2017). https://www.gartner.com/smarterwithgartner/top-trends-in-the-gartner-hype-cycle-for-emerging-technologies-2017/. Accessed 18 Jan 2019
36. Gartner Inc.: 5 Trends Emerge in the Gartner Hype Cycle for Emerging Technologies (2018). https://www.gartner.com/smarterwithgartner/5-trends-emerge-in-gartner-hype-cycle-for-emerging-technologies-2018/. Accessed 18 Jan 2019
37. Bordegoni, M., Cugini, U., Caruso, G., Polistina, S.: Mixed prototyping for product assessment. A reference framework. International Journal on Interactive Design and Manufacturing (IJIDeM) (2009). https://doi.org/10.1007/s12008-009-0073-9
38. Reinemann, J., Hirschter, T., Mandel, C., Heimicke, J., Albers, A.: Methodische Unterstützung zur Produktvalidierung in AR-Umgebungen in der Frühen Phase der PGE – Produktgenerationsentwicklung. In: Krause, D., Paetzold, K., Wartzack, S. (eds.) Design for X. Beiträge zum 28. DfX-Symposium Oktober 2018, Tutzingen, 25 September 2018 (2018)
39. Kohler, K., Hochreuter, T., Diefenbach, S., Lenz, E., Hassenzahl, M.: Durch schnelles Scheitern zum Erfolg. Eine Frage des passenden Prototypen? In: Usability Professionals 2013, Bremen, 8 September 2013, pp. 78–84 (2013)
40. Steiger, L., Mehler-Bicher, A.: Augmented Reality. Theorie und Praxis, 2nd edn. de Gruyter Oldenbourg, München (2014)
41. Geier, M., Jäger, S., Stier, C., Albers, A.: Combined real and virtual domain product validation using top-down strategies. In: Proceedings of the ASME 2012 Verification and Validation Symposium (V&V 2012). Verification and Validation Symposium (V&V 2012), Nevada, 2–4 Mai 2012, p. 2012 (2012)
42. Rudd, J., Stern, K., Isensee, S.: Low vs. high-fidelity prototyping debate. Interactions (1996). https://doi.org/10.1145/223500.223514

43. McCurdy, M., Connors, C., Pyrzak, G., Kanefsky, B., Vera, A.: Breaking the fidelity barrier. In: Olson, G., Jeffries, R. (eds.) Proceedings of the SIGCHI Conference 2006, Montreal, Quebec, Canada, 22–27 April 2006, p. 1233. ACM Press, New York (2006). https://doi.org/10.1145/1124772.1124959
44. Lim, Y.-K., Stolterman, E., Tenenberg, J.: The anatomy of prototypes. ACM Trans. Comput.-Hum. Interact. (2008). https://doi.org/10.1145/1375761.1375762
45. Albers, A., Walter, B., Wilmsen, M., Bursac, N.: Live-labs as real-world validation environments for design methods. In: Marjanović, D., Štorga, M., Škec, S., Bojčetić, N., Pavković, N. (eds.) Proceedings of the DESIGN 2018 15th International Design Conference, 21–24 Mai 2018, pp. 13–24. Faculty of Mechanical Engineering and Naval Architecture, University of Zagreb, Croatia; The Design Society, Glasgow (2018). https://doi.org/10.21278/idc.2018.0303

# Assessing the Effect of Sensor Limitations in Enhanced Flight Vision Systems on Pilot Performance

Ramanathan Annamalai, Michael C. Dorneich[(⊠)], and Güliz Tokadlı

Industrial and Manufacturing Systems Engineering Department,
Iowa State University, Ames, IA, USA
dorneich@iastate.edu

**Abstract.** Enhanced Flight Vision Systems (EFVS) enables approaches to altitudes closer to the runway that would otherwise be precluded due to low visibility ceilings. EFVS in flight cockpits has the potential to augment the safety in flight operations and enable improved crew performance during approach and landing phases of flight irrespective of the visibility conditions. EFVS utilizes imaging sensors capable of penetrating through obscuring weather conditions, thereby providing forward vision of the runway environment in real-time for display on a heads-up display (HUD). As EFVS potentially moves into use in general aviation operations, it is necessary to evaluate the associated human performance implications, especially during off-nominal conditions as most of the previous studies were primarily limited to nominal cases. The study of off-nominal cases was limited to only HUD failures. The objective of this paper is to present a detailed experimental plan, with preliminary results, to evaluate the human factors implications in using the EFVS under off-nominal conditions. A human-in-the-loop experiment will be conducted in a fixed-base simulator modeled with EFVS. Evaluation pilots will fly six different experimental trials with two visibility levels and three levels of information quality: No-EFVS, EFVS with correct information, and EFVS with degraded information. Measures of performance include approach and landing performance, visual performance, workload, and decision-making.

**Keywords:** Enhanced Flight Vision System · Off-nominal situation ·
Human factors implications · Pilot performance · Sensor technology · Aviation

## 1 Introduction

According to the National Transportation Safety Board report on flight accidents (NTSB 2014), most fatalities are related to the Part 91 general aviation (GA) flight operation with a rate of 6.51 fatalities per 100,000 flight hours. The average annual cost associated with these accidents' ranges from 1.5 to 4.5 Billion USD with 645 fatalities per year. Bad weather is the primary instigating factor and accounts for 23% of GA fatalities (Fultz and Ashley 2016). In 2014, ceiling and low visibility conditions contributed to 27% of these accidents with 70.6% fatalities (Fultz and Ashley 2016). Low visibility/ceilings present a significant challenge to GA pilots during approach and

© Springer Nature Switzerland AG 2019
J. Y. C. Chen and G. Fragomeni (Eds.): HCII 2019, LNCS 11575, pp. 449–465, 2019.
https://doi.org/10.1007/978-3-030-21565-1_30

landing, as small GA aircraft are not equipped with advanced onboard technologies due to expense, size, and power constraints. In a typical low visibility operations, pilots must be able to observe the runway marking at the mandated decision height to continue the approach. In other words, they must be able to transition from Instrument Flight Rules (IFR) to Visual Flight Rules (VFR) at the proscribed decision height to continue the approach (Doc, I.C.A.O 2006). If the crew is not able to acquire the appropriate visual cues, the crew must initiate the go-around procedure.

The U.S. air transportation seeks to improve the safety and reliability in the Part 91 GA Operations through technologies that enable equivalent vision operation (EVO) (Joint Planning and Development Office 2008). Successful implementation of EVO requires installation of advanced equipment within the cockpit or the development of airport infrastructure. EFVS is an onboard sensor system designed to detect visual cues in the forward environment. The sensor information is processed and presented on a HUD to conformably display the sensor output overlaid on the pilot's out-the-window view. It is employed in the visual segment of an instrument approach to obtain the visual cues needed to continue the approach. EFVS systems are aircraft-based, and do not require airport infrastructure. EFVS offers enhanced vision of the forward topography with the help of real-time imaging sensors such as millimeter-wave radar (MMWR), forward looking infrared (FLIR) and Light detection and ranging (LiDAR). According to Federal Aviation Administration (FAA) (2016), EFVS, as a head-up display (HUD)-based guidance/navigation system, supports the pilot during low visibility approach and landing. Thus, EFVS has the potential to augment flight safety and improve crew performance as it provides the equivalent visual cues needed to operate in low visibility conditions (Etherington et al. 2015). The EFVS capabilities address concerns in safety by enhancing situation and position awareness, allowing pilots to conduct a stabilized approach, and reduce the number of missed approaches. Moreover, the FAA revised its existing regulations and mandated additional requirements in §91.176 for EFVS that enables pilots to perform the touchdown and rollout operations, relying solely on the EFVS sensor imagery (FAA 2017). This revision enables the use of EFVS in a wider range of operations, including GA operations, and motivates this evaluation into the associated human performance implications in using EFVS, especially during off-nominal conditions.

Between 2004 and 2017, NASA conducted several flight tests and simulator-based studies to evaluate various aspects of EFVS. These studies focused on human factors and system performance related issues such as pilot performance, visual advantage, operational feasibility, and workload for varying visibility conditions. Flight test conducted by NASA has analyzed numerous performance measures (e.g. landing vs. go-arounds) (Kramer et al. 2014), lateral and vertical landing position (Bailey et al. 2010; Kramer et al. 2015; Kramer et al. 2014; Kramer et al. 2017), sink rate (Kramer et al. 2015; Kramer et al. 2017), airspeed variations (Kramer et al. 2017), and flight path, localizer, and glideslope deviations (Arthur et al. 2005; Kramer et al. 2015; Kramer et al. 2017). The flight tests were performed under nominal conditions and demonstrated improvements in pilot performance while using EFVS for conducting approach and landing operations. Workload assessments showed no significant differences (Kramer et al. 2009; Kramer et al. 2014). One simulator-based study was conducted to investigate the impact on pilot performance due to an EFVS HUD failure, an off-nominal condition (Etherington et al. 2015). The results indicated that the pilots did not perform a go-around when the HUD was intentionally failed by the experimenters well above decision height (DH). The crew ignored the failure messages displayed by EFVS. This suggests that the situational awareness of the pilot above and below the DH needs to be assessed for different EFVS and subsystem failure modes. NASA has also tested a few off-nominal scenarios, but the assessments were limited to the impact of the loss of HUD information and sensor imagery (Kramer et al. 2013). The implications of the quality of the EFVS information over pilot performance has not been studied fully.

Moreover, the sensors in EFVS have known limitations. For instance, infrared sensors work based on detecting temperature difference. It functions well during smoke and haze, but produce degraded visuals in fog, rain, and snow (Etherington et al. 2015). Furthermore, sensor output based on temperature differences between the runway and the adjacent ground is subjected to thermal reversals, where the runway and ground temperatures are equal twice a day, rendering the image of the runway indistinct from the adjacent ground (Yang and Hansmen 1994). The MMWR sensor in EFVS works well for most of the operationally relevant atmospheric conditions, but the images are not as high resolution as natural vision (Etherington et al. 2015). The performance of the MMWR sensor is generally measured through image contrast. Contrast is the ratio of difference in signal between runway and background divided by the background signal, and thus the ratio varies from −1 to 1. Signal level refers to the amplitude of the calibrated sensor. If the signal level of runway and background has no significant difference (zero contrast), then EFVS system cannot detect the runway; negative numbers indicate contrast of the runway is darker than the surrounding terrain; and larger positive numbers indicate contrast of the runway is brighter than the surrounding terrain (Burgess et al. 1993). From a tower test on MMWR sensor performance (Burgess et al. 1993), it was determined that the acceptable contrast range for MMWR sensor imagery lies between −0.6 to −0.8 on a clear day and the contrast for an unacceptable degraded sensor imagery is ranged between −0.2 to −0.6 on a foggy day. This is a clear limitation that MMWR sensor is likely to produce degraded imagery on foggy conditions.

Accordingly, the objective of this study is to evaluate the human performance implications associated in using EFVS due to sensor limitation. This study will evaluate the effects of EFVS with degraded sensor imagery on a pilot's approach and landing performance, decision-making, workload, situation awareness and visual performance. A human-in-the-loop experiment will be conducted in a fixed-based flight simulator with GA pilots. The next section will describe the experimental methods. Preliminary results are presented as the experiment is still underway.

## 2  Methodology

### 2.1  Hypothesis

The evaluation will test the hypothesis that the use of EFVS with degraded information during final approach and landing will decrease the pilot's visual and landing performance compared to the EFVS with no sensor-based limitations. It is also expected that the use of EFVS will improve the pilot's landing and approach performance compared to the conditions of when the final approach performed by the pilot where he/she does not use an EFVS or uses an EFVS displaying degraded visual cues for landing in a degraded visual environment.

### 2.2  Participants

The participants will be GA pilots with more than 10 h of flight experience. Preliminary testing has begun, and this paper will present the results of conducted with two participants. The mean of participant's age was 24 years ($SD = 0.7$). The average hours of flight experience were 63 h ($SD = 22.6$).

### 2.3  Independent Variable

The independent variables of this study are *Visibility* and the *Sensor Information Quality*. These variables are manipulated for each experimental trial to analyze the pilot performance during the approach and landing phases of flight.

**Visibility**

Visibility was expressed as two different Runway Visual Range (RVR) levels: 600 ft and 1000 ft. RVR is defined as "the range over which the pilot of an aircraft on the center line of a runway can see the runway surface markings or the lights delineating the runway or identifying its center line" (FAA-Pilot Controller Glossary 2014, pp. V-3). These visibilities levels were chosen based on the visibility levels assigned for CAT-II and CAT-III precision approach as per IFR rules.

**Sensor Information Quality**

The sensor information quality has three conditions: (a) No-EFVS (b) EFVS, and (c) EFVS with degraded information. For No-EFVS condition, the pilots will not have enhanced forward visibility due to the absence of EFVS, but a HUD is provided as guidance system with all essential symbology. For the EFVS condition, the EFVS displayed essential flight information and expected sensor imagery to complete the flight. The FAA approved 94 GHz MMWR sensor equipped EFVS was utilized as a reference model for the displays implemented within the flight simulator. The HUD symbology is designed as mandated in FAA advisory circular for EFVS (FAA Advisory Circular AC-90A 2010). For the EFVS with degraded sensor information condition, the participants will be provided with an EFVS setup displaying low-resolution sensor imagery. The contrast of the sensor imagery is set at negative (−0.2) with respect to the background. Depicting a degraded runway environment may make it challenging for pilots to visually confirm the runway during the approach and landing phases.

## 2.4    Dependent Variables

The dependent variables capture visual performance, pilot approach and landing performance, workload, and decision making during the approach and landing. Table 1 gives an overview of dependent variables, metrics, units and data collection utilized in this study.

**Table 1.** Dependent variables

| Dependent variables | Metrics | Units | Collection method | Frequency |
|---|---|---|---|---|
| Visual performance | Area of focus | Percentage | Eye-tracker data | During trial |
| | Direction of head-eye respect to HUD | Degrees | | |
| | Verbally identified cues by pilots | Subjective measure | | |
| Pilot performance (Approach) | Glideslope deviation | Measured with respect to 1 scale deviation | Flight sim data | During trial |
| | Localizer deviation | | | |
| | Sink rate | Feet per minute (FPM) | | |
| | Approach airspeed | KIAS | | |
| Pilot performance (Landing) | Successful landings | Count & Percentage | Flight sim data | During trial |
| | Vertical speed at touchdown | Feet per minute (FPM) | | |
| | Distance from centerline and touchdown location | Feet | | |
| Workload | NASA TLX | TLX: Likert scale 0-21 | Post-task questionnaire | After trial |
| Situation awareness | SART techniques | SART: Likert scale 1-7 | Post-task questionnaire | After trial |
| Decision making | Decision height for the flight | Feet | Flight sim recordings | During trial |
| | Retrospective interview | Subjective measure | Post experiment questionnaire | Post-experiment |

**Visual Performance**

A head-worn eye-tracking device will collect quantitative data on the area of focus and the direction of eye movements to evaluate the critical cues exploited by participants in completing the tasks.

**Pilot Performance (Approach)**

For instrument approaches, the FAA (2017) defines evaluation criteria to analyze pilot performance for instrument flight ratings. For evaluating approach performance, the metrics of glideslope deviation, localizer deviation and vertical speed at touchdown will be utilized. These metrics will be evaluated against the FAA standards; maintaining a stabilized final approach from the 1000 ft AGL to touchdown allowing no more than ¾-scale deflection of either the vertical or lateral guidance indications and maintain the desired approach airspeed of the aircraft ±10 knots.

**Pilot Landing (Approach)**

For evaluating landing performance, data on the number of successful and unsuccessful landings, distance away from centerline, and sink rate (feet per minute) will be collected and evaluated against FAA acceptable limits. Post experiment, subjective assessment and human error rate analysis will be also performed based for captured errors and failures during the trials.

**Workload and Situation Awareness**

Workload and Situation Awareness data will be collected using NASA-TLX (Hart and Staveland 1988) and SART techniques (Endsley 1995), respectively. Participants will complete NASA-TLX and SART questionnaires at the end of each task.

**Decision-Making**

The decision to initiate a missed approach or proceed for landing should be made at the decision height/decision altitude (DH/DA) for a precision approach. Screen recordings and the experimental log from the flight simulation software will be reviewed with the participants in the post-experiment interview to allow the participants to elaborate in their decision-making.

## 2.5 Experimental Design

The study utilized a 2 × 3 experimental design for approach and landing tasks. The experimental is a within-subject design with two independent variables; runway visual range (600 ft and 1000 ft) and information quality (No-EFVS, EFVS and EFVS with degraded imagery). Six experiment trials are listed below and can be seen in Fig. 1 and will be counterbalanced across participants.

1. 600 ft RVR with No-EFVS
2. 1000 ft RVR with No-EFVS
3. 600 ft RVR with EFVS
4. 1000 ft RVR with EFVS
5. 600 ft RVR with EFVS with degraded imagery
6. 1000 ft RVR with EFVS with degraded imagery

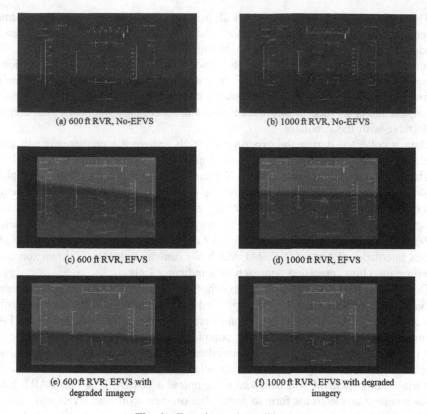

(a) 600 ft RVR, No-EFVS

(b) 1000 ft RVR, No-EFVS

(c) 600 ft RVR, EFVS

(d) 1000 ft RVR, EFVS

(e) 600 ft RVR, EFVS with degraded imagery

(f) 1000 ft RVR, EFVS with degraded imagery

**Fig. 1.** Experimental conditions.

## 2.6 Experimental Procedure

All the participants will be given a 45-minute briefing on the flight test details with a training session before the experimental flight. The duration of experiment for each participant is 2 h. The experimental procedure is represented in the flowchart below (Fig. 2).

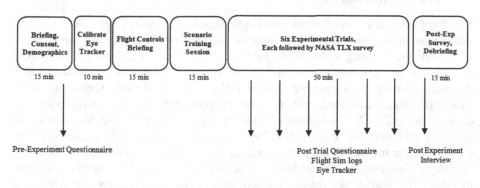

**Fig. 2.** Experiment procedure

The experimental procedure begins with participant briefing followed by informed consent the process, demographics survey, and eye-tracker setup. Pilots will then be introduced to the flight simulator and flight simulator, followed by flight training. The training sessions consist of two approach and landing tasks: (a) Normal Vision – Instrument approach (b) Normal Vision – Instrument approach with HUD. The training is provided to the participants to familiarize with flight controllers and display needed to complete the tasks successfully. Participants can repeat the approaches until they are comfortable with the simulator.

Data is collected during the experimental trials, where the participants will complete a six approach and landing tasks under assigned visibility and ceiling levels. In each trial, pilots will fly Cessna Citation X aircraft. The scenario stars with the airplane on autopilot and lined up with a runway five nautical miles away. The flight begins from the fixed approach point (5000 ft AGL), and airspeed is set at 160 in KIAS with no flaps. The runway environment is set at foggy condition with constant ceiling height of 200 ft. All the approach and landings tasks are conducted in the runway 05 of Des Moines International Airport (KDSM), which has runway lights, touchdown zone, and centerline markings, precision approach path indicator lights.

During each trial, the participants can either initiate the missed approach procedure or conduct the stabilized approach and proceed for the landing if the runway is visible at or above the DH/DA. These operations were conducted and evaluated under FAA Instrument Flight Rules. Once the pilot completes the stabilized approach, he or she must proceed to the landing phase and complete the flight successfully. For the missed approach procedure, the participant is instructed to climb to 3100 ft and hold. After each trial, the participant will be asked to complete a NASA TLX and SART based questionnaire in an electronic form to gather data on their workload levels and situation awareness of that trial. For each experimental trial, the flight was screen recorded and the eye-tracker measurements were also captured. After all the trials were completed, the participants will participate in the post-experiment interview. In this session, a retrospective interview will be conducted by replaying the video recordings and participants are asked to recount their decision-making during the flight. Finally, they will be debriefed about their role in the experiment and thanked for their participation.

## 2.7   Testing Environment

The flight simulator is configured with Flight Gear (v 3.2 2018, Flight Gear, Canada) which is an open source flight simulation software. Flight Gear software can integrate 3D models and the integration of a 3D modeled HUD glass to represent an EFVS-HUD installed aircraft. The hardware configurations for this simulator facility include Saitek (Logitech, Switzerland) controls: Rudder-Pedals, Saitek Throttle Quadrant, 4-axis Yoke Controller, Saitek Radio Panels, Saitek Instrument Panels. The forward view was depicted on a 82", TV screen, and two monitors support the pilot and co-pilot view of the flight deck displays (Fig. 3). The Tobii eye-tracker glasses will be utilized in this study to determine the visual performance of pilots. Tobii Pro Glasses 2 (Tobii AB, Danderyd, Sweden) is a wearable eye-tracking device with a wireless live view function. The glasses are mainly utilized for its visual analyzation capability and automated real-world mapping feature which enable us to streamline and map the eye tracker output, allowing immediate visualization of the quantified data.

**Fig. 3.** Flight simulator

# 3 Preliminary Results

This section includes the results of the pilot testing of the experimental design. Test data were evaluated for the impact of EFVS sensor quality (no-EFVS, EFVS, and EFVS with degraded information) for two runway visual range (RVR): 600 ft and 1000 ft. Evaluation results include pilot performance during approach and landing with respect to FAA acceptable standards, workload, and situation awareness.

## 3.1 Approach Performance

### Localizer and Glideslope RMS

The lateral and vertical path error were used as the measures for flight path control performance during approach. The root means square of glideslope and localizer needle deflection were determined and evaluated from 1000 ft AGL to touchdown. Figure 4 depicts the glideslope RMS for the six conditions. The no-EFVS ($M = 0.84$, $SD = 0.1$) condition glideslope RMS was greater compared to the both the EFVS ($M = 0.75$, $SD = 0.13$) and the EFVS with degraded imagery ($M = 0.76$, $SD = 0.14$) condition. The average glideslope RMS was somewhat smaller for 1000 ft RVR ($M = 0.75$, $SD = 0.11$) compared to 600 ft RVR ($M = 0.82$, $SD = 0.02$). For a stabilized approach, pilots are not allowed to exceed more than 0.75 out of 1 on either the vertical guidance (FAA 2017). Out of 12 approaches conducted across two participants, the participant exceeded glideslope acceptable limits for 58.3% of approaches (seven out of 12 approaches). The participants exceeded deviation limits in the No-EFVS condition for both RVR levels ($M = 0.95$, $SD = 0.03$ for 600 ft RVR and $M = 0.77$, $SD = 0.16$ for 1000 ft RVR) and EFVS with degraded information conditions ($M = 0.78$, $SD = 0.01$) for 600 ft.

Figure 5 depicts the localizer RMS value for all six trials. On comparing the localizer RMS values for different sensor information quality levels, it was observed that RMS value for no EFVS ($M = 0.82$, $SD = 0.19$) condition is greater than EFVS ($M = 0.45$, $SD = 0.12$) and EFVS with degraded imagery condition ($M = 0.53$, $SD = 0.19$) condition. Across different RVR levels, it was observed that the localizer RMS value at 1000 ft RVR ($M = 0.61$, $SD = 0.27$) is similar to 600 ft RVR ($M = 0.58$, $SD = 0.19$). For a stabilized approach, lateral path error (localizer RMS) should exceed more than 0.75 on a 1 scale division as per FAA guidelines (FAA 2017). Out of 12

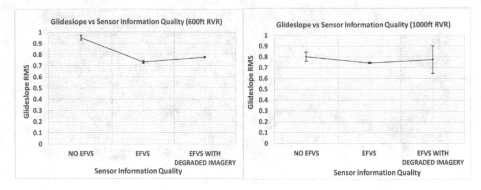

**Fig. 4.** Glideslope RMS for 600 ft (left) and 1000 ft RVR

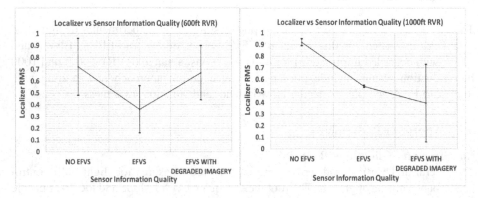

**Fig. 5.** Localizer RMS for 600 ft (left) and 1000 ft RVR (right).

approaches flown, the participants exceeded the acceptable limits on 42% of approaches (five out of 12). The participants exceeded the limits on approaches conducted under No EFVS condition with 1000 ft RVR ($M = 0.90$, $SD = 0.02$). All approaches conducted at 600 ft ($M = 0.39$, $SD = 0.13$) and 1000 ft RVR with EFVS ($M = 0.56$, $SD = 0.01$) were well with the FAA acceptable limits.

**Sink Rate**

Figure 6 describes the sink rate for all six trials. The sink rate was determined as a measure to evaluate pilot approach performance and represented as a negative number for descending aircraft. The sink rates of EFVS condition ($M = -590.4$, $SD = 11.2$) were lower compared to no EFVS ($M = -890.3$, $SD = 165.2$) and EFVS with degraded imagery condition ($M = -716.4$, $SD = 72.0$). For 600 ft RVR ($M = -755.7$, $SD = 218.1$), the sink rate was higher compared to 1000 ft RVR levels ($M = -708.1$, $SD = 108.2$). As per FAA guidelines, acceptable limit is below 1000 fpm for a stabilized approach conducted under IFR rules (ICAO 2008). Out of 12 approaches conducted, the participants were within FAA acceptable limits for 92% of the approaches (11 out of 12 approaches). From the 12 approaches, the exceedance on sink

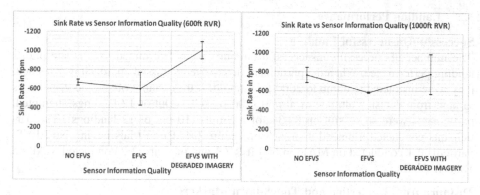

**Fig. 6.** Sink rate for 600 ft (left) and 1000 ft RVR (right).

rate was found only once on EFVS with degraded information condition for 600 ft RVR (*Sink rate* = −1100 fpm).

## Approach Airspeed

Figure 7 describes the approach airspeed for all six trials. The approach airspeed is also determined as a measure to evaluate pilot approach performance. On comparing the sensor information quality levels, the no EFVS condition ($M = 175.4$, $SD = 8.1$) has a higher sink rate compared to EFVS ($M = 147.4$, $SD = 0.87$) and EFVS with degraded imagery ($M = 156.4$, $SD = 17.9$). On evaluating the approach airspeed with respect to visibility levels, the approach airspeed for 1000 ft RVR ($M = 160.8$, $SD = 12.41$) is higher compared to 600 ft RVR ($M = 156.6$, $SD = 21.9$). As per FAA guidelines, acceptable limit is $V_{ref} + 20$ KIAS (Knots in Indicated Airspeed) for stabilized approach conducted under IFR rules (ICAO, 2008). For Cessna Citation X, the stalling airspeed, $V_{stall}$ is 113 KIAS (for landing configuration). The reference airspeed, $V_{ref} = 1.3 * V_{stall} = 146.9$ KIAS. The acceptable range is 147 to 167 KIAS approximately. Out of 12 approaches conducted, the participant exceeded the FAA acceptable limits for 25% approaches (3 out of 12). The non-compliant cases occurred on the No-EFVS conditions; both 600 ft RVR ($M = 181.6$, $SD = 33.8$) and 1000 ft RVR ($M = 170.2$, $SD = 34.0$) levels.

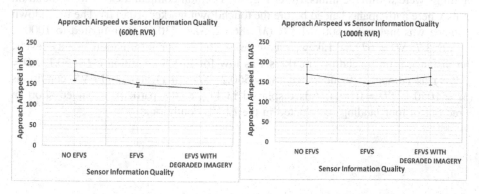

**Fig. 7.** Approach airspeed for 600 ft (left) and 1000 ft RVR (right).

## 3.2    Landing Performance

**Successful/Unsuccessful Landing**

The number of successful/unsuccessful landings were determined to evaluate pilot's landing performance. When the participant determined a missed approach was needed, they were instructed to climb to 2000 ft and hold, if they cannot obtain the visual cues to land from decision altitude of airport (200 ft AGL). Out of 12 landings attempted, participants were successful on 83.3% of attempts (10 out of 12 landings). The participants conducted a missed approach procedure (MAP) on trials having No-EFVS; participant 1 conducted on MAP on 600 ft RVR and participant 2 conducted MAP on 1000 ft RVR.

**Distance from Centerline and Touchdown Markers**

The trials were conducted on runway 05 of Des Moines Intl. Airport. The runway is 9003 ft long and 150 ft wide. Figure 7 represents 1/3 of the runway approximately (3150 ft) from the runway threshold line. The touchdown location for all 12 trials conducted among two participants were marked as P1 and P2 in figure; depicting the touchdown location of participant 1 and participant 2 respectively. The distance participants landed away from centerline for 600 ft ($M = 52.2$, $SD = 18.1$) was higher compared to 1000 ft ($M = 47.3$, $SD = 18.0$). On comparing the sensor information quality levels, the landing distance from centerline is less for EFVS condition ($M = 33.0$, $SD = 14.1$) as compared to degraded ($M = 60.2$, $SD = 4.1$) and no EFVS conditions ($M = 61.6$, $SD = 15.2$). Pilots are instructed that their landing point must not exceeds $\pm 75$ ft lateral deviation from the centerline. For 10 out of 12 successful landings (2 missed approaches were conducted on trials with No EFVS condition; both 600 ft and 1000 ft RVR levels), the participant successfully landed the aircraft within the evaluation criteria.

Distance from touchdown marker is a measure how far down the runway the pilot travelled before landing with respect to touchdown point. Distance from touchdown is measured as an absolute value. For KDSM airport, the threshold crossing height (TCH) for the runway was determined as 55 ft. The location of touchdown markers for Runway 05 was estimated as 1050 ft for 55 ft TCH. The Cessna Citation X has landing distance of 3300 ft. So, the evaluation criteria for pilot's landing performance were set at touchdown marker location (1050 ft) to 3300 ft. Of 10 successful landings, 6 of 10 landings were within the limits. (refer Fig. 8). The non-complaint cases were found on trials where participants landed before the touchdown marker (1050 ft). The touchdown distance was higher for 600 ft RVR ($M = 863.2$, $SD = 730.6$) as compared to 1000 ft ($M = 623.7$, $SD = 672.8$). Likewise comparing the sensor information quality levels, the distance from touchdown markers was low for EFVS condition ($M = 50.1$, $SD = 230.1$) as compared to degraded ($M = 560.2$, $SD = 4.1$) and no EFVS conditions ($M = 1050.1$, $SD = 0.001$). Ads displayed in Fig. 8, the participant landed short in three out of four landings conducted in the EFVS condition.

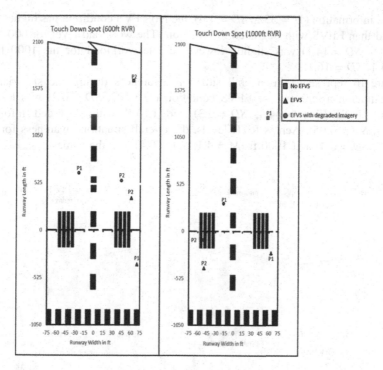

**Fig. 8.** Touchdown location for 600 ft (left) and 1000 ft RVR (right)

## 3.3 Workload and SART

Figure 9 depicts the overall workload assessment conducted for all six trials. The overall workload for each participant was obtained on a 21-point scale and normalized to a 100-point scale from the data analysis. The workload level for EFVS ($M = 17.7$, $SD = 0.03$) was lower than for No-EFVS ($M = 45.5$, $SD = 9.2$) and EFVS with

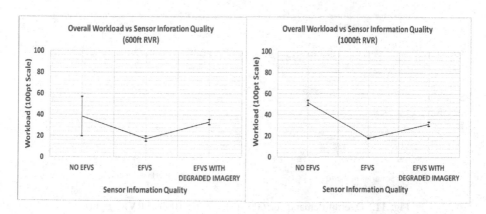

**Fig. 9.** Overall Workload (WL) for 600 ft (left) and 1000 ft RVR (right)

degraded information ($M = 33.2$, $SD = 1.4$), the No EFVS condition has higher overall workload than EFVS with degraded information. The workload level for 600 ft RVR ($M = 29.8$, $SD = 14.1$) was slightly lower than the workload for the 1000 ft RVR ($M = 34.1$, $SD = 16.1$).

Figure 10 represents the overall situation awareness during the six trials. The overall situation awareness for EFVS condition ($M = 3.7$, $SD = 0.2$) was less compared to No-EFVS ($M = 4.4$, $SD = 0.3$) and EFVS with degraded information ($M = 4.4$, $SD = 0.05$). Across RVR levels, the overall situation awareness for 600 ft ($M = 4.1$, $SD = 0.4$) and 1000 ft ($M = 4.1$, $SD = 0.4$) was the same

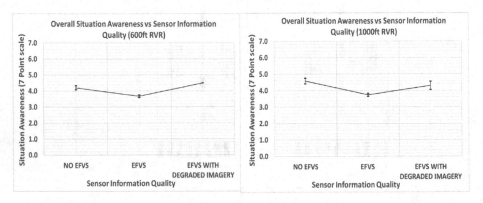

**Fig. 10.** Overall Situation Awareness (SA) for 600 ft (left) and 1000 ft RVR (right).

Figure 11 represents the overall demand during the six trials. The overall demand level for No- EFVS condition ($M = 4.4$, $SD = 0.2$) was higher compared to EFVS ($M = 3.3$, $SD = 0.6$) and EFVS with degraded information ($M = 3.3$, $SD = 0.3$). The demand level for 600 ft RVR ($M = 3.7$, $SD = 0.6$) and 1000 ft RVR ($M = 3.7$, $SD = 0.8$) was same.

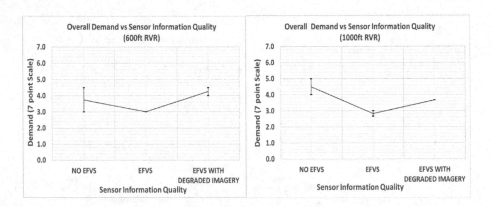

**Fig. 11.** Overall demand for 600 ft (left) and 1000 ft RVR (right).

Figure 12 depicts the overall understanding during the six trials. The overall understanding level for EFVS ($M = 5.3$, $SD = 0.4$) was greater than No EFVS ($M = 5.0$, $SD = 0.7$) and EFVS with degraded information ($M = 4.9$, $SD = 0.2$). The overall understanding level for 600 ft RVR ($M = 5.2$, $SD = 0.3$) was slightly greater to 1000 ft RVR ($M = 4.9$, $SD = 0.5$).

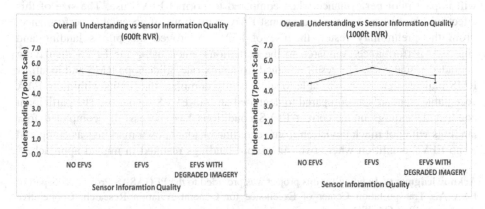

**Fig. 12.** Overall understanding for 600 ft (left) and 1000 ft RVR (right).

Figure 13 depicts the overall supply during the six trials. The overall supply level for EFVS with degraded information ($M = 4.4$, $SD = 0.2$) was greater than EFVS ($M = 2.9$, $SD = 0.1$) and similar to No EFVS ($M = 4.1$, $SD = 1.0$). For different RVR levels, the overall supply for 600 ft RVR ($M = 3.5$, $SD = 0.6$) was less than in 1000 ft RVR ($M = 4.0$, $SD = 1.0$).

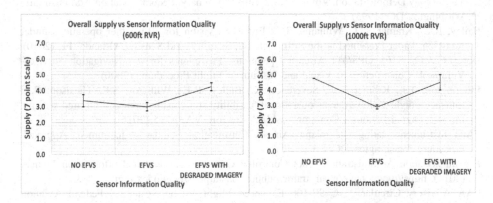

**Fig. 13.** Overall supply for 600 ft (left) and 1000 ft RVR (right).

# 4  Conclusion

The objective of the evaluation is to assess the effect of sensor limitations of EFVS on pilot performance. The paper has presented an experimental design and presented preliminary results. Since the results are preliminary, no conclusions can be drawn. The preliminary data trends in the way hypothesized where EFVS with degraded imagery will impact pilot performance when compared to normal EFVS use. The size of this effect will be assessed compared against FAA regulations of acceptable performance. From the preliminary result, the use of EFVS improved the pilot's landing and approach performance compared to the conditions when using the EFVS displaying degraded visual cues. The result obtained from sink rate, glideslope RMS and localizer RMS indicate that pilots was able to successfully complete the flights within the FAA acceptable standards as compared to degraded and no-EFVS scenarios. The participant conducted landings under correct EFVS conditions has successfully completed four landings with not much deviation from centerline or touchdown markings as compared to no-EFVS condition where two out of four landings resulted in missed approach.

**Acknowledgment.** Funding for this project was provided to the PEGASAS Project 24 as part of FAA Air Transportation Center of Excellence for General Aviation Research, Cooperative Agreement 12-C-GA-ISU.

# References

Arthur, J.J., Kramer, L.J., Bailey, R.E.: Flight test comparison between enhanced vision (FLIR) and synthetic vision systems. Paper presented at the Defense and Security 2005, Orlando, FL (2005)

Burgess, M., Chang, T., Dunford, D., Hoh, R.H., Home, W.F., Tucker, R.F.: Synthetic Vision Technology Demonstration. Volume 1. Executive Summary. Federal Aviation Administration Washington DC (1993)

Bailey, R.E., Kramer, L.J., Williams, S.P.: Enhanced vision for all-weather operations under NextGen. Paper Presented at the SPIE Defense, Security, and Sensing, Orlando, FL (2010)

Doc, I.C.A.O.: 8168 OPS/611 Aircraft Operations: Procedures for Air Navigation Services-Volume II Construction of Visual and Instrument Flight Procedures (2006)

Etherington, T.J., Kramer, L.J., Severence, K., Bailey, R.E., Williams, S.P., Harrison, S.J.: Enhanced flight vision systems operational feasibility study using radar and infrared sensors. In: 34th Digital Avionics Conference, AIAA, Reston, VA, p. 15 (2015)

FAA: Instrument Rating - Airplane: Airmen Certification Standards. Instrument Approach Procedure. Washington DC. 8A (2017)

Federal Aviation Administration: Pilot Controller Glossary. Aeronautical information Manual (2014). https://www.faa.gov/air_traffic/publications/atpubs/pcg/index.htm

FAA Advisory Circular, "AC 90-106 Enhanced Flight Vision Systems," Federal Aviation Administration (2010)

FAA: 90-106A: Enhanced Flight Vision Systems. J. Barbagallo, US Department of Transportation (2017)

Fultz, A.J., Ashley, W.S.: Fatal weather-related general aviation accidents in the United States. Phys. Geogr. **37**(5), 291–312 (2016)

Hart, S.G., Staveland, L.E.: Development of NASA-TLX (Task Load Index): results of empirical and theoretical research. In: Advances in Psychology, vol. 52, pp. 139–183. North-Holland (1988)

Joint Planning and Development Office: Next generation air transportation system integrated work plan: A functional outline. Technical report, Joint Planning and Development Office, Washington, DC (2008)

Kramer, L.J., Bailey, R.E., Prinzel III, L.J.: Commercial flight crew decision making during low-visibility approach operations using fused synthetic and enhanced vision systems. Int. J. Aviat. Psychol. 19(2), 131–157 (2009)

Kramer, L.J., Bailey, R.E., Ellis, K.K.: Using vision system technologies for offset approaches in low visibility operations. Procedia Manufact. 3, 2373–2380 (2015)

Kramer, L.J., et al.: Enhanced Flight Vision Systems and Synthetic Vision Systems for NextGen Approach and Landing Operations, NASA TP-2013-218054, November 2013

Kramer, L.J., Harrison, S.J., Bailey, R.E., Shelton, K.J., Ellis, K.K.: Visual advantage of enhanced flight vision system during NextGen flight test evaluation. In: Degraded Visual Environments: Enhanced, Synthetic, and External Vision Solutions 2014, vol. 9087, p. 90870G. International Society for Optics and Photonics, June 2014

Kramer, L.J., Etherington, T.J., Severance, K., Bailey, R.E., Williams, S.P., Harrison, S.J.: Assessing dual-sensor enhanced flight vision systems to enable equivalent visual operations. J. Aerospace Inf. Syst. 14(10), 533–550 (2017)

Endsley, M.R.: Measurement of situation awareness in dynamic systems. Hum. Factors 37(1), 65–84 (1995)

National Transportation Safety Board: General aviation: Identify and communicate hazardous weather (2014). http://www.ntsb.gov/safety/mwl/Pages/mwl7_2014.aspx

Yang, L.C., Hansman, R.J.: Human performance evaluation of enhanced vision systems for approach and landing. In: Sensing, Imaging, and Vision for Control and Guidance of Aerospace Vehicles, vol. 2220, pp. 267–282. International Society for Optics and Photonics, July 1994

# Use of an Enhanced Flight Vision System (EFVS) for Taxiing in Low-Visibility Environments

Dennis B. Beringer[1(✉)], Andrea Sparko[2], and Joseph M. Jaworski[3]

[1] FAA Civil Aerospace Medical Institute, Oklahoma City, OK 73169, USA
Dennis.Beringer@faa.gov
[2] Volpe National Transportation Systems Center, Cambridge, MA 02142, USA
[3] Cherokee CRC, LLC, Oklahoma City, OK 73125, USA

**Abstract.** Two studies (Boeing 777 and 737 simulators) examined flight crews' use of an Enhanced Flight Vision System (EFVS) for taxiing in low-visibility conditions in lieu of infrastructure for Low-Visibility Operations/Surface Movement Guidance and Control Systems (LVO/SMGCS). Twenty-five flight crews completed 21 short taxi scenarios under combinations of the following variables and levels: Runway visual range (RVR; 300, 500, 1000 ft); Enhanced-Flight-Vision System in head-up display (on/off); airport infrastructure - 3 levels. Two scenarios dealt with detecting obstacles near the taxi path. In both studies, the use of EFVS resulted in fewer route deviations, the majority of which occurred at 300 feet RVR with edge lights and either a standard painted centerline (Level 1) or a painted centerline with LVO/SMGCS "enhancements" but without centerline lights (Level 2). Deviation from taxiway centerline was variable, but was consistent between display conditions (EFVS/no EFVS) (mean <4 ft). Larger turn angles and lower visibilities were associated with slower rates of travel. Flight crews in both studies detected the right-side obstacle the majority of the time, and about twice as often as they detected the left-side obstacle. Regardless of EFVS, flight crews in both studies made more route deviations on larger turns and right turns. Pilot feedback suggested the issue was loss of visual references to the turn, particularly without centerline lights. Recommendations are provided regarding the benefits and limitations of EFVS for low-visibility taxi operations, procedures for low-visibility taxi operations in general, and suggestions for future research.

**Keywords:** Enhanced flight vision systems · Pilot performance · Transport aircraft

## 1 Introduction

### 1.1 Background

The Federal Aviation Administration (FAA) Low-Visibility Operations/Surface Movement Guidance and Control System (LVO/SMGCS) voluntary program has supported safer taxi operations in low visibilities of less than 1200 feet runway visual range (RVR) since 1996. Approximately 70 U.S. airports have FAA-approved

J. Y. C. Chen and G. Fragomeni (Eds.): HCII 2019, LNCS 11575, pp. 466–475, 2019.
https://doi.org/10.1007/978-3-030-21565-1_31

LVO/SMGCS plans, which comprise a combination of airport infrastructure and procedures as outlined in Advisory Circular (AC) 120.57A (FAA 1996) and FAA Order 8000.94 (2012). The current LVO/SMGCS program has two levels: Level 1 is at visibilities from 1200 to 500 feet RVR and Level 2 is at visibilities from 500 to 300 feet RVR. A Level 3 (<300 feet RVR) is proposed once FAA/industry can jointly demonstrate that aircraft will operate safely with emerging technologies like an Enhanced Flight Vision System (EFVS), a sensor-based system, based upon light in the infrared spectrum, which display a sensor image of the outside scene on a head-up display (HUD). Additionally, a proposed Protected Low Visibility Taxi Routes program change provides support for suitably equipped aircraft operating via procedural mitigations at participating airports.

To gain a better understanding of how the proposed changes may be implemented, the FAA is interested in whether an EFVS can aid pilots in taxiing safely in low-visibility conditions when LVO/SMGCS infrastructure is reduced or not present. If such operations were demonstrated to be safe, it might increase access to airports that do not currently have an LVO/SMGCS plan. Although the FAA does not regulate taxi operations, the FAA is interested in understanding how to better support taxi operations without compromising safety, particularly in reduced-visibility and reduced-infrastructure conditions.

There have been a number of studies that have looked at the use of forward-looking perspective displays and map displays to support low-visibility taxi operations. These fall into several categories which include: forward-looking synthetic-vision displays (head down, HDD, or head up, HUD), forward-looking sensor-based displays (HDD or HUD), and map displays (plan-view or exocentric perspective). Each of the various types, some in isolation and some in conjunction with other displays, has shown a potential for improving the safety and efficiency of aircraft operations.

The focus of this examination was limited, however, to a sensor-based display in light of (1) the fact that there have been numerous studies performed using data-base oriented displays to facilitate low-visibility operations (maps: Lorenz and Biella, 2006; Battiste et al. 1996; Yeh and Chandra 2003, and perspective forward-looking displays: McCann et al. 1997; Beringer et al. 2018), (2) a lesser number on use of EFVS (e.g. Kramer et al. 2013), and (3) some inherent limitations in displays generated from a database (accuracy of registration with the outside world, and obstacles or momentary obstructions that are unlikely to be contained and thus displayed). Thus, it has been suggested that a sensor-based system that can provide surveillance ahead of the aircraft at distances greater than that possible with the unaided eye is preferred for this type of operation. A number of EFVS systems have now become available and are, as such, candidates for supporting low-visibility operations.

The intent of this study was to identify any potential safety decrements that might be encountered during the use of EFVS for taxiing in low-visibility conditions under likely airport infrastructure variations with less than that presently required for LVO/SMGCS. The manipulations included a wide range of turn angles along the taxi paths, some unconventional paths, and trials where there were obstructions/hazards in order to fully exercise the potential use of the sensor/display system and the crews' abilities to perform the task. Additionally, data were collected for simulated wide-bodied aircraft (Boeing 777) and narrow-bodied aircraft (Boeing 737) operations given that how crews anticipate turns is dependent upon the placement of the nose wheel relative to the pilot's viewpoint.

## 2 Method

### 2.1 Participants

Twenty-four B-777 pilots (12 two-person flight crews) participated in Phase 1 and 26 B-737 pilots (13 flight crews) from various airlines participated in Phase 2. Both pilots in each crew were required to have at least 10 h flight time within the past 30 days. The pilot flying was required to have a least 100 h of head up display (HUD) experience. For the B-777 pilots, required HUD experience was as pilot-in-command in an aircraft equipped with an EFVS. At least one crewmember was required to be Category (CAT)-III qualified for the previous five years. Each individual flight crew was comprised of pilots from the same company to minimize differences in standard operating procedures. On average, B-777 pilots had 17 years of CAT-III experience (SD = 10, Range = 0–35) and B-737 pilots had 12 years (SD = 9, Range = 0.5–30). All pilots were compensated for their participation.

### 2.2 Simulation Environment

Phase 1 was conducted in a CAE B-777F level D full-flight simulator operated at the FedEx Flight Training Center in Memphis, TN, and Phase 2 was conducted in a CAE Boeing 737-800NG level D full-flight simulator operated by Flight Standards Flight Operations Simulation Branch at the Mike Monroney Aeronautical Center in Oklahoma City, OK. Both simulators used a version of the same Rockwell-Collins EP-8000 visual model for the infrared (IR) based EFVS image and airport simulation. The simulators were operated with the motion on to provide additional feedback (operational realism) to the pilots.

Enhanced Flight Vision System (EFVS). The IR-based EFVS simulated image was displayed on a Rockwell-Collins HUD in front of the left-seat pilot. The right-seat pilot did not have an EFVS. Pilots were able to control the pilot-adjustable settings (e.g., brightness) for the EFVS and HUD. All other EFVS settings were preset prior to the taxi trials. EFVS display features, characteristics, flight information, flight symbology, and sensor imagery were based on regulatory requirements (14 CFR §§ 91.176 and 25.773), minimum aviation system performance standards for EFVS (RTCA 2011; FAA 2016), guidance for EFVS operations (FAA 2017), and/or as recommended by LVO/SMGCS subject matter experts (SMEs). One exception was that the HUD FOV in both simulators was greater than the minimum requirement of 20° horizontally by 15° vertically (Study 1 FOV was 30° × 15° and Study 2 was 32° × 15°).

Example out-the-window and HUD/EFVS views are depicted in Figs. 1A and B.

**Fig. 1.** (A) Example out-the-window view from simulator left seat and (B) example view of the HUD EFVS image.

## 2.3 Design

The study measured the effect of three variables on pilot performance:

1. RVR (3 levels): 300, 500, or 1000 feet
2. Airport infrastructure (3 levels):
   a. Level 1 (L1): Standard centerline (6" wide) with edge lights
   b. Level 2 (L2): Level 1 plus centerline with LVO/SMGCS "enhancements" (12" wide with black border)
   c. Level 3 (L3): Level 2 plus centerline lights
3. EFVS (2 levels): on or off (when 'off', EFVS image turned off, HUD symbology left on).

These variable levels were combined to create a $3 \times 3 \times 2$ fully-crossed within-subject factorial design with flight crew as the replication factor (Table 1). That is to say, each flight crew performed one taxi trial for each of the experimental conditions.

**Table 1.** Experimental conditions (taxiway edge lights were always present). Heavily shaded cells with hite text indicate the 18 cells of the $3 \times 3 \times 2$ factorial design.

| RVR (ft) | Infrastructure | EFVS | |
|---|---|---|---|
| | | On | Off |
| 300 | Standard centerline + edge lights (L1) | **300-L1-on** | **300-L1-off** |
| | +centerline enhancement (L2) | **300-L2-on** | **300-L2-off** |
| | +centerline lights (L3) | **300-L3-on** | **300-L3-off** |
| 500 | L1 | **500-L1-on** | **500-L1-off** |
| | L2 | **500-L2-on** | **500-L2-off** |
| | L3 | **500-L3-on** | **500-L3-off** |
| 1000 | L1 | **1000-L1-on** | **1000-L1-off** |
| | L2 | **1000-L2-on** | **1000-L2-off** |
| | L3 | **1000-L3-on** | **1000-L3-off** |

## 2.4   Task/Scenarios

Pilots performed taxi scenarios at a simulation of KSLC (Salt Lake) at night. Nighttime conditions were chosen based on SME input to represent the more commonly encountered difficult low-visibility condition, compared to worst-case dusk or dawn times. Because the study examined minimal infrastructure, the KSLC simulator airport model was altered to remove LVO/SMGCS lights and markings along the taxi routes other than the specific LVO/SMGCS route used as a baseline reference. Twelve taxi scenarios were constructed such that: (1) each contained at least one turn each of <90°, 90°, and >90°, (2) scenarios were balanced between left and right turns, (3) all began on a taxiway or runway. Some were repeated within an order, but those that were repeated were placed near the beginning and near the end of the counterbalanced orders. Three additional scenarios were included as supplemental conditions. Two were designed to pass near a truck parked at the edge of the taxiway to assess to what degree an object that might pose a potential hazard might be detected. A third was conducted that used LVO/CMGCS centerline enhancements and centerline lighting only designated route lighted) in 300 feet RVR with the EFVS off to provide a baseline reference condition.

## 3   Procedure

Due to simulator availability, Phase 1 flight crews began the study at night (starting at approximately 7:30 PM) local time. For Phase 2, pilots began the study in the morning (8:00 AM) or early evening (5:00 PM), local time. The entire study took between 4–5 h for each flight crew to complete.

When crews arrived at the simulator facility, they were seated in a briefing room with a researcher to complete the pre-experiment paperwork and briefing. Each pilot read and signed an Informed Consent Form, filled out the background questionnaire concerning general pilot experience as well as LVO/SMGCS and EFVS, and viewed a PowerPoint briefing describing the EFVS (Phase 2 only), and a short verbal briefing which outlined the basic study procedures (Phase 1 and 2). Pilots were told that they would be asked to traverse some non-standard routes, including some with extreme turns. During the briefing, each pilot was also given paper sheets for each scenario that contained the ATC instructions, EFVS setting (on or "hide"), and the aircraft's starting position on a portion of the airport chart. Pilots were informed that they would not be able to use an airport moving map during the taxi scenarios.

After the briefing, pilots entered the simulator and completed a practice taxi scenario with the EFVS on in 500 feet RVR with LVO/SMGCS "enhanced" painted centerlines, centerline lights, and edge lights. The purpose of the practice trial was to generate pilot familiarity with the simulator and EFVS settings. Following the practice scenario, pilots were given a chance to ask questions before beginning the 21 experimental trials. Each taxi trial took approximately 5–10 min to complete. A 15 to 20 min break was provided halfway through the scenarios. Two researchers sat in the simulator cab during the scenarios—one acted as "live" ATC and the other observed and took notes.

At the completion of the trials, the flight crew returned to the briefing room where each pilot completed their own post-experiment questionnaire. Once these had been completed, the researcher asked the pilots for general comments or questions, and provided an overview of the purpose of the study. The entire session required between 4 and 5 h. As the results of both phases were similar, they will be presented together by type of performance measure.

# 4   Results

**Performance Metrics**

Centerline tracking. Although the means for centerline tracking were consistent and all averages were within 3.5 to 5 feet of the centerline, slightly more variability was evident when RVR was 300 than in the other visibilities, with 1000 RVR showing the narrowest variability. There was also slightly more variation with EFVS off than there was with it on, but the means were essentially the same. A similar pattern was observed for infrastructure but was somewhat anomalous with slightly less variation in conditions with the least infrastructure (Level 1).

Route Deviations. The majority of route deviations occurred at 300 feet RVR (Fig. 2). This was expected as a function of the reduced visibility. The maximum percentage of scenarios on which uncorrected deviations occurred was just over 15% for 777 at 300 RVR. About half as many deviations were detected soon enough to correct them. The 737 crews had roughly an equal proportion of uncorrected and corrected deviations in same visibility conditions (9% and 11.5% respectively). There were no uncorrected errors with either aircraft when EFVS was on at 300 RVR. This may also be related to the fact that crews taxied slightly slower in the lowest visibility than in the two higher visibilities. Overall, the percentage of deviations roughly linearly decreased as visibility increased.

Interestingly, the pattern of deviations relative to increasing taxiway infrastructure was not entirely as anticipated. Level 3 did exhibit the lowest number of deviations (Fig. 3). The nonintuitive result was that Level 2 exhibited the most, with Level 1 having the middle frequency of deviations. One can also see across the two figures that the percentage of deviations with EFVS on (which averaged 2.2%) was smaller than when EFVS was off (4.3%).

Obstacle detection. Obstacle detection was defined as the pilot verbally indicating seeing the truck during the scenario. Flight crews in both studies detected the right-side truck the majority of the time, and about twice as often as they detected the left-side truck (Fig. 4). In fact, the detection rate was approximately 90% for the 777 crews when the truck was on the right of the taxiway. If pilots did not verbally acknowledge seeing the truck, researchers asked the pilot about it during the post-test questionnaire and interview. However, for the purposes of analysis, only verbal indications of seeing the truck were included. The first officer frequently detected the obstacle, as the captain was often looking out the left-side window trying to keep the taxiway edge line in sight. The left-side truck was at a 90-degree turn to the left, and thus was not in the simulated sensor field of view during the turn, which possibly led to a lesser chance of

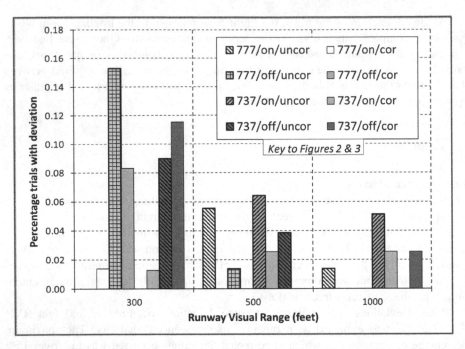

**Fig. 2.** Percentage of trials with corrected or uncorrected taxi deviations by RVR, EFVS on/off, and flight simulator type.

being detected. This represented a situation where objects outside the sensor's field of view could potentially pose a hazard not immediately apparent in the EFVS. Descriptive statistics are presented here because the events were not independent due to the repeated-measures design.

### Pilot Opinions

Boeing 737 pilots felt that reduced infrastructure contributed to increased workload. Moreover, Captains reported difficulty making right turns, particularly in the B-777, because they would lose visual reference to the centerline under the aircraft. Pilots did not feel that EFVS contributed to their position awareness above what their own direct observations provided. Although a moving map was not used in this study, pilots also felt that a moving map in addition to EFVS would provide improvements in position awareness. Some pilots had concerns about the use of EFVS in low-visibility operations, including the restricted EFVS FOV, limitations regarding EFVS visuals (e.g., parallax, blue lights showing up as green), and the limited effectiveness of EFVS under certain environmental conditions (e.g., precipitation or dense fog). Despite their concerns, both groups of pilots generally felt that an EFVS repeater should be made available to the First Officer.

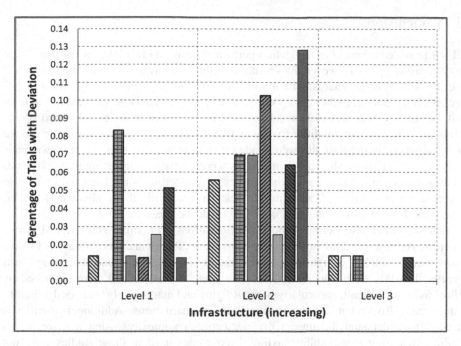

**Fig. 3.** Percentage of trials with corrected or uncorrected taxi deviations by level of infrastructure, EFVS on/off, and flight simulator type.

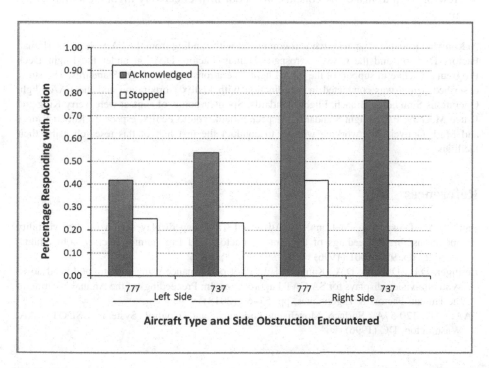

**Fig. 4.** Pilot responses (percentages) to an obstacle near the taxiway by aircraft type and object location.

## 5  Conclusions

EFVS provided a benefit to navigation performance at 300 feet RVR when there were no centerline lights. However, EFVS had no effect on navigation performance at 500 feet RVR and above. That is, with minimal taxiway infrastructure in visibilities of 500 feet RVR or greater, flight crews were generally able to navigate successfully with or without EFVS. Note that these results should not be taken to suggest that taxi operations are safe in these conditions without EFVS. Almost all of the wrong or missed turns observed in these studies were made on right turns. However, flight crews made very few wrong turns when centerline lights were available, suggesting that difficulties finding the centerline may be alleviated when the centerline is lit. The EFVS may also increase the probability of detecting obstacles in low-visibility conditions. However, obstacles that are outside the sensor's FOV could be missed.

These studies also examined potential limitations on taxiing with reduced infrastructure. As mentioned previously, right turns were difficult and were observed to have more errors, notably without centerline lighting. It was also found that sharp turns greater than 90° were associated with more route deviations and were described by pilots as being difficult, particularly without lights and markings. In wide-body aircraft, pilots may also find it difficult to oversteer on sharp turns. Additional research is needed to understand the impact of intersection complexity (using a more robust definition) during low-visibility taxiing. Taxi routes used in these studies were not designed to be complex. Although some complex intersections were noted, there were too few of them to make any conclusions about how effectively flight crews navigated them.

**Acknowledgments.**  This research was completed with funding from the FAA NextGen Human Factors Division and the CAMI Aerospace Human Factors Division under the Flight Deck Program Directive in support of the FAA Flight Operations Branch, Flight Standards. The study described herein was conducted in coordination with FedEx Corporation and the FAA Flight Operations Simulation Branch, Flight Standards. Sponsor points of contact were Terry King and Bruce McGray, FAA Flight Standards. A special thank you to FedEx, especially Robert Riding and Mark Gouveia, for working with us to conduct the first half of this research using their facilities.

## References

Battiste, V., Downs, M., McCann, R.: Advanced Taxi map display design for low-visibility operations. In: Proceedings of the Human Factors and Ergonomics Society 40th Annual Meeting, pp. 997–1001 (1996)

Beringer, D.B., Domino, D.A., Kamienski, J.: Pilot performance using head-up and head-down synthetic-vision displays for SA CAT I approaches. In: Proceedings of the Annual Meeting of the Human Factors & Ergonomics, pp. 57–61 (2018)

FAA: AC 120-57A, Surface Movement Guidance and Control System. USDOT FAA, Washington, DC (1996)

FAA: Order 8000.94, Procedures for Establishing Airport Low-Visibility Operations and Approval of Low-Visibility Operations/Surface Movement Guidance and Control System Operations. USDOT FAA, Washington, DC (2012)

FAA: AC 20-167A, Airworthiness Approval of Enhanced Vision System, Synthetic Vision System, Combined Vision System, and Enhanced Flight Vision System Equipment. USDOT Federal Aviation Administration, Washington, DC (2016)

FAA: AC 90-106A, Enhanced Flight Vision Systems. USDOT Federal Aviation Administration, Washington, DC (2017)

Kramer, L.J., et al.: Enhanced flight vision systems and synthetic vision systems for NextGen approach and landing operations. NASA/TP-2013-218054 (2013)

Lorenz, B., Biella, M.: Evaluation of onboard taxi guidance support on pilot performance in airport surface navigation. In: Proceedings of the Human Factor and Ergonomics Society 50th Annual Meeting, pp. 111–115 (2006)

McCann, R.S., Andre, A.D., Bebgault, D., Foyle, D.C., Wenzel, E.: Enhancing taxi performance under low visibility: are moving maps enough? In: Proceedings of the Human Factors and Ergonomics Society 41st Annual Meeting, pp. 37–41 (1997)

Pilot compartment view, 14 C.F.R. § 25.773 (2016)

RTCA: DO-315B, Minimum Aviation System Performance Standards (MASPS) for Enhanced Vision Systems, Synthetic Vision Systems, Combined Vision Systems and Enhanced Flight Vision Systems. RTCA, Inc., Washington, DC (2011)

Straight-in landing operations below DA/DH or MDA using an enhanced flight vision system (EFVS) under IFR, 14 C.F.R. § 91.176 (2017)

Yeh, M., Chandra, D.: Air transport pilots' information priorities for surface moving maps. In: Proceedings of the Human Factors and Ergonomics Society 47th Annual Meeting, pp. 129–133 (2003)

# The Measurement of the Propensity to Trust Automation

Sarah A. Jessup[1], Tamera R. Schneider[1], Gene M. Alarcon[2(✉)],
Tyler J. Ryan[3], and August Capiola[2]

[1] Wright State University, Dayton, OH, USA
jessup.11@wright.edu
[2] Air Force Research Laboratory, Wright-Patterson AFB, Dayton, OH, USA
gene.alarcon.1@us.af.mil
[3] General Dynamics Information Technology, Dayton, OH, USA

**Abstract.** In recent years, there has been a focus on not just how people work with automation, but how humans interact with and rely on automation in human-automation teams. Few studies have examined how propensity to trust in automation influences trust behaviors. Of the published studies, there are inconsistencies in how propensity to trust automation is conceptualized and thus measured. Research on attitudes and intentions has discerned that reliability and validity of measures can be increased by using language that is more specific for a particular context, which reduces respondent ambiguity and increases the ability to predict behavior. This study examined traditional measures of propensity to trust automation, and whether adapting measures could enhance our ability to predict beliefs about automation trustworthiness (perceived trustworthiness) and behaving in a trusting manner when interacting with automation (behavioral trust). Participants ($N = 55$) completed three propensity to trust in automation surveys including Propensity to Trust Technology, an adapted propensity measure, and the Complacency-Potential Rating Scale. Participants played a modified investor/dictator game, where people thought they were teaming with a NAO robot. This study demonstrated that compared to a more generally-worded measure, the context-specific measure of propensity to trust automation was more reliable and better predicted perceived trustworthiness and behavioral trust. Furthermore, the adapted measure was the only significant predictor of both beliefs about the trustworthiness of the automation and the actual trusting behaviors of participants. By decreasing the ambiguity of measures of propensity to trust automation, the reliability and predictive validity are increased.

**Keywords:** Trust · Automation · Propensity to trust · Personality · Measurement

## 1 Introduction

As systems, tasks, and machines become increasingly automated, researchers need to better understand how people and automation work together. Automation refers to technology that allows for data to be collected, selected, computed, and analyzed [1].

J. Y. C. Chen and G. Fragomeni (Eds.): HCII 2019, LNCS 11575, pp. 476–489, 2019.
https://doi.org/10.1007/978-3-030-21565-1_32

Automation helps users control processes in a systematic way and make decisions; it can decrease cognitive workload and reduce human error [2–4]. However, automation is irrelevant if humans do not use automated systems because of a lack of trust.

Propensity to trust is the general tendency and willingness of one person to trust another person [5]. Research has examined the relationship between propensity to trust and trust in interpersonal situations. People's tendency to trust another (propensity to trust) predicts initial beliefs about how trustworthy another person is (initial trustworthiness) [6–8]. Recently, researchers have adapted and extended the interpersonal trust literature to understand trust in automation, and there are some parallels. However, few studies have examined how the influence of propensity to trust automation influences user reliance on that automation (behavioral trust). Of those published, there are inconsistencies in measures of propensity to trust. With reliable and valid measures of personality, researchers can better predict behavior [9, 10]. This study examined various measures of propensity to trust automation and their ability to effectively predict perceived trustworthiness and behavioral trust of automation. With the increasing prevalence of automation, understanding the ways humans trust and work with automation will help us to design more effective human-machine partnerships.

## 1.1  Trust Models

**Interpersonal Trust.** Mayer and colleagues [5] proposed an interpersonal trust model, where the outcome is risk taking in the relationship. The model includes a trustee or referent of trust, and a trustor or the person or group engaging in trusting intentions or behaviors. Perceived characteristics of the trustee and the trusting disposition of the trustor influence the interaction differently. There are three trustee characteristics that influence perceived trustworthiness. These trustee characteristics are (1) ability, the level of domain-specific knowledge or the skills of the trustee, (2) benevolence, the extent to which the trustor's best interests are in the trustee's mind during decision-making, and (3) integrity, that the trustee behaves ethically and lawfully. Characteristics of ability, benevolence, and integrity of the trustee do not necessarily reflect ground truth. That is, the trustor perceives these characteristics in the trustee, and these perceptions shape the trustor's subsequent willingness to be vulnerable. Both these trustee characteristics and the trustor's dispositional propensity to trust the trustee influence what transpires in a given interaction in distinct and significant ways.

A trustor's propensity to trust is a general willingness and tendency to trust another [5]. This propensity is a relatively stable trait that is developed over time. The interactions that people have with others, including events they witness others experiencing, and the experiences that individuals learn about through media and cultural stories, all shape their own tendency to trust others [11]. Propensity to trust others is especially predictive of trusting behavior in novel situations compared to situations that are more predictable [12]. McKnight and colleagues [13] suggested this is also especially predictive of trusting beliefs in novel or ambiguous situations. As more information about a trustee becomes available, propensity to trust is less likely to predict trusting beliefs and behaviors [14]. The trustor will rely on characteristics of the trustee, such as whether she adheres to her word, reciprocates trust in subsequent interactions, or acts in a trustworthy manner. This type of information from trustor-trustee interactions will be a better predictor of trust than propensity to trust. Propensity to trust and perceived trustworthiness are antecedents of trust that should influence an action or behavior that informs whether one will be more or less vulnerable to another. Lee and See [1] adapted Mayer's model of interpersonal trust to that of trusting automation.

**Trust in Automation.** Lee and See [1] proposed three characteristics of automation that convey perceived trustworthiness, which are similar to ability, benevolence, and integrity. The three automation characteristics are performance, purpose, and process [15]. Performance refers to what the automation does and is capable of doing. Purpose refers to the reason the automation is used by people and whether it performs those functions. Process refers to how well and reliably the automation functions. Their model also accounts for individual differences of the user.

The authors [1] described the predisposition to trust in much the same way as Mayer and colleagues [5]. Similarly, Lee and See describe the predisposition to trust automation as an individual difference that influences initial trust intentions prior to any specific interaction with or knowledge of the automation. This propensity to trust is influenced by past interactions with automation and influences how new information about subsequent interactions will be interpreted. These characteristics are inherent to the trustor and not directly related to characteristics of the automation. Lee and See's model also accounts for the consequences of trusting automation, such as reliance on automation, which is defined as trusting behaviors demonstrated by using the automation.

## 1.2 The Evolution of Measuring Propensity to Trust

**Interpersonal Propensity to Trust.** Research on interpersonal propensity to trust has shown that it predicts both perceived trustworthiness and behavioral trust. Alarcon and colleagues [6] used a modified version of the prisoner's dilemma task to investigate propensity to trust and perceived trustworthiness in dyads with familiar compared to unfamiliar partners. They used both Mayer and Davis' [16] propensity to trust measure and their perceived trustworthiness scale. The researchers found that with unfamiliar dyads, propensity to trust significantly predicted greater perceived trustworthiness amongst partners. Similar research [17] found that propensity to trust (measured with a scale developed for that study) predicted greater behavioral trust during an investment game, such that people with greater propensity to trust invested more money in their partners over the course of the experiment.

**Propensity to Trust Automation.** Compared to interpersonal trust, research investigating the propensity to trust automation is sparse. As such, there are few scales to measure this construct. Two measures that have been developed are the Complacency-Potential Rating Scale [CPRS; 18] and the Propensity to Trust Technology [PTT; 19]. The CPRS has been used in several studies, but the PTT is newer and less used. The CPRS has an empirical base, but the items are broad and reference different types of automation (e.g., ATMs, cruise control, automated devices involved in aviation). Conversely, the PTT has general items with only one referent - technology.

*Complacency-Potential Rating Scale.* In developing the CPRS to assess attitudes toward automation, complacency was defined as a state of low suspicion [18]. That is, when automation is performing as it should and the users are satisfied with the performance of the automation, users may be less alert and attentive to the system, which is characterized as complacency. The researchers sought to measure attitudes about relying more or less on automated systems.

To test the properties of the CPRS, a cross-sectional study ($N = 139$) was conducted [18]. Both internal consistency ($\alpha = .90$) and test-retest reliably (3-month time lag; $\alpha = .87$) were high. This study found that the CPRS was not correlated with age, education, attitudes towards computer use, or computer experience, but it was novel in examining trust in automation as reflected in complacency attitudes. Alas, trust behaviors were not investigated in this study.

Others have also used the CPRS to predict trust behaviors during human-automation interaction. A luggage screening task was used to examine trust in automation [20]. The researchers used 12 items of the CPRS to measure propensity to trust machines. The automation was an x-ray screening task equipped with an automated weapon detector to examine luggage for potential threats, such as guns and knives. The CPRS predicted greater initial trustworthiness ($r = .23$, $p < .05$), but not post-task trustworthiness ($r = -.04$, $p > .05$) or behavioral trust (use of automation) ($r = .14$, $p > .05$). This study found that propensity to trust machines predicted initial perceived trustworthiness of automation, but more research on predicting behavioral trust is needed.

*Propensity to Trust Technology.* The Propensity to Trust Technology [PTT; 19] was developed to measure the general tendency to trust in technology. The creation of the scale was driven by theory related to trust in automation and factors purported to influence trust [see 1]. The items were designed to measure stable characteristics in individuals, attitudes towards technology, and whether people were likely to collaborate with technology.

The measure was developed to examine human-automation collaboration [19]. Before task engagement, participants ($N = 44$) completed the PTT ($\alpha = .64$), and then were introduced to a virtual spaceship wherein the human-automation task would commence. The participant, a virtual robot teammate (CEP), and the captain of the spaceship were avatars in the virtual world. The captain explained that the participant would be working with a robot who had prior task experience. The captain informed the participant that an emergency landing to the moon was inevitable and she should rank, from a list of 10 items, what they would need on the moon. She could work with CEP and the captain would evaluate their rankings relative to other teams. First, the participant and CEP independently ranked the items. Unbeknownst to participants, CEP's rankings remained the same across participants. After submitting rankings, participants could compare their and CEP's individual rankings. During this comparison, CEP's rankings also included a rationale for the ranking order (fact-based information, which was static across participants). Participants could change their rankings and were to submit the final ranked list. Change in participant ranking was calculated as the absolute difference between the participant's initial and final rankings ($P_i - P_f$ Rank), and they computed the difference between the participants' final and

CEP's rankings ($P_f$-CEP Rank). The PTT was marginally related to $P_i$-$P_f$ Rank ($r = .27$, $p = .09$) but not related to $P_f$–CEP Rank ($r = .22$, $p = .18$), demonstrating that initial trust levels tended to predict a change in ranking, but not reliance on CEP's ranking. As more information about CEP became available across the task, including the rationale for CEP's rankings, propensity to trust was less important for predicting behavioral trust [14]. Participants may have been influenced by their perceived trustworthiness of CEP, rather than initial trust propensities. This study did not measure perceived trustworthiness, and the PTT had relatively low scale reliability ($\alpha = .64$). We might enhance reliability by using language related to the measurement context.

### 1.3    General vs Specific Scale Specificity

Using specific and contextually relevant language in measurements of attitudes and intentions can reduce ambiguity and increase behavioral prediction [21]. Research has demonstrated that enhancing the contextual precision of wording for survey items also increases our ability to predict behavior [22]. In addition, providing respondents with a frame of reference improves the reliability and validity of measurement. A frame of reference effect occurs when respondents are provided with more context when given personality tests [23]. For example, providing the workplace as a reference for employees to respond to personality tests increased measurement precision and predictive utility [24]. These researchers added "at work" to general personality items and found that the specific measure of personality accounted for more variance in predicted workplace outcomes over and above the original personality measure. When participants were given a narrower context about which to focus and the outcomes were also related to that context, the reliability of the measure increased presumably due to less ambiguity about responding and the ability to predict context-relevant (i.e., work) outcomes increased. Given the match between the referent context and the outcome context, both the reliability and the predictive validity of the measure for that context increase [25].

Using this information, we adapted the PTT so that the referent was "automated agent" rather than the more general "technology". Technology refers to broad "practical applications of knowledge" [26] that might be automated, but by definition, technology does not necessarily refer to automation. For example, a light bulb would be considered technology, and incites ambiguity. Our more focused frame of reference should improve both reliability and validity of the PTT.

### 1.4    Hypotheses

This study examined the ability of measures of the propensity to trust automation to predict initial perceived trustworthiness and initial behavioral trust. We hypothesized that propensity to trust automation would predict perceived trustworthiness (H1), and predict behavioral trust (H2). We also hypothesized that an adapted, enhanced referent in a propensity to trust measure would better predict perceived trustworthiness (H3), and also behavioral trust (H4), compared to scales used in past research after controlling for other un-adapted scales.

## 2  Method

### 2.1  Participants

Participants were 55 adults recruited from a Midwestern university. Ages ranged from 18–41 years ($M = 24.11$, $SD = 5.36$). Ethnicities included 41.8% Black, 36.4% White, 16.4% Asian, and 5.5% Biracial. Most (64%) were female and native English speakers (72.7%). Participants were recruited from an introductory psychology course, flyers, email, and word of mouth, and received a $30 gift card and cash payment for all money earned during the task.

### 2.2  Task

Checkmate [27] is a modified investors/dictator game [28] played between two players. In this study, the participant was the "banker" (investor) and a robot was the "runner" (dictator). The banker's role was to loan money to the runner over five rounds. The runner's role was to collect as many boxes as possible in a virtual maze over five rounds. Participants were informed that all money exchanged in the task represented real money. The amount of money the banker had in his/her virtual bank at the end of the session belonged to the banker, and the earnings were paid out in the form of cash, rounded up to the nearest quarter.

The banker initially had $50 in her account, and loaned money to the runner each round in anticipation of earning interest on her investment based on the runner's performance. For each round, the banker chose a loan amount range: small ($1–$7), medium ($4–$10), or large ($7–$13). Given the initial loan range, the runner then chose a risk level to potentially earn more money by choosing a higher risk level, but the runner risked not earning any money at all if his performance was poor. Risk levels could be low (75–150%), moderate (50–200%), or high (0–300%). For example, if the risk level was low then the maximum loss would be 25% (100%–75% = 25%) if the runner did not collect any boxes, but the maximum gain would be 50%.

At the beginning of the round, the runner chose a risk level. The runner then promised to return the initial loan plus an additional 50% of the earnings to the banker. The banker was notified about the risk level and promised rate of return via a pop-up message. Then, the banker selected an actual amount to loan to the runner: small ($1–$7), medium ($4–$10), or large ($7–$13). Money was then transferred into the runner's virtual wallet and the maze-running task of two minutes commenced. The banker could watch the runner's performance in the task. After two minutes, the runner decided how much money to return to the banker. The banker received the exact amount to be returned via a pop-up message. These steps were repeated over five rounds. However, this study was part of a larger research effort. For this study, we were only interested in perceptions of perceived trustworthiness prior to round one and behavioral trust during round one.

For this study, the participant was always assigned to the role of banker and the runner was always a Nao robot (see Appendix 2). The runner's risk level was set to medium for each round and the robot always returned the promised amount of money to the banker. All runner data, including maze performance and return to the banker, was prerecorded so we could focus on participant trust of the automated partner in stable conditions. Participants were led to believe they were interacting with the robot.

## 2.3   Measures

### Propensity to Trust Automation

*Complacency-Potential Rating Scale.* The CPRS [18] is a 20-item scale to measure attitudes towards automation that could influence the potential for complacency, including 4 filler items. The scale has high reliability ($\alpha = .90$), internal consistency ($r > .98$), and three-month test-retest reliability ($\alpha = .87$). The full scale is not published, but we were able to secure 14 of the 20 items through published reports. A 14-item version was used for the present study, where respondents rated their agreement on 5-point scales (1 = *Strongly Disagree* to 5 = *Strongly Agree*). An example item is, "If I need to have a tumor in my body removed, I would choose to undergo computer-aided surgery using laser technology because it is more reliable and safer than manual surgery". Items 7 and 8 were reversed and an average was computed. The scale had poor reliability; all alphas are reported along the diagonal in Table 1.

*Propensity to Trust Technology.* The PTT [19] scale has 6-items that measure the general propensity to trust technology ($\alpha = .64$). The measure was developed to measure stable characteristics regarding attitudes towards technology, and the potential for collaboration with technology. Items included: "Generally, I trust technology"; "Technology helps me solve many problems"; "I think it's a good idea to rely on technology for help"; "I don't trust the information I get from technology" (R); "Technology is reliable"; and "I rely on technology". Responses were on a 5-point agreement scale. An adapted version included scale instructions that defined automated agent: "An automated agent can be defined as an entity that runs by computerized algorithms and that interacts with humans," and replaced "technology" with "automated agent" as the referent in each item. An adapted item is, "Automated agents help me solve many problems." The scale demonstrated adequate reliability.

**Perceived Trustworthiness.** Perceived trustworthiness of the runner was measured using the Trust in Automated Systems scale [29] [$\alpha = .96$; 30]. An 11-item scale measures trust in a specific type of system, and references "the system". For this study, we modified items so they referred to "the runner". An example item is, "I can trust the runner". Participants selected the option best describing their feeling or impression of the runner during the interaction using a 7-point range scale (1 = not at all, to 7 = extremely). The scale demonstrated adequate reliability.

**Behavioral Trust.** Behavioral trust was assessed with banker loan amounts (small, medium, or large), as described in the task section above.

## 2.4   Procedure

Participants were run in an experimental laboratory where they were consented then were introduced to the Nao robot, Rufus. Participants were told they were going to meet the other study participant, and when the experimenter tapped Rufus on the head, he stood up and became animated, stating "Thanks for waking me up [experimenter name]. Hi, I'm Rufus. It's nice to meet you. Time to get to work". Participants were then seated at a computer in an adjacent room to commence with the experiment, and completed surveys. Next, participants completed an endowment earning task that included five, medium-difficulty, multiple choice math problems. They were told that their performance would determine how much money they would earn toward their main task, and each earned $50 regardless of their performance. Then, participants completed the adapted PTT questionnaire. The experimenter read a backstory on Rufus aloud to participants (Appendix 1). Next, participants were trained on playing the task and they played two practice rounds; one the Banker and the other as the Runner. Then, participants were told they were randomly selected to play the Banker and Rufus was selected to play the runner for their session. Following practice, the perceived trust-worthiness questionnaire was completed. Each round lasted approximately three to five minutes. After the competition of the fifth round, participants were debriefed and paid for their time with a $30 gift card along with cash in the amount of their virtual wallet.

## 3  Results

To test the hypothesis that propensity to trust automation would predict perceived trustworthiness, we computed Pearson's product-moment correlations (see Table 1). The CPRS was not related to perceived trustworthiness, $r(53) = .08$, $p = .56$, but the PTT predicted greater perceived trustworthiness, $r(53) = .48$, $p < .001$, as did the adapted PTT, $r(53) = .47$, $p < .001$. Hypothesis 1 was partially supported.

To test the hypothesis that propensity to trust automation would predict behavioral trust, we used a combination of Spearman's rank-order correlations and discriminant analyses, as the outcome data are ordinal. The CPRS did not predict behavioral trust, $r_s(53) = .15$, $p = .27$, nor did the PTT, $r_s(53) = .17$, $p = .23$. However, the adapted PTT predicted greater behavioral trust, $r_s(53) = .30$, $p = .03$.

Discriminant function analysis was conducted to examine whether each measure of propensity to trust automation could predict whether participants would bet high, medium, or small loan amounts. Results indicated that the CPRS did not predict loan amounts, Wilk's $\lambda = .98$, $\chi^2 (2) = 1.32$, $p = .52$, accounting for only 3% of the variance in behavior. Approximately 29% of the participants in each group were correctly classified. The original PTT did not predict loan amounts, Wilk's $\lambda = .96$, $\chi^2 (2) = 2.19$, $p = .34$, accounting for only 4% of the variance in behavior. Approximately 33% of the participants in each group were correctly classified. However, the adapted PTT significantly predicted category of loan amount, Wilk's $\lambda = .88$, $\chi^2 (2) = 6.49$, $p = .04$, accounting for 12% of the variance in behavior. Approximately 42% of the participants in each group were correctly classified. Hypothesis 2 was partially supported.

Hierarchical regression was computed to test whether the adapted propensity to trust technology scale would better predict perceived trustworthiness controlling for the other two propensity to trust automation scales. The first step regressing perceived trustworthiness onto CPRS and PTT was significant, $R^2 = .24$, $F(2, 52) = 8.36$, $p = .001$, accounting for 24% of the variance in perceived trustworthiness

484    S. A. Jessup et al.

**Table 1.** Descriptive statistics and correlations for demographic and scale variables

|  | M | SD | 1 | 2 | 3 | 4 | 5 | 6 |
|---|---|---|---|---|---|---|---|---|
| 1. Age | 24.11 | 5.36 |  |  |  |  |  |  |
| 2. Gender |  |  | −.24 |  |  |  |  |  |
| 3. CPRS | 3.79 | 0.42 | .11 | −.32* | (.67) |  |  |  |
| 4. PTT (original) | 4.00 | 0.49 | .10 | −.12 | .43** | (.76) |  |  |
| 5. PTT (adapted) | 3.58 | 0.59 | .16 | −.12 | .33* | .52** | (.84) |  |
| 6. Perceived trustworthiness | 4.84 | 0.81 | .04 | −.07 | .08 | .48** | .47** | (.83) |
| 7. Behavioral trust | 1.04 | 0.69 | .09 | −.07 | .15 | .17 | .30* | .36** |

*Note.* $N = 55$ (except age $N = 54$). * $p < .05$, ** $p < .01$. Cronbach's α are on diagonals. Gender was coded: Males = 0, Females = 1. CPRS = Complacency-Potential Rating Scale, PTT = Propensity to Trust Technology. Behavioral Trust was coded: Small = 0, Medium = 1, Large = 2.

(see Table 2). The second step included adapted PTT, and was significant, $R^2 = .33$, $\Delta R^2 = .08$, $F(3, 51) = 8.21$, $p < .001$, adding another 9% to account for 33% of the variance in perceived trustworthiness. The adapted PTT accounted for a significant amount of variance in perceived trustworthiness, beyond the CPRS and PTT. Hypothesis 3 was supported.

**Table 2.** Hierarchical regression predicting perceived trustworthiness

| Predictor | Perceived trustworthiness | | | |
|---|---|---|---|---|
|  | Step 1 | | Step 2 | |
|  | B | β | B | β |
| Constant | 2.38* |  | 2.09* |  |
| CPRS | −0.28 | −.15 | −0.37 | −.20 |
| PTT | 0.89** | .54 | 0.63* | .38 |
| Adapted PTT |  |  | 0.46* | .34 |
| $R^2$ | .24 |  | .33 |  |
| F | 8.36* |  | 8.21* |  |
| $\Delta R^2$ |  |  | .08 |  |
| $\Delta F$ |  |  | 6.22* |  |

*Note.* $N = 55$. * $p < .05$, ** $p < .001$. CPRS = Complacency-Potential Rating Scale; PTT = Propensity to Trust Technology.

A combination of hierarchical regression and discriminant function analysis examined whether adding the adapted PTT improved the prediction of behavioral trust beyond that of CPRS and PTT. For the regression, the first step regressed behavior onto CPRS and PTT, and did not predict behavior, $R^2 = .05$, $F(2, 52) = 1.28$, $p = .29$ (see Table 3). The combination of CPRS and PTT accounted for only 5% of the variance in behavioral trust. The second step included the adapted PTT, and was not significant,

$R^2 = .09$, $\Delta R^2 = .05$, $F(3, 51) = 1.71$, $p = .18$, adding only 4% and accounting for a total of 9% of the variance in behavioral trust.

**Table 3.** Hierarchical regression analysis predicting behavioral trust

| Predictor | Behavioral trust | | | |
|---|---|---|---|---|
| | Step 1 | | Step 2 | |
| | $B$ | $\beta$ | $B$ | $\beta$ |
| Constant | −0.44 | | 0.62 | |
| CPRS | 0.15 | .09 | 0.09 | .05 |
| PTT | 0.23 | .16 | 0.07 | .05 |
| Adapted PTT | | | 0.29 | .25 |
| $R^2$ | .05 | | .09 | |
| $F$ | 1.28 | | 1.71 | |
| $\Delta R^2$ | | | .05 | |
| $\Delta F$ | | | 2.50 | |

Note. $N = 55$. * $p < .05$, ** $p < .001$.
CPRS = Complacency-Potential Rating Scale; PTT = Propensity to Trust Technology.

Hierarchical discriminant function analysis was conducted to examine whether propensity to trust automation predicts participants' behavioral trust. Step one including both the CPRS and the PTT was not significant, Wilk's $\lambda = .95$, $\chi^2$ (4) = 2.54, $p = .64$, accounting for 5% of the variance in behaviors. Just over 38% of the participants in each group were correctly classified. For step two, the adapted PTT was added to the model, Wilk's $\lambda = .86$, $\chi^2$ (6) = 7.73, $p = .26$, accounting for a nonsignificant 12% of the variance. Almost half (45.5%) of the participants in each group were correctly classified. The addition of the adapted PTT into the model accounted for an extra 7% of the variance in behavioral trust beyond that of the CPRS and PTT, but this was not significant. In the small loan category, 50% of the cases were predicted, in the medium loan category, 34.5% of the cases were predicted, and in the high loan category, 64.3% of the cases were predicted. Across all categories 45.5% of the original grouped cases were correctly classified. Hypothesis 4 was not supported. The adapted PTT did not predict behavioral trust categories over and above the other two measures of propensity to trust automation.

# 4 Discussion

We compared three measures of propensity to trust automation to ascertain their reliability and predictive validity for both perceived trustworthiness and behavioral trust. The CPRS did not predict perceive trustworthiness as it did in past research. Additionally, it did not it predict behavioral trust, which is consistent with previous research [20]. In the present study, the CPRS was only marginally reliable ($\alpha = .67$), nor was it in prior research [$\alpha = .61$; 20]. An acceptable reliability for Cronbach's alpha is .70 or higher [31]. The CPRS may not be reliable or predictive because it is too broad as a measure and the items reference many different types of automation, such as ATMs, automated medical equipment, and cruise control. Each type of automation entails a certain level of risk associated with it and that risk may not be equally dispersed across the different types of automation, which may influence responses. For example, if cruise control on a car is faulty, the owner might be issued a ticket for speeding. In contrast, if a person is undergoing open heart surgery and the surgery is augmented with a robotic arm for additional assistance, then the risk would be higher and a person's reliance may be affected. If the automation fails in this second scenario, the consequences could be fatal. Measurement that is more consistent with the referent of interest, such as the adapted PTT, which references "automated agent," increases reliability and predictive validity of the measure. When people are given a more specific referent, then researchers can increase the precision of measurement [23]. In this study, not only was the adapted PTT more reliable, it was also more predictive in some cases.

The PTT and the adapted PTT both predicted perceived trustworthiness. This is the first study to examine the use of the PTT to predict perceived trustworthiness of automation. As in past research [19], the PTT did not predict behavioral trust. The initial tendency to trust technology did not influence the amount of money participants chose to loan to the robotic runner. However, the adapted PTT did predict behavioral trust. When enhancing the specificity of the measure, to refer to the automated agent, which matched the context of the behavior, we aimed to predict initial disposition to trust automated agents. This is the first study to show that propensity to trust automation predicts behavior toward an automated agent. Although researchers in the interpersonal trust literature [17] have found that propensity to trust predicts behavioral trust with other people, this phenomenon has not been previously established in the automation domain.

Adapting the PTT to the trust context increased reliability of the measure from an alpha of .76 to .84. Furthermore, its capacity to predict both perceived trustworthiness and behavioral trust were increased. The adapted PTT accounted for a significant amount of variance in perceived trustworthiness, even after controlling for the PTT and the CPRS. This shows that, as we expected, adapting a measure to make it more specific to the context enhances predictability of perceived trustworthiness. It is interesting to note, however, that both terms "technology" and "automated agent" were responded to by participants as separate referents, yet both predicted unique variance in the perceived trustworthiness of the robot. However, this was not the case with behavioral trust. In this case, only the adapted PTT predicted behavioral trust. Although the adapted PTT scale did not account for a significant additional variance when controlling for the other measures, it should be noted the adapted scale accounted for 9% of the variance in behaviors. The final regression model accounted for 9% of the variance, indicating any variance in behavior the CPRS and un-adapted PTT scale account for are subsumed in the variance of the adapted PTT scale.

This study demonstrated that contextually specific measures are more reliable, can account for more variance in perceived trustworthiness, and can better predict behavioral outcomes of trust. Armed with these insights and this new measure, researchers can better predict perceived trustworthiness of automated systems and better understand human reliance on automated systems.

# 5   Conclusion

In conclusion, past research has inconsistently measured propensity to trust automation, and available measures have low reliabilities. This study demonstrated that context-specific measures of propensity to trust automation are more reliable and more predictive of perceived trustworthiness and behavioral trust. With better measures in hand, researchers can embark upon their future research to better understand the relationship between humans and their automated partners. As more systems and machines in the workplace and everyday life become automated, it is important that researchers understand how individual factors, such as propensity to trust automation, influence trust and use of those systems.

**Acknowledgements.**   This research was part of a larger study conducted in the Human-Centered Science Laboratory, supported by the Air Force Research Laboratory. This work was completed while one of the authors (TS) served at the National Science Foundation. The views expressed in this poster are solely those of the authors and do not necessarily represent those of NSF.

# Appendix 1

Backstory for Rufus
"The military currently integrates automation into dangerous scenarios alongside humans. Automation is useful in high-risk scenarios, such as disabling explosive devices, navigating unmanned aerial vehicles (UAVs), and carrying heavy equipment. However, automation is expensive and takes time to develop. As such, the military is testing automated robots containing self-preservation algorithms. This means the military is creating robots that should be able to make decisions to protect themselves, as well as other humans around them. If a situation is too dangerous, the robot should take proper precautions to minimize damages to itself. The current study uses the same algorithms to aid the robot's decision-making when teamed with another human in a maze-running task. Keep in mind that Rufus the robot may act self-interested, meaning he may prioritize himself over you".

## Appendix 2

NAO Robot

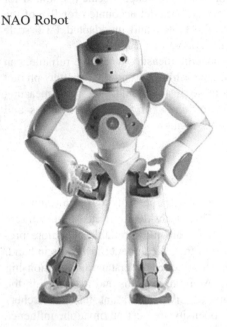

## References

1. Lee, J.D., See, K.A.: Trust in automation: designing for appropriate reliance. Hum. Factors **46**(1), 50–80 (2004)
2. Hoff, K.A., Bashir, M.: Trust in automation: integrating empirical evidence on factors that influence trust. Hum. Factors **57**(3), 407–434 (2015)
3. Huang, H., Bashir, M.: Personal influences on dynamic trust formation in human-agent interaction. In: 5th Proceedings of the International Conference on Human Agent Interaction, pp. 233–243. ACM, New York (2017)
4. Harvard Business Review. https://hbr.org/2018/07/want-less-biased-decisions-use-algorithms. Accessed 30 Dec 2018
5. Mayer, R.C., Davis, J.H., Schoorman, F.D.: An integrative model of organizational trust. Acad. Manag. Rev. **20**(3), 709–734 (1995)
6. Alarcon, G.M., Lyons, J.B., Christensen, J.C.: The effect of propensity to trust and familiarity on perceptions of trustworthiness over time. Pers. Individ. Differ. **94**, 309–315 (2016)
7. Colquitt, J.A., Scott, B.A., LePine, J.A.: Trust, trustworthiness, and trust propensity: a meta-analytic test of their unique relationships with risk taking and job performance. J. Appl. Psychol. **92**(4), 909–927 (2007)
8. Gill, H., Boies, K., Finegan, J.E., McNally, J.: Antecedents of trust: establishing a boundary condition for the relation between propensity to trust and intention to trust. J. Bus. Psychol. **19**(3), 287–302 (2005)
9. Funder, D.C., Ozer, D.J.: Pieces of the Personality Puzzle: Readings in Theory and Research. Norton & Co., New York (2010)

10. Wiggins, J.S.: Personality and Prediction: Principles of Personality Assessment. Addison-Wesley, Boston (1973)
11. Van Lange, P.A.M.: Generalized trust: four lessons from genetics and culture. Curr. Dir. Psychol. Sci. **24**(1), 71–76 (2015)
12. Rotter, J.B.: Interpersonal trust, trustworthiness, and gullibility. Am. Psychol. **35**(1), 1–7 (1980)
13. McKnight, D.H., Cummings, L.L., Chervany, N.L.: Initial trust formation in new organizational relationships. Acad. Manag. Rev. **23**(3), 473–490 (1998)
14. Jones, S.L., Shah, P.P.: Diagnosing the locus of trust: a temporal perspective for trustor, trustee, and dyadic influences on perceived trustworthiness. J. Appl. Psychol. **101**(3), 392–414 (2016)
15. Lee, J., Moray, N.: Trust, control strategies and allocation of function in human-machine systems. Ergonomics **35**(10), 1243–1270 (1992)
16. Mayer, R.C., Davis, J.H.: The effect of the performance appraisal system on trust for management: a field quasi-experiment. J. Appl. Psychol. **84**(1), 123–136 (1999)
17. Evans, A.M., Revelle, W.: Survey and behavioral measurements of interpersonal trust. J. Res. Pers. **42**(6), 1585–1593 (2008)
18. Singh, I.L., Molloy, R., Parasuraman, R.: Automation-induced "complacency": development of the complacency-potential rating scale. Int. J. Aviat. Psychol. **3**(2), 111–122 (1993)
19. Schneider, T.R., Jessup, S.A., Stokes, C., Rivers, S., Lohani, M., McCoy, M.: The influence of trust propensity on behavioral trust. Poster session presented at the meeting of Association for Psychological Society, Boston, May 2017
20. Merritt, S.M., Ilgen, D.R.: Not all trust is created equal: dispositional and history-based trust in human-automation interactions. Hum. Factors **50**(2), 194–210 (2008)
21. Ajzen, I., Fishbein, M.: Attitudinal and normative variables as predictors of specific behaviors. J. Pers. Soc. Psychol. **27**(1), 41–57 (1973)
22. Schneider, T.R., et al.: The effects of message framing and ethnic targeting on mammography use among low-income women. Health Psychol. **20**(4), 256–266 (2001)
23. Lievens, F., De Corte, W., Schollaert, E.: A closer look at the frame-of-reference effect in personality scale scores and validity. J. Appl. Psychol. **93**(2), 268–279 (2008)
24. Bowling, N.A., Burns, G.N.: A comparison of work-specific and general personality measures as predictors of work and non-work criteria. Pers. Individ. Differ. **49**(2), 95–101 (2010)
25. Schmit, M.J., Ryan, A.M., Stierwalt, S.L., Powell, A.B.: Frame-of-reference effects on personality scale scores and criterion-related validity. J. Appl. Psychol. **80**(5), 607 (1995)
26. Merriam-Webster. https://www.merriam-webster.com/dictionary/technology. Accessed 30 Dec 2018
27. Alarcon, G.M., et al.: The effect of propensity to trust and perceptions of trustworthiness on trust behaviors in dyads. Behav. Res. Methods **50**(5), 1906–1920 (2018)
28. Berg, J., Dickhaut, J., McCabe, K.: Trust, reciprocity, and social history. Games Econ. Behav. **10**(1), 122–142 (1995)
29. Jian, J., Bisantz, A.M., Drury, C.G.: Foundations for an empirically determined scale of trust in automated systems. Int. J. Cogn. Ergon. **4**(1), 53–71 (2000)
30. Chancey, E.T., Bliss, J.P., Proaps, A.B., Madhavan, P.: The role of trust as a mediator between system characteristics and response behaviors. Hum. Factors **57**(6), 947–958 (2015)
31. Nunnally, J.C.: Psychometric Theory, 2nd edn. McGraw-Hill, New York (1978)

# An Augmented Reality Shared Mission Planning Scenario: Observations on Shared Experience

Sue Kase[1][✉], Simon Su[1], Vincent Perry[2], Heather Roy[1],
and Katherine Gamble[1]

[1] US Army Research Laboratory, Aberdeen Proving Ground, MD 21005, USA
{sue.e.kase.civ,simon.m.su.civ,heather.e.roy2.civ,
katherine.r.gamble2.civ}@mail.mil
[2] Parsons Corporation, Aberdeen Proving Ground, MD 21005, USA
vincent.p.perry7.ctr@mail.mil

**Abstract.** The proliferation of immersive technologies has accentuated their potential utilization across a broad range of operational situations from strategic planning to the tactical edge. However, little is known about individual and team behavior associated with immersive technologies. We begin to address this challenge by conducting a user-based experiment comparing a 3D augmented reality (AR) device (HoloLens) to a traditional 2D flat screen display. Participant dyads used both technologies to interactively plan a mission to retrieve a repository of intelligence documents located within enemy-held territory. Survey and performance data were collected during the mission planning task. A survey instrument called the Shared Augmented Reality Experience (SARE) survey was developed to measure some aspects of "presence" as defined by factor categories from early virtual environment research. Tested during the mission planning task, a correlation analysis reveals several significant relationships between the survey items and the SARE total score. All relationships between the SARE total score and performance metrics are in the predicted direction; however, only one relationship is significant. Based on the limited data collected to date, experimental outcomes indicate that the level of shared AR experience should be associated with better performance and larger samples should be pursued.

**Keywords:** Shared Augmented Reality · Sensor fusion ·
User-based experiment

## 1 Introduction

The proliferation of immersive technologies (augmented reality (AR) and virtual reality (VR) systems) has accentuated their potential utilization across a broad range of operational situations from strategic planning to the tactical edge. The majority of immersive technology use in the U.S. Army focuses on meeting the needs of Soldier training consistent with existing doctrine. According to ADP 7-0 [1], the Army training process includes understanding, visualizing and describing the battlespace which is

J. Y. C. Chen and G. Fragomeni (Eds.): HCII 2019, LNCS 11575, pp. 490–503, 2019.
https://doi.org/10.1007/978-3-030-21565-1_33

often represented by creating training environments that mimic military operation conditions, also known as "training as you fight." Several examples of using immersive technologies for training purposes include: armored personnel carrier maintenance [2]; infantry operations, combat missions, and advanced mission rehearsals [3, 4]; and platoon leader communications [5]. Garneau et al. [6] have shown 3D models supporting tactical decision exercises. In cyber warfare, immersive technologies have been used to assist cyber defenders and analysts through visual tagging systems [7].

Unfortunately, continued advancements of immersive systems proceed as if all agree on the facets of human interaction within immersive environments for training or otherwise. There is a rush to assemble immersive platforms composed of mixed reality devices despite little scientific evidence that using immersive technologies produces any qualitative or quantitative benefit [8, 9]. In general, little is known about individual and team behavior associated with immersive environments. Empirical investigations of immersive technologies supporting collocated, remote, and distributed simultaneous shared visualizations are sparse. We begin to close this knowledge gap between human users and immersive technologies by applying a user-based experimentation approach in formulating a concept of shared visualization experience.

In the next section of the paper, we overview a user-based experimentation approach centered on a simulated mission planning scenario. This approach is used in formulating the concept of a shared AR experience. In Sect. 3, factors originating from very early virtual environment research are reviewed. These factors tap tendencies influencing a shared AR experience and form the foundation of an initial survey instrument, the Shared Augmented Reality Experience (SARE) survey. Section 4 details the SARE's scoring, a reliability analysis, and a preliminary correlation analysis of the survey items and performance measures. Section 5 discusses important points in the development of the SARE, and possible improvements applied to the next version of the survey. Section 6 concludes the paper.

## 2   User-Based Experimentation Approach

User-based empirical approaches are essential for understanding the shared AR experience offered by immersive technologies. User-based experimentation can inform future technology development and is obviously an important step in the evaluation process. In this experiment, we investigated two-member teams (dyads) performing a mission planning task with two different technologies, an AR technology (Microsoft HoloLens) and a large table-top multi-touch 2D display (Microsoft Surface table). The dyads used each of the technologies separately to interactively manipulate a subset of military symbology in the process of planning a simulated mission to retrieve a repository of intelligence documents located within enemy-held territory.

The HoloLens is a commercial off-the-shelf AR device with the capability to superimpose data collected and generated from modeling and simulation onto the actual physical environment of the HoloLens user in the form of a 3D holographic image. Team members can walk around the holographic image of the mission terrain, thereby changing their viewing perspective in reference to the image. Each team member's HoloLens allowed marking of symbols and routes on the terrain. By virtue of the mission being in AR, teammates could use their hands to point within the hologram, and the gestures could be seem by their teammates. In this version of the experiment, verbal communication within the dyads was collected while they interacted with the mission terrain. The dyads could optimize their mission plan using an iterative 'run and re-plan' workflow similar to running a wargame simulation with a specified set of model parameter values. Figure 1 shows the 3D holographic image of the mission terrain as viewed through a team member's Hololens. In Fig. 1, the vertical blue arrow in the center of the building model estimates the location of the targeted document repository. The blue lines are example routes decided by the team members to retrieve the documents and reach an extraction point on the waterfront. The black squares to the left of the building are an instruction menu for route planning.

**Fig. 1.** 3D holographic image of the mission terrain viewed from one of the Hololens devices.

Similar in capabilities to Microsoft Surface tablets and laptops, the Surface table is a Samsung SUR40 40" interactive multi-touch display positioned in a horizontal viewing angle. The SUR40 uses Microsoft Pixelsense enabling a more accurate touch recognition. The Surface table displays a 2D image of the mission terrain without rotate, pan, and zoom capabilities, making it similar to utilizing a static 2D representation of terrain in the form of a drawing on paper or a sand table representation. Similar to the Hololens condition, the dyads were collocated, enabling verbal communication and physical pointing to objects displayed on the 2D screen. Figure 2 shows the 2D representation of the mission terrain on the Surface table.

The visualization of the mission terrain was created in Unity using 3D assets and deployed to both devices (HoloLens and Surface table). The buildings, terrain, and

**Fig. 2.** 2D image of the mission terrain displayed on the Surface table.

other objects in the terrain were imported 3D models. Friendly forces were represented by blue diamond symbols; enemy forces were represented by red diamond symbols. Friendly forces moved along the planned route when the mission was executed. Enemy forces dynamically patrolled the interior and perimeter of the building.

An important aspect of formulating a concept of shared AR experience was reducing the registration error to ensure proper 3D holographic object placement for all team members' views. Our experience with using the HoloToolkit Sharing Service provided by Microsoft indicated a noticeable differential in the 3D holographic object placement when the same object was viewed by different HoloLens users [10]. 3D holographic object registration was only accurate for the HoloLens user doing the placement. For other HoloLens users, the same 3D holographic object was slightly misplaced in the actual environment resulting in a less than ideal shared AR experience.

Because the HoloLens is a single-user AR device, a more accurately placed 3D holographic object for a shared AR experience required additional 3D positioning information that is not available from the array of sensors incorporated into existing HoloLens devices. We developed a framework using the OptiTrack motion capture system to add positional tracking data of the different HoloLens users to improve the 3D holographic object registration in a shared AR application [10]. Initial use of this Unity-based sensor data fusion framework showed a vast improvement in the accuracy of the holographic object placement for all users compared to the holographic object placement based only on the Microsoft HoloToolkit Sharing Service.

# 3 Factors of Presence

With the registration error correction, the dyads had an accurately synchronized view of the model terrain and its components. This enabled an investigation of shared AR experience to be conducted with a user-based experimentation approach. In addition to collecting a variety of human performance data during the experiment (i.e., total mission planning time, boat wait time, mission success, length of route, fewest enemy encounters, and avoidance of obstacles) several frequently used survey instruments measuring system usability and perceived workload were incorporated into the experimental design (i.e., System Usability Scale [11]; NASA Task Load Index [12]) including a trial version of the Shared Augmented Reality Experience (SARE) survey developed by the authors.

The SARE survey draws heavily on factors identified in early virtual environment research conducted by Witmer and Singer [13] as part of the Virtual Environments for Combat Training and Mission Rehearsal (VIRTUE) program. Witmer and Singer developed two survey instruments to measure a phenomenon referred to as *presence*. At the time, the U.S. Army was increasing their use of distributed simulations for providing realistic training and rehearsal environments. Vehicle and equipment simulators were under development and being integrated to support battlefield training and rehearsal for Soldiers. The term *presence* can be traced back to telerobotics or teleoperations in experiencing a situation as if one were at the robot's location, or were present at the robot's remote task site. In the early 1990s, a generalized concept of presence was associated with experiencing a computer generated environment rather than the actual physical environment.

At the time, Witmer and Singer [13] reviewed literature that broadly addressed the concept of presence pertaining to the focusing of attention on a stimulus. Drawing from theoretical concepts discussed by Sheridan [14], Held and Durlanch [15], and Barfield and Weghorst [16], Witmer and Singer developed factors within several major categories as being related to or forming the basis of the experience of presence. The factor categories included: control, sensory, distraction, and realism. Each factor category contained a lower layer of sub factors which informed the development of an Immersive Tendencies Questionnaire and a Presence Questionnaire [13].

The *control factor* category captures the level of control a person has interacting with the task environment. Overall, it is thought that more control increases the experience of presence [14]. For example, the user would expect to manipulate and modify objects in the virtual environment giving the impression of controlling the model space and leaving a user-defined footprint. Another aspect of control is the immediacy of consequences resulting from an action. The interaction between the user and the virtual environment should be appropriately coupled based on the model used by the environment [17]. It is thought that a noticeable delay between action and the result of the action diminishes the sense of presence in a virtual environment [15]. The mode in which the user interacts with the environment is also an important control-based consideration. If a new mode of control for interacting with the environment is required, any dependent learning on the part of the user may diminish the sense of

**Table 1.** SARE questions associated with the control factor.

| |
|---|
| *Overall, how capable did you feel interacting with the virtual space by gaze/selection?* |
| *How well did the user interface (buttons) attribute to a shared interaction experience?* |
| *How successful do you think you were in planning the mission?* |

presence until the mode can become well-learned [15]. The SARE survey contains three questions pertinent to the control factor category (Table 1).

The *sensory factor* category concerns the modality of the information presented to the user. In a virtual environment much of the information is attained through visual channels, therefore the type and relevance of information presented to the user visually may strongly influence presence. For example, an environment that contains a considerable amount of information to stimulate the senses would generate a stronger sense of presence than a stimulus poor environment that conveys little information. The quality of the interface should be considered as well; this partially overlaps with the control factor category. Use of unnatural or clumsy interface devices can interfere with the interpretation of visual information presented in the virtual environment requiring excessive user effort and cognitive resources. The extent that the interface allows the user to modify their viewpoint of the environment, or to change what they see by repositioning their head, contributes to the perception of movement. Overall, the environmental richness of the virtual environment in containing a level of detail which appears "real" is important to the user's level of attenuating the surrounding virtual stimulus. Any disjunct visual information detected by the user can cause distraction and potentially lower presence [15]. The SARE survey contains two questions pertaining to the sensory factor category (Table 2).

**Table 2.** SARE questions associated with the sensory factor.

| |
|---|
| *How much did you enjoy the experience?* |
| *How well did the feedback on the menu buttons and in the scene attribute to knowing what your partner was doing?* |

The *distraction factor* category broadly focuses on the user's ability to ignore distractions external to the virtual environment such as local ambient noise and visual triggers (music, text messages, phone calls, and social interaction). The type of input device naturally affects distraction factors, for example, isolating the user from the real world by using a head mounted display compared to a 2D flat-screen. The ability or willingness of the user to ignore externally produced and unnatural or clumsy interface intrusions is an important individual behavioral characteristic to consider. In general, isolating the user from the real-world may increase the sense of being present in the virtual environment. The SARE survey contains two questions pertaining to the distraction factor category (Table 3).

**Table 3.** SARE questions associated with the distraction factor.

| |
|---|
| *How capable did you feel collaborating with your partner through visual perception and audible communication while wearing the HoloLens device?* <br> *How likely would you be to choose augmented reality to conduct mission planning?* |

The *realism factor* category contributes several positive aspects to the sense of presence such as the level of scene realism, consistency of information in the virtual environment, and meaningfulness of experience. Negative aspects associated with the realism factor are disorientation, simulator sickness, and a general feeling of anxiety upon entering and returning from the virtual environment. It seems the more consistent the information conveyed by the virtual environment is with what the user has learned in the real-world, the larger the increase in the positive aspects of presence [13]. Additionally, the more stable components of the scene appear to the user, the less likely simulator sickness or disorientation will detract from the feeling of presence. A shaky virtual environment fractures consistency of information, represses sensations of realism, and potentially leads to disorientation and oculomotor distress [13]. The SARE survey contains three questions pertaining to the realism factor category (Table 4).

**Table 4.** SARE questions associated with the realism factor.

| |
|---|
| *How stable did your gaze feel when trying to focus on a specific location in the scene, either for selection or for placement?* <br> *How stable did the scene appear during movement?* <br> *In your opinion, how close did your scene appear to be to your partner's scene?* |

Witmer and Singer [13] found that increased levels of presence tended to occur with decreased levels of simulator sickness. The Simulator Sickness Questionnaire (SSQ) [18] was used in their study as well as this experiment after a dyad completed the mission planning task with the HoloLens devices. Although not reported in this paper, we would expect a negative relationship between a shared AR experience and simulator sickness. The SARE survey was composed of 11 questions constructed from the four factor categories described above, and is included in the Appendix.

## 4 Shared Augmented Reality Experience Survey

Witmer and Singer [13] administered their Immersive Tendencies and Presence questionnaires to participants performing perceptual, locomotion, and manipulation tasks while wearing a helmet-mounted display unit and using either a joystick or spaceball to navigate a virtual environment. Despite the relatively poor state of the art in virtual environment equipment, Witmer and Singer determined their first attempts at constructing survey instruments measuring presence were promising.

The SARE survey was administered as part of the experiment protocol following completion of the HoloLens condition by the dyads. The objective of the survey was to provide a research instrument measuring a shared AR experience while also identifying and measuring possible individual differences in perception of a shared AR experience. In future experiments the data collected by the SARE survey could be used to stratify individual users into more evenly matched dyads, or even to predict an individual user's shared experience and the dyad's task performance in an AR environment. SARE does not attempt to investigate possible underlying abilities or skills that could influence a shared AR experience. Neither does it attempt to investigate major dimensions such as age, gender, educational background, or field of employment. Some data on these factors were collected through a separate demographic question-naire to be reported in later publications.

The SARE survey used a 5-point scale with semantic descriptions for the anchored ends and the midpoint. The semantic descriptors were based on the content of the question stem. The left anchor (identified as 'not' an instance of the variable) up to the first interval mark was scored as one (1). Any marks appearing in the right-most segment (identified as a 'very' instance of the variable) were scored as five (5). The survey did not contain accompanying instructions.

This version of SARE was analyzed as a single scale. It was hoped that several subscales associated with the presence factor categories would be identified; however, the current sample size was not large enough to support this. Before the survey results were examined in detail, an internal consistency measure of reliability was calculated. Construct validity is a requirement for surveys and questionnaires [19]. The internal consistency of the SARE survey was calculated using Cronbach's Alpha for all 11 survey items and was determined to be 0.65. Removing questions 1 and 9 from the reliability analysis increased the Cronbach's Alpha to 0.72 which is considered an acceptable level of internal consistency [20, 21].

The first question removed from the Cronbach's Alpha analysis is a direct elici-tation of the user's current level of experience with AR technology (1. How experi-enced are you with augmented reality technology?). The user's level of AR experience likely influences all of the factors discussed in the previous section. The second question removed from the Cronbach's Alpha analysis, Question 9 (How stable did the scene appear during movement?), is associated with the realism factor category. Question 9's context is similar to question 3 (How stable did your gaze feel when trying to focus on a specific location in the scene, either for selection or for place-ment?). Both questions (3 and 9) assess the user's interpretation of visual stability in the AR environment. Question 9 is more broadly focused on stability during "movement" whereas Question 3 focused more specifically on interface actions such as "selection" and "placement". It is unclear why removal of item 9 increased internal consistency but removal of item 3 did not.

The scoring method for the SARE survey was to sum the responses on the 5-point scales yielding a total score for each team member representing the magnitude of a shared AR experience. The average SARE total score was 41.16 ($SD$ = 5.23). To investigate whether there was an association between each survey item and the total SARE score a Spearman's rank-order correlation [22] was performed on the 18 team members (9 dyads) participating in the mission planning experiment. Seven of the 11 items correlated significantly with the total SARE score in the positive direction. Items 3, 4, and 8 are significant at the $p$ = .01 level. Items 2, 6, 7, and 11 are significant at the $p$ = .05 level. The statistically significant correlations are presented in Table 5.

The strongest correlations with the SARE total score were items 3 and 8 (realism factor category) and item 4 (control factor category). Item 3 (How stable did your gaze feel when trying to focus on a specific location in the scene, either for selection or for placement?) was discussed earlier with the removal of Question 9 from the reliability analysis. This item focused on the user's interpretation of visual stability in reference to actions such as "selection" and "placement". A feeling of visual stability when using the HoloLens to complete the mission planning task would have a positive effect on an overall shared AR experience. Visual stability was needed to accurately manipulate the components in the terrain model and efficiently utilize the menu capabilities to plan and execute the mission route. Item 8 (In your opinion, how close did your scene appear to be to your partner's scene?) benefited from the addition of the OptiTrack positional tracking data to reduce the holographic object registration across multiple HoloLens users. The dyad members had a synchronized view of the mission terrain model which supported a shared experience. Item 4 (Overall, how capable did you feel interacting with the virtual scene by gaze/selection?) overlaps with Item 3 especially when gaze was involved in completing an action using the HoloLens. The user's impression of how quickly and accurately the HoloLens responded to attempts to control or interact with it influenced the level of the user's shared AR experience.

**Table 5.** Correlations between SARE items and the SARE total score.

| | Total | Q2 | Q3 | Q4 | Q5 | Q6 | Q7 | Q8 | Q10 | Q11 |
|---|---|---|---|---|---|---|---|---|---|---|
| Total | – | | | | | | | | | |
| Q2 | .57* | – | | | | | | | | |
| Q3 | .70** | | – | | | | | | | |
| Q4 | .69** | .67** | .75** | – | | | | | | |
| Q5 | | | | | – | | | | | |
| Q6 | .48* | | | | | – | | | | |
| Q7 | .50* | | | | | | – | | | |
| Q8 | .62** | | | | | | | – | | |
| Q10 | | | | | | | | | – | |
| Q11 | .47* | .76** | | .63** | | | | | | – |

Note: N = 18; * = $p$ < .05; ** = $p$ < .01

There is also a strong significant relationship between items 2 (sensory factor category) and 4 (control factor category). If the user found the HoloLens responsive during planning the mission, this should contribute to a more enjoyable experience. Items 2 and 4 showed a strong relationship with item 11 (distraction factor category) which asked the user if they would choose AR to conduct mission planning. If the user found HoloLens interactions natural and responsive and the overall experience of completing a mission planning task enjoyable, then choosing the HoloLens to conduct mission planning would be expected to be a positive relationship. The positive relationships between these items should be tied to better performance measures in completing the task.

Mission planning task performance measures included: total time to complete the mission, mission time execution, number of obstacles hit, number of sightings by hostiles, total mission route distance, number of path segments making up route, number of path segments deleted, and patrol wait time for extraction. Better performance would be associated with less time required for completion of the task, shorter route distances, and fewer interactions with hostiles and obstacles. If a significant negative correlation occurred between the SARE total score and any of the performance measures then we could conclude there was a higher overall level of shared AR experience on the mission planning task.

Unfortunately, the total SARE score was only significantly correlated with one performance measure. There was a weak negative correlation between the total SARE score and the length of the mission route, $r_s(18) = -.484$, $p < .05$. The length of the mission route was calculated by summing the path segments plotted on the terrain to avoid physical obstacles and detection by hostiles in retrieving the repository of intelligence documents and then arriving at the extraction point. Although 100% of the correlations were in the predicted negative direction, it is not clear why there was only one significant relationship between the SARE score and the performance measures. Possible reasons for the lack of correlations are discussed in the next section. It is important to keep in mind that these results should be considered preliminary and interpreted with caution because of the small number of dyads participating in the mission planning experiment.

## 5  Discussion

Building on early virtual environment research measuring the subjective feeling of presence, a shared AR experience (SARE) survey was developed and tested with a user-based experimentation approach applied to a simulated mission planning task. Dyads performed the task comparing two technologies: the HoloLens instrumented with a sensor framework, and a 2D Surface table display. The HoloLens provided the dyad with an interactive 3D holographic image of the mission terrain overlaid on their physical environment. The Surface table offered the dyad a traditional flat screen display with touch recognition. In addition to administering the SARE survey and other questionnaires, performance measures from the dyad utilizing both technologies were collected.

Dyad team members completed the SARE survey after using the HoloLens in the mission planning task. Items making up the survey emerged from four categories of factors (control, sensory, distraction, realism) identified by Witmer and Singer [13] and other presence researchers [14–17]. The SARE items were analyzed as a single scale because subscales associated with the four categories of factors could not be identified. Most likely a larger sample size, a minimum of 150 or 5 to 10 samples per factor category would be required for item clustering to occur. After removing two of the 11 survey items, a reliability analysis yielded an acceptable level of internal consistency. However, there is certainly room for improvement in subsequent versions of the SARE survey by reducing redundancy and overlap across the factor categories.

The SARE items were summed to produce a total score for each team member. A correlation analysis was performed between individual items and the total score identifying several strong significant relationships. A feeling of visual stability by the user appeared important when manipulating mission planning components on the 3D terrain. A natural feeling of control in how the HoloLens responded to user interactions also appeared important. Both visual stability and naturalistic control showed a positive relationship with the SARE total score contributing to a shared AR experience. The addition of positional tracking data offered by the OptiTrack motion capture system maximized a synchronized view of the terrain model across dyad members creating a strong positive relationship with the SARE total score. An interesting across item relationship occurred between enjoying the overall experience and choosing to use AR (i.e., HoloLens) again for mission planning. A follow-up question specifying broader categories of tasks not limited to mission planning would have been informative. Does "enjoying" a shared AR experience during a particular task instance (i.e., mission planning) transfer to positive outcomes in future AR experiences across a broad range of tasks?

A somewhat disappointing result—only one weakly significant relationship between the SARE total score and the task performance measures was identified. All the performance measures were in the predicted direction but non-significant. The expected relationship was that the better the visual stability, control response, view synchronization, overall enjoyment, the more efficiently the mission planning task would be performed (e.g., shorter mission route, less mission execution time) and fewer errors made (e.g., hitting obstacles, sightings by hostiles). At the least, the limited data collected during this experiment provided indications that the hypothesis (level of shared AR experience is associated with better performance) should be pursued using larger samples.

# 6 Conclusion

The U.S. Army is increasing their use of virtual environments for providing realistic training and rehearsal environments. Advancements in immersive technologies are accelerating with limited information and empirical evidence on the actual effectiveness of learning and skill acquisition in these environments. Early virtual environment research questioned whether task performance of users was tied to their feeling of *presence*. Potential factor categories involved in a *being there* experience were identified by several presence researchers [13–17]. A Shared Augmented Reality Experience (SARE) survey was developed drawing from these factors and tested with a user-based experimentation approach. Dyads wearing HoloLens devices equipped with a positional tracking framework to enhance scene synchronization performed a mission planning task. Results from this preliminary administration of the SARE survey suggested satisfactory internal consistency on a single scale. Significant item correlations with the total SARE survey scores were identified as well as several significant inter-item correlations focused on the level of enjoyment of the AR experience, the responsiveness of the device, and scene stability which supported the dyad's perception of realism. Correlations between the SARE total score and performance measures were all in the predicted direction; however, only one correlation was found to be significant possibly due to the small sample size and too few survey items per factor category. Based on this limited data collection effort, analysis results indicated that the level of shared AR experience was associated with better performance and larger sample sizes should be pursued.

**Acknowledgments.** This work was supported in part by the DOD High Performance Computing Modernization Program at The Army Research Laboratory (ARL), Department of Defense Supercomputing Resource Center (DSRC).

# Appendix: Shared Augmented Reality Experience (SARE) Survey

1. How experienced are you with augmented reality technology?
   (Not experienced) 1 2 3 4 5 (Very experienced)
2. How much did you enjoy the experience?
   (Don't enjoy) 1 2 3 4 5 (Very much enjoy)
3. How stable did your gaze feel when trying to focus on a specific location in the scene, either for selection or for placement?
   (Not stable) 1 2 3 4 5 (Very stable)
4. Overall, how capable did you feel interacting with the virtual scene by gaze/selection?
   (Not capable) 1 2 3 4 5 (Very capable)
5. How well did the user interface (buttons) attribute to a shared interaction experience?
   (Not well) 1 2 3 4 5 (Very well)
6. How well did the feedback on the menu buttons and in the scene attribute to knowing what your partner was doing?
   (Not well) 1 2 3 4 5 (Very well)
7. How capable did you feel collaborating with your partner through visual perception and audible communication while wearing the HoloLens device?
   (Not capable) 1 2 3 4 5 (Very capable)
8. In your opinion, how close did your scene appear to be to your partner's scene?
   (Not close) 1 2 3 4 5 (Very close)
9. How stable did the scene appear during movement?
   (Not stable) 1 2 3 4 5 (Very stable)

10. How successful do you think you were in planning the mission?
    (Not successful) 1 2 3 4 5 (Very successful)
11. How likely would you be to choose augmented reality to conduct mission planning?
    (Not likely) 1 2 3 4 5 (Very likely)

# References

1. ADP 7-0 (FM 7-0): Training Units and Developing Leaders. Headquarters, Department of Army. Washington, DC (2012)
2. Henderson, S., Feiner, S.: Evaluating the benefits of augmented reality for task localization in maintenance of an armored personnel carrier turret. In: Proceedings on IEEE International Symposium on Mixed and Augmented Reality, pp. 135–144. IEEE Press, New York (2009)
3. Hamilton, R.N., Holmquist, J.P.: Training in virtual and augmented realities: an interview with Bruce Knerr. Ergonomics Des. **13**, 18–22 (2005)
4. Kaber, D.B., Riley, J.M., Endsley, M.R., Sheik-Nainer, M., Zhang, T., Lampton, D.A.: Measuring situation awareness in virtual environment-based training. Mil. Psychol. **25**, 330–344 (2013)
5. Khooshabeh, P., Choromanski, I., Neubauer, C., Krum, D.M., Spicer, R., Campbell, J.: Mixed reality training for tank platoon leader communication skills. In: Proceedings on IEEE Virtual Reality Conference, pp. 1–2. IEEE Press, New York (2017)
6. Garneau, C.J., Boyce, M.W., Shorter, P.L., Vey, N.L., Amburn, C.R.: The augmented reality sandtable (ARES) research strategy, ARL Technical Note ARL-TN-0875. U.S. Army Research Laboratory, Aberdeen Proving Ground, MD (2017)
7. Rekimoto, J., Ayatsuka, Y.: CyberCode designing augmented reality environments with visual tags. In: Proceedings on Designing Augmented Reality Environments Conference, pp. 1–10 (2000)
8. Raglin, A., Michealis, J., Dennison, M., Harrison, A., Trout, T., Schaffer, J.: MxR framework for uncertainty based explanation for uncovering adversarial behavior. In: Chen, J., Fragomeni, G. (eds.) VAMR 2018. LNCS, vol. 10910, pp. 354–368. Springer, Cham (2018). https://doi.org/10.1007/978-3-319-91584-5_28
9. Trout, T., et al.: Networked mixed reality (MxR) infrastructure for collaborative decision-making. In: Proceedings on International Society for Optics and Photonics (2018)
10. Su, S., Perry, V., Guan, Q., Durkee, A., Neigel, A.R., Kase, S.: Sensor data fusion framework to improve holographic object registration accuracy for a shared augmented reality mission planning scenario. In: Chen, J., Fragomeni, G. (eds.) VAMR 2018. LNCS, vol. 10909, pp. 202–214. Springer, Cham (2018). https://doi.org/10.1007/978-3-319-91581-4_15
11. Brooke, J.: SUS – A quick and Dirty Usability Scale. Digital Equipment Co., Reading (1986)
12. Hart, S.G., Staveland, L.E.: Development of NASA-TLX (Task Load Index): results of empirical and theoretical research. Adv. Psychol. **52**, 139–183 (1988)
13. Witmer, B.G., Singer, M.J.: Measuring presence in virtual environments. ARI Technical report 1014. U.S. Army Research Institute, Alexandria, VA (1994)
14. Sheridan, T.B.: Musings on telepresence and virtual presence. Presence **1**(1), 120–125 (1992)
15. Held, R., Durlach, N.: Telepresence. Presence **1**(1), 109–112 (1992)

16. Barfield, W., Weghorst, S.: The sense of presence within virtual environment: a conceptual framework. In: Salvendy, G., Simith, M.J. (Eds.) Proceedings on Fifth International Conference on Human-Computer Interaction (HCI) International, vol. 2, pp. 699–704 (1991)
17. Heeter, C.: Being there: the subjective experience of presence. Presence 1(2), 262–271 (1992)
18. Kennedy, R.S., Lane, N.E., Berbaum, K.S., Lillienthal, M.G.: A simulator sickness questionnaire (SSQ): a new method for quantifying simulator sickness. Int. J. Aviat. Psychology 3(3), 295–301 (1993)
19. Cronbach, L.J.: Coefficient alpha and the internal structure of the tests. Psychometrika 16, 297–334 (1951)
20. DeVellis, R.F.: Scale Development: Theory and Applications, 2nd edn. SAGE, Thousand Oaks (2003)
21. Kline, R.B.: Principles and Practice of Structural Equation Modeling, 2nd edn. Guildford, New York (2005)
22. Spearman, C.: The proof and measurement of association between two things. Am. J. Psychol. 15(1), 72–101 (1904)

# Human-Computer Interaction for Space Situational Awareness (SSA): Towards the SSA Integrated Sensor Viewer (ISV)

Mitchell Kirshner[(✉)] and David C. Gross[(✉)]

University of Arizona, Tucson, AZ 85721, USA
mkirshner@email.arizona.edu,
davidcgross@email.arizona.edu

**Abstract.** Systems intending to achieve any level of space situational awareness inevitably require operator interfaces that enable the operation of sensors and the utilization of sensor provided data. As sensors are frequently owned and operated by other agencies, significant modification of the individual sensor capabilities may be beyond the reach of the space situational awareness system designer. The utilization of the sensor data however is not limited by anything except the ability of the space situational awareness system designer to innovate.

The mission of the Architecture Driven Systems Laboratory (ADSL) at the University of Arizona's Systems and Industrial Engineering department is to explore such innovations in all aspects of system architecture- especially the operator interfaces. The ADSL has developed an initial operating capability encapsulated in the System Architecture Synthesis and Analysis Framework (SASAF). The SASAF's Operations Phase capabilities include separate instantiable tools modeling operation of sensors (i.e., the Sensor Tasking Tool), and utilization of sensor data (i.e. The Integrated Sensor Viewer).

The Sensor Tasking Tool provides little opportunity for innovation because it is limited by the available sensors. However, the Integrated Sensor Viewer (ISV) provides substantial opportunities for innovation to help operators visualize and understand Resident Space Object (RSO) ephemeris data. The ISV implements a dynamic ontology developed within the software Unity correlates RSO data to commercial SSA company LeoLabs data retrieval API, allowing users to access additional information in-situ, without disrupting their sensory immersion and situational awareness. Product documentation generated in the ADSL allow stakeholders to better understand the final product.

**Keywords:** Issues in development and use of VR and MR: situational awareness ·
Applications: virtual worlds and social computing ·
Interaction and navigation in VR and MR: immersion

## 1 Introduction

Space Situational Awareness (SSA) is a needed strategic and security capability, whose importance directly correlates with the increase in utilization of near/low-Earth orbit. Near/low-Earth orbit is accessible to over 70 space-faring nations, including even universities, businesses and startups [1]. Rapid advances in the use of near-Earth orbit

© Springer Nature Switzerland AG 2019
J. Y. C. Chen and G. Fragomeni (Eds.): HCII 2019, LNCS 11575, pp. 504–515, 2019.
https://doi.org/10.1007/978-3-030-21565-1_34

by this increasingly diverse set of players, has led to that space becoming competitive, contested, and congested [2]. As these organizations make ever more extensive use of space, their space-based capabilities become part of the foundation of their economic strength where SSA is critical [3].

SSA is often seen as the ability to observe, track, and predict natural and inactive man-made objects in a defined space environment. Natural objects include meteoroids and near-Earth asteroids. Inactive man-made objects include spacecrafts, atmospheric re-entry vehicles, and debris. Since both natural and inactive man-made objects are nonresponsive to stimuli, they are collectively referred to as space debris.

Research has focused on SSA for space debris since several orbital collisions occurred within years of one another. In 2007, a KT-2 missile and a non-functional Chinese weather satellite collided. Meanwhile, in 2009 an active Iridium communication satellite accidentally collided with a defunct Russian satellite. These events resulted in debris which will stay in orbit for hundreds of years. Whereas the number of natural objects is essentially stable, the number of inactive man-made objects is growing exponentially. This increase has created a need for SSA to track space debris, as well as utilize the resulting information to avoid damaging effects to active man-made objects.

From consideration of such challenges, a more complete view of SSA emerges as the ability to create knowledge (i.e., understand and predict) the current and future state of natural and manmade objects in orbit around the Earth whose purpose is not the knowledge as an end in itself, but the application of such knowledge in managing controllable behavior to create desired outcomes [4].

Careful consideration of several aspects of this more complete view of SSA make it clear that the human SSA operator is the key to unlocking the puzzle of achieving SSA:

1. Not just integration of data into information, but instead transformation of information into knowledge
2. Understanding and prediction of space events
3. Managing behavior (i.e., command and control)
4. Achieving desired outcomes (where do desires come from?) [5].

The continued advances of sensor and network-based technologies will provide the human operator with unprecedented volumes of data, as well as meta-data regarding its sources, quality, and uncertainties. It is neither clear however to what extent human computer interface technology will enable the operator to make meaningful and valid use of the information, nor is it certain that any specific solution will be sufficiently resilient to function in the face of simultaneous exponential growth in [4]:

1. The number of objects in low/near Earth orbit
2. The number of government and non-government organizations interacting with said objects
3. The economic value of all of this activity, raising the stakes for all concerned [4].

If the only difference between unique decisions is the state of the world and systems provide their users information about the state of the world solely through sensors (certainly the case for SSA), a system that either replaces or supports cognitive processes of manipulating sensor data can provide game changing assistance.

Many SSA systems have been developed by commercial agencies and governments, both of which have their own limitations. For example, currently operators mostly base their assessments based on messages that are provided by government-owned radars and systems. Such systems have associated issues, such as: transparency, timeliness, and machine-machine interactivity within an assessment system [5]. To address said issues, operators have begun to utilize commercial space debris mapping services, which eliminate deleterious human-feedback loops by enabling the sending of requests and receiving of information services [5].

Although automation is the proposed solution by many researchers, the Architecture Driven Systems Laboratory (ADSL) research team strongly believes user interaction with machines is critical to solving the challenges posted by SSA because unlike humans, machines do not value the relationships between items in an environment. Machines, however, can detect any potential human errors. Although current space operators are able to constantly render updated images of the space environment and gather orbital data, the need for an integrated picture remains crucial [4].

## 2    Related Work

An SSA system of systems with dynamic composition exercising variable levels of cooperation requires an intuitive Human Computer Interface (HCI) to observe, orient, decide, and act on the large volumes of data produced by heterogeneous sensor networks; no one sensor can overcome the challenges of space object tracking. As such, SSA necessitates leveraging of Sensor Fusion techniques including. One effective method to realize the intersection of these fields is creating relationships of SSA network data using a dynamic ontology, which can define set processes to visualize the relevant virtual data in a Virtual Reality/Augmented Reality (VR/AR) environment.

### 2.1    Sensor Fusion

Collaborative architectures and services can alleviate the complications caused by dynamic space environment. Such complications include: motion of objects, rapidly advancing technological capabilities, and uncertainty in object location. Acknowledging uncertainty and limiting the user's Situational Awareness (SA) so that it does not extend beyond the known situation is a critical aspect of the design of a system for sensor information fusion. Diminishing the risk of the user developing conjecture instead of awareness and exposing this disparity remains an active area of research.

### 2.2    Situational Awareness

The purpose of any SSA network is to create SA of some region of interest. Literature commonly refers to an SA framework consisting of those three levels, which was adopted in many domains including the space sector. This hierarchical structure propagates errors occurring in lower levels, yielding multiple errors in higher levels [6]:

4. Perceiving important data in the environment
5. Understanding the meaning of data and turning it in to information
6. Projecting the information to the near future [6].

## 2.3   Information Accessibility

Ontology is the study of the reality of an area; that is, it provides a definition of the objects and defines their inter-relationships. An ontological approach aims to formally represent knowledge components of the domain (also called a "knowledge model") [7]. Creating an ontology might involve concept development, theoretical and philosophical development, computational development, as well as informatics, data management, and artificial intelligence techniques [7].

**Machine Accessibility via Dynamic Ontologies.** Development of computational methods for ontology development helps researchers analyze and integrate data from different sources so that the fused sensor data is easier and faster to process. The literature related to collaborative SSA describes a lack of such integration in the field, which can and will be problematic for developing innovative SSA systems [7].

Despite a missing SSA industry standard dynamic ontology, some experimental ontologies are described in literature [7]. Capabilities afforded through the use of such ontologies included inference classifications for objects of interest, automated checks for relational consistency within the ontology, and renderings of the situation which aid in developing improved SA of a virtualized environment [7]. Therefore, to leverage these capabilities, SSA research should consider centering the design of an SSA system around the dynamic ontology to keep the system informed of the ever-changing situation in the overall scenario.

**Human Accessibility via Immersion in Virtual Reality.** VR/AR is the proper approach for engaging the user's sensory modalities as demonstrated by past work analyzing the hippocampal theta wave oscillations related to brain activity during navigation. Research using an EEG showed evidence for human movement-related theta low frequency cortical oscillations in immersive VR, and show that the most accurate measurements of navigation patterns come from real world immersion, then VR immersion, and then desktop VR [8].

Developing an SSA VR system centered on a dynamic ontology is a more "human" approach than one might think, as system users are already informally but constantly building ontologies in their heads about what is going on around them. They cannot help themselves – it is what people do to validate their encounters; psychology refers to such as a cognitive map. The more a user's cognitive map is consistent with "truth" (the ontology that reflects the reality of the surrounding contents of the environment), the more the user can accurately understand the relationships encompassed within the environment. Users that insist on acting on their own cognitive map will create a different kind of Virtual Realty – one that is particularly unhelpful and likely to be harmful.

Rendering a VR environment based on all available sensor data is an immediate type of sensor fusion problem. However, the quantity and quality of sensor data is limited by the SSA sensor information infrastructure and SSA network architectures; the sensor data will never provide a full virtual view of the real world. As such, to develop an accurate, immersive situation, an SSA data presentation system must project information from both the provided data and inferred data. VR approaches can overlay the projected data over the virtualized environment data to enable distinction and fusion of information viewpoints.

# 3 Methodology

The Architecture Driven Systems Laboratory proposes the Space Situational Awareness Integrated Sensor Viewer (SSA-ISV): an extendable, interoperable rendering application created to enhance and explore a prototype dynamic analysis and simulation environment. This viewer connects to public and private SSA databases to help a user access relevant information using a tool which queries the virtual reality environment in-situ. This knowledge-enabled ontology-based simulation design environment leverages computational techniques to rapidly compare and employ to the SSA-ISV an interactive data presentation architecture based on virtualized, federated, faceted, registered, Resident Space Object point data (Fig. 1).

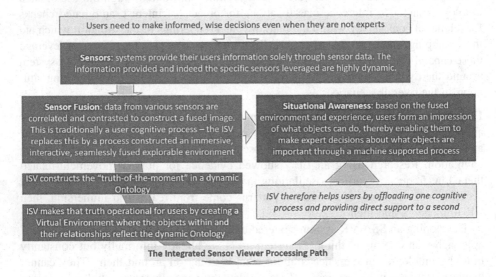

**Fig. 1.** Diagrammatic view of proposed approach

## 3.1   The University of Arizona Architecture Driven Systems Laboratory

The Architecture Driven Systems Laboratory's (ADSL) location at the University of Arizona enables collaboration with the SSA-Arizona program, which promotes international collaboration on a wide variety of SSA topics. Access to this expertise will allow for the development of a better-informed system if this project development is to continue; experts shall provide insights to enable space operators to tackle the numerous intricacies that arise in complex SSA.

**The Systems Architecture Synthesis and Analysis Framework (SASAF).** The Systems Architecture Synthesis and Analysis Framework (SASAF) is the core product of the University of Arizona's the Architecture Driven Systems Lab – but the real owner of SASAF is truly the interested technical community, which SASAF's development methodology ensures. The SASAF expressly accommodates discipline specific tools and techniques per the tenants of Model Based Engineering and promotes architecture reuse across a multitude of projects by enabling specialization of generic object classes. SASAF Operator hardware is shown in Fig. 2.

**Fig. 2.** ADSL SASAF operator station hardware

The SASAF core toolset allows for descriptions of countless possibilities of architectures by implementing software subdivided into three system life-cycle phases: the Architecture Creation Tool (ACT) and the Scenario Creation Tool (SCT) for the Design Phase, the Collaborative Command System (CCS), the Relevant Aspects of the World Emulator (RAW-E), the Integrated Sensor Viewer (ISV), and the Sensor Tasking Tool (STT) for the Operations Phase, and the Response Surface Analysis Tool (RSAT) for the Analysis Phase. For the purposes of Space Situational Awareness, the ADSL focuses on extending the ISV to develop the proposed SSA-ISV.

Figure 3 shows the functional flow block diagram for the three major portions of ISV and other parts of the SASAF and or the user community involved as much as they would like to be. Notice the upper branch feeding into ISV originates in the Air Force Research Lab (AFRL) and as such is opaque to those in the Space Situational Awareness (SSA) community who do not have immediate and in-depth access. It is not at all clear how AFRL generated the data files provided as part of the challenge. The motivation for incorporating this branch is to acknowledge that it is a necessary set of processing. Should AFRL decline to provide such data in the future, the SSA network instantiated by this study's efforts would have to continue to acquire and post the data and then post processes it to arrive at the current AFRL input.

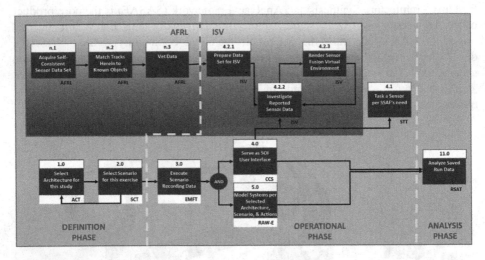

**Fig. 3.** The ISV functional flow block diagram

**Data Presentation Architecture Synthesis.** To create a dynamic analysis and simulation environment expressing data presentation architectures, the ADSL leverages architecture modeling techniques to represent data and its associated ontological semantic relationships within the ADSL ACT. The ACT defines the architecture at the start of system development through expression of many ontologies, the root of each being the different systems that are relevant to this study. One of these ontologies will always be the System of Interest (SOI), which will identify the sensors native to the SOI. But organic sensors may only be a small portion of the sensors the SOI can bring to bear. The other ontologies define the other systems in the study and must by their nature place their other systems in a range of relationship to the SOI.

Although the model structure required to frame a project may be well-understood and static, the parameters required for architecture execution, simulation, and analysis, may contain uncertainty, or be unknown altogether. These unknown characteristics can be fulfilled with the SCT, which shall identify remaining potential values that act as effectors or actuators to the environment. Iterating the chosen architecture through multiple scenario shall help the SSA-ISV operator develop awareness of how resilient each data presentation architecture is to a wide variety of conditions. With more scenarios, uncertainty in possible range of parameter values shall decrease. This decrease in uncertainty can be visualized in the SSA-ISV; users can react to this change by implementing dynamic alterations of object model behaviors, all while immersed within the virtual environment.

## 3.2    SSA-ISV VR Operations

This research aims to transform the ADSL capability to define and utilize presentation architectures for the provided AFRL data. Within systems engineering, this research is a key enabler for Model-Based Systems Engineering (MBSE) which is the international systems engineering community's objective, and beyond that to Model-Based Business, that is integrating technical, management fields for a revolution in how systems are developed and deployed. The SASAF aims to reduce the time and effort required to find suitable arrangements of hardware, software, procedures, and policies for a wide range of domains. This will enable addressing problems on a timely basis utilizing limited resources. To achieve this goal, this research has begun creation of an extensive ontology and prototype to properly handle industry provided object ephemeris data.

**Dynamic Ontology.** To generate contextually accurate results within the SSA-ISV, one must make sure to incorporate all relevant aspects of the simulation for tools. The SSA-ISV makes use of databases and other information technology but requires that every piece of information be available in a flat file, thereby reducing the information technology expertise demands on small players in the SSA industry. The ISV, which is inherently extendable, moves beyond the desktop to take full advantage of augmented and virtual reality interfaces. To enable users to utilize these capabilities, the ADSL develops a method by which to identify space objects within the provided AFRL dataset.

The Systems Tool Kit (STK) software by AGI Inc. contains a standard space object catalog. Most of the elements from this catalog are made public, but some are restricted. AGI provides the publicly available information for use with their STK software in the form of satellite database files and two-line mean element files (TLEs). The AFRL dataset also contain publicly available TLE elements. As such, if the ADSL can register each data object to real space object data found to more easily extract sensor and instrument data as needed.

**Sensor Fusion.** The commercial company LeoLabs was created to secure commercial operations in Low Earth Orbit (LEO). As the LEO ecosystem around the Earth is getting more crowded, the risk of collisions rises. To monitor this, LeoLabs installed a worldwide network of ground-based, phased-array radars that enable high resolution data on LEO objects. The LeoLabs platform delivers applications for operating in low Earth orbit; data products can be accessed through variety of interfaces such as web based, command line and REST API.

In the completed system, a user can specify which information they are seeking using filters related to common object parameters such as location, speed, size, etc. Furthermore, the user can even alter the virtual reality to view the effects that an actuation such as satellite repositioning would have throughout the multiple levels of Situational Awareness. The SSA-ISV shall then suggest views based on ontology recommendations formulated from user preferences and actual and projected data. Selecting a point of a view sends a signal to the simulation, actuating a response to the overall environment surface at that time, then simultaneously localizes and maps the frame of reference to the stakeholder's intended viewpoint.

Figure 4 shows a 3D virtual model of the Cassini satellite mission within the prototype environment. The ADSL posits that having an interactive virtual environment will increase the understanding this situation, and better allow for collaboration transdisciplinary collaboration compared to traditional document-based reporting.

**Fig. 4.** Sample 3D model in SSA-ISV prototype

## 4   Results and Discussion

The SSA-ISV prototype correlates object location, position, and velocity data from the provided CSV files to corresponding NORAD IDs within each object file name. The SSA-ISV compares the NORAD ID to the LeoLabs database based on user requests and returns both the LeoLabs object ID, as well as the object name to the virtual environment. An extended version of the prototype can allow for comparison of the object names to other science APIs and use similar methodologies to help both humans and machines develop SA of the data.

### 4.1   Situational Awareness Affordances

The ADSL has successfully created a Virtual Reality environment which allows a user to interact with the provided dataset. The enhancement of SSA using dynamic ontologies and virtual reality environments through procedures developed in the University of Arizona's Architecture Driven Systems Laboratory provides a means to fuse, observe, and augment the activities of AFRL/RY COMPASE Center's various services, including: Modeling and Simulation, the Sensor Data Management System, Test & Evaluation, and the Virtual Distributed Laboratory [9]. In this way, the ADSL's methodology enables both machine and human understanding of AFRL's data.

The prototype currently simulates a virtual reality environment using the software Unity comprising of three satellites in orbit using the provided AFRL dataset. The user can move through the space environment to position himself/herself near objects by facing a direction and touching the top portion of the HTC Vive right controller's trackpad. Clicking the trackpad moves the user faster through space. Selecting an object acquires information from LeoLabs using an API key. The returned JSON data is parsed into objects using regular expression, resulting in the ability for the user to see the NORAD ID, satellite name, and LeoLabs ID in VR. The user can select the object by pressing the grips on the right controller to start the selection and pulling the trigger to complete it. Information of the selected satellite is presented on a card above the left controller.

## 4.2    Sensor Fusion Affordances

If the SSA system design centers on ontologies that come into being through computational techniques, then one immediate advantage of this is that every part of the system can access and exploit the ontology; this is the key idea as to how the ACT communicates to the rest of the SASAF. Some systems will assert in their architecture that they are able and willing to share sensor data with the SOI; such systems amount in extensions of the SOI. Other systems will have no method by which to share sensor data, and still other systems may be ready and willing to reduce the effectiveness of the SOI's sensors through techniques such as radio and radar jamming across different bandwidths.

Depending on the driving objective of the study, the architecture definition may become quite detailed, especially because heterogeneous sensor networks have different procedures by which to exchange data. Once the architecture defines these procedures, data becomes accessible by every other component of the system as appropriate. At this point, the ADSL Sensor Tasking Tool (STT) enables the user to command only the sensors the architecture permit to better accomplish desired tasks and develop deeper SSA. Likewise, the SSA-ISV does not have to determine what sensors are available to make the fused sensor picture, because the architecture has been predetermined in the SASAF design phase.

## 4.3    Prototype Information

To ensure that the prototype meets the goals described in this research, the ADSL has created an ISV Specification document to keep track of requirements that shall be satisfied to accomplish the goals of the SSA-ISV. Furthermore, the ISV Verification document provides a scheme by which to verify that the proposed requirements are satisfied. Documentation for implementation are included within the Implementation document, which includes some steps taken towards verification of the Implementation with the requirements in the Specification. The SSA-ISV prototype executable is compatible with the HTC Vive and can also run on non-VR desktops. The prototype design allows the relevant files to be shared across research computers independent of the sizeable AFRL dataset.

## 5  Future Work and Conclusion

Currently the SSA-ISV prototype has demonstrated the potential to grow into a powerful tool for SSA purposes. Future work must be completed to enhance the working prototype, remove glitches, and add capabilities. Scaling the prototype using machine automation techniques will eventually allow for the full population of a novel, innovative, knowledge-based environment. Real-time capabilities shall be included as well, interfacing with sensor network information available throughout the scientific community. The ADSL's approach innovation involves gathering data from different sources and integrating them using Sensor Fusion technique into a holistic picture incorporated into a VR modality. This solution goes beyond visualizing the data: it provides an entirely virtual environment, within which the user develops a thorough SA.

The ADSL has generated the ISV Development Plan document to improve organizational transfer of the SSA-ISV prototype and better satisfy the needs of stakehodlers. This development plan also includes future activities to be performed to incrementally enhance the SSA-ISV prototype. Such plans include enabling the user to project the most likely complete view of all objects in cases where the available sensors are insufficient to create a full 3D view of an object in the virtual environment. Other future development plans include integration of the ADSL Sensor Tasking Tool to give the user control over any sensor available to the system of interest.

Virtual environments, based on dynamic ontologies which define relationships between system parameter evolutions over time, can act as a replacement for the natural environment. Using sensor data, a machine can construct a stable yet dynamic virtual environment via tasks such as projecting future states, evaluating courses of action, considering improbable outcomes, and so forth. As such, creating an immersive environment to analyze space system data enables space operators to develop a deep SSA through the ADSL's proposed SSA Integrated Sensor Viewer (SSA-ISV).

**Acknowledgments.** The authors would like to thank the following researchers for their crucial contributions to this publication: Vida Pashaei, Mostafa Lutfi, JT Dotzler, Sara Hohenstein, and Cody Jones.

## References

1. Ferguson, D.C., Worden, S.P., Hastings, D.E.: The space weather threat to situational awareness, communications, and positioning systems. IEEE Trans. Plasma Sci. **43**(9), 3086–3098 (2015)
2. O'Brien, T.E.: Space Situational Awareness CubeSat Concept of Operations, p. 87
3. McCall, D.G.H.: Space Situational Awareness: Difficult, Expensive–and Necessary, p. 11 (2014)

4. Gross, D.C.: Required Advances in Systems Engineering for Space Situational Awareness. University of Arizona, 11 April 2016
5. Archuleta, A., Nicolls, M.: Space Debris Mapping Services for use by LEO Satellite Operators, p. 16 (2018)
6. Durso, F.T., Sethumadhavan, A.: Situation awareness: Understanding dynamic environments. Hum. Factors **50**(3), 442–448 (2008)
7. Rovetto, R.J.: The Orbital Space Environment and Space Situational Awareness Domain Ontology–Towards an International Information System for Space Data (2016)
8. Bohbot, V.D., Copara, M.S., Gotman, J., Ekstrom, A.D.: Low-frequency theta oscillations in the human hippocampus during real-world and virtual navigation. Nat. Commun. **8**, 14415 (2017)
9. AFRL/RY - Compass Center: Wright-Patterson AFB. http://www.wpafb.af.mil/Welcome/Fact-Sheets/Display/Article/837762/afrlry-compase-center. Accessed 07 Jan 2019

# Image-Based Ground Visibility for Aviation:
# Is What You See What You Get?

## (Pilot Study)

Daniela Kratchounova[1(✉)], David C. Newton[2], and Robbie Hood[2]

[1] Federal Aviation Administration Civil Aerospace Medical Institute,
Oklahoma City, OK, USA
Daniela.Kratchounova@faa.gov
[2] Cherokee CRC, LLC., Oklahoma City, OK, USA

**Abstract.** Including a crowd in the weather-sensing loop has the potential for improving the availability of weather observations to Alaska's widely dispersed airfields where essential weather data sets are currently not available. One method of virtually expanding the existing weather-sensing infrastructure, at least in part, would be to pair the images taken by the large network of aviation weather cameras installed in Alaska with crowdsourced estimates of ground visibility (FAA 14 CFR 1.1 defines ground visibility as the prevailing horizontal visibility near the earth's surface as reported by the United States National Weather Service or an accredited observer [1]) derived from those images. In 2018, the Civil Aerospace Medical Institute (CAMI) conducted a pilot study of image-based ground visibility utilizing CAMI's cloud-based research platform at https://cbtopsatcami.faa.gov. The goal of this exploratory research was two-fold. First, make observations about the behavior of the different image-based and non-image-based visibility models across different weather conditions during daytime at airfields where a traditional weather sensor is collocated with an aviation weather-camera installation and on-staff expert human weather-observers. Second, survey the viability of deriving ground visibility from Alaska's weather camera network via crowdsourcing in applied settings. The models' behavior was examined using daily time-series plots. The recommendations for future research are founded on the observations of the models' behavior, participation rates and feedback from the pilot and expert human observer's communities.

**Keywords:** Aviation weather · Ground visibility · Image-derived visibility · Participatory sensing · Selective crowdsourcing

## 1 Background

General Aviation (GA) in Alaska suffers a disproportionately high accident rate [2]. Controlled flight into terrain (CFIT) accidents are a significant contributor to this rate, particularly fatal accidents. Most often, CFIT accidents occur when a pilot continues a flight planned under Visual Flight Rules (VFR) into unexpected or unknown Instrument Meteorological Conditions (IMC). Reliable, near-real-time data about the weather

J. Y. C. Chen and G. Fragomeni (Eds.): HCII 2019, LNCS 11575, pp. 516–528, 2019.
https://doi.org/10.1007/978-3-030-21565-1_35

conditions along a flight path during flight planning would likely reduce CFIT accidents. This could be particularly helpful along GA routes over long expanses of remote terrain between instrumented airfields and through heavily trafficked and treacherous mountain passes. One method of providing such data is to utilize the expansive network of aviation weather cameras installed in Alaska.

The notion of transforming the aviation weather cameras into weather sensors by using the images to derive ground visibility is not new. In the early 2000s, Massachusetts Institute of Technology (MIT) Lincoln Labs developed an edge detection algorithm that estimates the visibility based on a camera image. To date, MIT Lincoln Labs has completed initial testing of edge detection on a subset of Alaska camera archived data [3]. In the spring of 2017, Rockwell Collins conducted a laboratory image-based visibility demonstration using commercial crowdsourcing technology [4].

## 2 Ground Visibility Definitions and Measurement

According to the American Meteorology Society, ground visibility is determined by a human observer using natural vision to see and identify known landmarks and prominent objects at a known distance from the usual point of observation [5]. The National Weather Service (NWS) designates sector visibility as the visibility in a specific direction that represents at least a 45-degree arc of a horizontal circle. Prevailing visibility is defined as the visibility that is considered representative of the conditions at the field station at the greatest distance that can be seen over 90° of the horizontal circle even if the sector visibilities are not continuous across adjacent sectors [6].

Historically in the US, visibility at airfields and weather offices was reported by human observers. The development of automated visibility sensors began in the 1970s [7]. The technical goal was to correlate human-observed visibility with instrument measurements of the physical characteristics and properties of air. The challenge was to develop technology that would replace the inherently subjective nature of human observations with objective, consistent, and cost-effective observations irrespective of day or night conditions.

In the 1990s, the first operational Automated Surface Observing Systems (ASOS) network was deployed to provide surface observations for aviation operations. The FAA operates its own network of Automated Weather Observing Systems (AWOS) that provides continuous measurements of various weather parameters, including visibility [8]. ASOS and AWOS visibility sensors operating today were designed "to measure the prevailing visibility by assuming that the conditions between the sensors receiver and transmitter represent the nominal conditions around the horizon" [9]. Key advantages of the ASOS and AWOS network of visibility sensors are that placing the sensors at airfield touchdown zones provides precise visibility information for this critically important airfield feature. Automated visibility observations also provide consistency of observations between airfields without variations due to subjective human observations. However, a key drawback of automated visibility observations is that the sensor sample volume is generally only 0.75 cubic feet and may not accurately represent the airfield conditions if visibility is not homogenous [7].

All automated visibility observations greater than 10 statute miles (SM, mi) are reported as "10 SM" in FAA-defined Metrological Terminal Aviation Routine Weather Reports (METARs) even though the actual visibility may be much greater. This limit on reported visibility data may not affect some meteorological applications of the METAR observations but could be insufficient in the context of flight operations and pilots' go-no-go decision-making process.

## 2.1    From Distributed Human Computation to Participatory Sensing

**Distributed Human Computation.** The rapid expansion of information technologies and human computation applications in recent years has encouraged the research community to consider crowdsourcing as a viable human computation application for research, development and concept operationalization. Quinn and Bederson define distributed human computation (DHC) as a method of synergistically combining the strengths of computers and humans by assigning parts of the problem to a large group of geographically dispersed people who are connected via the Internet [10]. The authors provide a comprehensive overview of the different types and dimensions of DHC applications, including crowdsourcing. These applications have one thing in common: They rely on humans to perform elements of the task that are later aggregated to form the basis of some other computations that are performed by a computer [10].

**Crowdsourcing.** Jeff Howe coined the term crowdsourcing. According to his definition, it refers to a form of outsourcing of a function that is traditionally performed by employees, via an open call, to a network of people with diverse levels of experience, skills, and knowledge [11]. Crowdsourcing is often linked to the framework of collective intelligence and the idea that knowledge is the most accurate when it consists of inputs from a distributed population [12]. Furthermore, the idea of collective intelligence has been interpreted as the wisdom of crowds [13]. A key advantage of crowdsourcing is the harnessing of skills, knowledge, or other resources of a distributed crowd of workers to achieve an outcome at a lower cost and in a shorter time [14].

Some authors identify two distinct types of crowdsourcing: selective and integrative. According to Schenk and Guittard, selective crowdsourcing aims to involve selected experts with adequate skills. Alternatively, the goal of integrative crowdsourcing is to pool large amounts of relevant information from a large number of users [15].

Geiger, Rosemann, and Fielt identified four dimensions of crowdsourcing: (a) preselection of contributors, (b) accessibility of peer contributions, (c) aggregation of contributions, and (d) remuneration for contributions. They distinguish between qualification-based, where potential contributors must demonstrate their abilities before being allowed to participate, and context-specific preselection, where only certain individuals can contribute in a meaningful way [14].

**Participatory Sensing.** In the context of the overarching term of distributed human computing, today's proliferation of mobile smartphones, along with the ease of deployment of cloud-computing services for storage, processing, and visualization, have enabled a new pervasive data collection model: participatory sensing. Namely, tasking everyday mobile devices to form interactive sensor networks that enable users to gather, analyze, and share knowledge [14]. According to Ganti, Ye, and Lei, the transition to internet-enabled personal devices will bring about a host of benefits allowing for mobile crowd-sensing where data from device sensors is augmented with self-report data from users on their perceptions of the environment [17, 18].

## 2.2    The Role of Motivation

One of the most difficult challenges in the context of DHC is people's motivation to participate. The issue of motivation is somewhat alleviated, as these systems rely on networks of people connected via the Internet in the comfort of their homes. Oftentimes, participants are assigned tasks that do not directly benefit them. This may result in lessened motivation. Approaches that help with recruiting and motivating people to participate include monetary compensation, making the task interesting to complete online, highlighting the importance of the contribution, and integrating the task as much as possible into the regular workflow [10, 19, 20].

## 3    Method

For the research presented here, we applied a method containing elements from the definition of several DHC applications existing in the literature, as seen in Table 1.

**Table 1.**  Methodological elements of distributed human computing

| DHC elements | Reference |
| --- | --- |
| Context-specific preselection process was applied | Geiger et al. [14] |
| One group of paid volunteers<br>Two groups of unpaid volunteers<br>Participants provided estimates of numerical value of a variable (ground visibility) | Quinn and Bederson [10] |
| Hourly average was calculated for each group and type of ground visibility | Geiger et al. [14] |
| Study was conducted on cloud-computing research platform<br>Study user interface was available via both, a web-based and a mobile application | Burke et al. [16] |

The notion of involving participants with different levels of expertise and knowledge of aviation weather was motivated by previous research as well [21]. In this study, we were encouraged to explore different approaches to selective crowdsourcing that can sufficiently engage the aviation weather community and support an operationally sustainable concept in the future. With thousands of flight hours as compared to student-pilots, expert-pilots have developed specialized skills in assessing aviation weather. For this research, we focused on engaging the two ends of this spectrum. To obtain baseline data, expert human weather-observers on staff at the two participating sites were recruited.

## 3.1  Participants

Twenty-seven expert pilots, 27 student pilots, and two expert weather-observer representatives at two airfields in Alaska were preselected to participate in the pilot study. The expert-pilots and the expert weather-observers were unpaid volunteers; the student-pilots received monetary compensation for participating.

## 3.2  Design

For this exploratory research, the following *baseline* (non-image based) visibility values were collected for every hour during daytime at each participating site:

1. Prevailing visibility reported by the certified weather sensor (e.g., ASOS, AWOS);
2. Personal estimates of sector and prevailing visibility using natural vision by the expert weather observer (augmenter) on shift;
3. Prevailing visibility from the Aviation Digital Data Service (ADDS) METAR.

Image-based sector and prevailing visibility estimates constituted the *experimental* visibility values. They were collected via crowdsourcing from the expert-pilots and student-pilots. The pilots' visibility estimates were averaged across participants for each group. Daily time-series plots of all the baseline and experimental models were generated for each participating site and used to assess the models' behavior. Whether the experimental models converged toward, or diverged from the baseline models was the behavior of interest to us. This knowledge would contribute to the formulation of future research inquiries into the operationalizability of new and novel ways of collecting and distributing weather observations from remotely located airfields where no traditional weather-sensing infrastructure exists.

## 3.3  Procedure

For three months, beginning on July 1st, 2018, images taken by the aviation weather cameras at two airfields in Alaska were obtained and stored on CAMI's cloud-based research platform at https://cbtopsatcami.faa.gov. For operational consistency, from the six images taken per hour[1] by each aviation weather camera, only the images captured as close as possible to 50 min after the hour were used in this study. This timing was essential because at approximately 50 min after the hour, a reading from the traditional weather sensor is taken, and used (with or without augmentation) for generating the hourly METAR. The personal estimates of sector and prevailing visibility from the expert weather observers using natural vision were recorded at about the same time, as well.

## 3.4  Task

The participants in the two crowdsourcing-groups were asked to provide sector visibility and prevailing visibility estimates based on image-pairs (annotated Clear Day and the image taken closest to 50 min after the hour) from each participating site during daytime.

---

[1] The aviation weather cameras take images every 10 min.

The expert human observers' task was to log: (a) the type of report (METAR or SPECI), (b) the visibility value from the weather sensor, (c) their personal estimates of sector and prevailing visibility using natural vision, and (d) the prevailing visibility value submitted with the official METAR. They were asked to submit data for every hour on shift, at their discretion, and depending on their workload. For this study, a designated user interface was available for all participant groups at https://cbtopsatcami.faa.gov.

# 4   Results and Discussion

Of the twenty-seven expert pilots who were invited to participate in the study, sixteen (59%) provided data. Of those who provided data, five pilots (31%) provided a complete set of data (89 days). The remainder (69%) provided partial data. Twenty-seven student-pilots were invited to participate in the study. Twenty-three (85%) provided data. Of those who provided data, nine (39%) provided a complete set of data. The remainder (60%) provided partial data. For the three-month long study, approximately 16,000 image-pairs were posted for participants to evaluate. At each participating site, one of the expert human observers on shift provided a single data point hourly for each baseline model. The visibility values published in the METAR during daytime hours in Alaska were obtained from NOAA's ADDS.

## 4.1   Time-Series Plots

The daily time-series were plotted for the daytime hours in Alaska between July 1$^{st}$ and September 30$^{th}$, 2018. Plots generated from the crowdsourced image-based sector and prevailing visibility estimates contained the averaged values of the estimates from the expert-pilot and student-pilot groups. The expert weather observers on shift at each participating site provided the data for baseline plots. The data contained the single-value weather sensor reading, the weather observer's estimate of sector and prevailing visibility, using natural vision, and the visibility value entered in the METAR.

## 4.2   Observations Based on Models' Behavior

For the purposes of this research, the participants were given the option to enter higher than 10 statute miles visibility values when prominent landmarks or objects located at distances greater than 10 statute miles were clearly visible on either the camera images or using natural vision. This decision was inspired by feedback from pilot-experts and expert human observers who participated in the study. That is, it is just as operationally significant for pilots to know whether a prominent landmark located tens or even hundreds of miles away is clearly visible on a given day as it is to know whether the visibility is so low that no known landmarks or objects are visible, at all. Furthermore, FAA Order 7900.5 D Table 8-1 lists the reportable visibility values when observations are manual. The list includes visibility values between 10 and 15, in increments of 1 statute mile, and between 15 and 50, in increments of 5 statute miles [22]. For the purposes of this research, the maximum value participants could enter was 150 statute miles. The rationale was based on expert-pilots' feedback asserting that it is operationally significant to report it if, for example, a landmark such as Mount Denali is clearly visible from Fairbanks, AK at a distance of approximately 150 miles.

Looking at the time-series plots, several interesting patterns emerged. First, when the visibility was generally high, the averaged crowdsourcing values based on camera images were consistently higher than the METAR reported visibility (Fig. 1). Second, when the visibility was generally low (e.g., around or less than 3 statute miles), for a part of the day, the averaged crowdsourcing values based on camera images were frequently lower than the METAR reported visibility (Figs. 2 and 3). Third, when the visibility was variable throughout the day, the image-based estimates "anticipated" the changes especially if the visibility was trending low (Fig. 2).

One plausible explanation for these patterns is that the sensor sample volume of air ($\sim 0.75$ cubic feet) is very small in comparison to the weather cameras unobstructed, almost 360° combined field-of-view, of the airfield surroundings. That, and using the annotated Clear day images as a reference (Fig. 4), would have afforded the crowdsourcing participants the ability to derive prevailing visibility estimates somewhat different, yet moving in the same general direction, as the visibility values published in the METARs. In addition, pilots' ability to "read" weather based on training and operational experience would explain the experimental (image-based) models' "anticipating" behavior when the visibility was trending low.

Similar patterns, but to a lesser extent, were observed in the personal estimates data from the expert human observers using natural vision (Fig. 1 top and Fig. 3). According to the FMH, the expert human observers (augmenters) determine visibility using natural vision and through the ability to see and identify known landmarks and prominent objects at a known distance from the usual point of observation. Sometimes, very prominent landmarks or objects are located at distances well outside a radius of 10 statute miles around the airfield (Fig. 4). However, even though the expert human observers' personal estimates were very frequently higher than the weather-sensor reading, and while FAA Order 7900.5 D does allow manual reportable visibility values higher than 10 statute miles, no such values were reported in any of the METARs by any of the participating sites for the duration of the study [22].

In both cases, whether derived from the weather camera images or using natural vision, participants were able to assess ground visibility within a very large area around the airfields. While these data were limited to only a couple of airfields in Alaska, they provided an operationally significant insight. More specifically, they brought about the notions of (a) providing supplemental observations of ground visibility in addition to the observations made using the existing weather-sensing infrastructure; and (b) virtually extending the existing weather-sensing network to include remote, aviation weather camera equipped airfields and flight-routes, where such infrastructure does not exist.

In the context of pilots' level of aviation weather expertise, another interesting pattern emerged. For about 30 days, at the onset of the study, and when the weather was generally clear, on average, the student-pilots' estimates were higher than those submitted by the expert-pilots. However, over time, and for the remainder of the study, the estimates submitted by both groups became almost identical. We attribute this pattern to learning. As the student-pilots practiced more, they acquired valuable

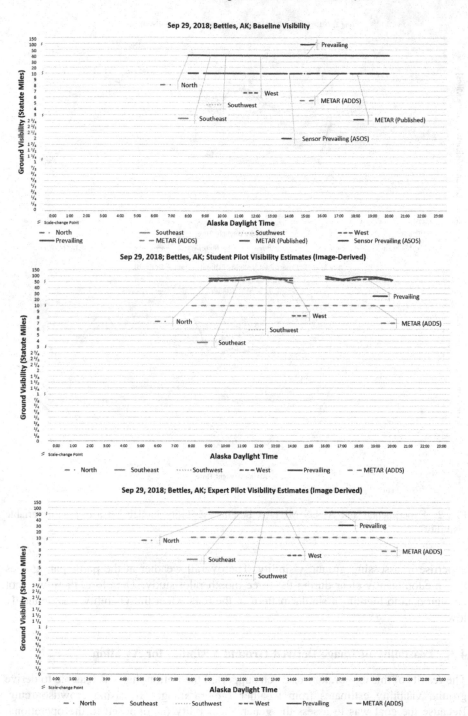

**Fig. 1.** Baseline (top) and experimental (image-derived) visibility models on a clear day

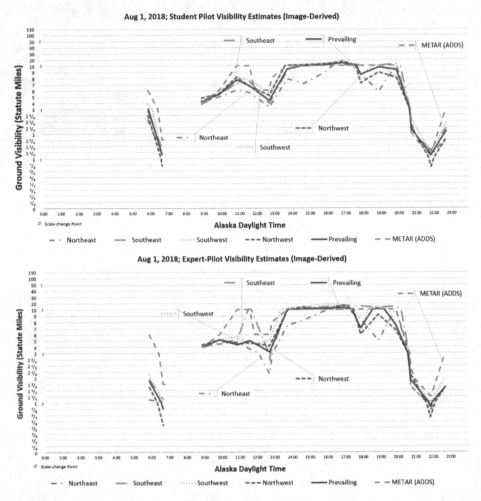

**Fig. 2.** Experimental and ADDS METAR baseline visibility models on a day with variable visibility

expertise in assessing ground visibility. The overall weather at the participating sites was predominantly clear during the three-month pilot study. Therefore, there was not enough data to identify a similar pattern in the data when the visibility was generally low.

### 4.3  Feasibility of Image-Derived Ground Visibility for Aviation

The results of this exploratory research supported the notion that it is feasible to derive ground visibility estimates from weather camera images by using crowdsourcing. Because the goal was to assess the general feasibility (as opposed to the operational feasibility) of image-derived visibility using crowdsourcing, this pilot study was conducted *without* requiring the expert-pilots and student-pilots to provide near real-time,

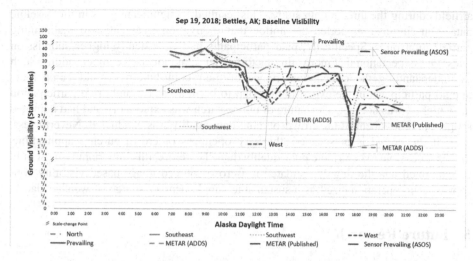

**Fig. 3.** Full set of baseline models on a day with variable visibility

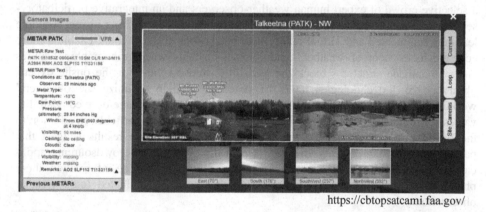

https://cbtopsatcami.faa.gov/

**Fig. 4.** METAR (left), annotated Clear Day image (center), and image from the NW camera at Talkeetna with Mt. Denali and Mt. Hunter clearly visible (right). Image from https://cbtopsatcami.faa.gov

hourly estimates online. For an operational feasibility assessment, a longer, "live" proof-of-concept evaluation will be required. Such evaluation will have to address the operational sustainability, as well. The success of any concept of operations that involves a crowd, even in part, will greatly depend on the crowd's motivation to participate continuously "live," hourly, and at around 50 min after the top of the hour.

### 4.4   Limitations

We acknowledge that there were some limitations of this pilot study that need to be addressed. Unforeseen logistical challenges caused two changes in the participating airfields during the three-month study. This resulted in significant gaps in the baseline data. Our findings supported the notion that motivation is essential to maintaining participation rates. Specifically, paid participants had consistently higher submission rates. Our expectation that motivating factors other than monetary compensation—such as understanding the critical importance of their contribution—would compel the unpaid participants in the expert-pilot group to be more active and drive participation rates higher, was not met. The nature of our research was exploratory and had a limited scope. No assessment of the crowdsourcing data quality was conducted. Nevertheless, even if the crowd is preselected, the very openness of crowdsourcing applications makes it possible to contribute poor-quality data. Therefore, this important issue should be examined and thoroughly validated if a crowdsourced image-based visibility concept is to be operationalized as a sustainable supplementary source of weather data.

## 5 Future Research

The results from this pilot study were encouraging to merit further investigation of a concept that is a hybrid between crowdsourcing and participatory sensing and involves a selective crowd of expert human weather-observers and an integrative participatory-sensing crowd. The deployment of advanced applications of machine vision, machine learning, augmented and virtual reality, and head-worn displays could enable a more accurate assessment of weather conditions at airfields where topographic features and/or manmade structures block the horizon-to-horizon view for the onsite expert-observers. Such technologies have the potential to help optimize the observers' workflow and enable routine and sustainable reporting of image-derived visibility values for remotely located, aviation weather-camera equipped airfields, in addition to the onsite observations using natural vision. Furthermore, the results suggest that participatory sensing could be the next step in the evolution of crowdsourcing applications and possibly an ideal system for allowing users to provide information about phenomena containing nuanced information that must be evaluated (e.g., weather observations).

The concepts of crowdsourcing and participatory sensing can be expanded to provide not only ground visibility for aviation but flight visibility, as well. Today, flight visibility may be included in pilot reports (PIREPs); however, the majority of PIREPs focus on reporting adverse weather phenomena such as turbulence and icing at altitude. Consequently, flight visibility is rarely included in these reports. Direct reporting of flight visibility data from onboard sensors, without involving the flight crew, has the potential to fill in some of the temporal and geospatial gaps in flight visibility coverage. Moreover, the participatory sensing model could be applied to enhance the coverage of flight visibility data by collecting images taken in-flight by the flight crew (e.g., image-based flight visibility) using certified for in-flight use devices. Further research is necessary for a systematic assessment of the viability and validity of these concepts.

# References

1. General Definitions. 14 CFR § 1.1 (1962)
2. AOPA Air Safety Institute: 27th Joseph T. Nall Report (2018). https://www.aopa.org/-/media/files/aopa/home/training-and-safety/nall-report/27thnallreport2018.pdf?la=en
3. Matthews, M., Colavito, J.: Alaska C&V camera imagery analytics. Presentation at Friends and Partners in Aviation Weather (FPAW), July 2017. https://ral.ucar.edu/sites/default/files/public/events/2017/friends-and-partners-in-aviation-weather/docs/matthews-presentation-v2-114682.pdf
4. Kronfeld, K.: Crowd sourced weather visibility using FAA Alaska weather cameras. Presentation at the First Annual Aviation Weather Human Factors Research Summit, Oklahoma City, OK, May 2018
5. Visibility [definition 1]. (n.d.). In: American Meteorology Society Meteorology Glossary. http://glossary.ametsoc.org/wiki/Visibility
6. NWS: National weather service glossary (2019). https://w1.weather.gov/glossary
7. National Oceanic and Atmospheric Administration, Federal Aviation Administration, Department of Defense, & United States Navy: Automated surface observing system (ASOS) user's guide (1998). https://www.weather.gov/media/asos/aum-toc.pdf
8. All Weather Inc.: AWOS 3000 User's Manual (2018). http://www.allweatherinc.com/wp-content/uploads/3000-0011.pdf
9. Hallowell, R., Matthews, M., Pisano, P.: An automated visibility detection algorithm utilizing camera imagery. Paper presented at the 23rd Conference on Interactive Information and Processing Systems for Meteorology, Oceanography, and Hydrology (IIPS), January 2007. https://ams.confex.com/ams/pdfpapers/120107.pdf
10. Quinn, A., Bederson, B.B.: A taxonomy of distributed human computation (Report No. HCIL-2009-23). University of Maryland, College Park (2009). http://www.alexquinn.org/papers/A%20Taxonomy%20of%20Distributed%20Human%20Computation.pdf
11. Howe, J.: The rise of crowdsourcing. Wired (2006). http://www.wired.com/wired/archive/14.06/crowds.html
12. Bonabeau, E.: Decisions 2.0: the power of collective intelligence. MIT Sloan Manag. Rev. 50(2), 45 (2009)
13. Surowiecki, J.: The Wisdom of Crowds: Why the Many are Smarter than the Few and How Collective Wisdom Shapes Business, Economies, Societies, and Nations. Doubleday & Co, New York (2004)
14. Geiger, D., Rosemann, M., Fielt, E.: Crowdsourcing information systems: a systems theory perspective. In: Proceedings of the 22nd Australasian Conference on Information Systems (ACIS 2011) (2011). https://aisel.aisnet.org/acis2011/33/
15. Schenk, E., Guittard, C.: Towards a characterization of crowdsourcing practices. J. Innov. Econ. Manag. 1, 93–107 (2011)
16. Burke, J., et al.: Participatory sensing. Presented at the Workshop on World-Sensor-Web (WSW): Mobile Device Centric Sensor Networks and Applications, Boulder, Colorado, October 2006. https://cloudfront.escholarship.org/dist/prd/content/qt19h777qd/qt19h777qd.pdf
17. Ganti, R.K., Ye, F., Lei, H.: Mobile crowdsensing: current state and future challenges. IEEE Commun. Mag. 49(11), 32–39 (2011)
18. Guo, B., Yu, Z., Zhou, X., Zhang, D.: From participatory sensing to mobile crowd sensing. In: 2014 IEEE International Conference Pervasive Computing and Communications Workshops (PERCOM Workshops), pp. 593–598. IEEE, Washington, D.C., March 2014

19. Hetmank, L.: Developing an ontology for enterprise crowdsourcing. Paper presented at Multikonferenz Wirtschaftsinformatik, Paterborn, Germany (2014)
20. Seidel, C.E., Thapa, B.E., Plattfaut, R., Niehaves, B.: Selective crowdsourcing for open process innovation in the public sector: are expert citizens really willing to participate? In: Janowski, T., Holm, J., Estevez, E. (eds.) Proceedings of the 7th International Conference on Theory and Practice of Electronic Governance, pp. 64–72. ACM, New York, October 2013
21. Zhai, Z., Sempolinski, P., Thain, D., Madey, G., Wei, D., Kareem, A.: Expert-citizen engineering: "crowdsourcing" skilled citizens. In: IEEE Ninth International Conference on Dependable, Autonomic and Secure Computing (DASC), pp. 879–886. IEEE, Washington, D.C., December 2011
22. U.S. Department of Transportation, Federal Aviation Administration: Surface weather observing (FAA Order No. JO 7900.5D), December 2016. https://www.faa.gov/documentLibrary/media/Order/7900_5D.pdf

# Examining Error Likelihood When Using Enhanced Vision Systems for Approach and Landing

Steven J. Landry[(⊠)], Denys Bulikhov, Zixu Zhang,
and Carlos F. Miñana

Purdue University, West Lafayette, IN 47907, USA
slandry@purdue.edu

**Abstract.** A flight simulator experiment simulating enhanced vision system approaches was conducted in which the dependent variable in question was the probability of large performance measure deviations, rather than the mean deviation of those measures. Prior work had established no mean deviation in performance measures, but the question of whether the enhanced vision system affected the probability of large errors was not answered. The results of the simulator study suggest that enhanced vision system approaches may not affect the probability of long error durations, but may reduce the probability of large error extents. While this appears to be a positive finding for enhanced vision approaches, it may suggest pilots are applying higher gain than strictly necessary in correcting for errors, which would raise concerns of unnecessarily increased workload. Such a concern is consistent with other work on enhanced vision system approaches.

**Keywords:** Enhanced vision · Error · Pilot performance ·
Aircraft approach and landing

## 1 Introduction

Past work done regarding human performance when using enhanced vision flight systems (EFVS) for approach and landing is fairly extensive and definitive, as it has included low-fidelity simulator studies and analysis (Beier and Gemperlein 2004; Endsley et al. 2000; Todd et al. 1992; Yang and Hansman 1994), high-fidelity simulator studies (Bailey et al. 2010; Kramer et al. 2017) as well as actual flight tests (Arthur et al. 2005; Kramer et al. 2014).

However, such past work's conclusions only applies to the effect of EFVS on nominal performance. That is, conclusions are drawn about the effect of EFVS on mean error or performance, but the effect of EFVS on the likelihood of deviation is not studied. This is an important gap, because it may be of interest whether the likelihood of significant deviation increases, especially if the use of EFVS in high volume commercial passenger operations becomes commonplace, whereas its use now is largely limited to cargo and business flight operations.

© Springer Nature Switzerland AG 2019
J. Y. C. Chen and G. Fragomeni (Eds.): HCII 2019, LNCS 11575, pp. 529–535, 2019.
https://doi.org/10.1007/978-3-030-21565-1_36

Unfortunately, no method has ever been applied to examine changes to the likelihood of a deviation for flight operations. In this work, a method to study this likelihood has been developed and is described. The method consists of collecting the same experimental data used in past studies, but examining the tails of the distribution of performance characteristics rather than the mean.

In this paper, the method is described and the results of the simulation experiment are provided. A discussion of those results and the recommended work going forward are also provided.

# 2 Method

Common statistical tests assume that the distributions of the dependent variables are symmetric, often normal, and then tests are conducted that investigate differences between the locations of the distributions, usually by tests on differences in means and/or medians. However, even similarly-shaped distributions may have nearly identical means and medians, but may differ in terms of the "fatness" of the tails.

Differences in the tails of distributions is potentially important, as it indicates that there are differences in the probabilities of significant departures from the center of the distribution. For example, the tails of the distribution that describes a manufacturing process can indicate how likely it is that the process produces defective products. The mean/median of that distribution only indicates the location of the distribution, which identifies the $50^{th}$ percentile or the "average" value.

For symmetric distributions, including normal distributions, such differences would likely appear as differences in the kurtosis of the distribution. However, if the shape of the distribution is not symmetric or is generally not well-behaved, such simple metrics may not provide sufficient insight. Moreover, even if a metric such as kurtosis is identified as different between two distributions, it is then left to determine what part of the tails are different and in what ways.

Therefore, a nonparametric, bootstrap-based method is used in this work to identify whether the areas under the tails of different probability density functions (PDFs) are significantly different or not. The particular portion of the tail to be studied is a parameter equal to the percentiles of interest, allowing one to make statistically-supported conclusions about the differences in the likelihood of specifically-large deviations from the mean of the performance parameter in question.

## 2.1 Bootstrapping to Compute Confidence Intervals on Percentiles of a Distribution

Simulation runs provide a sample of measures of an operators' performance. That sample, assuming it is representative of the population, can be over-sampled to produce numerous samples. Any particular statistic of the distribution of the sample can be computed such as mean, variance, and, most importantly in this case, the $n^{th}$ percentile. The range of that percentile within which 90% of the samples falls is the 90% confidence interval of the percentile.

Given two samples from different conditions, a conclusion that a sample whose median $n^{th}$ percentile does not fall within the other sample's 90% confidence interval comes from a different population would be accurate 90% of the time. This is equivalent to parametric testing with $\alpha = 0.10$.

One determination that must be made is the number of samples to produce in the bootstrapping procedure. With few samples, the estimates may vary widely and will not form a good distribution of estimates. So ideally one creates a large number of samples. In general, since computation is inexpensive, thousands to tens of thousands of samples are generated. In practice, it is only necessary to take sufficient samples that the estimate stops changing. This can be checked by examining the convergence of the estimates, and stopping when convergence within a desired range is achieved.

## 2.2  Performance Parameters Measured

In simulation, one can record a large number of performance parameters. In this study, as mostly a test and demonstration of a method, we focused solely on deviation from the desired glideslope and localizer course.

One complexity is that although a simulator can record such deviations at a high rate, often as much as 60 Hz, each such observation is not independent from the others and therefore cannot be used as an observation for statistical testing purposes. Such observations could only be analyzed using time-series methods.

Instead, a novel method was used in this study. Deviations were compiled into error events, which have a particular duration and maximum extent (extent). An example of this is shown in Fig. 1. Although there is no formal proof, such errors are likely independent from one another, and therefore the durations and extents can be considered different observations for statistical analysis purposes.

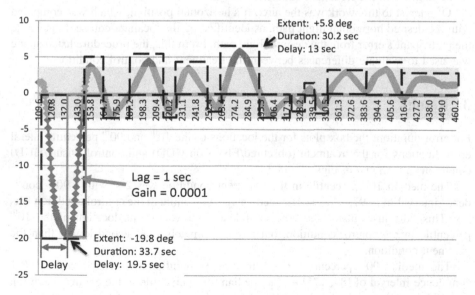

**Fig. 1.** Determination of error extents and durations.

In Fig. 1, each zero crossing is identified, and the regions between zero crossings are considered an error. Filtering should be done to eliminate errors of such small duration or extent that operators would not have corrected them. Duration is the time range over which the error occurred, and extent is the maximum magnitude of the deviation. Also shown in Fig. 1 are the "delay," "gain," and "lag." Delay refers to the time from error inception to the start of a correction. Gain and lag are parameters of the operator's response, calculated from applying a McRuer crossover model to each error (Landry 2014; McRuer and Graham 1965). These latter three parameters, however, were not examined in this work.

Of interest in this work is the location of the 90th percentile of error duration and error extent, and specifically the lateral error as compared to the localizer course. These correspond to long duration error events and large error extents. The analysis can therefore shed light on whether the use of enhanced vision systems have an effect on the likelihood of having errors of long duration or of large extent.

### 2.3  Specific Method Used

With reference to the above detail, five participants flew instrument landing system (ILS) approaches starting approximately 10 nautical miles (NMi) from the runway threshold. Pilots had a HUD that, in the treatment condition, showed the outside view as it would if an EFVS were in use. (In the baseline condition, the HUD operated normally, with the external view in sight through the HUD.)

Moreover, the visibility on the approach was unrestricted, but in the treatment condition, visibility outside of the HUD was zero, meaning the pilots had to rely only on the HUD with EFVS to fly the approach and landing. Obscuration of the view outside of the HUD was accomplished by manually blocking the external view portion of the monitor in the treatment condition.

Of interest to this work was the aircraft's horizontal position, which was compared with the desired horizontal flight path, as identified by the localizer course, to generate the participant's error from the desired flight path. From this, the procedure listed above was used to evaluate differences between the treatment and control conditions.

## 3  Results

For error duration, the box plots for the locations of the 10th and 90th percentile lateral error durations for the treatment (obscured/EFVS on HUD) and control (visual/HUD) conditions are shown in Figs. 2 and 3.

The median 10th percentile in the treatment condition was 2 s, with a 90% confidence interval of [1.97, 2.98] s. The median 10th percentile in the control condition was 3 s. This falls just outside the 90% confidence interval on the location of the 10th percentile in the control condition, but is approximately one second longer than the treatment condition.

The median 90th percentile in the treatment condition was 105 s, with a 90% confidence interval of [87, 175] s. The median 90th percentile in the control condition was 102 s.

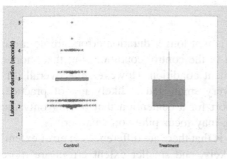

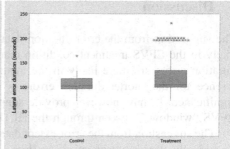

(a) Boxplots of the location of 10th percentile lateral (localizer) error duration for control and treatment conditions.

(b) Boxplots of the location of 90th percentile lateral (localizer) error duration for control and treatment conditions.

**Fig. 2.** Lateral error duration boxplots.

Of note is the larger number of "outlier" points in the treatment condition, shown as asterisks in Fig. 2. Since this is a boxplot of the location of the 90th percentile error duration, these asterisks represent samples where the 90th percentile was substantially higher than the median 90th percentile within the treatment condition.

For error extent, the box plots for the error extents in the treatment (obscured/EFVS on HUD) and control (visual/HUD) conditions are shown in Fig. 3.

For the 10th percentile extent, the median 10th percentile in the treatment condition is 0.0043 dots, with a 90% confidence interval of [0.0037, 0.0062] dots. The median 10th percentile in the control condition is 0.0093 dots.

For the 90th percentile extent, the median 90th percentile in the treatment condition is 0.46 dots, with a 90% confidence interval of [0.32, 0.56] dots. The median 90th percentile in the control condition is 0.79 dots.

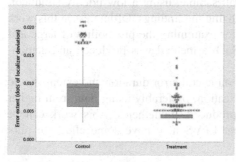

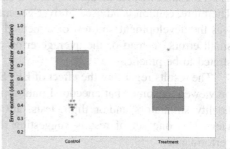

(a) Boxplots of the location of 10th percentile lateral (localizer) error extent for control and treatment conditions.

(b) Boxplots of the location of 90th percentile lateral (localizer) error extent for control and treatment conditions.

**Fig. 3.** Lateral error extent boxplots

## 4 Discussion

The suggestion from the error duration data is that longer duration errors are no more likely in the EFVS treatment condition than in the control condition, but that shorter duration errors are more likely in the treatment condition. However, the overall difference for the shorter duration errors is very small and is likely not of practical significance. It may, however provide support for a contention that having only the EFVS "window," as seen through the HUD, may focus pilots on small errors.

The suggestion from the error extent data is that there are differences in error extent. Specifically, larger extent errors are less likely, and smaller extent errors are more likely, when using EFVS. While this seems like a positive effect of using EFVS, the overall error extent differences are small – on the order of one-third to one-half a dot of localizer deviation. Depending on the distance at which these differences occur, such differences are not necessarily unsafe. This raises the concern, consistent with the error duration results, that the EFVS "window" focuses pilots on relatively small errors. While this may be an overall benefit from an accuracy perspective, since the errors in question are probably not significant from a safety standpoint, it may be that pilots are over-controlling, a situation that could lead to unnecessarily high workload during approach.

Overall, the suggestion from the data is that, when using EFVS, error duration is not strongly affected, but error extents are limited as compared to non-EFVS approaches. As suggested, this may be due to pilots' lack of contextual cues as to the safety of deviating from the desired flight path. If true, this suggests that EFVS could result in higher workload, although such a finding would be at odds with the subjective results of prior work using flight tests.

## 5 Conclusions and Future Work

The results described herein are from a small sample, using a low-fidelity simulator. Therefore, caution is advised in over-generalizing the findings. Of interest in this work was the development and test of a method for examining the probability of large and small errors, instead of the average error. Such a method was produced and demonstrated to be practical.

The results regarding the effect of EFVS on lateral error duration and extent should be viewed as somewhat anecdotal until replication, preferably using data from higher fidelity simulators and/or flight tests, are produced. Nonetheless, this work can be viewed as one set of results suggesting that EFVS may have some effect on pilot performance.

# References

Arthur, J.J., Kramer, L.J., Bailey, R.E.: Flight test comparison between enhanced vision (FLIR) and synthetic vision systems. In: Paper presented at the Defense and Security 2005, Orlando, FL, 25 May 2005

Bailey, R.E., Kramer, L.J., Williams, S.P.: Enhanced vision for all-weather operations under NextGen. In: Paper presented at the SPIE Defense, Security, and Sensnig, Orlando, FL, 23 April 2010

Beier, K., Gemperlein, H.: Simulation of infrared detection range in fog conditions for enhanced vision systems in civil aviation. Aerosp. Sci. Technol. **8**, 63–71 (2004)

Endsley, M.R., Sollenberger, R., Nakata, A., Stein, E.: Situation awareness in air traffic control: Enhanced displays for advanced operations, Report No. DOT/FAA/CT-TN00/01, Atlantic City, NJ (2000)

Kramer, L.J., Etherington, T.J., Severance, K., Bailey, R.E., Williams, S.P., Harrison, S.J.: Assesing dual-sensor enhanced flight vision systems to enable equivalent visual operations. J. Aerosp. Inf. Syst. **14**, 533–550 (2017)

Kramer, L.J., Harrison, S.J., Bailey, R.E., Shelton, K. J., Ellis, K.K.E.: Visual advantage of enhanced flight vision system during NextGen flight test evaluation. In: Paper presented at the Degraded Visual Environments: Enhanced, Synthetic, and Extended Vision Solutions 2014, 19 June 2014

Landry, S.J.: Modeling McRuer delay and gain parameters within recorded aircraft state data. In: Paper presented at the Human Factors and Ergonomics Society Annual Meeting, Chicago, IL (2014)

McRuer, D., Graham, D.: Human pilot dynamics in compensatory systems (AAFFDL-TR-65-15) (1965)

Todd, J.R., Hester, R.B., Summers, L.G.: Seeing through the weather: enhanced/synthetic vision systems for commercial transports. In: Paper presented at the IEEE/AIAA 11th Digital Avionics Systems Conference, Seattle, WA, 5–8 October 1992

Yang, L.C., Hansman, R.J.: Human performance evaluation of enhanced vision systems for approach and landing. In: Paper presented at the SPIE International Symposium on Optical Engineering and Photonics in Aerospace Sensing, Orlando, FL, 13 July 1994

# Towards a Mixed Reality Assistance System for the Inspection After Final Car Assembly

Marco Pattke, Manuel Martin[✉], and Michael Voit

Fraunhofer IOSB, Fraunhoferstr. 1, 76131 Karlsruhe, Germany
{marco.pattke,manuel.martin,michael.voit}@iosb.fraunhofer.de
http://www.iosb.fraunhofer.de

**Abstract.** Final manual inspection after vehicle assembly is a task that becomes more and more difficult because of the increasing number of customization options. We investigate how an assistance system based on mixed reality can help with this task. To this end we identify four major components that should help guide the worker and document his findings. We implement each component in three versions with increasing implementation complexity and immersion and investigate which version is most suitable in a user study.

**Keywords:** Interaction and navigation in VR and MR: Orientation and navigation · Presence in VR and MR: Design issues

## 1  Introduction

We investigate different interaction methods and graphical user interfaces for common tasks in mixed reality applications. We chose the final manual inspection after vehicle assembly as an example use case. This task is especially relevant because individual configuration options for customers are increasing and thus making the final quality assurance steps more complex.

To our knowledge, workers nowadays perform the final inspection of a car with either a paper checklist or a tablet computer. In some cases additional digital reports are filled out at the end of the inspection. The final inspection involves many different steps. These encompass for example functional checks, measuring gap dimensions, inspecting the paint for scratches, and checking for the installation of customizable hardware. The steps can vary greatly based on the choices of the customer. There are different aspects of this process that can be optimized with a wearable mixed reality based assistance system. The order of performed steps and the localization of the relevant parts of the car play a major role in the completion time of the task. A suitable guidance system can both help the worker find the relevant part of the car as fast as possible and can also indicate what needs to be done there. After performing a check, the worker can also continuously document his findings with the help of the

© Springer Nature Switzerland AG 2019
J. Y. C. Chen and G. Fragomeni (Eds.): HCII 2019, LNCS 11575, pp. 536–546, 2019.
https://doi.org/10.1007/978-3-030-21565-1_37

assistance system removing the need for additional reports. For documentation purposes, the worker could for example mark parts of the car with the assistance system or could use it to input numbers or text.

Based on this task description we identify four basic building blocks for a suitable assistance system: navigation, information display, highlighting of points on the car surface and numerical input. We investigate three versions of each building block with increasing immersion and difficulty to implement: 2D floating windows, 3D floating objects and mixed reality overlay. To evaluate the system we conduct a user study and measure task completion time, users workload with the NASA Task Load Index Questionnaire (NASA-TLX) and immersion of the system with the User Experience Questionnaire (UEQ).

## 2 Related Work

There are few assistance systems for the worker performing the inspection. Some approaches try to use smart glasses, like the Google Glass, to offer support for similar tasks [6–8]. However, the small screen is very limiting and does not allow overlying virtual objects with the real world as is necessary for mixed reality applications. Mixed reality glasses like the Microsoft HoloLens are however already used successfully for the training of assembly tasks [2,11].

Stocker et al. [10] develop a system for processing a checklist for car assembly using the head mounted display *Vuzix M100* (see Fig. 1). They evaluate the system for practical application and acceptance by the user. However, their results show that the head mounted display was too uncomfortable to wear for a prolonged time. In addition users criticized the detection rate of the user input. In general they still conclude a high application potential for head mounted displays for similar tasks.

Evans et al. [2] present an application for 3D assembly instructions for manual assembly using the Microsoft HoloLense. They investigate the feasibility and usability of the system for its use in industrial applications. They conclude that the Microsoft HoloLense is a promising system for this task. However, especially the tracking capabilities of the device caused problems. The built in tracking

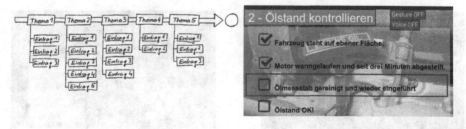

**Fig. 1.** Checklist for vehicle assembly, left: Concept, right: implemented Prototype [10].

methods were not able to reliably track the position of assembly parts and of the assembly station itself. To work around this shortcoming they use a marker based approach.

## 3   The Mixed Reality Assistance System

We develop a prototype system using the game engine Unity3d and the head-mounted display Microsoft HoloLens. For a mixed reality application to work it is necessary to have a suitable real world experimental setup to work with. We use the car integrated in our driving simulator for all experiments. It is an Audi A3 situated inside a room with normal indoor lighting. We use an accurate 3D model of this car to be able to augment the real environment properly. We focus on four key tasks: Navigation (see Fig. 3), selection (see Fig. 4), presentation of information (see Fig. 5) and numerical input (see Fig. 6).

Those groups where designed with the classification of Bowman et al. [1] in mind, where interaction techniques are divided into three groups: Navigation, selection/manipulation and system control. Because it is often important to show information like user instructions on the screen we add a fourth group to investigate how to best present information to the user. The manipulation group has been deliberately omitted, as it does typically not appear in the chosen application scenario and is more represented in application areas like games.

There are several ways to implement the above tasks with the Microsoft HoloLens. We choose to implement each task in three categories with increasing implementation complexity as well as increasing immersion: classic 2D, modern 3D and true world referenced (mixed reality).

The classic 2D category is very similar to a menu from a standard tablet computer. Interface elements are flat and fixed to the viewing area of the worker or on a spot on the car. This category can be implemented with small effort based on available user-interface tools. The modern 3D category represents each interface element as 3D object, floating in the scene. Implementing this category requires 3D models of suitable symbols. However, it does not require accurate tracking of the car. Elements in both categories either follow the user or are at a fixed position in his surrounding environment. The mixed reality category

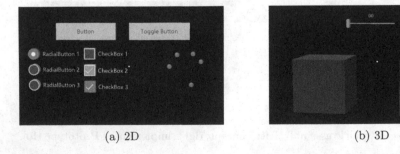

(a) 2D                                           (b) 3D

**Fig. 2.** Introduction scene where users can click and select buttons and move a slider with the air tap gesture.

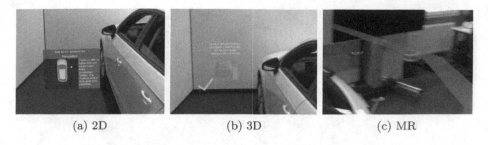

(a) 2D             (b) 3D             (c) MR

**Fig. 3.** Navigation assistance to find the right place around the car.

tries to integrate the interface as much as possible into the real world. Guidance information are located directly on the surface of the car and interactions are performed by interacting with the car and not with separate entities as in the two other categories. This requires accurate tracking of the inspected car so everything can be located precisely. It also requires the most effort in designing suitable input and output paradigms.

In the following we present each group and its three implementations in more detail.

## 3.1 Training Scenario

Head-mounted displays are still very novel devices which few people have experience with. We therefore develop an introduction task so users can get familiar with the device its limits and its input methods. This should help users perform the following tasks successfully. The training task is split in two parts (see Fig. 2).

The purpose of the first part of the task is to make the user familiar with the basic features of the Microsoft HoloLens. The user experiences the limited field of view, the basic method of information presentation (holograms) as well as the air tap gesture together with the head rotation that is used as the main input method of the device. For this purpose, the user is shown several buttons and a small 3D animation at a fixed location in the room. The second part introduces the manipulation gesture, which is an extension of the air tap gesture by presenting a slider that can rotate or scale a box.

## 3.2 Navigation

The goal of the navigation task is to guide the user around the car to the different inspection spots. To investigate how this can be achieved best we task the user to find various spots around the car and to walk to the indicated spot. As soon as the spot is reached, the next spot is displayed. In order to find the spots, the user needs a reference point, which is the vehicle in the task environment. Both reference point and the next spot that should be reached are represented in different ways for the three implementation options (see Fig. 3).

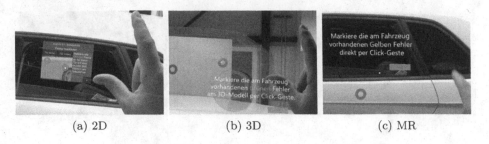

|         (a) 2D          |         (b) 3D          |         (c) MR          |

**Fig. 4.** Selection methods to mark paint defects.

The 2D category represents the reference point as the top down view of the car and the next spot to reach as a circle at the respective position around the top down view. The window follows the user around and stays in its viewing area.

The 3D category represents the reference point as the 3D model of the car and the next spot as a cylinder on the side of the model. The 3D model follows the user around.

The mixed reality category does not use a explicit representation of the reference point. Instead it uses the real car as the reference and displays a guide line at breast height that the user has to follow to reach the next spot. If the next spot is behind the car from the users point of view the end of the guide line is occluded and the user can only see the goal by following the line.

### 3.3   Selection

Selection can be used for different parts of the inspection task for example to indicate missing parts or defects in the finish of the car. To investigate how selection can best be performed we add stickers to the side of the car in three colors. The user has to select the stickers of one color for each of the three implemented versions. The input method for all categories is the *Gaze* in connection with the *Air-Tap* gesture, which are both built in the HoloLens as standard interactions. The three implemented versions are shown in Fig. 4.

For the 2D category the inspected area of the cars surface is shown as an image. The user first has to find a colored sticker on the surface of the car then he has to find the same position on the image to mark it. The window is at a fixed position in the environment.

The 3D category represents the car as the 3D model that is hovering above the real car. Similar to the 2D category the user first has to find a colored sticker then has to reference it on the 3D model above the car to mark it.

The mixed reality category does not represent the car as a separate entity. The user has to find a colored sticker on the surface of the car and can immediately select it on the surface. Selection is confirmed by highlighting the point on the surface of the car. We achieve this by superimposing the 3D model of the

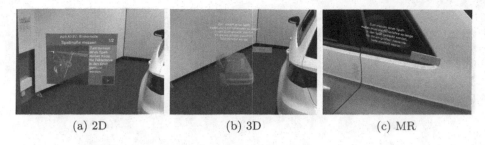

(a) 2D                    (b) 3D                    (c) MR

**Fig. 5.** Information display for the inspection step gap size measurement.

car over the real car without showing the 3D model to the user. This requires high tracking accuracy to ensure that the selection is at the right position.

### 3.4 Presentation of Information

Although text and other elements have already been presented in the previous tasks we specifically design an experiment to evaluate different display options. The user just has to evaluate which version he likes best without performing the described task. As an example task we choose the measuring of gap size on the side of the car with a special measuring device (feeler gauge). The measuring device was additionally printed in 3D so that the user could study it in parallel. It is also needed for the next task. Figure 5 shows the three representations of the task.

The 2D version describes the task with an image of a gap together with the feeler gauge and an explanatory text.

The 3D version replaces the image with an animated 3D model that rotates in front of the user.

The mixed reality version superimposes the feeler gauge over a gap on the side of the car and demonstrates its application with an animation.

### 3.5 Numerical Input

In order to enter numbers, the user must apply the knowledge from the previous task on how to use the feeler gauge to measure the gap dimensions at several points on the vehicle and enter the measured distance in the system. Figure 6 shows the designed input methods.

The 2D version of the interface presents an image to the user indicating the measurement position and uses a keypad as the input method. The window is located at a fixed position.

The 3D version of the interface uses the 3D model of the car to specify the measurement position and uses a slide as the input method.

The mixed reality version of the interface indicates the position superimposed on the surface of the car and presents a ring of possible numbers to enter the measured gap dimensions.

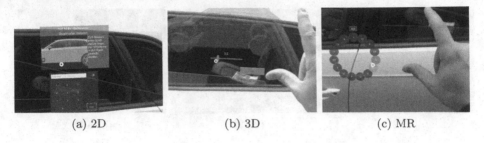

      (a) 2D               (b) 3D               (c) MR

**Fig. 6.** Method for the input of numbers.

## 4   Evaluation

We conduct a user study to evaluate all four interaction methods and their three different implementations. The goal of the user study is to find out which of the implemented versions are preferred by the users and are most effective.

The participants were first introduced to the use of the HoloLens and then performed the training task to become familiar with the device and its control paradigms. Afterwards, each test participant performed all four tasks in a fixed order. First the navigation task then the selection task, followed by the different information presentation methods and finally the task that involved the input of numbers. The order of the three categories (2D, 3D, MR) for each task were randomized to avoid training bias. After each task, the participant answered both the shortened *NASA-TLX* questionnaire [4] to measure workload, and the shortened user experience questionnaire (*UEQ-S*) [9] to measure the immersion and user experience. We also recorded the task completion time.

For both questionnaires, each question must be answered with a seven-point Likert scale, in which the user can more or less agree, or disagree with the statement. The answers to the questionnaires consists of ordinal scaled data on a scale from $-3$ to $3$ for the *UEQ-S*, and from $1$ to $7$ for the *NASA-TLX* questionnaire.

A total of 15 participants participated in the user study. Seven participants were between 20 to 30 years old, eight were between 30 and 40 years old. Eight participants wore glasses. Since this sample count can not be assumed to be normally distributed, the non-parametric data *Friedman test* is used [3]. It compares at least three or more samples, and the data must be metric or ordinal scaled. As a post-hoc test, the *Wilcoxon-Nemenyi-McDonald-Thompson test* is used, in which two categories are checked for statistical correlation among each other [5]. In the following we discuss the results for each interaction method.

The results of the navigation task are close together (see Fig. 7). There is no significant difference in the results of the *NASA-TLX* the scores where overall very low and the task not very demanding. The *UEQ-S* however shows significant differences for the hedonic quality and the overall quality. Here the scores are better with better immersion. So 3D scores better than 2D and MR scores better

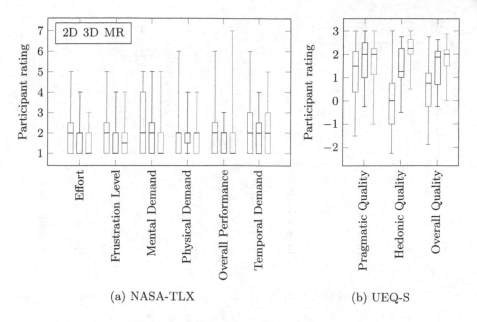

(a) NASA-TLX                    (b) UEQ-S

**Fig. 7.** Results of the navigation task.

than 3D. The task completion time was very similar between the three versions however users took slightly longer when using the MR implementation.

The results of the selection task show the biggest difference between the three categories. Figure 8 shows the results. The mixed reality implementation is overall significantly better than the other categories. The difference between the 2D and 3D representation is not as big, but still significant. The scores of the *NASA-TLX* questionnaire are very low for the mixed reality implementation and average for both other implementations. The reason for this is likely that these two categories require an extra step. Users first have to locate the sticker and then find this location again on the respective representation of the car. The scores of the *UEQ-S* are also significantly higher for the mixed reality implementation compared to the other categories showing the benefit of the increased immersion and ease of use of this implementation. The task completion time shows a similar result by eliminating the extra step in the mixed reality system users completed the task almost twice as fast compared to the 2D implementation.

The results of the information display experiment are close (see Fig. 9). There is no significant difference in the result of the *NASA-TLX*. Overall scores are very low however the frustration level is slightly increased for the 3D implementation. Participant commented that they wished the 3D implementation would have been interactive so they could rotate and scale it to get a better view. This likely caused the increased frustration level for this implementation. Similar to the navigation task, the *UEQ-S* shows significantly better scores for the 3D and MR implementations in hedonic and overall quality.

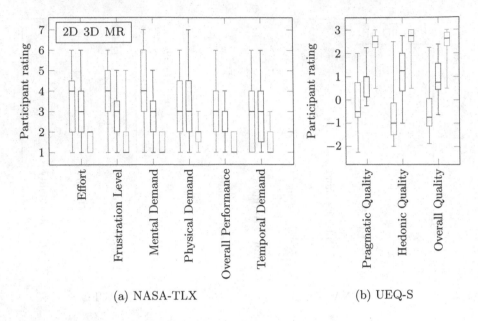

(a) NASA-TLX                    (b) UEQ-S

**Fig. 8.** Results of the selection task.

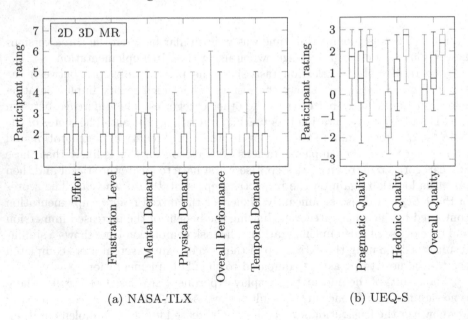

(a) NASA-TLX                    (b) UEQ-S

**Fig. 9.** Results of the information display task.

Figure 10 shows the results for the input task for numbers. *NASA-TLX* scores are close together. Scores are significantly lower for the mixed reality version for frustration level, mental demand, overall performance and temporal demand.

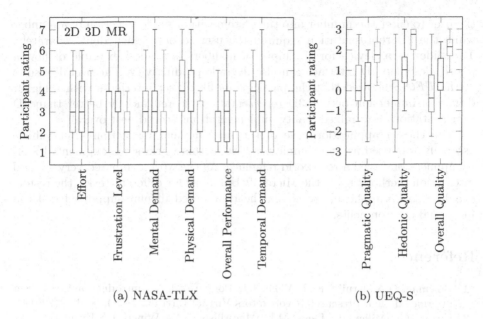

(a) NASA-TLX                    (b) UEQ-S

**Fig. 10.** Results of the input task for numbers.

This shows that overall the mixed reality implementation reduces the workload compared to the other to implementations. *UEQ-S* scores similarly also show overall significantly better scores for the mixed reality implementation. The task completion time was similar for the 2D and mixed reality implementation however participants needed twice the time with the 3D implementation. Many participants mentioned difficulties with the control of the slider. Often the Microsoft HoloLens did not recognize the end of the gesture correctly so the value changed even after the users intended to end the interaction.

## 5   Conclusion

We presented a prototype augmented reality assistance system for the application of manual inspection after final vehicle assembly using the Microsoft HoloLens. We implemented three different versions (2D, 3D, MR) for four building blocks of such an application: navigation, selection, information display and input of numbers. We investigated in a user study which of the implemented versions works best for each building block with regard to workload, user experience and task completion time.

Overall the user study showed that workload and task completion time did not change much with the tasks presentation except if the number of steps needed to complete the task changed for an implementation. This was the case for the selection task where the mixed reality implementation removed the need to reference the point on a separate representation of the car. In part this is also true for the mixed reality implementation of the input task because it enabled the user to enter the number into the system with a single selection of a number while the 2D representation required the user to enter each digit separately. The slider as a device for the input of numbers is a good example of how a poorly designed 3D interface can also degrade productivity. The overall results of the *UEQ-S* showed that the participants liked user interfaces with a higher degree of immersion better. 3D representations scored mostly better than 2D representations and mixed reality implementations scored best overall.

The chosen application case of the final manual inspection after vehicle assembly was used as an example use case in this work, since augmented reality applications need a real-world reference. As the work compared very general interaction methods using the Microsoft HoloLens for different tasks, the results should also be applicable to similar head-mounted display-supported tasks in industrial environments.

# References

1. Bowman, D.A., Kruijff, E., LaViola, J.J., Poupyrev, I.: An introduction to 3-D user interface design. Presence: Teleoperators Virtual Environ. **10**(1), 96–108 (2001)
2. Evans, G., Miller, J., Pena, M.I., MacAllister, A., Winer, E.: Evaluating the Microsoft HoloLens through an augmented reality assembly application. In: Degraded Environments: Sensing, Processing, and Display. International Society for Optics and Photonics (2017)
3. Friedman, M.: The use of ranks to avoid the assumption of normality implicit in the analysis of variance. J. Am. Stat. Assoc. **32**(200), 675–701 (1937)
4. Hart, S.G.: Nasa-task load index (NASA-TLX); 20 years later. Proc. Hum. Factors Ergon. Soc. Ann. Meet. **50**(9), 904–908 (2006)
5. Hollander, M., Wolfe, D.A.: Nonparametric Statistical Methods, p. 295. Wiley-Interscience, Hoboken (1999)
6. Meixner, G., et al.: Einsatz der google glass zur optimierung der manuellen inbetriebnahme und funktionsprüfung in der audi a8 fertigung. VDI-Bericht 2258: 16. Branchentreff der Mess-und Automatisierungstechnik, AUTOMATION 2015, Benefits of Change-the Future of Automation (2015)
7. Quint, F., Loch, F., Weber, H., Venitz, J., Gröber, M., Liedel, J.: Evaluation of smart glasses for documentation in manufacturing. Mensch und Computer (2016)
8. Rauh, S., Grauf, D., Schwager, S., Bolch, S., Meixner, G.: Optimising energy characteristics of head worn displays for active use in factory environments. In: 2016 8th International Congress on Ultra Modern Telecommunications and Control Systems and Workshops (ICUMT), pp. 219–224 (2016)
9. Schrepp, M., Hinderks, A., Thomaschewski, J.: Design and evaluation of a short version of the user experience questionnaire (UEQ-s). Int. J. Interact. Multimed. Artif. Intell. **4**(6), 103 (2017)
10. Stocker, A., Spitzer, M., Kaiser, C., Rosenberger, M., Fellmann, M.: Datenbrillengestützte Checklisten in der Fahrzeugmontage, vol. 40, pp. 255–263, June 2016
11. Werrlich, S., Lorber, C., Nguyen, P.-A., Yanez, C.E.F., Notni, G.: Assembly training: comparing the effects of head-mounted displays and face-to-face training. In: Chen, J.Y.C., Fragomeni, G. (eds.) VAMR 2018. LNCS, vol. 10909, pp. 462–476. Springer, Cham (2018). https://doi.org/10.1007/978-3-319-91581-4_35

# Interaction Paradigms for Air Traffic Control and Management in Mixed Reality

Syed Hammad Hussain Shah$^{(\boxtimes)}$, Kyungjin Han,
and Jong Weon Lee$^{(\boxtimes)}$

Department of Software Convergence, Sejong University,
Seoul, Republic of Korea
hammad.shah38@gmail.com, kjinn.han@gmail.com,
jwlee@sejong.ac.kr

**Abstract.** Mixed reality world overlays the real world with the 3D virtual objects. It provides 3D user interfaces placed within real world for better user interaction and operability. Hence making its way to a huge number of fields. This paper introduces the novel approach of controlling the air traffic using mixed reality's interaction mechanisms. Conventional user interfaces within control tower are hard to understand and could not provide better picture about various situations at airport and the traffic in air. This system provides the holographic displays for viewing the 3D information of air traffic from any angle in the mixed reality world. It provides view of multiple information and switching among them from a single see-through display which reduces the required number of computer screens at control tower. It also enables controllers to remotely control air traffic from any distant location with the help of a head mounted mixed reality display.

**Keywords:** Air traffic control · Mixed reality · Augmented reality

## 1 Introduction

Mixed reality is a world consisting of real world objects and virtual objects in a single environment. Unlike virtual reality, mixed reality enables the users to interact with virtual world along with feel of presence inside real world. It makes the human-computer interaction very effective. Due to this reason, concept of mixed reality is prevailing across various industries for creating highly interactive interfaces of their systems. Variety of industries from areas of engineering, marketing, entertainment etc. is using mixed reality for simulating their work and interactions in 3D environment. They found mixed reality as better source of medium to understand the information. If we analyze service of air traffic control and management, it also requires interactive mixed reality interfaces for better user experience [1]. Complexity in service of air traffic control is increasing day by day with the rise in air traffic [2]. It is becoming difficult to monitor and handle air traffic using conventional approaches in air traffic control tower. It needs interactive and more flexible interfaces for better quality of service. Main objective of this study is the provision of mixed reality interfaces for enhancing capabilities of air traffic controllers. The job of air traffic controllers is full of

© Springer Nature Switzerland AG 2019
J. Y. C. Chen and G. Fragomeni (Eds.): HCII 2019, LNCS 11575, pp. 547–556, 2019.
https://doi.org/10.1007/978-3-030-21565-1_38

stress because they need to monitor lot of information like airplane take-offs, landings, collision avoidance etc. There are multiple 2D displays representing different information within control tower (See Fig. 1). It is difficult for air traffic controllers to move around these screens for monitoring various information related to air traffic.

**Fig. 1.** Inside view of air traffic control tower    **Fig. 2.** Hindrance to the outside view from control tower due to fog

Moreover, 2D displays could not deliver full understanding of the situations at airfield. Therefore, controllers need to look outside of the window of control tower for visual monitoring of the runways. Sometimes, bad weather conditions come across, which limit the outside view of air traffic controllers from the tower (See Fig. 2). Due to this blocked view, controllers could not monitor the traffic on runways. We have developed this tool to overcome such limitations faced by the air traffic controllers within control tower. This tool assists air traffic controllers in monitoring and managing traffic at real time with the help of 4D view (3D Model + Time) of airfield in mixed reality world. It enables them to track the airplanes in more easy and interactive way. Target of the interaction models developed in this mixed reality tool is to increase the analysis power of air traffic controllers for better management of increasing air traffic. This tool presents two main views for monitoring and control of air traffic. First one is the 4D mixed reality view of whole airport including airport building, runways, taxiways, parking, traffic etc. for monitoring ground traffic. The second one is the map view within mixed reality for tracking the status of the traffic in air and having the globe view. Both can be categorized as the detailed view and broad view respectively. Furthermore, this study presents another concept which is based on provision of the easy and fast access to the information required by controller. Main contributions of this study are as follows:

1. Mapped flight trajectories using real world radar data into the mixed reality world of 4D airfield
2. Presented 4D view of airfield in mixed reality for providing more detailed and clear information of air traffic for better analysis.
3. Easy access to the multilevel information about air traffic's location in real world from a single see-through display at one place.

4. Weather independent air traffic control and management system in case of visual impairments due to bad weather conditions.
5. Facilitation of air traffic management service from any remote location with the help of interactive 4D view of airfield through wireless holographic display.

Better interactivity in work environment could increase the overall productivity. This proposed methodology could impact overall air traffic control systems on large extent. One of the significances of this tool is better interaction between air traffic controllers and system's interfaces of control towers. It reduces workload of controllers by providing easy access to required information on single holographic display in mixed reality. Concerned personnel do not have to switch between multiple screens for accessing various information based on requirements at runtime. Due to very interactive 3D display, this tool brings monitoring power of air traffic controllers beyond the limits of conventional 2D displays. Moreover, it helps air traffic controllers to analyze the complex airfield from different angles in mixed reality for better understanding of different situations at airfield. By using this tool, controllers would not be restricted by what the naked eye could see out of control tower's window. Due to this reason, it facilitates the efficient air traffic management in case of bad weather conditions like fog, heavy rain etc. In this way, such outside areas could also be analyzed well which may not be easily visible by human eye through the control tower's window at real time. Moreover, with the help of this tool, controllers could remotely monitor the air traffic and visualize ongoing situations at airfield using wireless head mounted display.

## 2 Related Works

Air traffic control is a very sensitive task and from last few decades lot of research is being done to make it efficient. Around 25 years ago, Lloyd Hitchcock of federal aviation administration (FAA) firstly proposed the idea of using augmented reality technology in air traffic control tower [3]. Prototype was not constructed at that time although many researchers recalled Mr. Hitchcock surmising on various methods that could facilitate controllers [4]. In 1996, Azuma and Daily presented advance human-computer interfaces of that time for air traffic management [1]. Furthermore, concept of remotely located air traffic service is also under focus. It includes real time rendering of recreated 360° tower view in virtual reality [5–8].

In 2010, Bagassi et al. presented a design of 4D interface on 2D screen for controllers to interpret the flight data [9]. This study also presented the method to estimate and display the airplanes at their future locations for detecting conflicts. In the mid of 2014, Reisman et al. executed a flight test for measuring registration error in the technology of augmented reality within the control tower [10]. In 2015, Arif Abdul Rahman et al. also proposed a method for 3D visualization of real time flight tracking data in 2D display [11]. They also aimed at providing better interaction mechanism to controllers using more focused visuals for clear interpretation of the flights around control tower.

In June 2016, Masotti et al. presented an idea of using augmented reality in the control tower [12]. In this study, they have proposed a rendering pipeline for multiple head-up displays for generating overplay between augmented reality layer and outside view from control tower. Afterwards, Bagassi et al. investigated different augmented reality systems in September 2016 for assessing their application to on-the-site control towers [13]. In their project, they have focused on the placement of the information on the actual windows of the control tower. In 2017, Zorzal et al. discussed the construction of a prototype which could place real time ground radar's information to airplane on the captured image from live IP camera [14].

All the existing systems which are discussed above, played a good role in betterment of air traffic control service. But if we observe them in terms of better human-computer interaction, many limitations are still existent. Although, 3D interfaces are being provided for visualizing traffic on airport but these systems are still using 2D screens for rendering [9, 11, 14]. Comparatively, analysis power of controllers has been increased by these systems but still they are unable to efficiently interpret the situations. It is because they are still limited to 2D screens. There is not such efficient and interactive interface provided for visualizing the radar data about traffic in air. Moreover, the proposed augmented reality based systems for overlaying the real windows with 3D information, require lot of complex apparatus [12].

However, our system presents remedies to these existent limitations. Three dimensional interfaces in our system are not restricted within 2D displays. As our proposed tool is mixed reality based, so controller can efficiently perform analysis of the traffic's situation by viewing the 4D information from multiple orientations. Possibility of viewing information from multiple angles by moving around the model induces more interactivity and controllers' interest in the system. Controller will not be restricted to the monitor screens and can move anywhere with the head mounted mixed reality display. It increases the capability of the air traffic controllers to analyze the information more efficiently in any situation. Effects of the bad weather conditions and other circumstances will be very low on the traffic management system.

Detailed view which is proposed in this paper presents very clear and complete information about traffic on the airport. However, in map view we have also made interpretation of the radar data very easy. We have provided these highly interactive interfaces under the single roof with the help of head mounted mixed reality display. Moreover, along with the very interactive interfaces, we have provided very easy management of these interfaces within the mixed reality environment. It is very easy for the controllers to switch between the interfaces without any extra effort in this system. If we talk about the air traffic management service from a distant location, this tool is very remote and helpful here also. Controllers can simply wear the head mounted mixed reality display and have 4D information of the air traffic anywhere. There is no need to setup the complex system for monitoring the air traffic from a distant location. One head mounted device can bear the whole load.

# 3 Proposed Mixed Reality Tool

We have presented a novel approach of 4D visualization of airfield in holographic mixed reality. Various information is used to be monitored by the controllers at airfield. That information includes airplane landings, takeoffs, ground traffic, traffic in air etc. If we closely observe the information tracked by the controllers, we can categorize it into two main levels; traffic on ground and the traffic in air. Ground traffic is usually monitored by watching outside view from the window of control tower while the traffic in air is monitored using radar data over 2D screens in control tower. Each one has its own limitations based on different circumstances. Outside view from tower could be blocked due to bad weather conditions while radar information on 2D screens could not provide interactive and clear interpretation of the status of air traffic. Moreover, switching among different interfaces and outside view of tower could be time taking and require more manpower. Hence, we come up with the 4D presentation of these two levels of information of air traffic through a single and very interactive holographic mixed reality display. We have proposed detailed view for ground traffic, map view for the distant traffic in air and real time fast switching among them based on requirement. 3D objects are used for representing airplanes in both views. On top of 3D object, it shows flight's information like flight number, airplane's speed etc. Detailed discussion about proposed interaction paradigms' design and development process are as follows:

## 3.1 Detailed View

As the name suggests, this view holds each minor detail of the airport as 3D scenery file. It includes airport's building, runways, taxiways, airport apron and major surroundings. In this mechanism, controller has a 3D airport lying on a real world surface. It presents clear details of ongoing activities of airplanes over the airport in mixed reality. Controller can clearly visualize the airplanes flying around the airport, landings, takeoffs, traffic on taxiways and the airplanes which are parked in airport's apron. Detailed view holds complete 4D mapping of airplanes' activities on ground and the traffic in air around control tower. Figure 3a and b shows the detailed view of airfield.

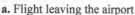

**a.** Flight leaving the airport                **b.** Flight landed on the airport

**Fig. 3.** Yellow circle is highlighting the Airplane in detailed view (Color figure online)

## 3.2   Map View

Map view gives a better and interactive visual presentation of the air traffic around the globe. It presents the abstract level view of the air traffic over the world map. Controller could view and monitor the air traffic on map. In map view, controller could see the 3D objects moving over the map which are actually representing air traffic. Controllers do not have to deeply analyze the radar data for extracting the useful information. Here because of 4D visual presentation of radar data, they could easily interpret that how many airplanes are going to approach the airport in coming duration. It gives an idea about distance of the airplane from airport and which city or location it has reached so far. Mapping of 3D objects over the map in mixed reality is based on the information retrieved from the radar. This view uses the 2D texture of the world map rendered over a surface in 3D mixed reality world as shown in Fig. 4a and b.

**a.** Map placed over a tabletop            **b.** Map placed loosely in environment

**Fig. 4.**  Map view of the air traffic

## 3.3   Design and Development Process

The process of mapping air traffic into the mixed reality world with respect to real world position consists of multiple steps. Detailed description of each step is as follows (First step is one time process):

**Calculation of Scaling Factor.** Calculated the scaling factor value to scale down real world distance in order to map it in mixed reality world. It means that how many units in mixed reality world represents the 1 unit of real world. If 'D1' represents the scale of distance you want to keep in mixed reality world and 'D2' represents the actual distance in real world then scaling factor is calculated as in Eq. 1.

$$\text{Scaling Factor} = \frac{\text{D1}}{\text{D2}} \qquad (1)$$

Way of acquiring the actual (real world) distance for detailed view and map view is slightly different as discussed below:

*Detailed View.* Here, we've considered the actual length of one of the runways of our target airport. Then calculated the scaling factor by substituting the two values required by Eq. 1. Runway's length that we wanted to keep for 3D model within mixed reality world and actual length of that runway.

*Map View.* For this view, we took a screenshot of map showing the location of our target airport and rendered it over a plane in mixed reality world. Afterwards, we calculated the scaling factor based on the actual distance from airport to top right location as shown in screenshot (see Fig. 5) and the scale we wanted to keep in mixed reality world.

**Fig. 5.** Arrow head representing the actual distance

**Conversion of WGS-84 Geodetic Locations (GPS Readings) to Cartesian Coordinates.** Radar data presents the location of airplane according to World Geodetic System (GPS readings). Whereas, for mixed reality world unity follows the Cartesian coordinates system. Hence, for getting the Cartesian coordinates as x, y and z coordinate, it is required to convert Geodetic coordinates to the local tangent plane [15]. Basis of this implementation is a book written by Farrell and Barth [16]. By using GPS information, the x, y and z coordinates can be derived by using following system of equations.

$$x = (h + N) \cos \lambda \cos \varphi \qquad (2)$$

$$y = (h + N) \cos \lambda \sin \varphi \qquad (3)$$

$$z = (h + (1 - e^2)N) \sin \lambda \qquad (4)$$

Here, 'h' represents height, '$\lambda$' is for latitude and '$\varphi$' represents the longitude. Whereas, 'N' and 'e' can be calculated as follows:

$$e = f (2 - f) \qquad (5)$$

'f' represents ellipsoid flatness and can be calculated as in Eq. 6.

$$f = \frac{(a - b)}{a} \qquad (6)$$

Where, 'a' is the WGS-84 Earth semimajor axis and 'b' represents the derived Earth semi-minor axis. Now, 'N' can be calculated using 'e' from Eq. 5 in Eq. 7.

$$N = \frac{a}{\sqrt{1 - e (s^2)}} \qquad (7)$$

Where, 's' can be calculated as follows:

$$s = \sin \lambda \qquad (8)$$

Hence, cartesian coordinates for airport's control tower and airplane's location are calculated using Eqs. 2, 3, 4 and other supporting equations as well.

**Directional Vector.** After finding the cartesian coordinates for both point/locations, we find the directional vector between both points. Let, $T(x_1, y_1, z_1)$ represents coordinates of control tower and $A(x_2, y_2, z_2)$ represents the coordinates of airplane, we can find the directional vector as follows:

$$\vec{TA} = \ <x_2 - x_1, y_2 - y_1, z_2 - z_1> \qquad (9)$$

Let, $\vec{TA} = \ <x_i, y_i, z_i>$. Now, we calculate the magnitude of this directional vector using Eq. 10 for finding the current distance between control tower and airplane.

$$M = \sqrt{x_i^2 + y_i^2 + z_i^2} \qquad (10)$$

After finding the magnitude, we multiply this with scaling factor (calculated in Eq. 1) to down scale the distance for mixed reality world.

**Mapping.** Afterwards, by using the directional vector and distance calculated in Step 3, we find the exact coordinates for the location of airplane in mixed reality world. After finding the exact location, we instantiate the 3D object and map it at derived location which represents the airplane in mixed reality world as shown in Figs. 3 and 4.

Our system performs the step 2, 3 and 4 against each airplane when GPS information of the air traffic is received over time.

## 4   Flight Tests

We have tested our system with real world flight trajectories. These trajectories were recorded during different departure and arrival flights from Jeju Airport, Republic Korea. Number of flights included in our test were 10 in total. Three of them were departure flights while remaining were the arrival flights. Flight codes were as; 9C8625, 9C8913, FE722, KE1237, OZ8995, MU5028, ZE228, ZE230, ZE551 and ZE706. These recorded flight trajectories are collected from an online source named as 'FlightRadar24' [17]. We retrieved the flight data from this web application as CSV file. Flight data was comprised of the latitude, longitude and altitude of airplane along with the timestamp during whole flight of each airplane.

# 5 Conclusion and Future Work

We have presented the interaction mechanisms for better control and management of air traffic. These interaction mechanisms consist of the mixed reality holographic 3D displays. With the help of these paradigms, air traffic controllers can easily understand the situation at airfield in more efficient and interactive way. It eliminates the barriers of bad weather conditions, fixed location for air traffic controller and less interactive interfaces in managing the air traffic. Although, we have not tested the system with the real air traffic controllers on the field, but we have tested our system with the real flight trajectories. Our system accurately mapped the recorded real flight trajectories and provided great interactivity for visualizing the traffic on airport in mixed reality world.

Our future work is planned to design the interaction mechanisms in mixed reality for conflict management in air traffic and aiding the situations caused by bad weather conditions. We have also planned to design the mechanisms using mixed reality technology to alarm the air traffic controllers about different alarming situations. These situations may include future bad weather conditions, airplanes deviation from actual path, flight trajectories which could cause collision, early or late arrivals as well as the departures of flights etc.

**Acknowledgment.** This work is supported by the Korea Agency for Infrastructure Technology Advancement (KAIA) grant funded by the Ministry of Land, Infrastructure and Transport (Grant 18CTAP-C142967-01-000000).

# References

1. Azuma, R., Daily, M.: Advanced human-computer interfaces for air traffic management and simulation. In: Proceedings of 1996 AIAA Flight Simulation Technologies Conference (1996)
2. Bagassi, S., De Crescenzio, F., Persiani, F.: Design and evaluation of a 4D interface for ATC. Proc. Inst. Mech. Eng. Part G: J. Aerosp. Eng. **224**, 937–947 (2010)
3. Weintraub, D.J.: Human factors issues in head-up display and design: the book of HUD. Crew System Ergonomics Information Analysis Center, Wright-Patterson AFB Ohio (1992)
4. Reisman, R.J., Brown, D.M.: Design of augmented reality tools for air traffic control towers. In: Proceedings of 6th AIAA Aviation Technology, Integration and Operations Conference (ATIO). American Institute of Aeronautics and Astronautics, Wichita, KS (2006)
5. Kunert, T., Krömker, H.: A pattern-based framework for the exploration of design alternatives. In: Jacko, J.A. (ed.) HCI 2007. LNCS, vol. 4550, pp. 1119–1128. Springer, Heidelberg (2007). https://doi.org/10.1007/978-3-540-73105-4_122
6. Ellis, S.R.: Towards determination of visual requirements for augmented reality displays and virtual environments for the airport tower. In: Virtual Media for Military Applications RTO-MP-HFM-136, pp. 31-1–31-10, RTO, Neuilly-sur-Seine (2006)
7. Fürstenau, N., Schmidt, M., Rudolph, M., Möhlenbrink, C.: Steps towards the Virtual Tower: Remote Airport Traffic Control Center (RAiCe). In: The ENRI International Workshop on ATM/CNS, Tokyo, Japan (2009)
8. Schulz-Rückert, D.: Future of aerodrome traffic control. In: The Aachen Aviation Convention, Aachen, Germany (2007)

9. Bagassi, S., De Crescenzio, F., Persiani, F.: Design and evaluation of a four-dimensional interface for air traffic control. Proc. Inst. Mech. Eng. Part G: J. Aerosp. Eng. **224**, 8 (2010)

10. Reisman, R.J., Feiner, S.K., Brown, D.M.: Augmented reality tower technology flight test. In: Proceedings of the International Conference on Human-Computer Interaction in Aerospace, HCI-Aero 2014. ACM, New York (2014)

11. Arif Abdul Rahman, A., Kirubakaran, P.S.B.: 3D simulation of real-time tracking of flights in ATC. Int. J. Res. Appl. Sci. Eng. Technol. (IJRASET), **3**(IV) (2015)

12. Masotti, N., De Crescenzio, F., Bagassi, S.: Augmented reality in the control tower: a rendering pipeline for multiple head-tracked head-up displays. In: De Paolis, L.T., Mongelli, A. (eds.) AVR 2016. LNCS, vol. 9768, pp. 321–338. Springer, Cham (2016). https://doi.org/10.1007/978-3-319-40621-3_23

13. Bagassi, S., De Crescenzio, F., Lucchi, F., Masotti, N.: Augmented and virtual reality in the airport control tower. In: 30th Congress of the International Council of the Aeronautical Sciences, ICAS 2016, Daejeon, South Korea (2016)

14. Zorzal, E.R., Fernandes, A., Castro, B.: Using augmented Reality to overlapping information in live airport cameras. In: 19th Symposium on Virtual and Augmented Reality (SVR) (2017)

15. Conversion of Geodetic coordinates to the (Portland State Aerospace) (2007). http://archive.psas.pdx.edu/CoordinateSystem/Latitude_to_LocalTangent.pdf

16. Farrell, J.A., Barth, M.: The Global Positioning System & Inertial Navigation. McGraw Hill Professional (1999)

17. Flightradar24 (2006). https://www.flightradar24.com

# Exploring Applications of Storm-Scale Probabilistic Warn-on-Forecast Guidance in Weather Forecasting

Katie A. Wilson[1,2(✉)], Jessica J. Choate[1,2], Adam J. Clark[2],
Burkely T. Gallo[1,3], Pamela L. Heinselman[2], Kent H. Knopfmeier[1,2],
Brett Roberts[1,2,3], Patrick S. Skinner[1,2], and Nusrat Yussouf[1,2]

[1] Cooperative Institute for Mesoscale Meteorological Studies,
University of Oklahoma, Norman, OK 73072, USA
Katie.Wilson@noaa.gov
[2] NOAA/OAR National Severe Storms Laboratory, Norman, OK 73072, USA
[3] NOAA Storm Prediction Center, Norman, OK 73072, USA

**Abstract.** The National Oceanic and Atmospheric Administration National Weather Service is responsible for issuing watches, warnings, and other forecast products related to hazardous weather. These products are intended to reach end users including government organizations, the media, emergency managers, and the public, such that decisions can be made to protect life, property, and the national economy. However, discontinuities currently exist in the guidance available to forecasters and in the products that are issued. Therefore, the NOAA Warn-on-Forecast program is developing and testing a convection-allowing ensemble analysis and prediction system. This system provides 0–6 h probabilistic forecast guidance for individual thunderstorms between the Watch and Warning timeframe. In addition to focusing research efforts on the development and testing of the Warn-on-Forecast system, a group of scientists are working closely with the weather forecasting community to establish ways in which Warn-on-Forecast guidance can be most useful during real-time operations. Two primary research questions being explored are: (1) How do meteorologists perceive, interpret, and understand Warn-on-Forecast guidance? (2) How can Warn-on-Forecast guidance be applied in the operational environment to enhance the forecast process? Research undertaken to address these two questions will be discussed.

**Keywords:** Probability · Forecast · Thunderstorm

## 1 Introduction

In the United States, the National Oceanic and Atmospheric Administration (NOAA) National Weather Service (NWS) is tasked with providing timely weather, water, and climate information that will protect life and property and enhance the national economy [1]. Most weather forecast information originates with the National Centers for Environmental Prediction, which is comprised of nine separate centers. Each center monitors and provides environmental predictions for various weather phenomena

© Springer Nature Switzerland AG 2019
J. Y. C. Chen and G. Fragomeni (Eds.): HCII 2019, LNCS 11575, pp. 557–572, 2019.
https://doi.org/10.1007/978-3-030-21565-1_39

across the United States. Additionally, many of these centers issue products to alert others to the possibility of impending hazardous weather. For example, as well as providing Convective Outlooks, the Storm Prediction Center assesses a variety of forecast guidance (e.g., the Global Forecast System model, High-Resolution Rapid Refresh model, and High-Resolution Ensemble Forecast system) to issue tornado and severe thunderstorm Watches. These products are issued typically hours ahead of when hazardous weather is expected to occur and for a broader area than what is usually impacted.

In addition to the national centers, 122 local Weather Forecast Offices (WFOs) provide localized short-term forecasts, advisories, warnings, and statements for their designated county warning area. In the case of a severe thunderstorm or tornado event, the local WFO is responsible for issuing warnings to alert their local community of the impending threat. Forecasters at local WFOs depend heavily on observations (e.g., radar and storm spotter reports) to make warning decisions about the real-time weather scenario. Warnings are typically issued minutes prior to when severe weather occurs, are valid for less than one hour [2], and cover a more specific area than what a Watch may have encompassed earlier in the day.

It is common for many hours with little or no official hazard guidance to occur between the issuance of a Watch and Warning. However, many important weather-related decisions are made by members of the general public and community officials during these hours. Therefore, a need exists for regularly updated information about the evolving weather scenario during the several hours that precede hazardous weather. Furthermore, enhancements to the current deterministic (yes/no) warning system are required to effectively communicate the evolving uncertainty of a weather event such that users of this information can make weather-related decisions according to their specific risk thresholds [3].

The need for a more continuous flow of probabilistic weather information across a broad range of temporal and spatial scales has been discussed at length over the past several years during the framing of NOAA's Forecasting a Continuum of Environmental Threats (FACETs) paradigm [4]. The FACETs paradigm describes seven stages of the forecast process that together encompass physical, social, and behavioral scientific challenges (Fig. 1). Although this paradigm is designed to address a wide variety of environmental threats, many of these challenges are first being explored within the context of severe weather. Furthermore, to date, much of the FACETS-related research effort has focused on demonstrating, testing, and evaluating methods and ideas at the warning scale. For example, during a series of studies at the NOAA Hazardous Weather Testbed in Norman, Oklahoma, a team of researchers have investigated NWS forecasters' use of probabilistic hazard information (PHI) within a new web-based prototype warning system for communicating the threat of severe weather [5]. Integrated warning teams have also been used to learn about applications of forecasters' PHI-driven guidance (in place of traditional deterministic warnings) to emergency managers' and broadcast meteorologists' decision making [5–7]. While this work will continue to evolve, efforts to explore the application of the FACETs paradigm at larger temporal and spatial scales is necessary. With respect to the NOAA Warn-on-Forecast program, these efforts are already underway.

**Fig. 1.** The seven components of the FACETs forecast process [4].

## 2  Warn-on-Forecast

The NOAA Warn-on-Forecast program is tasked with developing and testing a convective-scale ensemble analysis and forecast system that can provide probabilistic short-term guidance for individual thunderstorm hazards [8, 9]. While many sources of observations and guidance already exist within the NWS (e.g., radar, satellite, surface observations, models), advancements in numerical weather prediction have led to an increasing availability of real-time high-resolution forecast models capable of partially resolving convective storms known as convection-allowing models (CAMs) [10, 11]. More specifically, the NOAA Warn-on-Forecast program has led the development of a prototype CAM system. This system is currently in a testing phase and continues to evolve.

Unlike other CAMs, the Warn-on-Forecast system provides on-demand, rapidly-updating, short-term probabilistic forecast guidance for a variety of weather threats associated with individual convective storms. Technical descriptions and demonstrations of this system are available in several recent publications [12–15]. Warn-on-Forecast guidance is generated in an on-demand basis for a regional forecast domain (approximately 900 km × 900 km with 3-km horizontal grid spacing) within the Watch-to-Warning timeframe (0–6 h). Guidance from national centers is used to identify the most appropriate forecast domain, such as the Day 1 Convective Outlook from the Storm Prediction Center and the Day 1 Excessive Rainfall Outlook from the Weather Prediction Center (Fig. 2).

When run in experimental real-time settings, the Warn-on-Forecast system has provided 3-h probabilistic forecasts every 30 min (for severe hazards) or 6-h probabilistic forecasts every hour (for heavy rainfall and flash flooding). Guidance products from these forecasts are produced every 5-min during the forecast period, which enables detailed observation of the predicted storm evolution. A wide range of forecast products have been developed for operational use. These products include both environmental and storm-specific products. While the environmental products are similar to output from other CAMs, the storm-specific products provide probabilistic predictions of different hazards within individual thunderstorms. For example, guidance on the rainfall intensity and rotational characteristics of thunderstorms is provided using simulated radar reflectivity and updraft helicity [16], respectively. The distribution of

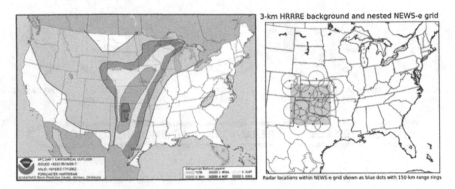

**Fig. 2.** The Storm Prediction Center Day 1 Convective Outlook for 16 May 2017 provided guidance for the placement of the Warn-on-Forecast domain, which is indicated by green shading in the right panel. (Color figure online)

forecast solutions provided by the 18-member ensemble allows for the generation of probabilistic products tailored to specific forecast problems. For example, the likelihood and severity of a predicted hazard may be assessed using probability of exceedance or percentile products. Additionally, ensemble guidance may be viewed similarly to deterministic forecasts using products such as the probability matched mean [17, 18], or paintball plots [19]. More recently, verification products using radar-derived proxies for severe thunderstorm hazards have been added for real-time assessment of forecast performance.

A Warn-on-Forecast web interface was created to view the forecast products (Fig. 3). This website has been through many iterations of improvement based on users' feedback and is designed to enable users to rapidly access and interrogate real-time guidance. The core web interface capabilities include: viewing both real-time and archived forecasts, navigating different forecast times, viewing a variety of ensemble forecast products, scrolling through the 5-min increments of each forecast product, and accessing individual ensemble member forecasts. The web viewer is used both in research and by operational meteorologists who may wish to access the guidance in real time and apply it experimentally to their forecast process.

In addition to the creation of a web viewer, a web-based forecast drawing tool was developed so that users can both view and interact with data from CAM ensemble forecast systems (Fig. 4). This tool was designed to support the transition of CAM ensemble systems from experimental to operational status [19], and has been used heavily in the NOAA Hazardous Weather Testbed Spring Forecast Experiment [20, 21]. The drawing tool allows forecasters and other research participants to draw polygons representing hazard probability thresholds over the model data and issue experimental forecasts. These experimental forecasts are prototypes representing the types of products which may be issued by the NWS Storm Prediction Center in the coming years. The tool also allows users to view, compare, and verify forecasts from multiple CAMs and CAM ensembles, including the prototype Warn-on-Forecast ensemble system.

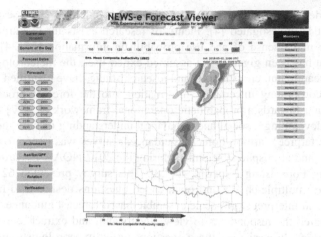

**Fig. 3.** The Warn-on-Forecast web viewer, which can be accessed at wof.nssl.noaa.gov.

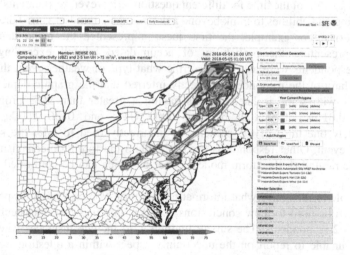

**Fig. 4.** Web-based forecast drawing tool for viewing and interacting with CAM ensemble forecast systems.

## 3 Perceptions and Interpretations of Warn-on-Forecast Probabilistic Guidance

### 3.1 Meteorologist Survey

In addition to investing research efforts into the development of a Warn-on-Forecast CAM ensemble system and suitable viewing tools, studies have been crafted to explore users' perceptions and interpretations of Warn-on-Forecast guidance. This area of research is also an identified challenge in the FACETs paradigm, such that social and behavioral understanding of how weather forecasters interpret and use probabilistic guidance must be investigated [4]. Plenty of research exists for examining how the general public make sense of and use probabilistic information [22–24], but not as much attention has been given to the assumed expert user, the meteorologist. Despite this lack of research, numerous reports and research studies have identified the potential benefits of incorporating uncertainty information into the forecast process and recommend moving towards a probabilistic operational framework [25–27].

To begin developing a social and behavioral understanding of how meteorologists perceive and interpret Warn-on-Forecast guidance, a survey was issued to participating meteorologists and atmospheric scientists during the 2017 NOAA Hazardous Weather Testbed Spring Forecasting Experiment [28]. This survey presented 62 participants with a series of multiple-choice and open-ended questions designed to measure how they perceive and interpret storm-scale ensemble-based forecast guidance. Many of the questions required the respondents to view, understand, and extract relevant information from graphics. In particular, these questions tested meteorologists' understanding of probability and percentile concepts.

Overall, respondents' answers were encouraging, with correct answers provided between 60%–96% of the time for different questions. However, respondents' depths of understanding and abilities to think beyond a deterministic mindset varied drastically in some questions. For example, the first question presented the respondents with a forecast representing the probability of accumulated rainfall exceeding 0.01 in. (Fig. 5). Respondents were asked to describe what type of weather event this graphic depicted. Many of the respondents correctly inferred that the graphic depicts a widespread area, with some isolated regions having a greater than 90% probability of exceeding 0.01 in. of rainfall between 0000 UTC and 0130 UTC. However, approximately one third of the participants incorrectly tried to infer the severity of the rainfall event. Other respondents tried to explain the forcing mechanisms responsible for the rainfall or the storm mode, neither of which can be confirmed using this graphic.

Being able to recognize what information Warn-on-Forecast products provide and how they can be used to draw conclusions is a skill that was not consistently applied among the 62 respondents. The survey findings [28] include instances when respondents were unable to report on the uncertainty aspect within a question when it was called for, and by comparison, inferred uncertainty when the graphic did not support it. Respondents also demonstrated an inconsistent application of knowledge, such that conceptual understanding of Warn-on-Forecast products varied depending on familiarity with the meteorological variable being presented. This finding demonstrates the importance in ensuring the user understands how products are calculated. Additionally, respondents displayed a tendency to focus on the worst-case scenario when presented with a combination of probabilistic and percentile representations of meteorological variables. These findings provide a base level understanding of the current strengths and gaps in meteorologists' knowledge of storm-scale ensemble guidance, and will form the basis for training recommendations that will soon be tried and tested among other meteorologists.

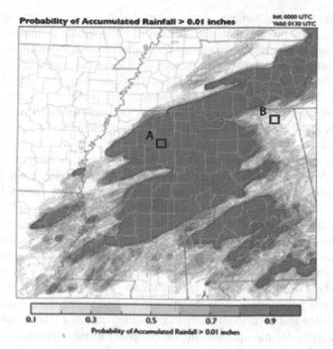

**Fig. 5.** Probability of accumulated rainfall exceeding 0.01 in. [28].

## 3.2 Spring Forecast Experiment

The NOAA Hazardous Weather Testbed Spring Forecast Experiment provides opportunities to present new data and products in front of operational and research meteorologists. These participants provide invaluable testing, evaluation, and feedback that help to improve and guide future research and development [10, 20, 21]. During the five-week 2018 Spring Forecasting Experiment, all attendees were provided with a one-hour training session on their first day that introduced Warn-on-Forecast and gave an overview of the task they would participate in during the rest of the week. This task assigned participants to one of two groups. Each group had approximately four participants and efforts were made to balance forecasting expertise between them. During each afternoon, the two groups each worked with a facilitator to view Warn-on-Forecast guidance, and collectively issue severe weather outlooks for two, 1-h periods, then update the outlooks when new Warn-on-Forecast guidance became available. These outlooks identified areas with contours of varying probability for experiencing severe weather during the valid 1-h period. An example of a 1-h severe weather outlook is shown in Fig. 4. Survey questions were designed to learn about forecasters' use, understanding, and attitudes about Warn-on-Forecast guidance while participating in this activity.

Participants' use of Warn-on-Forecast guidance was analyzed by tracking each group's product usage. The data collected provided information on the most popular products used to create outlooks each day. The most used product, regardless of which group participants were assigned to or what day they were forecasting for, was paintball plots. This product plots the location of all ensemble members (in different colors) that exceed a threshold value for a particular variable. Paintball plots allow for the visualization of model uncertainty, such that users can assess the location and extent of overlap of the 18 ensemble members. This deterministic assessment differs to viewing overall probabilistic information. The next four preferred products, in order of most to least requested, were for assessment of: hail (probabilistic), composite reflectivity (probabilistic), environment (deterministic), and individual member viewers (deterministic).

All 1-h severe weather outlooks were verified the next morning using the local storm report driven practically perfect method [29]. The reliability diagrams (Fig. 6), while only measuring one aspect of forecast quality, show that Group 1 performed slightly better than Group 2 (although overall both groups provided skillful forecasts). One explanation for this result is that Group 2's forecast outlooks covered a broader area than Group 1's forecast outlooks. Therefore, while Group 2 forecasted for more areas impacted by severe weather than Group 1, their forecasts also encompassed a larger false alarm area. Furthermore, when comparing all preliminary and updated outlooks for both groups combined, the preliminary outlooks verified slightly better. This finding was unexpected, since the updated outlooks used more recent Warn-on-Forecast guidance and participants' satisfaction ratings of their team's outlook tended to improve slightly for the updated outlook compared to the preliminary outlook. As can be seen in Fig. 6b, this slight degradation in reliability occurred for higher probability thresholds, and therefore it is possible that participants were operating with higher levels of confidence. Further research needs to assess what and why modifications are made to the outlook after receiving the latest Warn-on-Forecast guidance, and in what instances they benefit the outlook.

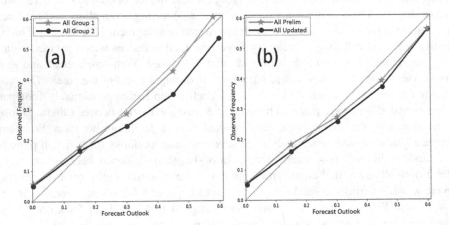

**Fig. 6.** Reliability diagrams for (a) Group 1 and Group 2 outlooks and (b) combined Group 1 and Group 2 preliminary and updated outlooks.

### 3.3  Hydrometeorology Testbed

The potential applications of Warn-on-Forecast guidance for the prediction of heavy rainfall and flash flooding events is also being explored within the NOAA Hazardous Weather Testbed [30]. For the first time in 2018, nine NWS forecasters evaluated probabilistic flash flood products to examine how the inclusion of 3-h Warn-on-Forecast quantitative precipitation forecasts (QPFs) affected forecasters' understanding of a possible flash flooding event. Forecasters reported on their perceptions of the flash flooding risk, where they chose to prioritize attention, and what they expected their subsequent action would be if in real-time operations (e.g., issuing a warning or statement).

Early analysis of forecasters' feedback from one scenario indicated that access to Warn-on-Forecast QPF driven guidance increased the area forecasters attended to from 2.8 counties per hour to 5.2 counties per hour. The additional areas attended to were mostly associated with the first 2 h of the 3-h Warn-on-Forecast QPF driven guidance. This heightened awareness of potential downstream impacts resulted in most participants keying into the region that later experienced flash flooding several hours earlier than when Warn-on-Forecast was not used. Furthermore, when comparing participants' expected actions, several warning decisions were made 2–3 h earlier and a handful of participants began communicating the potential threat to officials a few hours earlier also.

The findings from the early analysis of the 2018 study suggest that the use of Warn-on-Forecast QPFs in hydrologic modeling will be beneficial to the forecast process. To further explore these benefits, a follow-on study in the 2019 hydrometeorology testbed will evaluate use of Warn-on-Forecast for flash flood prediction in simulated real-time operations, such that forecasters will view data and issue products like they would in the real world, and their actions will be compared to the decisions that forecasters made during the actual event.

## 4  Operational Applications

In addition to investigating uses of Warn-on-Forecast in controlled settings such as the NOAA Hazardous Weather Testbed, experimental demonstrations within operational settings have also been conducted. These demonstrations are made possible through collaborative efforts with NWS offices, such that forecasters integrate the probabilistic Warn-on-Forecast guidance into real-time decision making and later provide feedback on whether the guidance was useful and why, in what way it was applied, and how it can be improved for future uses. Below are some examples of these operational demonstrations with NWS National Centers and local forecast offices.

### 4.1  National Centers

The NOAA NWS's Weather Prediction Center is responsible for providing forecasts and guidance for high-impact precipitation events. In particular, the Met Watch desk at the Weather Prediction Center monitors the potential for heavy rainfall and flash flood events, and issues Mesoscale Precipitation Discussions (MPDs) that indicate the likelihood of flash flooding should the threat exist over approximately two county warning areas during a 1–6-h period. The regional and short-term aspects of this forecast product make Warn-on-Forecast a potentially useful source of guidance for Met Watch responsibilities. Therefore, following a collaborative visit in which scientists learned about Met Watch forecasters' workflow, provided training on the Warn-on-Forecast concept, and introduced the web viewer, Met Watch forecasters agreed to use Warn-on-Forecast guidance experimentally in real time and provide feedback using a survey designed by both the scientists and the lead Met Watch forecaster.

Feedback from five Met Watch forecasters provided over 24 different weather events gave insight into when Warn-on-Forecast both did and did not positively impact their forecast process. In total, forecasters reported Warn-on-Forecast as benefiting their forecast process for 15 of the 24 events, of which MPDs were issued for nine events. Qualitative feedback described Warn-on-Forecast as being useful for determining the placement, timing, and persistence of heavy rainfall. This information supported forecasters' conceptual models and provided confidence in deciding the spatial extent, duration, and wording of MPDs. For example, on 20 July 2018, a Met Watch forecaster observed an organized convective event in the Upper Ohio Valley (Fig. 7). The Warn-on-Forecast guidance brought attention to where backbuilding and repeated convection would occur, and provided confidence that the wording "flash flooding likely" was justified. The forecaster also viewed that the early model runs were verifying well against observations, which encouraged him to weight the Warn-on-Forecast guidance more heavily in his decision-making process. In the six instances in which Warn-on-Forecast was useful but MPDs were not issued, forecasters reported that the guidance confirmed the lack of convective coverage and provided confidence that an MPD was not needed.

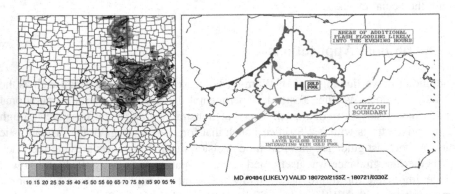

**Fig. 7.** (Left) Warn-on-Forecast 6-h rainfall probabilities >1 in. verified with the National Center for Environmental Prediction Stage IV 6-h rainfall probability >1 in. (black contours). (Right) The MPD issued on 20 July 2018, indicating the area where flash flooding is likely. Later in the evening, numerous flash flood warnings were issued in this area and local storm reports were received.

Warn-on-Forecast was not found to benefit the forecast process for nine of the 24 events reported. Of these events, MPDs were issued for seven events. Forecasters' feedback described both model limitations and logistical limitations as reasons why. For example, in some instances the Warn-on-Forecast guidance was slow to initiate organized convection or it did not match observations. Therefore, the guidance did not aid the forecast process and observations were relied on to make real-time decisions. In other instances, the guidance was either unexpectedly unavailable or the forecaster coming on shift did not have adequate time to assess all model guidance before issuing urgent MPDs. For the two events in which the guidance was not helpful nor did forecasters issue MPDs, they simply reported that there was not sufficient convection in the area to be concerned about flash flooding.

The Warn-on-Forecast group is also beginning to work with the NOAA Storm Prediction Center to explore utility of this guidance for severe convective weather prediction. Similarly to the MPDs issued by the Weather Prediction Center, the Storm Prediction center issues Mesoscale Discussions (MDs) on severe thunderstorm hazards and winter precipitation. These MDs often cover a similar or smaller area than a Watch, and include information about current observational trends and short-term guidance such as that provided by the Warn-on-Forecast system. Currently, the Warn-on-Forecast system has been used informally when available within the Storm Prediction Center, and its guidance was used in the issuance of an MD related to the tornado threat from Hurricane Florence. Moving forward, the guidance will be used in simulated real-time forecaster training activities, to give all Storm Prediction Center forecasters increased familiarity with the system and the effects of the rapid update cycles. Efforts are also underway to engage scientists and Storm Prediction Center forecasters more closely, including shadowing activities and co-development of guidance for the time period within the Watch to Warning scales. Finally, the system will be available in real-time to forecasters during the peak spring severe convection season, to help them refine their probabilistic forecasts and identify corridors of heightened risk.

## 4.2    Local NWS Forecast Offices

Given the co-location of federal, university, and operational partners at the National Weather Center, scientists have worked closely with the Norman WFO to experimentally explore applications of Warn-on-Forecast guidance within the Watch-to-Warning timeframe. On 16 May 2017, the Norman WFO used this guidance to assess the increasing tornado threat. After viewing notably high values of 2–5 km updraft helicity (a measure of mesocyclone intensity), the Norman WFO decided to issue a Significant Weather Advisory to indicate a "high probability that tornado warnings will be issued." Sharing expectations for later warning activity is very unusual, and represents the potential enhancements in weather threat communication that Warn-on-Forecast could provide to the traditional Watch and Warning products (Fig. 8).

The Norman WFO continued to use Warn-on-Forecast experimentally during the 2018 severe weather season, and further demonstrated enhanced messaging between the Watch and Warning products on 2 May 2018, when a forecaster disseminated five graphics to their official social media accounts as the event evolved (Fig. 9) [31]. These graphics provided greater specificity in the timing, location, and type of weather

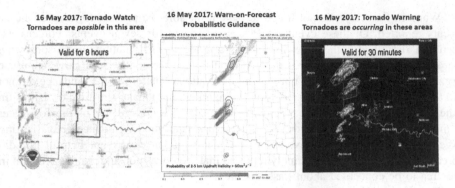

**Fig. 8.** Warn-on-Forecast guidance was provided for the temporal and spatial scales that span between the Watch and Warning products issued on 16 May 2017.

hazards expected than what the Watch provided, and were primarily based on the ensemble 90th percentile value of 2–5 km updraft helicity product. During this event, the forecaster was focused initially on the severe weather threat. As storms evolved and the Warn-on-Forecast guidance suggested an increasing likelihood of tornadoes, the forecaster switched the focus of the graphics to emphasize the tornado threat. In the final graphic, the storm system had grown upscale from supercellular storms into a mesoscale convective system, and the forecaster communicated the continued threat for possible hail, wind, and brief tornadoes. These graphics were issued spontaneously and were not based on learned best practices. Therefore, many questions remain regarding what the most effective methods are for translating and disseminating Warn-on-Forecast guidance to the general public as well as to official community members.

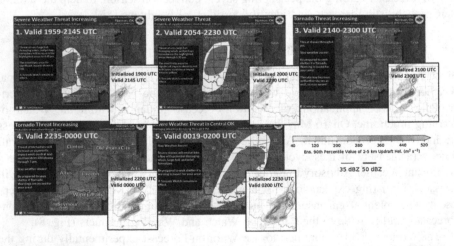

**Fig. 9.** Graphics issued by the Norman WFO during 2 May 2018 weather event in Oklahoma. The inset boxes show the Warn-on-Forecast product primarily used to create these graphics: the ensemble 90th percentile value of 2–5 km updraft helicity.

In addition to working with the Norman WFO, scientists have collaborated with the Topeka WFO to learn about their experimental use of Warn-on-Forecast guidance during real-time operations. On 1 May 2018, forecasters from this office reported that Warn-on-Forecast guidance provided "critical information to refine the spatiotemporal precision of forecast information pertaining to severe thunderstorm and tornado threats across the NWS Topeka county warning area." This guidance influenced forecasters to provide high-confidence messaging of severe and tornado threats in Enhanced Short-term Weather Outlooks. As can be seen in the ensemble 90th percentile values of 2–5 km updraft helicity (Fig. 10), Warn-on-Forecast identified a location favorable for tornado development, and as the model runs approached valid time, the guidance homed in on the location where an EF-3 tornado occurred. Furthermore, forecasters from the Topeka WFO reported that not only did Warn-on-Forecast guidance alert them to the most intense storms, but it also accurately predicted the weakening of other storms. Together, this information aided forecasters in assessing expectations for how this event would evolve.

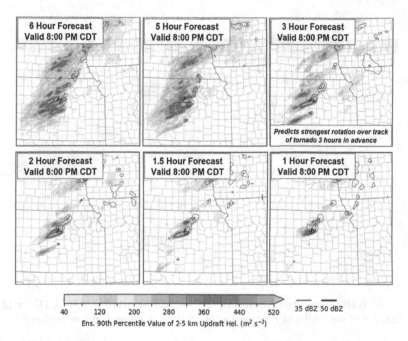

**Fig. 10.** Warn-on-Forecast ensemble 90th percentile value of 2–5 km updraft helicity for forecast hours preceding an EF-3 tornado in Culver, KS on 1 May 2018. The bold black line indicates the EF-3 tornado track.

## 4.3   Aviation

The short-term probabilistic forecast guidance provided by Warn-on-Forecast for individual storm hazards has potential to benefit the aviation community for air traffic planning. Assessment of numerous Warn-on-Forecast products can help determine the likelihood for storms growing upscale, their location, mode, and intensity, potential areas of dissipation, expected cloud top heights and cloud base heights, and the most likely types of weather hazards (e.g., hail, wind, or tornado). Use of this guidance may help determine feasible flight routes based on the extent of convection and potential gaps in coverage between storms.

An informal first demonstration of how Warn-on-Forecast guidance can aid decision making within the aviation community occurred on 12 May 2018. The Federal Aviation Administration (FAA) Air Traffic Control System Command Center used Warn-on-Forecast to guide decisions regarding possible severe weather in the northeast United States. The aviation meteorologist viewed paintball plots of 45-dBZ composite reflectivity to assess the expected location of storms, and reported that the guidance "pretty much nailed the solid line over MD/DE," and although the forecast members over MD/PA were not in as good consensus, they felt that "there was lots of value in seeing the spread." The meteorologist used this information to justify including this line of convection when issuing a Traffic Flow Management Convective Forecast (TCF) (Fig. 11).

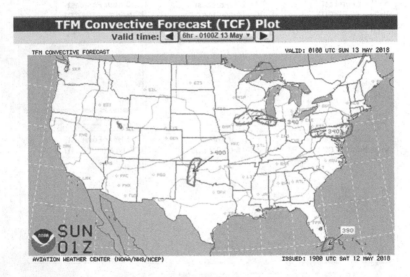

**Fig. 11.** The Traffic Flow Management Convective Forecast issued at 1900 UTC on 12 May 2018. Inclusion of the northeast corridor was justified by Warn-on-Forecast guidance.

## 5  Summary

The Warn-on-Forecast program is working to develop short-term probabilistic guidance for individual thunderstorms. No other guidance on this spatial and temporal scale currently exists. The goals of Warn-on-Forecast support the FACETs vision of providing a more continuous flow of probabilistic hazard information for various environmental threats, specifically between the temporal and spatial scales typical of a Watch and a Warning. Initial testing of the Warn-on-Forecast concept has been conducted in experimental conditions, through surveys, and in operational centers and local offices. This initial testing is crucial for obtaining early feedback on the strengths and limitations of the system, and is planned to continue in the coming years. In addition to exploring operational applications of Warn-on-Forecast, other research questions that need to be addressed include: how to visualize and interact with Warn-on-Forecast guidance in order to maximize forecaster experience; what types of real-time verification metrics are useful to the forecast process; how forecasters in National Centers and local WFOs should best work together to utilize the Warn-on-Forecast guidance; how forecasters can effectively communicate and disseminate Warn-on-Forecast guidance to stakeholders and the general public.

# References

1. NOAA NWS. https://www.weather.gov/about/nws. Accessed 30 Jan 2019
2. Brooks, H.E., Correia, J.: Long-term performance metrics for National Weather Service tornado warnings. Weather Forecast. **33**, 1501–1511 (2018)
3. Murphy, A.H., Winkler, R.L.: Probability forecasting in meteorology. J. Am. Stat. Assoc. **79**, 489–500 (1984)
4. Rothfusz, L.P., et al.: FACETs: a proposed next-generation paradigm for high-impact weather forecasting. Bull. Am. Meteorol. Soc. **99**, 2025–2043 (2018)
5. Karstens, C.D., et al.: Development of a human-machine mix for forecasting severe convective events. Weather Forecast. **33**, 715–737 (2018)
6. Nemunaitis-Berry, K.L., et al.: Broadcast meteorologist decision-making in the 2016 hazardous weather testbed probabilistic hazard information project. In: Fourth Conference on Weather Warnings and Communication, Kansas City, MO (2017)
7. LaDue, D.S., et al.: Temporal and spatial aspects of emergency manager use of prototype probabilistic hazard information. In: Fifth Symposium on Building a Weather-Ready Nation: Enhancing Our Nation's Readiness, Responsiveness, and Resilience to High Impact Weather Events, Seattle, WA (2017)
8. Stensrud, D.J., et al.: Convective-scale Warn-on-Forecast system: a vision for 2020. Bull. Am. Meteorol. Soc. **90**, 1487–1499 (2009)
9. Stensrud, D.J., et al.: Progress and challenges with Warn-on-Forecast. Atmos. Res. **123**, 2–16 (2013)
10. Clark, A.J., et al.: An overview of the 2010 hazardous weather testbed experimental forecast program spring experiment. Bull. Am. Meteorol. Soc. **93**, 55–74 (2012)
11. Benjamin, S.G., et al.: A North American hourly assimilation and model forecast cycle: the Rapid Refresh. Mon. Weather Rev. **144**, 1669–1694 (2016)
12. Sobash, R.A., Kain, J.S., Bright, D.R., Dean, A.R., Coniglio, M.C., Weiss, S.: Probabilistic forecast guidance for severe thunderstorms based on the identification of extreme phenomena in convection-allowing model forecasts. Weather Forecast. **26**, 714–728 (2011)
13. Wheatley, D.M., Knopfmeier, K.H., Jones, T.A., Creager, G.J.: Storm-scale data assimilation and ensemble forecasting with the NSSL experimental Warn-on-Forecast system. Part I: radar data experiments. Weather Forecast. **30**, 1795–1817 (2015)
14. Jones, T.A., Knopfmeier, K., Wheatley, D., Creager, G.: Storm-scale data assimilation and ensemble forecasting with the NSSL experimental Warn-on-Forecast system. Part II: combined radar and satellite data experiments. Weather Forecast. **31**, 297–327 (2016)

15. Yussouf, N., Kain, J.S., Clark, A.J.: Short-term probabilistic forecasts of the 31 May 2013 Oklahoma tornado and flash flood event using a continuous-update-cycle storm-scale ensemble system. Weather Forecast. **31**, 957–983 (2016)
16. Kain, J.S., et al.: Some practical considerations regarding horizontal resolution in the first generation of operational convection-allowing NWP. Weather Forecast. **23**, 931–952 (2008)
17. Ebert, E.E.: Ability of a poor man's ensemble to predict the probability and distribution of precipitation. Mon. Weather Rev. **129**, 2461–2480 (2001)
18. Clark, A.J.: Generation of ensemble mean precipitation forecasts from convection-allowing ensembles. Weather Forecast. **32**, 1569–1583 (2017)
19. Roberts, B., Jirak, I.J., Clark, A.J., Weiss, S.J., Kain, J.S.: Post-processing and visualization techniques for convection-allowing ensembles. Bull. Am. Meteorol. Soc. (in press)
20. Kain, J.S., Baldwin, M.E., Janish, P.R., Weiss, S.J., Kay, M.P., Carbin, G.W.: Subjective verification of numerical models as a component of a broader interaction between research and operations. Weather Forecast. **18**, 847–860 (2003)
21. Gallo, B.T., et al.: Breaking new ground in severe weather prediction: the 2015 NOAA/hazardous weather testbed spring forecasting experiment. Weather Forecast. **32**, 1541–1568 (2017)
22. Murphy, A.H., Winkler, R.L.: Forecasters and probability forecasts: some current problems. Bull. Am. Meteorol. Soc. **52**, 239–248 (1971)
23. Gigerenzer, G., Hertwig, R., Van Den Broek, E., Fasolo, F., Katsikopoulos, K.V.: "A 30% chance of rain tomorrow": how does the public understand probabilistic weather forecasts? Risk Anal. **25**, 623–630 (2005)
24. Joslyn, S., Nadav-Greenberg, L., Nichols, R.M.: Probability of precipitation: assessment and enhancement of end-user understanding. Bull. Am. Meteorol. Soc. **90**, 185–194 (2008)
25. NRC: Completing the Forecast: Characterizing and communicating uncertainty for better decisions using weather and climate forecasts. National Academies Press (2006)
26. AMS: Enhancing weather information with probability forecasts. American Meteorological Society (2008)
27. Hirschberg, P.A., et al.: A weather and climate enterprise strategic implementation plan for generating and communicating forecast uncertainty information. Bull. Am. Meteorol. Soc. **92**, 1651–1666 (2011)
28. Wilson, K.A., Heinselman, P.L., Skinner, P.S., Choate, J.J., Klockow-McClain, K.E.: Meteorologists' interpretations of storm-scale ensemble-based forecast guidance. Weather Clim. Soc. **11**, 337–354 (2019)
29. Hitchens, N.M., Brooks, H.E., Kay, M.P.: Objective limits on forecasting skill of rare events. Weather Forecast. **28**, 525–534 (2013)
30. Martinaitis, S., Gourley, J.J., Heinselman, P., Wilson, K., Yussouf, N.: Probabilistic precipitation forecasts and hydrologic modeling for improving flash flood warnings: the 2018 HMT-hydro experiment. In: National Weather Association 43rd Annual Meeting, St. Louis, MO (2018)
31. Wilson, K.A., Skinner, P.S., Lindley, T., Bowers, R., Speheger, D.: An observational study: real time use of the NSSL experimental Warn-on-Forecast system for ensembles during NWS severe weather operations. In: National Weather Association 43rd Annual Meeting, St. Louis, MO (2018)

# Author Index

Printed in the United States
By Bookmasters